THE BEST PLAYS OF 1935-36

EDITED BY

BURNS MANTLE

THE BEST PLAYS OF 1909-19
(*With Garrison P. Sherwood*)
THE BEST PLAYS OF 1919-20
THE BEST PLAYS OF 1920-21
THE BEST PLAYS OF 1921-22
THE BEST PLAYS OF 1922-23
THE BEST PLAYS OF 1923-24
THE BEST PLAYS OF 1924-25
THE BEST PLAYS OF 1925-26
THE BEST PLAYS OF 1926-27
THE BEST PLAYS OF 1927-28
THE BEST PLAYS OF 1928-29
THE BEST PLAYS OF 1929-30
THE BEST PLAYS OF 1930-31
THE BEST PLAYS OF 1931-32
THE BEST PLAYS OF 1932-33
THE BEST PLAYS OF 1933-34
THE BEST PLAYS OF 1934-35
THE BEST PLAYS OF 1935-36

THE NEW YORK DRAMA CRITICS' CIRCLE

Standing: The late *Percy Hammond, Richard Lockridge, Gilbert Gabriel, John Anderson, Whit*ney Bolton, Rowland Fields, John Mason Brown, Arthur Pollock. Seated: *George Jean Nathan* *Burns Mantle, Robert Garland, Kelcy Allen, Brooks Atkinson.* Upper left: *Maxwell Anderson* re*ceives a plaque. Upper right: *Burgess Meredith* and *Margo* in a scene from "Winterset."

THE BEST PLAYS
OF 1935-36

AND THE
YEAR BOOK OF THE DRAMA
IN AMERICA

EDITED BY
BURNS MANTLE

With Illustrations

DODD, MEAD AND COMPANY
NEW YORK - - - 1936

"Winterset," copyright, 1935, by Maxwell Anderson
Copyright and published, 1935, by Anderson House, Washington, D. C.

"Idiot's Delight," copyright, 1935, by Robert E. Sherwood
Copyright and published, 1936, by Charles Scribner's Sons, New York

"End of Summer," copyright, 1935, by S. N. Behrman
Copyright and published, 1936, by Random House, New York

"First Lady," copyright, 1935, by Katharine Dayton and George Kaufman
Copyright and published, 1936, by Random House, New York

"Victoria Regina," copyright, 1935, by Laurence Housman
Copyright and published, 1936, by Charles Scribner's Sons, New York

"Boy Meets Girl," copyright, 1935, by Samuel and Bella Spewack
Copyright and published, 1936, by Random House, New York

"Dead End," copyright, 1935, by Sidney Kingsley
Copyright and published, 1936, by Random House, New York

"Call It a Day," copyright, 1935, by Dodie Smith
Copyright and published, 1936, by Samuel French, New York and London

"Ethan Frome," copyright, 1935, by Owen Davis and Donald Davis
Copyright and published, 1911-22-26, by Charles Scribner's Sons, New York

"Pride and Prejudice," copyright, 1935, by Helen Jerome
Copyright and published, 1936, by Doubleday, Doran & Co., Garden City, N. Y.

COPYRIGHT, 1936,

BY DODD, MEAD AND COMPANY, INC.

INTRODUCTION

THIS eighteenth volume of The Best Plays series may boast as fine a collection of plays, in the estimation of the editor, as any one of the volumes that has gone before. At least the average of quality seems to him to be consistently higher.

What influence the free investment of Hollywood capital may have had upon this contribution of drama is a debatable subject to which some attention is given in a review of the season hereinafter included.

Seven of the plays are by American authors and three are from England. Which signifies nothing in particular save that it gives both nationalists and Anglophiles something to talk about.

There were, for the first time in the native drama's history, two first prizes awarded to American dramatists. New York drama reviewers having been irked on occasion by the selections of the committee organized under the provisions of the late Joseph Pulitzer's will to select the best play of the year of American authorship, determined to make a similar selection of their own. Now all men and women may know which play they, the critics, consider of first importance.

This year the critics' prize, a silver plaque, was given to Maxwell Anderson for his poetic modern tragedy, "Winterset." The Pulitzer committee a few weeks later declared its independence by voting for Robert Emmet Sherwood's "Idiot's Delight." The two plays lead the list of ten from which excerpts have been taken and are here included to indicate the trend and quality of the year's drama. Each of you who read the two may appoint himself an individual prize-awarding committee and make your own decision. It will not be necessary, however, to write the editor. Nothing can be done about it now.

Both prize-winning plays represent serious, purposeful efforts and are a credit to the native craftsmen whose numbers are annually increasing and the quality of whose work, it seems to me, is constantly approaching that of the masters of written drama of all time. Mr. Anderson's drama is a plea for social justice, Mr. Sherwood's an exposé of the idiocy of war.

A third play of definite importance, in that it also invades a recognizable section of the American scene and truthfully and observantly discusses its most timely problems, is S. N. Behrman's "End of Summer," which was runner-up to the prize-winning dramas.

Sidney Kingsley's "Dead End" is a third drama of purposeful social criticism, revealing city environments which cradle those of our public enemies engaged in gangster activities. A bold but honest exposé of the vicious and the profane.

Of the lighter plays, Katharine Dayton's and George Kaufman's "First Lady" is timely and incisive satire. A particularly happy choice in subject and treatment for a presidential campaign year. Bella and Samuel Spewak's "Boy Meets Girl," the most riotous of the season's light comedy successes, is a satirical cartoon of the cinema industry keenly observed, truthfully reported and expertly transferred to the stage. Owen and Donald Davis' "Ethan Frome" is a sympathetic and understanding transferral of a native classic from book covers to the theatre.

Of the three plays of English authorship Laurence Housman's "Victoria Regina" is a sentimental tour de force built around selected episodes from the life of a universally beloved royal lady; Dodie Smith's "Call It a Day" is a simple and appealing domestic comedy notable for its homely detail and normal family decencies, and Helen Jerome's "Pride and Prejudice" is, like "Ethan Frome" a supremely good example of the transferral of a popular story from the pages of a classic novel to the stage of a playhouse. Where the Davises excelled in the expansion of Miss Wharton's reasonably thin story of New England, Miss Jerome's achievement is one of an expert condensation which misses giving offense either to the Jane Austen loyalists or those playgoing critics who normally contend against the dramatized novel.

No major change has been made in the general character of the year book's contents. It has been deemed advisable to group the Federal Theatre plays given under the auspices of the Works Progress Administration rather than to insert them chronologically.

In response to frequent affirmations and denials respecting the table of birth dates included, I most respectfully repeat that they have been as carefully confirmed as possible. I should not advise A's betting B large sums on the positive correctness of any given date. The players are quite as human and as forgetful in such matters as other folk. Frequently the dates are altered from year to year to bring them up to date and to correct errors previously and unfortunately made.

B. M.

Forest Hills, L. I., 1936.

CONTENTS

viii
CONTENTS

ILLUSTRATIONS

THE BEST PLAYS OF 1935-36

THE BEST PLAYS OF 1935-36

THE SEASON IN NEW YORK

IT is quite generally admitted by those most familiar with the situation that this theatrical season has been the most exciting and the most satisfying of any New York has enjoyed since the years that preceded the crash of '29. I see no particular reason why we should stop at '29. Except in the matter of those statistics that boast the number of plays produced it would be possible to go back even farther without coming upon a record of plays more satisfying or more worthy of enthusiastic endorsement.

Some say the greater number of better plays is explained by the fact that the motion picture interests have this season invested more heavily in acted plays than they ever have before. I think this may account for the improved quality revealed in the physical production of the plays, but I fail to see where it reasonably can be held responsible for the literary quality or the entertainment value of the plays produced. There were as many plays backed by "movie money" that failed as there were that succeeded, which would seem to strengthen the argument, always obvious, that while money may make the mare go faster, it adds little to the judgment shown in the selection of the mare.

A further test of the value of Hollywood backing in the conduct of the legitimate theatre seems likely to be made the coming season. Hurt in their pride by the provisions of a new contract which the play producers have made with the Dramatists' Guild, picture producers have defiantly declared that they will back no more plays.

They may or may not hold to this determination. It is my personal conviction that they will back as many plays as they think will make them money, even though they make no more open agreements with producers such as Metro-Goldwyn-Mayer made this season with Max Gordon and Sam H. Harris. But if they should hold to their decision it will make little difference to Broadway. Backing for promising plays will always be forthcoming. Not, perhaps, in as generous amounts as the cinema Midases are able to supply it, but in sufficient amounts to give any good play a chance.

The new Dramatists' Guild-League of New York Theatre agreement is for five years. It provides a division of the money paid by the motion picture producer for the rights to a play that shall give the author of the play 60 per cent and the producer of the play 40 per cent of the total. If the play has been financed by a picture producer the picture rights are still to be offered in the open market, and the terms of sale agreed upon by a joint committee presided over by an official arbiter. The dispute ran on for two months, but the compromise was never very much in doubt.

An incident of the early season that involved producers and dramatists was that of the picketing of theatres in which Theatre Guild attractions were being shown. Virgil Geddes and Paul Sifton, playwrights who had sold scripts to the Guild, were incensed when the Guild took over the management of Elizabeth Bergner, an Austrian actress, and "Escape Me Never," an English play, for the length of the New York engagement. Geddes and Sifton, with their wives, wearing placards protesting the Theatre Guild's unfairness to American playwrights, weaved in and out of the first night crowds and passed out circulars informing the public that, even though it had its shelves well stocked with American plays, the Guild continued to promote the works of foreign authors. The demonstrations continued for two or three nights and were then discontinued. Results were doubtful. The picketing may have made the Guild more acutely conscious of the Messrs. Geddes and Sifton, but the Guild subscribers apparently took little interest.

The activities of the Federal theatre project were a factor of considerable interest during the season. An organization that had its beginnings the year before took definite form under the direction of Hallie Flanagan, for some years director of drama at Vassar College. Mrs. Flanagan appointed 12 regional directors who were to have charge of the work in different sections of the country. Elmer Rice accepted the post for New York, and did much good work until preparations for the first production of a Living Newspaper division uncovered to the powers in Washington a suggested inclusion of diplomatic dynamite. The proposed dramatized news story, "Ethiopia," contained references to the European situation in which Mussolini of Italy and Haile Selassie of Ethiopia were at grips that might, in the belief of the WPA executives, cause unpleasant complications. Rice made a fight for freedom of action in his work and, not being satisfied with the answer given him, resigned his post. Philip W. Barber was appointed his successor. A substitute Living Newspaper called "Triple-A Plowed Under" was issued in place of "Ethiopia" and the WPA went on.

What the future holds for this first experiment of the government in subsidizing theatre entertainment no man may completely vision. At the moment it does not appear reasonable that it can be suddenly discontinued, either in the cause of economy or by the power of political pressure, without leaving a variety of problems to be disposed of and a newly created public demand that will one day have to be met. After a year of low-cost and free entertainment brought to millions who have heretofore been denied these satisfying contributions to their restless lives it is not likely the Federal theatre's patrons will be content to give it up. Nor does it seem reasonable that the politicians of any party seeking the people's favor will fail to capitalize this freshly awakened interest. It is possible the states may take over the work from the national government, adding the cost to their educational budgets on the theory that a people's theatre may become of as great importance to its happiness and advancement as its libraries and its art galleries. In any event, we, as a nation, have apparently taken on in the cause of a relief that found jobs for thousands of distressed citizens a cultural crusade that cannot easily or reasonably be put aside.

The major productions of the WPA in the New York sector, which, naturally, was the most important of all, being the nation's center of theatrical activity, included an exceptionally satisfying production of T. S. Eliot's poetic drama, "Murder in the Cathedral"; a West Indian version of Shakespeare's "Macbeth," staged by the Negro unit; two mildly propagandic human documents called "Chalk Dust," which protested the regimentation of High School teachers, and "Class of '29," which spoke for the Lost Generation that inherited the world the year it went economically to smash, and two biographical dramas, "Battle Hymn," relating the adventures of John Brown of Osawatomie, and "Jefferson Davis," recalling the chief episodes in the life of the Confederacy's War President. Statistical facts concerned with these, and other major activities of the Federal theatre, will be found in a separate division of the season's record in this volume.

To go back to the beginning of the season, the Summer of 1935 was a dull affair in the theatre. Nothing in June worth remembering. Nothing in July. Nothing in August, except the resumed engagement of "The Great Waltz," which took up practically where it left off at the Rockefeller Center Theatre and continued for another forty-nine performances.

The new season swung into its stride in September, however, and there was a good deal of cheering here and there. Mr. A. H. Woods offered a melodrama by Ayn Rand called "Night of January 16." It was a good melodrama concerned with a murder trial, but it was made especially interesting to the experienced theatregoing crowd because (1) it gave Mr. Woods (who had gone down in the 1929 crash) another chance and (2) because the jury that tried the heroine accused of the crime was selected from the audience at each performance. Given a chance to render its own verdict, too. If the jury voted "Guilty!" the Judge granted a new trial. If "Not Guilty!" the heroine was dismissed with love and kisses.

The Messrs. Shubert organized another musical revue, "At Home Abroad," generously studded with names. Those of Beatrice Lillie, Ethel Waters, Eleanor Powell and Herb Williams were the best known, with that of Reginald Gardiner, an English monologist, shortly lifted to prominence because of the hit he made. The Guild brought in two productions, the Rev. John Haynes Holmes-Reginald Lawrence "If This Be Treason," and a version of Shakespeare's "Taming of the Shrew" that Alfred Lunt and Lynn Fontanne had fashioned for their own use. The crusading drama, though making a sometimes eloquent plea for peace, failed of Broadway approval, but the rowdy riot that was "The Shrew" ran on and on to become an uproarious success.

There was a second thriller, "Blind Alley," written by James Warwick and played principally by Roy Hargrave and George Coulouris, revealing a contest of wits and psychology, that was popular; a sentimental comedy, "Remember the Day," in which Philo Higley and Philip Dunning attempted to recapture those nostalgic reminiscences associated with puppy love, which found an interested public for several months. But September will be longest remembered as that month in which the Maxwell Anderson modern tragedy in verse, "Winterset," was revealed to a lightly startled but duly impressed populace. More of which appears in other pages of this edition.

There was an honest adaptation made by Sidney Howard of Humphrey Cobb's novel, "Paths of Glory," produced by Arthur Hopkins. The mechanics of the theatre got between the story and its listeners, resulting in the drama's failure. A comedy that was intelligently done and filled with interesting character studies of essentially unattractive people was called "A Touch of Brimstone." Leonora Kaghan and Anita Phillips wrote it and Roland Young and Mary Philips played it. Another was a simple something called "Moon Over Mulberry Street," which was frankly in the "Abie's Irish Rose" tradition and tried for a similar record. Nicholas Cosentino was the author.

The promise of September was in a measure sustained in October, but nothing was added to it. The Guild, for its third subscription performance, gave us the Gershwin musicalized version of DuBose Heyward's "Porgy," now called "Porgy and Bess." George Gershwin provided the score and his brother, Ira, worked with Mr. Heyward on the lyrics. The result was a success that was a shade overpowering. Audiences enthused but also wilted under the tension of it.

Close upon the heels of this musical excitement came "Jubilee," a musical comedy the Messrs. Cole Porter and Moss Hart had taken a trip around the world to write. "Jubilee" startled the Broadway natives somewhat. They had been accustomed to musical comedies of the revue order, usually studded with irrelevant interpolations, both musical and textual. "Jubilee" revealed an intelligent and coherent story of a royal family that escapes the confinements of its palaces and royal routine and goes in search of adventure. It was handsomely staged, splendidly acted by a cast headed by Mary Boland, and played to crowded houses for several months. It was finally withdrawn when Miss Boland was forced to return to Hollywood and an equally popular successor could not be found to take her place. Laura Hope Crews, who courageously tried to fill in, even though she had had no previous musical comedy experience, was more the Queen and less the comedienne.

A third major success in the October list was Sidney Kingsley's "Dead End." Mr. Kingsley, having won the Pulitzer award with "Men in White" two years before, took his time in the preparation of this newer opus. If the text failed to justify this additional care, the setting fitted to the play by Norman Bel Geddes supplied the lack. It was one of the outstanding stage pictures of the season and contributed no little to the drama's popularity. "Dead End" ran the season through and was set for a continued summer run as this record was compiled.

There were several interesting failures this month. "Sweet Mystery of Life," for one. "Sweet Mystery" had to do with life insurance, the story seeking to prove that any middle-aged hypochondriac who will buy himself an annuity and quit worrying can extend his expectancy a dozen years at least. The farce had three

authors—Richard Maibaum, Michael Wallach and George Haight
—and was provided with an extravagant setting in which mul-
tiple scenes were moved in and out like pieces of a jigsaw puzzle
(Donald Oenslager designed it). But the incidental scenes did
not hold well together and the plausibilities were too severely
stretched. Herman Shumlin, the producer, withdrew "Sweet Mystery" after eleven performances.

Arthur Hopkins produced Philip Barry's "Bright Star," this
being that usually sure playwright's first play in a season or two,
but withdrew it after a single week of disappointed audiences.
The play offered an interesting study of essentially uninteresting
characters, and this is a combination that rarely produces appealing drama. By contrast there was a drama called "Mulatto" concerned with racial prejudice. Written by a Negro poet, Langdon
Hughes, from the Negro's point of view, this one developed a
sufficient following, due to the boldness of its statement and the
artificial intensity of its dramatic climaxes, to hang on for several
months. "Mulatto" presents the problem of unhappy half-castes,
children in this instance of a plantation owner and his colored
housekeeper, after they achieve adolescence and sufficient education to unfit them for life with either the whites, who spurn them,
or the blacks, who resent them.

Walter Hampden brought a Martin Flavin play, "Achilles Had
a Heel," back from several successful trial performances in California, but New York would have none of it. Mr. Hampden's
character was that of a colored elephant keeper in a municipal
zoo and the play presumably exposed the human as well as the
animal race as victim of its baser instincts. It served rather to
expose Mr. Hampden as being sadly miscast.

There were major hits in November also. Helen Jerome's
adaptation of the Jane Austen classic, "Pride and Prejudice," the
first among them, found the playgoing public a little hungry for
the sentiment and grace of the older comedies. By emphasizing
the Jane Austen touch of irony and gift of wit in the casting of
the play Max Gordon succeeded in establishing a hit that ran for
two hundred and twenty-one performances.

Later in the month the George Kaufman-Katharine Dayton
"First Lady" applied the modern touch of social satire to the life
of such a politically minded somebody as Alice Roosevelt Long-
worth might have been and this, too, found great favor among
the lovers of high comedy and incisive wit.

Within the week this success was surpassed by that of an out-
and-out farce—Bella and Samuel Spewack's "Boy Meets Girl,"

which may be quite accurately described as a howling satire of the Hollywood scene—less extravagant than was the Kaufman-Hart "Once in a Lifetime" and equally as true to its subject.

A satisfying historical drama was Elsie Schauffler's "Parnell," for the playing of which two English actors of prominence, Margaret Rawlings and George Curzon, were imported by the Messrs. Robinson Smith and Frederick Ayer, a youthful firm of producers recently come into the theatre. A substantial hit was scored by "Parnell," which served to intensify the deep regret felt by the playwright's friends that she could not have lived to be witness to it. Mrs. Schauffler, the wife of a Kansas City physician, was taken from the rehearsals of "Parnell" to a hospital, where she died a few weeks before the play was produced. She had done some playwriting previously, but this was the Broadway recognition for which she had long waited.

Albert Bein extracted "Let Freedom Ring," a vivid social document, from a novel of Grace Lumpkin. A study of labor conditions in the cotton mills of the South, a good acting play as well, and one that was given a forceful performance by an organization of actor-enthusiasts. A little too strong on the propaganda side for uptown appreciation, though it did get twenty-nine performances, the play was withdrawn and later taken over by the Theatre Union, which is frankly radical in its drama preferences. Revived at the Provincetown Theatre a fortnight later it continued for seventy-nine additional performances.

Holiday time sweetened the play list. Helen Hayes brought "Victoria Regina" to town and immediately set the Hayes public cheering, both because this episodic biography of the beloved Victoria is thick with appealing sentiment, and because Miss Hayes, an an actress, achieved one of those exciting moments in which a surprised and delighted audience rises to acclaim a trick of the actor's trade. Covering the period following the death of Prince Albert and the discovery of Her Majesty at Balmoral Castle some sixteen years later Queen Victoria changes from a slim young matron to a somewhat dumpy old lady. To achieve this metamorphosis convincingly Miss Hayes resorted to dental accessories to puff out her cheeks, and this, with the padding of her clothes, presented so complete an alteration of physical appearance that audiences invariably stopped the performance to indicate their admiration for the artist. "Victoria Regina" was played through the remainder of the season to a succession of sold-out houses and was withdrawn in June because Miss Hayes insisted on a ten-week vacation.

Katharine Cornell, who had been touring again with "Romeo and Juliet," brought her company back to New York for a holiday fortnight before she began rehearsals for a revival of Bernard Shaw's "Saint Joan." The original Cornell Juliet success was repeated, but the fortnight was sufficient to satisfy those who had overlooked the first engagement.

A third lady of standing in the theatre, Alla Nazimova, who had been touring the country with a revival of Henrik Ibsen's "Ghosts," slightly modified in spirit and text, brought her production to the Empire Theatre and was received with considerable enthusiasm. Mme. Nazimova had long wanted to play Mrs. Alving, but had been denied the opportunity until Robert Henderson, promoter of the annual Dramatic Festivals at the University of Michigan in Ann Arbor, made the revival possible. Her success in the role has continued, the Broadway engagement being twice extended and a supplemental Spring engagement being played in May.

Clifford Odets, hailed, with reason, as a promising dramatist of the immediate future, following the success of his "Awake and Sing" and "Waiting for Lefty," was represented now by a new social drama entitled "Paradise Lost." Both the Group Theatre and the young playwright's admirers had set great store by this opus. It proved a disappointment to many, but more than a few found it a drama of first importance. Its weakness appeared to center in a confused statement, joined with a determination on the playwright's part to be simple and Chekovian at any cost. A cast crowded with types and a play crowded with irrelevant incidents was the result.

A spectacular failure, stemming from the new interest of the motion picture capitalists, and one proving that even a great deal of money cannot make a bad play good, was that of Martin Flavin's "Tapestry in Gray." B. P. Schulberg of Hollywood provided sufficient backing for a massive setting and a star cast. Everything that could be done for the drama, in the understanding of its promoters, was done. And yet so muddled was the story in the telling, and of so little appeal when clarified, the play lived only through a forced run of four weeks. It would reasonably have died in one without innumerable financial transfusions.

The new year started with a succession of failures. Pathetic failures, many of them, inspiring frequent doubt as to the sanity of the producers. Which is not an uncommon but always a depressing experience. Before January was passed, however, the Owen and Donald Davis adaptation of "Ethan Frome," Dodie

Smith's "Call It a Day" and Lynn Riggs' "Russet Mantle" had done much to restore the playgoers' normal state of mind. Both the Davises' "Ethan Frome" and the English playwright's "Call It a Day" are included in this volume's collection of important contributions to the season. Mr. Riggs' "Russet Mantle" wavered a little unsteadily between an exhibit of character comedy and the dramatist's natural liking for social drama. It met with fair success.

The interesting quasi-successes and quicker failures included James Hagan's first play since he had a season's success with "One Sunday Afternoon." This was an honest study of modern problems facing Kansas farmers, not necessarily because they are farmers, but because they are farmers in Kansas with Kansas convictions. This one worked himself to death, educated a son who turned communist and lost his crops through dust storms and drought.

The late Jobyna Howland, hungry for a re-establishment of her Broadway prestige after years in the motion pictures, came East to play the heroine of a comedy written for her by Zoe Akins, called "O, Evening Star." The story, based on the life adventures of three of Miss Akins' actress friends, Marie Dressler the best known among them, provided Miss Howland with a part somewhat beyond her histrionic range. This, added to a none too convincing story, proved the undoing of "O, Evening Star."

Morris Gest, after years of inactivity following the death of his father-in-law, the late David Belasco, decided to bring from London a Chinese classic done over by Dr. S. I. Hsiung, entitled "Lady Precious Stream." The play, a romance of the high-born lady and the lowly gardener's son, is given in the Chinese manner, plus a reader to explain the plot. It has moments of great charm and is weakened only by its length and repetitions.

The Federal theatre began to function in February. Its first production was that of a play by the Negro actor, Frank Wilson, called "Walk Together Chillun." Being lightly a play of propaganda, praying for racial unity among the colored people, it proved interesting but a little heavy for colored audiences. The Federals tried again a few weeks later with "Jefferson Davis," a biographical drama written in a series of episodes by John McGee. Only the Daughters of the Confederacy were definitely moved by this one, though it gave work to a large number of idle actors, stagehands, etc. In that same week the WPA forces did score something resembling a success with a satirical comedy written by Edwin and Albert Barker called "American Holiday." This one took the American mob for a ride through such a typically American scene as that developed by the Hauptmann trial in Flemington, N. J., when the newspaper photographers landed and soon thereafter had the situation well in hand.

The one major success scored in February was that of S. N. Behrman's "End of Summer," with Ina Claire and Osgood Perkins its featured players. This indictment of rich as well as radical units of our citizenry is also included by excerpt in these pages. A minor success, sustained largely by the popularity of Peggy Conklin, was the comedy called "Co-respondent Unknown," written by Mildred Harris and Harold Goldman. In the matter of an inoffensive boldness this piece was a worthy successor to the bundling comedy, "The Pursuit of Happiness," which Miss Conklin played successfully a year ago.

An English folk comedy, "Love on the Dole," revealed a good job of honest writing and honest character drawing, exposing the effect of the dole in England on what is still the sterling English character, even among the lower classes. Heading the cast was Wendy Hiller, an importation from Lancashire, who added definitely to the appeal of the play.

Richard Barthelmess, long absent from the living theatre, which he left as a lad and to which he returned as a plump young man, made a Broadway re-entry in James Cain's dramatization of his own novel, "The Postman Always Rings Twice." Mr. Barthelmess and Mary Philips played the leading characters, those of a tramp of the road and a restless wife married to the Greek proprietor of a gas station in California. The tramp helps the lady murder the Greek to clear the way to their marriage. She is killed in a car smash and he is hung for the Greek's murder. This is the type of play that, whatever its technical perfections, is pretty sure to miss popularity, again for the simple reason before stated that it is hard to write an appealing story about repellent humans.

Katharine Cornell was ready with her revival of Shaw's "Saint Joan" in March. The play was first done by the Theatre Guild in 1911, and well done, with Winifred Lenihan playing the Maid of Domremy. The Cornell production had none of the earmarks of a revival, being backed by a handsome new Jo Mielziner setting and superbly cast in all its parts. A sextet of fine actors assigned to its chief male roles included Arthur Byron, Charles Waldron, Brian Aherne, Maurice Evans, Eduoardo Cianelli and George Coulouris. Miss Cornell's personal triumph was again complete and, true to her vow not to neglect the minor theatre centers, she set forth on a Spring tour after eleven weeks of playing in

New York.

Alfred Lunt and Lynn Fontanne also decided in March to come in from the road with the new Robert Sherwood comedy, "Idiot's Delight." Their success was immediate and the popularity of the new play, a devastating arraignment of the idiocy that is war, as more fully appears in other pages of this issue, exceeded that of any play in which the Lunts have appeared under Theatre Guild auspices.

This was also a good month for the reappearance of stage veterans. William Gillette, who, at 80, had been traipsing defiantly about the Eastern country in a revival of Austin Strong's "Three Wise Fools," had a farewell week in town, opening on Sunday night to permit some of his old pals of the theatre to come and see him. George M. Cohan, who was among those on the welcoming committee, followed Mr. Gillette the same week with a new number he had dashed off during the Winter and called "Dear Old Darling." Not a bad comedy, but not up to the Cohan standard and played in much too large a theatre (the Alvin). George wisely withdrew it in two weeks.

The Group Theatre, which had failed with Odets' "Paradise Lost," hoped to recover prestige with a new version of Theodore Dreiser's "The American Tragedy." This was called "The Case of Clyde Griffith" and was a modernized translation by Erwin Piscator and Lena Schmidt which has been successfully staged in Europe, and which employs a Speaker (or Chorus) as a leading character. The Speaker stands in the orchestra pit and both analyzes and explains the social significance of successive scenes. The Group Theatre production was attractive and Morris Carnovsky gave an eloquent reading as Speaker, but save for the enthusiasm of the few, there was little audience response.

Joyce Carey, daughter of Lillian Braithwaite of England and herself an actress well known to the English theatre, turned playwright a year ago and, under the nom de theatre of Jay Mallory, wrote a sentimental drama entitled "Sweet Aloes." It boasted a good old-fashioned melodramatic plot in which an indiscreet English girl, about to bear the son of Lord Farrington a child, agrees to turn the infant at birth over to the childless wife of his young lordship that the family line may be carried on. Financed by the Farringtons the unhappy young woman comes to America to start life afresh. Years later, after she has married an American lawyer, the Farringtons visit America and a meeting between the real and the adopted mothers of the Farrington heir is arranged. Their mutual understandings and confessions clear the situation emotionally and dismiss the audience in tears. A too obvious drama, it may be. Broadway, at least, turned thumbs down.

April and May brought the season to an end, as usual, and brought little that was new and worthy into the theatre. One good musical play, "On Your Toes," made sport of the interpretive dancers and their modern ballets without sacrifice of good nature in the spoofing. Ray Bolger, who has come closer than any of his fellows to filling the place of the late Jack Donahue as a dancer-comedian of the better class, had the lead, with the exciting Tamara Geva, Prof. Monty Woolley and Luella Gear to help him.

There was a bit of excitement caused also by the production of "Bury the Dead" as a regular Broadway attraction. This impressive one-act protest written by a twenty-three-year-old Brooklynite, Irwin Shaw, had been given on numerous occasions as a special benefit feature. Alex Yokel, who had had a season's success with "Three Men on a Horse," read it and, becoming enthused, decided to reassemble its cast and produce it properly. The result was a barrage of laudatory reviews and a few weeks of excellent business. "Bury the Dead" is a reflection of "Miracle at Verdun" in that it relates the protest against war of soldiers killed in battle. A burial detail lays six cadavers in a trench (the same being the orchestra pit in the theatre), and is about to cover them with earth when the six rise in their burial clothes and refuse to be buried. Neither pleas nor high commands can alter their determination. When their womenfolk are summoned to beg them, for the sake of peace and harmony, now that they are dead please to remain dead, they still refuse. At the play's end they are crawling over the side of the trench to begin a march across the world that shall, by inference, voice the protest of all dead men killed in war against the foolishness of war.

Walter Hampden, who had revived "Cyrano de Bergerac" on tour to recoup his losses with "Achilles Had a Heel," brought that sturdy poetic romance of Rostand's, in the Brian Hooker adaptation, to Broadway for a final farewell. He planned playing a fortnight but was induced to stay on for four weeks, which brought his total Cyrano performances over a thousand. He insists that he is getting too old to caper as the nimble swordsman and will not play Cyrano again. We shall see.

The WPA scored one of its major financial successes in April with a production of "Macbeth" by the Negro theatre unit. The version was one arranged by Orson Welles and John Houseman for a Haitian setting, with all the company representing gaily costumed West Indian natives in place of hardy Scots. The text was unchanged. There were thirty weird sisters in place of three, and much was made of the "jungle" scenes. The production created a good deal of talk, gave vast satisfaction to the colored colony and continued for many weeks.

Ann Nichols, still hoping to achieve another "Abie's Irish Rose," produced a comedy called "Pre-Honeymoon" which she wrote with Alfred Van Ronkel. It was bad, but not bad enough. A revival of "Parnell" introduced Dennis King and Edith Barrett in the roles of the Irish statesman and Katie O'Shea. The play was thus frankly reduced to the stature of a simple love romance, with less emphasis placed upon its value as historical drama. It lingered briefly. Nazimova returned for her final engagement in "Ghosts," which had been to the Pacific coast and back. There was a new musical revue, "New Faces," which Leonard Sillman staged. This being fairly original entertainment, and there being only "On Your Toes" by way of musical competition, lasted well into the summer.

The Players Club revived George Ade's "The County Chairman" as its annual gesture toward remembered favorites, and, for the first time in its recent history, came a cropper. Whether it was because the Ade comedy was neither old enough to be a curiosity nor of recent enough date to give it contemporary interest, or because the cast was not as star-studded as the Players usually provide, is a debatable question, but the revival lost money for its promoters.

"Winterset," in order to capitalize the winning of the drama critics' award, came back for a fortnight's engagement before being retired for the season. And that proved a fitting finish for the season's activities. The play closed to a succession of large audiences. Burgess Meredith was starred now in the role of Mio, the hero; Lee Baker played Judge Gaunt, vice Richard Bennett, retired because of illness, and Eva Langbord substituted for Margo, who was the original Miriamne. They were credited with giving the best reading the play had been given.

Statistically it was a less flourishing season than that of the year before, there being only 102 new productions as opposed to 132 the season of 1934-35. But, those of us who went through it, are quite content.

THE SEASON IN CHICAGO

By Charles Collins
Dramatic Critic of the *Chicago Tribune*

THE history of the Chicago stage during the theatrical year of 1935-1936 does not make severe demands upon the keepers of the archives. This period marked a new "low" in the number of play titles—a precipitous decrease of fifty per cent when compared to the score of the preceding year. Before 1929 the annual catalogue would run to well over 100 items; but my count for the season which expired early in June, 1936, contains only 21.

Taken by themselves, these figures are ominous. They suggest that the legitimate stage in Chicago is rapidly dying out and that in a few more years it will become totally extinct, as it now is in many other American cities of major rank. This may come to pass, and I am prepared to accept the threatened catastrophe with a fatalistic shrug of the shoulders. I see no remedy for the major cause of the decline of the living stage in this country—the competition of the movies and their predatory interference with dramatic productions by offers of opulent Hollywood contracts to every promising actor in sight. But I am a die-hard in this matter and refuse to give up the ship, although she seems to be badly riddled.

Chicago's distressing score for 1935-1936 is only a part of the story. The picture was not as dark as the tally-card proclaims; it contained certain high-lights of promise, certain auguries of improvement. Although the quantity was slight, the quality of productions was superior. The audit sheets of the box-offices told of increasing patronage, a renewal of the habit of playgoing, a passing of the six-year-old fog from the economic skies. People in general who did not bother about keeping score regarded the season as a marked advance over its immediate predecessors.

The plays and musical shows whose Chicago premières fell within the year ending June 8, 1936, were as follows:

"Tobacco Road," with Henry Hull. (Closed after five weeks by the civic authorities.)

"Dodsworth," with Walter Huston. (Ten weeks.)

"Rose Marie" in revival. (Two weeks.)

16

"Her Master's Voice" in revival. (Three weeks; Chicago management.)

"Romeo and Juliet," with Katharine Cornell. (Two weeks.)

"Personal Appearance," with Gladys George. (Eleven weeks.)

"Anything Goes," with William Gaxton and Victor Moore. (Five weeks.)

"The Old Maid," with Judith Anderson and Helen Menken. (Three weeks.)

"Squaring the Circle," with Glenn Hunter. (Two and one-half weeks.)

"The Great Waltz," with Guy Robertson, Marion Claire and Gladys Baxter. (Fifteen weeks.)

"Boy Meets Girl," with special Chicago cast. (Fifteen weeks.)

"Ghosts," with Alla Nazimova. (Two weeks.)

"The Taming of the Shrew," with Alfred Lunt and Lynn Fontanne. (Two weeks.)

"Porgy and Bess," with Theatre Guild cast. (Three weeks.)

"Cyrano de Bergerac," with Walter Hampden. (Two weeks.)

"At Home Abroad," with Beatrice Lillie, Ethel Waters, and full Broadway company. (Six weeks.)

"From Out of the Darkness," under Chicago management. (Two performances only.)

"Winterset," with Burgess Meredith. (Three weeks.)

"Awake and Sing," by New York Group Theatre company. (Five weeks.) Also special matinee of "Waiting for Lefty."

"Three Men on a Horse," return engagement, with Jack Sheehan. (Two weeks.)

"Saint Joan," with Katharine Cornell. (Two weeks.)

This list contained only four failures. They were the once famous "Rose Marie," whose revival with a third-rate cast for "the road" in its more benighted aspects proved that American taste in operetta has advanced greatly during the past ten years; "Her Master's Voice," Clare Kummer's comedy of several seasons ago, bluntly acted by a middle class cast with most of its irresponsible feminine flutter lost in the interpretation; "Squaring the Circle," a specimen of Soviet humor hopefully brought out to Chicago under the management of a New York dentist because it had a cut-rate success among the Russophiles of New York; and "From Out of the Darkness," a drama of war's horrors, juvenile of authorship and amateur of management.

The other titles formed an exceptionally choice collection and were welcomed with enthusiasm by the playgoing element, which seemed to have come to life with a hunger for the stage after a

long period of sleeping sickness or economic stupefaction. Short
runs were the custom of the season, except in the cases of "Dodsworth," "The Great Waltz," "Personal Appearance" and "Boy
Meets Girl"; but this was due to the mysterious arrangements of
the booking offices on Broadway rather than to box-office reactions. All of the two- and three-week engagements, it seemed,
could have been doubled.

Katharine Cornell figured twice on the Chicago schedule, and
this was counted as an unusual blessing. She brought her brilliant
production of "Romeo and Juliet" here in the fall, on the last leg
of her transcontinental tour; and she returned early in June with
Shaw's "Saint Joan," to the accompaniment of hosannahs from
the press and an energetic scramble for tickets by the public. She
had avoided Chicago during the year of 1934-1935, but not her
Chicago admirers, for many of them made a pilgrimage to Milwaukee to observe her Shakespearean début; and thus her two
visits of 1935-1936 had an air of squaring of her account. Her appearance in Shaw's fine historical interpretation of the medieval
mind might easily be taken as a parable of the American theatre;
for she is its Saint Joan, she finds it in a deplorable condition,
and she crusades for its salvation—hearing voices, perhaps, in the
bells of locomotives that carry her about the country, but shutting her ears to the temptations of Satan, who in this elaborate
metaphor would be the movies.

After "Romeo and Juliet" in the swift, vivid Cornellian production—generally regarded here as the best in a lifetime—Chicago saw another tour de force in Shakespearean interpretation,
also representing leadership in acting. This, of course, was the
Lunt-Fontanne "Taming of the Shrew," in the Theatre Guild's
dizzy stylization. Alfred and Lynn can do no wrong in the eyes
of their admirers here, and if a few of the elder Shakespearean
connoisseurs lifted eyebrows at this daft extravaganza, they were
like the few conservatives who stood aghast in the flood-tide of
admiration for the New Deal's early political eccentricities. No
one dared to tell Lynn's lord and master that he slapped her
bottom often enough to suggest an obsession or a complex; or to
hint to Alfred's consort that a protruded lower lip can become a
bad habit, even among the birthmarked Bourbons. It was all good,
blowzy fun, however, bearing the glad tidings that Shakespeare
is more amusing than a night club.

Ibsen came to life with Nazimova's staging of "Ghosts," and
had a *succès fou*. Praise by superlatives was the order of the
year, and this Mrs. Alving was pronounced the best to be seen

on the American stage in our native language. Playgoers who had
never seen "Ghosts" before read this in the newspapers and sagely
nodded assent. It was an interpretation of the character which
recalled to some the Duse whom they had seen in youth in Italian
travels; and to many others the aged Duse of her last American
tour.

Two prize plays, much publicized because of their blue ribbons,
were also on the catalogue. The first-comer was "The Old Maid,"
in all its original glory of period costumes, with the smoldering
Judith Anderson and the emotional Helen Menken as the strange,
frustrated sisters—Pultizer choice for first honors in 1934-1935.
Women playgoers thought it was too, too divine. It is not my
practice to nag at awards of prizes and call shrilly for a new
trial; therefore I will let "The Old Maid" pass as a premiated
article with the statement that I did not find it a notable contribution to dramatic literature.

This same point of view applies to Maxwell Anderson's
"Winterset," which arrived with a badge pinned on its chest by
the ink-stained fingers of New York's dramatic critics. There was,
I understand, a negative minority vote of three when the gentlemen of the press came to the balloting—a bitter, cynical and vocal
minority which hooted vigorously in print at the award. I arrayed
myself with this minority when "Winterset" came to Chicago, but
my colleagues went into dithering ecstasies over the play, and
the public voted strongly in favor at the box-office.

My arguments against "Winterset" are, briefly, these: Its mood
is bilious with the synthetic ire that well-fed American literary
men affect when they go in quest of "social justice" and royalties;
that it is merely a gangster melodrama with pretentious trim-
mings; that in striving for poetic expression in a new medium—
the American vernacular and the contemporary American scene—
the author has been haunted with discordant echoes from the
classic edifice; and that the verse, when it is not striking Elizabethan gestures in underworld slang, is patterned after the
drugged and entranced style of Swinburne in rhythm and
metaphor. As poetry, I felt that "Winterset" was merely artifice
and *pastiche*. In acting, stage direction and scene design, I agree
that the production had high value.

The Group Theatre of New York, whose name had already been
borrowed by gatherings of local amateurs (gatherings that ought
to be lanced, according to a wisecrack of thirty years ago), came
to Chicago late in the spring to make its bow and to form diplomatic relations prefatory to a longer residence next season. It

offered "Awake and Sing," by Clifford Odets, the young man from its own ranks whom it seeks to canonize as a literary Messiah, seeking to lead the world into a Bronxian Utopia. He has the gift of stirring speech in his native idiom; and a keen eye for the characters of his environment. He also has the reformatory mania of a college sophomore who has just discovered Karl Marx. After searching "Awake and Sing" closely for its message of importance to the world, I begin to suspect that its strongest argument is in favor of the suppression of the maternal instinct in the Bronx, for it is the greedy, grasping, protective matriarchism of the Momma in the story which causes most of the woe. Master Odets will outgrow this mood, I believe, when he becomes a Poppa.

Chicago reacted favorably to the acting of the Group company. Two of the able players in the cast, incidentally, are alumni of the extinct Goodman Theatre repertory company, formerly under the management of the Art Institute of Chicago. They are Roman Bohnen and Art Smith.

Various miscellaneous and unclassifiable items have been omitted from the scoring. They were: Cornelia Otis Skinner (one week) and Ruth Draper (two weeks), lyceum entertainers; three plays on a summer suburban program with professional casts— "Marie Rose," with Edith Barrett; "The Crime at Blossom's," with Jessie Royce Landis and Eric Dressler; and "Noah," with Burgess Meredith; two benefit performances of operettas in German—"Das Dreimaederlhaus" and "Die Csardasprinzess"; a number of old-school melodrama revivals on the showboat "Dixiana," which went into bankruptcy in mid-season; and two engagements, of eight days each, of Col. W. de Basil's Ballet Russe.

To complete the picture and assure the world that Chicago is, after all, a metropolis where the theatre arts may be found in some abundance, one should glance at the operatic stage. The year has been brightened with the following opera activities: Chicago City Opera Company, in the Civic Opera House, five weeks, plus one pre-season and one post-season performance; the San Carlo Opera Company, four weeks in the Auditorium Theatre in two engagements; the Detroit Civic Opera Company, three performances in the Auditorium.

The longest run of the season was that of "Three Men on a Horse," which is statistically entered in the records of the preceding year. This comedy opened on March 31, 1935, and ran until December 14, achieving a record for non-musical shows since 1929 —37 weeks.

The most notable engagement of the season from the box-office point of view was that of "The Great Waltz." This operetta-spectacle from Radio City, New York, ran for 15 weeks in the Auditorium to an attendance which would represent a full year's capacity business at any of the smaller Chicago theatres. So far as public enthusiasm was concerned, this was the most striking event of the year. There was general enthusiasm for this brilliant musical diversion.

The censorship of "Tobacco Road" also made history. Here are the facts in this *cause célèbre:* After the play had been in performance for five weeks, Mayor Kelly went to see it, accompanied by his wife. The next day the license of the Selwyn Theatre was revoked on his order. He stated that he found the play to be "a mass of filth and obscenity" in violation of the city ordinances. The management of the company promptly secured a temporary injunction, restraining the city from interference with the play, from United States District Judge William H. Holly. The city then took the case into the United States Circuit Court of Appeals (Judges Lindley, Alschuler and Sparks), which sustained Mayor Kelly's action and ordered the injunction dissolved. This decision was based upon the court's view of the mayor's motive: "It cannot be said that he acted without justification or arbitrarily."

The liberals raged; the free speechers foamed at the mouth; the censor-chasers, the minor intelligentsia, the college profs, the star-eyed idealists, the socialists, the communists, the rakes, bawds and Rabelaisians were highly indignant. But the Chicago air smelled sweeter after the departure of "Tobacco Road." I agreed that it was properly banished as an example of blazing impudence and a case of disorderly conduct. Oddly enough, "Tobacco Road" was the first play to be closed by the authorities in Chicago since 1929 and its predecessor, "Frankie and Johnny," was written by the same Jack Kirkland who dramatized Erskine Caldwell's study of total depravity among the Georgia peasantry.

Federal theatricals sponsored by the Works Progress Administration have been omitted from my statistics because they fall outside the normal history of the stage as an institution. Two downtown playhouses of the obsolescent type—the Blackstone and the Great Northern—were opened on March 8 under WPA auspices, the Blackstone with an average stock company point of view, the Great Northern with an "art theatre" or "experimental" policy. They are still in operation at the date of writing (June 8), and promise to continue through the summer. Their performances thus far have been mediocre. The Blackstone has staged "A Texas Steer," "Secret Service," "On Trial" and "Three Wise Fools." The Great Northern has presented Ibsen's "An Enemy of the People," a version of Goethe's "Urfaust" which was largely travesty; and "Chalk Dust," an example of WPA playwriting with metropolitan high school administration as its theme.

As a sidelight upon Chicago's stage activity during the past year, statistics on weeks of operation per theatre may be of value. Here is the count: Grand Opera House, 21 weeks; Harris, 45 weeks; Selwyn, 30 weeks; Erlanger, 20 weeks; Auditorium Theatre (excluding opera, ballet and concerts), 15 weeks; Blackstone, 2½ weeks regular, 14 weeks WPA; Great Northern, 13 weeks WPA; Studebaker, 3 weeks plus 2 performances.

THE SEASON IN SAN FRANCISCO

By Fred Johnson

Drama Editor of *The Call-Bulletin*

WITH "Go West" as their slogan, New York producers made the season of 1935-36 the period of their most intense cultivation of the greener pastures they had visioned on this California coast.

A year also of the greatest number of Broadway play successes to visit San Francisco—nearly all within the season's latter half—it witnessed four of the original producers personally launching their attractions for coast premières. Of these, three supervised the recasting from New York and Hollywood talent, while Brock Pemberton, the fourth, made San Francisco his first visit as the season ended for Gladys George's opening in "Personal Appearance," with his Broadway cast intact. The two weeks' engagement brought him no disappointment.

Here he completed arrangements for Miss George's few weeks' screen interlude at Paramount, starring in "Valiant Is the Word for Carrie," before resuming her stage role in London.

J. J. Shubert led the adventurous band in October with his coast production of Noel Coward's "Bitter Sweet," starring Evelyn Laye in her original London role, but with inferior support. Her name drew fair patronage at the Curran Theatre for three weeks, but the succeeding "Blossom Time," featuring Paul Keast and Diana Galen, fared worse during a fortnight's run. Meanwhile Shubert backed at the Columbia a play brought up from Hollywood, titled "Common Flesh" and of reputed authorship by Mae West. Its death came after five nights.

A. H. Woods and Arch Selwyn appeared next in person with Ayn Rand's "The Night of January 16," its able Pacific Coast cast headed by Nedda Harrigan, Edwin Maxwell and Herbert Rawlinson. The run of five weeks at the Geary, lengthened by word of mouth over its locally chosen trial juries, exceeded that of any other Broadway hit of the season in San Francisco.

Walter Huston's coincident four weeks at the Curran in "Dodsworth" might have been extended as much longer but for the pressure of bookings.

Herman Shumlin completed the quartet of visiting producers,

23

directing his Hollywood and Broadway cast in "The Children's Hour," headed by Barbara Leeds as the schoolgirl menace, after playing a different role in the New York production. Alma Kruger was cast as the grandmother, Sally Bates and Marion Burns as the teachers. The drama's much discussed theme met with less than the expected interest, although the play's 19 days' run at the Curran exceeded by three days that of "The Old Maid," co-starring Judith Anderson and Helen Menken.

Mme. Alla Nazimova in "Ghosts" received enthusiastic patronage for a late-winter fortnight at the same theatre, supported by McKay Morris, Harry Ellerbe and Beatrice de Neergaard.

Further evidence of Broadway producers' interest in the Pacific Coast field is Lee Shubert's announcement of plans to stage new plays in San Francisco and Los Angeles, as well as in New York. First of his projected California offerings will be George Kelly's new play, "Reflected Glory," set to open at the Curran Theatre in San Francisco, July 20, and planned for a New York booking in the fall.

The problem of New York casting, which he has found increasingly difficult, and the availability of Hollywood talent, are reasons given by Shubert for his westward move.

San Francisco's discriminating theatre-goers have enjoyed the first fruits of a nation-wide road revival as well as continuous activity by the coast-defending producers. They are set for another Katharine Cornell feast early in July, when she returns after a three years' absence for a fortnight's engagement in "Saint Joan," to be followed by "Russet Mantle," with Martha Sleeper and others of the original company.

Homer Curran's production activities for the season were more limited than usual. His presentation of May Robson in "Kind Lady," with Ralph Forbes and Granville Bates, was disappointing, due to public preference for the star in the serio-comedy roles of her old popularity. In association with Melville Brown, Curran presented Ina Claire in "Ode to Liberty," with Robert Warwick and Alexander Clark. Her two weeks failed of the patronage she received here in "Rebound" and "Reunion in Vienna."

With Edwin Lester as associate, he ended the season with a revival of "The Merry Widow," starring Helen Gahagan, with John Ehrle as Prince Danilo. The offering received a two weeks' fair patronage. Its successor, "The Desert Song," with George Houston, Francia White and Bobby Jarvis, failed pitifully, despite its recognized merit in voices and production.

The season's end marked the return of Henry Duffy to his old theatre, the Alcazar, which in 1924 became the nucleus of his chain of coast theatres, abandoned several years ago. For its re-opening he brought back Charlotte Greenwood in "Leaning on Letty," originally "Post Road," for a four weeks' run prior to her London appearance in the play under Duffy's management. His productions of "Three Men on a Horse," featuring Chester Clute and Matt Briggs, and the Theatre Guild success, "Call It a Day," were scheduled to follow.

Duffy's earlier offerings of the season were staged in Louis Lurie's Geary Theatre. They included his most pretentious musical, "Anything Goes," with Hugh O'Connell, George Murphy and Shirley Ross, for an unprofitable fortnight's engagement; "Accent on Youth," with Otto Kruger and Martha Sleeper, and "Petrified Forest," with Conrad Nagel, Lois Moran and Roger Pryor. The dramatic offerings were also of short duration.

Jack Kirkland and Sam H. Grisman's "Tobacco Road," starring Henry Hull, ended five weeks of successful business at the Curran as the season began, with similar success for Alex Yokel's "Three Men on a Horse" in opposition at the Geary.

The Old Globe Theatre Players achieved three lusty weeks of streamlined Shakespearean repertoire at the Alcazar, following a summer at the San Diego Exposition.

Drama in the open air had its summer revival across the bay in the Greek Theatre (University of California) productions of "The Taming of the Shrew" and Sean O'Casey's "Within the Gates," under the festival management of Carol Eberts of New York, with Julius Evans as director. Rollo Peters and Peggy Wood headed a worthy cast of local players. Both these offerings and the university Little Theatre's later production of "Elizabeth the Queen" were the year's outstanding non-commercial attractions and were well patronized. Stanford University's contribution was a production of "Othello" as the finale of its summer drama course under the direction of William Thornton, Shakespearean actor of western note.

The Federal Theatre Project of this area made a belated start in an unpopular play, Andreyeff's "Sabine Women." Its costly production of "The Taming of the Shrew" and the locally authored "Woman Hate" did little better. But on moving into the downtown Columbia Theatre the group won a more general following with productions of "The First Legion," "Lady Say Yes" and "Chalk Dust." The latter has been an emphatic hit.

The San Francisco Museum Theatre, organized to feature

plays of historic California interest, succumbed after a brief run of "Gold Eagle Guy" in a remote Lincoln Park playhouse above the Golden Gate. Other little theatre groups carried on, however, the Wayfarers of waterfront loft fame among the more tenacious, opening its new home with a production of Robert Nathan's "Jonah." And Baldwin McGaw, of the Fairmont Playhouse, greeted the summer with an impressive "Hamlet."

A loss to the San Francisco Rialto and to readers of his seasoned comments was caused by the illness and retirement of George C. Warren, for many years drama critic of the San Francisco *Chronicle*. He had completed in this newspaper his recollections of players he had known through many years of devotion to the theatre as manager and reviewer.

THE SEASON IN SOUTHERN CALIFORNIA

BY EDWIN SCHALLERT

Drama Editor of the *Los Angeles Times*

THE inception of Federal activities in the field of the stage was the most important new event during the theatrical season of 1935-1936 in Southern California. More than thirty productions were given under WPA auspices. The subjects were many and varied. Some new plays were offered, and revivals ranged to the classics, early American, a farce of Hoyt, and other vintage expressions in the dramatic art.

It is estimated that expenditures have so far totaled in excess of $800,000. Some fifteen hundred persons are employed in the work, of whom between 400 and 500 are actors. Ninety per cent of the money spent goes into salaries, and about 10 per cent into materials.

To date, very little has come out of the whole undertaking, except the employment feature. One divertisement of revue type, "Follow the Parade," scored a hit, moving from a downtown showhouse to Hollywood, with a later presentation at the Greek Theatre, an open-air establishment. "Black Empire," which gave prominence to colored actors, "Censored," "Chalk Dust," "A String of Pearls," "Enemy of the People," "Knight of the Burning Pestle," and "Mary Stuart" were other plays, which had double engagements either in Los Angeles and Hollywood, or in some other locality. A revival of "Seventh Heaven" merited praise. "Six Characters in Search of an Author," "Noah," "Our

American Cousin," "The Bishop's Candlesticks," "Under Two Flags," "Twelfth Night" and "The Octoroon" were presented.

One of the difficulties seems the developing of an audience. There is no existent one as, say, might be found in Russia for a theatre of the people. Routined showgoers appear, in some cases, hardly cognizant of the enterprise. It's off the beaten path. Yet there are certain indices in it all which can't be ignored. The prices, for example, are in direct competition with the film theatres. There is a certain ambulatory character to the activity that is particularly fitting to the geographical situation in the Los Angeles vicinity, which has always been so perplexing. What is meant by this is that the city spreads over so much territory that it is difficult to get people from one section to visit another, except for an inspiring reason. The Federal theatre, evidencing apparently some recognition of this fact, and possessing the facilities through its control of playhouses, moves its attractions about, and may do this in a larger way in the future. The circus has long been aware of the necessity of shifting from one location to another during its visits if it expects to appeal to the maximum audience.

Today, outside of the Federal theatres, there is very little if anything going on in downtown Los Angeles. Henry Duffy holds the fort in Hollywood, though he is practically alone there. Homer Curran productions are still given at the Belasco Theatre, with some thought also of the Biltmore, which is still the home of the road company—when and if there are such!

The 1935-36 season was a lean year in the professional realm, unless a WPA project is to be thus classified. Most effort was sporadic, and again the community theatres carried the beacon for the original type of activity. That, of course, has its great disadvantages, but it is, at any rate, a definite attempt at some sort of progress. Notable progress, of course, in the instance of the Pasadena Community Playhouse, which still is far in the lead.

Of the New York stage plays chosen by Mr. Mantle, as the ten best for the 1935-36 season, only "Call It a Day," presented by Duffy, was seen. It opened within a month of the end of the fiscal year. Violet Heming and Conway Tearle played the leading roles of wife and husband. Kay Linaker, as the elder daughter; Lauri Beatty, as the younger; Catherine Doucet, as the garrulous friend of the wife; May Beatty, Valerie Cossart, Clare Vedera, Eily Malyon, Colin Hunter and Leona Maricle were other principals who made a good impression. The quality of the work of

Joan Fontaine, sister of Olivia de Havilland of the films, as the girl next door, was delightful. The production was admirably staged.

Duffy's chief hit during the season was "Leaning on Letty," adapted to the needs of Charlotte Greenwood from the "Post Road," seen last season in New York. This ran for ten weeks. Other Duffy plays registered as follows: "Three Men on a Horse," which visited on tour last season, nine weeks; "Accent on Youth," with Otto Kruger, eight weeks; "Anything Goes," seven weeks; "Night of January 16," which had its first presentation as "The Woman on Trial" in Hollywood, six weeks. "Petticoat Fever" with Dennis King also had a short run.

"The Drunkard," of course, still holds forth as an institution, having passed its 1100th performance. Galt Belt, its sponsor, tried another experiment with "Murder in the Red Barn," not very fortunately, mingling cabaret and play. Also he was associated with two performances in the Greek Theatre that had Rollo Peters as their moving spirit.

One must applaud Mr. Peters for a superior presentation of "Within the Gates." Though it only was staged for one night, the results were brilliant. Peggy Converse gave a most creditable interpretation of the girl, who is dignified by no very pleasant name, and the ensemble was remarkable. Less fortunate was the Peters-Peggy Wood venture into Shakespeare with "Taming of the Shrew," though Miss Wood endowed her work with a great deal of personal charm.

Visiting companies were headed by Walter Huston in "Dodsworth," from which Fay Bainter was greatly missed; Helen Menken and Judith Anderson in the Pulitzer-prize-winning "The Old Maid," Ina Claire in "Ode to Liberty," and Gladys George in "Personal Appearance." Katharine Cornell arrived with "Saint Joan" almost at the close of the fiscal year, and had probably one of the biggest first nights in Southern California annals. Her company and the staging were excellent. Alla Nazimova in "Ghosts," arriving earlier in the season, was also a sensation. Of the other touring attractions "Dodsworth" pleased the most.

Of Coast origin were a rather weak production of "Bury the Dead," "Kind Lady" with May Robson starred, and Ralph Forbes as the menace, which only lasted a week; "The Children's Hour," a fair presentation, which held the stage for three weeks, and various other short-lived ventures of such nondescript character as hardly to justify a mention. It was evident that money is lacking for any casual activities.

While the "Pilgrimage Play" was given last summer at its theatre in the hills, a second Max Reinhardt spectacle in the Hollywood Bowl could not be matured. The production was discussed for both the early summer and late fall. Reinhardt particularly desired Katharine Hepburn for the role of Viola, but her film commitments prevented. This season because of Reinhardt engagements in Europe, the California Festival Association has been considering Johannes Poulsen, leading Danish theatrical director. The production will be classical in its attributes.

There has been nothing lacking of Shakespeare, owing to the Pasadena Community Playhouse's ambitious programs for sequences of plays. The cycle last summer included the English chronicle plays from "King John" to "Henry VIII," with the rarely offered "Henry VI," Parts I, II and III, presented in full panoply. This year the Greco-Roman cycle brings "Pericles, Prince of Tyre" to the American stage for presumably the first time. Such comparative rarities as "Timon of Athens," "Coriolanus," "Troilus and Cressida," which opened the series; "Cymbeline" and "Antony and Cleopatra" were seen from mid-June to August. "Julius Caesar" was the only true familiar in the sequence. The remarkable program commenced a little less auspiciously than in the summer of 1935, but in toto redounded again to the credit of a unique institution. It takes enormous courage and large resources to offer the lesser known plays, especially a "Pericles," but then the Pasadena Community is the only theatre in the land to have done Eugene O'Neill's "Lazarus Laughed"—and right successfully!

No discussion of Shakespeare in Southern California could be complete without some reference to the Globe Players at the San Diego exposition. Their "rapid transit" performances—for they give a play in a little over an hour—are amazingly diverting. The condensed versions preserve the spirit of the plays to an extraordinary degree. Furthermore the company does them with great gusto. The professional crowd was often quite in evidence at the replica of the old Globe, situated in the midst of an Elizabethan garden, fronted by a greensward, with a Falstaff Inn on one side, and booths where old lavender and mementos were sold scattered about. It proved a delightful tourist attraction, and probably brought Shakespeare to thousands of people who were unacquainted with the staging of the Bard.

Before bidding adieu to the more professional realm of the theatre, it would be well to take token of the light opera experiments, which were conducted during the fall and the spring.

J. J. Shubert attempted to bring this type of entertainment to the ample spaces of Shrine Auditorium late in 1935, but it was almost an acoustic impossiblity. His several productions began with Noel Coward's "Bitter Sweet," Evelyn Laye starred, continued with "Rose Marie," featuring Nanette Guilford and Paul Gregory, and finally faded with the "Countess Maritza," starring Peggy Wood, with Gregory. In the spring Helen Gahagan, a favorite, delighted in "The Merry Widow," which was followed by "Naughty Marietta," with Francia White; "Maytime," with Charles Purcell, Paul Keast and Charlotte Lansing, and "The Desert Song" with George Houston. There was a small loss on the spring season, while the fall also chalked up a deficit.

Gala entertainment to start the new theatrical year eventuated in the Actors' Fund benefit, which, taking the form of a "Cavalcade of the Theatre," gathered together a huge representation of talent from new days and old days in pictures, not to speak of the stage. It was the first benefit of the type to take place on the Coast in about fifteen years.

Held over from last season was "Tobacco Road," with James Barton substituting for a brief while for Henry Hull in a Hollywood presentation. More or less unclassifiable were such efforts in the theatre as "Her Majesty the Prince" with Barbara Barondess; "The King Sleeps," featuring the youngster, Jackie Moran; "Romeo and Juliet," in skeleton version, with Evelyn Venable; "The Wilder Beauty," with Helene Costello and a few others.

As the tumult and shouting that prevailed during the first years after the introduction of talking pictures settles down, it is evident that the playwrights and very incidentally the players are taking a greater interest in the theatre which is right about them. About the only places where they are assured of tests for their wares are the community groups, which will apparently chance anything, in so far as they are able. One hears mostly talk of what is to come, rather than what actually exists. But the general tendency is toward more intelligent goals.

The Pasadena Playhouse gave "Hollywood Holiday" by Benn Levy and John Van Druten, which met with pleasing response. Discovery of the film subject "Every Saturday Night," by Katherine Kavanaugh, was made at the Gateway Theatre. At the Bliss-Hayden William A. Brady picked "Night on Earth" by Julian Lamothe for New York production.

"I Am Laughing" by Edwin Justus Mayer, "Doc Lincoln" by Leo A. Levy and Harold Daniels, "Not for Children" by Elmer Rice, "Fly Away Home" by Dorothy Bennett and Irving White, and "The Dominant Sex" by Michael Egan were interestingly performed at Pasadena. Very commendable was "The Virgin Queen" by Will Whalen as given at the Bard Theatre. "No. Nine Pine Street" by John Colton was offered by the Beverly Hills Theatre for Professionals.

Other plays and productions that drew attention were: At Pasadena: "Queen Victoria" by David Carb and Walter Pritchard Eaton, with Doris Lloyd; "The Guardsman" with Mischa Auer, as directed by Ilya Motyleff; "Rain from Heaven" by S. N. Behrman, "Yellow Jack" by Sidney Howard; "The Cherry Orchard" by Anton Chekov; "Squaring the Circle" by Valentine Katayev; "Noah" by André Obey, and "The Rose and the Ring" by Thackeray. "The Pursuit of Happiness" was well given with Frederick Giermann in the masculine lead by the Beverly Professionals.

"Green Grow the Lilacs" at the Jean Muir Workshop, "Thirsty Soil" by Raymond Bond, "Sunday" by Martin Flavin, and "Portrait of a Lady" at the Bliss-Hayden; "Clean Beds" at the Hollytown; the much-banned "Maya," Eugene Walters' adaptation of Louis Verneuil's "Jealousy," featuring Baron de Gunsborg; "Dear Brutus" as given by the Uplifters Players, Goldoni's "Mistress of the Inn," as presented by the Westwood Village Players; "Saint Joan," as offered by the University of California at Los Angeles, were all distinctive. While The Mission Play has remained in obscurity the past several seasons, the Little Theatre of Padua Hills continues a bright center of Spanish-accented entertainment.

If there is aught that is needed in Southern California it is crystallization of the many and diversified endeavors, so comparatively few of which appear to attain the true professional status.

WINTERSET

A Drama in Three Acts

BY MAXWELL ANDERSON

THE first drama of the theatre season of 1935-36 designed for what is frequently classified as the intelligent minority was Maxwell Anderson's "Winterset." This proved a somber tragedy of a hate as strong as any that moved young Hamlet to thought of revenge, frustrated by such a love as welded the lives of the Capulet daughter and the Montague son.

Intelligent minorities are frequently turned into enthused majorities by such a play, and so it proved, or partly proved, in the case of "Winterset." The drama's start in late September was slow, but gradually, as word of its quality as to text, setting and superior performances by the actors engaged spread over the city, attendance increased and "Winterset" ran well past those first hundred performances that are by the tradition of Broadway the accepted test of a drama's right to be called a success in the commercial theatre. In the Spring it was given the first annual prize award of the New York Drama Critics' Circle as the best play of the year by an American author.

"Winterset" is as free an expression of the Anderson thought, and is written with a conviction as deeply felt as was his Pulitzer-prize-winning drama, "Both Your Houses." In that drama he flayed with satire and ridicule the nation's political setup and the politicians who disgrace it. In "Winterset" he goes back to the case of the State of Massachusetts *vs.* Sacco and Vanzetti to vindicate, by implication, a similarly strong personal conviction that the great New England Commonwealth erred gravely in that prosecution.

His story is of the son of such an alleged anarchist as he believes either of these unfortunates might have been and the son's quest for evidence that shall by one stroke clear his father's name and give rest to his own tortured soul. The play is written in that inspiring verse which gave so much beauty and eloquence to "Elizabeth the Queen" and "Mary of Scotland" and is, by the author's confession, an experiment of sorts.

"When I wrote my first play, 'White Desert,' I wrote it in

32

verse because I was weary of plays in prose that never lifted from the ground," the dramatist writes in the preface to the play as published. "It failed, and I did not come back to verse again until I had discovered that poetic tragedy had never been successfully written about its own place and time. There is not one tragedy by Aeschylus, Sophocles, Euripides, Shakespeare, Corneille or Racine which did not have the advantage of a setting either far away or long ago. With this admonition in mind I wrote 'Elizabeth the Queen' and a succession of historical plays in verse, some of them successful, and found myself immediately labeled a historical and romantic playwright, two terms I found equally distasteful. 'Winterset' is largely in verse, and treats a contemporary tragic theme, which makes it more of an experiment than I could wish, for the great masters themselves never tried to make tragic poetry out of the stuff of their own times. To do so is to attempt to establish a new convention, one that may prove impossible of acceptance, but to which I was driven by the lively historical sense of our day—a knowledge of period, costume and manners which almost shuts off the writer on historical themes from contemporary comment. Whether or not I have solved the problem in 'Winterset' is probably of little moment. But it must be solved if we are to have a great theatre in America. Our theatre has not yet produced anything worthy to endure—and endurance, though it may be a fallible test, is the only test of excellence."

It is an early, dark December morning when "Winterset" opens. The scene is a river bank, directly beneath a mighty bridgehead. "A gigantic span starts from the rear of the stage and appears to lift over the heads of the audience and out to the left." The foreground is shadowed and cluttered. There is a gloomy apartment house at one side. A pile of original rock at the other. A couple of sheds have been thrown up against the masonry of the bridge tower at the rear. A scattering of apartment house lights can be seen across the river beyond.

Trock Estrella, a slim, wiry man of ashen face, and a companion known as Shadow, slide into the scene from the left. Two others would follow, but are curtly sent back to watch the car. Trock is in command and this is as far as he cares for company. Being, as we gather, recently released from prison and still bitter against the forces, social and political, that put him there, Trock is of a mind to indulge a brooding melancholy.

"They've soaked me once too often in that vat of poisoned hell they keep up-state to soak men in, and I'm rotten inside," he

mutters. "And now they want to get me and stir me in again—
and that'd kill me—and that's fine for them. But before that
happens to me a lot of these healthy boys'll know what it's like
when you try to breathe and have no place to put air—they'll
learn it from me!"

"They got nothing on you, chief," encourages Shadow.

"I don't know yet. That's what I'm here to find out. If they've
got what they might have it's not a year this time—no, nor ten.
It's screwed down under a lid. I can die quick enough without
help."

"You're the skinny kind that lives forever," suggests Shadow.

"He gave me a half a year, the doc at the gate."

"Jesus!"

"Six months I get, and the rest's dirt, six feet. . . ."

Lucia, the street piano man has come for his piano, which he
keeps in one of the sheds at back. Piny, an apple woman, also
drifts in, ready to begin her day. They're friendly, but their
greetings are ignored.

The scene changes to a room in the cellar of the apartment
building, a room "floored with cement and roofed with huge boa-
constrictor pipes that run slantwise." A table and a few chairs
make up the furnishing.

Garth, a good-looking boy in his early twenties, is studying
a crack that has appeared at the base of his violin. The steam
does that, he explains to Miriamne, his sister, a frail, ethereal
child of fifteen. The steam does it and a dollar could mend it,
if Garth had a dollar.

But Miriamne is worried about more serious things than
cracked violins. Worried because her brother has sat at home
for three days now and started at strange sounds. And because
her father, Esdras, "reads without knowing where," and covertly
watches those that pass. Miriamne has found a letter, too, that has
added to her fears. A letter from a lawyer, reading: "Don't get
me wrong, but stay in out of the rain the next few days, just for
instance."

"I thought I burned that letter," exclaims the startled Garth.

"Afterward you did," admits Miriamne. "And then what was
printed about the Estrella gang—you hid it from me, you and
father. What was it—about this murder?"

GARTH—Will you shut up, you fool!

MIRIAMNE—But if you know why don't you tell them, Garth?
If it's true—what they say—you knew all the time Romagna

wasn't guilty, and could have said so—

GARTH—Everybody knew Romagna wasn't guilty! But they weren't listening to evidence in his favor. They didn't want it. They don't want it now.

MIRIAMNE—But was that why they never called on you?—

GARTH—So far as I know they never'd heard of me—and I can assure you I knew nothing about it—

MIRIAMNE—But something's wrong—and it worries father—

GARTH—What could be wrong?

MIRIAMNE—I don't know.

GARTH (*after a pause*)—And I don't know. You're a good kid, Miriamne, but you see too many movies. I wasn't mixed up in any murder, and I don't mean to be. If I had a dollar to get my fiddle fixed and another to hire a hall, by God I'd fiddle some of the prodigies back into Sunday School where they belong, but I won't get either, and so I sit here and bite my nails—but if you hoped I had some criminal romantic past you'll have to look again!

MIRIAMNE—Oh, Garth, forgive me—but I want you to be so far above such things nothing could frighten you. When you seem to shrink and be afraid, and you're the brother I love, I want to run there and cry, if there's any question they care to ask, you'll be quick and glad to answer, for there's nothing to conceal!

GARTH—And that's all true—

MIRIAMNE—But then I remember—how you dim the lights— and we go early to bed—and speak in whispers—and I could think there's a death somewhere behind us—an evil death—

GARTH (*hearing a step*)—Now for God's sake, be quiet!

It is Esdras, the father, who has entered from the outside. He is "an old rabbi with a kindly face," hurried and troubled. Esdras would speak alone with someone who is following. Before Miriamne and Garth can leave, the door bursts open. Trock stands menacingly inside. He, too, would clear the room of all save Garth. The others are to go into the inner room, and if they listen Trock will riddle the door—

Trock, out of prison, has come first to Garth, he explains. Someone has started looking up a case with which he and Garth were both vitally concerned. Trock would know about that. Perhaps it's Garth—turning state's evidence—

"Hell, Trock! Use your brain!" protests Garth. "The case was

closed. They burned Romagna for it and that finished it. Why
should I look for trouble and maybe get burned myself?"

"Boy, I don't know, but I just thought I'd find out."

"I'm going straight, Trock. I can play this thing, and I'm
trying to make a living. I haven't talked and nobody's talked
to me. Christ—it's the last thing I'd want!"

"Your old man knows."

"That's where I got the money that last time when you needed
it. He had a little saved up, but I had to tell him to get it. He's
as safe as Shadow there."

Trock has a feeling that there could be a lot of people safer
than Shadow; a feeling that Shadow would be safer dead, along
with a lot of other gorillas and "Jesus-bitten professors."

"There's no evidence to reopen the thing," protests Garth.

"And suppose they called on you and asked you to testify?"
demands Trock.

"Why, then I'd tell 'em that all I know is what I read in the
papers. And I'd stick to that."

Garth is also sure there is no danger of Miriamne's telling.
She's too scared and too loyal. Besides, no one wants another
trial except the radicals, and they have nothing new to take to
court. Let them yell. Nobody gives a damn.

But Trock isn't satisfied. There is also the trial judge to
reckon with. He, by the papers, has gone off his nut and is
wandering the streets trying to prove to everybody that he was
right; that the radicals were guilty. The police of three cities
are looking for Judge Gaunt.

Shadow can't see why that should worry Trock. After all the
Judge is crazy, and if he weren't he is arguing on Trock's side.
Trock's got the jitters and will damn well give himself away if
he isn't careful—a statement that irritates the jumpy Trock.

"Maybe you're lying to me, and maybe you're not," he says,
turning to Garth. "Stay at home a few days."

"Sure thing. Why not?"

"And when I say stay home I mean stay home. If I have to go
looking for you you'll stay a long time wherever I find you. . . ."

Trock and Shadow have gone. Garth has called Miriamne and
Esdras from the outer room. They are anxious for him, and
frightened, and would know who Trock is—

"He'd kill me if I told you who he is, that is, if he knew," says
Garth.

"Then don't say it," pleads Miriamne.

GARTH (*excitedly*)—Yes, and I'll say it! I was with a gang one time that robbed a pay roll. I saw a murder done, and Trock Estrella did it. If that got out I'd go to the chair and so would he—that's why he was here today—

MIRIAMNE—But that's not true—

ESDRAS—He says it to frighten you, child.

GARTH—Oh, no, I don't! I say it because I've held it in too long! I'm damned if I sit here forever, and look at the door, waiting for Trock with his sub-machine gun, waiting for police with a warrant!—I say I'm damned, and I am, no matter what I do! These piddling scales on a violin—first position, third, fifth, arpeggios in E—and what I'm thinking is Romagna dead for the murder—dead while I sat here dying inside—dead for the thing Trock did while I looked on—and I could have saved him, yes—but I sat here and let him die instead of me because I wanted to live! Well, it's no life, and it doesn't matter who I tell, because I mean to get it over!

MIRIAMNE—Garth, it's not true!

GARTH—I'd take some scum down with me if I died—that'd be one good deed—

ESDRAS—Son, son, you're mad—someone will hear—

GARTH—Then let them hear! I've lived with ghosts too long. God damn you if you keep me from the truth!—(*He turns away.*) Oh, God damn the world! I don't want to die! (*He throws himself down.*)

ESDRAS—I should have known. I thought you hard and sullen, Garth, my son. And you were a child, and hurt with a wound that might be healed.—All men have crimes, and most of them are hidden, and many are heavy as yours must be to you. (GARTH *sobs.*) They walk the streets to buy and sell, but a spreading crimson stain tinges the inner vestments, touches flesh, and burns the quick. You're not alone.

GARTH—I'm alone in this.

ESDRAS—Yes, if you hold with the world that only those who die suddenly should be revenged. But those whose hearts are cancered, drop by drop in small ways, little by little, till they've borne all they can bear, and die—these deaths will go unpunished now as always. When we're young we have faith in what is seen, but when we're old we know that what is seen is traced in air and built on water. There's no guilt under heaven, just as there's no heaven, till men believe it—no earth, till men have seen it, and have a word to say this is the earth.

GARTH—Well, I say there's an earth, and I say I'm guilty on it, guilty as hell.

It is not old Esdras' arguments that it were neither wise nor merciful for Garth to confess his crime, nor Miriamne's bewilderment, that weigh most heavily upon the boy's mind. It is his fear—

"Oh, I'm a coward—I always was!" shouts Garth. "I'll be quiet and live. I'll live even if I have to crawl. I know."

"Is it better to tell a lie and live?" Miriamne would know, when Garth has gone.

"Yes, child. It's better," answers Esdras, solemnly.

"But if I had to do it—I think I'd die," says Miriamne.

"Yes, child. Because you're young."

"Is that the only reason?"

"The only reason. . . ."

The scene again has changed. It is evening of the same day. Under the bridge Miriamne is sitting alone. A street lamp is flickering. A tramp wanders in looking for a place to sleep. He has no luck. Both sheds are locked. He coils up finally on a pile of rags and shavings in the corner.

Two young girls are crossing the alley. One is listening intently to the other's recital of an adventure with a young man who cried so hard when she kicked a hole through the windshield of a borrowed car that she was sorry for him and surrendered.

Judge Gaunt, "an elderly, quiet man, well dressed but in clothes that have seen some weather," wanders in. He is studying a clipping from a newspaper. He would know of the startled tramp what street this is and would explain with rambling particularity why he is there. He is a stranger, from another city, he says, and not the man the hobo may think, though the hobo has thought of nothing save his own discomfort at being disturbed.

"Yet, why should I deceive you?" persists Judge Gaunt. "Before God, I held the proofs in my hands. I hold them still. I tell you the defense was cunning beyond belief, and unscrupulous in its use of propaganda—they gagged at nothing—not even— No, no— I'm sorry—this will hardly interest you. I'm sorry. I have an errand. . . ."

Two young road boys of seventeen or so, Mio and Carr, appear at the corner. They have just met for the first time since they were together in the Northwest and pause as they exchange reminiscences.

Mio had spent a good deal of his time fishing with a family of
Greeks—Greeks who sang as they fished. After that he had
worked south and gone to the Hollywood High School for a
while—or until they had kicked him out because he had no
permanent address. Now Mio has caught sight of Miriamne, who
has been crying. He inquires sympathetically as to the cause
of her tears. The girl only looks at him wonderingly as she passes
them and disappears. . . .

"Last time I saw you you couldn't think of anything you
wanted to do except curse God and pass out," Carr is saying, as
Mio turns back from gazing after Miriamne. "Still feeling low?"

"Not much different," answers Mio. "Talk about the lost
generation, I'm the only one fits that title. When the State exe-
cutes your father, and your mother dies of grief, and you know
damn well he was innocent, and the authorities of your home town
politely inform you they'd consider it a favor if you lived somewhere else—that cuts you off from the world—with a meat-ax."

Carr—They asked you to move?

Mio—It came to that.

Carr—God, that was white of them.

Mio—It probably gave them a headache just to see me after
all that agitation. They knew as well as I did my father never
staged a holdup. Anyway, I've got a new interest in life now.

Carr—Yes—I saw her.

Mio—I don't mean the skirt.—No, I got wind of something,
out West, some college professor investigating the trial and turning up new evidence. Couldn't find anything he'd written out there,
so I beat it East and arrived on this blessed island just in time to
find the bums holing up in the public library for the winter. I
know now what the unemployed have been doing since the depression started. They've been catching up on their reading in
the main reference room. Man, what a stench! Maybe I stank,
too, but a hobo has the stench of ten because his shoes are poor.

Carr—Tennyson.

Mio—Right. Jeez, I'm glad we met up again! Never knew
anybody else that could track me through the driven snow of
Victorian literature.

Carr—Now you're cribbing from some half-forgotten criticism
of Ben Jonson's Roman plagiarisms.

Mio—Where did you get your education, sap?

Carr—Not in the public library, sap. My father kept a newsstand.

Mio—Well, you're right again. (*There is a faint rumble of thunder.*) What's that? Winter thunder?

Carr—Or Mister God, beating on His little tocsin. Maybe announcing the advent of a new social order.

Mio—Or maybe it's going to rain coffee and doughnuts.

Carr—Or maybe it's going to rain.

Mio—Seems more likely. (*Lowering his voice.*) Anyhow, I found Professor Hobhouse's discussion of the Romagna case. I think he has something. It occurred to me I might follow it up by doing a little sleuthing on my own account.

Carr—Yes?

Mio—I have done a little. And it leads me to somewhere in that tenement house that backs up against the bridge. That's how I happen to be here.

Carr—They'll never let you get anywhere with it, Mio. I told you that before.

Mio—I know you did.

Carr—The State can't afford to admit it was wrong, you see. Not when there's been that much of a row kicked up over it. So for all practical purposes the State was right and your father robbed the pay roll.

Mio—There's still such a thing as evidence.

Carr—It's something you can buy. In fact, at the moment I don't think of anything you can't buy, including life, honor, virtue, glory, public office, conjugal affection and all kinds of justice, from the traffic court to the immortal nine. Go out and make yourself a pot of money and you can buy all the justice you want. Convictions obtained, convictions averted. Lowest rates in years.

Mio—I know all that.

Carr—Sure.

Mio—This thing didn't happen to you.

> They've left you your name
> and whatever place you can take. For my heritage
> they've left me one thing only, and that's to be
> my father's voice crying up out of the earth
> and quicklime where they stuck him. Electrocution
> doesn't kill, you know. They eviscerate them
> with a turn of the knife in the dissecting room.
> The blood spurts out. The man was alive. Then into
> the lime pit, leave no trace. Make it short shrift
> and a chemical dissolution. That's what they thought
> of the man that was my father. Then my mother—

I tell you these county burials are swift
and cheap and run for profit! Out of the house
and into the ground, you wife of a dead dog. Wait,
here's some Romagna spawn left.
Something crawls here—
something they called a son. Why couldn't he die
along with his mother?
Well, ease him out of town,
ease him out, boys, and see you're not too gentle.
He might come back. And, by their own living Jesus,
I will go back, and hang the carrion
around their necks that made it!
Maybe I can sleep then.
Or even live.

CARR—You have to try it?

MIO—Yes.
Yes. It won't let me alone. I've tried to live
and forget it—but I was birthmarked with hot iron
into the entrails. I've got to find out who did it
and make them see it till it scalds their eyes
and make them admit it till their tongues are blistered with
saying how black they lied!

The street is filling again. A gawky salesman comes in search
of the two girls who had passed. Lucia, with the piano, and
Piny, the apple woman, are back. The decree has gone forth that
there shall be no more street music. The Mayor has heard the
sextette once too often. Lucia is distressed but philosophical.
Perhaps he may play back in the shadows, if not in the street.
Perhaps people can dance the rumba there, this last night at
least.

Now a crowd of urchins has drifted in and is dancing. A
sailor weaves his way out of the shadows and applauds the
scene. But soon a policeman has wandered in and commanded
that the music stop. Let them dance if they want to, but without
music. Nor is he of a mind to argue the point.

"And there you see it, the perfect example of capitalistic
oppression," shouts a Radical, jumping on top a rock. "In a land
where music should be free as air and the arts should be encouraged, a uniformed minion of the rich, a guardian myrmidon
of the Park Avenue pleasure hunters, steps in and puts a limit on
the innocent enjoyments of the poor! We don't go to theatres!
Why not? We can't afford it! We don't go to night clubs, where

women dance naked and the music drips from saxophones and leaks out of Rudy Vallée—we can't afford that either!—But we might at least dance on the river bank to the strains of a barrel organ—!"

"It's against the law," protests the officer.

"What law? I challenge you to tell me what law of God or man—what ordinance—is violated by this spontaneous diversion? None! I say none! An official whim of the masters who should be our servants!—"

Now Judge Gaunt has shuffled in from the shadows and is interested. He would protest mildly when the Policeman is of a mind to haul the Radical from his rostrum—

"One moment, Officer," protests the Judge. "There is some difference of opinion even on the bench as to the elasticity of police power when applied in minor emergencies to preserve civil order. But the weight of authority would certainly favor the defendant in any equable court, and he would be upheld in his demand to be heard."

The Policeman would roughly question this interference, and is suspicious of this man who claims to be a Judge of some standing in another city, a city of similar statutes—

"I ask this for yourself, truly, not for the dignity of the law nor the maintenance of precedent. Be gentle with them when their threats are childish—be tolerant while you can—for your least harsh word will return on you in the night—return in a storm of cries!—Whatever they may have said or done, let them disperse in peace! It is better that they go softly, lest when they are dead you see their eyes pleading, and their out-stretched hands touch you, fingering cold on your heart!—I have been harsher than you. I have sent men down that long corridor into blinding light and blind darkness! (*He suddenly draws himself erect and speaks defiantly.*) And it was well that I did so! I have been an upright judge! They are all liars! Liars!"

But the Policeman has no time to listen to such a crazy fool. Nor any time to waste with such a crowd. He listens as Mio enters the argument, for Mio's words would indicate a sympathy with "the badge," who's only doing what he's paid to do.

"Buddy, I tell you flat I wish I was from Ireland, and could boast some Tammany connections," says Mio. "There's only one drawback about working on the force. It infects the brain, it eats the cerebrum. There've been cases known, fine specimens of manhood, too, where autopsies, conducted in approved scientific fashion, revealed conditions quite incredible in policemen's upper layers. In some, a trace, in others, when they've swung a stick too long, there was nothing there!—but nothing! Oh, my friends, this fine athletic figure of a man that stands so grim before us, what will they find when they saw his skull for the last inspection? I fear me a little puffball dust will blow away rejoining earth, our mother—and this same dust, this smoke, this ash on the wind, will represent all he had left to think with!"

The Policeman, Mio thinks, may, on later reflection, conclude that he is being "kidded out of his uniform pants," and "smack his wife down" by way of retaliation when he gets home, but at the moment the Policeman would fight the crowd on the theory that someone is trying to start a riot. There is considerable confusion as the officer puts his hand on his gun and backs toward a defensive position. The crowd, a little awed by the move, melts slowly away. Shortly the Policeman and the Judge are alone. Trock and the two young men in serge have appeared in the shadows at back and Miriamne is standing wonderingly at one side.

"Yes, but should a man die," the Judge is saying to the belligerent officer, "should it be necessary that one man die for the good of many? Make not yourself the instrument of death, lest you sleep to wake sobbing! Nay, it avails nothing that you are the law—this delicate ganglion that is the brain, it will not bear these things—!"

The Policeman has gone. Garth has sidled up to his father and urged him to get Judge Gaunt in the house. "He's crazy as a bedbug and telling the world," warns Garth. "Get him inside."

The Judge does not object to going with Esdras. Old men have a common bond and understanding. Trock and his men have also disappeared. And now Mio comes back alone, and finds Miriamne still in the shadow. A fine sleet has begun to blow across the street lights.

Mio is not surprised to find Miriamne. He had asked her lightly to meet him there and evidently she had thought he meant it. But now he would have her go inside out of the threat of rain and forget it.

"I'm not your kind," he says. "I'm nobody's kind but my own. I'm waiting for this to blow over." And then, as she rises to go, he adds quickly: "I lied. I meant it—I meant it when I said it—but there's too much black whirling inside me—for any girl to know. So go on in. You're somebody's angel child and they're waiting for you."

"Yes. I'll go."

MIO—And tell them when you get inside where it's warm, and you love each other, and mother comes to kiss her darling, tell them to hang on to it while they can, believe while they can it's a warm safe world, and Jesus finds his lambs and carries them in his bosom. I've seen some lambs that Jesus missed. If they ever want the truth tell them that nothing's guaranteed in this climate except it gets cold in winter, nor on this earth except you die sometime.

MIRIAMNE—I have no mother. And my people are Jews.

MIO—Then you know something about it.

MIRIAMNE—Yes.

MIO—Do you have enough to eat?

MIRIAMNE—Not always.

MIO—What do you believe in?

MIRIAMNE.—Nothing.

MIO—Why?

MIRIAMNE—How can one?

MIO—It's easy if you're a fool. You see the words in books. Honor, it says there, chivalry, freedom, heroism, enduring love— and these are words on paper. It's something to have them there. You'll get them nowhere else.

MIRIAMNE—What hurts you?

MIO—Just that. You'll get them nowhere else.

MIRIAMNE—Why should you want them?

MIO—I'm alone, that's why. You see those lights, along the river, cutting across the rain—? those are the hearths of Brooklyn, and up this way the love-nests of Manhattan—they turn their points like knives against me—outcast of the world, snake in the streets.—I don't want a hand-out. I sleep and eat.

MIRIAMNE—Do you want me to go with you?

MIO—Where?

MIRIAMNE—Where you go.

MIO (*a pause. He goes nearer to her*)—Why, you god-damned little fool—what made you say that?

MIRIAMNE—I don't know.

MIO—If you have a home stay in it. I ask for nothing. I've schooled myself to ask for nothing, and take what I can get, and get along. If I fell for you, that's my look-out, and I'll starve it down.

MIRIAMNE—Wherever you go, I'd go.

MIO—What do you know about loving? How could you know? Have you ever had a man?

MIRIAMNE (*after a slight pause*)—No. But I know. Tell me

your name.

Mio—Mio. What's yours?

Miriamne—Miriamne.

Mio—There's no such name.

Miriamne—But there's no such name as Mio! M. I. O. It's no name.

Mio—It's for Bartolomeo.

Miriamne—My mother's name was Miriam, so they called me Miriamne.

Mio—Meaning little Miriam?

Miriamne—Yes.

He would have her leave him now, for all his great longing for her. There is still the memory of his father between them, and all the misery that the world has spun. "Enduring love!" he cries; "oh, gods and worms, what mockery!—And yet I have blood enough in my veins. It goes like music, singing, because you're here. My body turns as if you were the sun, and warm. This men called love in happier times, before the Freudians taught us to blame it on the glands."

"I will take my hands and weave them to a little house, and there you shall keep a dream," promises Miriamne.

"God knows I could use a dream and even a house," answers Mio.

And now he has kissed her lips lightly and drawn away to look at her.

"Why, girl, the transfiguration on the mount was nothing to your face. It lights from within—a white chalice holding fire, a flower in flame, this is your face."

"And you shall drink the flame and never lessen it," says Miriamne. "And round your head the aureole shall burn that burns there now, forever. This I can give you. And so forever the Freudians are wrong."

Again she is conscious of the attraction that has drawn them together and repeats her wish that he take her with him. But Mio is conscious, too—conscious of the man he is and the oath he has sworn; conscious of a memory of what he has been through—and of what he still has to do.

"I have no house, nor home, nor love of life, nor fear of death, nor care for what I eat, or who I sleep with, or what color of calcimine the Government will wash itself this year or next to lure the sheep and feed the wolves. Love somewhere else, and get your children in some other image more acceptable to the State!

This face of mine is stamped for sewage!"

Miriamne is worried now, as she senses his plan. He must not stop there; he must not seek out the Garth Esdras he has come in search of; there is death lurking in that locality and he must fly from that. She is still pleading as Trock and Shadow reappear and she pulls Mio back into the shadow where they listen.

Shadow is still trying to turn Trock from his purpose. There is nothing gained in plugging a guy, and then another, and another, to free the world of witnesses.

But Trock is angry and will not listen. If that is the way Shadow figures it he's through. He can go. Shadow goes, after he has taken the precaution to see that Trock is not armed. But he has not gone far before the men in serge appear and, at a sign from Trock, follow after. A minute or two later shots are heard.

Soon the road boy, Carr, is running back to tell Mio and Miriamne that a man has been shot and his body has fallen into the river.

"You know a man really ought to carry insurance living around here," says Carr. "God, it's easy, putting a fellow away. I never saw it done before."

Miriamne has gone into the house. Carr has left; Lucia comes back to recover his piano and to put it in the shed. Mio, with a last look at the tenement, goes again into the street and disappears. The curtain falls.

ACT II

That same evening, in the Esdras basement, Miriamne is listening to her father read. The door to the inner room is open, and strains from Garth's playing of a theme from Beethoven's Archduke trio are heard.

Miriamne is not very intent upon her father's words. She is listening as though she expected a step at the outer door. Soon Garth's violin is heard no more and the boy comes into the room, closing the door carefully after him.

Garth has left Judge Gaunt asleep inside and it is his conviction that when the Judge wakes again he should be kept quiet during the night and shipped off first thing in the morning. Let someone else pick him up.

Miriamne is anxious for Garth. He would, she is sure, be safer from Trock any other place in the city than he is there. But Garth is of no mind to move. He has no money, for one thing, and for another he could not get around the first corner without being shot down.

Judge Gaunt appears in the doorway of the inner room. He is a little surprised to find himself there; grateful for their hospitality but curious as to who they are and how he had met them. Being told the name is Esdras he is vaguely conscious of a new interest stirring in his mind—the name Garth Esdras is not a usual name and lately it has been connected with a case with which the Judge was familiar—but probably this is not that Garth Esdras.

Now the Judge would have one of them set him on his way, and is lightly vexed when Garth advises him, for his own good, to stay where he is. He is protesting his distaste for his surroundings when suddenly a flash of memory brings back the purpose of his coming to the neighborhood.

"Professor Hobhouse—that's the name," he exclaims, turning to Garth. "He wrote some trash about you and printed it in a broadside.—Since I'm here I can tell you it's a pure fabrication—lacking facts and legal import. Senseless and impudent, written with bias—with malicious intent to undermine the public confidence in justice and the courts. I knew it then—all he brings out about the testimony you might have given. It's true I could have called you, but the case was clear—Romagna was known guilty, and there was nothing to add. If I've endured some hours of torture over their attacks upon my probity—and in this torture have wandered from my place, wandered perhaps in mind and body—and found my way to face you—why, yes, it is so—I know it—I beg of you say nothing. It's not easy to give up a fair name after a full half century of service to a state. It may well rock the surest reason. Therefore I ask of you say nothing of this visit."

The Esdrases have no intention of saying anything. They are content to let things stay as they are for all their sakes. Now again Judge Gaunt is eager to be off, but before he can go there is a knock at the door. When it is opened Mio is standing there. Mio, too, has come in search of information he believes the Esdrases are in a position to give him.

"I'll be quick and brief," promises Mio, once he has their attention. "I'm the son of a man who died many years ago for a pay roll robbery in New England. You should be Garth Esdras, by what I've heard. You have some knowledge of the crime, if one can believe what he reads in the public prints, and it might be that your testimony, if given, would clear my father of any share in the murder. You may not care whether he was guilty or not.

You may not know. But I do care—and care deeply, and I've
come to ask you face to face."

GARTH—To ask me what?

MIO—What do you know of it?

ESDRAS—This man Romagna, did he have a son?

MIO—Yes, sir, this man Romagna, as you choose to call him,
had a son, and I am that son, and proud.

ESDRAS—Forgive me.

MIO—Had you known him, and heard him speak, you'd know
why I'm proud, and why he was no malefactor.

ESDRAS—I quite believe you. If my son can help he will. But
at this moment, as I told you—could you, I wonder, come tomorrow, at your own hour?

MIO—Yes.

ESDRAS—By coincidence we too of late have had this thing
in mind—there have been comments printed, and much discussion
which we could hardly avoid.

MIO—Could you tell me then in a word?—What you know—
is it for him or against him?—that's all I need.

ESDRAS—My son knows nothing.

GARTH—No. The picture-papers lash themselves to a fury
over any rumor—make them up when they're short of bedroom
slops.—This is what happened. I had known a few members of a
gang one time up there—and after the murder they picked me
up because I looked like someone that was seen in what they
called the murder car. They held me a little while, but they
couldn't identify me for the most excellent reason I wasn't there
when the thing occurred. A dozen years later now a professor
comes across this, and sees red and asks why I wasn't called on
as a witness and yips so loud they syndicate his picture in all
the rotos. That's all I know about it. I wish I could tell you more.

ESDRAS—Let me say too that I have read some words your
father said, and you were a son fortunate in your father, whatever
the verdict of the world.

MIO—There are few who think so, but it's true, and I thank
you. Then—that's the whole story?

GARTH—All I know of it.

MIO—They cover their tracks well, the inner ring that dis-
tributes murder. I came three thousand miles to this dead end.

ESDRAS—If he was innocent and you know him so, believe it,
and let the others believe as they like.

MIO—Will you tell me how a man's to live, and face his life,

if he can't believe that truth's like a fire, and will burn through
and be seen though it takes all the years there are? While I
stand up and have breath in my lungs I shall be one flame of
that fire; it's all the life I have.

ESDRAS—Then you must live so. One must live as he can.

MIO—It's the only way of life my father left me.

Now Judge Gaunt would have a word. If it is the case of
Bartolomeo Romagna of which they speak he knows the case and
knows Romagna to have been guilty. Also that his trial was fair
and that he had every chance to prove his innocence—

MIO—What chance? When a court panders to mob hysterics,
and the jury comes in loaded to soak an anarchist and a foreigner, it may be due process of law but it's also murder!

GAUNT—He should have thought of that before he spilled
blood.

MIO—He?

GAUNT—Sir, I know too well that he was guilty.

MIO—Who are you? How do you know? I've searched the records through, the trial and what came after, and in all that
million words I found not one unbiased argument to fix the crime
on him.

GAUNT—And you yourself, were you unprejudiced?

MIO—Who are you?

ESDRAS—Sir, this gentleman is here, as you are here, to ask
my son, as you have asked, what ground there might be for this
talk of new evidence in your father's case. We gave him the same
answer we've given you.

MIO—I'm sorry. I'd supposed his cause forgotten except by
myself. There's still a defense committee then?

GAUNT—There may be. I am not connected with it.

ESDRAS—He is my guest, and asks to remain unknown.

MIO (after a pause, looking at GAUNT)—The Judge at the trial
was younger, but he had your face. Can it be that you're the
man?—Yes—Yes.—The jury charge—I sat there as a child and
heard your voice, and watched that Brahminical mouth. I knew
even then you meant no good to him. And now you're here to
winnow out truth and justice—the fountain-head of the lies that
slew him! Are you Judge Gaunt?

GAUNT—I am.

MIO—Then tell me what damnation to what inferno would
fit the toad that sat in robes and lied when he gave the charge,

and knew he lied! Judge that, and then go to your place in that hell!

GAUNT—I know and have known what bitterness can rise against a court when it must say, putting aside all weakness, that a man's to die. I can forgive you that, for you are your father's son, and you think of him as a son thinks of his father. Certain laws seem cruel in their operation; it's necessary that we be cruel to uphold them. This cruelty is kindness to those I serve.

MIO—I don't doubt that. I know who it is you serve.

GAUNT—Would I have chosen to rack myself with other men's despairs, stop my ears, harden my heart, and listen only to the voice of law and light, if I had hoped some private gain for serving? In all my years on the bench of a long-established commonwealth not once has my decision been in question save in this case. Not once before or since. For hope of heaven or place on earth, or power or gold, no man has had my voice, nor will while I still keep the trust that's laid on me to sentence and define.

MIO—Then why are you here?

GAUNT—My record's clean. I've kept it so. But suppose with the best intent, among the myriad tongues that come to testify, I had missed my way and followed a perjured tale to a lethal end till a man was forsworn to death? Could I rest or sleep while there was doubt of this, even while there was question in a layman's mind? For always, night and day, there lies on my brain like a weight, the admonition: see truly, let nothing sway you; among all functions there's but one godlike, to judge. Then see to it you judge as a god would judge, with clarity, with truth, with what mercy is found consonant with order and law. Without law men are beasts, and it's a judge's task to lift and hold them above themselves. Let a judge be once mistaken or step aside for a friend, and a gap is made in the dykes that hold back anarchy and chaos, and leave men bond but free.

MIO—Then the gap's been made, and you made it.

There is not, in Judge Gaunt's defense of his own action, any chance for an unjust decision. There was nothing to justify his reopening of the case on Garth Esdras' testimony, as Mio has heard. And all other evidence and rumor of evidence he has examined faithfully and fully. If it had been otherwise he would, he feels, have gone quite mad.

"It's no light thing when a long life's been dedicate to one end to wrench the mind awry," says the Judge.

"By your own thesis you should be mad," answers Mio, "and

no doubt you are."

By similar reasoning, thinks the Judge, Mio, too, could have
suffered madness. He has brooded day and night on one theme
until he can see but one side of it—

"I've seen it happen with the best and wisest men," insists
Judge Gaunt. "I but ask the question. I can't speak for you. Is
it not true wherever you walk, through the little town where you
knew him well, or flying from it, inland or by the sea, still walking
by your side, and sleeping only when you too sleep, a shadow
not your own follows, pleading and holding out its hands to be
delivered from shame?"

"How you know that, by God, I don't know."

"Because one specter haunted you and me—and haunts you
still. But for me it's laid to rest now that my mind is satisfied.
He died justly and not by error."

Mio has stepped forward menacingly, a light of hatred burning fiercely in his eyes.

"Do you care to know you've come so near to death it's miracle
that pulse still beats in your splotchy throat? Do you know there's
murder in me?"

"There was murder in your sire, and it's to be expected! I say
he died justly, and he deserved it!"

"Yes, you'd like too well to have me kill you! That would
prove your case and clear your name, and dip my father's name
in stench forever! You'll not get that from me! Go home and die
in bed, get it under cover, your lux-et-lex putrefaction of the
right thing, you man that walks like a god!"

"Have I made you angry by coming too near the truth?"

"This sets him up, this venomous slug, this sets him up in a
gown, deciding who's to walk above the earth and who's to lie
beneath! And giving reasons! The cobra giving reasons; I'm a
god, by Buddha, holy and worshipful my fang, and can I sink
it in!"

Mio has turned to go. He is quiet now. "This is no good," he
mutters. "This won't help much," and sinks into a chair.

It is not until Esdras has taken Judge Gaunt away and
Miriamne comes again into the room that Mio knows that she,
too, is a member of this family that he has hunted down, and
that Garth is her brother. The knowledge is disturbing. He would
leave now. He feels that his quest has ended in failure, his interest
in living has been destroyed.

"It was bad enough that he should have died innocent, but
if he were guilty—then what's my life—what have I left to do—?"

"Never believe them, Mio, never."

"But it was truth I wanted, truth—not the lies you'd tell yourself, or tell a woman, or a woman tells you! The Judge with his cobra mouth may have spat truth—and I may be mad! For me—your hands are too clean to touch me. I'm to have the scraps from hotel kitchens—and instead of love those mottled bodies that hitch themselves through alleys to sell for dimes or nickels. Go, keep yourself chaste for the baker bridegroom—baker and son of a baker, let him get his baker's dozen on you!"

"No—say once you love me—say it once; I'll never ask to hear it twice, nor for any kindness, and you shall take all I have!"

When Garth comes, and would break up this love scene, as Mio is agreed he should, it is Miriamne who argues otherwise.

"I've always loved you and tried to help you, Garth. And you've been kind. Don't spoil it now."

"Spoil it how?"

"Because I love him. I didn't know it would happen. We danced together. And the world's all changed. I see you through a mist, and our father, too. If you brought this to nothing I'd want to die."

Still Mio is of a mind it is time for him to go. Nor will he kiss the waiting Miriamne as she pleads.

"When it rains, some spring on the planet Mercury, where the spring comes often, I'll meet you there, let's say. We'll wait for that. It may be some time till then," says Mio.

The outer door has burst open. Esdras and the Judge are back, as though driven into the room by Trock, who follows. Trock makes a hurried count of those present. He is startled when he discovers Mio to be the Romagna son. This may be some trick of Garth's and not, as Garth explains, an accidental appearance because of the stuff in the papers.

Trock, however, is too intent upon the business in hand to worry long. He has come to take Judge Gaunt home. To take him in a car, with chauffeurs and everything done in style. "Don't worry about the Judge," advises Trock. "He'll be taken care of. For good."

They are stopped for awhile. The storm has broken fiercely again and there is a good deal of lightning.

"We were born too early," Judge Gaunt muses philosophically as Esdras listens. "Even you who are young are not of the elect. In a hundred years man will put his finger on life itself, and then he will live as long as he likes. For you and me, we shall die soon—one day, one year more or less, when or where, it's no matter. It's what we call an indeterminate sentence. . . ."

In another blinding flash of light Shadow appears suddenly at the door, bursting in out of the storm, gun in hand. Now he has faced the thoroughly frightened Trock and held him where he stands with his hands in the air.

"You said the doctor gave you six months to live—well, I don't give you that much. That's what you had, six months, and so you start bumping off your friends to make sure of your damn six months. I got it from you. I know where I got it. Because I wouldn't give it to the Judge. So he wouldn't talk."

"Honest to God—"

"What God? The one that let you put three holes in me when I was your friend? Well, He let me get up again and walk till I could find you. That's as far as I get, but I got there, by God! And I can hear you even if I can't see!"

Shadow staggers as he gropes blindly for his enemy. He sways and falls and his gun drops from his hand. Mio picks up the gun.

"You will hear it said that an old man makes a good judge, being calm, clear-eyed, without passion," Judge Gaunt is saying as Garth and Esdras carry Shadow into the inner room. "But this is not true. Only the young love truth and justice. The old are savage, wary, violent, swayed by maniac desires, cynical of friendship or love, open to bribery and the temptations of lust, corrupt and dastardly to the heart. I know these old men. What have they left to believe, what have they left to lose? Whorers of daughters, lickers of girls' shoes, contrivers of nastiness in the night, purveyors of perversion, worshipers of possession! Death is the only radical. He comes late, but he comes at last to put away the old men and give the young their places. It was time."

Trock is pacing the room, wild-eyed with a new terror, calling hysterically to Esdras to close the door.

"He won't come back again," promises Esdras.

"I want the door shut," shouts Trock. "He was dead, I tell you. And Romagna was dead, too, once! Can't they keep a man underground?"

"No. No more!" cries Mio, springing in front of Trock, gun in hand. "They don't stay under ground any more, and they don't stay under water! Why did you have him killed?"

Trock—Stay away from me! I know you!

Mio—Who am I, then?

Trock—I know you, damn you! Your name's Romagna!

MIO—Yes! And Romagna was dead, too, and Shadow was dead, but the time's come when you can't keep them down, these dead men! They won't stay down! They come in with their heads shot off and their entrails dragging! Hundreds of them! One by one—all you ever had killed! Watch the door! See!—It moves!

TROCK (*looking, fascinated, at the door*)—Let me out of here! (*He tries to rise.*)

MIO (*the gun in hand*)—Oh, no! You'll sit there and wait for them! One by one they'll come through that door, pulling their heads out of the gunny-sacks where you tied them—glauming over you with their rotten hands! They'll see without eyes and crawl over you—Shadow and the paymaster and all the rest of them—putrescent bones without eyes! Now! Look! Look! For I'm first among them.

TROCK—I've done for better men than you! And I'll do for you!

GAUNT (*rapping on the table*)—Order, gentlemen, order! The witness will remember that a certain decorum is essential in the courtroom!

MIO—By God, he'll answer me!

GAUNT—Silence! Silence! Let me remind you of courtesy toward the witness! What case is this you try?

MIO—The case of the State against Bartolomeo Romagna for the murder of the paymaster.

GAUNT—Sir, that was disposed of long ago.

MIO—Never disposed of, never, not while I live.

GAUNT—Then we'll have done with it now! I deny the appeal! I have denied the appeal before and I do so again! (*A flash of lightning.*) Who set that flash! Bailiff, clear the court! This is not Flemington, gentlemen! We're not conducting this case to make a journalistic holiday! (*The thunder rumbles faintly.* GARTH *opens the outside door and faces a solid wall of rain.*) Stop that man! He's one of the defendants! (GARTH *closes the door.*)

MIO—Then put him on the stand!

GARTH—What do you think you're doing?

MIO—Have you any objection?

GAUNT—The objection is not sustained. We will hear the new evidence. Call your witness.

MIO—Garth Esdras!

GAUNT—He will take the stand!

GARTH—If you want me to say what I said before I'll say it!

MIO—Call Trock Estrella to the stand!

GAUNT—Trock Estrella to the stand!

Trock—No, by God!

Mio—Call Shadow, then! He'll talk! You thought he was dead,
but he'll get up again and talk!

Trock (*screaming*)—What do you want of me?

Mio—You killed the paymaster! You!

Trock—You lie! It was Shadow killed him.

The light in Mio's eyes is one of exultant victory. "And now
I know!" he shouts. "Now I know!"

"Again I remind you of courtesy toward the witness," solemnly
prompts Judge Gaunt.

Mio—I know them now!
    Let me remind you of courtesy toward the dead!
    He says that Shadow killed him! If Shadow were here
    he'd say it was Trock! There were three men involved
    in the new version of the crime for which
    my father died! Shadow and Trock Estrella
    as principals in the murder—Garth as witness!—
    Why are they here together?—and you—the Judge—
    why are you here? Why, because you were all afraid
    and you drew together out of that fear to arrange
    a story you could tell! And Trock killed Shadow
    and meant to kill the Judge out of that same fear—
    to keep them quiet! This is the thing I've hunted
    over the earth to find out, and I'd be blind indeed
    if I missed it now!
        (*To* Gaunt.)
    You heard what he said:
    It was Shadow killed him! Now let the night conspire
    with the sperm of hell! It's plain beyond denial
    even to this fox of justice—and all his words
    are curses on the wind! You lied! You lied!
    You knew this too!

Gaunt (*low*)—Let me go. Let me go!

Mio—Then why did you let my father die?

Gaunt—Suppose it known,
    but there are things a judge must not believe
    though they should head and fester underneath
    and press in on his brain. Justice once rendered
    in a clear burst of anger, righteously,
    upon a very common laborer,
    confessed an anarchist, the verdict found

and the precise machinery of law
invoked to find him guilty—think what furor
would rock the State if the court then flatly said;
all this was lies—must be reversed? It's better,
as any judge can tell you, in such cases,
holding the common good to be worth more
than small injustice, to let the record stand,
let one man die. For justice, in the main,
is governed by opinion. Communities
will have what they will have, and it's quite as well,
after all, to be rid of anarchists. Our rights
as citizens can be maintained as rights
only while we are held to be the peers of those who live
    about us. A vendor of fish
is not protected as a man might be
who kept a market. I own I've sometimes wished
this was not so, but it is. The man you defend
was unfortunate—and his misfortune bore
almost as heavily on me.—I'm broken—
broken across. You're much too young to know
how bitter it is when a worn connection chars
and you can't remember—can't remember. (*He steps for-
    ward.*)
You
will not repeat this? It will go no further?
MIO—No.
No further than the moon takes the tides—no further
than the news went when he died—
when you found him guilty
and they flashed that round the earth. Wherever men
still breathe and think, and know what's done to them
by the powers above, they'll know. That's all I ask.
That'll be enough.
GAUNT—Thank you. For I've said some things
a judge should never say.
TROCK (*he has risen and looks darkly at* MIO)—Go right on
talking.
Both of you. It won't get far, I guess.
MIO—Oh, you'll see to that?
TROCK—I'll see to it. Me and some others.
Maybe I lost my grip there just for a minute.
That's all right.
MIO—Then see to it! Let it rain!

What can you do to me now when the night's on fire
with this thing I know? Now I could almost wish
there was a god somewhere—I could almost think
there was a god—and he somehow brought me here
and set you down before me here in the rain
where I could wring this out of you! For it's said,
and I've heard it, and I'm free! He was as I thought him,
true and noble and upright, even when he went
to a death contrived because he was as he was
and not your kind! Let it rain! Let the night speak fire
and the city go out with the tide, for he was a man
and I know you now, and I have my day!

There is a heavy knock at the outside door. It is the Policeman in oilskins. He is followed by a Sergeant and they are looking for Judge Gaunt. They have come to take the old man home.
The Sergeant recognizes Trock; knows that he is just out of
prison and advises him to take care of himself. If there are any
stiffs found along the river bank the police will know whom to
look for—
"Then look in the other room!" shouts Mio. "I accuse that
man of murder! Trock Estrella! He's a murderer! . . . It was
Trock Estrella that robbed the pay roll thirteen years ago and
did the killing my father died for! You know the Romagna case!
Romagna was innocent, and Trock Estrella guilty!"
"Oh, what the hell! That's old stuff—the Romagna case."
"The boy's a professional kidder," chimes in the Policeman.
"He took me over about half an hour ago. He kids the police
and then ducks out."
The Sergeant goes into the room finally, after Garth and even
Miriamne have denied there are any corpses about. In the room
he finds nothing. It must be right that Mio is a kidder; the kind
that puts in fire alarms to see the engine.
"By God, he was there! He went in there to die!" persists
Mio.
"I'll bet he did. And I'm Haile Selassie's aunt! What's your
name?" queries the Sergeant.
The Sergeant and the Policeman have taken Judge Gaunt. The
mystery of Shadow's disappearance is cleared. He had fallen in
the hall beyond the room and died there. Trock is much relieved
by the news. Trock is going now. He advises Garth to turn Mio
loose and let him go as far as he likes. There is an ominous ring in
the suggestion. It frightens Miriamne. She would have Mio get

away while there is time.

As for Garth, he doesn't care what Mio does. He can run his own campaign, tell whatever story he wants to tell. But he had better beware of Trock.

"My father died in your place. And you could have saved him! You were one of the gang!" accuses Mio.

"Why, there you are. You certainly owe me nothing," agrees Garth.

MIRIAMNE (*moaning*)—I want to die. I want to go away.

MIO—Yes, and you lied! And trapped me into it!

MIRIAMNE—But, Mio, he's my brother. I couldn't give them my brother.

MIO—No. You couldn't. You were quite right. The gods were damned ironic tonight, and they've worked it out.

ESDRAS—What will be changed if it comes to trial again? More blood poured out to a mythical justice, but your father lying still where he lies now.

MIO—The bright, ironical gods! What fun they have in heaven! When a man prays hard for any gift, they give it, and then one more to boot that makes it useless. (*To* MIRIAMNE.) You might have picked some other stranger to dance with!

MIRIAMNE—I know.

MIO—Or chosen some other evening to sit outside in the rain. But no, it had to be this. All my life long I've wanted only one thing, to say to the world and prove it: the man you killed was clean and true and full of love as the twelve-year-old that stood and taught in the temple. I can say that now and give my proofs—and now you stick a girl's face between me and the rites I've sworn the dead shall have of me! You ask too much! Your brother can take his chance! He was ready enough to let an innocent man take certainty for him to pay for the years he's had. That parts us, then, but we're parted anyway, by the same dark wind that blew us together. I shall say what I have to say. (*He steps back.*) And I'm not welcome here.

MIRIAMNE—But don't go now! You've stayed too long! He'll be waiting!

MIO—Well, is this any safer? Let the winds blow, the four winds of the world, and take us to the four winds.

The three are silent. He turns and goes out as the curtain falls.

ACT III

Outside the Esdras tenement the rain still sweeps mistily past the street lamps. The young men in serge who are usually to be found with Trock Estrella are leaning against the masonry of the bridgehead engaged in a game of matching bills. Occasionally they stop long enough to check the scene carefully and then resume their play.

Presently Trock appears, coming from the tenement. He walks rapidly over to them, speaks to them in tones too low to be heard and goes on out toward the street. The young men momentarily resume their game and then, hearing a noise at the tenement door, move away and are lost in the shadows.

Mio comes out the door, starts to walk briskly away. What he sees up the path ahead of him causes him to hesitate. He is leaning against the tenement when Miriamne comes through the door. She, too, is anxious for his safety. Miriamne would have him hide there, somewhere. Perhaps with Lucia, the piano man, or in the tenement. But Mio is afflicted with claustrophobia—he prefers to die in the open, seeking air.

Shortly the door of the tenement again opens and Garth, after a hurried look around, comes forth bearing the body of Shadow. He passes on silently toward the river. Mio looks musingly after him—

MIO—This is the burial of Shadow, then;
    feet first he dips, and leaves the haunts of men.
    Let us make mourn for Shadow, wetly lying,
    in elegiac stanzas and sweet crying.
    Be gentle with him, little cold waves and fishes;
    nibble him not, respect his skin and tissues—

"Must you say such things?" demands Miriamne.

MIO—My dear, some requiem is fitting over the dead, even
    for Shadow. But the last rhyme was bad.

Whittle him not, respect his dying wishes.

That's better. And then to conclude:

His aromatic virtues, slowly rising
will circumnamb the isle, beyond disguising.

He clung to life beyond the wont of men.
Time and his silence drink us all. Amen.

Garth has returned from his errand and gone again silently
into the house. Presently Esdras appears, bent on calling the police, whatever may result. Let them know the story; let Garth
be implicated, still Esdras is determined.

"I don't ask help, remember," says Mio, firmly. "I make no
truce. He's not on my conscience, and I'm not on yours."

"But you could make it easier, so easily. He's my only son.
Let him live."

"His chance of survival's better than mine, I'd say."

As the old man goes Miriamne would kiss his hands. But he
would deny the gesture. His are guilty hands, he says, and hurries out. From the tenement come strains from Garth's violin.

MIO—There was a war in heaven
   once, all the angels on one side, and all
   the devils on the other, and since that time
   disputes have raged among the learned, concerning
   whether the demons won, or the angels. Maybe
   the angels won, after all.
MIRIAMNE—And again, perhaps
   there are no demons or angels.
MIO—Oh, there are none.
   But I could love your father.
MIRIAMNE—I love him. You see,
   he's afraid because he's old. The less one has
   to lose the more he's afraid.
MIO—Suppose one had
   only a short stub end of life, or held
   a flashlight with the batteries run down
   till the bulb was dim, and knew that he could live
   while the glow lasted. Or suppose one knew
   that while he stood in a little shelter of time
   under a bridgehead, say, he could live, and then,
   from then on, nothing. Then to lie and turn
   with the earth and sun, and regard them not in the least
   when the bulb was extinguished or he stepped beyond
   his circle into the cold? How would he live
   that last dim quarter-hour, before he went,
   minus all recollection, to grow in grass
   between cobblestones?

MIRIAMNE—Let me put my arms around you, Mio.
Then if anything comes, it's for me, too. (*She puts both arms
around him.*)
MIO—Only suppose
this circle's charmed! To be safe until he steps
from this lighted space into dark! Time pauses here
and high eternity grows in one quarter-hour
in which to live.
MIRIAMNE—Let me see if anyone's there—
there in the shadows. (*She looks to the right.*)
MIO—It might blast our eternity—
blow it to bits. No, don't go. This is forever,
here where we stand. And I ask you, Miriamne,
how does one spend a forever?
MIRIAMNE—You're frightened?
MIO—Yes.
So much that time stands still.
MIRIAMNE—Why didn't I speak—
tell them—when the officers were here? I failed you
in that one moment!
MIO—His life for mine? Oh, no.
I wouldn't want it, and you couldn't give it.
And if I should go on living we're cut apart
by that brother of yours.
MIRIAMNE—Are we?
MIO—Well, think about it.
A body lies between us buried in quicklime.
Your allegiance is on the other side of that grave
and not to me.
MIRIAMNE—No, Mio! Mio, I love you!
MIO—I love you, too, but in case my life went on
beyond that barrier of dark—then Garth
would run his risk of dying.
MIRIAMNE—He's punished, Mio.
His life's been torment to him. Let him go,
for my sake, Mio.
MIO—I wish I could. I wish
I'd never seen him—or you. I've steeped too long
in this thing. It's in my teeth and bones. I can't
let go or forget. And I'll not add my lie
to the lies that cumber his ground. We live our days
in a storm of lies that drifts the truth too deep

for path or shovel; but I've set my foot on a truth
for once, and I'll trail it down!

Carr comes around the corner of the tenement. He has come
looking for Mio, being worried. Up the street Carr has just come
upon those young men in serge. He does not like the looks of
them, nor their curiosity regarding him.

Mio is grateful for Carr's interest, but will not be needing his
help. Not even to take a message, as Miriamne suggests he should.
Nor will he let her send a message.

"No. Let it go the way it is. It's all arranged another way,"
Mio insists. "You've been a good scout, Carr, the best I ever
knew on the road."

"That sounds like making your will."

"Not yet, but when I do I've thought of something to leave
you. It's the view of Mt. Rainier from the Seattle jail, snow over
cloud. And the rusty chain in my pocket from a pair of hand-
cuffs my father wore. That's all the worldly goods I'm seized of."

"Look, Mio, hell—if you're in trouble—"

"I'm not. Not at all. I have a genius that attends me where
I go, and guards me now. I'm fine."

Miriamne would know, after Carr has gone, why Mio would
not send a message by him. It was his chance. But the words,
says Mio, stuck in his throat.

Mio—I've lost
   my taste for revenge if it falls on you. Oh, God,
   deliver me from the body of this death
   I've dragged behind me all these years! Miriamne!
   Miriamne!
Miriamne—Yes!
Mio—Miriamne, if you love me
   teach me a treason to what I am, and have been,
   till I learn to live like a man! I think I'm waking
   from a long trauma of hate and fear and death
   that's hemmed me from my birth—and glimpse a life
   to be lived in hope—but it's young in me yet, I can't
   get free, or forgive! But teach me how to live
   and forget to hate!
Miriamne—He would have forgiven.
Mio—He?
Miriamne—Your father.
Mio (a pause)—Yes.

You'll think it strange, but I've never
 remembered that.
MIRIAMNE—How can I help you?
MIO—You have.
MIRIAMNE—If I were a little older—if I knew
 the things to say! I can only put out my hands
 and give you back the faith you bring to me
 by being what you are. Because to me
 you are all hope and beauty and brightness drawn
 across what's black and mean!
MIO—He'd have forgiven—
 Then there's no more to say—I've groped long enough
 through this everglades of old revenges—here
 the road ends.—Miriamne, Miriamne,
 the iron I wore so long—it's eaten through
 and fallen from me. Let me have your arms.
 They'll say we're children— Well—the world's made up
 of children.
MIRIAMNE—Yes.
MIO—But it's too late for me.
MIRIAMNE—No. (*She goes into his arms and they kiss for the
 first time.*) Then we'll meet again?
MIO—Yes.
MIRIAMNE—Where?
MIO—I'll write—
 or send Carr to you.
MIRIAMNE—You won't forget?
MIO—Forget?
 Whatever streets I walk, you'll walk them, too,
 from now on, and whatever roof or stars
 I have to house me, you shall share my roof
 and stars and morning. I shall not forget.
MIRIAMNE—God keep you!
MIO—And keep you. And this to remember!
 if I should die, Miriamne, this half-hour
 is our eternity. I came here seeking
 light in darkness, running from the dawn,
 and stumbled on a morning.

One of the young men in serge wanders idly in, takes count of
what he sees, and disappears. Now old Esdras is back, his hat
gone, his face bleeding. They wouldn't let him pass on the bridge
and had kicked and beat him back. Trock was there, and soon

Trock will be coming here. He had said so.

Now Mio would think of some way to escape the trap. He might get through the tenement to the roof and out that way. Esdras goes ahead to see if that were possible, and is to signal them when he reaches an upper window. They stand, Miriamne and Mio, looking upward for a sign from Esdras as he climbs—

"Now all you silent powers that make the sleet and dark, and never yet have spoken, give us a sign," prays Mio. "Let the throw be ours this once, on this longest night, when the winter sets his foot on the threshold leading up to spring and enters with remembered cold—let fall some mercy with the rain. We are two lovers here in your night, and we wish to live."

Now they can see Esdras at the window, but he waves them back.

"Mio, see, that path between the rocks—they're not watching that—they're out at the river—I can see them there—they can't watch both—it leads to a street above."

Mɪo—I'll try it then.
    Kiss me. You'll hear. But if you never hear—
    Then I'm the king of hell, Persephone,
    and I'll expect you.
Mɪʀɪᴀᴍɴᴇ—Oh, lover, keep safe.
Mɪo—Good-by. (*He slips out quickly between the rocks. There is a quick machine gun rat-tat. The violin stops.* Mɪʀɪᴀᴍɴᴇ *runs toward the path.* Mɪo *comes back slowly, a hand pressed under his heart.*) It seems you were mistaken.
Mɪʀɪᴀᴍɴᴇ—Oh, God, forgive me! (*She puts an arm around him. He sinks to his knees.*) Where is it, Mio? Let me help you in! Quick, quick, let me help you!
Mɪo—I hadn't thought to choose—this—ground—but it will do. (*He slips down.*)
Mɪʀɪᴀᴍɴᴇ—Oh, God, forgive me!
Mɪo—Yes? The king of hell was not forgiven then,
    Dis is his name, and Hades is his home—
    and he goes alone—
Mɪʀɪᴀᴍɴᴇ—Why does he bleed so? Mio, if you go
    I shall go with you.
Mɪo—It's better to stay alive.
    I wanted to stay alive—because of you—
    I leave you that—and what he said to me dying:
    I love you, and will love you after I die.
    Tomorrow I shall still love you, as I've loved

the stars I'll never see, and all the mornings
that might have been yours and mine. Oh, Miriamne,
you taught me this.

MIRIAMNE—If only I'd never seen you
then you could live—

MIO—That's blasphemy— Oh, God,
there might have been some easier way of it.
You didn't want me to die, did you, Miriamne—?
You didn't send me away—?

MIRIAMNE—Oh, never, never—

MIO—Forgive me—kiss me—I've got blood on your lips—
I'm sorry—it doesn't matter—I'm sorry—

MIRIAMNE (ESDRAS *and* GARTH *come out*)—Mio—
I'd have gone to die myself—you must hear this, Mio,
I'd have died to help you—you must listen, sweet,
you must hear it—(*She rises.*)
I can die, too, see! You! There!
You in the shadows!—You killed him to silence him!
But I'm not silenced! All that he knew I know,
and I'll tell it tonight! Tonight—
tell it and scream it
through the streets—that Trock's a murderer
and he hired you for this murder!
Your work's not done—
and you won't live long! Do you hear?
You're murderers, and I know who you are! (*The machine
gun speaks again. She sinks to her knees. GARTH runs to her.*)

GARTH—You little fool! (*He tries to lift her.*)

MIRIAMNE—Don't touch me! (*She crawls toward* MIO.)
Look, Mio! They killed me, too. Oh, you can believe me
now, Mio. You can believe I wouldn't hurt you,
because I'm dying! Why doesn't he answer me?
Oh, now he'll never know! (*She sinks down, her hand over
her mouth, choking. GARTH kneels beside her, then rises,
shuddering.*)

ESDRAS—It lacked only this.

GARTH—Yes.
Why was the bastard born? Why did he come here?

ESDRAS—Miriamne—Miriamne—yes, and Mio,
one breath shall call you now—forgive us both—
forgive the ancient evil of the earth
that brought you here—

GARTH—Why must she be a fool?

Esdras—Well, they were wiser than you and I. To die
when you are young and untouched, that's beggary
to a miser of years, but the devils locked in synod
shake and are daunted when men set their lives
at hazard for the heart's love, and lose. And these,
who were yet children, will weigh more than all
a city's elders when the experiment
is reckoned up in the end. Oh, Miriamne,
and Mio—Mio, my son—know this where you lie,
this is the glory of earth-born men and women,
not to cringe, never to yield, but standing,
take defeat implacable and defiant,
die unsubmitting. I wish that I'd died so,
long ago; before you're old you'll wish
that you had died as they have. On this star,
in this hard star-adventure, knowing not
what the fires mean to right and left, nor whether
a meaning was intended or presumed,
man can stand up, and look out blind and say:
in all these turning lights I find no clue,
only a masterless night, and in my blood
no certain answer, yet is my mind my own,
yet is my heart a cry toward something dim
in distance, which is higher than I am
and makes me emperor of the endless dark
even in seeking! What odds and ends of life
men may live otherwise, let them live, and then
go out, as I shall go, and you. Our part
is only to bury them. Come, take her up.
They must not lie here.

Lucia and Piny come near to help. Esdras and Garth stoop to
carry Miriamne.

THE CURTAIN FALLS

IDIOT'S DELIGHT

A Drama in Three Acts

By Robert E. Sherwood

THERE were two prize plays this theatre season of 1935-36. One, and the first to be named, was Maxwell Anderson's "Winterset." The second Robert Emmet Sherwood's "Idiot's Delight." The Anderson drama, as heretofore recorded, was awarded the first annual prize of the New York Drama Critics' Circle. The Sherwood comedy won the longer-established Pulitzer prize.

The citation of the drama critics named "Winterset" as a drama "interpreting a valid and challenging contemporary theme dealing with the pursuit of human justice in terms of unusual poetic force." The Pulitzer committee selected "Idiot's Delight" as "the most distinguished play of the year by an American author, preferably dealing with an American theme."

In box-office appeal Mr. Sherwood's play was the more popular, advantaged as it was by the presence of two favorite Theatre Guild players, Lynn Fontanne and Alfred Lunt, in its principal roles. "Idiot's Delight" offers a vigorous arraignment of the war madness at present both afflicting and threatening the world, and in particular those countries which have already succumbed to Fascist domination or tendencies. It is essentially a comedy with a definite overlay of philosophic conviction covering the war theme, as "The Petrified Forest," the Sherwood drama of the year before, was essentially a gunman melodrama shot through with a philosophy of life and tied in with modern social problems.

The Sherwood comedy was a late production of the Theatre Guild, coming in March at the end of a season that had included such other Guild successes as the Gershwins' musicalized "Porgy and Bess," the English domestic comedy of Dodie Smith, "Call It a Day," and S. N. Behrman's "End of Summer."

"Idiot's Delight" opens at the Hotel Monte Gabriele, which originally was a sanatorium in the Austrian Alps. Following the treaty of Versailles, when this section of Austria was ceded to Italy, the sanatorium was partially rebuilt and reopened as a hotel. The newer part, into which we are now ushered, includes a rather ornate Cocktail Lounge.

Through a wide doorway at the back of the lounge a glimpse
may be had of the reception desk of the hotel. At one side of the
lounge there is an entrance to the American bar. An attractively
wide stairway at back leads from the lounge to the newer section
of the hotel above, and from a tall, broad window at the back of
the stairway it is possible to look into three countries—Switzerland, Austria and Bavaria.

At the moment Donald Navadel, "a rather precious, youngish
American, suitably costumed for Winter sports by Saks Fifth
Avenue," is standing on the stairway landing gazing dolefully at
the view. "Experienced in the resort business, he was imported
this year to organize sporting and social life at Monte Gabriele
with a view to making it a Mecca for American tourists. He is
not pleased with the way things have turned out."

On the floor of the lounge a four-piece orchestra is doing what
it can, though that isn't much, with a tune entitled "June in
January." It is Mr. Navadel's idea that the orchestra should de-
sist. There are no guests present, nor any likely to arrive; let the
musicians "grab themselves a smoke."

The orchestra is quite willing to stop, but Signor Pittaluga, the
proprietor of the Monte Gabriele Hotel, is considerably disturbed
by Mr. Navadel's impudence in issuing the order. Not only is the
orchestra paid to play until 3 o'clock, but Mr. Navadel is not yet
the manager of the hotel, even though it is his custom to give
himself the airs of a manager. Mr. Navadel, Signor Pittaluga
would point out, was engaged on the theory that he would be
followed from St. Moritz, Muerren and Chamonix by many of his
rich friends. But where are the friends? Mr. Navadel has his own
opinion as to that, and adds a conviction that the Hotel Monte
Gabriele is "a deadly, boring dump."

The screech of sirens interrupts the exchange of pleasantries
between Signor Pittaluga and his Social Manager. This is a warning of air raids and comes from a nearby aviation field. From
the window it is possible to see a number of the bigger bombers
taking off from the field. But, as Captain Locicero, the officer in
charge of this frontier station just entering the lounge is pleased
to explain, it is not really a raid. It is only a test of the sirens,
to see how fast the combat planes can go into action.

"This is a crucial spot, Dr. Waldersee," the captain continues,
in answer to the somewhat anxious query of a hotel guest come
excitedly from above stairs. "We must be prepared for visits from
the enemy."

"Enemy, eh? And who is that?"

"I don't quite know, yet. The map of Europe supplies us with a wide choice of opponents. I suppose, in due time, our government will announce its selection—and we shall know just whom we are to shoot at."

"Nonsense! Obscene nonsense!"

"Yes—yes. But the taste for obscenity is incurable, isn't it?"

"When will you let me go into Switzerland?"

"Again I am powerless to answer you. My orders are that no one for the time being shall cross the frontiers, either into Switzerland or Austria."

"And when will this 'time being' end?"

"When Rome makes its decision between friend and foe."

"I am a German subject. I am not your foe."

"I am sure of that, Dr. Waldersee. The two great Fascist states stand together, against the world."

"Fascism has nothing to do with it! I am a scientist. I am a servant of the whole damn stupid human race. If you delay me any longer here, my experiments will be ruined. Can't you appreciate that? I must get my rats at once to the laboratory in Zurich, or all my months and years of research will have gone for nothing."

Don Navadel has reappeared, escorting two prospective guests, a Mr. and Mrs. Cherry, a "pleasant young English couple in the first flush of their honeymoon." The attractions of the Hotel Monte Gabriele—named for the Italian poet and warrior, Gabriele d'Annunzio—are eloquently detailed by Mr. Navadel, and the Cherrys are duly impressed. They have just been turned over to Signor Pittaluga to be shown their rooms when another group of guests arrive, led by Harry Van, "a wan, thoughtful, lonely American vaudevillian promotor, press agent, book-agent, crooner, hoofer, barker or shill, who has undertaken all sorts of jobs in his time, all of them capitalizing his powers of salesmanship, and none of them entirely honest. He wears a snappy, belted, polo coat and a brown felt hat with brim turned down on all sides."

Mr. Van is pleased to recognzie a fellow American in Mr. Navadel and quick to explain his position. Mr. Van has just come in on the train from Fiume and been told that the border is closed. He is extremely anxious to get to Geneva. Mr. Van is traveling with six dancing girls, Shirley, Beulah, Bebe, Francine, Edna and Elaine, who now come swarming into the lounge in response to his call. He wants Captain Locicero to know them.

"Allow me to introduce the girls, Captain. We call them 'Les Blondes,' " explains Harry. "We've been playing the Balkan circuit—Budapest, Bucharest, Sofia, Belgrade and Zagreb. (*He turns to* DON.) Back home, that would be the equivalent of 'Pan Time.' (*He laughs nervously, to indicate that the foregoing was a gag.*) . . . The situation in brief is this, Captain. We've got very attractive bookings at a night spot in Geneva. Undoubt-edly they feel that the League of Nations needs us. (*Another laugh.*) It's important that we get there at once. So, Captain, I'll be grateful for prompt action."

The Captain is interested, both in the girls and in their indi-vidual accomplishments. Shirley, Mr. Van explains, is a fan dancer. Beulah is a bubble dancer, and therefore more of a dreamer. Elaine and Francine, Edna and Bebe are just dancers. The girls are inclined to turn on their charm and everything is pleasant, but—there isn't anything the Captain can do about helping them get to Geneva.

"I'm as powerless as you are, Mr. Van. I, too, am a pawn," explains the Captain, picking up his coat and hat. "But, speaking for myself, I shall not be sorry if you and your beautiful com-panions are forced to remain here indefinitely."

The situation is a rather delicate one. After the way they have been betrayed in the Balkans there is very little money in the Van treasury and it is important that "Les Blondes" should be permitted to go about their legitimate business. On the other hand it is apparent that Mr. Van is not fully aware of the present international situation. The world, as Don Navadel sees it, stands on the brink of war. Whether Mr. Van believes it or not, that is the situation. And it has to be accepted. A moment taler Van is negotiating with Signor Pittaluga for rooms.

"Come on, girls," he calls, and adds: "Now I want two girls to a room, and a single room for me adjoining. I promised their mothers I'd always be within earshot. . . ."

Van has come back into the Cocktail Lounge after seeing "Les Blondes" well bestowed. He is, as he later explains to "a small, dark, brooding radical-socialist" whom he meets there, he is look-ing for somebody to talk to. It gets pretty trying traveling with a group of blondes. The dark young man, it transpires, is Quillery, a Frenchman, who was on the train with Harry and his girls from Zagreb. . . .

A voluble two come from the bar and pass through the room talking excitedly. "I get an awful kick hearing Italian," admits Harry. "It's beautiful. Do you speak it?"

"Only a little. I was born in France. And I love my home. Perhaps if I had raised pigs—like my father, and all his fathers,

"IDIOT'S DELIGHT"

Irene: Somewhere in that funny, music-hall soul of yours is the spirit of Leander, and Abelard, ad Galahad. You give up everything—risk your life—walk unafraid into the valley of the adow—to aid and comfort a damsel in distress. Isn't that the truth?
Harry: Yes—it's the truth—plainly and simply put.

(Lynn Fontanne, Alfred Lunt)

back to the time when Caesar's Roman legions came—perhaps, if I had done that, I should have been a Frenchman, as they were. But I went to work in a factory—and machinery is international."

HARRY—And I suppose pigs are exclusively French?

QUILLERY—My father's pigs are! (HARRY *laughs*.) The factory where I worked made artificial limbs—an industry that has been prosperous the last twenty years. But sometimes—in the evening—after my work—I would go out into the fields and help my father. And then, for a little while, I would become again a Frenchman.

HARRY (*takes out his cigarette case*)—That's a nice thought, pal. (*Offers* QUILLERY *a cigarette*.) Have a smoke?

QUILLERY—No, thank you.

HARRY—I don't blame you. These Jugo-Slav cigarettes are not made of the same high-grade quality of manure to which I grew accustomed in Bulgaria.

QUILLERY—You know, my comrade—you seem to have a long view of things.

HARRY—So long that it gets very tiresome.

QUILLERY—The long view is not easy to sustain in this short-sighted world.

HARRY—You're right about that, pal.

QUILLERY—Let me give you an instance: There we were—gathered in Zagreb, representatives of the workers of all Europe. All brothers, collaborating harmoniously for the United Front! And now—we are rushing to our homes to prevent our people from plunging into mass murder—mass suicide!

HARRY—You're going to try to stop the war?

QUILLERY—Yes.

HARRY—Do you think you'll succeed?

QUILLERY—Unquestionably! This is not 1914, remember! Since then some new voices have been heard in this world—loud voices. I need mention only one of them—Lenin—Nikolai Lenin! (*A ferocious-looking Major of the Italian flying corps comes in and goes quickly to the bar. As he opens the door, he calls "Attention!" He goes into the bar, the door swinging to behind him.*)

HARRY—Yes—but what are you going to do about people like *that!*

QUILLERY—Expose them! That's all we have to do. Expose them—for what they are—atavistic children! Occupying their undeveloped minds playing with outmoded toys.

HARRY—Have you *seen* any of those toys?

QUILLERY—Yes! France is full of them. But there is a force more potent than all the bombing planes and submarines and tanks. And that is the mature intelligence of the workers of the world! There is one antidote for war—Revolution! And the cause of Revolution gains steadily in strength. Even here in Italy, despite all the repressive power of Fascism, sanity has survived, and it becomes more and more articulate. . . .

HARRY—Well, pal—you've got a fine point there. And I hope you stick to it.

QUILLERY—I'm afraid you think it is all futile idealism!

HARRY—No—I don't. And what if I did? I am an idealist myself.

QUILLERY—You too believe in the revolution?

HARRY—Not necessarily in *the* revolution. I'm just in favor of any revolution. Anything that will make people wake up, and get themselves some convictions. Have you ever taken cocaine?

QUILLERY—Why—I imagine that I have—at the dentist's.

HARRY—No—I mean, for pleasure. You know—a vice.

QUILLERY—No! I've never indulged in that folly.

HARRY—I have—during a stage of my career when luck was bad and confusion prevailed.

QUILLERY—Ah, yes. You needed delusions of grandeur.

HARRY—That's just what they were.

QUILLERY—It must have been an interesting experience.

HARRY—It was illuminating. It taught me what is the precise trouble with the world today. We have become a race of drug addicts—hopped up with false beliefs—false fears—false enthusiasms . . .

A moment later Quillery has overheard two Italian officers, also coming from the bar, admit that war, so far as Italy and France are concerned, has already begun. This is exciting news to Quillery. He hurries away to make arrangements about getting across the border. Which leaves Harry Van with only Dumptsy, the waiter, to talk to. Dumptsy accepts the war situation philosophically. Originally he was an Austrian, but when Italy took over this mountain he went with it. "In one day I became a foreigner," recites Dumptsy. "So now my children learn only Italian in school, and when I and my wife talk our own language they can't understand us."

A new guest to arrive is Irene. "She is somewhere between thirty and forty, beautiful, heavily and smartly furred in the Russian manner. Her hair is blonde and quite straight. She is a

model of worldly wisdom, chic, and carefully applied gracious-
ness. Her name is pronounced 'Ear-ray-na.' "

Irene is interested in the view from the tall window when Don
Navadel calls it to her attention, and momentarily stirred by the
discovery of the aviation field and the big bombers that are being
exercised. She can see little sense in their testing the sirens, however. She is quite sure there is not going to be any war, a statement which she seeks to have confirmed by her friend, Achille
Weber, who has just arrived with Signor Pittaluga. Weber (pronounced "Vay-bair") "is a thin, keen executive, wearing a neat
little mustache and excellent clothes. In his lapel is the Legion
of Honor."

"Achille—there will be no war, will there?" demands Irene.

"No, no—Irene," answers the amused Weber. "There will be
no war. They're all much too well prepared for it."

Signor Pittaluga has taken Irene and Weber to inspect their
rooms. Harry Van, his curiosity greatly piqued by the newcomers,
would know more of them.

"Who was that?" he demands of Don.

"That was Achille Weber. One of the biggest men in France.
I used to see him a lot at St. Moritz."

"And the dame? Do you assume that is his wife?"

"Are you implying that she's not?"

"No, no—I'm not implying a thing. I'm just kind of—kind of
baffled. . . ."

Harry is at the piano idly strumming a Russian song, "Kak
Stranna," when Dr. Waldersee comes again into the lounge.
The Doctor sits at table listening to the music and presently
would start a conversation. He speaks first of the song, "Kak
Stranna," which Harry explains means "How Strange!" and then
about music in general. What music Harry knows he admits he
learned playing a piano in a moving picture theatre, but he is
pretty proud of his skill. Particularly is he proud of a trick arrangement of "The Waters of the Minnetonka." "It is suitable for
Scenics," he explains—" 'Niagara Falls by Moonlight.' Or—if
you play it this way—it goes fine with the scene where the young
Indian chief turns out to be a Yale man, so it's O.K. for him to
marry Lillian ('Dimples') Walker."

Presently, after they have had a drink, the Doctor grows both
talkative and confidential. He is greatly wrought up over the
prospect of impending war.

"You are familiar with the writings of Thomas Mann?" he
demands, more as a challenge than a question.

"I'm afraid not, pal," Harry answers.

With which encouragement the Doctor opens a copy of "The Magic Mountain" and reads aloud: " 'Backsliding,' he said, 'spiritual backsliding to that dark and tortured age—that, believe me, is disease! A degradation of mankind—a degradation painful and offensive to conceive.' True words, eh?"

HARRY—Absolutely! (DUMPTSY *comes in with the Scotch.* HARRY *sits down with the* DOCTOR.)

DOCTOR—Have you had any experience with the disease of cancer?

HARRY—Certainly. I once sold a remedy for it.

DOCTOR (*exploding*)—There *is* no remedy for it, so far!

HARRY—Well—this was kind of a remedy for everything.

DOCTOR—I am within *that* of finding the cure for cancer! You probably have not heard of Fibiger, I suppose?

HARRY—I may have. I'm not sure.

DOCTOR—He was a Dane—experimented with rats. He did good work, but he died before it could be completed. I carry it on. I have been working with Oriental rats, in Bologna. But because of this war scare, I must go to neutral territory. You see, nothing must be allowed to interfere with my expermients. Nothing!

HARRY—No. They're important.

DOCTOR—The laboratory of the University of Zurich has been placed at my disposal—and in Switzerland, I can work, undisturbed. I have twenty-eight rats with me, all in various carefully tabulated stages of the disease. It is the disease of civilization—and I can cure it. And now they say I must not cross the border.

HARRY—You know, Doctor, it *is* funny.

DOCTOR—*What's* funny? To you, everything is funny!

HARRY—No—it's just that you and I are in the same fix. Both trying to get across that line. You with rats—me with girls. Of course—I appreciate the fact that civilization at large won't suffer much if *we* get stuck in the war zone. Whereas with you, there's a lot at stake. . . .

DOCTOR—It is for me to win one of the greatest victories of all time. And the victory belongs to Germany.

HARRY—Sure it does!

DOCTOR—Unfortunately, just now the situation in Germany is not good for research. They are infected with the same virus as here. Chauvinistic nationalism! They expect all bacteriologists to work on germs to put in bombs to drop from airplanes. To fill

people with death! When we've given our lives to *save* people.
Oh—God in heaven—why don't they let me do what is good?
Good for the whole world? Forgive me. I become excited.

HARRY—I know just how you feel, Doctor. Back in 1918, I
was a shill with a carnival show, and I was doing fine. The boss
thought very highly of me. He offered to give me a piece of the
show, and I had a chance to get somewhere. And then what do
you think happened? Along comes the United States Government and they drafted me! You're in the army now! They
slapped me into a uniform and for three whole months before
the Armistice, I was parading up and down guarding the Ashokan
Reservoir. They were afraid your people might poison it. I've
always figured that that little interruption ruined my career. But
I've remained an optimist, Doctor.

DOCTOR—*You* can afford to.

HARRY—I've remained an optimist because I'm essentially a
student of human nature. You dissect corpses and rats and similar
unpleasant things. Well—it has been my job to dissect suckers!
I've probed into the souls of some of the God-damnedest specimens. And what have I found? Now, don't sneer at me, Doctor—but above everything else I've found Faith. Faith in
peace on earth and good will to men—and faith that "Muma,"
"Muma" the three-legged girl, really has got three legs. All my
life, Doctor, I've been selling phoney goods to people of meager
intelligence and great faith. You'd think that would make me
contemptuous of the human race, wouldn't you? But—on the
contrary—it has given *me* Faith. It has made me sure that no
matter how much the meek may be bulldozed or gypped they *will*
eventually inherit the earth.

Two of the blondes, Shirley and Bebe, are down from upstairs
a little excited by the discovery of printed cards in all languages
in each of their rooms. These are headed: "What to do in case
of air raids." Shirley is going to send hers to her mother. "It'll
scare the hell out of her," prophesies Shirley.

Now Beulah has arrived, and with a request. Beulah would
like Harry's permission to go out with Mr. Navadel and learn
how to do skiing. But Harry is not for that. Risk Beulah's beautiful legs? "Not for me, dear. Those gams of yours are my bread
and butter."

Captain Locicero is back and plainly worried. He has been
trying to get through to headquarters. Now the best he can
promise M. Weber is that he will be able to leave next day. There

is no other word. The wires are crowded. The whole nation is in a state of uproar. The report has just come through that a state of war already exists between Italy and France.

"Germany has been mobilized," adds the Captain; "but I don't know if any decision has been reached. Nor do I know anything of the situation anywhere else. But—God help us—it will be serious enough for everyone on this earth."

"But I thought they were all too well prepared, Achille," says Irene, looking pointedly at Weber. "Has there been some mistake somewhere?"

WEBER (*confidentially*)—We can only attribute it to spontaneous combustion of the dictatorial ego.

IRENE (*grimly*)—I can imagine how thrilling it must be in Paris at this moment. Just like 1914. All the lovely soldiers— singing—marching—marching! We must go at once to Paris, Achille.

HARRY (*rising*)—What's the matter with the music, professor? Us young folks want to dance.

ELAINE (*coming in with* FRANCINE)—Can we have a drink, now, Harry?

HARRY—Sure. Sit down. (DON *enters, exuding gratification at the sight of this gay, chic throng. The Orchestra starts to play "Valencia."*)

WEBER—Will you have a drink, Irene?

IRENE—No, thank you.

WEBER—Will you, Captain Locicero?

CAPTAIN—Thank you. Brandy and soda, Dumptsy.

DUMPTSY—Si, Signor.

BEBE (*yells*)—Edna! We're going to have a drink! (EDNA *comes in.*)

WEBER—For me, Cinzano.

DUMPTSY—Oui, Monsieur. (*He goes into the bar.*)

DOCTOR—It is all incredible.

HARRY—Nevertheless, Doctor, I remain an optimist. (*He looks at* IRENE.) Let doubt prevail throughout this night—with dawn will come again the light of truth! (*He turns to* SHIRLEY.) Come on, honey—let's dance.

"They dance. Don dances with Beulah. The Orchestra continues with its spirited but frail performance of 'Valencia.' There are probably 'border incidents' in Lorraine, the Riviera, Poland, Czecho-Slovakia and Mongolia."

The curtain falls.

ACT II

Early the same evening the Cherrys are in the Cocktail Lounge having a pre-dinner apéritif. Mr. Cherry is considerably concerned about the latest news to come through the wireless, but even more concerned with assuring and reassuring Mrs. Cherry that her husband loves her very deeply, that he thinks she is beautiful and that he is being moved constantly by an impulse to kiss her. Mrs. Cherry is happily receptive, but less demonstrative than Mr. Cherry.

Harry Van idles into the room and would have idled out again if Mr. Cherry had not asked him to play something. Harry sits again at the piano and strums a bit, but he is in no mood for playing. He is pleased with the Cherrys' confession that they have been married but two days, and is prepared to agree with them that their chances of getting along fine are very good. Especially, as Mrs. Cherry points out, because they are both independent— Mr. Cherry being a painter of murals and Mrs. Cherry a clerk in the gift department at Fortnum's.

Now Quillery has joined them. Quillery, too, is in search of news, which you cannot expect to find in any of the patriotic journals obtainable in the hotel. It is Quiller's opinion that the only person in this hotel who really knows anything about what is happening is the great Achille Weber of the Comité des Forges. "He can give you all the war news. Because he made it," declares Quillery, with mounting excitement. "You don't know who he is, eh? Or what he has been doing here in Italy? I'll tell you. (*He rises and comes close to them.*) He has been organizing the arms industry. Munitions. To kill French babies. And English babies. France and Italy are at war. England joins France. Germany joins Italy. And that will drag in the Soviet Union and the Japanese Empire and the United States. In every part of the world, the good desire of men for peace and decency is undermined by the dynamite of jingoism. And it needs only one spark, set off anywhere by one egomaniac, to send it all up in one final, fatal explosion. Then love becomes hatred, courage becomes terror, hope becomes despair. (*The* DOCTOR *appears on the gallery above.*) But—it will all be very nice for Achille Weber. Because he is a master of the one *real* League of Nations— (*The* DOCTOR *slowly comes down the steps.*) The League of Schneider-Creusot, and Krupp, and Skoda, and Vickers and Dupont. The League of

Death! And the workers of the world are expected to pay him for it, with their sweat, and their life's blood."

DOCTOR—Marxian nonsense!

QUILLERY—Ah! Who speaks?

DOCTOR—I speak.

QUILLERY—Yes! The eminent Dr. Hugo Waldersee. A wearer of the sacred swastika. Down with the Communists! Off with their heads! So that the world may be safe for the Nazi murderers.

DOCTOR—So that Germany may be safe from its oppressors! It is the same with all of you—Englishmen, Frenchmen, Marxists —you manage to forget that Germany, too, has a right to live! (*Rings handbell on the table.*)

QUILLERY—If you love Germany so much, why aren't you there, now—with your rats?

DOCTOR (*sitting*)—I am not concerned with politics. (AUGUSTE *enters from the bar.*) I am a scientist. (*To* AUGUSTE.) Mineral water! (AUGUSTE *bows and exits into the bar.*)

QUILLERY—That's it, Herr Doctor! A scientist—a servant of humanity! And you know that if you were in your dear Fatherland, the Nazis would make you abandon your cure of cancer. It might benefit too many people outside of Germany—even maybe some Jews. They would force you to devote yourself to breeding malignant bacteria—millions of little germs, each one trained to give the Nazi salute and then go out and poison the enemy. You—a fighter against disease and death—you would come a Judas goat in a slaughter house. (DON *has appeared during this.*)

CHERRY—I say, Quillery, old chap—do we have to have so much blood and sweat just before dinner?

QUILLERY (*turning on him*)—Just before dinner! And now we hear the voice of England! The great, well-fed, pious hypocrite! The grabber—the exploiter—the immaculate butcher! It was *you* forced this war, because miserable little Italy dared to drag its black shirt across your trail of Empire. What do *you* care if civilization goes to pieces—as long as you have your dinner—and your dinner jacket!

CHERRY (*rising*)—I'm sorry, Quillery—but I think we'd better conclude this discussion out on the terrace.

MRS. CHERRY—Don't be a damned fool, Jimmy. You'll prove nothing by thrashing him.

QUILLERY—It's the Anglo-Saxon method of proving everything! Very well—I am at your disposal.

Don—No! I beg of you, Mr. Cherry. We mustn't have any of that sort of thing. (*He turns to* Quillery.) I must ask you to leave. If you're unable to conduct yourself as a gentleman, then . . .

Quillery—Don't say any more. Evidently I cannot conduct myself properly! I offer my apologies, Mr. Cherry.

Cherry—That's quite all right, old man. Have a drink. (*He extends his hand. They shake.*)

Quillery—No, thank you. And my apologies to you, Herr Doctor.

Doctor—There is no need for apologizing. I am accustomed to all that.

Quillery—If I let my speech run away with me, it is because I have hatred for certain things. And you should hate them, too. They are the things that make us blind—and ignorant—and—and dirty.

Quillery has gone. A moment later he is followed by the Cherrys and the Doctor. Now there are two matters about which Harry would like to talk with Don Navadel. First, has Don learned anything more as to the identity of the "dame" with Weber? Did Weber register her as his wife?

As it happens, Weber and Irene are registered separately. But so far as Don can see, it is none of Harry's business anyway. It isn't. Harry admits as much. But still he can't help wondering "where have I seen that face before."

Secondly, how would Don like to have "Les Blondes" and their leader put on a part of their act this evening for the entertainment of the hotel guests? "What kind of an act is it?" demands Don, suspiciously.

"Don't say 'What kind of an act' in that tone of voice," snaps Van. "It's good enough for this place. Those girls have played before the King of Rumania. And if some of my suspicions are correct—but I won't pursue that subject. All that need concern you is that we can adjust ourselves to our audience, and tonight we'll omit the bubble dance and the number in which little Bebe does a shimmy in a costume composed of detachable gardenias, unless there's a special request for it."

"Do you expect to be paid for this?"

"Certainly not. I'm making this offer out of the goodness of my heart. Of course, if you want to make any appropriate adjustment on our hotel bill . . ."

The act, it is agreed, shall be free of all vulgarity and shall go on at 11 o'clock.

And now Irene has come to take command of the lounge for a moment. First she would know of Monsieur Weber, who has followed her, just what the situation is likely to develop. It is most serious, Weber is quick to admit. The bombers that left the airport earlier in the afternoon were headed for Paris. Italy is in a hurry to strike the first blow. After that there are quite likely to be reprisals on the part of France, and France will know where the bombers came from. If that happens it is not likely that anyone will be able to get away soon. . . .

Irene is drinking vodka alone when the Cherrys join her. She would introduce them to this national drink of her country, which, she assures them, is quite as wonderful as a liqueur as it is as a stimulant to the appetite. When they admit being somewhat depressed by all that is happening Irene is quick to understand.

"It's the altitude," says she. "After the first exhilaration there comes a depressive reaction, especially for you, who are accustomed to the heavy, Pigwiggian atmosphere of England."

"Pigwiggian?"

"Yes, Pigwig—Oliver Twist—you know, your Dickens?"

"You know England, Madame?" Mr. Cherry is interested.

IRENE (*fondly*)—Of course I know England! My governess was a sweet old ogre from your north country—and when I was a little girl I used to visit often at Sandringham.

CHERRY (*impressed*)—Sandringham?

MRS. CHERRY—The palace?

IRENE—Yes. That was before your time. It was in the reign of dear, gay King Edward, and the beautiful Alexandra. (*She sighs a little for those days.*) I used to have such fun playing with my cousin David. He used to try to teach me to play cricket, and when I couldn't swing the bat properly, he said, "Oh, you Russians will never be civilized." (*Laughs.*) When I went home to Petersburg I told my uncle, the Tsar, what David had said, and he was so amused! But now—you must drink your vodka. (*They rise, and lift their glasses.*) A toast! To His Most Gracious Majesty the King. (*They clink glasses.*) God bless him.

CHERRY—Thank you, Madame. (*All three drink and MRS. CHERRY coughs violently.*)

IRENE (*to MRS. CHERRY*)—No—no! Drink it right down. Like this. (*She swallows it in a gulp.*) So! (*Refills the glasses from the bottle.*) The second glass will go more easily. (*They sit.*) I used to laugh so at your funny British Tommies in Archangel. They all hated vodka until one of them thought of mixing it with beer.

MRS. CHERRY—How loathsome!

IRENE—It was! But I shall be forever grateful to them—those Tommies. They saved my life when I escaped from the Soviets. For days and nights—I don't know how many—I was driving through the snow—snow—snow—snow— in a little sleigh, with the body of my father beside me, and the wolves running along like an escort of dragoons. You know—you always think of wolves as howling constantly, don't you?

CHERRY—Why, yes—I suppose one does.

IRENE—Well, they don't. No, these wolves didn't howl! They were horribly, confidently silent. I think silence is much more terrifying, don't you?

CHERRY—You must have been dreadfully afraid.

IRENE—No, I was not afraid for myself. It was the thought of my father. . . .

MRS. CHERRY—Please! I know you don't want to talk about it any more.

IRENE—Oh, no—it is so far away now. But I shall never forget the moment when I came through the haze of delirium, and saw the faces of those Tommies. Those simple, friendly faces. And the snow—and the wolves—and the terrible cold—they were all gone—and I was looking at Kew Gardens on a Sunday afternoon, and the sea of golden daffodils—"fluttering and dancing in the breezes." (WEBER *has come in with the daffodils.*)

WEBER—Shall we go in to dinner now, Irene?

IRENE—Yes, yes, Achille. In a minute. I am coming. (WEBER *goes.* IRENE *rises.*) Now—we must finish our vodka. (CHERRY *rises.*) And you must make another try to eat something.

CHERRY—Thank you so much, Madame. (*They drink.*)

IRENE—And later on, we must all be here for Mr. Van's entertainment—and we must all applaud vigorously.

MRS. CHERRY—We shall, Madame.

CHERRY—He's such a nice chap, isn't he?

IRENE (*going*)—Yes—and a real artist, too.

CHERRY—Oh—you've seen him?

IRENE—Why—yes—I've seen him, in some cafe chantant, somewhere. I forget just where it was.

"The three of them have gone out together. The light is dimmed to extinction." The curtain falls.

Two hours later Achille Weber, in the lounge for a drink of brandy, is trying to learn from Captain Locicero what is happening in the war zone. The Captain has little information. The radios are in a state of utter bedlam, with each government enforcing the strictest censorship. There is, however, an ominous silence in Paris. Only one station active and that one transmitting exclusively in code.

Presently the drone of airplanes is heard. It is the bombers returning. Seven out of eighteen, as the Captain counts them. Which is not bad—for Italians, concludes Monsieur Weber.

Irene has come to join her friend. She would congratulate him, though there is a veiled sarcasm in her tone. All this "great, wonderful death and destruction everywhere" that Weber has promoted—

"Don't give me too much credit, Irene," Weber protests.

"But I *know* what you've done," she answers, sweetly.

WEBER—Yes, my dear. You know a great deal. But don't forget to do honor to Him—up there—who put fear into man. I am but the humble instrument of His divine will.

IRENE (*looking upward, sympathetically*)—Yes—that's quite true. We don't do half enough justice to Him. Poor, lonely old soul. Sitting up in heaven, with nothing to do, but play solitaire. Poor, dear God. Playing Idiot's Delight. The game that never means anything, and never ends.

WEBER—You have an engaging fancy, my dear.

IRENE—Yes.

WEBER—It's the quality in you that fascinates me most. Limitless imagination! It is what has made you such an admirable, brilliant liar. And so very helpful to me! Am I right?

IRENE—Of course you are right, Achille. Had I been bound by any stuffy respect for the truth, I should never have escaped from the Soviets.

WEBER—I'm sure of it.

IRENE—Did I ever tell you of my escape from the Soviets?

WEBER—You have told me about it at least eleven times. And each time it was different.

IRENE—Well, I made several escapes. I am always making escapes, Achille. When I am worrying about you, and your career. I have to run away from the terror of my own thoughts. So I amuse myself by studying the faces of the people I see. Just ordinary, casual, dull people. (*She is speaking in a tone that is sweetly sadistic.*) That young English couple, for instance. I was watching them during dinner, sitting there, close together, holding hands, and rubbing their knees together under the table. And I saw him in his nice, smart, British uniform, shooting a little pistol at a huge tank. And the tank rolls over him. And his fine strong body, that was so full of the capacity for ecstasy, is a mass of mashed flesh and bones—a smear of purple blood—like a stepped-on snail. But before the moment of death, he consoles himself by thinking, "Thank God *she* is safe! She is bearing the child I gave her, and he will live to see a better world." (*She walks behind* Weber *and leans over his shoulder.*) But I know where she is. She is lying in a cellar that has been wrecked by an air raid, and her firm young breasts are all mixed up with the bowels of a dismembered policeman, and the embryo from her womb is splattered against the face of a dead bishop. That is the kind of thought with which I amuse myself, Achille. And it makes me so proud to think that I am so close to you—who make all this possible. (Weber *rises and walks about the room. At length he turns to her.*)

Weber—Do you talk in this whimsical vein to many people?

Irene—No. I betray my thoughts to no one but you. You know that I am shut off from the world. I am a contented prisoner in your ivory tower.

Weber—I'm beginning to wonder about that.

Irene—What? You think I could interest myself in someone else—?

Weber—No—no, my dear. I am merely wondering whether the time has come for you to turn commonplace, like all the others?

Irene—The others?

Weber—All those who have shared my life. My former wife, for instance. She now boasts that she abandoned me because part of my income is derived from the sale of poison gas. Revolvers and rifles and bullets she didn't mind—because they are also used by sportsmen. Battleships too are permissible; they look so splendid in the news films. But she couldn't stomach poison gas. So now she is married to an anemic Duke, and the large fortune that she obtained from me enables the Duke to indulge his principal passion, which is the slaughtering of wild animals, like rabbits, and pigeons and rather small deer. My wife is presumably happy with him. I have always been glad you are not a fool as she was, Irene.

Irene—No. I don't care even for battleships. And I shall not marry an anemic Duke.

Weber—But—there was something unpleasantly reminiscent in that gaudy picture you painted. I gather that this silly young couple has touched a tender spot, eh?

IRENE—Perhaps, Achille. Perhaps I am softening.

WEBER—Then apply your intelligence, my dear. Ask yourself: why shouldn't they die? And who are the greater criminals— those who sell the instruments of death, or those who buy them, and use them? You know there is no logical reply to that. But all these little people—like your new friends—all of them consider me an arch-villain because I furnish them with what they want, which is the illusion of power. That is what they vote for in their frightened governments—what they cheer for on their national holidays—what they glorify in their anthems, and their monuments, and their waving flags! Yes—they shout bravely about something they call "national honor." And what does it amount to? Mistrust of the motives of everyone else! Dog in the manger defense of what they've got, and greed for the other fellow's possessions! Honor among thieves! I assure you, Irene— for such little people the deadliest weapons are the most merciful.

The Cherrys are back from dinner. They have eaten everything offered, thanks to the vodka. Don Navadel is in to announce Mr. Van's entertainment of the evening, a cabaret show, for which Don does not vouch, but which he thinks may prove unintentionally amusing. Irene is quite sure she will love it, knowing Mr. Van to be an artist.

Gradually the guests gather. The musicians find their places. There is a good deal of pushing chairs about to make room for the dancers. Harry Van precedes his girls. He is wearing a tight-fitting dinner jacket and carrying a straw hat. His mood is spirited and professional.

"Before we start, folks, I just want to explain that we haven't had much chance to rehearse with my good friend, Signor Palota, and his talented little team here. (*He indicates orchestra with a handsome gesture.*) So we must crave your indulgence and beg you to give us a break if the rhythm isn't all strictly kosher. (*He waits for his laugh.*) All we ask of you, kind friends, is 'The Christian pearl of Charity,' to quote our great American poet, John Greenleaf Whittier. We thank you. Take it away!"

Harry has bowed elaborately and started his song, a rhythmic ditty entitled "Puttin' on the Ritz"—

> "Have you seen the well-to-do
> Up on Lenox Avenue?
> On that famous thoroughfare
> With their noses in the air—

High hats and colored collars
White spats—and fifteen dollars—
Spending every dime
For a wonderful time—"

The girls prance in and join in the chorus:

"If you're blue and you don't know
Where to go to
Why don't you go
Where Harlem sits
Puttin' on the Ritz.
Spangled gowns
Upon a bevy
Of the high browns
From down on the Levee, all misfits,
Puttin' on the Ritz."

There is a round of applause and Harry at the piano sings an encore to the tune of "Suwanee River." Then, with two of the girls, he adds a ditty called "Pardon My Southern Accent":

"It's a universal moon above you,
Ask the Irish, ask the Greek—
They can always understand
I love you
No matter how they speak.

"Pardon my Southern accent
Pardon my Southern drawl;
It may sound funny,
Ah, but honey,
I love y'all!"

Four flying corps officers have drifted into the room. They "are dirty and in a fever of heroically restrained excitement." The show and the girls fascinate them. Harry orders the Fascist anthem, "Giovinessa."

In the midst of a second song, while the girls have gone to sit with the military, the excitable Quillery dashes into the lounge. His face is flushed with excitement. The fact that these people can sit calmly through an entertainment when Paris has just been bombed by the Fascisti is too much for Quillery.

"For the love of God—listen to me!" he shouts. "While you

sit here eating and drinking, tonight, Italian planes dropped twenty thousand kilos of bombs on Paris. God knows how many they killed. God knows how much of life and beauty is forever destroyed! And you sit here, drinking, laughing, with *them*—the murderers. (*Points to the flyers, who ask each other, in Italian, what the hell is he talking about.*) They did it! It was their planes, from that field down there. Assassins!"

The Italian officers make a move toward Quillery. Harry Van, striving to act as pacifier, grabs Quillery and calls the Captain to take care of his men. But Quillery is not to be quieted—

"You see, we stand together! France—England—America! Allies!"

"Shut up, France! It's O.K., Captain. We can handle this—"

QUILLERY—They don't dare fight against the power of England and France! The free democracies against the Fascist tyranny!

HARRY—Now, for God's sake stop fluctuating!

QUILLERY—England and France are fighting for the hopes of mankind!

HARRY—A minute ago, England was a butcher in a dress suit. Now we're Allies!

QUILLERY—We stand together. We stand together forever. (*Turns to Officers.*) I say God damn you. God damn the villains that sent you on this errand of death.

CAPTAIN (*takes a few steps toward* QUILLERY)—If you don't close your mouth, Frenchman, we shall be forced to arrest you.

QUILLERY—Go on, Fascisti! Commit national suicide. That's the last gesture left to you toy soldiers.

HARRY—It's all right, Captain. Mr. Quillery is for peace. He's going back to France to stop the war.

QUILLERY (*turns on* HARRY)—You're not authorized to speak for me. I am competent to say what I feel. And what I say is "Down with Fascism! Abbasso Fascismo!"

CAPTAIN (*ordinarily gentle, is now white hot with rage—there is an uproar from the Officers*)—Attenzione!

QUILLERY—Vive la France! Viv—

CAPTAIN—E agli arresti.

QUILLERY—Call out the firing squad! Shoot me dead! But do not think you can silence the truth that's in me.

CAPTAIN (*grabs* QUILLERY *from the left and calls the First Officer*)—Molinari! (*First Officer grabs* QUILLERY *from the right. They start to take him out.*)

QUILLERY (*as he is being led out*)—The Empire of the Fascisti will join the Empire of the Caesars in smoking ruins. Vive la France! Vive la France! (WEBER *goes upstairs and exits. They have gone.*)

CHERRY (*to* HARRY)—You'd better carry on with your turn, old boy.

HARRY—No, pal. The act is cold. (*To the orchestra leader.*) Give us some music, Signor. (*The orchestra starts playing.*) Let dancing become general.

CHERRY—Let's dance, my sweet.

MRS. CHERRY—I can't bear to, Jimmy.

CHERRY—I think we should.

MRS. CHERRY—Very well, darling. (*They dance. The Officers dance with the Girls.*)

HARRY (*goes over to* IRENE)—Would you care to dance?

IRENE—Why—why, thank you. (*She stands up, and they join the slowly moving mob.* SHIRLEY *is singing as loud as she can.*)

"The color wheel turns so that the dancers are bathed in blue, then amber, then red," as the curtain falls.

It is quite late the same night. Irene and Harry are still in the Cocktail Lounge. At the moment they are alone. Irene has been telling the story of her life and Harry has listened "with fascination and doubt."

"My father was old," Irene is saying. "The hardships of that terrible journey had broken his body. But his spirit was strong —the spirit that is Russia. He lay there, in that little boat, and he looked up at me. Never can I forget his face, so thin, so white, so beautiful, in the starlight. And he said to me, 'Irene—little daughter,' and then—he died. For four days I was alone with his body, sailing through the storms of the Black Sea. I had no food—no water—I was in agony from the bayonet wounds of the Bolsheviki. I knew I must die. But then—an American cruiser rescued me. May God bless those good men! (*She sighs.*) I've talked too much about myself. What about you, my friend?"

"Oh—I'm not very interesting. I'm just what I seem to be."

"C'est impossible!"

"C'est possible. The facts of my case are eloquent. I'm a potential genius—reduced to piloting six blondes through the Balkans . . . I worked my way through college selling encyclopaedias."

"I knew you had culture! What college was it?"

"Oh—just any college. But my sales talk was so good that I

fell for it myself. I bought the God-damned encyclopaedia. And I read it all, traveling around, in day coaches, and depot hotels, and Fox-time dressing rooms. It was worth the money."

"And how much of all this have you retained?"

"I? I never forget anything."

Achille Weber is mentioned. Irene corrects Harry's impression that she is the wife of the munitions agent. She is associated with Monsieur Weber in a sort of business way only. Monsieur Weber is a very distinguished man who has rendered distinguished services to many governments and been generously decorated—with the Legion of Honor, the Order of the White Eagle, the Order of St. James of the Sword and the Military Order of Christ.

The talk turns to America. Irene knows America well. She has flown across the continent, she has met many Americans. She recognizes Harry as being typical. He is just like all Americans—an ingenuous, sentimental idealist.

"You believe in the goodness of human nature, don't you?"

"And what if I do? I've known millions of people, intimately—and I never found more than one out of a hundred that I didn't like, once you got to know them."

"That is very charming—but it *is* naïve."

"Maybe so. But experience prevents me from working up much enthusiasm over anyone who considers the human race as just so many clay pigeons, even if he does belong to the Military Order of Christ."

Still Irene holds a little patronizingly, that M. Weber is quite necessary to civilization as it exists. "Stupid people may consider him an arch-villain because it is his duty to stir up a little trouble here and there to stimulate the sale of his products," but—

"Monsieur Weber is a true man of the world. He is above petty nationalism; he can be a Frenchman in France—a German in Germany—a Greek—a Turk—whatever the occasion demands."

"Yes—that little Quillery was an internationalist, too. He believed in brotherhood, but the moment he got a whiff of gunpowder he began to spout hate and revenge. And now those nice, polite Wops will probably have to shut him up with a firing squad."

"It is a painful necessity."

"And it demonstrates the sort of little trouble that your friend stirs up." Harry does not like Monsieur Weber.

They have come to the matter of Harry's staring so persistently at Irene, and his explanation that he has noticed from his first meeting with her a strange resemblance to someone he used to know; someone who occupies "a unique shrine in the temple of my memory." Irene is interested but would change the subject. She would know just why he degrades himself "touring about with those obvious little harlots." Harry, she believes, is fitted for something requiring more mentality. Besides, he is a very bad dancer.

"The King of Rumania thought I was pretty good," counters Harry.

"He is entitled to his opinion—and I to mine."

HARRY—I'll admit that I've done better things in my time. Would it surprise you to know that I was once with a mind-reading act?

IRENE—Really?

HARRY—Yeah.

IRENE—Now you're staring at me again.

HARRY—Have you ever been in Omaha?

IRENE—Omaha? Where is that? Persia?

HARRY—No. Nebraska. That's one of our states. I played there once with the greatest act of my career. I was a stooge for Zuleika, the Mind Reader. At least she called me her stooge. But I was the one who had to do all the brain work.

IRENE—And she read people's minds?

HARRY—I did it for her. I passed through the audience and fed her the cues. We were sensational, playing the finest picture houses in all the key cities. Zuleika sat up on the stage, blindfolded—and usually blind drunk.

IRENE—Oh, dear. And was *she* the one that I resemble?

HARRY—No! There was another act on the same bill. A troupe of Russians. . . .

IRENE—Russians?

HARRY—Singers, mandolin players, and squat dancers. One of them was a red-headed girl. She was fascinated by our act, and she kept pestering me to teach her the code. She said she could do it better than Zuleika.

IRENE—Those poor Russians. There are so many of them all over the world. And so many of them completely counterfeit!

HARRY—This dame was counterfeit all right. In fact, she was the God-damnedest liar I ever saw. She lied just for the sheer artistry of it. She kept after me so much that I told her finally to come up to my hotel room one night, and we'd talk it over.

IRENE—I hope you didn't tell her the code.

HARRY—No. After the week in Omaha the bill split. The Russians went to Sioux Falls and we went on the Interstate Time. I played with Zuleika for another year and then the drink got her and she couldn't retain. So the act busted up. I've always hoped I'd catch up with that red-headed Russian again sometime. She might have been good. She had the voice for it, and a kind of overtone of mystery.

IRENE—It's a characteristic Gypsy quality. And you never saw her again?

HARRY—No.

IRENE—Perhaps it is just as well. She couldn't have been so clever—being duped so easily into going to your room.

HARRY—She wasn't being duped! She knew what she was doing. If there was any duping going on, she was the one that did it.

IRENE—She *did* make an impression!

HARRY (*looking straight at her*)—I was crazy about her. She was womanhood at its most desirable—and most unreliable.

IRENE—And you such a connoisseur.

It is getting late. Harry has gone to the piano and is playing "Kak Stranna" again. He drifts into other Russian compositions. Suddenly he would know how "Ear-ray-na" spells her name. She spells it out. I-R-E-N-E! Now he knows! Everything fits! *She* is that red-headed liar!

"Irene is a very usual name in Russia," she says, laughing heartily.

HARRY—I don't care how usual it is. Everything fits together perfectly now. The name—the face—the voice—Chaliapin for a teacher! Certainly it's you! And it's no good shaking your head and looking amazed! No matter how much you may lie, you can't deny the fact that you slept with me in the Governor Bryan Hotel in Omaha in the fall of 1925. (IRENE *laughs heartily again.*) All right—go ahead and laugh. That blond hair had me fooled for a while—but now I know it's just as phoney as the bayonet wounds, and the parachute jumps into the jungle. . . .

IRENE (*still laughing*)—Oh—you amuse me.

HARRY—It's a pleasure to be entertaining. But you can't get away with it.

IRENE—You amuse me very much indeed. Here we are—on a mountain peak in Bedlam. Tonight, the Italians are bombing Paris. At this moment, the French may be bombing Rome, and the English bombing Germany—and the Soviets bombing Tokyo, and all you worry about is whether I am a girl you once met casually in Omaha.

HARRY—Did I say it was casual?

IRENE—Oh—it *is* amusing!

HARRY (*angrily*)—I know you're amused. I admit it's all very funny. I've admitted everything. I told you I was crazy about you. Now when are you going to give me a break and tell me—

IRENE—You! You are so troubled—so—so uncertain about everything.

HARRY—I'm not uncertain about it any more, Babe. I had you tagged from the start. There was something about you that was indelible . . . something I couldn't forget all these years. (WEBER *appears on the gallery, wearing his Sulka dressing gown.*)

WEBER—Forgive me for intruding, my dear. But I suggest that it's time for you to go to bed.

IRENE—Yes, Achille. At once. (WEBER *treats* HARRY *to a rather disparaging glance and exits.* IRENE *starts upstairs.*) Poor Achille! He suffers with the most dreadful insomnia—it is something on his mind. (*She goes up a few more steps.*) He is like Macbeth. Good night, my friend—my funny friend.

HARRY—Good night.

IRENE—And thank you for making me laugh so much—tonight.

HARRY—I could still teach you that code.

IRENE—Perhaps—we shall meet again in—what was the name of the hotel?

HARRY—It was the Governor Bryan.

IRENE—Oh, yes! The Governor Bryan! (*Laughing heartily, she exits.* HARRY *goes to the piano, sits down and starts to play* "Kak Stranna." DUMPTSY *enters from the bar.*)

DUMPTSY—That was wonderful—that singing and dancing.

HARRY (*still playing*)—Thanks, pal. Glad you enjoyed it.

DUMPTSY—Oh, yes, Mr. Van—that was good.

HARRY (*bangs a chord*)—Chaliapin—for God's *sake!*

DUMPTSY—I beg your pardon, sir?

HARRY (*rises*)—It's nothing. Good night, Dumptsy. (*He goes out into the lobby.*)

DUMPTSY—Good night, sir.

He starts for the bar as the curtain falls.

ACT III

Van has called a rehearsal of "Les Blondes" the following afternoon in the Cocktail Lounge. At the moment, however, the blondes are not doing much rehearsing. Harry is at the piano strumming through Kreisler's "Caprice Viennois." Shirley is darning stockings. Bebe is plucking her eyebrows. Beulah is telling Elaine's fortune with cards and Francine and Edna are looking on.

They successfully absorb Beulah's news that Elaine is going to marry again, and probably again after that, before Harry calls them to order. When he does he is a little peevish. He has not liked their performance of the night before. He is determined that before they strike the big time in Geneva, where their audiences will be important, they have got to brighten their act.

"Now, listen to me, girls. Geneva's a key spot, and we've got to be good," warns Harry. "Your audiences there won't be a lot of hunkies, who don't care what you do as long as you don't wear practically any pants. These people are accustomed to the best. They're mains—big people, like prime ministers, and maharajahs and archbishops. If we click with them, we'll be set for London and Paris. We may even make enough money to get us home."

Furthermore, that the act may be still more definitely improved, Harry has decided to retire from the dance routine. This statement rather worries the girls, but Harry sticks to it.

"I've decided that I'm a thinker, rather than a performer. From now on, I shall devote myself to the purely creative end of the act, and, of course, the negotiation of contracts."

Shirley is decidedly suspicious. Just what was it that Harry spent so much time discussing with that Russian dame last night? And why this sudden decision—

Don Navadel is there dressed for traveling. The train is due to leave about four o'clock. Don has other news, too. The Italians had shot Quillery the night before.

"Of course, he asked for it," admits Don, "but even so, it's pretty sickening to see one of your fellow human beings crumpled up in horrible, violent death. Well—there'll be plenty more like him, and right here, too. The French know all about this air base, and they'll be over any minute with their bombs. So—it's California here I come!"

"But I can't understand—why did they have to shoot that

poor boy?" Beulah wants to know.

"It's hard to explain, Beulah," admits Harry. "But it seems there's some kind of argument going on over here, and the only way they can settle it is by murdering a lot of people."

Mr. and Mrs. Cherry are ready for the four o'clock train. Their honeymoon is over. Mr. Cherry will have to get back to England to do his bit for civilization. "Perhaps he'll join in the bombardment of Florence, where we were married," says Mrs. Cherry, bitterly.

"You know—after the ceremony we went into the Baptistry and prayed to the soul of Leonardo da Vinci that we might never fail in our devotion to that which is beautiful and true. I told you we were a bit on the romantic side. We forgot what Leonardo said about war. Bestial frenzy, he called it. And bestial frenzy it is."

"But we mustn't think about that now. We have to stand by France. We have to make the world a decent place for heroes to live in. Oh, Christ!" (*She starts to sob.* CHERRY *rushes to her.*)

"Now, now, darling. We've got to make a pretense of being sporting about it. Please, darling. Don't cry."

"Let her cry, the poor kid," speaks up Harry. "Let her sob her heart out—for all the God-damned good it will do her. You know what I often think? (*He is trying to be tactful.*) I often think we ought to get together and elect somebody else God. Me, for instance. I'll bet I'd do a much better job."

"You'd be fine, Mr. Van."

"I believe I would. There'd be a lot of people who would object to my methods. That Mr. Weber, for instance. I'd certainly begin my administration by beating the can off him."

"Let's start the campaign now! Vote for good old Harry Van, and his Six Angels."

Captain Locicero has brought a briefcase full of passports. He is apologetic for the state of affairs, but he is not responsible.

Achille Weber is pleased to learn that everything is in order so far as he is concerned. There has, however, been some little difficulty about Madame Irene's passport, the Captain reports. It has been issued by the League of Nations, which is often done when there is doubt as to a traveler's nationality. But so long as Madame is traveling with Monsieur Weber, and Monsieur will vouch for her, the Captain will be quite willing—

"Vouch for her," interposes Weber, with cold authority; "it is not necessary for anyone to vouch for Madame! She is entirely capable of taking care of herself. If her passport is not entirely in order, it is no affair of mine."

"But—I must tell you, Monsieur Weber—this is something I do not like. This places me in a most embarrassing position. I shall be forced to detain her."

"You are a soldier, my dear Captain, and you should be used to embarrassing positions. Undoubtedly you were embarrassed this morning, when you had to shoot that confused pacifist, Quillery. But this is war, and unpleasant responsibilities descend upon you and on me as well. However . . . (*He sees* HARRY, *who is coming in.*) I shall attend to my luggage. Thank you, Captain."

Monsieur Weber has gone. Harry Van is back, and soon Doctor Waldersee is down from his room with his arms filled with luggage. Harry is hoping the Doctor has the rats safely packed and that he (Harry) will yet have the chance to boast of having known the man who saved the world from cancer. The Doctor, however, is bitter. He is going back to Germany. With Germany at war he may be needed—

"Why should I save people who don't want to be saved—so that they can go out and exterminate each other?" demands the Doctor, fiercely. "Obscene maniacs! Then I'll be a maniac, too. Only I'll be more dangerous than most of them. For I know all the tricks of death! And—as for my rats, maybe they'll be useful. Britain will put down the blockade again, and we shall be starving—and maybe I'll cut my rats into filets and eat them."

It is an added disappointment to Harry that the Doctor should go back on his convictions as to the degradation of mankind, but there seems nothing he can do about it. He stands wearily contemplating this thought when Irene appears on the balcony. Soon she is joined by Monsieur Weber and the matter of the irregularities respecting her passport are taken up with Captain Locicero. Irene is not deeply concerned. Monsieur Weber will settle the problems, whatever they are.

"There is some question about your nationality," Weber reports, coldly.

"It states here, Madame, that your birthplace is uncertain, but assumed to be Armenia," adds the Captain.

"That is a province of Russia!"

"You subsequently became a resident of England, then of the United States, and then of France."

"Yes—it's all there—clearly stated," insists Irene, angrily. "I have never before had the slightest difficulty about my passport. It was issued by the League of Nations."

"I'm afraid the standing of the League of Nations is not very high in Italy at this moment."

"The fact is, Madame, the very existence of the League is no longer recognized by our government," concludes Captain Locicero. "For that reason we cannot permit you to cross the frontier at this time."

Monsieur Weber is mildly sympathetic. He would also wait over, but Irene knows how dangerous delays are in his case. He would advise her to go on to Vienna and hands her such money as she will need. Irene thanks Monsieur for his tact in managing everything.

"You are a genuinely superior person, my dear," explains Monsieur; "it is a privilege to have known you." He has kissed her hand and is gone.

Harry watches Irene as she puts Weber's money in her handbag. Then he, too, would be sympathetic. "Tough luck, babe," he ventures, moving toward her. "I just talked to the Captain and he isn't going to be as brutal as the Bolsheviks were. I mean, you won't suffer any bayonet wounds. He'll fix it for you to get through tomorrow."

IRENE—You want to be encouraging, my dear friend. But it's no use. The Italian government has too many reasons for wishing to detain me. They'll see to it that I disappear—quietly—and completely.

HARRY—Yes—I know all about that.

IRENE—All about what?

HARRY—You're a person of tremendous significance. You always were. (SHIRLEY *appears*.)

SHIRLEY—Hey, Harry! It's time for us to go.

HARRY—I'll be right out. (SHIRLEY *goes*.)

IRENE—Go away—go away with your friends. If I am to die, it is no concern of yours!

HARRY—Listen, babe—I haven't any wish to . . .

IRENE (*flaming*)—And please don't call me *babe!* (*She stands up and walks away from him. He follows her.*)

HARRY—My apologies, Madame. I just call everybody "babe."

IRENE—Perhaps that's why I do not like it!

HARRY—Even if I don't believe anything you say, I can see pretty plainly that you're in a tough spot. And considering what we were to each other in the old Governor Bryan Hotel—

IRENE—Must you always be in Omaha?

HARRY—I'd like to help you, Irene. Isn't there something I can do?

IRENE—I thank you, from my heart, I thank you, for that offer. But it's useless. . . .

HARRY—You don't have to thank me. Tell me—what can I do?

IRENE—You're very kind, and very gallant. But, unfortunately, you're no match for Achille Weber. He has decided that I shall remain here and his decision is final!

HARRY—Is he responsible for them stopping you?

IRENE—Of course he is. I knew it the moment I saw that ashamed look on Captain Locicero's face, when he refused to permit me . . .

HARRY—So Weber double-crossed you, did he! What has the son of a bitch got against you?

IRENE—He's afraid of me. I know too much about his methods of promoting his own business.

HARRY—Everybody knows about his methods. Little Quillery was talking about them last night . . .

IRENE—Yes—and what happened to Quillery? That's what happens to everyone who dares to criticize him. Last night I did the one thing he could never forgive. I told him the truth! At last I told him just what I think. And now—you see how quickly he strikes back! (SHIRLEY and BEBE appear.)

SHIRLEY—Harry! The bus is going to leave.

HARRY—All right—all right!

BEBE—But we got to go this minute!

HARRY—I'll be with you. Get out!

SHIRLEY (as they go)—Can you imagine? He stops everything to make another pass at that Russian. (They have gone.)

IRENE—Go ahead—go ahead! You can't help me! No one can! (He picks up his coat and hat.) But—if it will make you any happier in your future travels with Les Blondes, I'll tell you, yes—I did know you, slightly, in Omaha!

HARRY (peering at her)—Are you lying again?

IRENE—It was Room 974. Does that convince you?

HARRY (ferociously)—How can I remember what room it was?

IRENE (smiling)—Well, then—you'll never be sure, Mr. Van.

BEBE'S VOICE—Harry!

SHIRLEY'S VOICE—For God's sake, Harry!

DON (appearing)—We can't wait another instant! (DON goes.)

SHIRLEY'S VOICE—Come on!

HARRY (*turns and starts for the door, addressing the Girls en route*)—All right, God damn it!

Harry has gone. Irene has found her vanity case and done something to her face. Dumptsy, the waiter, is in. He wears the Italian uniform and is both conscious and amused. His friends are going to laugh loudly when they see him. Irene thinks she would like to drink a bottle of champagne with Dumptsy. . . . Signor Pittaluga is ready to show Madame back to her suite. Irene has decided to take a smaller room at the other side of the hotel. Captain Locicero is also eager to be of service to Madame, if she will permit— But there is nothing the Captain can do.

Irene has put aside her hat and coat and is at the piano trying to pick out a sketchy accompaniment to "Kak Stranna." She may be crying a little when Harry comes back. He is wearing a snappy overcoat and his hat and lays both quickly aside. He helps himself to some of the champagne. In answer to Irene's anxious queries, Harry reports that he had put the girls on the train and asked Mr. and Mrs. Cherry to look out for them. He has come back to help Irene, but mostly to tell her that now he is sure it *was* Room 974 at the Governor Bryan Hotel. Or pretty close to it.

"I couldn't help feeling rather flattered, and touched, to think that with all the sordid hotel rooms you've been in, you should have remembered that one," Harry says, between drinks of champagne. And Irene is pleased. The Chevalier Bayard is not dead!

"Somewhere in that funny, music-hall soul of yours is the spirit of Leander, and Abelard, and Galahad," she says to him. "You give up everything—risk your life—walk unafraid into the valley of the shadow—to aid and comfort a damsel in distress. Isn't that the truth?"

"Yes—it's the truth—plainly and simply put," he admits. "Listen to me, babe—when are you going to break down and tell me who the hell are you?"

"Does it matter so very much who I am?"

"No."

"Give me some more champagne. My father was not one of the Romanoffs. But for many years, he was their guest—in Siberia. From him I learned that it is no use telling the truth to people whose whole life is a lie. But you—Harry—you are different. You are an honest man."

"I am—am I?"

Harry has ordered another bottle of champagne and closed the door to the bar. He wants to talk seriously to Irene. He wants her to know that if she is hooking up with him it is only for professional reasons. Moreover he is going to be the manager. He will fix it so they can cross the border and rejoin the girls. In Geneva they can rehearse the mind-reading code. If Irene is smart and will apply herself she can master that in six months or so. More than that, if she is to qualify as a mind reader she has got to lay off liquor, after, of course, they have finished their last bottle. Booze and science won't mix.

"I don't think I shall use my own name," muses Irene. "No— Americans would mispronounce it horribly. No, I shall call myself—Namoura . . . Namoura the Great—assisted by Harry Van."

"You've got nice billing there."

"I shall wear a black velvet dress—very plain—my skin ivory white. I must have something to hold. One white flower. No! A little white prayer book. That's it. A little white . . . (*The warning siren is heard.*) What's that?"

"Sounds like a fire!"

It is the airplane warning. Soon the Captain and a Major burst in from the bar. Gazing excitedly from the stairway window they decide French war planes are staging an attack in reprisal. The French are coming to destroy the air base. They will probably miss the hotel—but there might be an accident.

The room is filling with the help. The blinds are lowered. Captain Locicero would have them all take to the cellar. Irene would prefer to stay and watch the bombardment. She is not frightened. Death and she are old friends.

Now there is a bursting of bombs that shakes the hotel. Signor Pittaluga would also excitedly urge them into the cellar, for which he is evidently headed himself.

"Ridiculous!" protests Irene, with spirit. "Here we are, on top of the world—and he asks us to go down into the cellar. . . . Do you want to go into the cellar?"

"Do you?"

IRENE—No. If a bomb hits, it will be worse in the cellar. (*He holds her close to him. She kisses him.*) I love you, Harry.

HARRY—You do, eh!

IRENE—Ever since that night—in the Governor Bryan Hotel— I've loved you. Because I knew that you have a heart that I can trust. And that whatever I would say to you, I would never

—*never* be misunderstood.

HARRY—That's right, babe. I told you I had you tagged, right from the beginning.

IRENE—And you adore me, don't you, darling?

HARRY—No! Now lay off—

IRENE—No—of course not—you mustn't admit it!

HARRY—Will you please stop pawing me? (*She laughs and lets go of him.*)

IRENE (*going to the window, opens the slats of the blinds, and looks out. There is now a great noise of planes, machine guns and bombs.*)—Oh, you must see this! It's superb! (*He crosses to the window with his glass and looks out. The light on the stage is growing dimmer, but a weird light comes from the window. The scream of many gas bombs is heard.*) It's positively Wagnerian—isn't it?

HARRY—It looks to me exactly like "Hell's Angels." Did you ever see that picture, babe?

IRENE—No. I don't care for films.

HARRY—I *do*. I love 'em—every one of them. (*He is dragging her to the piano—a comparatively safe retreat.*) Did you know I used to play the piano in picture theatres? Oh, sure—I know all the music there is. (*They are now at the piano—*HARRY *sitting.* IRENE *standing close by him. She is looking toward the window. He starts to accompany the air-raid with the "Ride of the Walkyries." There is a loud explosion.*)

IRENE—Harry . . .

HARRY—Yes, babe?

IRENE—Harry—do you realize that the whole world has gone to war? The *whole world!*

HARRY—I realize it. But don't ask me why. Because I've stopped trying to figure it out.

IRENE—I know why it is. It's just for the purpose of killing *us* . . . you and me. (*There is another loud explosion.* HARRY *stops playing.*) Because we are the little people—and for us the deadliest weapons are the most merciful. . . . (*Another loud explosion.* HARRY *drinks.*)

HARRY—They're getting closer.

IRENE—Play some more. (*He resumes the "Walkyrie."*) Harry —do you know any hymns?

HARRY—What?

IRENE—*Do you know any hymns?*

HARRY—Certainly. (*He starts to play "Onward, Christian Soldiers," in furious jazz time, working in strains of "Dixie." There*

*is another fearful crash, shattering the pane of the big window.
He drags her down beside him at the piano.* HARRY *resumes
"Onward, Christian Soldiers" in a slow, solemn tempo.*) Onward,
Christian Soldiers—(IRENE *joins* HARRY *in the loud singing.*)

> Marching as to war—
> With the cross of Jesus
> Going on before . . .

The din is now terrific! Demolition—bombs, gas-bombs, air-planes, shrapnel, machine guns!

THE CURTAIN FALLS

END OF SUMMER

A Drama in Three Acts

By S. N. Behrman

SAMUEL NATHANIEL BEHRMAN, who greatly prefers the simple S. N. as a handle to his surname, is the American drama-tist whose work of late seasons has been most frequently com-pared with that of the Bernard Shaw of the eighteen nineties, and he the despair of the dramaturgic action and conflict theorists a quarter century ago. Doubtless because Mr. Behrman, like Mr. Shaw, is much more deeply concerned with what his characters have to say than he is with the method of their saying it. His dramas are quite frequently condemned as "talky," but just as frequently extolled as "brilliant."

This was true of "End of Summer," which, in any fair rating, is entitled to be classified as the second outstanding hit of the Theatre Guild's list of four—the others being Robert Sherwood's "Idiot's Delight," Dodie Smith's "Call It a Day" and the Hey-ward-Gershwin musicalized "Porgy and Bess."

"S. N. Behrman, the dramatist who has discovered a virtually critic-proof method of saying wise and important things in an amiable way, is a one-play-a-year craftsman," wrote Whitney Bolton in the *Literary Digest*. "Season by season he adds to his score and his stature with witty exercises in flinty philosophy. Last season it was 'Rain From Heaven.' This season it is 'End of Summer.' Last season it was compassion and truth. This season it is surrender and doubt. And there are not three persons in the whole grasp of the New York theatre who can agree which is the better of the two plays."

Mr. Behrman is also interested definitely in the problems of the intelligent minority. He has the gift of moving naturally about the drawing rooms of the well-to-do and of reporting their ob-servations with a grace and conviction which the listener may feel flatters them extravagantly, but seldom sounds either forced or didactic.

The veranda-living room of Bay Cottage, the Frothinghams' summer place in Northern Maine, is a charmingly furnished room, with beautiful old distinguished pieces. The chintz coverings give

101

the room an air of informality. On this particularly lovely afternoon in May, when "End of Summer" opens, silver birch and maple trees, seen through windows that look out on the gardens at back, are just beginning to put out their leaves. Woodbine and Virginia creeper are sprawling over the fences of native stone. The sea is beyond.

There are two people in the room at the moment, Mrs. Wyler, a very old lady, and Will Dexter, a very young man. From Mrs. Wyler young Dexter, by a process of polite but eager cross-questioning, is learning something of the history of the Wyler pioneers. It was through their discoveries of oil that the family dynasty was established. Mrs. Wyler can remember when an oil gusher broke forth directly in their backyard in Oil City. She does not remember, however, that the discovery of oil was particularly exciting to anybody, certainly not to the young people. Excitements of that sort were left to the men.

"As I look back over my life the principal excitement came from houses—buying and building houses," she says. "The shack in Oil City to the mansion on Fifth Avenue. We had houses everywhere—houses in London, houses in Paris, Newport and this—and yet, it seemed to me, we were always checking in and out of hotels."

"It seems strange to think—" Will begins.

"What?"

"This golden stream—that you stumbled on so accidentally—it's flowing still—quenchless—and you on it—all you dynastic families—floating along in it—in luxurious barges."

Mrs. Wyler is not impressed by the politely critical attitude of her young friend. Nor by the attitude of the authors of so-called debunking books attacking the monied leaders of her time. The Wylers and their kind did as well as anybody could, according to their lights. At least their young men didn't moon about. They made opportunities for themselves.

"Or did the opportunities make them?" queries Will. "All you had to do was to pack your week-end bag and pioneer."

Will is free to admit that he is one of those young radicals the colleges are full of these days. If he doesn't know exactly what he stands for he is reasonably certain of what he is against. Will is greatly interested in the past. He loves talking to Grandma Wyler. And when it comes her turn to ask questions he is ready to answer. No, he is not staying on at Bay Cottage. He must go back to Amherst to get his degree. What, after that? Probably the dole. Mrs. Frothingham has been kind enough to invite Will's father

"END OF SUMMER"

Leonie: You are such a comfort. Really it is too much now to expect me to do without you. Kenneth?

Kenneth: Yes, Leonie.

Leonie: Will you be a darling—and marry me?

(*Osgood Perkins, Ina Claire, Doris Dudley*)

down, and that will be interesting. The elder Dexter is a physicist out of a job just now because his inventions have been too successful. Their application would greatly increase technological unemployment. Another young friend who is expected is Dennis McCarthy. It is with McCarthy that Will has some hope of starting a magazine.

"A national magazine for undergraduate America," Will explains. "You see, Mrs. Wyler, before the rift in our so-called system, college men were supposed to live exclusively in a world of ukuleles, football slogans, and petting parties—*College Humor* sort of thing. But it was never entirely true. Now it is less true than ever. The magazine—if we can get it going—would be a forum for intercollegiate thought. It would be the organ of critical youth, as opposed—to the other."

"What other?"

"The R.O.T.C., the Vigilantes and the Fascists—the Youth Movement of guns and sabers—"

Paula Frothingham has joined them. Paula "is a lovely young girl in gay summer slacks." She is amused to hear that her grandmother and Will have been discussing "life with a capital L." And pleased that Will has made such a conquest of Granny. He is way ahead of all her other beaus, she tells him, after Mrs. Wyler has left them.

"I'm crazy about her," Will admits. "You feel that she has been through everything and that she understands everything. Not this, though. Not the essential difference between her times and ours."

"Oh, dear! Is it the end of the world, then?"

"The end of this world."

"Such a pretty world," mutters Paula, at the window. "Look at it! Too bad it has to go. Meantime before it quite dissolves let's go for a swim."

Will is ready for a swim but there is something he must settle first. It is something about Paula's mother. Paula is not surprised. Mother is always up to something. Or is it that Will has fallen in love with Mother? Most of Paula's boy friends do.

Mother, it appears, has left Will a note, under his breakfast plate, inclosing a check for a hundred dollars and a request that he spend it giving her little girl a good time. Paula is not surprised. But if Mother thinks her little girl can have a good time with *that* she doesn't know her little girl. Nor has she any intention of helping Will return the check—

"Catch me!" protests Paula. "Don't take it too seriously. She slips all the kids something every once in a while. She knows my friends all are stony. You overestimate the importance of money, Will—it's a convenience, that's all. You've got a complex on it."

WILL—I have! I've got to have. It's all right to be dainty about money when you've lots of it, as you have. . . .

PAULA—Rotten with it is the expression, I believe. . . .

WILL—I repudiate that expression. It is genteel and moralistic. You can't be rotten with money—you can only be *alive* with it.

PAULA—You and the rest of our crowd make me feel it's bad taste to be rich. But what can I do? I didn't ask for it!

WILL—I know. But look here . . . I've got a brother out of college two years who's worked six weeks in that time and is broke and here I am in an atmosphere with hundred-dollar bills floating around!

PAULA (*with check*)—Send him that!

WILL—Misapplication of funds!

PAULA (*warmly*)—Mother would be only too . . .

WILL—I know she would—but that isn't the point. . . . You know, Paula—

PAULA—What?

WILL—Sometimes I think if we weren't in love with each other we should be irreconciliable enemies—

PAULA—Nothing but sex, eh?

WILL—That's all.

PAULA—In that case— (*They kiss.*)

WILL—That's forgiving. But seriously, Paula—

PAULA—Seriously what?

WILL—I can't help feeling I'm here on false pretenses. What am I doing with a millionaire family—with you? If your mother knew what I think, and what I've let you in for in college—she wouldn't touch me with a ten-foot pole. And you too—I'm troubled about the superficiality of your new opinions. Isn't your radicalism—acquired coloring?

PAULA—I hope not. But—so is all education.

WILL—I know but—!

PAULA—What are you bleating about? Didn't I join you on that expedition to Kentucky to be treated by that sovereign state as an offensive foreigner? My back aches yet when I remember that terrible bus ride. Didn't I get my name in the papers picketing? Didn't I give up my holiday to go with you to the Chicago Peace Congress? Didn't I?

WILL (*doubtfully*)—Yes, you did.

PAULA—But you're not convinced. Will darling, don't you

realize that since knowing you and your friends, since I've, as you say, acquired your point of view about things, my life has had an excitement and a sense of reality it's never had before? I've simply come alive—that's all! Before then I was bored—terribly bored without knowing why. I wanted something more—fundamental—without knowing what. You've made me see. I'm terribly grateful to you, Will darling. I always shall be.

Will is still worried about the money. If Paula should turn it all over to him, as she threatens to do, he swears he will use it in every way he can to make it impossible for anyone ever to have so much again. That, too, would be all right with Paula.

A telephone message from Paula's father announces his approach, and Paula is quite thrilled. Troubled a bit, as well. Her father doesn't know about Mother's latest. Not a certain Russian. The Russian dates from last winter. But a new one, a Dr. Rice, a psychoanalyst from New York, who is also arriving today—

And now Mother comes in, "running a little and breathless, like a young girl." Leonie Frothingham "is slim, girlish, in a young and quivering ecstasy of living and anticipation. . . . There is something, for all her gaiety, heartbreaking about Leonie, something childish and child-like—an acceptance of people instantly and uncritically at the best of their own valuation. She is impulsive and warm hearted and generous to a fault. . . . A spirituelle amoureuse she is repelled by the gross or the voluptuary; this is not hypocrisy—it is, in Leonie, a more serious defect than that. In the world in which she moves hypocrisy is merely a social lubricant, but this myopia—alas for Leonie!—springs from a congenital and temperamental inability to face anything but the pleasantest and the most immediately appealing and the most flattering aspects of things—in life and in her own nature."

At the moment Leonie is thrilled with the radiance of the day. A little startled to hear that Sam, her husband, has telephoned; a little piqued that he is on his way to Selena Bryant's; a little disturbed at Paula's attitude—

LEONIE (*her most winning smile on* WILL)—Does she bully you, Will? Don't let her bully you. The sad thing is, Paula, you're so charming. Why aren't you content to be charming? Are you as serious as Paula, Will? I hope not.

WILL—Much more.

LEONIE—I'm sorry to hear that. Still, for a man, it's all right, I suppose. But why are the girls nowadays so determined not to be feminine? Why? It's coming back you know—I'm sure of it—femininity is due for a revival.

PAULA—So are Herbert Hoover and painting on china.

LEONIE—Well, I read that even in Russia . . . the women . . . (*She turns again to* WILL *whom she feels sympathetic.*) It isn't as if women had done such marvels with their masculinity! Have they? Are things better because women vote? Not that I can see. They're worse. As far as I can see the women simply reinforce the men in their mistakes.

WILL (*to* PAULA)—She has you there!

LEONIE (*with this encouragement warming to her theme*)—When I was a girl the calamities of the world were on a much smaller scale. It's because the women, who, after all, are half the human race, stayed at home and didn't bother. Now they do bother—and look at us!

PAULA—Well, that's as Victorian as anything I ever—

LEONIE—I'd love to have been a Victorian. They were much happier than we are, weren't they? Of course they were.

PAULA (*defending herself to* WILL)—It's only Mother that brings out the crusader in me— (*To* LEONIE.) When you're not around I'm not like that at all.

Leonie is quite excited about her psychologist friend, Dr. Rice. A man of astounding achievements. He had psychoanalyzed Leonie's friend, Sissy Drake, and cured her absolutely of a terrible blinking habit she had. The Doctor proved that it was due to Mrs. Drake's inability to look at her husband without blinking. She divorced the husband, married Bill Wilmerding and is now as normal as anyone. Leonie hopes Dr. Rice will be able to help her Russian friend, Boris. Boris, who has been writing the memoirs of his father, the great Count Mirsky of Russia, is giving signs of being overworked—

"Isn't it strange that Count Mirsky's son should find himself in this strange house on this odd headland of Maine—Maine of all places—writing his father's life? It's fantastic!" declares Will.

"Is Dr. Rice going to help you acclimate him?" Paula asks Leonie, with some malice.

"I hope so." (*To* WILL.) "You and Paula will have to entertain him—you young intellectuals. Isn't it a pity I have no mind?" . . .

The matter of the note and the check has come up. Leonie hopes that Will understood. Will is sure it was very generous of Leonie. She would not have him think that, either—

"Generous! Please don't say that. After all—we who are in the embarrassing position nowadays of being rich must do something with our money, mustn't we? That's why I'm helping Boris to write this book. *Noblesse oblige.* Don't you think so, Will? Boris tells me that the Russians—the *present*—Russians—"

"You mean the Bolsheviks?"

"Yes, I suppose I do. He says they don't like his father at all any more and won't read his works because in his novels he occasionally went on the assumption that rich people had souls and spirits, too. You don't think like that, too, do you, Will—that because I'm rich I'm just not worth bothering about at all— No, you couldn't!"

"Mrs. Frothingham—I love you!"

"Isn't he sweet?" Leonie has risen from the arm of the sofa and found herself a place next to Will. "And I love you, Will. Please call me Leonie. Do you know how mother happened to name me Leonie? I was born in Paris, you know, and I was to be called Ruhama after my father's sister. But Mother said no. No child of mine, she said, shall be called Ruhama. She shall have a French name. And where do you think she got Leonie?"

"From the French version of one of those Gideon Bibles."

"Not at all. From a novel the nurse was reading. She asked the nurse what she was reading and the nurse gave her the paper book and Mother opened it and found Leonie!"

"What was the book?"

"Everyone wants to know that. . . . But I don't know. Mother didn't know. She kept the book to give to me when I grew up. But one day she met M. Jusserand on a train—he was the French Ambassador to Washington, you know—and he picked up the book in Mother's compartment and he read a page of it and threw it out of the window because it was trash! You see what I have had to live down."

Leonie has gone now. She is still a problem to Paula. "She makes me feel like an opinionated old woman. . . . She arouses my maternal impulse," confesses Paula.

"She relies rather too much on charm," Will thinks. If she does, Paula is convinced, it certainly has worked. What happened to all Will's fine indignation about the check? What became of the insult to his pride? Will's only defense is that it just seems cruel to face Leonie with realities. . . .

Sam Frothingham, Paula's father, has arrived. "A very pleasant-faced, attractive man between forty-five and fifty," Sam is deeply devoted to his daughter and she to him. Paula sends Will to wait for her at the beach while she sets her father right as to the more recent Frothingham family activities. Sam knows about the Russian, Boris, but Dr. Rice, who has been invited up, Paula says, "to massage the Russian's complexes," is new. Sam, usually worried as to just what is going to happen to Leonie, is more anxious than usual this day. He has come to tell Paula that he has fallen in love. Sounds absurd—romance at his age—but there it is. He will, of course, have to divorce Leonie.

"Do you feel I am deserting you?" Sam asks, as Paula turns her head away to cover her emotion.

"No—you know how fond I am of you—I want you to be . . . happy," Paula manages to answer.

"I must make you see my side, Paula."

"I do."

"It isn't only that—you're so young—but, somehow—we decided very soon after you were born, Leonie and I, that our marriage could only continue on this sort of basis. For your sake we've kept it up. I thought I was content to be an—appendage—to Leonie's entourage. But I'm not—do you know what Selena—being with Selena and planning with Selena for ourselves has made me see—that I've never had a home. Does that sound mawkish?"

"I thought you loved Bay Cottage?"

"Of our various menages this is my favorite—it's the simplest. And I've had fun here with you—watching you grow up. But very soon after I married Leonie I found this out—that when you marry a very rich woman it's always *her* house you live in."

"I'm awfully happy for you, Sam, really I am. You deserve everything, but I can't help it, I . . ."

"I know!"

It is Sam's hope that, if Leonie should marry again, as she undoubtedly will, Paula will want to come and live with him and Selena. Selena admires Paula enormously and she likes Selena. Sam and Selena expect to live in New York, where Selena will keep up with her work. Paula is grateful, but she, too, is hoping for a sort of independence; she wants to feel that she is standing on her own feet; that she is justified.

"I mean it—really I do," Paula goes on, as Sam smiles understandingly. "It's curious—how—adrift—this makes me feel. As if something vital, something fundamental had smashed. I wonder how Mother'll take it? I think—unconsciously—she depends on you more than she realizes. You were a stabilizing force, Sam, in spite of everything."

It is Sam's opinion that Paula is the stabilizing force, but she is afraid not. Some of these days someone may come along who is not as harmless as Boris, and then—

Leonie is back, bringing with her Dr. Kenneth Rice, Dennis McCarthy and Will Dexter. "Dr. Rice is handsome, dark, magnetic, quiet, masterful. He is conscious of authority and gives one the sense of a strange, genius-like intuition. Dennis is a flamboyant Irishman, a little older than Will, gawky, black-haired, slovenly, infinitely brash."

The greetings, under Leonie's direction, are gay and friendly. She is ever so pleased to see Sam, and glad to hear of Selena. Leonie envies Selena above all women; Selena is so attractive and self-sufficient; Leonie is so dependent on other people. Dr. Rice might make Leonie self-sufficient, the Doctor admits, but he would never dream of doing it. "It would deprive your friends of their most delightful avocation," he assures his hostess.

It now appears that Leonie has been hearing great argument all the way in from Ellsworth. Dr. Rice and the younger generation have been at grips. "Statistics and theology—with some metaphysics thrown in," as Dennis phrases it, have been given a considerable going over.

"Dr. Rice still believes in the individual career," explains Will.

"I hang my head in shame," admits Kenneth.

DENNIS—He doesn't know that as a high officer of the National Student Federation, I have at my fingers' ends the statistics which rule our future, the statistics which constitute our horizon. Not your future, Paula, because you are living parasitically on the stored pioneerism of your ancestors.

PAULA—Forgive me, Reverend Father!

DENNIS—I represent, Doctor, the Unattached Youth of America—

KENNETH—Well, that's a career in itself! (*They laugh.*)

DENNIS (*imperturbable*)—When we presently commit the folly of graduating from a benevolent institution at Amherst, Massachusetts, there will be in this Republic two million like us. Two million helots. (*Leaning over* LEONIE.) But Dr. Rice pooh-poohs statistics.

LEONIE (*arranging his tie*)—Does he, Dennis?

DENNIS—He says the individual can surmount statistics, violate the graphs. Superman!

WILL—Evidently Dr. Rice got in just under the wire.

KENNETH—I'd never submit to statistics, Mr. Dexter—I'd submit to many things but not to statistics.

LEONIE—Such dull things to submit to—

DENNIS—You must be an atheist, Dr. Rice.

KENNETH—Because I don't believe in statistics?—the new God?

LEONIE—Well, *I'm* a Protestant and I don't believe in them either.

DENNIS—Well, Protestant is a loose synonym for atheist—and I, as an Irishman—and a—

KENNETH—Young man—

DENNIS—Yes?

KENNETH—Have you ever heard Bismarck's solution of the Irish problem?

DENNIS—No. What?

KENNETH—Oh, it's entirely irrelevant.

LEONIE—Please tell us. I adore irrelevancies.

KENNETH—Well, he thought the Irish and the Dutch should exchange countries. The Dutch, he thought, would very soon make a garden out of Ireland, and the Irish would forget to mend the dikes. (*They laugh.*)

LEONIE—That's not irrelevant.

DENNIS—It is an irrelevance, but pardonable in an adversary losing an argument.

KENNETH (*to* PAULA)—Miss Frothingham, you seem very gracious. Will you get me out of this?

PAULA—No, I'm enjoying it.

LEONIE—Whatever you may say, Dennis, it's an exciting time to be alive.

DENNIS—That is because your abnormal situation renders you free of its major excitement.

LEONIE—And what's that, Dennis?

DENNIS—The race with malnutrition.

KENNETH—But that race, Mr.—?

DENNIS—McCarthy.

KENNETH— —is the eternal condition of mankind. Perhaps mankind won't survive the solution of that problem.

WILL (*with heat*)—It's easy to sit in this living room—and be smug about the survival of the fittest—especially when you're convinced you're one of the fittest. But there are millions who won't concede you that superiority, Dr. Rice. There are millions who are so outrageously demanding that they actually insist on the right to live! They may demand it one day at the cost of your complacency.

LEONIE—Will! We were just chatting.

WILL—I'm sorry! The next thing Dr. Rice'll be telling us is that war is necessary also—to keep us stimulated—blood-letting for the other fellow.

KENNETH—Well, as a matter of fact, there's something to be said for that too. If you haven't settled on a career yet, Mr. Dexter, may I suggest evangelism?

DENNIS—But, Dr. Rice—!

KENNETH—And now, Mrs. Frothingham, before these young people heckle me too effectively, may I escape to my room?

LEONIE (rising)—Of course. Though I don't think you need be afraid of their heckling, Doctor. You say things which I've always believed but never dared say.

Leonie has taken Dr. Rice to his room. The next arrival is Will's father, Dr. Dexter, "a dusty little man with a bleached yellow Panama hat" who doesn't hear very well. The elder Dexter is barely introduced before he and Dennis McCarthy have plunged into what evidently has been a sort of running argument covering the length of their acquaintance—Dennis contending that Science, as represented by the technologically expert Dr. Dexter, is starving and breaking the workers of the world; Dr. Dexter replying, with force and logic, that there is no present evidence that anyone starved and broken deserved a better fate.

". . . From the illimitable icebergs of the unknown I have chipped off a fragment of knowledge," earnestly concludes Dr. Dexter as he definitely puts the slightly startled Dennis in his place; "a truth which so-called practical men may put to a use which will make some of your numbers unnecessary in the workaday world. Well—what of it, I say?—who decrees that you shall be supported? Of what importance are your lives and your futures and your meandering aspirations compared to the firmness and the beauty and the cohesion of the principles I seek, the truth I seek? None—none whatever! Whether you prattle on an empty stomach or whether you prattle on a full stomach can make no difference to anybody that I can see. (To PAULA.) And now, young woman, as I have been invited here to spend the night, I'd like to see my room."

The butler has taken Dr. Dexter to his room. Dennis, smarting a little under the Scientist's charge, has gone into the garden and Will follows to soothe his friend's injured pride. Paula and Sam are left to face again their immediate problem. What of Leonie after Sam draws away from the family?

Leonie has come bounding back, impressed afresh with the charm and achievements of Dr. Rice. Paula promptly leaves them and now Sam, having heard of Paula's friends, and how radical they are; of how radical Paula is trying to be, and how amused Leonie is at being looked upon "as a hopeless kind of spoiled Bourbon living away in a never-never land—a kind of Marie Antoinette," has reached the point of his lightly embarrassing confession.

"I am in love with Selena Bryant. We want to get married," Sam says.

For a moment Leonie stares straight ahead of her. When she speaks she says, quite simply: "Human nature is funny! Mine is!"

"Why?"

"I know I ought to be delighted to release you. Probably I should have spoken to you about it myself before long—separating. And yet—when you tell me—I feel—a pang. . . ."

"That's very sweet of you."

"One's so possessive—one doesn't want to give up anything."

"For so many years our marriage has been at its best—a friendship. Need that end?"

"No, Sam. It needn't. I hope truly that it won't."

Their thoughts turn naturally to their daughter. Sam is frank to confess that he had spoken to Paula about coming with him and Selena. Leonie is resentful. She sees no reason why Paula should leave her, even if she should marry again. Nor any reason to believe Paula would not be as drawn to whomever she did marry as Sam seems to feel she has been drawn to Selena. Nor will she admit that Selena, being a working woman and of serious mind, could help her. Leonie suddenly feels very martyrish.

"Well, this sort of thing isn't good for Paula," persists Sam.

"What sort of thing?" demands Leonie, very cold, very hurt. "Be perfectly frank. You can be with me. What sort of thing?"

"Well, Leonie— You've made a career of flirtation. Obviously Paula isn't going to. You know you and Paula belong to different worlds. And," Sam adds, with considerable heat, "the reason Paula is the way she is is because she lives in an atmosphere of perpetual conflict."

"Conflict? Paula?"

"With herself. About you."

But that is too subtle for Leonie. It must have been suggested by Selena, she thinks, and is doubtful of Sam's denial. Leonie is sorry for anything she may have done to interfere with Paula's happiness—she is sorry for everything—and pretty close to tears as she runs out of the room. . . .

Paula has been showing Dr. Rice the rock-bound coast. She has found it a little difficult to make up her mind about the doctor. Finds him rather inscrutable. Still she is not prepared to accept Selena's estimate of him as a brilliant charlatan. She has, however, decided definitely about going with Sam and Selena after they are married. She thinks she will stay with Leonie, if Sam doesn't mind. Somebody has got to look after Leonie—

Dr. Rice is duly impressed with the Maine coast. "A masculine Riviera" he calls it. He hopes to see more of it, under Paula's guidance, whenever she has the time.

Leonie has sent for Dr. Rice. She would like to see him in her study. Paula and Sam turn to look at each other questioningly as the Doctor goes to answer the summons and the curtain falls.

ACT II

It is late afternoon the following midsummer. In the veranda-living room Kenneth Rice is working out a chess problem by himself. When he hears Boris and Leonie approaching he is quick to get out of the way, standing by the garden door until they have come in and then slipping into the garden unobserved.

Boris, Count Mirsky, "is very good looking, Mongoloid about the eyes. His English is beautiful, with a slight and attractive accent. He is tense, jittery, a mass of jangled nerves—his fingers tremble as he lights one cigarette after another."

Boris is not in a particularly agreeable mood. He is convinced that Leonie has come in from the garden because she thought someone was in the house. Just as, when they are in the house, she would go into the garden because she thinks someone is there. And Leonie knows quite well whom he means. Also Boris would call Leonie's attention to the fact that she has been divorced for several weeks. Her divorce was all they were waiting for— So? But Leonie refuses to be "coerced."

Now Dr. Rice has joined them. The Doctor has been in his room all day slaving away at a scientific paper. A paper on shadow-neurosis, "a sensation of non-existence. . . . The victim knows that he exists, and yet he feels that he does not!"

"In a curious way I can imagine a sensation like that—do you know I actually can," admits Leonie, brightly. "Isn't it amusing?"

"The doctor is so eloquent," agrees Boris. "Once he describes a sensation it becomes very easy to feel it."

"That's an entrancing gift," bubbles Leonie. "Why are you so antagonistic to Kenneth? He wants to help you, but you won't let him. I asked him here to help you."

"Your skepticism about this particular disease is interesting, Count Mirsky," ventures Kenneth; "because, as it happens, you suffer from it."

"Has it ever occurred to you that you are a wasted novelist?" asks Boris.

The conversation has turned to the book that Boris is writing. He is rather vague as to how well he is getting along with it, and more than a little startled when Dr. Rice charges that there is no such book, nor ever has been. He challenges Count Mirsky to produce the book, or any part of it. Kenneth could, however, suggest a title for such a book, if there were one. He would call it: "The Memoirs of a Boy Who Wanted to Murder His Father!"

"I am not a hysterical woman, Doctor—and I'm not your patient!" snaps Boris.

"But, Kenneth—Boris worshiped his father," adds Leonie.

"No, he hated him," persists Kenneth. "He hated him when he was alive and he hates him still. He grew up under the overwhelming shadow of this world-genius whom, in spite of an immense desire to emulate and even to surpass—he felt he could never emulate and never surpass—nor even equal— Did you worship your father, Count Mirsky?"

"It's true! I hated him!" admits Boris. And in answer to Leonie's repeated request that he let them see the book, he adds a further confession, "You might as well know it then. There isn't any book. There never will be. Not by me."

"But I don't understand—every day—in your room working —all these months! . . . protests Leonie.

"One wants privacy!" answers Boris, facing her. "Possibly you can't realize that. You who always have to have a house full of people. . . ."

Leonie considers Dr. Rice's skill in revealing Boris' character as nothing less than uncanny, but the Doctor considers it no more than an incident of the day's work. He is convinced, however, that she is the last woman in the world whom Count Mirsky should marry.

"I don't think I understand you, Kenneth—really I don't— and I do so want to understand things," pleads Leonie.

"Well—your charm, your gaiety, your position, your wealth, your beauty—these would oppress him. Again, he cannot be himself. Or, if he is himself, it is to reveal his nonentity, his inferiority—again the secondary role—Leonie Frothingham's husband—the son of Count Mirsky—the husband of Leonie Frothingham. Again the shadow—again, eternally and always—nonexistence. Poor fellow."

Leonie is ever so grateful to Kenneth. She would like to express her gratitude in some tangible form. She has been thinking a lot about that. She remembers once, when he had taken her to dinner in a little restaurant where he went with his doctor friends, that he had confessed to her his dream of one day having a sanitarium of his own. She should like to give him that.

Kenneth is not prepared to accept so generous a gift, particularly not from one who really knows him so little. Nor is he swayed by Leonie's argument that it would mean so much to her to do something that would be helpful to so many people.

"I distrust impulsive altruism," declares Kenneth, quite frankly. "You will forgive me, Leonie, but it may often do harm."

"How do you mean, Kenneth?"

"I gather you are about to endow a radical magazine for the *boys*—"

"Will and Dennis! I thought it would be nice to give them something to do."

"Yes. You are prepared to back them in a publication which, if it attained any influence, would undermine the system which makes you and people like you possible."

"But it never occurred to me anyone would read it."

"There is a deplorable high literacy in this country. Unfortunately it is much easier to learn to read than it is to learn to think."

Leonie is prepared to give up the magazine idea, if Kenneth doesn't approve, but she is still eager to go ahead with the sanitarium, if for no other reason than because it would be helping him, and he the first strong man who has ever come into her life. . . .

Will and Dennis are back from New York. Paula brings them in. Neither of the young men has anything in the way of luck to report. Neither has found anything to do. Yet neither is willing to accept Leonie's suggestion that they stay there for a time and rest. They might as well do nothing there as in New York.

"Yes, but it's an ethical question," explains Dennis. "When we're in New York doing nothing we belong to the most respectable vested group going! The unemployed. As such we have a status, position, authority. But if we stay here doing nothing—

what are we? Low-down parasites."

Still, Leonie doesn't see. Supposing Dennis has been rejected by no less than twenty-eight newspapers and magazines in one week in New York, why shouldn't he stay on at Bay Cottage and be rejected by mail?

"Doesn't give you that same feeling somehow—that good, rich, dark-brown sensation of not being wanted!" insists Dennis. . . .

Dennis and Leonie have decided to go for a swim. Kenneth follows to look on. Will and Paula have their first visit in some days. It has been lonesome in town without Paula, Will confesses, but he has made some progress. He has managed to collect eleven dollars for book reviews in *The Times* and *The Masses*.

So far as Paula is concerned, the time has arrived for a decision. She does not like the reports of Will's adventures in town. Doesn't care for the thought of his haunting the Public Library, nor the comfort he may have gained from seeking an occasional shoulder to lean on. If there is to be a shoulder from now on she will provide it.

"You know, the way you're avoiding the issue is all nonsense," says Paula.

"You mean my gallant fight against you?"

PAULA—I've decided that you are conventional and bourgeois. You're money-ridden.

WILL—Eleven dollars. They say a big income makes you conservative.

PAULA—I don't mean your money. I mean—my money. It's childish to let an artificial barrier like that stand between us. It's also childish to ignore it.

WILL (*rising*)—I don't ignore it. That's what worries me. I count on it. Already I find myself counting on it. I can't help it. Sitting and waiting in an office for some big-wig who won't see me or for some underling who won't see me, I think: "Why the hell should I wait all day for this stuffed shirt?" I don't wait. Is it because of you I feel in a special category? Do I count on your money? Is that why I don't wait as long as the other fellow? There's one consolation: the other fellow doesn't get the job either. But the point is disquieting!

PAULA—What a Puritan you are!

WILL (*sitting beside her again*)—Will I become an appendage to you—like your mother's men?

PAULA—You're bound to—money or no money.

WILL (*taking her in his arms*)—I suppose I might as well go on the larger dole—

PAULA—What?

WILL—Once you are paid merely for existing—you are on the dole. I rather hoped, you know—

PAULA—What?

WILL—It's extraordinary the difference in one's thinking when you're in college and when you're out—

PAULA—How do you mean?

WILL—Well, when I was in college, my interest in the—"movement"—was really impersonal. I imagined myself giving my energies to the poor and the downtrodden in my spare time. I didn't really believe I'd be one of the poor and downtrodden myself. In my heart of hearts I was sure I'd break through the iron law of Dennis's statistics and land a job somewhere. But I can't—and it's given a tremendous jolt to my self-esteem.

PAULA—But you'll come through. I'm sure of it. I wish you could learn to look at my money as a means rather than an end.

WILL—I'd rather use my own.

PAULA—You're proud.

WILL—I am.

PAULA—It's humiliating but I'm afraid I've got to ask you to marry me, Will.

WILL—It's humiliating but considering my feelings I see no way out of accepting you.

PAULA—You submit?

WILL (*kisses her hand*)—I submit.

PAULA—After a hard campaign—victory!

WILL—You *are* a darling.

Paula could sigh with relief at the thought of getting away from Bay Cottage. Affairs there are becoming complicated. What with Leonie, and Boris, and Dr. Rice—Paula can't stand Dr. Rice, and yet she is fascinated by him. . . .

Grandmother Wyler is wheeled in in her chair. She is much wasted since the preceding summer. Her mind is as alert as ever, even though her memory isn't as good as it was. "Now I just live from day to day," she tells Will. "The past is just this morning."

Mrs. Wyler has sent for Sam Frothingham. When he comes she loses little time in getting the others out of the room. She has sent for Sam, she explains, because he is one on whom she knows she can count. "Louise, you know you're the love of my life," says Sam.

"I'm dying, Sam. And I'm dying alone," says Granny. "I have

to talk to somebody. You're the only one."

There are plenty of things worrying Granny. The future particularly—Leonie's future, and Paula's. Granny feels she is surrounded by aliens. The house is full of strangers. The Russian! The Doctor? What do they want?

Is she worried about the boy, Dexter, and Paula, Sam would know.

"I like the boy," says Granny. "But Paula—I'm worried about what the money'll do to her. We know what it's done to Leonie. You know, Sam, in spite of all her romantic dreams Leonie has a kind of integrity. But I often wonder if she's ever been really happy."

"Oh, now, Louise, this pessimism's unlike you—"

MRS. WYLER—This money we've built our lives on—it used to symbolize security—but there's no security in it any more.

SAM—Paula'll be all right. I count on Paula.

MRS. WYLER—In the long run. But that may be too late. One can't let go of everything, Sam. It isn't in nature. That's why I've asked you to come. I want you to remain as executor under my will.

SAM—Well, I only resigned because—since I'm no longer married to Leonie—

MRS. WYLER—What has that got to do with it?

SAM—All right.

MRS. WYLER—Promise?

SAM—Certainly.

MRS. WYLER—I feel something dark ahead, a terror—

SAM—Now, now, you've been brooding.

MRS. WYLER—Outside of you—Will is the soundest person I'll leave behind me, the healthiest—but in him too I feel a recklessness that's just kept in—I see a vista of the unknown—to us the unknown was the West, land—physical hardship—but he's hard and bitter underneath his jocularity—he isn't sure, he says, what he is— Once he is sure, what will he do?—I want you to watch him, Sam, for Paula's sake.

SAM—I will.

MRS. WYLER—They're all strange and dark. . . . And this doctor. A soul doctor. We didn't have such things—I am sure that behind all this is a profound and healing truth. But sometimes truths may be perverted, and this particular doctor—how are we to know where his knowledge ends and his pretension begins? Now that I am dying, for the first time in my life I know rear. Death seems easy and simple, Sam—a self-indulgence—but can I afford it? (*She smiles up at him. He squeezes her hand.*)

SAM—Everything will be all right. Trust me.

MRS. WYLER—I do. (*A pause.*) You'll stay the night?

SAM—Of course.

MRS. WYLER—Now I feel better.

SAM—That's right. (*Pause.*)

MRS. WYLER—I'd like to live till autumn.

SAM—Of course you will. Many autumns.

MRS. WYLER—Heaven forbid. But this autumn. The color—the leaves turn. (*Looking out window.* SAM *looks too.*) The expression seems strange. What do they turn to?

SAM (*softly, helping her mood*)—Their mother. The earth.

MRS. WYLER—I'm happy now. I'm at peace.

SAM (*puts arm around her, draws her to him*)—That's better.

MRS. WYLER (*smiling up at him*)—It's very clever of me to have sent for you, Sam. I'm pleased with myself. Now, Sam, let 'em do their worst—

SAM (*smiling back at her and patting her hand*)—Just let 'em! . . .

The curtain falls.

It is just before dinner. Leonie and Boris are at the end of an emotional review of their affair, which Leonie would end beautifully. Boris finds some difficulty in accepting her decision. They have nothing more for each other, Leonie has concluded. She has failed. But she would have Boris less bitter.

"You're eating yourself up. You're killing yourself," she says to him. "There's the great lovely world outside and you sit in your room hating—"

"What do you recommend? Cold showers and Swedish massage? What does the man of science prescribe for me?"

"Why do you hate Kenneth so?"

"I'm jealous, my dear."

"Poor Boris. You're beyond a simple emotion like that, aren't you?"

"I envy you, Leonie. All like you."

"Do you?"

"I envy all sentimental liars who gratify their desires on high principle. It makes all your diversions an exercise in piety. You're sick of me and want to sleep with the man of science. (*He seizes her arms and turns her to him.*) Does this suffice for you? No. It must be that you can no longer help me. (*Little silent laugh.*)

My sainted father was like that. God!"

Boris recognizes that this is the end, but he would warn Leonie against the man of science. Let her beware of him. All she knows of him is what he tells her—

Kenneth has come to deliver a message from Mrs. Wyler. She has sent for Leonie. And Boris is ready for a grand exit. "Don't worry about me," he says. "A magazine syndicate has offered me a great deal for sentimental reminiscences of my father. Imagine that, sentimental! They have offered me—charming Americanism—a ghost-writer. It will be quaint—one ghost collaborating with another ghost. (*Raising his hand like Greek priest.*) My blessings, Leonie. (*Kisses her hand.*) You have been charming. Dr. Rice—"

And he has gone.

"He's part of the past. You must forget him," Kenneth advises. And so it stands. Boris is exorcised. . . .

Now Leonie has turned to Kenneth, not only for counsel, but for help. He is, she feels, the only one in the world on whom she can count.

She and Paula are poles apart, probably because she has always encouraged Paula to be independent. But Paula has taken on such superiority that she dares to criticize even her mother's technique with men.

"She said it was lousy," admits Leonie. "Isn't it delicious? She said I threw myself at men instead of reversing the process."

"But I should think she would have approved of that. She makes such a fetish of being candid!"

"That's just what I said, exactly. I said I couldn't pretend—that I couldn't descend to—technique. I said that when my feelings were involved I saw no point in not letting the other person see it. I reproached her for deviousness. Strange ideas that child has—strange."

"I'm afraid her generation is theory-ridden," observes Dr. Rice.

But Paula was right about Leonie. She can't conceal her feelings. Least of all from Kenneth.

"You are such a comfort," she is saying to him a moment later. "Really it is too much now to expect me to do without you. Kenneth?"

"Yes . . . Leonie?"

"Will you be a darling—and marry me?"

The Doctor is not one to make too quick a decision. He would know first whether or not Leonie has given the matter due thought. She is so impulsive! Before he can answer her Paula has come to remind Leonie again that her mother is still expecting her. . . .

Now Paula, determined "to get rid of the tantalizing and irritating mixed feelings she has about Kenneth . . . is playing a game to discover what it is, and yet she becomes increasingly conscious that the game is not unpleasant to her because of her interest in her victim."

She would know what it is that has set Leonie all a-flutter. She hopes that Kenneth's intentions are honorable and she would like to know his motive. Yet if he were to tell her she wouldn't believe him.

"Now, why is that?" Paula asks. "Even when you are perfectly frank your frankness seems to me—a device. Now why is that?"

"Because you yourself are confused, muddled, unsure, contradictory. I am simple and co-ordinated. You resent that. You dislike it. You envy it. You would like such simplicity for yourself. But, as you are unlikely to achieve it, you soothe yourself by distrusting me."

Dr. Rice would expand his analysis. Paula is muddled because she "has accepted a set of premises without examining them or thinking about them." She is a walking contradiction in terms— her radicalism—her friends—her point of view— Borrowed! Unexamined! Insincere!

"You are rich and you are exquisite. Why are you rich and exquisite? Because your forebears were not moralistic but ruthless. . . . Your own origins won't bear a moralistic investigation. You must know that. Your sociology and economics must teach you that."

To repudiate her origins would take more courage than Paula has, insists Kenneth. And why should she? She is neither gifted with a special talent nor is she a crusader. "Instead of repudiating your origins you should exult in them and in that same predatory system that made you possible."

And what were Kenneth's origins? They were anonymous. Kenneth was discovered on a doorstep. He was brought up in a foundling asylum in New England. He remembers as a kid of twelve going to the library in Springfield and getting down the Dictionary of National Biography and hunting out the bastards.

"Surprising how many distinguished ones there were and are. I allied myself early with the brilliant and variegated company of the illegitimate," says Kenneth.

He had got himself through college and medical school and for a little had practiced medicine.

"I devoted myself—when the victims would let me—to their noses and throats. It was a starveling occupation. But I gave up tonsilectomy for the soul. The poor have tonsils but only the rich have souls. My instinct was justified—as you see."

Kenneth has come an incredible journey. He admits it. And it has not developed the least sympathy in him for the underdog. The herd bores him. Dexter would say that he had been lucky. "It always satisfies the mediocrity to call the exceptional individual lucky." No, he doesn't like Will. He despises him in fact. "I detest these young firebrands whose incandescents will be extinguished by the first job. I detest radicals who lounge about in country houses." He regrets that Paula has committed herself to Will.

"I see precisely the effect your money will have on him," he says. "He will take it and the feeling will grow in him that in having given it you have destroyed what he calls his integrity. He will even come to believe that if not for this quenching of initiative he might have become a flaming leader of the people. At the same time he will be aware that both these comforting alibis are delusions—because he has no integrity to speak of nor any initiative to speak of. Knowing they are lies he will only proclaim them the louder, cling to them the harder. He will hate you as the thief of his character—petty larceny, I must say."

Kenneth has come close to Paula now and is speaking in a changed voice, softly calling her name. Paula backs away. She is looking at him fixedly, listening, fascinated, as he asks if she does not know and trust him better now, when Will comes into the room.

Kenneth's manner quickly changes. He asks Paula's permission to congratulate Will. They, he and Paula, have been discussing the European and American points of view toward money marriages, he explains.

"The European fortune-hunter, once he has landed the bag, has no more twinge of conscience than a big-game hunter when he has made his kill. The American—"

"Is that what you think I am, Doctor?"

"You see (*turning to* PAULA), he resents the mere phrase. But, my dear boy, that is no disgrace. We are all fortune-hunters—"

"Not all, Kenneth—!" Paula's inference is pointed.

"But I see no difference at all between the man who makes a profession of being charming to rich ladies—or any other—specialist. The former is more arduous. . . ."

Kenneth has excused himself and withdrawn, leaving Will flushed with rage. He never could stand Kenneth and he would curse him now as a sneering cynic, a marauder, an adventurer with a cure-all— And he is right. Will admits that.

"While he was talking I felt like hitting him. At the same time a voice inside me said: Can you deny it?"

Will is suspicious of the whole situation, as it has developed. Evidently Kenneth hasn't quite decided whom he wants. Doubtless Paula will enjoy helping him decide.

"It's lucky for both of us that one of us has some self-control," suggests Paula.

"No, I won't stay here. I hate the place, I hate Dr. Rice, I hate myself for being here!"

"Don't let me down, Will—I need you terribly just now—"

"I haven't quite the technique of fortune-hunting yet—in the European manner. Which of the two is he after—you or Leonie? Will he flip a coin?"

"I hate you! I hate you!"

"Well, we know where we are at any rate."

"Yes. We do!"

Leonie has come running in. She is wearing an exquisite summer frock and is alive with enthusiasm. She has a surprise for Will. She loves Will. She likes all the people who like her. Will's surprise is his father. Leonie, hearing Will say he had to leave to visit his father, had sent for Dr. Dexter so they both can spend the week-end at Bay Cottage.

Now Dennis has joined them and cocktails are to be served. In her present mood Leonie is even willing to make the effort to like Dennis. Dennis, she is quite sure, could be quite charming if he wanted to. But Dennis doesn't want to be charming—to anyone except Leonie. He is soon in another argument with Dr. Rice.

"You really must treat him, Kenneth," declares Leonie, despairing of Dennis. "He has no censor at all."

"My censor is the Catholic tradition," answers Dennis, cheerfully. "We Catholics anticipated both Marx and Freud by a little matter of nineteen centuries. Spiritually we have a Communion in the Holy Ghost—Communion. As for Dr. Rice, he offers confession without absolution. He is inadequate."

"It seems such bad taste to discuss religion at cocktail time. Try a stuffed olive," suggests the worried Leonie.

"By the time you get your beautiful new world, true science will have perished," ventures Dr. Dexter.

"Aren't you too pessimistic, Dr. Dexter?" questions Leonie. "Too much science has made you gloomy. Kenneth, the depression hasn't stopped your work, has it? Depression or no depression—"

"That's right, Leonie," interjects Will, tensely, as everyone turns and faces him. "Depression or no depression—war or peace—revolution or reaction—Kenneth will reign supreme!"

"Will!"

"Yes, Leonie. His is the power and the glory."

"Dennis, this is your influence—"

"I admire you unreservedly, Doctor. Of your kind you are the best. You are the essence."

"You embarrass me," smiles Kenneth.

"Some men are born ahead of their time, some behind, but you are made pat for the instant. Now is the time for you—when people are unemployed and distrust their own capacities—when people suffer and may be tempted—when integrity yields to despair—now is the moment for you!"

"When, may I ask, is the moment for you—when if ever?" Kenneth has strolled over and is facing Will.

"After your victory," shouts Will. "When you are stuffed and inert with everything you want, then will be the time for me."

Will has rushed from the room. He pays no heed to the calls of Paula, who follows after him. Leonie cannot understand. She turns to Kenneth to set her right. Should she go after Will and Paula? Kenneth thinks not. After all it is their problem.

"You are so wise, Kenneth," Leonie murmurs, taking the Doctor's arm to follow the others in to dinner. "How did I ever get on without you? I have that secure feeling that you are going to be my last indiscretion. When I think how neatly I've captured you—I feel quite proud. I guess my technique isn't so lousy after all."

The curtain falls.

ACT III

It is late in the fall. "The trees have turned. The sumach have put out the brilliant red flowers of autumn." Will Dexter and Dennis McCarthy have just arrived at Bay Cottage, coming from New York. Leonie and Sam Frothingham have come to the veranda-living room to meet them. Sam, Leonie explains, has driven over from Blue Hill to talk business with her.

Leonie has sent for the boys as a little surprise for Paula. Paula hasn't been herself. Leonie thought Will might cheer her up. She is grateful for their coming.

"Well, as a matter of fact, Leonie, it wasn't easy to get away from the office," admits Dennis.

"Are you in an office?"

"Sometimes as many as fifteen in a day," boasts Dennis. "But when I got your appealing letter—*and* the return tickets—I'm chivalrous at heart, you know, Leonie—"

Leonie was afraid Will might be angry with them—he has not been there in so long. Not since Granny died. Did Paula write him about Granny's funeral? No?

"Of course I hate funerals—I can't bear them—but this was so—natural," Leonie is saying. "Mother wanted to live until the fall and she did. It was a dreaming blue sky and there was that poignant haze over the hills and over the bay, and the smell of burning wood from somewhere. Burning wood never smells at any other time the way it does in Indian summer. And the colors that day! Did you ever, Sam, see such a day?"

"It was beautiful."

"They say the colors of autumn are the colors of death, but I don't believe that. They were in such strength that day. I cried—but not on account of Mother—that kind of day always makes me cry a little bit anyway. You couldn't cry over consigning anyone you loved to an earth like that—on a day like that. . . ."

Sam thinks he would like to talk with Will for a moment, and Leonie will take Dennis to his room in the tower. An ivory tower, Dennis is hoping. He would feel uncomfortable in any other.

It is about Will and Paula that Sam wants to talk, though he finds it pretty hard to say so. There are certain things to which he thinks Will should give some thought—

"Hang it all, Will, I like you, and I don't like to preach to you, you know," blurts Sam.

"Go on."

SAM—Well, there are—from my point of view at least—a lot of nonsensical ideas knocking about. I'd like to point out just one thing to you. Your radicalism and all that— Well, the point is this—if you marry Paula—and I hope you do, because I like you—and what is more important, Paula likes you—you'll have responsibilities. Paula will be rich. Very rich. Money means responsibility. Now I shouldn't, for example, like you to start radical magazines with it. I shouldn't like you to let the money drift through your fingers in all sorts of aimless, millennial directions that won't get anywhere.

WILL—Who told you that was my intention?

SAM—A little bird.

WILL—With a black mustache?

SAM—Does that matter?

WILL—No.

SAM (*putting hand on* WILL's *shoulder*)—As a matter of fact, I'm not worried about you at all. Money, I expect, will do to you what getting power does to radical opposition, once it gets office—

WILL—Emasculate me, you mean?

SAM—Well, hardly. Mature you. Once you're rich yourself, I have no doubt you'll be—

WILL—Sound.

SAM—Yes. Sound. But your friends—this McCarthy boy—

WILL—Well, I can easily cut Dennis—all my poor and unsound friends—

SAM (*quietly*)—I'm sorry you're taking this tone with me, Will. I'm the last person in the world to ask you to drop anybody. I'd be ashamed of you if you did. Only—

WILL—Only?

SAM—I must tell you that I am in position—by virtue of the will left by Mrs. Wyler—to keep Paula's money from being used for any purpose that might be construed as—subversive.

WILL—From whose point of view?

SAM (*quietly*)—From mine.

WILL—I see.

SAM—Possibly you may not believe this—but I trust you, Will. Mrs. Wyler trusted you.

WILL—You needn't worry. Paula seems to have other interests apparently.

SAM—What do you mean?

WILL—Sounder interests—

Dennis is back. Dennis feels sorry for Leonie—the last of the lovely ladies. But the inheritance taxes will get them all in the end. Dennis is anxious about Will, too. He would like to help Will with Paula, but if Will will not make a confidant of him Dennis can do nothing—nothing except to fire him from his job on the magazine that isn't yet started. . . .

Paula is in from a walk with Kenneth Rice and amazed to find Will and Dennis there. Amazed and delighted, though the boys are rather cool. Paula is particularly glad to see Will. She was just going to write him—

"I'm afraid it's my fault, Dexter. I do my best to keep Paula so busy that she finds no time to write letters," says Kenneth.

"I was sure I could count on you, Doctor," answers Will, leaving them abruptly.

Being accused of liking to hurt Will, Dr. Rice admits that whenever he finds an obstacle in his path he does his best to remove it. Paula is curious to know just why he thinks that, with Will removed, she would turn to him—

"Because it is true," answers Kenneth, confidently. "Were it not for the squids of idealistic drivel spouted around you by Will and his friends, there would be no issue at all between us. I resent even an imputed rivalry with someone I despise."

"Rivalry?"

"Paula— There's no reason any longer why I shouldn't tell you the truth."

"What is it, Kenneth?"

There's a moment's pause. When Kenneth answers he speaks quite slowly. "Do you know what I feel like? I feel like a man on a great height, irresistibly tempted to jump over. Do you want the truth really?"

Again Paula has the feeling of being drawn into a game. "Somehow his words, his voice, his attitude make her feel that really now he may reveal something which before he wouldn't have revealed . . . somehow, though she distrusts him utterly, some instinct tells her that at this moment actually he is tempted by a force, disruptive to himself, to tell her the truth."

"Don't you know it? Don't you feel it?" Kenneth is saying. "Haven't you known it? Haven't you felt it?" He pauses a moment. "I love you."

Paula for the moment is too stupefied to speak. She, too, is under a spell. She walks away from him. She supposes she should be afraid of him, she says, but she is not afraid. She listens as he goes on telling her of the plan of his life that has now matured.

"Don't you love Mother?" she says, faintly.

"No," he answers. "You are the youth I have never had, the security I have never had—you are the home I have hungered for." He has moved over beside her. "That I am standing near you now, that I have achieved a share in your life, that you are listening to me, that you are thinking of me and of what I am, to the exclusion of everything else in the whirling universe—this is a miracle so devastating that it makes any future possible—Paula—"

He is leaning over her, repeating her name "as if he got a sexual joy from saying her name." Suddenly Paula does feel afraid and would draw away. But he continues, even after she has admitted his charge that she thinks him insane—

"Because I am ambitious, because I am forthright, because I deal scientifically with the human stuff around me—you think me insane. Because I am ruthless and romantic you think me insane. This boy you think you love—who spends his time snivelling about a system he is not strong enough to dominate—is he sane?"

Before Paula can answer the Doctor has gone on to justify his claim and belittle the pretensions of his inferiors. In a world in which the opportunity for the individual career has never been more exalted, at a time when house painters and minor journalists have become dictators of great republics, he, Kenneth, has come from an impossible distance to her, so that when he speaks she can hear—

"What might we not do together—Paula—you and I—"

Paula "loathes the strange fascination she feels in this man, and yet is aware it might turn to her advantage."

"We don't want the same things," she is saying, and a moment after: "I keep thinking—what you want now—what you're after now?"

"I am simple, really. I want everything. That's all."

"And you don't care how you get it."

"Don't be moralistic, Paula—I beg you. I am directly in the tradition of your own marauding ancestors. They pass now for pioneers—actually they fell on the true pioneers and wrested what they had found away from them, by sheer brutal strength. I am doing the same thing—but more adroitly."

"Why are you so honest with me?"

"Perhaps because I feel that, in your heart, you, too, are an adventurer." Kenneth has summoned his most charming smile.

A thought has been forming slowly in Paula's mind. "This man is the enemy. This man is infinitely cunning, infinitely resourceful. Perhaps—just the possibility—he really feels this passion for her. If so, why not use this weakness in an antagonist so ruthless?"

She should not listen to him, Paula assures Kenneth. What reason has she to trust him? Isn't he going to marry her mother? Only as an alternative? Will he tell her mother that?

"You say you love me! If you feel it—really feel it— You haven't been very adventurous for all your talk! Taking in Mother and Sam! Give up those conquests. Tell her! Tell Mother! Then perhaps I will believe you."

"And then?"

"Take your chances!"

Paula has gone to the foot of the stairs and called her mother. When Leonie comes she is a vision of enchantment in an exquisite old-fashioned wedding dress "which billows around her in an immense shimmering circle." It was Granny's. Leonie had found it poking around in Granny's room, while Sam was talking to her about bonds. It has brought a nostalgic glow to Leonie, that exquisite old dress. But Paula is in no mood to be diverted. Kenneth has something to say to Leonie. Paula would have him say it.

"I love Paula. I want to marry Paula," Kenneth tells Leonie. There is a pause. (*Granny's wedding-dress droops.*)

"Do you mean that, Kenneth?"

"Yes."

"This isn't very nice of you, Paula." Leonie's voice is piteous.

"I had nothing to do with it. I loathe Kenneth. But I wanted you to know him. Now you see him, Mother, your precious Lothario—there he is! Look at him!"

Leonie sways slightly. When she would force the subject back to the styles of Granny's day her voice is faint and uncertain. She agrees with Paula that she had better go upstairs and lie down.

Paula calls the butler. Dr. Rice is leaving. His bags are to be packed.

"You, Miss Frothingham, are my *last* miscalculation. I might even say my first. Fortunately not irreparable." Dr. Rice's voice is low and even, but tense with hate. "Forgive me for having overestimated you."

Dr. Rice has left. Paula is suffering a reaction from all she has been through. She is trembling physically and on the verge of tears when Will Dexter comes into the room. She rushes into Will's arms.

"Put your arms around me, Will—hold me close—"

"What's happened?"

"I've tricked him. I made him say in front of Mother that he loved me, that he wanted to marry me. Poor Leonie! But it had to be done! And do you know, Will—at the end I felt—gosh, one has so many selves, Will. I must tell you—for the—well, for the completeness of the record—at the end I felt I had to do it— not only to save Leonie—but to save myself. Can you understand that? I felt horribly drawn to him, and by the sordid thing I was doing— But it's over. Thank God it's over—"

Now Paula's mind is made up. Six weeks without Will have been hell. She cannot wait longer. She needs him too terribly. Will is torn with his longing for Paula, too, but he is firm in his decision that he cannot marry her, despite his longing; he cannot face what he would become.

"But, Will, I'll give up the money," cries Paula. "I'll live with you anywhere."

"I know that, Paula. But I mustn't. You mustn't let me. I've thought it all out. You say you'd live with me anywhere. But what would happen? Supposing I didn't get a job? Would we starve? We'd take fifty dollars a week from your Grandmother's estate. It would be foolish not to. Taking fifty, why not seventy-five? Why not two hundred? I can't let myself in for it, Paula. (*A long pause*). Paula, darling—do you hate me?"

"No."

"Supposing you weren't rich? Is it a world in which, but for this, I'd have to sink? If it is, I'm going to damned well do what I can to change it. I don't have to scramble for the inheritance of dead men. That's for Kenneth—one robber baron—after the lapse of several generations—succeeding another. I don't want this damned fortune to give me an unfair advantage over people as good as I am who haven't got it. (*Torn with pity for her.*) Paula—my dearest—what can I do?"

"I see that you can't do anything. I quite see. Still—"

"I love you, Paula, and I'll be longing for you terribly, but I can't marry you—not till there's somebody for you to marry. When I've struck my stride I won't care about Sam, or the money, or anything, because I'll be on my own. If you feel the way I do, you'll wait."

"Of course, Will. I'll wait." Her voice is very still.

"Darling—darling—" Will, overcome with gratitude and emotion, seizes Paula in his arms passionately and, as Leonie appears in the doorway, dashes out of the room. . . .

Leonie has tried lying down but has been unable to control the thoughts that assail her.

"Kenneth's going. He's leaving." Leonie's voice is piteous. "I suppose you're happy. It's the end—the end of summer!"

Paula, torn with her own emotions, would talk to her mother, but there is the barrier of Leonie's own distress. Suddenly Leonie finds it cold and hateful there. She is going to sell the place. "I suppose the thing about me that is wrong is that love is really all I care about. I suppose I should have been interested in other things. Good works. Do they sustain you? But I couldn't, somehow. I think when you're not in love—you're dead."

Paula has sunk at her mother's feet, burying her face in her lap. She is crying bitterly. It's Will! He's going away! It's the money! Leonie knows. The money will always work against them. "It gives you the illusion of escape—but always you have to come back to yourself."

"What shall I do, Mother?"

"You and Will want the same things," answers Leonie. "In the end you will find them. But don't let him find them with someone else. Follow him. Be near him. When he is depressed and discouraged, let it be your hand that he touches, your face that he sees."

"Mother—you're right—he told me last summer—'you must have a shoulder to lean on'—"

"Let it be your shoulder, Paula; follow him. Be near him."

Dennis and Will have come for their farewells. Dennis is gay with banter, Will solemn and preoccupied. Now they have said their good-bys and left, Will without looking at Paula. But Paula, taking the hint from Leonie, has kissed her mother gratefully and run after him.

Leonie walks sadly over to the chair in which Granny Wyler had sat so often. She is looking out at the darkening sea when Kenneth Rice suddenly reappears. Kenneth has come back to explain—to explain how it was that he had, for a moment, at least, found Leonie and Paula interchangeable. He was attracted by Paula's resemblance to Leonie, for one thing. He hated Paula for that. She probably hated him—

"This fused emotion of love and hate. It had to be brought out into the open. It's a familiar psychosis—the unconscious desire of the daughter to triumph over the mother."

Leonie doesn't understand and Kenneth undertakes to explain to her how he had planned it all; how he told Paula that he loved her; how she insisted that he should repeat that in front of Leonie; of how, after experiencing her great moment, Paula had been freed and was able to go to Will.

Leonie is not convinced. She had heard what Kenneth said, and she cannot believe now that everything he had said and everything he did was to cover what he felt. "I must trust my instinct," Leonie says.

"That, Leonie, is your most adorable trait," agrees Kenneth; "that trust, that innocence. If it weren't for that you wouldn't be you—and everyone wouldn't love you—"

Dennis has forgotten his briefcase. He is back for it now. Leonie fastens rather desperately upon Dennis—"this straw in the current." She would have Dennis stay, even if it means that he will miss the boat. Kenneth is going and Leonie cannot bear to be alone. But, Dennis is enlisted in a cause—he can't live a personal life—

"Stay for dinner," pleads Leonie. "After dinner we can talk about your magazine."

"Oh, well—that makes it possible for me to stay," decides Dennis.

"Send me your magazine, Dennis. I shall be honored to be the first subscriber." Kenneth is going.

"I'll be glad to," agrees Dennis. "Your patients can read it in the waiting-room instead of the *National Geographic*."

"Your first subscriber—and very possibly your last," continues Kenneth, starting out. "Good-by, Leonie. Good luck, Dennis. We who are about to retire—salute you."

Neither of them turns to see him go.

"Trouble with that fellow is—he lives for himself. No larger interest," concludes Dennis from the sofa. "That's what dignifies human beings, Leonie—a dedication to something greater than themselves."

"Yes?" questions Leonie, coming to hand Dennis a whiskey and soda and to sit beside him. "I envy you, Dennis. I wish I could dedicate myself to something—something outside myself."

DENNIS—Well, here's your opportunity, Leonie—it's providential. You couldn't do better than this magazine. It would give you a new interest—impersonal. It would emancipate you, Leonie. It would be a perpetual dedication to Youth—to the hope of the world. The world is middle-aged and tired. But we—

LEONIE (*wistfully*)—Can you refresh us, Dennis?

DENNIS—Refresh you? Leonie, we can rejuvenate you!

LEONIE (*grateful there is someone there—another human being she can laugh with*)—That's an awfully amusing idea. You make me laugh.

DENNIS (*eagerly selling the idea*)—In the youth of any country, there is an immense potentiality—

LEONIE—You're awfully serious about it, aren't you, Dennis?

DENNIS—Where the magazine is concerned, Leonie, I am a fanatic.

LEONIE—I suppose if it's really successful—it'll result in my losing everything I have—

DENNIS—It'll be taken from you anyway. You'll only be anticipating the inevitable.

LEONIE—Why—how clever of me!

DENNIS—Not only clever but graceful.

LEONIE—Will you leave me just a little to live on—?
DENNIS—Don't worry about that—come the Revolution—you'll have a friend in high office.

Leonie accepts gratefully this earnest of security. They touch glasses in a toast.

THE CURTAIN FALLS

FIRST LADY
A Comedy in Three Acts

By Katharine Dayton and George S. Kaufman

IT has become a common custom to credit George S. Kaufman with being the chief inspiration of all those plays to which his name is linked with that of a collaborator. On occasion Mr. Kaufman has modestly but emphatically disclaimed his right to this credit. He would, I think, prefer to be credited with being no more than a co-creator. If his public, which has become a pretty sizable body, would kindly think of him merely as one of two or more authors who, from certain fairly nebulous beginnings, gradually evolve a certain play he would be completely satisfied.

As it happens in the case of "First Lady" the idea of Miss Dayton's writing a play of Washington life was born in the mind of Miss Dayton's literary agent after Miss Dayton had won considerable distinction as a Washington commentator. Miss Dayton received the suggestion with a smile, and a shrug as well, but the agent was persistent. Miss Dayton decided, she explained later in a brochure she wrote for the New York *Times*, that she could not be bothered, at her time of life, with the writing of a play without the help of George Kaufman, and Mr. Kaufman had said he did not want any new collaborators. Even that did not discourage the enthusiast and, much to the surprise of both, a luncheon was arranged. "So we had lunch," explains the authoress, "and agreed there might be a play in the importance of the social trivia of Washington, and the next day or so he came up and we started planning it."

Kaufman, being the most alert and successful of contemporary satirists working in the theatre, was a natural choice for this particular job. His recent connection with the universally admired "Of Thee I Sing" served to intensify the choice. Miss Dayton's knowledge of Washington's social foibles served perfectly to provide the framework. Her knowledge of such social rivalries as might easily stem from political conspiracies of potentially national significance was also a help.

There were, at the time of casting, several actresses mentioned

"FIRST LADY"

cy: How I envy your knack with older men. . . . That reminds me. How's your husband? idn't come with you, did he?

ne: No, Carter's busy. He's writing a minority opinion.

cy: Again? I'm so sorry.

(Jane Cowl, Lily Cahill)

as possibilities for the leading part of Lucy Chase Wayne, grand-daughter of a former President of the United States and wife of a current Secretary of State. Jane Cowl, Ina Claire, Laura Hope Crews—all were possibilities, but all were contractually tied to previous engagements. Finally Miss Cowl found herself free to accept the part and the comedy was placed in rehearsal for a New York opening November 26, 1935.

"First Lady" is a lively piece that does not place too great stress upon probability. But, as Brooks Atkinson wrote, "although the story is improbable it is not impossible, for Washington is the capital of improbability."

The living room of Secretary of State Wayne's house in Washington, D. C., in which the comedy has its beginning, is "a cluttered, homelike room—not 'done' in any particular period, but a mixture of three generations. Charming, old-fashioned, solid American."

Over the fireplace, and dominating the room, "is the portrait of a vigorous, middle-aged man. . . . Somehow you sense that from this old fellow have stemmed the family traditions and position." Across the hall at the back of the room a glimpse of the dining room shows it set for tea, "with silver service, candles, flowers, etc."

The first person we meet in the living room is Sophy Prescott, "an attractive, poised woman, somewhere in her thirties." She brings with her a stack of small ash trays and her activity at the moment is to check with the butler, Charles, to see that everything is in readiness. The ash trays are common little affairs intended to replace those in ordinary use.

"If they must have souvenirs let them steal these," explains Sophy. "I'm not going to have them carrying off bits of jade and ivory, the way they usually do."

Charles is helpful. He has thought to put Persian cigarettes where the Persian minister will see them, and Egyptian cigarettes in the next compartment. He is able to report the whereabouts of Mrs. Wayne, who will be the hostess of the occasion if she manages to get home in time. At the moment Mrs. Wayne is in the Senate gallery listening to a speech by Senator Keane, where she has been practically all afternoon.

"I don't see how Aunt Lucy can sit in that old Senate all the time," protests Emmy Paige, Mrs. Wayne's niece, "a soft and fluffy young woman, very young, naïve, Southern," who has just come in. "I think I'd just scr-ream! I was talking to Paul Starrett about her and he says she knows what those old senators are saying when they don't even know themselves."

Sophy has phoned the Senate Press Room and asked a friend to warn Mrs. Wayne that she is expected home. The situation is not serious, Sophy mumbles to herself as she hangs up the phone, but after all it *is* the official day at home of the wife of the Secretary of State, and practically any minute everybody in Washington will be pouring in, "from ex-Presidents' widows to Armenian atrocities." Not to mention dozens of delegates representing the Women's Peace, Purity and Patriotism League, now in session at the Mayflower.

Emmy knows about the delegates, too. She has been talking with Paul Starrett about them. Which reminds Sophy that Emmy has been doing a great deal of talking to Paul Starrett lately. That's probably where Starrett got Lucy Wayne's remark about Irene Hibbard being the "Ten Least-Dressed Women in Washington—"

"Well, Aunt Lucy did say it, and everybody laughed," declares Emmy, defensively. "She says terribly wrong things and people always laugh."

"But she says them at the right time, Emmy, and to the right people."

"Well, down in Mississippi everybody tells everybody everything, and nothing happens except once in a while somebody shoots somebody."

"Well, if that's all they did here . . ."

"I declare I think Washington's awful confusin'. All that about where you sit, and who sits next to who—I don't see how you ever learned it. Aunt Lucy says you're the best secretary in Washington. She says if it wasn't for you she doesn't know what she'd do."

"The same as she does now, probably—whatever she feels like."

Lucy Wayne may be one of the two most glamorous women in Washington, agrees Sophy (the other being Irene Hibbard, according to Mr. Starrett), and it may be perfectly natural that these two should be enemies, but Lucy is also the most spoiled, the most maddening, self-willed, unreliable White House baby who ever had a one-time President of the United States for a grandfather.

At about which moment Lucy Chase Wayne arrives home. "Having spent her girlhood in the White House, a hundred and twenty million people know her age, but you would never think it to look at her. She has good looks, but they are subordinate to her vitality, charm, distinction. Over the years every newspaper and magazine in America has printed her picture—not once, but again and again. Everything she does, everything she says, is News. Should her dog bite the most obscure man in the world, it gets a box on Page One. She is LUCY CHASE WAYNE."

"Oh, how lovely everything looks," explodes Lucy, with high enthusiasm. "How nice, Charles! The table looks beautiful! You've arranged everything divinely! Emmy, child, you look charming! Thanks, Charles. I never saw so many flowers. Looks like a gangster's funeral. (*As she gets rid of her coat.*) Now, Sophy darling, don't say it! You'll only be sorry, and besides I can take the words right out of your mouth. Such an unhygienic phrase, I always think. 'It was all very well when you were Lucy Chase or even Lucy Chase Wayne,' etc., etc.,—curtain lowered to denote the passing of two hours—" 'but now that you are the wife of a cabinet member'—Sophy, don't look so grim—can't you ever forget you were General Prescott's daughter?"

Lucy is also convinced that she must have a breathing spell and a cigarette. She has been sitting in the Senate gallery for two mortal hours and she is tired. But she has also been saving the country. Otherwise Senator Keane would have been attacking Stephen's treaties. Senator Keane, it develops, is a "boy Senator" from one of the Western States and a particular friend of Irene Hibbard's.

Lucy knows that; knows that Mrs. Hibbard and Keane have been having lunch together practically every day. But not today! Lucy got there first. She and Senator Keane had lunch together and he agreed not to mention the treaties. . . . Also Irene Hibbard saw them and was perfectly furious. "Her nostrils positively breathed fire," Lucy reports. "You could have cooked crêpes suzettes over them."

It is Lucy's conviction that there is something behind the Hibbard interest in Senator Keane. Probably an attempt to jab at Lucy through her husband. But Lucy is going to fix that. She is going to fix it to have Stephen meet Senator Keane this afternoon and have a talk with him. That would bring the young man into the Wayne camp. . . .

Now Stephen Wayne has appeared in the doorway. He is "of a thoroughly dignified yet pleasing appearance" with "that bit of gray at the temples," and he is very tired. It is Lucy's plan that the minute the treaties are signed she and Stephen shall go away to some place where there are neither foreigners nor Americans and where they cannot be reached even by cable. To Lucy official cables are especially silly things. "What do they say, anyhow?"

she wants to know. " 'Love and kisses—Mussolini.' 'Wish you were here—Haile Selassie!' "

Stephen is amused to hear about Senator Keane and his speech, although he disapproves of Lucy's ghost-writing for Senators. It is sure to get her into trouble sometime. Nearly did when she got Senator Whozis to propose a sailors' bonus as well as a soldiers' bonus.

"You know, it's really a good thing you weren't around when the Constitution was written," says Stephen. "Lord knows what you would have done to *that*."

Lucy—Well, if I had been it wouldn't need so much work today. . . . Darling, why don't you lie down a few minutes, with this mob coming? You look *so* tired. I'll bet you didn't have a bite of lunch, did you?

Stephen—Yes, I did.

Lucy—What? One of those brought-in sandwiches?

Stephen—Not at all. I had lunch with the President.

Lucy—Really? What did he say?

Stephen—Nothing.

Lucy—Now, Stephen, he couldn't have a whole lunch and say nothing.

Stephen—Well, he—said it was a nice day. Asked after *you*—

Lucy—Stephen, you're *so* aggravating. You only tell me the things you want me to know.

Stephen—Well, that's all we tell Great Britain.

Lucy—Really, it's terrible being married to the Secretary of State. His whole business is not telling things.

Stephen—I'd tell you anything I could, Lucy. You know I *want* to tell you *every*thing.

Lucy (*suddenly serious*)—Then why don't you?

Stephen (*taken aback*)—What?

Lucy—Oh, I don't mean state secrets, Stephen. What did the President say about *you?* Because I know, Stephen—I *feel* it. It *was* about *you*, wasn't it? He wants you to succeed him. We've never talked about it, Stephen—all these years. It's been—too deep down to talk about. Whenever anybody's mentioned it— you're being President, I mean—we've just laughed. We've never really talked about it.

Stephen (*with quiet dignity*)—And we never *must* talk about it, Lucy.

Lucy—But I want to talk about it, Stephen. I want you to have it. So much. You've worked so hard, Stephen. You've been so good. You *are* so good. (STEPHEN *looks at her for a moment, the ghost of a smile on his lips. Then he leans forward and kisses her, ever so gently.*)

STEPHEN—Do you want it so very much, my dear?

LUCY—Oh, not for myself. It'd be no treat for me—I know what mother went through. But I want it for you, Stephen—for you and the country. They need you, Stephen.

STEPHEN—Oh, I think they'll stagger along, even without me. But I appreciate your giving me the nomination. I'd rather be your choice than the people's any day.

The first reception guests we meet are a couple of seasoned tea pourers, Mrs. Belle Hardwick and Mrs. Mary Ives. "The former is an ample woman somewhere in her fifties; Mrs. Ives is younger." Mrs. Hardwick is the wife of a senator, Mrs. Ives' husband is in the Cabinet. Which, on occasion, is a bothersome distinction. Mrs. Ives can smoke freely, but Mrs. Hardwick can't. Let her smoke a few cigarettes in her state and Senator Hardwick would lose his senatorship.

Ann Forrester is next to arrive. She is young and chatty, a State Department wife who has just been packing her husband to go down the bay and meet the President of Haiti.

"You know, I just love this room," bubbles Ann. "There are just three rooms in Washington that have real American atmosphere—the little old Supreme Court chamber—I don't know why they ever left it—and the Blue Room at the White House, and this. And I think I like this best of all."

MRS. IVES—It's that portrait of old President Chase. Somehow he's still presiding.

ANN—Well, that's part of it, of course. (*Her eyes linger on it for a moment.*) You know, Mrs. Wayne has that same look around the eyes, hasn't she? Or rather, behind the eyes. But of course she gets her beauty from her mother. That heavenly portrait in the drawing room.

BELLE—Mm—she was an angel if ever there was one.

MRS. IVES—I wish I'd been here then. She must have been a very clever woman.

BELLE—Mm. She handled the old President like nobody's business. And she had something else besides cleverness. Kindness. It's a combination that's rare in Washington—cleverness and kindness. But it makes wonderful hostesses.

ANN—What makes us so unkind, anyhow? I suppose nobody

else lasts here long enough to feel that it really matters. The whole place shifting with every administration. . . . You know the people you meet aren't going to be here a couple of years from now, and you aren't either. So why bother.

MRS. IVES—But it's a lot of fun while you *are* here. Of course it's a lot like home in some ways—every bit as hick, really, and always a feud going on, with everybody in town lining up on one side or the other. You've got to be for either the first or the second wife in every divorce, just like at home. But the difference is that everybody's *somebody* here—it puts gossip on a much higher plane, somehow. There's a finish to it, if you know what I mean.

BELLE—And yet the dirt's all there, underneath.

MRS. IVES—Exactly. Take Lucy and Irene, for instance. Back home they'd just be any two Methodists, but here it's Lucy Chase Wayne and the wife of a Supreme Court Justice. My dear, I trembled at the Rumanian Legation the other night. They just missed each other by two minutes.

ANN—You should have seen them up at the Capitol today— nobody listened to poor Senator Keane. Every eye in the place was on the gallery.

MRS. IVES—What do you mean? They weren't together, surely?

ANN—Heavens, no!

MRS. IVES—I guess it's one feud we can count on year after year. What started it, anyhow? A man?

BELLE—Naturally.

MRS. IVES—Really?

ANN—Secretary Wayne?

BELLE—No, indeed. Taking a woman's husband—that's fair enough—everybody expects that—but Irene did worse. She took Lucy's cook. And, my dear, it simply isn't done.

MRS. IVES—Why, I never heard that.

BELLE—Well, that's how it started. He was a colored chef. He made the most heavenly omelets . . . popovers . . . batter-bread and roe-herring . . . you'd wake up in the night dreaming about them. They made Lucy's Sunday breakfasts the most potent political force in Washington—Presidents were made and unmade, right between popovers. . . . And then Irene came along. She'd just divorced that foreign prince of hers—what was his name?

MRS. IVES—Gregoravitch.

BELLE—That's it. I never can remember.

MRS. IVES—I don't see how you can forget. He's always marrying somebody. He and his brothers.

BELLE—Anyhow, she took that house on Massachusetts Avenue, and started in to splurge with the Baker millions—she was born Irene Baker in Mansfield, Ohio—her father made those old Baker Steamers—you know, the wrong kind of automobile, while Henry Ford was making the right kind—but they made an awful lot of money before too many of them blew up.

MRS. IVES—Oh, I'll never catch up on Washington. But of course I've only been here two administrations.

BELLE—Well, man and boy, I've seen eight, which makes me practically a Neanderthal woman. When you've seen only two you think they're different, but by the time you see eight you know they're all alike.

ANN—But so much happens.

BELLE—Yes, a lot happens, but nothing changes. No matter how big the personality it always passes. It's Washington itself that stays.

Lucy, finally dressed, appears in the doorway, "charming, dignified, beautifully gowned." She has a pleasant word for each of them, and the right word. Now the outside rooms are beginning to fill and the hostess and her helpers advance to the fray.

"Come on, girls—up and at 'em," commands Lucy. "Belle, I want you near me. Mary, you'd better start in the hall. You too, Ann. And remember, keep people moving. That's the secret of the whole thing. It doesn't matter where they go, so long as they keep moving." (MRS. IVES *and* ANN *open the center doors a little and squeeze through. There is a glimpse of arriving guests in the hallway; the buzz of conversation.*) "Ooooh! Sounds like a bird store! Keep those closed—we'll use this room as a haven. Sophy, *don't* let that Peace and Purity woman get past me. Once I accidentally snubbed a temperance woman and it delayed repeal three years."

Some of the crowd, which is beginning to mill about in the dining room, filters through to the living room. Mrs. Wayne herself brings in two ladies who have asked to see President Andrew Wayne's picture. They are just thrilled with the experience. A frock-coated foreigner bows his way in, nervously, and bows out again. Evidently, decides one lady, a minister from one of the rug countries.

Those in the fore part of the crowd include a Baroness seeking a moment's rest from the crush. And a General in full uniform who is trying to explain to his companion that an army travels on its stomach, but that it is not as uncomfortable as she persists in believing. There are two who are souvenir hunters, and one—the one that got a napkin at the White House—manages to add an ashtray from the Secretary of State's.

Now we have Mrs. Louella May Creevey, President of the Women's Peace, Purity and Patriotism League, "every inch a clubwoman—all bust and flowers and blue and gold sash. The minute she comes in you know you are up against something."

Ann Forrester has brought Mrs. Creevey in, turned her over to Mrs. Ives and escaped. Mrs. Creevey is delighted to meet Mrs. Ives—Mrs. Postmaster General Ives!

"I'm such an admirer of your husband, Mrs. Ives," Mrs. Creevey is saying. "As you know, I have the honor to represent five million women, including affiliated bodies, and we are not going to rest until we make it ten. And of course next year we celebrate our quadri-centennial—doubtless you've read about it —and we have petitioned the Postmaster General to issue a special stamp in honor of the occasion."

"I'm sure that would be most appropriate."

"I'm *so* glad you think so, but the question is: What should be the design on the stamp? The executive committee is divided— some think it should be a simple dove of peace, and others think it should be *me*. (*She laughs a little.*) Since the quadri-centennial occurs during my presidency."

Senator Hardwick wanders in and is promptly gathered in by Mrs. Creevey. She had been looking all day for the Senator. She and her six million women in forty-seven states are hoping to learn just where he stands, and just whom the party is going to nominate for President. "We want a man who had a mother, Senator Hardwick," warns Mrs. Creevey. "The women of America—"

But Lucy, having been duly tipped off, swoops down on Mrs. Creevey before she can tell the Senator more. He takes advantage of the swoop to make his escape.

"*Mrs.* Creevey! So nice of you to come!" burbles Lucy. "With all the *terrific* responsibilities you have, and this *marvelous* convention. I hear it is the most inspiring one you've ever had."

Lucy "is just exuding charm at every pore" when Sophy sidles up back of her with a floral horror tied with red, white and blue ribbon that the WPPP has sent. Lucy manages to get her hand on the flowers without Mrs. Creevey's knowing it, and continues with new enthusiasm: "And to *think* of your sending me these beautiful flowers! *So* lovely!"

"Oh, thank you. . . . I've just been telling the Senator—

where'd the Senator go?— (*She looks around. No Senator.*) Oh, well!—that we must have a President that the six million women of the WPPP can get behind."

"Well, of course that takes a big man."

"Indeed it does, Mrs. Wayne. The women of America *demand* such a man. The hand that rocks the cradle must also be the mailed fist. Don't you agree with me?"

"Oh, absolutely! And now I want *everyone* to meet you! Baroness, may I present Mrs. Creevey? Mrs. Creevey is behind six million women."

"No, no! They're behind *me*."

The circulation of the crowd continues. And then Senator Keane arrives. "He is a good-looking man, tall, well set-up," and he seems a little doubtful about adventuring further. Emmy Paige sees and recognizes him. Introducing herself as Mrs. Wayne's niece, Emmy explains that she has seen Senator Keane in the Senate, knew him at once because, looking down from the gallery, he is the only one on the floor with that much hair.

Lucy, greeting the Senator, is properly pleased and complimentary. She liked the Senator's speech very much. What little she had to do with it really didn't amount to anything. She is hoping that when the crowd thins out it will be possible for the Senator and her husband to have a good long talk. They are quite certain to like each other. Senator Keane can heartily subscribe to a hope that they will. He admires the Secretary very much, even though he does not always see eye to eye with him.

The Senator is also duly impressed sitting beneath the picture of Andrew Wayne, whom he, as a boy, remembers having heard speak from the rear platform of a train. It must have been quite wonderful to be as close to him as Lucy was. And how old Andrew must have loved her—

"Well, my father was his only child, you know, and he adored my mother," Lucy explains. "Of course, I ate it up—there was always something exciting going on. But it had its drawbacks— I was patted on the head by practically every member of the party. Maybe that's what's the matter with me."

Senator Hardwick, Mrs. Hardwick and Mrs. Ives are back. The crowd is beginning to thin out a bit in the other rooms. Suddenly Sophy comes in a state of considerable repressed excitement to whisper to Lucy. A second later Ann Forrester appears in the doorway with Irene Hibbard in tow.

Mrs. Hibbard "was born Irene Baker of Mansfield, Ohio, but Europe was her finishing school. She can be described only in

French. Elégante, soignée, chic."

"Irene! How like you to give us this pleasure!" is Lucy's welcome.

"I'm sorry to be so late. But I had no idea I could make it," Irene answers, sweetly.

"Neither had I," admits Lucy.

Irene knows everybody there and is *so* pleased to see them all again. And *so* surprised to find Senator Keane there.

"Won't you sit down, Irene? You look tired," suggests Lucy, sweetly.

"Thank you," smiles Irene, dropping her bag as she settles herself into a chair. "You're looking—better, Lucy."

"Only two pounds."

"But it's becoming."

"Thank you. . . ."

"Really, it must be frightful for you to have to do this sort of thing, Lucy—these terrible crowds," Irene is saying as the buzz of conversation comes through from the inner rooms. "People who don't care anything about you, or you about them. Politics would simply kill me. But then, I'm too sincere."

"*You* seem to be taking an interest in politics lately, Irene," says Lucy. "I saw you lunching with old Senator Taylor today—you were having a wonderful time."

"Oh, were you there?"

"And Senator Taylor, too—I never saw him so captivated. How I envy you your knack with older men. (IRENE's *silence is eloquent*.) That reminds me, how's your husband? He didn't come with you, did he?"

"No, Carter's busy. He's writing a minority opinion."

"Again? I'm so sorry."

"Well, at least Carter can afford to express an opinion. The bench is permanent."

"Yes, it must give you such a comfortable feeling, like royalty, almost. But you *were*, almost, weren't you? Of course! What was that fascinating little country you lived in?"

"If you mean Prince Gregoravitch's country, it was Slovania."

"Of course! (*Addressing this mainly to* KEANE.) She had the most beautiful crest—a gorgeous crown, and unicorns sitting on sweet-breads—that's one thing you got out of it, anyhow, Irene. That crest. I remember when you had the place at Middleburg, how beautiful it looked on the bed linen! Of course it left welts on the funniest places."

Stephen Wayne has arrived. Irene's greeting is in quite her

most alluring manner and Stephen, too, is momentarily impressed. But now Irene must take Senator Keane away. They are driving into Maryland, and time is short. If Lucy is surprised at this move she does not show it. It probably would be well for them to get an early start, she agrees. Irene's car so frequently breaks down.

"Mrs. Wayne was going to show me some old photographs," protests Senator Keane, politely.

"Not really?" chuckles Irene. "Dragging out the memoirs again, Lucy? 'My Life and Times in the White House.' Oh, you can see those any time—can't he, Lucy? They're *always* on exhibition."

"Well—then if I may come again?" Keane is saying.

"May he, Irene?" smiles Lucy.

"Of course! I wouldn't dream of his missing those photographs! With you in bloomers, playing basketball, or riding piggy-back on dear old Grandpa! . . . Well, good-by, everybody! We just *must* run! Good-by, Lucy! You're so fortunate to have a past, my dear. It gives you something to talk about."

They have swept out of the house. A ghastly silence follows. It is the first time any of this group has seen Lucy downed.

"I would have put two to one on you, Lucy," says Senator Hardwick. "Something's happened to your footwork."

"'Piggy-back!' Did you hear that?" snaps Lucy to Belle Hardwick, when the others have gone back to the reception. "What about *her* picture in one of those Baker Steamers that buttoned up the back! The nerve of her!"

But Belle is not at all surprised at anything Irene Hibbard has said or done, considering what's back of it. This, Lucy should remember, is a Presidential year. Irene Hibbard holds the Western crowd in the hollow of her hand, and she means to put Senator Keane in the White House.

Lucy is virtually flabbergasted at the thought. Keane! White House! With the possibility of Irene—

"Think a minute," counsels Belle. "She's through with Carter Hibbard—you know that. This is her big chance. Keane is younger, and attractive, and it just *may* happen that he gets it. You know politics."

"But *Irene*, Belle! Irene in the White House! It's too funny."

"Nothing is too funny for this town. And Keane is just the kind they might fall for. Good-looking, Western, and doesn't know a thing. Am I right or wrong?"

Sophy is back to warn Lucy the party is beginning to break up.

Lucy, wide-eyed and flushed of face, turns suddenly upon her, bursting with Belle's deductions.

"It's so simple when you really get hold of it," she cries, a little hysterically. "She's going to divorce Carter, and marry Keane, and make him President. Just like that."

"I wish you'd talk English, Lucy."

LUCY—Only I'm not going to let her, Sophy. Keane in the White House when they could have a man like Stephen! Why doesn't she mind her own business, anyhow? What if she is sick of Carter Hibbard and that Supreme Court black night gown of his? When I think of Stephen—(*She stops suddenly as she slowly gets an idea.*) Sophy!

SOPHY—What?

LUCY—Sophy!

SOPHY—What is it?

LUCY—Sophy!

SOPHY—If you say that again, Lucy—

LUCY—Sophy, if she thought Carter had a chance to be President—a bigger chance than Keane, Sophy—what would she do? She'd stick to him, wouldn't she? You bet she would!

SOPHY—Now, Lucy!

LUCY—So what we've got to do, Sophy, is make Irene think that Carter's *going* to be President! We're going to launch a Presidential boom. For Carter Hibbard! Get it, Sophy?

SOPHY—But they'd never *think* of picking Carter!

LUCY—Of course they wouldn't—that's the whole point. But we've got to make Irene *think* they would.

SOPHY—Lucy—

LUCY—Just a little bit of a boom, Sophy—just big enough to make Irene stay with Carter—happily with Carter. And incidentally sidetrack Gordon Keane. . . . Piggy-back, eh? Well, she'll wish *she* was piggy-back before I get through with her!

SOPHY—Lucy, you're out of your mind!

LUCY—The only question is: How are we going to go about it? How do you launch a Presidential boom, Sophy? How do you launch a Presidential boom? (*At which point the whole thing is happily solved by the entrance of—you've guessed it—* MRS. CREEVEY.)

MRS. CREEVEY—Oh, *here* you are, Mrs. Wayne!

LUCY (*As she puts two and two together*)—Mrs. Creevey!

MRS. CREEVEY—I'm *so* sorry I have to rush. You see, ex-officio I am a member of every committee, and—

Lucy—My dear Mrs. Creevey, I'm so sorry I didn't get a real chance to talk to you—why don't you have lunch with me here tomorrow, just we two?

Mrs. Creevey—Why, Mrs. Wayne, I'd be delighted.

Lucy—Oh, that'll be fine! Just the two of us and not *any* affiliated bodies! Because I know *just* the man for you to get behind!

Mrs. Creevey—Really, Mrs. Wayne?

Lucy—The *very* man! You see, you'll get *behind him* and then *I'll* get behind you—Sophy can get behind me—why, the possibilities are endless! (*Butlers are opening the dining room door; a babble of conversation is heard from the Guests grouped around the tea table.*) Shall we say one o'clock? Or if you'd prefer, one-fifteen, Mrs. Creevey! One-twenty, one-twenty-five. . . .

The curtain falls.

ACT II

Carter Hibbard's study is lined with books—"books that are obviously 'in re' or 'vs.' something"—and there are classical busts on top of the bookcases. Also, by way of contrast, on the wall a huge mounted fish, "a particularly homely fish so realistically stuffed that you can almost hear it gasp."

The Hibbards have finished dinner. Carter Hibbard, Associate Justice of the Supreme Court, is in his sixties, dignified and solemn. Settled in the largest chair in the room, suffering some little discomfort with an overful stomach, Carter is preparing to devote the time he is waiting for a particular radio program to the reading of the evening newspaper.

Irene Hibbard, resplendent in evening clothes, sits across the room regarding her husband with something less than intense interest. The "jeweled sandals that reveal glistening burnt-orange toes" are beginning to tap the floor nervously as Bleecker, the butler, brings the coffee—coffee for Irene, Sanka for the Associate Justice. Sanka and soda tablets.

With a few final and characteristic adjustments, including the producing and clipping of a cigar, the fumbling with a keychain heavy with gadgets, the shaking out of the newspaper, the turning on the radio, and a scattering of stomach rumbles, Carter Hibbard is ready to settle for the evening.

It is too much for Irene. She is up and pacing the floor before the radio can warm up. She does not like the room. She does not like the books in the room. She does not like the fish. And she has no intention of listening to the further adventures of Snooky-Wookums and Dimple-Face on the radio.

Bleecker is in with the brandy, but the interruption is brief and the spat goes on. Irene is waiting for the car. She is to pick Senator Keane up at the Racquet club. Hibbard is of the opinion that she has been going out a good deal lately, and tonight he had hoped she would be there when George Mason called. George had made rather a point of it. Irene is sorry, but she has made other plans. She is also planning a week-end with the Anthonys in Middleburg. The fact that the Chief Justice is giving a dinner Saturday night does not interest her.

The radio is announcing the eight o'clock program over JDK. Irene is furious. She demands that it be turned off.

"Turn it off?" protests Carter. "Irene, you know very well that after the grind of the day's work the clean, wholesome fun of the Whoops family—"

"Relaxes you!" shouts Irene. "I know! And when you're relaxed you stay relaxed until Bleecker brings your ovaltine, and that relaxes you *again!* And then you go to bed, and GOD! how you relax!"

"That is an unreasonable contention, my dear. The greatest minds in history required relaxation. Take Abraham Lincoln. He, too, relished an occasional bit of humor."

"Yes, Carter. But you have all of Lincoln's annoying qualities and none of his great ones."

The radio has taken over the conversation but gets no farther than the announcement that Dr. McIntosh's Sweetie-Wheaties are fine for little tousle-heads when Irene springs to the dials and snaps them off. Instantly, his face flushed, the Judge is on his feet protesting such unseemly conduct.

"I'm through, Carter," calmly announces Irene.

"What's that?"

IRENE—I'm through. Through, done, finished!

HIBBARD—My dear, this is a most unseemly exhibition.

IRENE—Oh, come down off that bench! Stop being a Supreme Court judge and be a human being just long enough to understand this. I'm leaving you, Carter. I'm leaving you because I can't stand it—*one—minute—longer!*

HIBBARD—You don't know what you're saying! Because I turned on the radio?

IRENE (*in an unnatural voice*)—Yes! Because you turned on the radio. That's as good a reason as any.

HIBBARD—But that's absurd. That's no reason. That wouldn't stand in a court of law.

IRENE—Law, law! What's law got to do with marriage? What's law compared to the Whoops Family, and those briefs you bring home, and that fish up on the wall, and that kit of tools that you carry in your pocket, and your stomach, stomach, stomach! Answer me that!

HIBBARD—So this is a case of incompatibility!

IRENE—And sitting here night after night! Night after night after night after night after night! Relaxing!

HIBBARD (*finally stung*)—You haven't sat here very many nights. Traipsing around with young Keane all over the place! How about *that?* Is it my stomach or Senator Keane that's at the root of this? I suppose he hasn't *got* a stomach!

IRENE—I never should have married a man so much older.

HIBBARD—You're not so young any more. You haven't been able to look up a telephone number for five years.

IRENE—Leave my age out of this!

HIBBARD—You tried marrying a younger man. That didn't work so well either.

IRENE—Leave my marriage out of it, too!

HIBBARD—You bought your rotten little Prince Gregoravitch and then you had to buy the filthy Slovanian courts to get rid of him—when I think of myself mixing in that mess! You were just as eager then for respectability as you are now to escape from it! Well, I've given it to you! The daughter of Sockless Sam Baker is the wife of a Supreme Court Justice!

IRENE—You leave my father out of this!

HIBBARD—Sockless Sam Baker! Never took a spoon out of a coffee cup! And I've given you a social position second to none!

IRENE—Thank you so much. And I suppose I didn't *buy you*, too! All those years you were counsel for Baker Steamers. Doing *their* dirty work!

HIBBARD—Irene, you know my stomach. You know what these scenes do to me, a man with my constitution.

IRENE—Constitution! If it isn't *your* constitution it's the country's—I don't know which is the more deadly! All I know is that I'm sick of them both! I'm sick of *you*, if you must know! And you don't want me! You've got your Supreme Court and your fish—that's all you care about! Just be careful that you don't get them mixed up!

HIBBARD—That will do, Irene. You have chosen to cast aspersion upon my calling—the highest and noblest in all the world.

It is an offense I can neither forgive nor condone.

IRENE—That suits me, as long as you understand the situation.
I want a divorce and I want it quickly. You got me one when
you were a dinky Cleveland lawyer; it ought to be easy for a
Supreme Court judge.

HIBBARD—You'll get your divorce—go! Go! And take that
fancy chef with you. No one will reproach *me;* before the bar of
public opinion, the onus will be borne by you.

IRENE—Onus! Onus! Do you think anyone cares what the
wife of a Supreme Court judge does? Do you think anyone even
knows that a Supreme Court judge *has* a wife? Do you suppose
a Supreme Court Justice is credited with any passion stronger
than *heartburn!*

HIBBARD (*with enormous dignity*)—The discussion is at an
end.

Bleecker has announced Judge Mason. Irene thinks to escape,
but it is too late. Mason is in the door, smiling happily. With
him is Louella May Creevey and back of her Ellsworth T.
Ganning, "a gentleman of decided presence." *The* Ellsworth T.
Ganning, it transpires, of the Ganning newspapers.

Both Mrs. Creevey and Mr. Ganning are long-time admirers
of Justice Hibbard, and are pleased with an opportunity of telling him so. Again Irene tries to escape, but this time it is Mrs.
Creevey who blocks the way. And now the object of the visit is
disclosed.

"Carter, we feel that these are pretty ticklish times," begins
Judge Mason, trying to put the whole thing on an informal basis.
"When Mrs. Creevey came to me—as a boyhood friend of yours
—with the suggestion that I am about to present to you, my
first reaction was: George Mason, why didn't *you* think of that
long ago? Then I said to myself, now, who is the man who can get
behind this thing and put it over? Well, sir, there was only one
answer—Ellsworth T. Ganning, of the Ganning newspapers.
Carter, we feel that what the country needs—and when I say 'we'
I am speaking for the Bar Association—we feel that with all the
changes made in the Constitution latterly, it wouldn't be a bad
idea to have a President who understood administering it, let
alone had read it. And I speak for the State Association, too."

HIBBARD—Presidency? You mean—of the Bar Association?

MRS. CREEVEY—Ah, what modesty!

MASON—No, Carter. I mean the Presidency of the United

States.

HIBBARD—Why—why—

MASON—Now don't say a word yet. Not a word. We want you to think seriously before answering.

MRS. CREEVEY—And you too, Mrs. Hibbard. I know what your first thought is—it is of *him*. The strain, the burden of it all. Can he bear it?

MASON—Say! Anybody that can wade all day in a trout stream —eh, Carter?

HIBBARD (*still in a daze*)—What's that? Oh, yes, yes. . . . Well, may I say that this is—pretty overwhelming?

MASON—I don't blame you. It overwhelmed me at first.

HIBBARD—But—does this mean I would have to resign from the Supreme bench?

MASON—Oh, not for a long while. Nobody's to know about this for weeks—we're not breathing a word.

MRS. CREEVEY—Not even a syllable! Millions of women are keeping perfectly quiet.

MASON—All we want now is permission to sound people out —very quietly.

GANNING—Then, when the time comes, we shoot! Announcement, publicity—why, I'll put your picture on the front page of twenty million newspapers every day, right opposite my signed editorial. You can't lose, Mr. Justice. *Now!* What do you say?

MASON—It's up to *you*, Carter.

MRS. CREEVEY—The women of America are hanging on your words.

HIBBARD—Gentlemen—and Mrs. Creevey—I am of course engrossed in the honorable position I occupy. I regard with repugnance the strifes and partisanships of political life. Also, in the last analysis, there is a personal element involved. Any decision of this magnitude must rest with—my dear wife.

MRS. CREEVEY—How sweet! How too, too sweet!

GANNING (*with a flourish*)—Well, Mrs. Hibbard?

MASON—First Lady of the Land, Irene!

MRS. CREEVEY—America waits!

IRENE—What can I say? My husband's interests are mine; his life is mine. I can but follow him, even though it means giving up the peace and quiet of our own fireside. (*And, with that sweet dignity which is so much a part of* IRENE, *she embraces him.*)

The thing is settled. Already Ganning is planning a first picture for his newspapers, a picture of Associate Justice and Mrs. Hibbard sitting cozily in this very room, just the way millions of American couples sit every night, listening to the radio. It is all so beautifully human to Mrs. Creevey—it would be difficult for a less sturdy type to stand the beauty of it. Carter's love of fishing suggests a second picture to Editor Ganning, and that reminds Irene—

"That's an American amberjack," she tells them, proudly indicating the atrocity on the wall. "Caught off the Coast of Florida, February twenty-sixth, nineteen hundred and seventeen."

MRS. CREEVEY—Think of it! She knows the very date!

GANNING—A real American wife, that's what she is! You know what I want from you, Mrs. Hibbard? A daily feature article on home-making. How to put up quince preserves, make your own dresses, apple pie, all the good old American dishes!

IRENE—I'd be delighted.

MRS. CREEVEY—She'll be another Dolly Madison!

GANNING—Wonderful, wonderful!

IRENE—But of course I only know the simplest dishes. Because Carter has such a delicate stomach. Haven't you, dear?

GANNING—A delicate stomach! That's marvelous! That'll appeal to people all over the country! Do you know how many people in this country have got bad stomachs? Millions! Millions!

MRS. CREEVEY (beaming)—Mr. Creevey has one!

IRENE (gathering up the bottle on the desk)—Darling, you mustn't forget your tablets! You know, if I don't look after him he just doesn't do a thing for himself! (She shakes a handful of the tablets out of the bottle.) Just a great big baby, really! (It is the real American wife at her best, her most uxorial. MRS. CREEVEY and the others look on in worshipful admiration as the curtain falls.)

It is late evening a month later. The Stephen Wayne living room is dimly lighted. The dining-room doors are closed, but the sound of masculine laughter can be heard. Presently Secretary Wayne comes through the doors looking for an evening newspaper to point a joke he has told. A glimpse of several men sitting around the table, the table in disarray and the room heavy with cigar smoke, is seen. Finding the newspaper, Wayne returns to the dining room, closing the doors behind him.

Presently Lucy Wayne and Senator Keane come in through the hall. They are in evening clothes, having been to dinner and the theatre. The Senator is of a mind to stop awhile, if Lucy will listen to his proposed agricultural bill—

Emmy Paige and a good-looking young man named James Fleming have arrived. Emmy has been to dinner at the Italian Embassy. She has had a most marvelous time and met positively the most beautiful attaché in the Embassy, if not in the world.

"I told her to relax, Mrs. Wayne," reports Jason. "Mussolini makes them resign from the Diplomatic Service if they marry out of their country."

"That's one law of his I approve of," agrees Senator Keane.

Senator Keane thinks he had better be going. He still has his bill in mind, however, and there is to be a hearing on it at 9 next morning. Perhaps Lucy will be there—

Lucy would love to, but unfortunately she has another engagement. She proposes Emmy as a substitute and Emmy is quite delighted. So, apparently, is Senator Keane.

Sophy is still up. She has been doing invitations for Lucy's Diplomatic Corps dinner, and is amused to hear about Lucy's evening at the play. Lucy, suggests Sophy, appears to be picking up with Senator Keane where Irene Hibbard left off.

"Sophy, she was at the theatre," reports Lucy, brightening perceptibly. "Sitting in a box with her Presidential timber. They were so beautifully connubial. She actually believes it, Sophy. It was a *great* success, Sophy, the whole idea. And it was worth doing, in spite of Gordon."

"Speaking of Gordon, what are you going to do with him now that you've got him? Salvation Army?"

"Well, I had a little inspiration there. At least I think I did, Emmy."

"Why don't you open a day nursery? . . ."

The men's dinner is breaking up. The guests have included Senator Hardwick, Ellsworth Ganning and Herbert Sedgwick, a banker. Ganning appears to be the only one enthused. Hardwick has been a little staggered by what has happened, and Secretary Wayne also. Lucy is all curiosity. What have they been doing? If they have agreed upon a candidate, why can't she know who it is? A little reluctantly Hardwick admits that the candidate is to be Carter Hibbard. In answer to Lucy's exclamation of complete amazement, uttered in the voice of a stricken woman, he goes on to explain:

"It seems we need a man who can interpret the laws of the country, and we got so God-damned many now that it takes a Supreme Court Justice to do it."

"But—Carter Hibbard! How—how did you ever come to select *him?*" demands Lucy, recovering a normal poise. The answers are not very satisfying.

"He's the logical candidate, that's all," says Ganning.

"Well, maybe. I'm not crazy about him, but there's no denying he's got the jump on us," admits Hardwick.

"There just seems to be a lot of Hibbard sentiment, Lucy," adds Stephen. "We don't know how it started—"

"Spontaneously, I assure you," beams Ganning.

"Anyhow, it certainly exists," continues Stephen, "and it's sort of taken us by surprise. The women's clubs are back of him solid, and the bar associations. Taking the whole thing together, it looks as though he's got a head start."

"Well, I don't see where you'd get a better man," says Ganning. "A poor boy, born in Kentucky—there's a doubtful State to begin with, Kentucky. Studied law in Ohio—there's the Lincoln touch. Fishes every year in Wisconsin and Florida—there's the West and the South. Country home in Virginia—another doubtful State. I tell you, he's a natural."

Lucy's subtle protests sound feeble. It may take years to build up a Presidential candidate, as she suggests, but the fact remains that Hibbard seems to be the man. He has already as good as accepted. In a letter written for the Ganning papers the Associate Justice has protested modestly that, although he is not a candidate for the nomination, such is his respect for the wishes of what he has been told is a decided majority of the better element that if these are insistent he will, of course, deem it his duty to accept.

Now Ganning and Sedgwick have gone, Stephen seeing them to the door. Emmy, after wondering naïvely if what she has heard presages the appearance of Mrs. Hibbard in the White House as the First Lady of the Land, has been persuaded by her aunt that she should really be in bed.

Senator Hardwick and Lucy, alone, are still a little stunned. The Senator is free to admit now that it was the intention of his group of party leaders to keep Stephen a little ahead of all other possibilities for the nomination.

"Hadn't been for this Hibbard business we could have done it, too," insists Hardwick. "Even had the President with us. Then Ganning crashed through with all these clubwomen behind him— God, I wish women would keep out of politics."

"So do I," admits Lucy, ever so quietly.

"Well—too bad. Would have been kind of right—Stephen in the White House. And *you* there again, Lucy—it would have been kind of right." (*He looks at the portrait.*) "Andy would have liked it, too."

The Senator is ready to leave. Stephen is back. He thinks perhaps he and Hardwick will go and thresh things out a little. Would Lucy like to come?

Lucy would not. Lucy is still numb from shock. Impulsively she calls Stephen back as he is about to follow Hardwick. He comes back and stands for a second looking at her.

"Stephen, you know I love you, don't you?" she asks.

"Well, I hope so." He is smiling.

"No, I mean it. I do love you, Stephen. I do love you."

"Why, Lucy!" The depth of her tone has surprised him.

LUCY—I just wanted to say it, that's all. I love you.

STEPHEN—Now, Lucy, it's all right. You mustn't feel badly about *me*. I won't say I wouldn't have liked it—at least I'd be sure then that the work of these last years wouldn't be tipped over. But—you've just got to put it out of your mind. It's all right.

LUCY—I wish I could take it like you, Stephen. But I can't—I can't! It kills me.

STEPHEN—We've got to be sports about it—that's all there is to it. . . . Funny it has to be Irene, isn't it?

LUCY—Yes, isn't it?

STEPHEN—I'm sorry, my dear. I'm sorry to have failed you.

LUCY (*holding back the tears*)—Stephen, my darling! Don't! Don't!

STEPHEN—Come now—this isn't like you.

LUCY—Oh, Stephen! Stephen! Stephen!

STEPHEN (*comforting her*)—I know. I know.

LUCY (*slowly coming out of it*)—I'm all right now.

STEPHEN—Of course you are. . . . I ought to run along. Sure you're all right? (*She smiles at him.*) Coming up?

LUCY—In a minute. Finish up with Tom. (*He kisses her— tenderly, affectionately. A little smile passes between them when it's all over. He goes.*)

Lucy hardly sees Sophy as she comes back into the room. She is standing thoughtfully looking up at the portrait of Andrew Chase. Suddenly she turns:

LUCY—How could I, Sophy? How could I have done it? Poor Stephen! That's what I can't forgive myself—what I've done to

Stephen!

Sophy—Well, you might have known something like this would happen. You just got caught, that's all.

Lucy—How was I to know? Do you think for a minute I would have deliberately jeopardized Stephen's chances if I'd known? Who'd ever *believe* they'd do a thing like this? Carter Hibbard! Oh, if only I'd never met that woman!

Sophy—What woman?

Lucy—You know, with the affiliated bodies. (*With a gesture she generously outlines the Creevey figure.*) If only I'd never met her!

Sophy—Anyhow, it's done. But it ought to be a lesson to you.

Lucy—Yes. . . . Yes. . . . I've got nothing to say for myself, Sophy. Nothing at all. But to think of *me* turning out to be one of those meddling Washington women—the kind I've always despised, Sophy—and then I go and do the same thing myself! To think of *me* being responsible for putting Carter Hibbard in the White House! I won't have it, Sophy—that's all. I won't have it!

Sophy—Well, it looks as though you're *going* to have it!

Lucy—Well, I won't! And Irene, Sophy! Irene as First Lady— I won't have it! I tell you I won't have her in those rooms!

Sophy—Now, Lucy—

Lucy—I won't, I won't! I'd use anything. (*She looks up at the portrait.*) Do you think *he'd* have stood by and let a thing like this happen? NO!! Because first and last he was a politician! Do you know what he did once? He locked his delegates in a hotel room and walked around with the key in his pocket! For two days! And do you know what Abraham Lincoln did? He jumped out of a window so he wouldn't have to have his vote recorded! Because *he* was a politician too! And so am *I!* Grandpa, Lincoln and *me*, Sophy! And if we can't beat Irene Hibbard with a ticket like that, there's something wrong with Lincoln and Grandpa!

The curtain falls.

ACT III

It is early Spring in Washington. In the Wayne sitting room Emmy Paige, becomingly dressed in riding togs, is reading and waiting. Reading the Congressional Record and waiting for Senator Keane. The Record is pretty slow going for Emmy, and when she considers the number of them she may have to wade through the outlook is not cheering.

Sophy Prescott has arrived to check with Charles on this evening's dinner and is presently absorbed with a small rack representing the table and a handful of markers representing the guests, the trick being to seat everybody diplomatically. Emmy is not expected, but she may be called upon to fill in.

Presently Senator Keane arrives, also in riding clothes, and Emmy drags him into Sophy's table problem by demanding to know where he has been placed, and with whom. Keane, as Sophy has seated him, is to be between Mrs. Archibald Wellington, the Vice-President's daughter, and Madame von Langendonck, wife of the Dutch chargé d'affaires. Two terribly brainy women, Emmy fears, and quite likely to put all thoughts of her out of the Senator's mind.

"I'm not bright the way they are," pouts Emmy; "there's nothing interesting about me."

"Oh, but there is. You don't know how interesting you are to me," protests the gallant Keane.

"But they're so much older than I am—they've had so much experience. All I know is just to be myself."

At which point Sophy, having stood all she could, brings a heavy paper weight down on the desk with disturbing emphasis. Fortunately Belle Hardwick appears in the door at the same moment. Emmy and her Senator decide to start immediately for their ride.

Belle has come hoping to have a few minutes with Lucy. Lucy, it appears, has been absent much of the time the last month, working mysteriously on something. Belle is hoping it is Irene. She still cannot accustom herself to the thought of Irene Hibbard in the White House.

"It isn't a pleasant prospect," admits Sophy.

"Pleasant? It's fantastic!" snaps Belle. "Can you imagine her sweeping down those White House stairs at the State receptions, bowing graciously to the peasantry while the Marine Band blares out 'Hail to the Chief!' I hope they don't forget some night and play 'I Wonder Who's Kissing Her Now.' . . . Oh, well! . . ."

Lucy arrives in a state of anxious excitement. She is looking for an important letter, or, missing that, a long distance call. Neither has come. Lucy's excitement is intensified. The committee is meeting this afternoon, she admits finally, and is planning to announce Carter Hibbard's candidacy for the Presidency in the morning.

"Well, what of it? You knew they were going to, sooner or later," says Belle.

"But if I could have more time!" protests Lucy. "Once he's

before the public it's ten times as hard—you know that. Even a *little* thing might stop him now, if we had the right one. I'm on the track of it, but if it doesn't come today—"

"What have you got? What is it?"

"Oh, well, it's not here, so what's the use? . . . And just to make it perfect, who do you think is coming with him this afternoon? With Carter, I mean. The little woman to whom he owes it all, who has stood so bravely at his side through all these years."

"Not really? Irene?"

"Exactly. Irene."

Lucy is of a mood to throw things. She does take up a tray of calling cards and hurls them in the air. "Asinine calling cards," she calls them; "obsolete everywhere else! Washington theme song: 'I hear you ca-alled on me-e-e!' " The cards flutter down like snow, and the faithful Sophy is on her knees picking them up.

Charles suddenly recalls that there are some bundles in the cellar that recently arrived for Mrs. Wayne. Came from Cleveland. Immediately Lucy is galvanized into action. Here is what she has been waiting for. Now they're saved! At least Lucy thinks they're saved.

"Lucy, you're driving me crazy," interrupts Belle Hardwick. "Will you tell us what this is all about?"

LUCY—All right! Do you want to know what I've been doing all these weeks? Well, I'll tell you. I've been sitting in the Congressional Library, and I've read every decision handed down by the Supreme Court since Carter Hibbard went on it.

BELLE—Well, I don't see—

LUCY—Oh, of course you do! Because I felt pretty sure that somewhere along the line he'd stubbed his toe. I wanted a case that had to do with women—where he affronted American Womanhood. So I just sat in that mausoleum, and I read, and I read, and I read—all about easement, and chattels, and depositions—do you know that a wife can't sue her husband for a personal tort, Sophy? Well, she can't, no matter who the tort is—and I learned about competency, and estoppel, and fiduciaries, and nolle prosse, and ad nauseam—there's nothing I don't know! I could pass the bar examination in any State in the Union—but I found what I was after! That's the important thing!

BELLE—What did you find?

SOPHY—Yes—what?

LUCY—The case of Mary Haggerty, God bless her. The case

of Mary Haggerty versus—where's my bag? (*She reaches for the huge bag; dumps out its contents in one great pile. Papers and general riff-raff are scattered over the table. A pair of dice roll out.*) I've got it written on a slip of paper. (*She dives into the pile.*) Belle, help me.

BELLE—I never saw such a mess. (*Picking up a card.*) "Sir Arthur Erskine. Minister Plenipotentiary." (*She finds another.*) "Nathan Feldstein. Send Me Your Old Rugs."

LUCY—Please, Belle!

BELLE—You've got everything here but golf sticks. . . . What's this?

LUCY—Let me see. Oh, those are Stephen's original notes on the Trans-Bulgania treaty. I want to keep those.

SOPHY—Keep them? You've never thrown anything away.

LUCY—Well, you never can tell.

BELLE—Mrs. Mary Haggerty. Is this it?

LUCY (*grabbing it*)—That's it! (*She reads.*) "Mrs. Hary Haggerty vs. Cleveland Interurban Railways, Inc., Ohio, 1912-13. A.L.R., 2586." Whatever that means. (*She calls out.*) Charles, where are those bundles?

CHARLES (*in the distance*)—Right away, Mrs. Wayne.

LUCY—Oh, if I'm only right about this! Now here's the case. Mary Haggerty got on a Cleveland trolley car—this was way back in 1912, when Carter was on the Appellate bench out there. Anyhow, Mary got on the car, and it seems she was in what's called a delicate condition. Anyhow, too delicate for a Cleveland trolley car. Well, they came to Euclid Avenue or some place, and along came a beer truck, which was *not* in a delicate condition. Motorman James J. Monahan stopped the trolley car abruptly to avoid hitting the truck, and what happened? Mrs. Haggerty's baby was born in the trolley car. Prematurely, and it died. Mrs. Haggerty sued the street car company, and the Appellate Court decided against her! How's that for justice? Six to one, and you can't tell me Carter was the one! He isn't built like that!

BELLE—Well, I don't know, Lucy—

LUCY—Nonsense! Of course it was appealed to the Supreme Court—that's how *I* got hold of it. Only *their* records didn't name the judges—I mean out in Ohio. All it said was six to one. So I sent to Cleveland for the full report—used my pull with the Attorney General. Charles! (*But CHARLES is already staggering in—tugging a great roped bundle in each hand.*) Good heavens, they didn't send all that!

CHARLES—There are two more outside, Mrs. Wayne.

Lucy—Not really? But I only asked them— Sophy, where are the scissors? You open that one.

Belle—Lucy, this was an awfully long time ago. Do you really think—

Lucy—You bet I do! Oh, it may have been according to law, but an awful lot of women have got babies, don't forget that. Including those affiliated bodies. It's only a little bit of a thing, Belle, but it's the kind that matters to a candidate.

Feverishly the three women attack the bundles. Charles is still bringing in others. It isn't the report of a single case, it's the state archives they have sent her, Lucy decides. Finally Sophy comes upon the Haggerty case. Lucy grabs it and reads—

" 'Public carrier for hire . . . not imputable to a passenger riding *in* said public carrier . . . really, they put in more talk . . . eminent domain . . . annotation' . . . here we are!"

"What's it say?"

" 'Decision of the court . . . liability under constitution' . . . my God, they keep *on* . . . 'in consideration of'—I've got it! 'Concurred in the result: Sloane, MacKenna, McGivney—dissenting—Justice Carter Hibbard'—the dirty dog!"

"He voted for Mary Haggerty. He was the only one that did. The skunk!" Lucy's voice is sunk. She drops into a chair, licked.

Let Charles take the bundles out and burn them. Let Sophy worry about the dinner seatings. Lucy is for the moment all through.

Then Belle Hardwick has an idea. Wouldn't it have been easier to have got something on Irene rather than Carter? Lucy had thought of that, too. But there wasn't anything. That South American? A week-end party, no hotel register, nothing. That Spaniard? He's back in Madrid and no one else knows anything about it.

"I tell you I've been over everything," insists Lucy. "Those years in Slovania, or whatever it's called—when she was married to Gregoravitch—there must be something there, but how do you find out? Even the country's lost now—you can't *find* it since the war. It isn't on the map—I looked. . . . There's no use Belle—she's going to be First Lady, and that's that."

Belle (*shaking her head*)—Have you seen her lately? She's practically in the White House already. Drives Carter to his office every day, walks around the golf links with him—

Lucy—Don't tell me about it. When I think what it'll do to

Stephen. His whole career.

BELLE—But surely there'll always be a place for Stephen. The party can't get on without him.

LUCY—Belle, I can't let it happen. I—I just can't, that's all.

BELLE—You know, it's all wrong, really—letting a woman be First Lady just because she happens to be married to a President.

LUCY—Of course it is. They ought to elect the First Lady and then let her husband be President.

BELLE—You know what she was doing today? Guest of honor at the Girl Scout House. They were cooking her a model lunch.

LUCY—Girl Scout! If I ever see that woman toasting a hot dog, I'll not be responsible.

BELLE—Well, every First Lady has to have a pet charity, and it was a toss-up between the Scouts and the Wayward Girls. She finally plunked for the Scouts.

LUCY—Too bad—she and the Wayward Girls could have had such fun swapping stories.

BELLE—Anyhow, she's getting all ready for the job. She's started to tone down the make-up—much lighter on the lipstick, and I think she'll have eyebrows again in another week.

LUCY—Oh, Belle, I don't really care about Irene any more—it's gone beyond that. But Carter, Belle! Carter Hibbard as President! We can't do that to the country! Even Keane would have been better. Oh, why did you ever tell me about Keane, anyhow? That's what started the whole business.

BELLE—What? What did that have to do with it?

LUCY (*realizing she has gone too far*)—Nothing. Nothing at all—I was just talking.

In Lucy's bag Belle has found Stephen's notes on the Trans-Bulgania treaty. And from these notes Lucy suddenly acquires a new inspiration. The next minute she is at the phone. When she gets Jason Fleming at the State Department she tells him that Secretary Wayne wants him to bring the Trans-Bulgania treaty to the house as soon as possible. He is to bring it over personally.

Now Stephen and Hardwick have arrived. Stephen is anxious about the afternoon, on Lucy's account. He knows it is going to be hard on her. They have to fix up an announcement—one of those "In response to an overwhelming demand," as Hardwick explains—and they'll hurry all they can. It was Carter's idea that Irene should come—

"Carter's nothing!" corrects Lucy. "It was *hers!* Do you think she'd miss a chance like this?"

Lucy is all for starting a new party, but time is a little short. Irene and Carter Hibbard and Ellsworth Ganning are already on the stairs.

"Don't worry, Stephen," Lucy reassures her husband, "I'll behave. How can I do anything else?" She kisses him as Charles appears at the door, followed by the company.

It is decided that the men shall go upstairs with Stephen, and have their drinks up there, and that Irene will stay with Lucy and have tea. As the men are leaving Ganning pauses for another look at the wall portrait of Andrew Chase.

"You know," he says, soberly, "it seems eminently fitting that our announcement should be made from this very house, the home of Andrew Chase. Eh, Hardwick?"

"I suppose so," mutters Hardwick.

"I hope, Mrs. Wayne," joins in Carter Hibbard, "that I'm able to fill his shoes."

"Oh, I'm sure you can," answers Lucy, sweetly. "But of course it was the other end of grandfather that mattered."

The men have gone. Lucy and Irene, the atmosphere lightly ruffled, are settling to their tea when Sophy quietly slips in "as though she had been waiting for just such a dangerous moment, as, indeed, she had been." Lucy greets her with mock formality, which Sophy accepts in kind.

"Ah, if you only knew how heavenly it is to have a quiet moment," Irene is saying. "I've really had the most exhausting day. Receiving this person and that. When I allow myself to think of what's ahead of me, it—it rather overwhelms me."

"Nonsense!" protests Lucy, with spirit. "You mustn't feel that way about it. With your years of experience."

IRENE—Ah, but it's a real challenge—a challenge to any woman. Because I don't think the White House has ever been done properly, do you?

LUCY (leaning forward, rapt)—How's that?

IRENE—Oh, I don't mean any reflection, my dear, but no one has ever preserved all its democratic traditions—because after all, this is a democracy—and still given it the flavor and distinction of a European court. Which it should have. Because Europe sees us through her diplomats' eyes, and judges accordingly. You see, having lived abroad for so many years, I know.

LUCY—Oh, yes, I'd forgotten about that. Whatever became of that country, anyhow? It seems to have just disappeared after you left.

IRENE (*with a sigh*)—Oh, that horrible war! What it did to Slovania! Poor Gregoravitch lost everything—it was only a year after we were married.

LUCY—Dear me! He didn't keep it long, did he?

SOPHY (*doing just a little bit of rescue work*)—For my part, I think it will be very nice—having someone in the White House who really knows the ropes. I know it will make *my* life easier.

LUCY—Oh, I'm sure it will, Sophy. (*She turns to* IRENE.) You know, Sophy doesn't care who makes the laws of a nation, so long as the dinners are correctly seated.

IRENE—At least that's *one* thing you won't have to worry about for the next four years, Lucy—where you sit at the dinner table. Because, of course, you're not remaining in Washington?

LUCY—I beg your pardon?

IRENE—Really, I don't know what we're going to do without you here. It'll be like Washington without the monument. Because to most people you have become a monument.

LUCY—Why, that's sweet of you, Irene.

IRENE—I'm sure you'll find it such a relief—living back in New York again, where no one will notice you. It'll be so restful just to be nobody.

LUCY—Well, of course you know more about that than I do.

IRENE—Where you can do anything you like without having it matter. Where every time anyone says something witty it won't be attributed to you—unjustly, of course.

LUCY—Some more lemon, Irene?

IRENE—No, thank you. And Stephen, too. Freed from the pressure of public life. I do hope he'll find something to interest him.

LUCY—It's awfully good of you, Irene, to have thought so much about us.

IRENE—Oh, not at all.

LUCY—Because it isn't what happens to *us*, of course—it's what happens to *you* that counts.

Irene has no idea how many things are likely to happen to her, according to Lucy. Nor will she ever have until she has experienced them. For one thing she will have to be right with Carter for four whole years. She will have to campaign with him, which means getting up at all sorts of hours in all sorts of places. She will have to lay wreaths and launch battleships in the most awful weather. All her Paris frocks will have to be sacrificed. As a candidate's wife she will be obliged to buy American and

dress American. And on New Year's Day she will have to stand
in the reception line practically forever. And let her not forget
the musicales and those little gilt chairs that always leave a line
across you right there—

Irene, if she could, would laugh such dire predictions off as
more of Lucy's absurdities, but she does not find laughing easy.

"Oh, but that isn't the worst of it," concludes Lucy with accumulated conviction. "It's those years after you *leave* the White
House—they're what really hurt. Because there isn't any place to
go after *that*. And you can't lie about your age any more, because a hundred and thirty million people know all about you.
Once you've lived in the White House you're a dated egg."

Now Jason Fleming has arrived with the Trans-Bulgania
treaty for Secretary Wayne. Lucy has him in to tea while Sophy
is sent to see if the Secretary is still in conference. While Jason
waits Lucy would have him tell her all the gossip of the department—all those interesting little inside facts that she never can
get from Stephen.

There does not appear to be much gossip. As to routine, the
Trans-Bulgania treaty is finally ready for signing, after the better
part of a year's work on it—

"I know—it seems forever that Stephen's been talking about
it," agrees Lucy. "I'd no idea it was so important."

JASON—Oh, it isn't, exactly. But it makes things a lot easier
for *us* boys. Business men know where they stand, for example—
we don't have to answer a lot of questions every day. Such as: If
I import tiddly-winks sets from Trans-Bulgania, do I have to
stamp "Made in Trans-Bulgania" on every tiddly-wink?

LUCY—Well, it goes further than that, doesn't it? I was just
taking a look at Stephen's notes—doesn't it have something to
do with marriage laws, too?

JASON—Yes, it covers everything. It just means that from now
on they recognize our laws and we recognize theirs. And boy!
they've got some funny ones. Church and State are just like that
over there. (*He holds up two fingers in close juxtaposition.*)

LUCY (*thoughtfully*)—Trans-Bulgania. Where *is* that, anyhow?

JASON—Oh, it's one of those jigsaw puzzle countries that they
put together after the war. It's a union of four pre-war States,
really.

LUCY—Oh, I know—sort of bits and pieces that didn't fit any
place else.

JASON—That's right. Their old names were—ah—Carpathia, Vladisoya, Hohlenburg, and Slovania.

LUCY (*salvation in sight*)—Really? Did you say Slovania?

JASON—Oh, yes, indeed. Slovania is the largest of the four.

LUCY—Why, isn't that interesting? Irene, did you know that? (CHARLES *appears*.)

CHARLES—I beg pardon, Mr. Fleming. The Secretary wants to know if you'll come up now.

JASON—Oh, thank you, Charles. . . . If you'll excuse me—

LUCY—Wait a minute, Jason. Tell me—you mean we never had a treaty with them before? Slovania.

JASON—No. Sounds funny, but we didn't.

LUCY—Well—what did we *do?* Suppose something happened to an American over there, what did we *do?*

JASON—Well, nothing, really. So far as we were concerned, it didn't happen.

LUCY—You know, this interests me awfully. I was noticing on Stephen's notes—it said something about divorce. You mean, if somebody was divorced over there, that we didn't recognize it?

JASON—That's right. Of course it'll be different from now on.

LUCY—Then if she married someone else afterwards, would that mean—

JASON—Well, strictly speaking, she couldn't do it. It wouldn't be a marriage.

LUCY—But if she went ahead and did it anyhow, then she's been— (*She rolls the phrase pleasurably on her tongue.*)—living in sin?

JASON—That's right. (*A light laugh.*) So you see we *needed* a treaty.

LUCY—Yes.

JASON—Pardon me. (*He goes.*) (IRENE, *of course, has stood riveted as this revelation has come forth. A caged tigress.*) (*For a moment the two women face each other, while a white-faced* SOPHY *stands in the background.*)

IRENE—You—wouldn't—dare!

LUCY—Wouldn't dare *what?*

IRENE—Wouldn't dare come out with it! With what's going on in that devilish mind of yours. It's a lie! A lie, I tell you! And I can prove it!

LUCY—Oh, no, you can't! You've been living with Carter Hibbard all these years without being married to him, and that's all there is to it. Of course, *why* you would want to *do* that I haven't any idea.

IRENE—It's not true! Because this little squirt comes in here and says so—it's nothing but a technicality, that's all it is!

LUCY—Technicality or not, wait till the opposition paper comes out with dates, and names, and places—with your marriage to Gregoravitch and a phony divorce! And photostatic copies of the phony divorce! With an interview with Gregoravitch, and another with his four wives—I'm sure the one that's in the movies will talk—and *pictures, pictures!* They'll print pictures of everything except you and Carter—ah—you know—and they may even print *those!* (*Her tone changes.*) After that, Irene, *nothing* will matter. You could explain till you were blue in the face, but the damage will be done. Because if a man's going to run for President of the United States, there mustn't be even a *whisper* about him! And you know it!

IRENE—It's—it's an outrage! It's unfair!

LUCY—All right, it's unfair. But it'll do the trick, just the same. How about the Church vote? Why, the party would be crazy to go ahead with him.

IRENE (*taking a long moment*)—I've got to think about it. I've got to have time.

LUCY—*No.* He's got to tell them today. This afternoon.

IRENE—I know why you're doing this. Don't think I don't. You want it yourself, that's why. You want it for Stephen. You've always been in my way, wherever I turned. You've traded on that family name of yours—you think you *own* Washington. That precious grandfather of yours! (*She looks at the portrait.*) What *was* he, anyhow? Nothing but a dirty politician! And so are you!

LUCY (*quite pleased*)—You bet I am. Or you'd be in the White House.

The men are down from their conference, ready to announce the selection of a candidate. Ganning is beaming. Hibbard is worried. Stephen is pleasantly resigned. Hardwick is morose. Before they can make their announcement Irene has gone quickly to Carter and drawn him into the drawing room.

Jason Fleming has made his farewells. Lucy, "apparently for no reason at all" has burst into song. She sings, she explains to the mystified Stephen, because she is the happiest girl in the world. Ganning can understand. Or thinks he can. He changes his mind, however, when Hibbard comes back into the room, followed at some distance by Irene—

"Gentlemen—I don't know quite how to tell you this," the

Associate Justice begins, painfully, his face ashen. "I thought that I had been fully restored—to health—but I regret to announce that—my stomach has gone back on me. Gentlemen, I am not a candidate for the nomination."

Stephen and Hardwick are startled into exclamations of surprise. Ganning is quite convinced that Hibbard is crazy, and says so.

"I simply say that I do not feel equal to the strain of a Presidential campaign," continues Hibbard. . . . "Don't try to dissuade me. I have made up my mind, and there is no appeal from my decision. Are you coming, Irene?"

Irene, after pausing for a moment to survey the room belligerently, follows after. Ganning is still bewildered. Stephen is trying to figure just how the Trans-Bulgania treaty fitted in and Lucy smilingly assures him that he is not old enough to know.

"Well, this sort of leaves you out on a limb, doesn't it," ventures the beaming Senator Hardwick to the puzzled Ganning. "A king maker, and no king!"

"It's—it's monstrous," snorts Ganning. "What are we going to do?"

"You know damned well what we're going to do! There's your candidate, right there! And he hasn't got a stomach, either!"

"Why, thank you, Tom. That's one of the nicest things I've ever had said about me," admits Stephen, turning happily to Lucy, who is already on the verge of tears, and adding, "Don't cry, don't cry! I haven't been elected yet!"

"Kiss me anyway," commands Lucy. And he does.

"So, what do you say, Ganning? Here's your chance to get aboard the bandwagon," Hardwick goes on.

Ganning hesitates no longer than it takes him to frame an acceptance and a suggestion.

"Aye—yes. Yes," he agrees. And adds—"You understand, Mr. Secretary, I don't want anything for myself, but Mrs. Ganning has always wanted to live in England. So, if you see your way clear—"

Before he can finish Emmy Paige has rushed into the room, flushed and excited. Senator Keane follows after, a little embarrassed. Emmy has come to announce their engagement, and that is a second pleasant bombshell to strike Lucy this afternoon. She is almost as happy about the engagement as Emmy. Little Emmy, a Senator's wife! There's no telling what that may lead to, insists Stephen. The White House, perhaps. But Emmy promptly squelches that idea. Her Gordon can never be President. He wasn't born in the United States.

"What was that?" demands Lucy, coming slowly to life. "You weren't born in the United States?"

"No, I was born in Canada. British Columbia," answers the Senator.

"Oh, my God!"

"Why, what's the matter?"

"You know, I'm just beginning to see daylight," puts in Stephen.

At that moment Belle Hardwick has rushed in, breathlessly demanding to know what has happened.

"Not a thing, Belle—not a thing," answers Lucy. "Except that Senator Keane was born in Canada, Belle, and he can't ever be First Lady. Of course he can be Queen of England, Belle, but you never told me about that."

THE CURTAIN FALLS

VICTORIA REGINA
A Drama in Three Acts

By Laurence Housman

ONE of those truly gala events in the theatre—gala in that they produce an outpouring of excited playgoers who proceed to revel in the adventure of acclaiming a favorite player and a new play—was provided by Gilbert Miller at Christmas time. This was his introduction to America of Laurence Housman's "Victoria Regina," a series of dramatic vignettes covering ten interesting and reasonably important episodes in the life of the late Queen Victoria of the British Empire, with Helen Hayes starring in the name part.

It was Miss Hayes' second recent experience with European Royalty. The season of 1934-35 she played Mary, in Maxwell Anderson's "Mary of Scotland," and was highly successful in that role. Her Mary of Scotland and her Victoria of England are no more than sisters under the make-up but, thanks to her gifts as an actress and the affection in which she is held, the two queens were so successfully merged in the Hayes personality that no one was of a mind to question the complete authenticity of either likeness. Audience enthusiasm was as strong for the Hayes characterization of the gentle and sentimental "Vicky" as it was for that of the theatrically vigorous and more dramatic Mary.

The Housman play was taken from the author's published volume containing no less than thirty similar short sketches revealing the life of the Queen from the morning of her ascension to the celebration of her Diamond Jubilee. The stage version, which was denied production in England because the English censor held the personality of Victoria as too sacred for stage representation, employs ten of the sketches. They are concerned for the most part with Victoria's meeting with, marriage to, and felicitous though occasionally tempestuous domestic life with Albert of Saxe-Coburg. It leans rather frankly, and a little heavily, upon the romantic reactions of the pair. After Albert is taken from the picture Victoria is little more than an important manikin in two pictorial episodes. She never ceases, however, with Miss Hayes' personal attractions added, to be an interesting and

169

inspiring historical figure. Victoria earned the respect and affection of the world, as did the grandson who recently followed her in death, by the sheer decency of her life and her oustanding courage and firmness of character.

THE SIX O'CLOCK CALL

As "Victoria Regina" opens, it is six o'clock in the morning of that June day in 1837 when the young Princess Victoria was told of her accession to the throne of the British Empire. Lord Conyngham and the Archbishop of Canterbury have arrived in an outer hall at Kensington Palace. It is still quite dark. The window shutters have not yet been opened and only a dim light relieves the shadows of the vaulted hall.

Admitted by a sleepy footman, Lord Conyngham is quick to insist that Her Royal Highness' maid be sent at once to awaken her. The footman is hesitant about carrying out the order. The maids sleep where he is not supposed to go. To awaken one it will be necessary for him to stand outside and throw pebbles at the window. Lord Conyngham is not particularly interested as to how the footman proceeds, but he does wish Her Royal Highness to be summoned at once on a matter of some urgency.

It is Lord Conyngham's opinion, expressed to the Archbishop while they are waiting, that one of the first duties of the new Queen's advisers will be to get her married, and to the right man. There is her cousin, Prince George of Cambridge. George would be very suitable, is of a proper age, and by report has learned to talk English like a native. But, thinks Canterbury, the Queen's mother, the Duchess of Kent, would never agree to Prince George. The Duchess, undoubtedly, has planned a marriage more to her own liking.

"She has two nephews," recalls the Archbishop, "through her brother, the Duke of Saxe-Coburg—Prince Ernest and Prince Albert."

"But that won't do," protests Conyngham. "Tainted blood! Tainted blood!"

"Indeed!"

"Ye-es; bleeding skins—haemophilia. It's in the family. Cousins. No! It won't do!"

"But Prince George is her cousin, also."

"Ah, but it's not on that side. It's on the mother's—the Coburgs. And, you know, it comes through the women. The males have it; the women don't; but they pass it on. Do you know her brother, the Duke, once nearly bled to death?"

"Dear me! Is that so?"

"Yes. Marrying her daughter to *his* son would be fatal! You know, it's all very well, on the way, Royalty to make itself a class all by itself. But it's a German notion. 'Tisn't English. And when it leads to so much inbreeding, it gets dangerous. English kings have married commoners in the past; they'd better do it again—if the Duke of Wellington had been—well, twenty years younger, I'd have married her to him."

A maid has finally appeared. She comes to tell Lord Conyngham that she had gone to awaken Her Royal Highness, but had found her sleeping so beautifully she lacked the heart. Again Conyngham is insistent. Let Her Royal Highness be awakened immediately and told that he and the Archbishop of Canterbury await an audience.

Now the Duchess of Kent arrives, "robed rather than dressed," and in some excitement. The King is dead! Princess Victoria is now Queen! She flutters with the news. But that she, the Duchess, is also now the Queen Mother, Lord Conyngham is quick to deny. She is the Queen's mother, and that is the distinction. Only had she been Queen in her own right could she be the Queen Mother. Nor will it be possible, as she thinks, for her to force her daughter to confer the honor of Queen Mother upon her.

"Madam, we are here to see Her Majesty, the Queen, on urgent business, and we must not be delayed," adds Conyngham, with some firmness. "Your presence at the interview, Madam, will not be required, unless Her Majesty sends for you."

The Archbishop, confirming his lordship's statement, has opened a side door for the Duchess, through which she withdraws, "compelled, but reluctant."

A light has appeared on the stairway. The shadow of the Princess Victoria is projected upon the wall of the lobby as she descends the stairs. She is wearing a long robe; her hair falls over her shoulders; she is a very young, a very little queen. The Archbishop and Lord Conyngham kneel to kiss her hand. The Duchess has thrust her head back through a partly opened door and is watching spellbound.

"Your Majesty, it is our painful duty to announce to Your Majesty the death of His Majesty, King William," says Lord Conyngham. "Following upon which sad event, by right of succession Your Majesty is now sovereign Queen of the United Kingdom of Great Britain and Ireland. Defender of the Faith."

"We beseech God, by whom Kings and Queens do reign, to

bless the Royal Princess Victoria with long and happy years to reign over us," intones the Archbishop.

"May we have Your Majesty's gracious permission to take our leave?" asks Conyngham.

As though still a little mystified, Victoria nods. The royal messengers ceremoniously withdraw. A moment later the sound of a closing door is heard. Immediately the side door opens and the Duchess of Kent "advances rapturously to claim her daughter's homage."

"Mamma!" Victoria calls out, wonderingly.

"My child! My child! Oh, my child!" The Duchess has embraced her daughter.

VICTORIA—They came to tell me that I am Queen.

DUCHESS—Yes; you are Queen at last!

VICTORIA—But really Queen—*now:* before I have been crowned?

DUCHESS—Yes: now, at once! The King is dead: you are Queen!

VICTORIA—Then my reign has already begun? I can do—as I like?

DUCHESS—Yes: as you like! Do not mind what anyone says. If you want to do it—do it!

VICTORIA—Oh! . . . Then . . . Mamma. There *is* something I would like.

DUCHESS—Ah, yes! Say it! It shall be done.

VICTORIA—How strange that it should have all come—so suddenly!

DUCHESS—Yes, so suddenly—after we have waited so long. But now, my love—do not stay here to catch cold. Come back to your own mother's bed!

VICTORIA—No, Mamma dear. As I may now do as I like, I wish in future to have a bed, and a room of my own.

DUCHESS—*Of your own?*

VICTORIA—Yes—please, Mamma.

DUCHESS—Oh! So you have been waiting for *that?*

VICTORIA—I should be very glad, if you don't mind—now that I am my own mistress. Yes, I would rather be alone. (*She does not wait to hear more.*)

DUCHESS—Oh, God, what is going to become of me? (*She stands and watches, while* VICTORIA, *mistress henceforth of her own destiny, turns and goes quietly upstairs again, having im-*

posed, even now, her wish to be alone for a while. The DUCHESS *snuffs the candles.*) Mind! . . . Glad! . . . Alone! . . .

The curtain falls.

SUITABLE SUITORS

We have moved into a sitting room at Windsor Castle. A year has passed. The Queen, animated and happy, is still in mourning, although she does not mourn. She is talking with her Prime Minister, Lord Melbourne, "a gentleman of breeding, worldly, witty, and to a certain extent wise."

"She is not clever; she cannot say clever things; but the mingled strain of artlessness and self-possession, of dignity and simplicity, which he finds in his Royal Mistress's character—a character which he is artfully molding, not so much to his own ends as his own convenience—attracts and delights him."

The Queen, continuing quite unaffectedly with her wool-work, would know many things of Lord Melbourne. How, for instance, does he begin his day? And how does he continue it? When, with so many things to do, does he find time to say his prayers?

As to prayers, his Lordship is pleased to confess that he says them whenever he can find time for them, as often and as long as possible. Such a custom may be, as Her Majesty suggests, a little irregular, but it is as he would have it.

And now they have come to weightier and more important matters. "Certain things which will have soon to be decided, and one or two in which delay is inadvisable."

"Oh, yes; there are many, I'm sure," Victoria is quick to confess.

MELBOURNE—There is one especially, which Your Majesty graciously deigned to mention the other day. You then said, Ma'am—with a courage which I thought remarkable in one so young—"Some day we must marry" . . . Has Your Majesty given that matter any further thought?

VICTORIA—Oh, yes, Lord Melbourne, I have thought of it a great deal.

MELBOURNE—Is Your Majesty prepared yet to take me into Your Majesty's gracious confidence?

VICTORIA—You mean?

MELBOURNE—As to the possible recipient of so overwhelming an honor.

VICTORIA—Oh, I have not thought of any person—in particular. I mean, I have made no decision.

MELBOURNE—I am relieved to hear it, Ma'am. Then Your Majesty has still an open mind!

VICTORIA—An open mind? Oh, *of course*. I shall make my own choice, Lord Melbourne.

MELBOURNE—Why, of course, Ma'am. I would not suggest otherwise, for a moment.

VICTORIA—But there are certain things as to which I am quite resolved.

MELBOURNE—As for instance?

VICTORIA—My marriage, Lord Melbourne, must be a marriage of affection.

MELBOURNE—That, I am sure, Ma'am, can be arranged without difficulty.

VICTORIA—Someone, I mean, whose character I can respect; one whom I can love and look up to.

MELBOURNE—Look up to?

VICTORIA—Yes, Lord Melbourne, it may sound strange to you; but I must have as my husband one whom I can eventually look up to—when I have trained him for the position he will have to occupy.

MELBOURNE—Oh, quite so, quite so. I trust that such a person will be found. And as Your Majesty has owned to an open mind on the subject, I have here with me a list of—of possibles.

VICTORIA—Oh, Lord Melbourne, how interesting! . . . How many?

MELBOURNE—Well, at present, Ma'am, only five. But more are coming.

VICTORIA—Coming?

MELBOURNE—That is, I am making inquiries about them.

VICTORIA—What kind of inquiries?

MELBOURNE—All kinds of inquiries, Ma'am: my bounden duty. I would not wish to present Your Majesty with one to whom there could be any possible objection.

VICTORIA—And you have already found *five!* Lord Melbourne, how clever of you!

MELBOURNE—"Possibles," I said. The inquiry is still going on; I am making it now. After inquiry of Your Majesty, possibly there will be only one left.

VICTORIA—I would like to see your list, Lord Melbourne.

MELBOURNE—If Your Majesty will pardon me a moment. When I have fully explained the considerations which guided me

"VICTORIA REGINA"

"Now Victoria has come to stand back of Albert. As he begins the second verse of 'Drink to Me Only with Thine Eyes' her hand falls gently on his shoulder."

(Helen Hayes, Vincent Price)

in my selection, I will submit my list for Your Majesty's judgment, and (as I hope) approval.

VICTORIA—I cannot approve all five!

MELBOURNE—Just as a preliminary, Ma'am, why not? From five in the running select your favorite—the winner.

VICTORIA—Perhaps I shall not choose one for a long time. But go on; I am quite interested and excited.

Lord Melbourne proceeds to enumerate the "special and particular conditions" that should be observed in the choosing of a suitable consort of Her Majesty's throne. He must be of Royal blood, but neither the direct nor likely heir of any foreign king or reigning prince. This to avoid entangling alliances. He must be of the Protestant faith. The Act of Settlement demands that. He must know the English language or be capable of learning it; "capable also of adapting himself to English customs, habits and prejudices," the most difficult condition of all, Lord Melbourne concludes, "since the English have a prejudice against foreigners."

He must have a presence suited to his station, a certain amount of brains (though not too much) and he must understand that he is not to interfere in politics. He must have health and a sound constitution and come of good stock.

"That, Ma'am, has been our main difficulty," admits Lord Melbourne. "Good stock, in the Royal Families of Europe, is rare."

"Please explain, for I don't quite understand," pleads Victoria. " 'Good stock'—I thought that meant cattle."

"It does, Ma'am, in certain connections. But it also means— what comes from father to son. You find it referred to in the Second Commandment where we are told that the sins of the fathers are visited on the children: also their virtues. In certain Royal lines the sins and the virtues have been mixed: and one has to be careful that they shall not be more mixed. For that reason the marriage of Royal cousins is generally inadvisable."

"Oh!"

"Generally, I say. In the case of a certain branch of Your Majesty's family connections it is unfortunately true in a rather special degree. For that reason I have *not* included two of Your Majesty's cousins, who might otherwise have been desirable candidates—Their Serene Highnesses Prince Ernest and Prince Albert of Saxe-Coburg Gotha."

"But they both looked quite strong and healthy when I last saw them two years ago."

"Apparently, Ma'am. But appearances are sometimes deceptive. It is, of course, a delicate—even a painful subject. But, acting under medical advice, and with a due sense of responsibility, I have *not* included either of those young Princes in the list which I have now the honor to submit."

Victoria recognizes but one of the five names—that of Prince George. He is her cousin, too, but, Lord Melbourne explains, of a different branch. There is no objection to Prince George on Lord Melbourne's part, but considerable objection on the part of Victoria. She never could marry her cousin George.

Lord Melbourne is again at pains to assure Her Highness that her choice shall be her own. But he would call her attention to the fact that were any attempt to be made by anyone to influence that choice in a certain direction, then it would be necessary for him to impose opposition. Which, Victoria is as quick to answer, she would not allow.

"I see. I understand. I sympathize," gracefully agrees Lord Melbourne. "I shall say no more. I will only commend the matter to Your Majesty's good sense—and conscience."

"Oh, how kind you always are to me, Lord Melbourne," enthuses Victoria. "What a lot you are teaching me!"

"What a lot you are teaching *me*," responds Melbourne. "I have served under old sovereigns—under two. But I have never served under one who listened to advice so wisely or so well. . . ."

The list of possible suitors has been torn up and thrown aside. It is Victoria's wish now that she might see portraits of those candidates named. She cannot decide on anyone until she knows what he is like.

"Portraits are sometimes deceptive, Ma'am," protests Melbourne.

"Yes," agrees Victoria; "I saw a portrait of my cousin George of Cambridge the other day; quite handsome he looked."

MELBOURNE—I can get their portraits, Ma'am, if you wish. But Court Painters, like Prime Ministers, know their duty; and they only do what is expected of them. If they can't do that, they have to go.

VICTORIA (*going towards a table, on which stands a framed portrait*)—Here is a portrait that was sent to Mamma the other day—of my cousin, Prince Albert.

MELBOURNE (*who has followed to the table*)—Oh! Ah! Yes. H'm.

VICTORIA—Surely *he must* have grown very handsome! It

would not be possible for a Court Painter to *imagine* anyone like that.

MELBOURNE—You never know, Ma'am, you never know. Imagination sometimes goes a long way. Well, the list having gone, am I now to make a collection of portraits for Your Majesty?

VICTORIA—Oh, no, Lord Melbourne. I wasn't speaking seriously when I said that.

MELBOURNE—No more was I, Ma'am. But I do ask Your Majesty to *think* seriously. The future welfare of this country is now in this little hand. (*He stoops and kisses it.*)

VICTORIA—Indeed, Lord Melbourne, I pay great attention to everything that you say. And I shall continue to take your advice, whenever I find it—possible. Good-by. (LORD MELBOURNE *bows himself out.* VICTORIA *goes and sits, takes up the portrait and kisses it.*) Albert . . . Albert . . . Albert . . . Will you marry me?

WOMAN PROPOSES

In the same sitting room of Windsor Castle, the year following, Prince Albert of Saxe-Coburg Gotha is standing looking out the window. "The outside prospect is beautiful; but some other prospect seems to depress him." He is a tall, handsome young man, a blond Teuton of modest but assured presence. Shortly Albert is joined by his brother Ernest, a darker, smaller man, but likewise of good presence and agreeable appearance. When they speak their English is very good, but still there are traces of foreign accent. It is English they speak mostly, as Ernest insists, for the practice. Soon one of them, Ernest reminds Albert, will have to speak English always, if he is chosen as Victoria's consort.

The thought is a little depressing to Albert. To Ernest it is exciting. To be almost a king!

"No! The English people will never allow a foreigner—you or me—to be King; nor anything like one," insists Albert.

"We are hardly more foreigners than some of their own Royalty," protests Ernest. "We speak as good English."

"But we were not *born* in England."

"What real difference does that make to a man—where he was born?"

"Real? None. But—to the English—all the difference. Has it never occurred to you, Ernest, that the English are a very romantic nation?"

"Rather materialistic, I should say."

"Yes, but very romantic over their material—some of it. I

have been reading English history lately. It is all a romance.
Their lost battles? Where are they? Except for one or two—they
do not exist."

"What about their lost countries—France, and America?"

"They don't know they have lost them—till it is such old history that it means to them—nothing. Why, for three hundred
years after they had been driven out, their kings still called themselves Kings of France. That is true, Ernest. Don't laugh!"

"Of France? Yet they do not like foreigners, you say?"

"Oh, they like *ruling* them. They do that as a favor. Here you
or I will only be—a puppet, kept to breed by."

The prospect does not worry Ernest, who now explains that it
is he who must be Victoria's choice. Albert was not told, but this
was their father's wish. It must seem to be Victoria's choice, but
for family reasons that choice must fall to Ernest.

Albert, admits Ernest, had always been their mother's favorite,
but Ernest was his father's choice. Their mother had left them
shortly after Albert was born. She had written afterward, but only
to Albert, and secretly. Albert was always more to his mother
than Ernest—and now, suddenly, Ernest knows why. And why
his father has insisted on his being Victoria's choice.

"Now I understand," he says, with repressed excitement.
"Yes . . . listen, Albert! . . . *It has got to be me!* You are my
brother, but you are not—"

"I am not—"

"*You are not the son of my father.* And *that* is why he says
now it must be *me.* Albert! You are very dear to me, but you
must obey my father."

It is a line of reasoning Albert refuses to accept. Why should
he obey a man who is not his father, even though he be his reigning Prince? If his father had wanted his obedience he should have
told him and not Ernest! If Victoria does ask him Albert will
accept.

In that case Ernest will feel it his duty to have Albert recalled.
Unless Albert will agree to do as Ernest says he will be sent home.
The brothers are facing each other defiantly as Victoria enters the
room. She notices their serious expressions, but takes little account
of them. Soon they will all go for a ride in the park.

First, however, she would have Ernest practice his music. There
will be plenty of time before they are ready to ride. Ernest has
told her that he always practices at home, and she would have
him feel quite at home where he is. Nor will she listen to Ernest's
excuses—that the piano is not in good tune, or that he and Albert

usually practice together.

Reluctantly, and with a final caution to Albert, Ernest goes to his music.

"How strangely Ernest spoke to you, then!" says Victoria. "Is anything the matter?"

"Oh, no; nothing serious," insists Albert.

VICTORIA—You haven't been quarreling, I hope?

ALBERT (*laughing*)—We never quarrel.

VICTORIA—I think it would be very hard to quarrel with *you*, Albert. *I* couldn't.

ALBERT—Please, don't ever try!

VICTORIA—Some people are able to quarrel without trying.

ALBERT—Yes.

VICTORIA—Maybe they like it. (*Pause.*) Won't you sit down, Albert? (*She sits on settee. He takes a distant seat.*) Why don't you sit nearer? Talking then is so much easier.

ALBERT (*rising and crossing to settee*)—You are very kind, Cousin, ever since we came: to both of us, I mean.

VICTORIA—I am very fond of—Ernest.

ALBERT (*sitting down*)—Yes, so am I.

VICTORIA—You've always been together, haven't you?

ALBERT—We've never been apart yet.

VICTORIA—How very nice that has been—for both. (*Pause.*) Would it be a great trial to you, if you had to live away from him?

ALBERT—Of course, the parting would be a trial. But one would get used to it—as to other things—if it had to be.

VICTORIA—In my life I have been so much alone, except, of course, with Mamma. I don't know what it can be like—to have a brother.

ALBERT—One gets very fond of a brother.

VICTORIA—Yes; but one can get fonder of someone else—can one not?

ALBERT—It does happen. (*Pause.*)

VICTORIA—Albert! What are you thinking?

ALBERT—I was listening to Ernest, practicing. It is Beethoven.

VICTORIA—Don't listen to Ernest! You must listen to me!

ALBERT—I beg your pardon, Cousin; I was listening. Please don't think that I am inattentive.

VICTORIA (*after a long pause*)—Albert . . . I have something to say to you.

ALBERT—Yes . . . what is it, Cousin?

VICTORIA—In my position, it is I who have to say it—unfortunately. Ordinarily it is not what a woman would wish to say herself. She would rather—*he* said it.

ALBERT—Is there anything you wish me to say?

VICTORIA—To hear you say you *can* love me, is all I can hope —yet. If you could say that you already *do* love me, that would be—almost like Heaven.

ALBERT—I do . . . love you, Cousin.

VICTORIA—Enough to marry me?

ALBERT—More than enough to marry you. For people in our position often marry without any love at all.

VICTORIA—I couldn't do that—Albert.

ALBERT—Nor could I—Victoria.

VICTORIA—Then you will marry me?

ALBERT—If it is still your wish—when you know me—I will, very gratefully and humbly, accept this dear hand that you offer me.

Quietly, seriously, Albert confesses the story of his origin that Ernest has told him. Now, if Victoria wishes him to he will leave her. But Victoria does not wish Albert to leave. She wishes him to stay. What he has told her makes no difference to Victoria. Besides, who knows? And if Ernest's father had sent both Albert and Ernest to see her, and had thought she ever could have chosen Ernest after seeing Albert, he was just silly.

"Oh, Albert! Albert! What does it matter?" she cries. "It is not your father that I shall marry; it is you."

She is in his arms now and, again at her suggestion, he has kissed her fondly. Now she has led him to the settee and asked to be kissed again. And now she is talking quite excitedly about their marriage, which must be soon, because everybody expects it.

"Expects it? They don't know!" a surprised Albert reminds her.

VICTORIA—Expects me to marry, I mean. I had to choose *some*body. But I wasn't going to choose *any*body.

ALBERT—Not even Ernest?

VICTORIA—Oh, I liked Ernest very much, from the first . . . I do still.

ALBERT—Is that why you sent him to practice? . . . He *knew*.

VICTORIA—That this was going to happen?

ALBERT—No; he did not know *that*.

VICTORIA—What, then?

ALBERT—That you were going to ask me.

VICTORIA—Well, then, what else could he suppose *would* happen?

ALBERT—He expected me to say no.

VICTORIA—But you couldn't have said "No" to a Queen—could you, Albert?

ALBERT—No, dear; one couldn't say "No" to a Queen.

VICTORIA—But did you want to?

ALBERT—No, Dearest One. All it means is that Ernest will be disappointed.

VICTORIA—Oh, I see. Poor Ernest! . . . Well, we must both try to be very nice and kind to him . . . and now it is quite time that we went for our ride.

ALBERT—Isn't Ernest to come, too?

VICTORIA—Why, yes, of course!

ALBERT—Then won't you send and say he may stop practicing? This hasn't taken an hour, you know. (ERNEST *enters.*)

VICTORIA—Nor has he, either; for here he is. Are you ready to come riding, Ernest?

ERNEST—Quite, if you are, Cousin.

VICTORIA—Oh, yes, we are quite ready *now*. Everything has been settled. Tell him, Albert.

ALBERT—Ernest, you told me to remember—I forgot.

(ERNEST *has only to look at them, and the awful situation is explained. It will also have to be explained elsewhere. For when* VICTORIA *says that a thing is settled, it* is *settled—for good.*)

The curtain falls.

MORNING GLORY

The scene has changed to Prince Albert's dressing room at Windsor Castle. An elderly valet has brought hot water, razors, soap, shaving-brush and towel and placed them before a shaving glass. He puts out the two candles still burning and opens the curtains. The hour is late and the sun streams in.

A moment later Prince Albert enters. He is wearing a fine brocaded dressing-gown and a silk night cap. Prince Albert has decided to shave himself this morning. The valet is dismissed. With some particularity His Highness applies the lather to his face and is about to proceed with the shaving when his attention is distracted by a gentle knocking on the door through which he has entered.

The intruder is Victoria. First she merely sticks in her head, covered with a pretty frilled nightcap, the strings hanging loose. "Presently she is all there, wearing a rose-colored dressing-gown, and over it a white cashmere shawl with long fringes. She looks very happy and charming."

The Queen is greatly interested in the shaving exercise. It is the first time she has ever seen a man with shaving soap on his face and it is an exciting experience. She hopes Albert will let her stay and watch the operation. How often does he have to shave? Once a day? How funny. She only has to cut her nails once a week!

Albert is amused at Victoria's curiosity. He would kiss her if it were not for the "soup." And after he has been taught that it isn't soup but soap, he wipes his lips and the kiss is delivered.

Now, as the shaving goes on, Victoria must know more about it. With what kind of an instrument is it accomplished? Does it hurt? Is it dangerous? Did Albert ever cut himself?

Albert seldom cuts himself—when he is alone. But there was a valet who used to shave him who did cut him one day, and rather badly. That had caused a good deal of excitement. The Court Physician came running in a terrible fright, thinking to find Albert bleeding to death.

"Because, my dear, my father—my brother Ernest's father—so nearly did," explains Albert, to the wondering, wide-eyed Victoria. "But that did not happen to *me*. . . . I am not that way, you see. Perhaps what I told you makes the difference."

THE QUEEN—Oh, Albert! Then that "difference" has, perhaps, saved your life? Albert, suppose you had died before we got married, I wonder if I *could* have married anyone else?

ALBERT—Of course, Dearest. You had to marry someone. You could not disappoint your people by not giving them an heir to the Throne.

THE QUEEN—Oh, Albert! Shall I? Will that really happen?

ALBERT—We will hope so, Dearest—in time.

THE QUEEN—In time? I hope it will be very *soon*. Oh, isn't it wonderful? We really are—married now, aren't we?

ALBERT—Yes, Weibchen, I think so.

THE QUEEN—Yesterday seems almost like another world—so different. All the crowds, and the cheering, and the firing, and the bells: and the thousands and thousands of people all looking at us, as if we belonged to them; as, of course, in a way, we do. . . .

And now we are all by ourselves—all alone—just we two.

ALBERT—Yes, all alone—just we two. Shall I be able to make you happy? . . . You are happy?

THE QUEEN—Happy? So happy, I can't—I can't tell you, Albert! . . . It's like Heaven!

ALBERT (*bends over and kisses her hair*)—No, Vicky, not just like this—that is not possible. That is not human nature.

THE QUEEN—But I shall never love you less than I do now, Albert.

ALBERT—No, Dearest, perhaps not. But you will be less excited about it—less romantic, perhaps.

THE QUEEN—No, I will not.

ALBERT—We love each other, but we have to learn each other's characters—and ways. That will take time. . . . (*She shakes her head fondly, confident that she knows him already—by heart.*) Oh, yes . . . You have come to see me shave today—for the first time. That pleases—that excites you. But it will not always excite you as much as today. You will not come, I think, to see me shave every day—for the next twenty years.

THE QUEEN—Why not?

ALBERT—That it should become less of a spectacle is only reasonable.

THE QUEEN—I don't want to be reasonable with *you*, Albert.

ALBERT—But you *will* want—in time, I hope, Vicky. So shall I. You have a great life of duties to perform, in which I am to share. Is it not so?

THE QUEEN—We can't share everything, Albert. Some things I shall have to do alone—affairs of state, in which it would not be right for you to concern yourself.

ALBERT—So?

THE QUEEN—You must take great care, Dearest. The English are jealous; and to them you are still a foreigner.

ALBERT—And—to you?

THE QUEEN—To me you are everything—life, happiness, peace, and comfort! When I am with you, I shall want to forget everything—except our love.

Victoria has thrown herself into Albert's arms. Suddenly, from outside, there comes a burst of music. In happy excitement Victoria draws her husband to the window to show him the band of the Royal Life Guard which she has given orders should play a few suitable pieces before they come down. The suitable piece with which the concert has begun is Mendelssohn's "Wedding

March" from the composer's new setting to Shakespeare.

Albert and Victoria are very young this day, and very happy. Victoria is childishly enthused by the demonstration in the yard. She can't keep away from the window.

"The people may see you," Albert protests.

"Well, why shouldn't they?" Victoria wants to know. "It would please them."

"Yes; too much. . . . That is why I say—do not." Albert is quite firm.

"Albert, darling, we have got to appear in public again almost at once," protests Victoria. "It's no use being shy. And why should we, when I'm so proud of having got you?"

"I want my breakfast, Vicky," continues Albert, rescuing modesty with common sense. "Please to go and get yourself ready— quick. I am going to ring now for my dresser to come."

"Order me to go, Albert!" pleads Victoria, reveling in wifely submission. "ORDER me!"

"Go, woman! He says to you, Go!"

Victoria is gazing at her lord and master adoringly as she drops a deep curtsey and retires. He stands looking fondly after her; then, with a sigh, turns and rings the bell, as the curtain falls.

ACT II

A GOOD LESSON

It is ten o'clock of a bright morning, two years later. In Prince Albert's writing room at Buckingham Palace His Highness' secretary, Mr. Anson, is sorting his mail when a gentleman arrives from the Queen. Her Majesty would like to know whether the Prince has yet returned, and, if not, where he is.

Mr. Anson is not able to answer. His Highness had attended the Royal Academy dinner the evening before; had delivered the speech he was expected to deliver, as is fully reported by the morning *Times*. That is all Mr. Anson is able to report.

Richards, Prince Albert's valet, is also a visitor, and similarly disturbed. Richard has not seen or heard from His Highness since he had dressed him for the dinner. He is quite relieved to be assured by Mr. Anson that His Highness is all right and quite likely to return to the castle at any moment.

A moment later Prince Albert, unusually calm and collected, has returned. He is pleased to report that the Academy banquet had gone off very well. Albert had found the company interesting and sympathetic to his suggestion that there should be a competition and a Fine Arts Commission appointed to decide upon the artists who should do the mural decorations for the new Houses of Parliament.

Presently the Queen's gentleman is back. His mistress is still eager to discover the whereabouts of her consort. Hurrying back to Her Majesty with the good news of Albert's return Her Majesty presently appears in person. Her entrance is a bit flamboyant and her irritation is apparent.

"Albert, where have you been?" Victoria demands with true wifely vigor.

"To Windsor, Victoria," Albert answers, quite calmly.

THE QUEEN—Impossible! Why did you not come back last night?

ALBERT—I did not come back last night, Victoria, because of the way in which you sent for me.

THE QUEEN—I told you before you went, that I wished you to be back by half-past ten at the latest.

ALBERT—Yes.

THE QUEEN—At half-past ten you had not come; so I sent for you.

ALBERT—Yes, I received from you this note. (*He produces it.*) . . . "Albert, it is quite time you were back. Please to come at once!"

THE QUEEN—Yes; I wrote it; I sent it; and my orders were that it should be put into your hand by the Messenger to whom I gave it.

ALBERT—It was put into my hand. (*Puts letter on desk.*) I sent back word that I had received it.

THE QUEEN—Yes; but you did not come!

ALBERT—I did not come, because I was not ready then to come.

THE QUEEN—Albert! When you go anywhere without *me* (as you *had* to do on this occasion), I do not expect you to be late.

ALBERT—No. But when I go without you, you must leave it for me to decide, myself, when I shall return.

THE QUEEN—But this time I had already told you my wishes, and decided *for* you, so I sent again.

ALBERT—Yes. At eleven o'clock I received this. (*He picks it up from desk.*) "Albert, I order you to return at once. Victoria Regina."

THE QUEEN—And still you did not!

ALBERT—I did not. (*Puts letter down.*)

THE QUEEN—So you disobeyed your Queen!

ALBERT—Yes, my dear; I disobeyed my Queen. Send me to the Tower for it, and cut off my head.

THE QUEEN—I do not regard this as a subject for amusement and jest, Albert.

ALBERT—No? Then it is lucky that *I* do.

THE QUEEN—And if you think . . .

ALBERT—For if neither of us thought it amusing, we might have quite a serious quarrel about it. But now—as it is only you who do not think it amusing—the quarrel will not be serious.

THE QUEEN—Albert, what did you do, after I had ordered you to return? Where did you spend the night?

ALBERT—At Windsor, as I have told you.

THE QUEEN—I don't believe it!

ALBERT—Don't you? (*Quietly he turns back to his letters.*)

THE QUEEN (*taking letter from his hand and putting it on desk*)—Albert, I will not be treated like this! Please to remember that, though I am your wife, I am also your Queen.

ALBERT—Sit down, my dear, sit down! There is nothing to stand up about. . . . Listen to me, my dear. When you married me, you made a promise that was strange for a Queen to make; but you made it. . . . To love, honor, and obey. And because it was so strange—so unlikely—I have never once told you to obey me, except for fun, when you wished it. Now, my dear, as I have not expected *you* to obey *me* in anything—so there are some things in which you must not expect *me* to obey *you*. That is why, when I started back—after having received your "orders"—I told the coachman to drive—not to Buckingham Palace, but to Windsor.

Victoria suffers further chagrin to think of what the coachman must have thought, but Albert is again reassuring. Whatever the coachman may have thought at the order to drive to Windsor, when they arrived he must have been convinced it was a good order. Albert had found the castle a blaze of lights and the servants enjoying a grand fancy dress ball in the Great Hall. Two of them were dressed as Victoria and Albert and they were having great fun.

Albert had stood for a moment looking at them severely. When the dancers saw him the dancing stopped, and then the music. Soon the hall was cleared.

THE QUEEN—But, Albert, that such a thing *could* happen without our knowing—well, it means that such a lot of other things may be happening, too.

ALBERT—Yes; I am afraid so . . . I think, my dear, that you had better make me your Manager of Windsor— They will not like it, because I have too much of a head for business; but it will be good for them. And for you, a great saving of unnecessary expense.

THE QUEEN—Yes; and if I do it at once, everybody will understand *why*.

ALBERT (*puts papers in drawer of desk*)—It was a good thing, Vicky, was it not, that I was brought up rather poor?

THE QUEEN—So was I.

ALBERT—Yes? But you had not to manage much for yourself, had you? (*Turning to her.*) What are you smiling at?

THE QUEEN—The coachman, Albert! It *was* funny! I'm so glad you went; for now they will all be thinking how clever it was of you to find out! And what a good lesson it was for them, to be sure!

ALBERT—Yes, my dear, it was a good lesson. . . . But, Weibchen, I have not had my morning kiss yet. . . . Please? (*And he says it so simply and sweetly that, quite forgetting now what she first came about, she kisses him with true wifely affection, very fondly and contentedly.*)

The curtain falls.

UNDER FIRE

On May 30, of the same year, 1842, Prince Albert is nervously pacing a room in Buckingham Palace, stopping frequently to gaze out the windows overlooking the park. He has been awaiting Mr. Anson, his secretary, who has now arrived. His excuse for being late is that he had been summoned by the Chief Inspector of Police. It is the Inspector's urgent request that Her Majesty shall not take her customary drive this day.

"But that is nonsense," protests Albert, with some spirit. "If Her Majesty does not drive to the park as usual the man will suspect that we know. So we shall not catch him."

"Isn't that a great risk, sir?"

"It is a risk. It has to be taken. It will be a greater risk if we leave him to choose his own time later, when the Police will not be so ready for him as they are today."

"He will choose his own time in any case, Sir."

"Yes; but now it will be the earliest possible. Yesterday, when his pistol missed fire, he did not know that he was seen by any-one." Anson looks at Albert sharply. "Her Majesty herself was looking the other way."

Her Majesty, reports Albert, is not alarmed. It was she who decided, when she had been told of what happened, that she should go out again today as usual. If the man is sure to make another attempt she would have it over with. That is very sensible, thinks Albert. "Sense is sometimes more *valuable* than courage," he tells Mr. Anson; "and much rarer where Kings are concerned."

The crowd is gathering and waiting for Her Majesty to start. Presently Victoria appears, in bonnet and shawl, "a little nervous, but very self-controlled."

"You are very punctual, my dear," is Albert's greeting.

"Yes; we mustn't be late today," answers Victoria, firmly.

ALBERT—You look very well—very charming! That bonnet suits you.

THE QUEEN (*crossing up to him*)—Kiss me, Albert.

ALBERT (*as he does so*)—You make a very good Queen, my dear.

THE QUEEN—With you to help me.

ALBERT—Even by yourself, I think, you would not do so badly.

THE QUEEN—That will never happen, Albert. I couldn't live without you.

ALBERT—You can do very unexpected things, my dear. You never expected that you would have to do anything like this. But you are going to. It is having to do that makes it possible.

THE QUEEN—Doing it with you, Dearest, I *like* doing it.

ALBERT—So do I. It makes our life mean so much more to us. . . . Look at all those friendly people, waiting for you to smile on them. . . . Rather amusing, is it not?—that none of them knows in the least—what *we* know.

THE QUEEN—Albert, this must be rather like going into battle.

ALBERT—Just a little, my dear. But we have to do it in cold blood, without any excitement. That makes it rather more diffi-cult, perhaps.

THE QUEEN—Oh, but it excites me very much, Albert. For this is really to be a Queen. And with you I feel quite safe that I can behave like one.

ALBERT—Yes; so do I, Weibchen; so do I.

Two ladies-in-waiting, Lady Grace and Lady Muriel, are an-nounced. They, too, are expecting to accompany the royal pair on their ride, but Albert and Victoria have decided that that would

be an unnecessary risk, and their ladyships are dismissed, plainly
to Lady Muriel's displeasure.

And now Victoria and Albert, calmly talking about the weather,
"go out to give Fate and its Fool their opportunity for ending
the Victorian Era before it has earned its name."

Lady Muriel and Lady Grace remain behind to express rather
freely their opinion of the decision that has defrauded them of
their ride with Royalty before admiring crowds. From the windows
they watch Victoria and Albert depart, driving out through the
park toward Constitution Hill.

It is Lady Muriel's belief that Their Majesties have had a
quarrel and that Victoria has taken Albert alone to have it out
with him. Lady Muriel knows that the Queen adores her Prince,
but she can be jealous, too, and when she is jealous she lets him
know it. Already there have been two or three frightful rows.

Suddenly, in the midst of their gossiping, there is a report that
might have been a pistol shot, but that does not stop them long.
Outside the crowd is still waiting. Not content with having seen
the royal personages once it must stand about for a second view.

But now the crowd is evidently greatly excited. People are
swarming over Constitution Hill. There must have been an
accident! The mounted police have appeared. Presently Victoria
and Albert can be seen returning. The people are shouting and
waving and there is great excitement.

Now a third lady-in-waiting bursts into the room with the
news that the Queen has been shot at! On Constitution Hill!
A man had fired at her—a madman, they think! He had tried to
do it before! Her Majesty knew; she had expected it to happen!

"Then that was why! Oh, my dear, she knew!—went, knowing
she was going to be shot at!" exclaims Lady Grace.

"*So didn't take us!* Oh, what a worm I feel myself, now!"
says Lady Muriel.

Now the police have pushed the crowd back and Victoria and
Albert have re-entered the house. Lady Grace and Lady Muriel
curtsey before the Queen "with an emotional reverence which
makes the formality almost beautiful."

"Lady Muriel, Lady Grace, why are you still here?" demands
Victoria. "Didn't I tell you that I should not want you again
till this evening? Now go at once!"

"Oh, Your Majesty! I'm so sorry, so ashamed of myself!"
pleads Lady Muriel.

THE QUEEN—Ashamed? Why?

LADY MURIEL—When Your Majesty said we were not to come

out with you this afternoon, I was foolishly cross; I didn't understand.

THE QUEEN—Of course not. It was not necessary that you should. But now you *do.* So that will help you to know better another time. Go. Please, Lady Muriel. I don't want you any more now. (LADY MURIEL *curtseys herself out after the others have gone.*)

ALBERT (*turning sharply*)—Another time!

THE QUEEN—Why, yes, Albert: there *may* come another time. Why not?

ALBERT—Oh, my dear, my dear! (*Crosses to her.*) And you can say that *now*—as if you did not mind if it *should* come again! (*Sits beside her.*) Is that really true?

THE QUEEN—Yes, Albert: it was wonderful! For, with you, I felt—so safe. . . . Didn't you?

ALBERT—No, Weibchen. I was afraid!

THE QUEEN—Afraid?

ALBERT—I was afraid that—if he missed *one* of us, it might be *me* that he missed. Ah, no, no, no! do not talk of another time! I could not bear it!

THE QUEEN—Oh, Albert, had I thought for a moment that it might be *you*—I *couldn't* have gone! But that *that* could happen I didn't think!

ALBERT—What a very good thing it was, then, my dear, that you did *not* think. Queens must not think too much about others —only about themselves! (*Having made that little joke, very much to his own satisfaction, he kisses her.*)

THE QUEEN (*relaxed*)—Dearest! Have I pleased you?

ALBERT—You have *more* than *pleased* me. You have behaved —like a *Queen!*

THE QUEEN—Then I must go and take off my things. (*Rises.*) Oh, dear! what a lot of letters I shall have to write *now.* To Uncle Leopold, and to everybody! (*And with this added inconvenience of attempted assassination upon her mind, off she goes, for there is no time to lose.*) How it will interest them. "Just think," I can hear them say, "poor Vicky's been shot at." After all when one has been shot at, it's worth writing about.

She goes out as the curtain falls.

THE ROSE AND THE THORN

Four years have passed. The year is 1846. The Queen is holding court at Windsor. We are in a small ante-chamber to the large
music room, in which the ladies and gentlemen of the Court are
now gathering. Presently four musicians, led by their conductor,
the John Oakley who is later to become Sir John, file into the
room, carrying their instruments. Now the doors to the music
room are closed. Soon the first strains of the opening number of
the program are faintly heard.

Into the ante-room a Duchess, the Queen's Mistress of the
Robes, followed by her cousin, Lady Jane, young and handsome,
bring the continuation of a discussion that evidently has been
quite animated. Lady Jane is protesting the difficulty of a situation in which she finds herself. The Duchess is attempting to convince her that most situations at Court are difficult. Difficult and
often humiliating. To accept them calmly and compose them with
dignity and grace is the larger part of the duties involved.

Lady Jane's particular concern of the moment is that she has
inspired the Queen's displeasure. Her Majesty is evidently jealous
of her, and for no reasonable cause. Merely because Prince Albert
may have shown her some slight attention in a most formal way.

"We were out riding in the park, and the Prince came and
rode beside me, just for a moment," explains Lady Jane. "My
reins had got caught, and he was putting them straight for me.
And the Queen pushed her horse right in between us; and she
said, 'Lady Jane, if you don't know how to ride properly, you
had better not come out with us!' And the Prince said (*mimick-
ing his accent*), 'Lady Jane rides very nicely and well.' Oh, you
should have seen the Queen's look then! And it's true; I *do* ride
nicely—better than she does; and she knows it!"

"And was that all that happened?"

"All that happened to *me*. But the Prince left the Queen, and
went straight off, and rode with one of his gentlemen. And then
the Queen suddenly turned round, and we all had to ride back
to the Castle. And of course everybody knew that something was
the matter, for we hadn't gone half our usual round. And now,
I believe, she has put Lady Maud to spy on me."

The Duchess is inclined to doubt that the Queen has even
mentioned the incident, Her Majesty is much too proud. But it
might be as well if it were arranged for Lady Jane to take a
little holiday, on the advice of her physician. Certainly she should

not think of giving up her position at Court. If Her Majesty should suggest dismissing her, then the Duchess will have something to say, probably with the endorsement of the Prince. Victoria is always much more easy to reason with when Albert is present.

"He is a very good corrective, and she knows it," explains the Duchess. "I'm very fond of her, but she needs managing and he is the only person who can do it."

The doors of the music room are opened. Members of the audience drift into the corridor, pausing frequently to congratulate Mr. Oakley. Soon the Queen and Prince Albert appear, the Prince crossing quickly into the ante-room, the Queen pausing to add her congratulations to those the conductor is receiving. Now Victoria has left her group and followed Albert, addressing him protestingly. Why has he been so cold to her? Has she offended him?

Victoria should not try to give him riding lessons especially before others, Albert suggests sharply, and walks away to rejoin the group at the music room door. For a few moments Victoria stands, angry and undecided. Then she, too, turns and is talking with her ladies when the Duchess and Lady Jane re-enter the room.

A rose has fallen from Lady Jane's hair. The Prince, seeing it on the floor, stoops to pick it up and returns it to her ladyship.

"Lady Jane, here is something that you have dropped," says he, presenting the flower with courtly grace.

"Oh, Your Highness, I am sorry!—sorry to have given Your Highness the trouble."

"No trouble . . . a pleasure. . . . It is a color that suits you."

The Duchess is observing the incident with an amused smile. The Queen's attention has also been attracted. Suddenly, pushing past the Duchess, the Queen advances on Lady Jane and snatches the flower from her hand.

"Your Majesty must pardon me; that flower is mine," protests Lady Jane.

"How dare you speak to me? Go! Go instantly!" responds Victoria, flushed with anger. She is crushing the flower in her hand.

Lady Jane curtseys formally and withdraws. Albert pauses briefly, then turns and leaves the room. The Queen would send the Duchess to bring the Prince back, but the Duchess first insists upon explaining what has happened. The Prince was not giving Lady Jane a flower, as Her Majesty might suspect. He merely had picked up a rose Lady Jane had dropped and courteously returned it to her.

"You saw that, you say? You know that for certain?" The Queen is greatly relieved by this explanation.

"I assure Your Majesty it was so."

THE QUEEN—Do you know, also, what happened this morning?

DUCHESS—I do, ma'am. My cousin has told me everything.

THE QUEEN—Did she try to explain it?

DUCHESS—There was hardly anything to explain, ma'am. It might have happened to anyone.

THE QUEEN—Then why did she tell you about it?

DUCHESS—She was very much upset by the way Your Majesty had taken what was a mere accident.

THE QUEEN—It may have been an accident: I don't know. What has happened now is much more serious.

DUCHESS—Very much more serious, Your Majesty. (THE QUEEN *looks at her in surprise. The* DUCHESS *does not flinch. A pause.*)

THE QUEEN—It was all so sudden—so unexpected. One hadn't time to think.

DUCHESS—That is so. Your Majesty gave yourself no *time* to think.

THE QUEEN—I was too hasty, you mean?

DUCHESS—Does Your Majesty wish me to say more than I have said?

THE QUEEN—I only wish you to tell me the honest truth.

DUCHESS—I will, ma'am. . . . At least, I will try. But the truth is sometimes difficult.

THE QUEEN—It should not be.

DUCHESS—Not even when it is—to a Queen, ma'am?

THE QUEEN—A Queen may need it sometimes, far more than others.

DUCHESS—If she knows that she needs it, ma'am, she is already on the side of truth.

THE QUEEN—I do know it—I do! . . . Tell me!—Is it possible that I have been unjust?

DUCHESS—It is possible, Your Majesty.

THE QUEEN—I did not intend to be.

DUCHESS—No one, who knows Your Majesty, would think that for a moment.

THE QUEEN—Thank you, dear Duchess, for saying that! In my position, I would wish never to be unjust to anyone. . . . Will

you—will you ask your cousin—Lady Jane—to come and speak
to me?

DUCHESS—I am not sure, ma'am, that she will come—now.

THE QUEEN—Will you say "please" for me?

DUCHESS—If I can say it, ma'am, as you have said it—

For a moment the Queen, left to herself, "sits rigid, facing an
ordeal which, for her, is of an almost unbelievable character.
Nevertheless she faces it."

When Lady Jane appears the expression of her face does not
make matters easier for the Queen.

"Lady Jane . . . I have sent for you to say . . . I am sorry.
. . . Forgive me. . . . I was quite wrong." Lady Jane curtseys
deeply. As she kisses Her Majesty's hand she bursts into tears.

"I am sorry, so sorry to have upset you," continues Victoria.
"You had better go to bed now, and rest. . . . And, Lady Jane,
if you would like—only if you would like—to go away for a little,
for a change—pray do so. I'm not asking you to go; but should
you at all wish to do so, you have my permission."

"I thank Your Majesty for so kindly suggesting it."

"Then that shall be arranged. . . . And now, will you tell the
Prince—I mean, will you ask someone to tell the Prince—that I
wish to see him?"

For a moment the Queen sits motionless, waiting. The Prince
does not come. Slowly Her Majesty's head sinks upon her breast.
She is shaken by sobs. The door opens softly. Albert moves quietly
toward Victoria. Standing beside her he gently strokes her hair.
As her sobbing is quieted Albert goes to the piano. Seated, he
plays a few bars and then, in a low, rich baritone, sings the first
verse of "Drink to Me Only with Thine Eyes."

Now Victoria has come to stand back of Albert. As he begins
the second verse her hand falls gently on his shoulder. She is
standing there, with her head resting against his beautiful hair as
the curtain falls.

INTERVENTION

It is the 30th of November, 1861. The scene is again that of
Albert's writing room. The Queen is there listening as General
Grey, her private secretary, reads a dispatch which Lord Russell,
the Foreign Secretary, has submitted to Her Majesty for approval.
It is a message his lordship is planning to send to Lord Lyons,
the British Ambassador at Washington, and refers to the seizure

upon the high seas of two Confederate officers from the British ship "Trent."

It is Lord Russell's suggestion that Her Majesty's government shall demand the liberation of the gentlemen captured, their delivery to the proper British authorities and an apology from the Government of the United States for the insult offered the British flag.

The Queen is dutifully impressed with the urgency of the situation, but she would like to consult with Prince Albert before she approves the dispatch. The fact that Lord Palmerston is now the Prime Minister, and liable to act quite without instructions, adds to Her Majesty's anxiety.

She is vastly relieved when Prince Albert arrives. He had stopped to change to dry clothes, Albert explains. His uniform had been wet through and he had been thoroughly chilled.

Albert does not approve Lord Russell's dispatch. It means war, he is quick to decide. Victoria is willing to concede the possibility but, as America is in the wrong, she doesn't see what they can do.

"Say it, but say it differently," Albert advises. "Often it is just the way a thing is said that decides whether it shall be peace or war. It is the same when two people quarrel. You and I, Weibchen, might often have quarreled had we said the same thing that we did say—differently. . . . (*Back to paper.*) Russell? Oh, no: this is Palmerston, I think! He is the man that would *like* to have war with America. He has worked for it; and this is his opportunity—that we are in the right! . . . He shall not have it! War? Oh, yes; and this time we should win. But another time would come, and we should *not* win."

"But we could always beat America now, Albert."

"Ah, so? What if we were fighting someone else, Vicky; and America chose her time then?"

America, as Albert sees it, knows that she has done wrong. It would be wise for England to accept the incident as a mistake and invite America to reconsider. America, in all probability, would in that case behave reasonably. But say "I order you" to her and she would not. Just as Britain would not.

"And we should call it 'Honor,'" says Albert. "And for that Honor we should send thousands and thousands to die. What a wicked, black thing Honor can become—when men make use of it—*so!*"

"And what are we going to do, Albert?"

"We are going to alter this, *now*. . . . Take your pen at once and write. Say that this dispatch is not to go, till he has heard from you. . . . And your messenger must go now, at once, and must see Lord Russell himself. . . . This will take me more time; but you write your letter at once!"

"Yes, Albert, yes!"

A messenger has been sent to tell Lord Russell to hold his dispatch. Victoria would now stand beside Albert as he writes the correction but Albert is sure he could work better alone. As Victoria goes, a little reluctantly, the lights fade. The clock on the mantel has just struck four. . . .

When the scene is resumed some hours have passed. The candles are lighted. Albert is still at the desk and writing, but is soon finished. The pen drops from his tired hand. He has summoned a gentleman and sent for the Queen. When he tries to rise from his chair he falls back. Victoria finds him leaning on the table, his head on his arms. It is with some difficulty that he raises himself and asks her to read what he has written. She hurries through the dispatch and is quick to approve its every word. It is, says Albert, to be sent at once. And then he reaches out to the Queen with a gesture of helplessness.

"Take me to bed! . . . Take me to bed, Weibchen," he pleads. "Ich bin so schwach. Ich habe kaum die Feder halten können!"

The Queen throws her arms about him and is holding him close as the curtain falls.

ACT III

THE QUEEN, GOD BLESS HER

In the summer of 1877 Queen Victoria is at Balmoral Castle in Scotland. She is sitting at the moment at a table in a gaily striped garden tent on the lawn. She has aged perceptibly. Her cheeks are full, round and reddened by the outdoor life she has been leading. Her figure has filled out until there is a marked rotundity. Her parasol is leaning against her, and on the table before her are writing materials, a fan and a dish of peaches. She is reading "The Scotsman" and continues reading until she is disturbed by some unseen object. That is what the parasol is for. She lifts it now and industriously beats a small dog that, lying against her skirts, has annoyed her by demanding more attention.

A moment later she has rung the handbell and summoned John Brown, "a fine figure of a man in Highland costume," who, standing in the door of the tent, "speaks in the strong Doric of his native wilds."

"Was Your Majesty wanting anything, or were you ringing only for the fun?" demands John Brown. (*To this brusque delivery* HER MAJESTY *responds with a cozy smile, for the special function of* MR. JOHN BROWN *is not to be a courtier; and, knowing what is expected of him, he lives up to it.*)

"Bring another chair, Brown. And take Mop with you; he wants his walk," orders Her Majesty.

"What kind of a chair are you wanting, ma'am? Is it to put your feet on?"

"No, no. It is to put a visitor on. Choose a nice one with a lean-back."

"With a lean-back? Ho! Ye mean one that you can lean back in. What talk folk will bring with them from up south, to be sure! Yes, I'll get it for ye, ma'am."

The Queen will also have her morning sherry brought, and with two glasses. There is a slight lifting of the Brown eyebrows at the suggestion, but he goes dutifully out with Mop. A moment later a liveried footman has brought the sherry. The Queen has resumed her reading when John Brown reappears with the chair. He is not at all disturbed by Her Majesty's complaint that there are wasps about. There usually are wasps about this time of year. It's the fruit they're after.

"Yes; like Adam and Eve," smiles Victoria. "You'd better take it away, Brown, or cover it; it's too tempting."

"Ah! Now if God had only done that, maybe we'd still all be running about naked," ventures Brown.

"I'm glad he didn't, then," answers Her Majesty, quickly. "The Fall made the human race decent, even if it did no good otherwise."

Brown is plainly interested in the expected visitor. He knows him for Lord Beaconsfield, and has given him a room that he, Brown, used to have, which has a good spring bed in it, and a kettle-ring for the whiskey. He remembers his lordship, too, as a nice gentleman who had the courtesy not to take back a tip after he had been reminded of the liberty he had taken in giving it. An ignorant man, so far as certain marvels of nature and custom are concerned, Brown is convinced, and not so well up on his Burns as a man should be who thinks to make laws for Scotland, but a good man withal.

"He's very innocent, ma'am, if you get him where he's not expecting you," concludes Brown.

"Well, Brown, there are some things you can teach him, I don't doubt; and there are some things he can teach you. I'm sure he has taught me a great deal."

"It's a credit to ye both, then," agrees Brown.

Going to call Lord Beaconsfield, Brown finds his lordship in the garden, talking with the Princess, which is a little flustering to the Queen. She is at pains to put a feminine touch or two to her dress and cap before having him in. "Put your bonnet straight, Your Majesty," is John Brown's parting advice, as he leaves the tent to summon Beaconsfield. She has resumed her writing when Beaconsfield appears and stands for a moment at the tent's entrance waiting for her to finish. Victoria's favorite Minister is "flawlessly arrayed in a gay frock suit suggestive of the period when male attire was still not only a fashion but an art."

"Despite, however, the studied correctness of his costume, face and deportment give signs of haggard fatigue; and when he bows it is the droop of a weary man, slow in the recovery."

Their exchange of greetings is felicitous and a little florid. Her Majesty is feeling "bonnie," as they say in Scotland, and Lord Beaconsfield has found compensation for the long journey to Balmoral in looking forward to that which is now before him. He is hesitant in answering Her Majesty's impatience to hear the political news only because there is almost nothing to tell. "Politics, like the rest of us, have been taking holiday," his lordship reports.

"I thought that Mr. Gladstone had been speaking," suggests the Queen.

"Oh, yes!" admits Beaconsfield, with an airy flourish of courtly disdain; "he has been speaking!"

QUEEN—In Edinburgh, quite lately.

LORD B.—And in more other places than I can count. Speaking—speaking—speaking. But I have to confess, Madam, that I have not read his speeches.

QUEEN—I have read some of them.

LORD B.—Your Majesty does him great honor—and yourself some inconvenience, I fear.

QUEEN—They annoy me intensely. I have no patience with him!

LORD B.—Pardon me, Madam; if you have read *one* of his speeches, your patience has been extraordinary.

QUEEN—Can't you stop it?

LORD B.—Stop?—stop what, Madam? Niagara, the Flood?

QUEEN—But, surely, he should be stopped when he speaks on matters which may, any day, bring us into war! (*Touching the newspaper.*) This morning's news isn't good, I'm afraid. The Russians are getting nearer to Constantinople.

LORD B.—They will never enter it, Madam.

QUEEN—No, they mustn't! We will not allow it.

LORD B.—That, precisely, is the policy of Your Majesty's Government. Nevertheless, we may have to make a demonstration.

QUEEN—Do you propose to summon Parliament?

LORD B.—Not Parliament; no, Madam. Your Majesty's Fleet will be sufficient.

QUEEN—Oh! There is something I would like to do, Lord Beaconsfield, on which I want your advice.

LORD B.—Always at Your Majesty's disposal.

QUEEN—I wish to confer upon the Sultan of Turkey my Order of the Garter.

LORD B.—Ah! How generous, how generous an instinct! How like you, Madam, to wish it!

QUEEN—What I want to know is, whether, as Prime Minister, you have any objection?

LORD B.—"As Prime Minister"; how difficult that makes it for me to answer! How willingly would I say "None!" How reluctantly on the contrary, I have to say, "It had better wait."

QUEEN—Wait? Wait till when? I want to do it *now*.

LORD B.—Yes, so do I. But can you risk, Madam, conferring that most illustrious symbol of honor, and chivalry, and power, on a defeated monarch?

QUEEN—But do you think, Lord Beaconsfield, that the Turks are going to be beaten?

LORD B.—The Turks are beaten, Madam. . . . But *England* will never be beaten. We shall dictate terms—moderating the demands of Russia; and under Your Majesty's protection the throne of the Kaliphat will be safe—once more. Some day, who knows? Egypt, (VICTORIA *nods, pleased at each name.*) possibly even Syria, Arabia, may be our destined reward. (*Like a cat over a bowl of cream, England's Majesty sits lapping all this up. But, when he has done, her commentary is shrewd and to the point.*)

QUEEN—The French won't like it!

LORD B.—They won't, Madam, they won't. But has it ever been England's policy, Madam, to mind what the French don't like?

QUEEN—No, it never has been, has it? (*They both smile satisfied.*) Ah! You are the true statesman, Lord Beaconsfield. Mr. Gladstone never talked to me like that.

LORD B.—No? . . . You must have had interesting conversations with him, Madam, in the past.

QUEEN—I have never once had a conversation with Mr. Gladstone, in all my life, Lord Beaconsfield. He used to talk to me as if I were a public meeting—and one that agreed with him, too!

LORD B.—Was there, then, any applause, Madam?

QUEEN—No, indeed! I used to cough sometimes.

LORD B.—Rather like coughing at a balloon, I fear. Only today I learn that he has been in the habit of addressing—as you, Madam, so wittily phrased it—of addressing "as tho' she were a public meeting" that Royal Mistress, whom it has ever been my most difficult task not to address sometimes as the most charming, the most accomplished, and the most fascinating woman of the epoch which bears her name. But I come to be consulted as Your Majesty's First Minister of State. If, therefore, your royal mind have any inquiries, any further commands to lay upon me, I am here, Madam, to give effect to them in so far as I can.

The visit grows increasingly intimate as Lord Beaconsfield is led to refer feelingly to the loneliness that came upon him with the loss of his wife. It is a loneliness that Victoria can understand. She is much moved by Beaconsfield's devotion to the memory of one he had loved deeply.

"In the history of my race, Madam, there has been a great tradition of faithfulness between husbands and wives," says Lord Beaconsfield. "When my wife died I had no thought to marry again. Circumstances that have happened since have sealed irrevocably that resolution."

"Oh, I think that is so wise, so right, so noble of you," answers Victoria.

Now Lord Beaconsfield has arisen, preparatory to taking his formal departure. He is courteously apologetic for having stayed so long, as he bends over Her Majesty's outstretched hand. Victoria would have him pause briefly to drink a glass of sherry with her.

While the servant is pouring the wine there is one other thing of which Victoria would speak to her Minister. That Order of the Garter which she had thought to confer upon the Sultan, she now has decided, again with his permission as Prime Minister, to confer nearer home—"on one to whom personally—I cannot say more—on yourself, I mean," Victoria concludes, emotionally moved. For a moment Beaconsfield stands "in an attitude of drooping humility." The eloquent silence is broken by the Queen's gentle demand for an answer.

"Oh, Madam! What adequate answer can these poor lips make to so magnificent an offer?" His lordship's voice is vibrant with feeling. "Let me come to you again when I have saved Constantinople, and secured once more upon a firm basis the peace of Europe. Then ask me again whether I have any objection, and I will own—I have none!"

QUEEN—Very well, Lord Beaconsfield. And if you do not remind me, I shall remind you. (*She points to the tray.*) Pray, help yourself! (*He takes up the decanter.*)

LORD B.—I serve you, Madam?

QUEEN—Thank you. (*He fills the two glasses; and takes up his own.*)

LORD B.—May I propose for myself—a toast, Madam? (*The* QUEEN *sees what is coming, and bows graciously.*) The Queen! God bless her! (*He drains the glass, then breaks it against the pole of the tent, and throws away the stem.*) An old custom, Madam, observed by loyal defenders of the House of Stuart. To my old hand came a sudden access of youthful enthusiasm— an ardor which I could not restrain. Your pardon, Madam!

QUEEN—Go and rest yourself, my friend.

LORD B.—Adieu, Madam.

QUEEN—Draw your curtains, and sleep well. (*For a moment he stands gazing at her with a look of deep emotion; he tries to speak. Ordinary words seem to fail; he falters into poetry.*)

LORD B.—"When pain and anguish wring the brow,
          A ministering Angel, thou!"

(*Silent and slow, with head reverentially bowed, he backs away from the Presence. The* QUEEN *sits and looks after the retreating figure, then at the broken fragments of glass. She takes up the hand-bell and rings. The attendant enters.*)

QUEEN—Pick up that broken glass. (*The attendant collects it on the hand-tray which he carries.*) Bring it to me! . . . Leave it! (*The attendant deposits the tray before her, and goes. Gently the* QUEEN *handles the broken pieces.*) Such devotion! Most extraordinary! (*And in the sixteenth year of her widowhood and the fortieth of her reign, the* ROYAL LADY *bends her head over the fragments of broken glass—and weeps happy tears.*)

The curtain falls.

HAPPY AND GLORIOUS

Twenty years have passed. We have come to 1897 and Victoria's Diamond Jubilee. It is late in the day of the great celebration. The scene is a chamber in Buckingham Palace adjoining a balcony from which Royalty has often addressed the people. In the chamber are gathered more than fifty of the Queen's direct descendants, "together with representatives of all the crowned heads of a Europe still at peace."

"The Triumphal Procession is over, and the large upper chamber becomes filled with Royalty. Bonnets, costumes, uniforms, mingle in a moving clash of colors; Orders sparkle, sword-chains clink, spurs jingle. Their owners step delicately, bowing their way from group to group; and—some now encountering for the first time—high form and ceremony are still the rule. But here and there members of the Royal Family, meeting each other, exchange remarks of a familiar character, though sometimes in a foreign accent. And as all (except an Official or two) who thus mix and converse are Royal Highnesses—if nothing more—there is no need to trouble about names. Nobody today, except the Queen herself (and perhaps the Heir-Apparent) is individually important."

The conversation rises in a steady hum from which may be extracted such conventional comment as: "How beautifully everything went!" "Nothing could have been better!" "I hope mamma enjoyed it as much as I did!" "What crowds!" "What cheering!" And so on.

Now footmen have opened the center doors. The crowd becomes a little more animated. From the inner room a voice is heard announcing the approach of Her Majesty. Now those gathered in the chamber stand at attention on either side of the window.

Presently the Queen enters, seated in her wheeled chair and accompanied by her two sons. The assembled family and guests bow low before Her Majesty. The one word "Congratulations!" rises above the continued hum of voices on every side.

Her Majesty, a little old lady sunk deep in her shawls, smiles gently and nods her head in acknowledgment. As the guests move toward the doors the Queen calls them back. She would have them remain.

"Mamma dear, how are you?" inquires the Princess Beatrice, a little anxiously.

"Very tired, my dear; but, oh, so happy. . . . To think that it is all over. . . . So glad that I had the strength for it!" Victoria's voice is still firm, the light in her eyes bright with excitement.

DUCHESS OF YORK—You were quite wonderful, Grandmamma!

THE QUEEN—Thank you! Oh, thank you!

PRINCESS BEATRICE—Won't you go and rest now, Mamma?

THE QUEEN—Not yet. . . . That cheering that I heard means that my dear people are expecting to see me again. . . . I must try not to disappoint them.

PRINCESS BEATRICE—It would be nice if you could, Mamma. Do you think that you can?

THE QUEEN—Yes. But I shall have to go as I am. I can't get up. It's very gratifying, very, to find—after all these years—that they do appreciate all that I have tried to do for them—for their good, and for this great country of ours. We have been so near together today—they and I; all my dear people of England, and Scotland, and Wales—*and* Ireland, and the dear Colonies, and India. From all round the world I have had messages. Such loyalty—such devotion! Most extraordinary! But tell Mr. Chamberlain how very much I approve of all the arrangements he made for the proper representation of all parts of my Empire in the Procession. Everything so perfectly in order. Most gratifying! . . . So happy! As we were coming back—you were in front, Beatrice, so perhaps you didn't see—it was just by Hyde Park Corner, there was a great crowd there; and a lot of rough men—of course it ought not to have happened, but it didn't matter—broke right through the lines of the police and troops guarding the route; and they ran alongside the carriage, shouting and cheering me. And I heard them say: "Go it, Old Girl! You've done it well!" Of course, very unsuitable—the words; but so gratifying! And oh, I hope it's true! I hope it's true! I must go to them now. Have the windows opened. (*A chamberlain orders a footman, who opens the windows.*) Hark! How they are cheering. Albert! Ah! if only you could have been here!

And, having said her say, the great, wonderful, little old lady gives the signal to her attendants, and is wheeled slowly onto the balcony.

THE CURTAIN FALLS

BOY MEETS GIRL

A Comedy in Three Acts

By Bella and Samuel Spewack

THE last week of November was a great help to the recovery program in the theatre of 1935-36. Two of the season's outstanding comedy successes were included in the contributions of that seven days. The Dayton-Kaufman "First Lady" stirred the villagers to shouts of joy on a Tuesday evening and the Spewacks' "Boy Meets Girl" set them shrieking with laughter the Wednesday following.

" 'Boy Meets Girl' is, I think, the best play that has yet appeared about Hollywood," writes George Abbott in the preface to the published text of the play. "It is the real thing. And it is the real thing because Bella and Samuel Spewack are reporters as well as dramatists and they report what they see and observe, not what convention would want them to see."

That sums up admirably both the virtues and the character of this comedy. Despite the admitted extravagances in which its authors have indulged, and the satirical subtleties included in their observations, the impression the play leaves is of a picture taken at first hand, of analyses of character and situation based intelligently on fact.

The added fact that the play was directed and produced by Mr. Abbott, himself one of the more keenly observing and intelligent men of the theatre, who also has had his experiences in Hollywood, proved of definite value to the comedy. It was, by the record, an overnight success that promised to run through the summer.

The Spewacks, approaching the theatre through practical experience as newspaper workers, had previously written "Clear All Wires" and "Spring Song," both well spoken of by professional play reviewers but lacking something of popular appeal. They had been working in Hollywood for some time previous to the appearance of "Boy Meets Girl" and were credited with having taken certain recorded adventures of the writing team of Ben Hecht and Charles MacArthur as the inspiration of their story. They were quick to issue the customary and expected denial of this charge.

The room into which we are ushered at the opening of "Boy Meets Girl" is one of a suite of three occupied by C. Elliott Friday, "a supervisor, sometimes called a producer, who is engaged in manufacturing motion pictures in Hollywood, California."

"In its present state the room is a happy combination of the Regency and Russell Wright periods," the authors explain, "given over to pale green, mauve and canary yellow, with Rodier-cloth-covered easy chairs and couch. A magnificent, be-French-phoned desk is at one end of the room. On it rests the inner-office dictograph, over which in the course of the play we hear the voice of the great B. K., chief executive of the studio. Beside it, appropriately, stands an amiable photograph of Mrs. C. Elliott Friday, a cultured if fatuous lady; a copy of 'Swann's Way' (leaves uncut), a bronze nude astride an ash tray, a bottle of Pyramidon and a copy of *Variety*. In the trash basket is a copy of *Hollywood Reporter*. (It was very unkind to Mr. Friday.)"

There are two windows, partially concealed by Venetian blinds ("a supervisor would lose cast without Venetian blinds") and through those Venetian blinds "you can feel the sweet sterility of the desert that is so essentially Southern California. The sun is bright, of course, and it pours endlessly through the windows. The time is two o'clock, and the boys have been at it since noon."

"One of the boys is Benson—J. Carlyle Benson, whom we discover prone on a couch. He is in his thirties and in his flannels. Years ago, as he will tell you, he worked as a scene painter and a property boy. He became a writer because he learned how bricks were made and laid. He knows every cliché, every formula, and in his heart of hearts he really believes the fairy tale is a credo of life. And he's a damned nice guy."

"The other member of the writing team is Robert Law, whom you will find listed in O'Brien's 'Best Short Stories' of five years ago. He came to Hollywood to make a little money and run right back to Vermont where he could really write. He is rather handsome, a little round-shouldered; smokes incessantly. He's a damned nice guy, too."

"There is a deep and abiding affection between the two men, even though Law's nostalgia for realism and sincerity and substance finds no echoing response in Mr. Benson. They have one great thing in common—their mutual love of a great gag, a practical joke to enliven the monotony of the writing factory."

In the room also are Larry Toms, a Western star, and one Rosetti, Mr. Toms' agent. "Mr. Toms is handsome, of course.

He is also parsimonious. He leads a completely righteous life, and if you don't like him it isn't our fault; in all respects he is an extremely admirable character."

Mr. Law has been telling Mr. Toms a story for a picture they would like to have him play. So far Mr. Toms has been unable to vision the picture and he is very anxious. This is to be his last picture under his present contract and it must be good. He is very glad to have this star team of writers assigned to him, but so far, to Mr. Toms, they have done nothing but clown around and the shooting date's only two weeks off.

"I've got to play this picture," concludes Mr. Toms, in something resembling a wail.

"Why?" callously demands Mr. Law.

LARRY (*swallowing*)—Tell me your story in a few simple words.

LAW—Mr. Benson, what's our story?

BENSON—How the hell do I know?

LAW (*sits up*)—Didn't you listen?

BENSON—No. We ought to have a stenographer.

LAW—But they won't wear tights. And I can't dictate to a stenographer who won't wear tights.

LARRY—Now listen, boys—

LAW—Don't speak to me. You don't like our story.

LARRY—I didn't say I didn't like it. I couldn't follow it. (*He slumps in disgust.*)

BENSON (*indignantly*)—You couldn't follow it? Listen, I've been writing stories for eleven years. Boy meets girl. Boy loses girl. Boy gets girl.

LAW—Or—girl meets boy. Girl loses boy. Girl gets boy. Love will find a way. Love never loses. Put your money on love. You can't lose. (*Rises and saunters to window.*) I'm getting hungry.

BENSON—It's a sorry state of affairs when an actor insists on following a story. Do you think this is a golf tournament?

ROSETTI (*earnestly*)—If I may make a point, I don't think you're showing the proper respect to one of the biggest stars in this studio. A man who's not only captivated millions of people but is going to captivate millions more—

BENSON (*wearily*)—With his little lasso—

LARRY—Just because I don't get Gable's fan mail don't mean I ain't got his following. A lot of those that want to write me ain't never learned how.

LAW—Benson, injustice has been done. We've been lacking

"BOY MEETS GIRL"

Susie: When I come into a room—does something happen to you?
Rodney: Eh? Of course—very much so.
Susie: When you come into a room, something happens to me, too.

(*Joyce Arling, James MacColl*)

in respect for the idol of illiteracy.

BENSON—Do we apologize?

LAW—No!

Mr. Rosetti would come to his star's defense by drawing attention to his, Mr. Toms', larynx, which could easily be that of a
singer. And that certainly should mean something. It might,
agree the Messrs. Law and Benson, but it doesn't. By which time
Mr. Toms has worked himself into such a state of disgust that
he proposes to wipe up the studio with these crazy writers who
"get fifteen hundred a week for acting like hoodlums."

"We're not writers, we're hacks," protests Law. "If we weren't,
would I be sitting here listening to your inarticulate grunts?
. . . For two cents, Benson, I'd take the next train back to
Vermont."

"That's all right with me," agrees the still angry Toms.

"Will you forget Vermont?" demands Benson.

"At least I wouldn't have to sit around with *that* in Vermont,"
continues Law, fervently. "I'd write—really write. My God, I
wrote once. I wrote a book. A darn good book. I was a promising young novelist. O'Brien reprinted three of my stories. 1928-
1929-1930. And in 1935 I'm writing dialogue for a horse!"

Again the excited Toms wants to settle the issue with a killing
and again Rosetti has some trouble restraining him. Presently
"C. F." who could be none other than C. Elliott Friday, comes
from his conference with "B. K." and the situation becomes
more composed.

C. F. is in a good deal of a bustle. This promises to be a heavy
day. He warns his secretary that he is not to be disturbed and
orders lunch which, to C. F., means raw carrots and raw milk
for everybody. Benson and Law cannot go that far. For themselves they will have chicken broth, ham hocks, cabbage, lemon
meringue pie and bicarbonate of soda. . . .

C. F.'s present state of mind has been influenced by many
things. Royal Studios, he reports, stands in danger of a reorgani-
zation. If that comes it probably will mean his job and Larry
Toms' job. Nor will Benson and Law be sitting any too securely.
So, this next picture they are to do for Larry Toms must be a
really big picture.

"I want to do something fine—with sweep, with scope—stark,
honest, gripping, adult, but with plenty of laughs and a little
hokum," enthuses C. F. "Something we'll be proud of. Not just
another picture, but the picture of the year. A sort of Bengal

Lancer, but as Kipling would have done it. Maybe we could wire Kipling and get him to write a few scenes. It would be darned good publicity."

The boys call his attention to the fact that nestling on his desk the last two weeks is a very excellent script—the one with Benson's fingerprints on the corner. The boys know this to be a good story because it is the same one Larry Toms has been doing for years.

"Griffith used it. Lubitsch used it. And Eisenstein's coming around to it," insists Law.

"Boy meets girl. Boy loses girl. Boy gets girl," prompts Benson.

"The great American fairy tale. Sends the audience back to the relief rolls in a happy frame of mind," adds Law.

"And why not?" demands Benson.

LAW—The greatest escape formula ever worked out in the history of civilization . . .

C. F.—Of course, if you put it that way . . . but, boys, it's hackneyed.

LAW—You mean classic.

C. F. (*triumphantly*)—"Hamlet" is a classic—but it isn't hackneyed!

LAW—"Hamlet" isn't hackneyed? Why, I'd be ashamed to use that poison gag. He lifted that right out of the Italians. (PEGGY, *a manicurist, enters and crosses to her chair and sits.*) Ask Peggy. (PEGGY *puts the bowl now half-filled with water down on the desk.*)

BENSON—Yes, let's ask Peggy . . . if she wants to see Larry Toms in a different story. She's your audience.

PEGGY—Don't ask me anything, Mr. Benson. I've got the damnedest toothache. (*She takes* C. F.'s *hand and looks up at him suddenly.*) Relax! (*She begins filing.*)

BENSON (*wheedling*)—But, Peggy, you go to pictures, don't you?

PEGGY—No.

BENSON—But you've seen Larry's pictures and enjoyed them?

PEGGY—No.

BENSON— . . . As millions of others have . . .

LAW—Why, one man sent him a rope all the way from Manila —with instructions.

C. F.—Boys, this isn't getting us anywhere.

BENSON (*assuming the manner of a district attorney; barking at* PEGGY)—Peggy, do you mean to sit there and tell me you haven't seen *one* Larry Toms picture?

PEGGY—I saw one.

BENSON—Ah!

PEGGY—"Night in Death Valley."

BENSON—This isn't getting us anywhere, eh? How would you like to see "Night in Death Valley" again—with a new title?

PEGGY—I wouldn't.

BENSON—That's all. Step down. (*Crosses to couch; slaps* LAW *on shoulder.*) May I point out to this court that the body was found only two feet away, in an open field, with every door and window shut? (*To* LAW.) Your witness. (*He exits.*)

LAW (*rises*)—I've got to see a man about a woman. (*He exits. Our writers have vanished. They love to vanish from story conferences.*)

C. F. (*rises*)—Come back here! (*Picks up phone.*)

LARRY—That's what I mean—clowning.

C. F. (*at phone*)—Miss Crews, leave word at the gate Benson and Law are not to be allowed off the lot. They're to come right back to my office. (*Hangs up.*)

LARRY—Why do you stand for it?

C. F.—Larry, those boys are crazy, but they've got something.

LARRY—They've been fired off every other lot.

C. F.—I'll fire them off this one, after they've produced a story. I've made up my mind to that. Meanwhile, patience.

LARRY—That's easy to say.

C. F.—You can't quibble with the artistic temperament when it produces.

LARRY (*grumbling*)—They've been producing nothing but trouble around here.

A handsome young actor in the resplendent uniform of the Coldstream Guards has put in an appearance. His name is Rodney Bevan and he has been sent, he explains, by the Wardrobe department to see if C. F. approves his uniform. It is for a picture to be known as "Young England."

There is for the moment considerable added confusion. Outside C. F.'s window a small band of midgets has assembled. They had been ordered, they insist, by C. F. but he remembers nothing about it and orders them sent away. To which they reply by throwing rocks through the window, causing a hasty lowering of the Venetian blinds. Getting back to Rodney and the uniform C. F. is greatly displeased with the busby which tops it.

"Well, it's very peculiar that you should take umbrage at the hat, as it happens to be the only correct item in the entire outfit," says Rodney, smiling diffidently.

"What's that?"

RODNEY—This coat doesn't hang properly—these buttons are far too large. These shoulder straps are absurd, of course. And the boots . . . if I may say so . . . are too utterly fantastic. Any Guardsman would swoon away at the sight of them.

C. F.—So!

RODNEY—The hat, however, *is* authentic.

C. F.—It is, eh? What's your salary?

RODNEY—As I understand it, I'm to receive seven dollars a day Monday and Tuesday, when I speak no lines, and fifteen dollars a day Thursday, Friday and Saturday, when I propose a toast.

C. F.—And you're telling a fifty-thousand-dollar-a-year man how to run his picture. Look here—I spent two weeks in London, my man, at the Savoy, and I watched them change the guards, personally.

RODNEY—At the Savoy?

C. F.—Young man, we have a technical adviser on this picture. And it doesn't happen to be you.

RODNEY—Quite. He's a splendid fellow, but he's a third generation Canadian. He's never even been to London.

C. F.—So you don't like the uniform and you don't like the technical expert. (*Smoothly.*) What's your name?

RODNEY—Rodney Bevan. Of course, it's a sort of nom de plume, or nom de guerre—

C. F.—Rodney Bevan. (*Picks up phone.*) Give me Casting. . . . This is C. F. . . . Extra here by the name of Rodney Bevan doesn't like his uniform. Fire him.

RODNEY (*aghast*)—Fire? Have you given me the sack?

C. F.—I've enough trouble without extras telling me how to make pictures. That's the trouble with this business. A man spends his life at it, and anybody can walk in and tell him how to run it.

RODNEY—But I merely suggested—

The distraction next following is occasioned by the sudden appearance of the Messrs. Green and Slade, song writers. They have just completed an opus for "Young England" which they insist C. F. shall hear. It is a touching little thing, explains

Green, but with great power, the title being "Pain in My Heart, and My Heart's on My Sleeve." Before they can be stopped Mr. Slade has glued himself to the piano and Mr. Green is singing the song "with all the fervid sincerity of Georgie Jessel with a cold. . . ."

The song is no more than finished when Benson and Law reappear. They are wearing the costumes of beefeaters. They're for "Young England" too, they announce, but they would like to be photographed in technicolor. This, thinks C. F., is no time to be masquerading!

"Now really, boys, I'm tolerant, but I've got to see results," he warns them. "I'm not one to put the creative urge in a straitjacket. But you've been fired off every other lot in this industry for your pranks. Perhaps you've forgotten, Benson, but when I hired you for this job you promised me to behave in no uncertain terms. And you promised me Law would toe the line. Now I'm warning you, boys. Let's get to work. Let's concentrate. Do you realize you boys are making more than the President of the United States?"

"But look at the fun he's having!" protests Law.

The song writers have given up. Law has danced a measure or two of "The Merry Widow" waltz with Miss Crews, C. F.'s surprised secretary, and C. F. is again prepared to halt everything and voice a final and definite protest when a young woman named Susie appears in the door with the lunch.

Susie is a waitress. A frail, blonde child whom it is easy to worship because of "the ineffable charm of her touching naïveté." Immediately the hungry men have surrounded her and are relieving her of her tray. She weakly protests that they should be careful and then neatly collapses at their feet. Immediately there is great excitement. C. F. is little less than flabbergasted that anything like that could happen in his offices. Benson has jumped to the phone to call the doctor. Law has taken Susie's head in his lap and is calling for water.

Presently Susie opens her eyes and inquires sweetly if they all have napkins. Now they have helped her into a chair. Her voice is still quavering, but she assures them she is quite all right. It wasn't necessary for them to send for a doctor.

"Do you get these epileptic fits often?" C. F. wants to know.

"I didn't have an epileptic fit," protests Susie.

C. F.—Then what's wrong with you?

SUSIE—There's nothing wrong . . . it's only natural.

C. F.—Only natural for you to come into my office and collapse on the floor.

Susie—Oh, no, sir . . . it's only natural for you to feel sick when you're going to have a baby.

Law—A baby!

Benson—Susie, you're not going to have a baby!

Susie—That's what they told me. . . .

Benson—Susie's going to have a baby!

Law—Let's get drunk!

C. F. (*into phone*)—Tell that doctor not to come. You heard me. I don't want him. (*He hangs up.*) I won't have my office converted into a maternity ward! (*He turns on* Susie.) I don't think much of your husband—letting you work at a time like this!

Susie—Oh, but I haven't got a husband.

C. F.—Huh?

Susie (*rises*)—You'd better eat your lunch before it gets cold. Have you all got napkins?

Law (*humbly*)—The new generation! Faces the facts of nature without squeamishness, without subterfuge. "I haven't got a husband," she says. "It's only natural," she says. "I'm going to have a baby." . . . Susie, you're magnificent.

Susie—I'm quitting at the end of the week so I thought I'd tell everybody why. I wouldn't want them to think I was discontented.

Law—Our little mother!

Susie—Oh, don't make fun of me.

Law (*rises*)—Fun? I've never been so touched in my life. Susie, I feel purified.

Benson—Susie—can we be godfather?

Susie—Do you mean it?

Benson—Do we mean it? We haven't got a baby. And we've been collaborating for years.

Susie—Oh, I think that would be wonderful for Happy to have writers for a godfather.

Benson—Happy?

Susie—I'm going to call him Happy—even if he's a girl. Because I want him to be happy—even if he's a girl.

Benson—Beautiful! A beautiful thought! Where are you going to have this baby, Susie?

Susie—In the County Hospital. It's all fixed. I was very lucky because I've only lived in the county three months and I'm not eligible.

C. F.—Now, listen, boys—enough of this.

LAW (*into phone*)—Give me the Cedars of Lebanon Hospital—and make it snappy.

BENSON (*jubilant*)—We've got a baby!

C. F.—Just a minute. Hang up that phone. (BENSON *good-naturedly brushes his arm down.*)

LAW—Dr. Marx, please. . . . Willy, this is Law of Benson and Law. Reserve the best suite in the house for us. I'm serious. Dead serious. A little friend of ours is going to have a baby and we want the goddamnedest confinement you've got in stock. . . .

BENSON—Day and night nurse.

LAW (*to* BENSON)—And not the one with the buck teeth either. She's dynamite. (*Into phone.*) We want everything that Gloria Swanson had—only double. What's that? Bill? Bill the studio, of course. (*He hangs up.*)

C. F. is again heavy with protest. He doesn't propose to stand for any such gag as this. He would send Susie peremptorily from the room, but Susie suddenly finds she has acquired a couple of determined protectors. Benson and Law have been conferring excitedly in the corner. Now they take charge of Susie to the further amazement of C. F.

The boys have also found their story! A story for Larry Toms and a baby. Larry finds a baby! The baby of a girl with a no-good gambler—out of Las Vegas— Gambler is killed! Girl leaves baby on ranger's doorstep—

" 'My God,' he says—'a baby,' " shouts Law, dramatizing the situation to the hilt. "The most precious thing in life. The cutest, goddam little bastard you ever saw!"

"Tugging at every mother's heart. And every potential mother," chips in Benson.

"And who isn't?" demands Law.

Before they have finished developing this "love story between Larry and the baby—the two outcasts," they have had Larry meet the mother, who now hates all men, and leave her to rejoin the Foreign Legion and forget. Finally, in the fire of a greater inspiration, they see Susie as the Mary Magdalen of the Foreign Legion and Larry a West Point man who wanted to forget.

"The baby brings them together, splits them apart, brings them together—" cries Benson.

And there they are. "Boy meets girl. Boy loses girl. Boy gets girl."

"Boys, I think you've got something!" C. F. capitulates with a will. "Let's go up and try it on B. K. while it's hot."

As they dash through the door they only hear a part of Larry Toms' protest. He is trying to tell them that he won't play any such part. A baby would take the picture away from him. Look at what happened to Chevalier! Larry is still protesting vehemently as he follows them out.

For a moment Susie is alone. She tries to rise, but quickly sits down again. Rodney, the Coldstream Guards actor, is back, seeking another interview with Mr. Friday. If Susie doesn't mind he thinks he had better wait.

Susie doesn't mind. Susie even goes so far as to suggest that the young man help himself to some of Mr. Friday's lunch. He looks hungry, and the men in that office are always sending things back that they ordered and never even touched. Presently they are both eating the lunch and having a pleasant visit. It is good broth because, Susie explains, it is made from nine chickens especially for B. K. The ham hocks are good, too. The chef himself eats them. Susie, however, cannot eat ham hocks. Happy doesn't like them. Happy likes milk.

Rodney is a little puzzled by Susie's confessions, but he thinks her an extraordinary girl, very direct, sincere and kind.

"Of course, I'm different on account of my condition," admits Susie. "Most girls aren't in my condition."

"Your condition?"

SUSIE—The minute I found out about Happy I said to myself: I'm going to be very good and very sincere, because then Happy will be very good and very sincere.

RODNEY—I'm afraid I don't quite follow.

SUSIE (*sighing*)—Nobody does.

RODNEY—Eh? Oh, yes. . . . As I was saying— What was I saying?

SUSIE (*looking into his eyes and feeling strangely stirred*)— Have some mustard.

RODNEY—Do you know, I must confess. I was hungry. As a matter of fact, I was close to wiring home for funds today. But I didn't. (*Looks very determined, righteous.*)

SUSIE—You mean you need money, and you can get it—and you won't wire for it?

RODNEY—I can't—and keep my pride. I told *them* I was on my own. You see, my family didn't want me to act. Not that they've any prejudices against the stage—or the films. Not at all. In fact, one of my aunts was a Gaiety girl. Quite all right. But they don't think I *can* act. That's what hurts.

SUSIE—Can you act?

RODNEY—No.

SUSIE—Not at all?

RODNEY—Not at all. I'm awful!

SUSIE—Oh, that's too bad.

RODNEY—But I only realized it in the stock company . . .
out in Pasadena. I was the worst member of the company. At
first I thought it was because they were always giving me
character parts—American gangsters—and that sort of thing.
And then one week I played a Cambridge undergraduate. And,
mind you, I've been a Cambridge undergraduate. And do you
know that I was utterly unconvincing?

Rodney would, he confesses, give up trying to act if it were
not for his pride. His ambition now is to go through with just
one part and then wire home that he has tried acting and chucked
it as not being good enough. That would save his pride. Susie
can understand that.

Susie and Rodney are still eating lunch when C. F., followed
by a still angry Larry Toms, barges back into the room. By
Gad, C. F. is all but thunderstruck to see what is happening in
his room. Drinking his milk, too. Susie tries to explain but is
shut up. Rodney tries to apologize. He has come with a book
from Research to prove his point about the costume, but C. F.
is mad enough to call the studio police. Brusquely he orders
them both out of the room.

Rodney, after expressing his eternal gratitude to Susie, is
gone, but Susie has not had time to pick up her dishes when
Benson and Law, down to their shirt sleeves, are back and all
excitement. They have been having a session with B. K.

"Sold! Lock, stock and baby!" shouts Benson, triumphantly.
"B. K. says it's the best mother-love story he's heard in years."

"What? What's that?" demands Larry.

LAW (*magnificently*)—Susie, put that tray down!

SUSIE—Please, Mr. Law, I've got to get back to the com-
misary.

LARRY—You sold him that story, huh?

BENSON—Lie down, actor!

LARRY—I'll see about this. (*He exits.*)

BENSON—Now listen, Susie—and listen carefully.

LAW—Let me tell her, will you? (*He faces her.*) Susie, nature meant you for a sucker. You were designed to get the short end of the stick. The girl who gets slapped.

BENSON (*quickly*)—But we're changing all that.

LAW—Susie, in real life, you'd have your baby in the County Hospital . . . get yourself a job, if lucky, with a philanthropic Iowa family of fourteen adults and twelve minors for twenty bucks a month. And when your grateful son grew up he'd squirt tobacco juice in your eye and join the Navy.

BENSON—There you go with your goddam realism. (*Turns to* SUSIE *with paper and pencil.*) Sign, please—

SUSIE—Here? (*She signs; and then turns brightly.*) What is it?

BENSON—Just a power of attorney authorizing us to deal for you in all matters with this studio.

C. F.—What power of attorney? What are you boys up to?

LAW—We said to ourselves upstairs—why shouldn't Susie have the good things of life?

BENSON—After all, we're godfathers.

SUSIE—I—I don't feel very good.

LAW—Get this, Susie. We've just sold a story about a baby.

BENSON—Sweetest story ever told!

LAW—A new-born baby.

BENSON—Brand new.

LAW—We're going to watch that baby—the first hair—the first tooth—the first smile—

BENSON—The same baby. No switching—first time in the history of pictures. That baby's going to grow before your eyes.

LAW—Open up like a flower. . . . Just like the Dionne quintuplets.

BENSON—Minute he's born we set the cameras on him. We stay with him—

LAW—That baby's going to gurgle and google and drool his way to stardom!

SUSIE—But—

LAW—And that baby, Susie, is Happy. Upstairs in B. K.'s office we put your unborn child into pictures!

SUSIE (*transported*)—Happy—in pictures! Oh—that's wonderful— (*Then, with a sudden gasp.*) Oh!

LAW (*quickly*)—Susie! What's the matter?

SUSIE—I don't know . . . I . . . I . . . I don't feel so good . . . I think . . . I . . . (*In these broken words,* SUSIE *tells all.* BENSON *helps* SUSIE *to lie on couch.* LAW *looks over* SUSIE's *shoulder; whistles; runs to phone.*)

LAW (*into phone*)—*Emergency! Get the ambulance over to Mr. Friday's office right away—get the doctor—get the nurse.* . . .

C. F. (*staring*)—What is it? In *my* office. Good Gad! Miss Crews!

MISS CREWS (*at door*)—The trumpets are here! (*Trumpets outside sound their triumphant clarion call.*)

LAW (*through the Wagnerian bass, to* BENSON, *awed*)— Happy's on his way!

The curtain falls.

ACT II

Briefly we are in our neighborhood theatres watching the screen and listening to the trailer announcement for the coming week. To the accompaniment of "Home on the Range" we read, in flashing, exciting, dancing, jiggly words, "If You Liked Happy in 'Wandering Hearts' You'll Adore Him in 'Golden Nugget.' "

"There are, of course, beautifully composed shots of horses, men and open spaces, and finally we come upon a series of close-ups of Happy, over which these titles dance:

"Happy!
HAPPY!
HAPPY!"

There is also an intimation that Happy is a "Crown Prince of Comedy," a "King of Tragedy," and an "Emperor of Emotion," and when the picture is finally explained as that of "The Desert Waif Who Made a Softie of a Bad Man," practically everything has been told, save that the story is by H. G. Wells, adapted by J. Carlyle Benson and Robert Law, directed by Serge Borodokov and produced by C. Elliott Friday.

As the screen lifts we are back in Mr. Friday's office, with Benson sitting on the couch beside Larry and his agent, Rosetti. Miss Crews is near by and C. F. at his desk.

Miss Crews is reading a list of figures representing the gross receipts of the last release of Happy and Larry Toms. Eighty-two thousand at the Music Hall; forty-eight thousand, five hundred and thirty-eight in Des Moines; twenty-eight thousand in Newark; forty-two thousand in San Francisco—

Larry is quick to recall these places as centers in which he always has gone big, but to Benson they only prove that Happy is worth the thirty-five hundred a week they are asking for him.

Such a salary is fantastic to C. F. And how about the people that came to see him, Larry Toms would like to know. Benson is prepared to satisfy him as to that. Didn't *Variety* say: " 'Wandering Hearts' socko in Minneapolis despite Larry Toms.' . . . And 'Mexico nuts about Happy but no like Larry Toms' "—

"This," concludes Benson, "is an accidental business in an accidental world. Happy is going to get it while it's hot."

C. F. offers three hundred a week for Happy. Benson laughs. The boys still have their power of attorney. If they are thrown out of the studio, as C. F. threatens, Happy goes with them—

"We're asking thirty-five hundred a week," says Benson. "We'll consider three thousand and settle for twenty-five hundred. But not a penny less. Incidentally, Fox'll pay twenty-five hundred for Happy. We promised to let them know by Saturday. No hurry, of course."

After Benson has left Rosetti has an idea. What was the date of the power of attorney that Susie signed with Benson and Law? It is just possible it is about to run out and the boys have forgotten all about it. The Rosetti theory is that you have to have vision in the picture business. He goes to do a bit of research. . . .

The nurse, followed by the doctor, has wheeled Happy into the studio in a stream-lined carriage. Happy is through for the day and looking for his mother. Mother has been attending high school.

A few moments later word has come from the legal department confirming Rosetti's opinion as to the power of attorney. It ran out a week ago! Happy is nobody's property but his mother's!

"Larry, there's been something developing in the back of my mind for some weeks," says Rosetti, catching the actor when he is bewailing the stupidity of a studio that gives up making moving pictures and devotes its time to shooting closeups of babies. "Why do you think I asked you to take Susie to the Trocadero?"

"She talked me deaf, dumb and blind about going to high school," replies Larry, belligerently. "Set me back fourteen bucks. Lucky she don't drink."

"I wanted you to get friendly with her because I visualized a way for you and me to get Happy—for life."

"Huh?"

"Larry, here's the tactical move. You marry Susie."

"Marry her?"

"That's what I said."

"I won't do it."

Rosetti does not press the matrimonial proposition, but he does call Larry's attention to the fact that B. K. is already dickering to borrow Clark Gable or Gary Cooper for Happy's next picture.

"If you marry her, you're Happy's legal guardian and we control the situation," continues Rosetti. "A father and son team off the screen as well as on! Is that practical or am I just an idealist? Look at Guy Lathrop! He argued with me when I told him to marry Betty Bird. But he finally had the sense to play along with me and we've been drawing top money ever since."

"I don't want to marry nobody," persists the cowboy.

"Larry, you're at the crossroads right now. One road leads to stardom and big pictures, with Happy and me. The other leads to Poverty Row and cheap Westerns. Will you put your hand in mine and let me guide you?"

Larry has not thought of an answer before he is called back to the set. As he is leaving Susie arrives. She is wearing a white middy blouse and a navy blue pleated skirt, because they had had gym at high school. She is pleased to hear that Happy is in the garden and that he is through for the day. She has not seen a great deal of Happy lately. Happy is working while mother goes to school.

Larry has decided to ask Miss Crews to telephone the set that he may be late. He wants to talk to Susie. She is busy looking over a batch of fan mail, but manages to find time to listen a little. First, Larry would like her to know that he is to have two tickets for the new De Mille picture at the Chinese theatre. Susie thinks that might be wonderful. But people are always doing wonderful things for her, muses Susie. She's a Cinderella, that's what Mr. Benson was saying. And he had added that all she needed was a Prince Charming. No, Benson had not suggested Larry. For that matter Susie isn't sure she'd know a Prince Charming if she met one. She does remember a very nice young man in a uniform who came into the office one day—but—

"Happy needs a father," announces Larry, with conviction.

"Do you think so?" questions Susie, a little surprised.

LARRY—Well, you want him to be able to look the whole world in the face, don't you?

SUSIE (*twinkling*)—He does!

LARRY—I mean when he grows up. He's gonna be ashamed

when he finds out he never had a father.

Susie—Of course he had a father.

Larry—I mean—a married father.

Susie—He was married—but I didn't know it. (Larry *winces*.)

Larry—Uh—listen, Susie—I'm mighty fond of you and Happy. (*He tries playing the bashful Western hero*.) Mighty fond.

Susie—Are you really, Larry?

Larry—Mighty fond.

Susie—Who would have thought six months ago that I'd be sitting in the same room with Larry Toms and he'd be saying to me he was—

Larry—Mighty fond.

Susie—Do you know something very odd? When I first came to California, it was raining very hard—oh, it rained for three weeks—it was very unusual—and I was looking for a job, and I couldn't find one—and I had fifteen cents—and I just had to get out of the rain—and I went into a theatre and there you were—on the screen—

Larry—Mighty fond—

Susie (*awed*)—That's just what you were saying to Mary Brian—and now you're saying it to me.

Larry—What was the picture?

Susie—"Thunder over Arizona." It was a beautiful picture. I don't remember what it was about, but I saw it four times. Until I got dry.

Larry—Susie, soon's this picture's over, how'd you like to come up to my ranch? You and Happy—

Susie (*rises*)—Ranch? Oh, that would be lovely! Maybe Mr. Benson and Mr. Law could come, too?

Larry—Maybe they could, but they won't.

Susie—But I couldn't go alone—without a chaperon.

Larry—Susie—you and Happy'll love that ranch. I got a mighty nice house, big and rambling. I got plenty of barns and a corral and plenty of livestock. But no baby.

Susie—I know Happy'll just love it.

Larry—Susie—I know you don't expect this, and I don't want you to get too excited—but, Susie, I been thinkin' about you and Happy—thinkin' a lot. Ever since the day you come into this office and fell on that there floor, I said to myself: Larry, there's your leadin' lady—for life.

Susie—Me?

Larry—Nobody else.

Susie—But I don't—you won't get mad?—but I'm not in love

with you.

LARRY—You shouldn't be thinking of yourself—I'm not thinking of myself—you should be thinking of Happy.

SUSIE—I guess you're right. I don't know what to say. (*Pause.*) I'll ask Mr. Benson and Mr. Law—

LARRY—Huh?

SUSIE—They've been so good to me.

LARRY—I'm not proposing to them!

SUSIE—I know, but—

LARRY—You don't mean nothing to them. Before you came along they had a Spanish snake charmer until they got tired of her. And before that they had a broken-down pug who wiggled his ears. They was groomin' him for my place. There ain't nothin' holy to them!

SUSIE—But they've done everything for me.

LARRY (*crosses to* SUSIE)—I'm offering you my ranch—my name—and a father Happy'll be proud of!

SUSIE—I know, but—

LARRY—Don't give me your answer now. Think it over. (*Pats her arm.*) Only don't think too long. I'll be waiting for your answer in the Legal Department.

Susie, who has asked Miss Crews to keep a lookout for the young man of the uniform, has inspected an extra man that Miss Crews thinks perhaps might be that person, but he isn't. This one isn't even English. It seems a vain search. Probably, sighs Susie, her young man had swallowed his pride and gone back to England.

And now Benson and Law come rushing in. They are in the throes of composition and they are looking for an opening scene for a new Larry Toms picture. They have got Larry started for a zoo carrying meat to a pet tiger, and about to be run down by a rich bitch from society, when Susie hesitantly interrupts to ask them if they think she should marry Larry. The boys are much too busy to be worried with Susie, but something of the shock registers. Law at least would like to know if, when Larry suggested matrimony, Susie had thought to spit in his face.

"He's taking me to the opening tonight," reports Susie. "He says he's mighty fond of Happy and me."

"Why shouldn't he be?" demands Law. "His contract depends on it. Even Wilkes-Barre doesn't want him, and they're still calling for Theda Bara—"

"Don't you think he'd be good for Happy? He's an outdoor

man."

"So's the fellow who collects my garbage," says Law.

Now they must get back to their scenario. They must think of a fiance for the heroine who shall suggest an anemic louse, thereby causing an audience reaction prompting many to yell: "Don't marry that heel!"

In the face of this detachment, and convinced that her former friends have quite forgotten her, Susie collects her fan mail and slips quietly into the garden where Happy is taking the sun.

Benson and Law return to Larry, the zoo, the tiger and Happy. Now they have Happy asleep in the paws of the tiger and Larry to the rescue before anything happens. Then Larry and his pal, who would be the comic, fumble awkwardly in an effort to adjust Happy's diapers, a sequence that ends when the tiger playfully grabs the diapers and runs away. The old diaper gag, according to Law, is always good.

Law fills in a little time telephoning the music department. In the name and voice of C. F. he suggests that someone write him a roundelay with a symphonic undertone—not a lullaby—a roundelay—"the sort of thing Beethoven dashes off," and have it ready in fifteen minutes. Agent Rosetti, flushed with something like success, rushes in to announce that he has just set Larry Toms to a long-term contract without a cut—a joint contract with Happy!

"The mother came to me just now and said you two were tired of her," explains Rosetti. "I happened to look up your power of attorney and it seems you didn't even care to get a new one when it expired."

There is a good deal of consternation at Rosetti's news. The added fact that he had got only three hundred a week for Happy, when the former guardians had turned down fifteen hundred from Fox, adds to their disgust, and the further announcement that Larry and Susie are going to the theatre to celebrate new family ties is a little more than the boys can stand.

"You'd better be careful how you talk to me," warns Rosetti, backing away from the menacing Law. "And you'd better be careful how you talk to Larry from now on. He'd fed up with your gags and insults. You got away with a lot of stuff around here because you had Happy. Well, Larry's got him now, and he's going to have plenty to say around here. I'm warning you. He'd like to see you boys off this lot. And he's in a position to do it— now. So be careful. If you want to keep your jobs."

Something pretty violent might have happened to Rosetti if

he had not at that moment dashed through the door and closed it quickly after him. What follows with Benson and Law, each charging the other with carelessness in forgetting about the power of attorney and refusing to listen to Susie, is at least a little violent. When it is over they have agreed on one thing: Something must be done to induce Larry to break the new contract—

"He's scared green of scandal," suggests Benson. "Suppose we show up at the opening tonight with a drunken dame! *Larry's deserted wife!*"

LAW—Has he got one?

BENSON—We'll get one of your tarts.

LAW—That's too damned obvious.

BENSON—Can you top it?

LAW—Let me think.

BENSON—How about a poor deserted mother? I'll bet he's got one.

LAW (*carried away*)—I know! *Happy's father.*

BENSON—Huh?

LAW—We're going to produce Happy's father on the air—tonight.

BENSON—Happy's father! That's swell! That's marvelous. . . . (*Pause.*) But where'll we get a father?

LAW (*into phone*)—*Central Casting, please.* . . . Hello. I want a handsome young extra, a gentleman, a little down at the heel, not too well fed, neat business suit—shiny but well pressed; quiet manner . . . (*Door opens and* RODNEY *enters.*)

BENSON—What do you want?

RODNEY—I received a message from Miss Crews but apparently she's stepped out. Is Mr. Friday here? I assume I've been called for a part.

LAW (*into phone, as his eyes refuse to leave* RODNEY)—Never mind—cancel it. (*Hangs up.*)

BENSON—Will you shut the door, please? (RODNEY *complies.*) So you're an actor, my boy? (*Paternally.*)

RODNEY—Of course, I haven't had much experience. As a matter of fact, I never appeared in a picture. I almost did. Since then I've been out of the profession, so to speak. Odd jobs—barbecue stand, and when that closed I offered to show tourists homes of the movie stars. Unfortunately I haven't a motor car and they won't walk. . . . I don't mind saying this call was an extremely pleasant surprise.

LAW—He's perfect!

RODNEY—Do you really think I'll do?

LAW (*inspired*)—Benson, take these lines. . . .

RODNEY—Oh, are there lines? Then the fee will be fifteen dollars, I assume?

LAW—Fifteen? One hundred for you.

RODNEY—I'm afraid I'm not worth that.

LAW—This is a trailer we're making tonight. We pay more for trailers.

RODNEY—Oh, I say!

BENSON (*at desk, with paper and pencil*)—We're going to shoot this at Grauman's Chinese in the lobby. There'll be a girl at the microphone. Her name is Susie. You come running up . . . you say . . .

LAW (*at downstage end of desk*)—"Susie, why did you leave me?" . . . Say it.

RODNEY—Susie, why did you leave me?

BENSON—With feeling.

RODNEY (*with feeling*)—Susie, why did you leave me?

LAW—I'm Happy's father.

RODNEY—I'm Happy's father.

BENSON—Louder.

RODNEY—*I'm Happy's father.*

LAW—I did not go down on the "Morro Castle." . . . Susie, I've searched for you in the four corners of the earth. . . . *Susie, why did you leave me?*

RODNEY (*who has been repeating the ends of the phrases in* LAW'S *speech*)—Susie, why did you leave me?

BENSON (*jubilant*)—Right!

The light fades as the curtain falls.

Again we are in a movie theatre, or in front of one. This time it is Grauman's Chinese theatre in Hollywood. The booming voice of a radio announcer is picturing the scene. "Folks, this is the première of Cecil B. De Mille's super-spectacle of Egyptian life— "King Saul"—at Grauman's Chinese. Your favorite stars, folks, in person—and the *crowds!* They're pushing and shoving and yelling for autographs—" . . .

Now the curtain rises. We are back in C. F.'s office. C. F. is busy with a cutter and the script of "Young England." Benson is sitting near the radio listening to the Grauman announcer—

". . . And now, folks, I'm told that none other than Larry Toms is with us tonight. And he's not altogether by his lone-

some for hanging on his manly arm is none other than Mrs. Susan
Seabrook, mother of America's Crown Prince—Happy!"

This is cheering news to Benson—

". . . And now I have the honor to present Mrs. Seabrook, the
mother of Happy. . . . Is it true, Mrs. Seabrook, that you and
Larry have been window shopping?"

"Well—" Susie's voice is very, very nervous. "I would like to
thank all of you for the thousands of letters and gifts that you've
sent my baby, Happy. I read all your letters and some of them
make me cry—they're so pathetic. I would like to send all of
you money only I haven't got that much and the studio won't let
me. I'd like to say a few words about the letters asking about
Happy's diet. You read a lot of advertisements of what he eats
but if Happy ate everything they said he ate I guess he'd be a
giant, and he's really got a very little stomach."

With further interruptions from the announcer Susie goes on to
explain why she is going to high school. She is going because she
wants to be able to keep up with Happy when he goes to college. Happy hasn't got a father—and—Susie is through. The
announcer cuts in quickly, introducing Larry Toms.

Larry stumbles through a few words. He has heard the rumors
the announcer has been mentioning and blushingly admits that
they may be right—

"I kinda missed the little fellow after the day's work was
done," admits Larry. "So I guess pretty soon I'll be Happy's
father off the screen as well as on—"

Suddenly there is a commotion in the crowd. A strange voice
takes over the microphone. It is Rodney's voice.

"Stop! I'm Happy's father!" shouts Rodney. "I did not go
down on the "Morro Castle." I've searched for you in the four
corners of the earth. Susie, why did you leave me?"

C. F. (*excitedly*)—Did you hear that?

BENSON (*softly*)—Yes. I wonder what that was . . . (*Cries
are heard of "Here, Officer"—inarticulate shouts—a siren.*)

RADIO ANNOUNCER—Folks, there was a slight interruption.
That voice you heard was a young man . . . he . . . well, he
threw his arms about Mrs. Seabrook and kissed her. There's some
confusion—a police officer is making his way through—they've
got the young man . . . no, they haven't got him . . . Folks,
this is the opening of Cecil B. De Mille's super-spectacle of
Egyptian life, "King Saul," at Grauman's Chinese . . . (BENSON
turns it off.)

C. F. (*stunned*)—Good Gad! (*Phone rings. He moves to it.*)

BENSON (*shakes his head*)—Strangest thing I ever heard.

C. F.—Oh, hello, B. K. . . . Yes, I've just heard it over the radio . . . (*Miserable.*) I'm sitting here trying to cut "Young England" . . . what? . . . But, B. K. . . . yes, of course, it's a serious situation . . . I agree with you . . . yes . . . yes . . . of course . . . I'll get hold of the mother immediately. (*He rises; hangs up, still dazed. To* BENSON.) B. K.'s coming down to the studio! (*Phone rings.*) Yes . . . Look here, I've nothing to say to the press. It's a canard. (*He hangs up.*) (*Phone rings again.*) I won't answer it. (MISS CREWS *enters.*)

MISS CREWS—Doctor Tompkins is calling you, Mr. Friday. He says it's important.

C. F.—What's he want? I'm not in. Call Mrs. Seabrook's house and have her ring me the minute she comes in.

MISS CREWS—Yes, Mr. Friday.

C. F.—Benson, do you think that young man was genuine?

BENSON—Search me.

C. F.—Well, we'll soon find out. B. K.'s set the police after him.

BENSON (*a little disturbed*)—Why do that? Best thing the studio can do is ignore it.

C. F.—We can't ignore it. This has brought up the whole paternity issue.

BENSON—What of it?

C. F.—Suppose Happy has a skeleton in his closet?

BENSON (*lies on couch*)—I don't even know if he's got a closet.

C. F.—Save your gags for your pictures. They need them. I've never heard B. K. so excited. What do you think the reaction will be in the sticks—in the provinces? An illegitimate baby!

BENSON—This is 1935.

C. F.—To me, yes. But how many intellectuals have we in America?

BENSON—One.

C. F.—You don't seem to realize—

BENSON—Why, this is going to send Happy's stock up one hundred per cent. From now on he's not only cute, he's romantic.

C. F.—He's illegitimate! I know America!

The excitement grows. In the midst of it the music boys are in and determined to play the roundelay C. F. has no recollection having ordered. C. F. has no sooner rid the office of the music boys than Rosetti and Larry Toms appear, wearing top hats, tails

and, so far as Mr. Toms is concerned, a deep-seated disgust. The
scandal of the radio drama has floored him. He wants it known
positively that he is not "going through with no contract to play
with no un-baptized baby!" Larry and Rosetti are dashing out,
headed for Larry's dressing room and a sedative, when they pass
Law coming in. Law has been to the Grauman opening, he reports, and was witness to all the excitement, including the rout
of the chivalrous Larry, whose exit was startling, though un-
gallant.

"Law, do you think the fellow was a crank?" C. F. wants to
know. "Or do you think he was really—"

"Hard to say," answers Law, weighing the matter judicially.
"He had a sinister underlip."

Miss Crews has been unable to locate Susie. Over the dictograph B. K. wants to know if any dope has been obtained on
the mysterious young man, and is pretty mad when C. F. admits
being baffled. B. K. summons C. F. over the dictograph.

Rodney, it now appears, has been in the custody of Law. At
the moment he is locked in an office across the hall. Law thought
he had to put him some place where he couldn't blab and where
the police department, stirred to excessive action by B. K., would
be least likely to look for him. But what is to be done with him
now, Law admits, he has not thought out.

"Get that guy out of the studio," pleads Benson. "Put him on
a plane to Mexico! Strangle him! I don't care what you do!"

"No—no. Murder leads to theft and theft leads to deceit.
Haven't you read De Quincey?" blandly asks Law, making for
the door. Two minutes later he comes rushing back. Rodney's
loose! A cleaning woman had let him out!

And now Susie, "magnificently decked out for the opening,"
has come in search of Benson and Law. Susie has been phoning
everywhere trying to get them. She is all upset because of what
has happened; she wishes she had never gone to the opening at
all; she wouldn't have gone if Larry Toms hadn't insisted.

Susie is terribly worried about Happy. Happy wouldn't eat his
formula and he wouldn't say good-by to her. And when she got
home and went to the Hospital they wouldn't let her see him—

"Hospital?" shouts Law.

"Hospital?" echoes Benson.

"They won't let me in . . . not for two weeks!"

BENSON—Happy's in the hospital?
SUSIE (*puzzled*)—Happy's got the measles.
LAW—What?

Susie—And they won't let me come near him.

Benson—Measles!

Law—He certainly picked the right time for it!

Susie—That's why he wouldn't eat his formula.

C. F.'s Voice (*off-stage; grimly*)—Well, we'll see— (*As he opens the door.*) I brought you some visitors, boys. Come in. (Rodney *enters with Studio Officer.*) (*To* Rodney.) Are these the men?

Rodney—They most certainly are.

Susie—You know you're not Happy's father.

Rodney—Of course not, but—

Susie—You couldn't be!

Rodney—Of course not! My dear, I'm very sorry. Look here, we always seem to meet under extraordinary circumstances . . . I never dreamt . . . I'd no idea . . . It was all so spectacular . . . And to do this to you— You were so kind to me . . . They said it was a trailer . . . I didn't realize until I was in the midst of it . . . And then I found myself in a car . . . with him . . . (*Indicates* Law.) I asked him to bring me to you at once. Instead, he locked me in a dusty office.

C. F.—So you boys put him up to it!

Law—Before you say anything you'll be sorry for, C. F. . . . (*Turns to* Officer.) Smitty, who called you tonight to tell you this unfortunate young man was loose in the studio?

Officer—*You* did, Mr. Law.

Law (*grandly*)—That's all.

Benson—Take him away.

Law—It's an obvious psychiatric case, C. F.

Benson (*to* C. F.)—I wouldn't be surprised if he's the boy that's been springing out of bushes.

Law—Certainly. Look at the way he kissed Susie!

Rodney (*appalled*)—But you coached me for hours. Both of you. Wait—here are my lines. (*He fumbles in his pocket.*) I know I have them—unless I've lost them.

Law—So you're an author, too! And I thought it was extemporaneous.

Rodney—Here—here they are! My dear, will you please read these lines? (*He hands the paper to* Susie.) They're the very words I spoke over the radio.

Susie (*reads and backs away from* Rodney)—You never said *these* lines. You *must* be a crank. Maybe you do spring out of bushes.

Rodney (*stares*)—Oh, I beg your pardon. My lines are on

the other side.

LAW (*grabs for paper*)—I'll take that! Susie—

C. F. (*taking paper out of* SUSIE's *hand brushes* LAW *aside*)—Just a minute. (*Reads.*) "She's a high-handed rich bitch."—"Tiger Tamer"!—There it is in the corner. "Tiger Tamer" by J. Carlyle Benson and Robert Law!

LAW (*hurt to the quick*)—It's a forgery. Benson, we've been framed.

C. F. (*grimly*)—This is the last prank you'll ever play.

MISS CREWS (*enters*)—The new trumpets are here. (*For once* C. F. *is not interested. The trumpets blare out.*)

C. F. (*into dictograph*)—B. K.? I just found out—Benson and Law put that young man on the radio.

B. K.'s VOICE—Are you sure of that?

C. F.—I have the proof. The young man is in my office.

B. K.'s VOICE—All right, fire them. I don't want them on this lot. If they think they can get away with that—

C. F.—Fire them? Of course I'll fire them. (LARRY's *voice is heard as he enters.*)

LARRY—Don't tell me nothing—let go of me. (DOCTOR *and* ROSETTI *enter, following* LARRY *and struggling with him.*)

C. F.—Quiet there—

LARRY—Let go of me!

C. F.—Larry, I have neither the time nor the patience to pander to actors!

LARRY (*bellowing with the hurt roar of a wounded bull*)—No? Babies, huh . . . (*Turns on* SUSIE.) You—you—

SUSIE (*frightened; runs to* BENSON)—What do you want?

LARRY—What do I want? That goddam baby of yours has given me the measles!

The curtain falls.

ACT III

Several weeks later, in a hospital, J. Carlyle Benson, formerly of the writing team of Benson and Law, has called to see Susie. She meets him in the corridor outside Happy's room and is a little shocked at his appearance. Benson looks as though he had not been getting any too much sleep and admits there is good reason for that conclusion.

Susie is still a little resentful because the boys played that joke on her, but feeling like a sister toward them, she is also forgiving and hopes they will give up drinking.

Now Robert Law has arrived to say hello and good-by to Susie. He is on his way back to good old Vermont, where a man can "touch life, and feel life, and write it." Law has chartered a plane to take him direct to Vermont, cutting out New York. And where did he get the money? Well, he grudgingly admits, there are twelve Rotarians flying with him.

"You won't drink too much in Vermont, will you, Mr. Law?" pleads Susie.

"Only the heady wine air that has no dregs," Law promises.

"Because you're crazy enough without drinking."

"I drank for escape . . . escape from myself . . . but now I'm free! I've found peace!" declares Law.

When Susie has gone to see if Happy is awake, Benson and Law have a few moments for confidences. Benson would, if he could, dissuade Law from his Vermont flight. And Law would feel better about going if Benson had a job in Hollywood. Law suggests as much to Rosetti, come to call upon Larry Toms. Larry has the room next to Happy's. Let Rosetti get Benson a job. Rosetti only smiles. He is not handling blacklisted writers for one thing, and for another he is completely immersed at the moment in a possible deal involving millions. Gaumont British is figuring on buying B. K.'s Royal studios. B. K. has already turned down an offer of three million.

"They won't touch you with a ten-foot pole," asserts Rosetti, getting back to the question of jobs. "You, Law or Happy."

"Or Happy?" Benson can't understand that.

"I gave B. K. a swell angle. Listen in on KNX this afternoon. The world is full of babies. You can get them two for a nickel," is Rosetti's significant reply.

A nurse brings Larry Toms through the door of his room in a wheel chair. The cowboy is on his way to his sun bath. He hasn't forgotten about the box of dead spiders Law had sent to him. He's just waiting until he gets through convalescing—

Now Law is ready to leave. He has seen Happy and kissed Susie fondly upon the forehead. The boys are alone and the silence is a little embarrassing.

"Well, you bastard—get out of here," Benson manages to say finally, and with some force.

"I'm going, stinker," replies Law, extending his hand for a farewell shaking.

BENSON (*without turning*)—Say— (LAW *stops.*) I don't sup-pose you'll be interested—Rosetti finally admitted Paramount wants us. Two thousand bucks a week to save Dietrich. We can close the deal in three or four days.

LAW (*turns slowly*)—My plane leaves in twenty-five minutes. And you're a liar!

BENSON—I'm not trying to hold you back. But I figured this time you might *save* your money and—

LAW—I can live on twelve dollars a week in Vermont—in luxury!

BENSON—It would kind of help *me* out— If I could lay my hands on some ready dough Pearl might listen to reason.

LAW (*casually*)—Well, we loaned out a lot of money in our time. Collect it. And send me my share.

BENSON—I thought of that. The trouble is I don't remember just who it was—and how much. The only one I remember is Jascha Simkovitch.

LAW—Who?

BENSON—Jascha Simkovitch. The fellow that came over with Eisenstein. Don't you remember? You made a wonderful crack about him. He said, "There's a price on my head in Russia." And you said, "Yeah—two roubles."

LAW—Sure, I remember him. Why, we gave that bedbug three thousand bucks! Get hold of him and collect it.

BENSON—He's in Paris. What's-his-name came over and said Jascha was living at the Ritz Bar.

LAW—Then you can't collect it. Well, I'm off. (*He moves to exit once more.*)

BENSON (*as if struck with sudden thought*)—Wait a minute! I've got a great gag for you! Let's call Jascha up in Paris—on Larry's phone! (*Chuckles, throws arms around* LAW. *Both laugh.*) Can you imagine Larry's face when he gets the bill? A farewell rib!

LAW (*hesitates*)—Have I got time?

BENSON (*reassuringly; looks at his watch*)—You've got plenty of time.

LAW—I'll work fast. Stand guard, Benson. (*He enters* LARRY'S *room.* BENSON *follows and partly closes door.*)

LAW'S VOICE—I'm talking for Mr. Toms. I want to put a call through to Paris, France. . . . I want Jascha Simkovitch . . . Hotel Ritz, Paris. . . . Listen, don't worry about the charges . . . That's right—Jascha, as in Heifetz . . . S-i-m-k-o-v-i-t-c-h. (BENSON *closes door on* LAW. NURSE *enters with registered letter, knocks on* SUSIE'S *door.* BENSON *looks at his watch.* SUSIE *appears.*)

Nurse—Registered letter for you, Mrs. Seabrook.

Susie—For me?

Nurse—You'll have to sign for it. There's a return receipt on it. (Susie *signs*.)

Susie—Now what do I do?

Nurse—Now you give me the receipt back and I'll give it to the postman. He's waiting for it. Here's your letter.

Susie (*cheerily*)—Why—it's from Mr. Friday. (Law *emerges, as she opens letter*.)

Law—The service had better be good or there'll be no farewell rib. I haven't got much time.

Susie—Oh, didn't you go yet, Mr. Law?

Law—I'm on my way!

Susie (*reading letter*)—What does Mr. Friday mean when he says they're taking advantage of Clause 5A?

Law—What? Let me see that. (*He reads the letter.* Benson *looks over his shoulder*.) Well, this is the goddamdest . . .

Susie—You mustn't swear so much. I don't mind—I'm used to it—but Happy might hear you. What does it mean?

Law (*reading*)—Clause 5A—when an artist through illness— for a period of more than fourteen days—

Benson—They're just using that for an excuse. It's the paternity issue!

Susie—What paternity issue?

Benson—They're crazy! That kid's going to be as good as he ever was—better.

Susie—What does it mean?

Law—It means, Susie—Happy is out.

Susie—Out?

Benson—Yeah. Finished—done. At the age of eight months— In his prime!

Susie—Out of pictures?

Benson (*turning on* Law)—And there's the man who did it. It was your brilliant idea!

Susie—Oh, no. After all, it was just like a dream. I had to wake up sometime.

Law (*as phone rings*)—I guess that's Paris.

Susie—What's Paris? (*Phone still rings*.)

Benson—Go ahead and have your farewell rib, and get out, author! (*Phone still rings.* Law *enters room*.)

Susie—What's Paris?

Benson—A city in France.

Law (*in room*)—Hello—right here.—Yes—yes—I'm ready.

Hello! . . . Hello—Jascha? Jascha Simkovitch? This is Bobby
Law. Is it raining in Paris? . . . well, it's not raining here!

BENSON—Wonderful age we're living in!

LAW (*in room*)—Listen, Jascha, are you sober? . . . How
come? . . . Oh, you just got there! . . . You're going to London? . . . Today? . . . Hold the wire. (LAW *enters*.) I've got
an idea! *Let's buy the studio!*

BENSON—What?

LAW—You heard Rosetti. Gaumont British is offering three
million. Let's get Jascha to send a cable—sign it Gaumont British
—offering four!

BENSON—Why be petty? Offer five!

LAW (*judicially*)—Right! (*Exits into room.*)

SUSIE—You boys are very peculiar.

LAW (*in room*)—Jascha—got a pencil and paper? Fine. Listen,
Jascha, we want you to send a cable from London as follows:
Quote . . . (LARRY *enters in his wheel chair.* BENSON *closes the
door hurriedly.*)

LARRY—Hey, that's my room!

BENSON (*firmly shutting the door*)—A private conversation
should be private.

LARRY—What's the idea of using my phone?

BENSON—Do you object?

LARRY—Certainly I object. I ain't gonna pay for your calls.

BENSON—All right, if that's the way you feel about it—here's
your nickel!

The lights fade as the curtain falls.

There is an interlude during which you hear, over the radio,
an announcement of the Royal Studios' Baby Star Contest to
find a successor to Happy, "who retired from the screen after his
illness."

"Ladies and Gentlemen, the lucky baby is Baby Sylvester Bur-
nett, infant son of Mr. and Mrs. Oliver Burnett of Glendale,
California," cheerfully intones the announcer. "Congratulations,
Mr. and Mrs. Burnett. Contracts for your baby are waiting in
Mr. C. Elliott Friday's office at the Royal Studios. Incidentally,
Mr. Friday asks that you bring your baby's birth certificate and
your marriage license. This is KNX, the Voice of Hollywood."
(Chimes are heard.)

The curtain lifts to reveal Mr. Friday's office the following day.
At the moment Mr. Friday is dictating to Miss Crews. He is

writing to Signor Pirandello, thinking perhaps that worthy Italian author has something in his trunk suitable for a baby star's use on the screen. He has started a second letter to Stark Young when there is an excited call over the dictograph from B. K. Gaumont British have cabled a new offer! He wants to see C. F. at once.

When C. F. returns from the conference he, too, is all excitement. He would have Miss Crews send roses to Happy. And orchids to Happy's mother. He would have Miss Crews get hold of Benson and Law as soon as possible. He would send a radio to Happy in the hospital and he would like to talk with Susie.

He has no time to waste on his music department or on Rosetti and Larry, who have a lot to take up with him. Finally he confides the big news. Gaumont British has offered five million dollars for the Royal Studios company intact, including all the stars except Larry. C. F. has got to sign Happy, who is the sensation of London, immediately.

It happens that Susie is in the outer office. They call her in. Benson and Law are already closeted with B. K. C. F. has started for that conference when he all but stumbles over Rodney Bevans at the door. Rodney has come with a large box of flowers and a check covering the cost of the lunch he had in C. F.'s office, including interest at 6 per cent. C. F. would throw Rodney out, but Rodney has something he wants to say to Susie. He can say it, C. F. agrees, but he had better be gone before C. F. gets back.

"I know you don't want to see me," Rodney begins, when he and Susie are alone. He is holding the flowers out to her. "I wrote, you know. I explained everything."

"Happy's not allowed to have flowers," says Susie, without looking up.

RODNEY—Oh, but they're for Happy's mother—from Happy's father.

SUSIE (*turning; aghast*)—Are you joking about what you did?

RODNEY—I'm not joking. Lord, no. I mean it. Look here—will you marry me? (SUSIE *stares at him.*) I've thought it all out. I owe it to you. Shall we consider it settled?

SUSIE—Did Mr. Law and Mr. Benson put you up to this, too?

RODNEY—Good Lord, no. I haven't seen them and, what's more, I don't intend to.

SUSIE—Then why do you want to marry me?

RODNEY—I owe it to you.

SUSIE (*angrily*)—That's no reason.

RODNEY—My visa's expired—I've two days' grace. I must get a train this afternoon. Are you coming with me?

SUSIE—I don't think you'd make a very sensible father for Happy. I don't think so at all.

RODNEY—I'm not at all sensible. I'm frightfully stupid—impulsive—emotional—but I'm not really at my best these days. Most people aren't when they're infatuated.

SUSIE—You couldn't be infatuated with me!

RODNEY—But I am. Look here, it's no good debating. My mind's made up. I don't frequently make it up, but when I do, I stick to the end.

SUSIE—But you don't know about my past.

RODNEY—I've been through all that, in my mind. It doesn't matter.

SUSIE—But it does. I'm ashamed to tell you.

RODNEY—Please don't, then.

SUSIE—Happy's father was a bigamist.

RODNEY—Eh?

SUSIE—He married twice.

RODNEY—Is that it?

SUSIE—What did you think?

RODNEY—It doesn't really matter.

SUSIE—I didn't know he was married before.

RODNEY—But, good Lord, nobody can blame *you*.

SUSIE—His wife did.

RODNEY—Naturally.

SUSIE—How was I to know? And it wasn't his fault, either. He got a Mexican divorce and he didn't know it wasn't good.

RODNEY—Oh!

SUSIE (*drawing herself up à la Fairfax*)—So I said to him, "Your duty is to your first wife." And I ran away. I didn't know I was going to have Happy, then.

RODNEY—Have you—heard from him?

SUSIE—Oh, no. Of course, he should have told me in the first place. But he was infatuated, too, and I didn't know any better.

RODNEY—Well, have you divorced him?

SUSIE—No.

RODNEY—You'll have to clear that matter up, I think—immediately.

SUSIE—I can't clear it up. He's dead.

RODNEY—Oh!

SUSIE—She shot him.

RODNEY—His wife?

SUSIE—Yes.

RODNEY—Good Lord!

SUSIE—I hear from her sometimes. She's awfully sorry.

RODNEY (*brightly*)—Well, then, you're free to marry, aren't you?

SUSIE—Oh, I'm free, but the point is—do I want to? After all, I don't know you very well, and every time we meet something terrible happens. I didn't know Jack very well, either, and look what happened to him. I've got to be careful.

RODNEY—But I'm not a bigamist.

SUSIE—Maybe not. You may be something else.

RODNEY—But the British Consul'll vouch for me. He knows my family. I haven't had much of a life, but it's an open book.

SUSIE—Oh, I believe you. But I can't listen to my heart. I've got to listen to my head.

RODNEY—Of course, I haven't much to offer you. I've just come into a little money, and on my thirtieth birthday I come into a great deal more. We can have a flat in London and one of my aunts is going to leave me a place in the country.

SUSIE—That's in Europe, isn't it?

RODNEY—Yes, of course.

SUSIE—Oh, I couldn't go to Europe.

RODNEY—But why not?

SUSIE—The boys want to put Happy back in pictures.

RODNEY—I wouldn't hear of it. That's no life for a baby. Thoroughly abnormal. And, furthermore, I don't like the California climate. Now in England we have the four seasons.

SUSIE—You have?

RODNEY (*ardently*)—Summer, winter, spring and fall.

SUSIE (*finally*)—I want to ask you something.

RODNEY—Certainly.

SUSIE—When I come into a room—does something happen to you?

RODNEY—Eh? Of course—very much so.

SUSIE (*turns away*)—Well, I'll think it over.

RODNEY (*takes* SUSIE's *arm*)—Look here, I couldn't possibly take no for an answer.

SUSIE—Of course, when you come into a room, something happens to me, too.

RODNEY—Does it really?

Susie is in Rodney's arms when Law and Benson come from the conference with B. K. The sight does not please them. Susie's further announcement that she is going to marry Rodney and go to England to live pleases them even less. They can't stand for that. They have just signed another contract to handle Happy's pictures for Royal. Law has sacrificed everything that Vermont means to him to be with Happy. And who is this Rodney person, anyway? The boys know who he is. He's English Jack! Confidence man! Ship's gambler! Petty racketeer! Bigamist!

Susie recoils before such charges, but Rodney is only lightly disturbed. The English Consul will vouch for him, says Rodney. And these blusterers are not going to intimidate Susie into signing any contract.

Benson is busily calling the Department of Justice and asking for operatives when the door opens and a man Larry Toms is bringing in turns out to be Major Thompson, the representative of Gaumont British in America.

The Major, puzzled no end when Larry had reported to him that his home office had cabled Royal Studios, was even more puzzled when he cabled his home office and discovered that no cable of any kind had been sent. The whole thing, says Larry, was phony.

Before the Major can explain further Rodney, who has been trying excitedly to attract his attention, finally makes contact and there is immediate mutual recognition.

"Well! Aren't you— Why, how do you do! I thought I recognized you!" exclaims the Major. "Met you with your brother. By the way, I saw him a few weeks ago just before I sailed. Particularly asked me to look you up."

"Is my name English Jack? Am I a ship's gambler? Have I served sentences for bigamy?" demands Rodney.

MAJOR—Good Gad, no!

RODNEY—Will you vouch for me?

MAJOR (*a bore of bores*)—Vouch for Puffy Bevan? Delighted! His brother—splendid chap— I met him first in India—he's a captain in the Coldstream Guards. His father is Lord Severingham. His sister is Lady Beasley—lectures, I believe. Now, let me see—

LAW (*interrupting*)—Did you say—Lord Severingham?

MAJOR—Yes.

BENSON—I beg your pardon, sir—*his* father? (*He indicates* RODNEY.)

MAJOR—Yes. (BENSON *shakes his head in wonder.*)

SUSIE—Is your father a lord?

RODNEY—It doesn't matter, does it?

SUSIE—If you don't care, I don't care.

MAJOR—If I can be of any further service—

RODNEY—No. I think we'll sail along beautifully now. Thanks.

MAJOR—Good afternoon. (*Shakes hands with* RODNEY.)

C. F.—Who sent that cable? That's all I want to know! Who sent that cable! (MAJOR *and* LARRY *exit.*) Who perpetrated this hoax? Who's responsible for this outrage? By Gad, I'll find out. (*Exits.*)

RODNEY (*turns to* SUSIE)—Shall we go?

SUSIE—Good-by, boys. Take care of yourselves.

LAW (*bows; bitterly*)—Thank you, milady.

SUSIE—Don't drink too much.

LAW—Thank you, milady.

SUSIE—You were awful good to me. Yes, they were, Rodney. They were awful good to me sometimes.

RODNEY—In that case, I don't mind shaking hands with you. (*Starts toward* LAW.)

LAW (*quickly*)—Don't shake hands. Just go. Dissolve—*slow fade-out!*

BENSON (*pantomiming*)—Shimmer away!

RODNEY—Eh? (*Shrugs.*) Well—come, Susie.

SUSIE (*waving a delicate little hand*)—Good-by, boys. (*Pause. They exit in silence.*)

LAW (*tense*)—I wonder what C. F.'s up to.

BENSON (*struck all of a heap*)—The hell with that. Look at it—it checks! Cinderella—Prince Charming— Boy meets girl. . . . Boy loses girl. . . . Boy gets girl! Where's your damned realism now? (C. F. *enters. He looks grimly at the boys.*)

C. F. (*finally*)—Well—it's a good thing you boys are not mixed up in this! (*He goes to desk.*)

BENSON (*slowly*)—What?

LAW (*slowly*)—What happened, C. F.?

C. F.—I don't understand it at all. The cable was sent from London all right. But B. K. should have known it was a fake. It was sent collect. (*He picks up phone.*)

LAW—Jascha always sends collect.

C. F.—Huh? (*Into phone.*) Miss Crews, get hold of the Burnett baby immediately. . . . Who? . . . The *what* is here? (*Puzzled. The answer comes in the clarion call of the trumpets, blaring their gay, lilting notes through the windows. Ta-ra-ta-ta-ta-ta-tata-tata-tata! So much pleasanter than a factory whistle, don't you think?*)

THE CURTAIN FALLS

DEAD END

A Drama in Three Acts

By Sidney Kingsley

BEING a meticulous and thoughtful craftsman, Sidney Kingsley worked two years after he had won a Pulitzer award for his first drama, "Men in White," before he was satisfied to offer a second. This was revealed as a study of human nature exposed to a variety of environmental influences and hereditary traditions which he called "Dead End." The setting, a notably fine one designed by Norman Bel Geddes, who was also producer of the play, is that of a dead end New York street running to the East River, and the theme circles the dead end of hope and opportunity that oppresses the poverty-stricken and underprivileged from whose ranks public enemies are recruited.

"Dead End" was received with a vigorously expressed enthusiasm by its first audiences. It was variously though generously debated by its critics. The chief point made against it was that it was a drama of colorful though frequently offensively realistic incidents dwarfed by the towering solidity of its setting. Yet the late Percy Hammond, writing observantly of the impression the drama had made upon him, took directly the contrary view. "To this observer it [the setting] is the play's most artificial component, half real and half palpably counterfeit," wrote Mr. Hammond. "I can believe in the characters and in everything they say and do, but Mr. Geddes' buildings, although imposing and as complete as the art of the theatre will allow, leave a doubter still doubting."

There were those, too, who resented the concession to the theatre's demands for romance found in Mr. Kingsley's contrasting sub-plot, that of an impecunious cripple and a girl who has risen to a life of luxury through the commercializing of her charms. But for the dramatist's integrity of purpose and sincerity of effort there was nothing but praise.

The Kingsley drama was fittingly produced in the theatre over which the late David Belasco presided for many years and on the stage of which he, too, had reveled in a lavish realism. It began its run in late October, and was promising to continue through the Summer when this record was compiled.

With the opening of "Dead End" we, as audience, are sitting on a raft in the East River facing the piling of a wharf. Looking on beyond the wharf we see the rear garden of the expensive East River Terrace on the left, and next to it the façade of a crumbling three-story tenement of red brick. Standing in the center of the street, where it has been temporarily abandoned, and shutting off a view of the street intersection beyond, is a caterpillar steam shovel. At the right is a huge red sand hopper superimposed on stilts of heavy timber and rising several stories high.

The touch of magnificence suggested by the gates of the apartment house, its posts surmounted by handsome ship lanterns, one red, the other green, is in marked contrast to the living quarters of the tenement dwellers.

The river at this point is brown and covered with a swirling scum. But this does not in the least deter the gang of urchins that we find swimming there. It is their habit to dive in above the sand hopper and swim with the current to the wharf, where they climb out of the water and onto the wharf by means of a ladder. However, they may seem to you to be coming up out of the orchestra pit. The boys are a tough crew, most of them wearing bathing trunks in various states of repair, but one or two, seen dimly in the shadows of the timbers supporting the sand hopper, are apparently nude. "Their speech is a rhythmic, shocking jargon that would put a truck driver to blush."

"There are a few onlookers. A fat, greasy woman leans out of a tenement window. She is peeling an orange and throwing the peels into the street. A sensitive-faced young man, in a patched frayed shirt, open at the neck, is sitting on one of the piles. In his lap is a drawing board. Occasionally he will work feverishly, using pencil and triangular ruler, then he will let the pencil droop and stare out over the river with deepset eyes, dream-laden, moody. A tubercular-looking boy about sixteen is up near the hopper, pitching pennies to the sidewalk."

The first of the boys to appear answers to the name of Tommy, "lean, lithe, long-limbed, snub-nosed." As Tommy climbs up out of the water his cheeks are puffed. At the top he turns and expels the water in his mouth into the face of another following and is raucous in boast of his marksmanship. From down the street two other boys join the gang, Angel, an Italian bootblack with a box swung over his shoulder, a small boy with a great shock of blue-black hair, and Dippy, "a gawky Polack, head shaven, cretinous and adenoidal." Out of the water crawls one known as Spit, whose ability to shoot saliva through a partition in his teeth and hit almost any mark aimed at keeps his companions dodging or fighting him a good part of the time. His target at the moment is the disrobing Dippy's navel and his aim is accurate. "Right inna belly-button!" gleefully shouts Spit.

Tommy would be leader of this gang, if a leader were acknowledged, and it is Tommy who forces Spit to lay off Dippy. The Doorman of the Terrace, coming through the gate and whistling for a taxi for two of his tenants, explains to the latter the necessity for using the garden entrance while the street in front of the Terrace is torn up. . . .

Two new men have come into the picture. "One tall, young, rather good-looking in a vicious way, the other older, shorter, squat, a sledge-hammer build. The first has thin nervous lips, narrow agate eyes, bloodshot. A peculiarly glossy face, as if the skin had been stretched taut over the cheekbones which are several sizes too large for the lean jaw underneath. Here is a man given to sudden volcanic violences that come and are gone in a breath. . . . He wears a gray, turned-down fedora, an expensive suit, sharpy style, the coat a bit too tight at the waist, pleated trousers, and gray suede shoes. His squat companion is dressed almost identically, but was not designed to wear such clothes."

Tommy and the others have been trying to beg cigarettes from Gimpty, the lad with the drawing board, and have given up in disgust. They will find their own butts. Spit's got a whole stack of butts he's picked up and been savin'. They'll smoke those.

Now the boys' attention is turned to Philip. Philip is "a well-dressed, delicate-featured little boy" just come out of the Terrace apartment with his French governess. She leaves him there with instructions in French to wait for her while she returns for a moment to the apartment. Philip's "Oui, oui, mademoiselle," delight's Tommy's gang.

"Wee-wee! He's godda go wee-wee!" yells Tommy, and while the boys are shouting with laughter he decides to put Philip further in his place. "Yuh wanna see sumpen? A swan-dive?" he challenges, handing his cigarette butt to Dippy to hold. "Watch!"

Tommy has dashed off under the hopper and a moment later, with a shrill "Whe-e-e" and a loud splash, is in the water. The gang clucks its approval.

"What's wonderful about that?" sneers Philip.

"Aw, yuh fat tub a buttuh, it's more'n yew kin do."

PHILIP—That shows how much you know.
T. B.—I bet a dollar he can't even swim.
PHILIP—I can too.

T. B.—Ah, bologny!

PHILIP—Bologny yourself! We've a pool in there and I swim every day . . . with instruction.

SPIT—Aw, bushwa! (TOMMY *appears on the ladder.* DIPPY *hands him his cigarette.*)

DIPPY—He sez dey godda pool in 'ere.

TOMMY—How wuzat swan-dive?

DIPPY—He sez it wuz lousy.

TOMMY (*climbing over the parapet and crossing to* PHILIP, *belligerently*)—Oh, yeah? What wuza mattuh wid it? Kin yew do bettuh?

PHILIP—A trillion times.

TOMMY—Awright. Lessee yuh.

PHILIP—Where?

TOMMY—Heah!

PHILIP—Here?

TOMMY—Yeah, heah. Yew hoid me. Yew ain' deef. (*Turns to the others.*) His eahs ovuhlap, dat's it! (*All the boys roar with laughter.*)

PHILIP—I wouldn't swim here.

T. B.—He's yelluh, dat's what! Dat's what! He's godda yelluh streak up 'is back a mile wide.

PHILIP—It's dirty here.

DIPPY (*shocked*)—Doity!

T. B. (*very indignant*)—Doity! He sez doity. He sez it's doity! I'll sock 'im!

ANGEL—Lil fairy!

SPIT—Wassamattuh? Yuh scaired yuh git a lil doit on yuh?

PHILIP—Besides, I haven't got my suit.

TOMMY—Well, go in bareass.

T. B.—Yeah, wassamattuh wid bareass?

PHILIP—And besides, I'm not allowed to.

DIPPY (*sing-song*)—Sissy, sissy, sucks his mamma's titty!

PHILIP—Sticks and stones may break my bones, but names will never hurt me. (*The boys crowd him back against the gate.*)

TOMMY—Ah, Ah'll spit in yuh eye an' drown yuh. Hey, what's 'at junk yuh got in yuh mout' . . . like a hawse?

PHILIP—It's a brace, to make my teeth straight.

TOMMY—Wha-a-at? I could do dat wit one wallop!

The gang roars with laughter, but Philip doesn't give way. Let them try anything like that and he'll get them arrested. Philip's uncle is a Judge. That doesn't frighten the gang any. T. B. has a friend who is a Judge, too. Judge Poikins. He sent T. B. to reform school oncet.

The Doorman has come to Philip's rescue and scattered the gang, to a chorus of boos and a lot of razzing.

Now the boys, having regathered, are hungry and wondering where they can get something to eat. They might snitch sumpin, but all the store keepers in the neighborhood are on to them. If they had a little money they could send one of the guys in to buy sumpin and while he was buyin' the udduh guys could be swipin' stuff. But they ain't got any money. They suspect Angel, the shine merchant, may be holding out on them and make a dash for his pants to search the pockets. They find nothing but a couple of stamps and a boy-scout knife. Spit takes the knife, but Tommy makes him give it up. Tommy needs a knife himself.

The tall stranger and his squat friend are back. They would send Dippy to an apartment in a tenement up the street to ask for a Mrs. Martin. Dippy's to tell her a friend wants to see her. Gimpty catches a tone in the Tall Man's voice that sounds startlingly familiar, but the strangers are quick to deny that there is any chance of their having met. . . .

Now Milton innocently appears around the corner. Milton is a new kid on the block and it occurs to Tommy that he might want to belong to the gang. If he does he's godda have some dough. He's godda have a quatuh, in fact, if he wants to be initiated, and he's only got "tree sants." Milton's surname is Schwartz and his parents are Jewish. Satisfied that Milton is not lying, Tommy suggests that he might get a quatuh from his ole lady if he knows where she keeps it. Stealin's a sin to Milty, however, and if they will give him back his tree sants he will withdraw from the gang. They couldn't do that, Tommy insists, so they decide to "cock-alize" Milty. Before he knows what is happening they have tumbled him to the ground, pinioned his arms and legs, torn his clothes open and smeared his body with dirt scooped up from the street. They are proceeding with a few added indecencies when the tattoo of running feet diverts them. A second later "a whirl-wind hits the group and the boys are dispersed right and left. The whirlwind is a girl not much bigger than Tommy, with a face resembling his—pushed up nose and freckles. She slaps and pulls and pushes the boys, who scatter away laughing and shouting."

"Aw, scram, will yuh, Drina! Scram!" pleads Tommy.

"Shut up!"

Drina helps Milty to his feet and brushes off his clothes. "Her simple dress, her hair combed back of the ears and held in place with a cheap celluloid clasp, her lithe boyish figure combine to create the illusion of a very young girl. When she comforts Milty, however, it is apparent in the mature quality of her solicitude that she is much older—in her earlier twenties."

"You ought to be ashamed of yourself, standing there and letting them pile up on this kid," she says to the Tall One, who is leaning against the wall of the tenement and laughing. "Why didn't you stop 'em?"

"What for? It'll do him good."

"Aw, Drina—why don'tcha butt outa my business?" wails Tommy.

But Drina has no intention of butting out. She has a lot of things to do. Tommy's scratching his head reminds her of one of them. She'll get him home and wash his head. Milton's wail that they still have his tree sants suggests another obligation. Drina finally pins the possession of the money on Spit, and when he boldly and profanely refuses to give it up she smacks him. Spit is about to smack back when Tommy comes hurriedly down from the hopper where he has climbed and rushes to Drina's defense. He is ready to fight his sister himself, but no other guy is going to touch her. Spit has to give up the tree sants, too, or take a punch in the nose. . . .

Dippy is back from trying to find Mrs. Martin. He hasn't been successful. The squat fellow decides he had better go himself and bring the lady back. And now Gimpty has remembered the Tall Man's voice! It's Babyface Martin!

"I ain't Martin, you bastard," snarls the Tall One.

"Don't you remember me?" persists Gimpty. "I'm Gimpty. . . . Remember?"

MARTIN—Gimpty?

GIMPTY—Sure, Babyface. I . . .

MARTIN—Sh! Shut up! My name's Johnson. Git it? Johnson.

GIMPTY—We were kids here. Don't you remember? I was one of the gang.

MARTIN (*squints at him carefully for a long time*)—Yeah.

GIMPTY—You don't have to worry about me.

MARTIN—I ain't worryin' about you. I'm worryin' about me. (*His hand emerges slowly from under his coat.*) You wuz dat funny kid who used to mind my clothes when I went swimmin'.

GIMPTY—Yeah!

MARTIN—Yeah. 'At's right. Kin yuh still keep yer lips buttoned up?

GIMPTY—I guess so.

MARTIN—Yuh guess so! Yuh better find out. And God damn quick!

GIMPTY—You know me, Marty, I . . .

MARTIN (*someone comes out of the East River Terrace and passes off*)—Sh! (*Relaxes.*) O.K. Ony, I'm tellin' yuh, if it wuz anybody else, so help me God, I'd . . . (*Gestures with thumb and forefinger as if reaching for his gun.*)

GIMPTY—Thanks. . . . What did you do to your face?

MARTIN—Operation. Plastic, dey call it.

GIMPTY—Oh! And you dyed your hair too.

MARTIN—Yeah. I guess yuh read about me.

GIMPTY—Sure. You're the headliner these days.

MARTIN—God damn right! (*Pauses. Looks around reminiscently and nods toward the East River Terrace Apartments.*) Hey, dat's something new, ain't it?

GIMPTY—No. It's been up a couple of years.

MARTIN—Yeah? What is it?

GIMPTY—One of the swellest apartment houses in town.

MARTIN—Yuh don' tell me! Well, what do yuh know!

GIMPTY—Yeah. You have to have blue blood, a million bucks, and a yacht to live in there, or else you have to . . .

Gimpty breaks off moodily and cannot be induced to finish his thought. He changes the subject by pointing out other changes the neighborhood has undergone—the floating dock where the millionaires tie up their yachts for one. He tells Martin something of himself. Gimpty is an architect, or would be if he could find work. Nine out of ten in that profession happen to be out of work right now. Nobody's building any more. Gimpty has been to both High School and College—six years of College—and—

"Six years?" echoes Martin, wonderingly. "Why, yuh son uv a bitch, you're marvelous!"

"Well, I won a scholarship, and Mom worked like hell . . . and here I am. I was doin' a little work for the government, but . . ."

"Oh, yeah?"

GIMPTY—No . . . don't get excited. . . . On a slum clearance project. But that folded up. I'm on home relief now.

MARTIN—Oh! (*A man comes down the street and enters the tenement.*)

GIMPTY—Say, is it so smart for you to come here? With that big reward.

MARTIN—I ain' here. I'm out West. Read da papers.

GIMPTY—Have you seen your mother yet?

MARTIN—No. Dat's one reason why I come back. I ain't seen da old lady 'n seven years. I kind a got a yen. Yuh know?

GIMPTY—Sure. . . . I saw her here day before yesterday.

MARTIN—Yeah? I t'ought she might be aroun'. How's she look?

GIMPTY—All right.

MARTIN—Gese. Seven years! Since da day I come outa reform school. Say, yew came down here wid her tuh meet me, didn' yuh?

GIMPTY—Yeah.

MARTIN—Sure. 'At's right.

GIMPTY—Well, you've gone a long way since then.

MARTIN—Yeah.

GIMPTY—You know, Marty, I never could quite believe it was you.

MARTIN—Why not?

GIMPTY—To kill eight men?

MARTIN—Say, what da hell a' yuh tryin' tuh do? Tell me off, yuh bastard. Why, I'll—

GIMPTY—No, Marty. . . .

MARTIN—Say, maybe yuh changed, huh? Maybe yuh become a rat. Maybe yuh'd like tuh git dat faw grand 'at's up fuh me. . . .

GIMPTY—You know better.

MARTIN—I'm not so sure. Forty-two hundred bucks is pretty big dough fer a joik like yew.

GIMPTY—You can trust me.

MARTIN—Den don' gimme any a dat crap! What da hell did yuh tink I wuz gonna do? Hang around dis dump waitin' fer Santa Claus tuh take care a me, fer Chris' sake. Looka you! What 'a' yuh got? Six years yuh went tuh college an' what da hell 'a' yuh got? A lousy handout a thoity bucks a month! Not fer me! I yain't like yew punks . . . starvin' an' freezin' . . . fuh what? Peanuts? Coffee an'? Yeah, I got mine, but I took it. Look! (*Pulls at his shirt.*) Silk. Twenty bucks. Look a' dis! (*Pulls at his jacket.*) Custom-tailored—a hundred an' fifty bucks. Da fat a da land I live off of. An' I got a flock a dames dat'd make yew guys water at da mout'. Dat'd make yew slobs run off in a dark corner when yuh see deir pichure an' play pocket-pool.

GIMPTY—Ain't you ever scared?

MARTIN—Me? What of? What da hell, yuh can't live forever. Ah, I don' know. Sure! Sometimes I git da jitters. An' sometimes I git a terrific yen tuh stay put, an' . . . Ah, da hell wid it! Say,

Photo by White Studio, New York.

"DEAD END"

"The ambulance men arrive to take the wounded G-man away. They leave Babyface, 'with
thing left to look at but chopped meat,' as the interne says, to wait for the wagon to trundle
body to the morgue. The Medical Examiner has marked it D.O.A., 'Dead on Arrival.'"

do you remember dat kid Francey?

GIMPTY—Francey?

MARTIN—She wuz my goil when we were kids.

GIMPTY—Oh, yeah. She was a fine girl. I remember.

MARTIN—Yew bet. Dey don' make no more like her. I know. I had 'em all. Yuh ain't seen her around, have yuh?

GIMPTY—No.

MARTIN—Hoid anythin' about her?

GIMPTY—No.

MARTIN—Gee, I got a terrific yen tuh see dat kid again. Dat's why I come back here. I wonder what she's doin'. Maybe she got married. Nah, she couldn't! Maybe she died. Nah, not Francey! She had too much on da ball, too much stuff . . . guts. Yeah, she wuz like me. Nuttin' kin kill Babyface Martin an' nuttin' kin kill her. Not Francey. Gese, I wonder what's become a her?

GIMPTY—She's the girl whose uncle owns a tailor shop around the corner, isn't she? (MILTY *strolls over to the parapet and stands looking into the water.*)

MARTIN—Yeah. Yew remember her now.

GIMPTY—Sure. I remember her all right.

MARTIN—I tole Hunk, he's one a my boys, tuh look in 'ere an' see if he could git her address. Gese. I gotta see dat kid again!

There is a suggestion of rebellion in the gang. Spit would add something to the cockalizing they have given Milty and Tommy orders him to lay off. Milty's had enough for one time. Spit, however, would question the authority of Tommy. He goes on questioning it until Tommy is obliged to give him a good sock in the nose that sends him sprawling. After that things are pretty quiet.

"Da kids aroun' here don' change," observes Martin.

Now his squat friend, Hunk, is back to report that the Babyface's mother ain't home and he couldn't find the girl, Francey. He got the address of Francey's aunt in Brooklyn, however, and Martin would have him hop a taxi and follow it up. . . .

Philip of the Terrace has reappeared on the parapet of the garden. Philip is still uncowed. It's a free country, so far as Philip is concerned, and he'll look where he pleases.

"Hey, Wee-wee, what ah yuh, a boy 'r a goil?" shouts Tommy.

"He's a goil, can'tcha see?" shouts back T. B.

"I'm a man!" corrects Philip.

To prove it Philip would name all the Presidents of the United States, and bet a dollar neither of them can do that. The fact that Philip has a dollar is startling news to T. B. and Tommy.

They haven't a dollar, even if Tommy could remember Presidents. So they decide to give Philip a "cockalizing" too. They are rushing the Terrace garden when the Doorman comes to Philip's aid and sends them running again.

"Wait till I git you—I'll fix your wagon," yells Tommy, derisively. Turning to the gang he calls them together. "Come here, guys. We gotta git dat kid away from deah. We gotta git him. . . ." And they go.

Drina is back looking for Tommy. The head washing has got to be done. It can't wait until night, because Drina has a strike meeting at night and won't have any time. But Tommy will have none of the washing, except what he gives himself in the river. He distracts Drina's attention until she loosens her hold on his shirt and in a second he's free and off under the pillars to dive again into the river.

"What are you gonna do with a kid like that?" asks Drina, helplessly.

"I don't know," laughs Gimpty.

DRINA (*seating herself on the parapet next to* GIMPTY)—It's not that he's dumb, either. I went to see his teacher yesterday. She said he's one of the smartest pupils she's got. But he won't work. Two weeks he played hookey.

GIMPTY—I don't blame him.

DRINA—I can't seem to do anything with him. It was different when Mom was alive. She could handle him . . . and between us we made enough money to live in a better neighborhood than this. If we win this strike, I'm gonna move, get him outa here the first thing.

GIMPTY—Yeah. That's the idea.

DRINA (*noticing his drawings*)—What've you got there? More drawings?

GIMPTY—Couple new ideas in community housing. Here! See? (*He passes the drawing pad to her.*)

DRINA (*studies them and nods admiration*)—Yeah. They're beautiful houses, Pete. But what's the good? Is anybody going to build them?

GIMPTY—No.

DRINA (*handing back the drawings*)—So what?

GIMPTY—All my life I've wanted to build houses like these. Well . . . I'm gonna build 'em, see? Even if it's only on paper.

DRINA—A lot of good they'll do on paper. Your mother told me you've even given up looking for a job lately.

GIMPTY (*suddenly bitter and weary*)—Sure. What's the use? How long have you been on strike now?

DRINA—A month.

GIMPTY—Picketing an' fighting an' broken heads. For what?

DRINA—For what? For two dollars and fifty cents a week extra. Eleven dollars a month, Pete. All towards rent. So's Tommy and I can live in a decent neighborhood.

GIMPTY—Yeah. You're right there. I've seen this neighborhood make some pretty rough guys. You've heard about Babyface Martin? He used to live around here.

DRINA—Yeah. I read about it.

GIMPTY—I used to know him.

DRINA—You did? What was he like? (TOMMY *climbs up out of the water, breathless. He lies on the parapet, listening.*)

GIMPTY—As a kid, all right . . . more than all right. Yeah, Drina, the place you live in is awfully important. It can give you a chance to grow, or it can twist you (*he twists an imaginary object with grim venom*), like that. When I was in school, they used to teach us that evolution made men out of animals. They forgot to tell us it can also make animals out of men.

TOMMY—Hey, Gimpty.

GIMPTY—Yeah?

TOMMY—What's evilushin? (*He clambers along the parapet and lies on his stomach in front of* DRINA.)

GIMPTY (*looks at* TOMMY *a moment, smiles, and comes out of his dark mood*)—What's evolution, Tommy? Well, I'll tell you. A thousand million years ago we were all worms in the mud, and that evolution made us men.

DRINA—And women!

GIMPTY—And women.

TOMMY—And boys and goils?

GIMPTY—And boys and girls.

TOMMY—Ah, I wuzn't even born a t'ousan' million years ago.

GIMPTY—No, but your great, great, great, great-grandfather and mother were; and before them their great, great, great, great, great-grandfather and mother were worms.

TOMMY—Blah-h-h!

DRINA (*impressed*)—It's like God!

GIMPTY—It is God! Once it made dinosaurs . . . animals as big as that house.

TOMMY—As big as that?

DRINA—Sure.

TOMMY—Wow!

GIMPTY—Then it didn't like its work and it killed them. Every
one of them! Wiped 'em out!

TOMMY—Boy! I'd like tuh see one a dem babies.

GIMPTY—I'll show you a picture sometime.

TOMMY—Will yuh?

GIMPTY—Sure.

TOMMY—'At'll be swell, Gimpty. (SPIT *appears on the ladder
and stops to listen, hanging from the top rung.*)

GIMPTY—Once evolution gave snakes feet to walk on.

TOMMY—Snakes? No kiddin'?

SPIT (*sings in mockery*)—Te-da-da-da-da-bushwa, te-da-da
bushwa!

TOMMY—Shut up! Right innee eye! (*He spits:* SPIT *jumps
back into the water.*)

DRINA—Tommy, cut that out! See? You're like an animal.

TOMMY—Well . . . he does it tuh all de uddah kids. . . .
Anyhow, what happened tuh duh snakes' feet?

GIMPTY—Evolution took 'em away. The same as ostriches
could once fly. I bet you didn't know that.

TOMMY—No.

GIMPTY—Well, it's true. And then it took away their power
to fly. The same as it gave oysters heads.

TOMMY—Oysters had heads?

GIMPTY—Once, yeah.

TOMMY—Aw-w!

DRINA—Sh, listen!

GIMPTY—Then it took them away. "Now men," says Evolution, "now men . . . (*nods to* DRINA, *acknowledging her contribution*) and women . . . I made you walk straight, I gave
you feeling, I gave you reason, I gave you dignity, I gave you a
sense of beauty, I planted a God in your heart. Now let's see
what you're going to do with them. An' if you can't do anything
with them, then I'll take 'em all away. Yeah, I'll take away your
reason as sure as I took away the head of the oyster, and your
sense of beauty as I took away the flight of the ostrich, and men
will crawl on their bellies on the ground like snakes . . . or die
off altogether like the dinosaur."

An attractive young woman has appeared at the Terrace gate.
She is smartly groomed in white linen. Kay is her name. "She
brings a clean coolness into this sweltering street. She has a distinctive, lovely face." As she comes through the gate the boys are
startled into expressions of "Gee!" "Wow!" and the like. Angel

recognizes Kay as Gimpty's goil friend, but that's a bit too much
for Dippy. How kin she be Gimpty's goil friend and live in there?
Is she a billionairess? Or a millionairess? No. Then she must be
a soivant goil!

Gimpty has been squirming with embarrassment, but he can't
get rid of the gang. Nor can Drina. She makes another attempt
to get Tommy home. Again he eludes her and is in the water.
Anyway, demands Tommy, if evilushin's God, and God made
everything, including bugs, what's Drina wanta kill 'em fer?

"He's very logical," suggests Kay.

"Yeah. That part's all right," admits Drina; "but he's very
lousy, too, an' that part ain't. . . ."

The boys have gone back to the water. Drina is forced to give
up capturing Tommy and go home. Now Gimpty and Kay are
alone. She picks up his drawing board and admires his work. She
has been talking to her friend Jack about him. Jack has given
her a card that Gimpty is to take to a man named Del Block.
It may be Block will be able to help him.

Gimpty, pleased and grateful, is staring a little helplessly at
Kay, as he tries to explain his emotions of the moment.

"I was telling Mom about you last night," Gimpty is saying.
"I been kind of going around the house like a chicken with its
head chopped off . . . and Mom asked me why. So I told her."
"What?"

GIMPTY—Oh, just a little about how we'd got to talking here,
and meeting every day, and what great friends we've become.
How you've been trying to help me. And . . . that I worship
you!

KAY—You didn't!

GIMPTY—Well, I do. Do you mind?

KAY (deeply touched)—Mind? You fool! What'd she say?

GIMPTY—She said you sounded like a very real, good person.

KAY—Good? Did you tell her all about me? About Jack?

GIMPTY—Yeah.

KAY—Your mother must be a sweet woman. I'd like to meet
her sometime.

GIMPTY (enthusiastically)—She'd be tickled. Will you?

KAY—Right now, if you like.

GIMPTY—Well, she's out for the afternoon.

KAY—Oh!

GIMPTY—Maybe I can get her down here day after tomorrow,
huh?

KAY (*pauses, then, a bit depressed*)—I may not be here then. I may leave tomorrow.

GIMPTY—Tomorrow?

KAY—Night. Jack's going on a fishing trip. He wants me with him.

GIMPTY—Isn't that sudden?

KAY—He's been planning it for some time.

GIMPTY—How long will you be gone?

KAY—About three months.

GIMPTY—That's a long time.

KAY—Yes.

Down the street strides a well-dressed, handsome man in his early forties. His face is hard, and at the moment he is hot, uncomfortable and irritated about having to use the back way. Neither is he too well pleased at seeing Kay there. He is less pleased and somewhat puzzled a minute later when Dippy, climbing out of the river, demands to know from "Gimpty's goil friend" whether he (Dippy) had done a good blackjack dive or had he?

Jack will want an explanation when he gets Kay inside, but Kay doesn't want to go in just yet. That makes Jack sore, too. Here he has been tearing around all day getting things ready for the fishing trip and he comes home to find her acting like a cheap—

Kay stops Jack at that point and he angrily turns and goes into the Terrace. Kay starts to follow, then changes her mind. Let him be mad if he wants to.

"Is that the guy?" demands Gimpty, after Jack has disappeared.

"Yes," admits Kay, but quickly adds, "Don't judge him by this. He's really not so bad. He's going to be sorry in a few minutes. He's so darn jealous. His wife gave him a pretty raw deal. You can't blame him for . . .

GIMPTY (*suddenly inflamed*)—All right! If it were anybody else, all right! But you? He can't treat *you* like that!

KAY (*sits there awhile in silence, thinking. Finally, she speaks, slowly, almost in explanation to herself.*)—I've been living with Jack a little over a year now. He isn't usually like this. You see, he really loves me.

GIMPTY—He has a funny way of showing it.

KAY—He wants me to marry him.

GIMPTY—Are you going to?

Kay—I don't know.

Gimpty—Do you love him?

Kay—I like him.

Gimpty—Is that enough?

Kay—I've known what it means to scrimp and worry and never be sure from one minute to the next. I've had enough of that . . . for one lifetime.

Gimpty (*intensely*)—But, Kay, not to look forward to love . . . God, that's not living at all!

Kay (*not quite convincing*)—I can do without it.

Gimpty—That's not true. It isn't, is it? (*He's sure it isn't.*)

Kay (*smiles. She's been caught.*)—Of course not.

The gang is reassembling. A fat lady has come from the garden trailed by a Pekinese and that is a laugh to Tommy. Tommy never seen a cockaroach like dat before. Where'd she git it? The fat lady is mad enough to burst.

"Get away from here, you little beasts!" she orders.

"In yuh hat, fat slob!" answers Spit.

The fat lady calls the Doorman. The Doorman chases the boys away, but he can't shut them up. They chatter from the timbers of the sand hopper into which they have climbed. In the midst of the row Philip comes out of the garden with his father and another man. Philip also has a complaint against the boys. They wanted to hit him. Mr. Griswald thinks they had better not try that. But, in case they do, Philip is to hit back. Perhaps he had better get Philip some boxing gloves and teach him how to defend himself.

As they disappear Tommy again calls the boys together. They've gotta get that Philip guy and cockalize him. Tommy thinks he has thought of a way. Foist they'll get Philip in the hallway, and then—

"The little savages! They'll all wicked! It's born in them. They inherit it," protests the fat lady.

That's too much for Gimpty. He turns suddenly and bursts out, a bitter personal note in his passion:

"Inheritance? Yeah! You inherit a castle thirty stories over the river, or a stinkin' hole in the ground! Wooden heads are inherited, but not wooden legs . . . nor legs twisted by rickets!"

The fat lady, completely taken aback, gathers her Pekinese to her capacious bosom and stamps away. Gimpty apologizes to the sympathetic Kay. Tommy's gang is still in a whisper huddle.

"Gosh, I wish we could be alone for a minute!" wishes Gimpty.

"Pete, I've thought of that so many times. I've wanted to invite you inside, but . . ."

"You couldn't, of course."

"Cockeyed, isn't it? Couldn't we get to your place?"

"Gee, I . . . ! No, you wouldn't like it."

"Why not?"

"It's an awful dump. It would depress you. I'd love to have you, Kay, but I'm ashamed to let you see it. Honestly."

"Oh, Pete, that's silly. I wasn't born in a penthouse. Come on!"

Gimpty rises with the aid of a cane, and as he moves away with Kay "we notice for the first time that one of his legs is withered and twisted—by rickets. . . ."

Milton has reappeared. He has been waiting for a chance to speak to Tommy. Now he edges over nearer the huddle. Milty thinks that he knows a way now how he can snitch that quatuh Tommy wants.

"O.K., Milt!" announces Tommy. "Den yuh're inna gang, see?" He turns to the others. "Anybody gits snotty wid Milt gits snotty wid me, see?" Then to Milt: "Now git dat quatuh. Come on, git duh lead outa yuh pants!"

Milt is off like a shot to snitch the quatuh. The chug-chug of an approaching tugboat breaks into the noises of the scene, growing louder as the tug approaches.

"See? He's a good kid," says Tommy, looking after Milt. "He loins fast. Remember da time I moved aroun' heah? I wuz wearin' white socks an' I wouldn' coise, so yuh all t'ought I wuz a sissy."

" 'Cept me, Tommy," Dippy reminds him.

"Yeah, 'cept yew. Everybody else I hadda beat de pants offa foist. (*Down to business again.*) Now, here's how we git Weewee: You, T. B. . . ."

His voice is drowned out by the chug-chug of the passing tugboat. The curtain falls.

ACT II

The next day the gang is again in session. This time the boys are concentrating on a poker game, with a puffed, blowsy deck of cards and matches for chips. Leaning against the wall Babyface Martin looks on "with grim nostalgia." Between times the gang hears the experience of Angel, who has appeared with a bump on his head. Angel's ole man had come home drunk the night before—Gese, wuz he drunk—and fuh nuttin' he had stahted beatin' hell outa Angel's ole lady—

"Boy, he socks 'er all ovah de place!" reports Angel. At which report Spit laughs.

"What da hell a' yuh laughin' at? Dat ain' so funny," protests Tommy.

"No, dat ain' so funny," echoes Angel; " 'cause den he picks up a chair and wantsa wallop me wid it."

"Whatcha do den?"

"So I grabs a kitchen knife . . . dat big . . . an' I sez, 'Touch me, yuh louse, an' I give yuh dis.' "

"Yeah?"

"Yeah, yeah, I did. So he laughs, so he laughs, so he falls on a flaw, an' he goes tuh sleep . . . so he snores . . . (*imitates a rasping snore*) like 'at. Boy, wuz 'e drunk! Boy, he wuz stinkin'!"

Milty has been on an errand for Martin. He is back with a message. "She said tuh meet huh down heah," reports Milty. For which pleasant word Martin tosses Milty a half dollar, and immediately precipitates a fight. Spit shouts, "Akey! Akey! Haffies!" and Milty has no idea of permitting any akey. Or any haffies either. Spit never had his fingers crossed. Tommy, as arbiter, agrees to this, and the fight's off.

Two tough boys appear suddenly up by the steam shovel. They go into a moment's conference and then advance belligerently. They represent the Second Avenya gang and they are looking for a fight. Tommy, answering as leaduh, treats the proposition with disdain until he is forced to answer. Then he is ready to fight them any way they want.

"Yuh wanna fight are gang?" demands the emissary from Second Avenya.

"Sure," answers Tommy, turning to his gang for confirmation. "O.K., felluhs? Yuh wanna fight de Second Avenya gang?" They are raucous with their approval. "Sure!" Tommy repeats to the emissaries.

"O.K. On are block?"

"Yeah. O.K."

"Satiday?"

"O.K. Satiday, fellahs? Faw o'clock? O.K. We'll be up deah Satiday faw o'clock an', boy, we'll kick de stuffin's outa youse!"

"Yeah?"

"Yeah! No bottles 'r rocks, jus' sticks 'n' bare knucks. Flat sticks. No bats."

"Sure."

"O.K.?"

"O.K.!"

The emissaries withdraw, turning when they are at a safe distance to suggest loudly that there isn't a guy among the enemy whose parentage is regular.

Martin has called Angel to shine his shoes. As he is being given this service he would give the boys a little instruction in gang fighting. It is Martin's advice that they get on the field earlier than they said, and start the fight by tossing over a few electric light bulbs and milk bottles. Then, when some of the enemy get hurt, let Tommy's gang charge in and finish it.

"Yeah, but we made up no milk bottles, ony bare knucks an' sticks," explains Tommy.

"Yuh made up! Lissen, kid . . . when yuh fight dee idea is tuh win," counsels Martin. "It don' cut no ice how. An' in gang fightin' remember, take out da tough guys foist. Tree aw faw a yuh gang up on 'im. Den one a yuh kin git behin' 'im an' slug 'im. A stockin' fulla sand an' rocks is good fuh dat. An' if 'ey're lickin' yuh, pull a knife. Give 'em a little stab in ee arm. 'Ey'll yell like hell an' run."

"Yeah, but we made up no knives. Gese, 'at ain' fair. . . ."

Gimpty has strolled in, whistling cheerfully. He hears a part of Martin's advice. Gimpty is against it and tells the boys so.

"We kin lick 'em wid bare knucks, fair an' square," promises Tommy.

"Lissen, kid . . . 'ere ain' no fair an' 'ere ain't no square. It's winnah take all. An' it's easier tuh lick a guy by sluggin' 'im fum behin' 'en it is by sockin' it out wid 'im toe tuh toe. 'Cause if yuh're lickin' 'im, 'en he pulls a knife on yuh, see? 'En wheah are yuh?"

"Den I pull a knife back on him."

Again Gimpty objects, and seems likely to get himself a sock in the puss, according to Martin. In the end Tommy agrees to use the knife if he can get one. Whereupon Milty buys Angel's boy-scout knife for a quatuh and gives it to Tommy. "Gese, 'at's swell . . . tanks!" says Tommy. "Aw, dat's nuttin'," insists the new member. . . .

Charles, the Griswalds' chauffeur, has brought Philip from the Terrace. They are on their way to the garage, but Philip thinks he will wait there for the car. Immediately the gang goes into an important conclave. T. B. would know the time and Philip consulting the Gruen watch on his wrist, tells him it is half-past four. It's a nice watch, all right, T. B. admits.

Now Tommy is calling to T. B. to come and see something

great. They are going in the hall to show it, and the gang is loud with a faked excitement. T. B. thinks maybe Philip would like to go, but Tommy rules against any outsiders. This is only for the gang. T. B. pleads for Philip, but Tommy and the gang stand firm.

"Too bad dey won't let yuh see it," sympathizes T. B. "Boy, yuh nevuh saw anyting like dat."

"Well, I don't care," answers Philip. "I can't anyway. I'm waiting for my father and mother. We're going to the country."

"It'll only take a minute. . . . Hey, felluhs, let 'im come 'n' see it, will yuh? He's O.K."

"Well . . . awright. Let 'im come!" calls Tommy, after a great show of reluctance. And Philip goes. . . .

Kay has come from the Terrace to meet Gimpty. There is a slight strain in her voice, a suggestion of overkindness, "as if she were trying to mitigate some hurt she was about to give him."

Gimpty reports his latest attempts to get a job. He is not discouraged, but nothing very hopeful has happened to him. Kay is distressed, and more determined than ever that he shall find something.

"I used to think we were poor at home because I had to wear a made-over dress to a prom," says Kay. "Yesterday I saw the real thing. If I hadn't seen it, I couldn't have believed it. I dreamt of it all night . . . the filth, the smells, the dankness! I touched a wall and it was wet. . . ."

"That house was rotten before I was born. The plumbing is so old and broken . . . it's been dripping through the building for ages."

"What tears my heart out is the thought that you have to live there. It's not fair! It's not right!"

"It's not right that anybody should live like that, but a couple of million of us do."

"Million?"

"Yeah, right here in New York . . . New York with its famous skyline . . . its Empire State, the biggest God-damned building in the world. The biggest tombstone in the world! They wanted to build a monument to the times. Well, there it is, bigger than the pyramids and just as many tenants. (*He forces her to smile with him. Then he sighs and adds hopelessly:*) I wonder when they'll let us build houses for men to live in? (*Suddenly annoyed with himself.*) Ah, I should never have let you see that place!"

"I'm glad you did. I know so much more about you now. And I can't tell you how much more I respect you for coming out of that fine, and sweet . . . and sound."

"Let's not get started on that." Gimpty's eyes have dropped to his withered limb.

From the tenement hallway comes the sound of Philip's sobbing. Suddenly the door is burst open and he rushes out. His clothes are all awry. The gang follows, yelling and laughing. Tommy is holding Philip's watch. It is his idea that they get dressed and beat it quick, but the others are for taking another quick swim first. Tommy turns the watch over to T. B. and follows the swimmers.

Gimpty and Kay have been quiet onlookers at this excitement. Now they resume their own affairs. Kay is more and more determined that Gimpty shall get out of this neighborhood, and he is ready to make the attempt. But—if he does get out and get a start, will she marry him? Kay is a little startled by the suggestion, but ready to answer it.

"Listen!" she says seriously. "First I want you to know that I love you . . . as much as I'll allow myself to love anybody. Maybe I shouldn't have gone with you yesterday. Maybe it was a mistake. I didn't realize quite how much I loved you. I think I ought to leave tonight."

Kay holds to that opinion through all Gimpty's excited opposition. Presently the sound of an approaching motor boat is heard. It is the boat that Kay will sail away in tonight. She hopes Gimpty will be there that she may see him before she goes.

Kay has gone now, and Martin, looking up from his newspaper with a lascivious smirk, would ride Gimpty for not taking advantage of the situation. Dames like Kay are pushovers if yuh know how to handle 'em. Gimpty objects to Martin's insinuations and gets set down for his pains. "Look what wantsa fight wid me!" sneers Martin. "Little Gimpty wantsa fight wid me! Whassamattuh, Gimpty? Wanna git knocked off?"

Before Martin can pursue the Gimpty matter further his friend Hunk has returned with word that the party is coming. A moment later Mrs. Martin shuffles into view, "a gaunt, raw-boned, unkempt woman, sloppy and disheveled. Her one garment an ancient house dress retrieved from some garbage heap, black with grease stains: her legs are stockingless, knotted and bulging with blue, twisted, cord-like veins. Her feet show through the cracks in her house slippers. In contrast to the picture of general decay is a face that looks as if it were carved of granite; as if infinite suffering had been met with dogged, unyielding strength. . . . She comes to a dead stop as she sees Martin. There is no other sign of recognition, no friendliness on her lips. She stares at him out of dull, hostile eyes."

MARTIN (*his face lights, he grins. He steps rapidly toward her.*)—Hello, Mom! How are yuh? (*Pause.*) It's me. (*No recognition.*) I had my face fixed. (*There is a moment of silence. She finally speaks in an almost inaudible monotone.*)

MRS. MARTIN—Yuh no good tramp!

MARTIN—Mom!

MRS. MARTIN—What're yuh doin' here?

MARTIN—Ain'tcha glad tuh see me?

MRS. MARTIN (*she suddenly smacks him a sharp crack across the cheek*)—That's how glad I am.

MARTIN (*he rubs his cheek, stunned by this unexpected reception. He stammers.*)—'At's a great hello.

MRS. MARTIN—Yuh dog! Yuh stinkin' yellow dog, yuh!

MARTIN—Mom! What kin' a talk is 'at? Gese, Mom. . .

MRS. MARTIN—Don't call me Mom! Yuh ain't no son a mine. What do yuh want from me now?

MARTIN—Nuttin'. I jus' . . .

MRS. MARTIN (*her voice rises, shrill, hysterical*)—Then git out a here! Before I crack yuh goddam face again. Git out a here!

MARTIN (*flaring*)—Why, yuh ole tramp, I killed a guy fer lookin' at me da way yew are.

MRS. MARTIN (*looks at him and nods slowly. Then quietly*)—Yeah. . . . You're a killer all right. . . . You're a murderer . . . you're a butcher, sure! Why don't yuh leave me ferget yuh? Ain' I got troubles enough with the cops and newspapers botherin' me? An' Johnny and Martha . . .

MARTIN—What's a mattuh wid 'em?

MRS. MARTIN—None a yer business! Just leave us alone! Yuh never brought nothin' but trouble. Don't come back like a bad penny! . . . Just stay away and leave us alone . . . an' die . . . but leave us alone! (*She turns her back on him and starts to go.*)

MARTIN—Hey, wait!

MRS. MARTIN (*pauses*)—What?

MARTIN—Need any dough?

MRS. MARTIN—Keep yer blood money.

MARTIN—Ah yuh gonna rat on me . . . gonna tell a cops?

MRS. MARTIN—No. They'll get yuh soon enough.

MARTIN—Not me! Not Martin! Huh! Not Babyface Martin!

MRS. MARTIN (*muttering*)—Babyface! Babyface! I remember. (*She begins to sob, clutching her stomach.*) In here . . . in

here! Kickin'! That's where yuh come from. God! I ought to be
cut open here fer givin' yuh life . . . murderer!!! (*She shuffles
away, up the street, weeping quietly.* MARTIN *stands there looking
after her for a long time.*)

Martin is bewildered but will have none of Hunk's sympathy.
Hunk is virtually slapped down and sent on his way when he
would discuss the Martin family surprise. Babyface is still puzzled and irritable when Gimpty asks what he expected—flags and
a brass band? For that Gimpty gets his face slapped, just for
shootin' off his mout', for talkin' outa toin.

"Gee, when I was a kid I used to think you were something,"
sneers Gimpty, jerking his head free of the clutch with which
Martin has pushed him against the wall; "but you're rotten . . .
see? You ought to be wiped out!"

Martin's face twists with anger. His foot shoots out and he
kicks Gimpty's crippled leg viciously.

"All right. O.K. Martin! Just wait!"

Martin has wheeled, his hand seeking his shoulder holster.
"What? What's dat?" he shouts, menacingly.

"Go on! Shoot me! That'll bring them right to you! Go on!"
shouts Gimpty, defiantly. Martin lowers his gun arm and starts
up the street with threats of finishing the business later.

And now Philip has reappeared with his father and Jeanne, the
governess. Philip is still crying and repeating the injuries that
have been done him. Griswald is muttering threats about sending
his son's assaulters to jail.

The gang is climbing out of the water. T. B. gives the danger
cry. They make a dash for their clothes under the sand hopper.
Griswald, urged on by Philip, starts in hot pursuit. Spit, Angel,
T. B. and Milty all get away. Tommy, who stumbles, is caught
by Griswald. Tommy wriggles and twists. Philip dances with joy
at sight of his captured enemy. Mr. Griswald hangs on, demanding Philip's watch, threatening to break Tommy's neck and calling
to the governess to summon an officer.

Now Tommy is pleading wildly with Griswald not to be turned
over to the cops, swearing he hasn't got Philip's watch. Between
pleas he yells lustily for help from the gang. A minute later Milty
comes running down the street, holding the watch in his out-
stretched hand and adding his pleas to Griswald to let Tommy
go. Tommy didn't do nuttin', yells Milty, and starts pummeling
Griswald viciously.

Griswald gets a strange hold on Tommy with one arm, and is

fighting off Milty with the other. With both arms free Tommy
manages to get his hand in his pocket and a hold of his knife.
Another second he has flashed the open blade and struck at his
captor's wrist. With a cry of pain Griswald loosens his hold.
Tommy and Milty dash wildly up the street. At the sight of his
father's blood Philip sets up a fresh howl.

When Griswald twists his handkerchief about his wrist the
blood quickly soaks through, indicating a deep wound. An officer
arrives. He suggests a tourniquet, but Griswald is sure that will
not be necessary. What he wants is to have the hoodlum who did
the stabbing arrested. The officer is willing, but he hasn't much
to go on in the way of description. Griswald can't remember how
his assailants looked, and the governess knows only that they were
practically naked and quite filthy. The officer is not impressed, but
takes a livelier interest when he learns from the Doorman that
Griswald is a brother of Judge Griswald. Even then he makes but
little progress with his investigations. Gets nothing at all out of
Gimpty, and less than nothing out of Drina, who has come from
her strike meeting with an ugly bruise on her forehead. Another
lousy cop had beaten her—when she and the others had a perfect
right to picket. Drina is unhappy and worried—about herself and
about Gimpty, but Gimpty is so worried about himself she doesn't
get much sympathy from him. Nor much understanding. . . .

The officer has got as far as the name of one of the gang. It's
Tommy. But neither Gimpty nor Drina can remember any boy by
that name around there. Because of the Griswalds' influence the
officer sees himself transferred to Harlem, if he doesn't make
headway with this case.

"Too bad," sympathizes Gimpty, as an idea takes form in his
mind. "Well . . . maybe you can catch Babyface Martin or one
of those fellows, and grab off that forty-two hundred dollars reward. Then you can retire."

"Yeah, you could do a lot on that."

"Yeah, I guess you could. . . . Say . . . tell me something.
. . . Supposin' . . . supposin' a fellow knew where that . . . er
. . . Babyface Martin is located. How would he go about reporting him . . . and making sure of not getting gypped out of
the reward?"

"Just phone police headquarters . . . or the Department of
Justice direct. They'd be down here in two minutes. (*He looks at*
GIMPTY *and asks ironically:*) Why? You don't know where he is,
do you?"

"Colorado, the newspapers say. . . . No, I was just wonderin'."

"Well, whoever turns that guy in is taking an awful chance. He's a killer."

"Well . . . you can't live forever."

At that moment Martin, cat-footed, walks down the street. He stops as he sees Gimpty and the cop. Gimpty, pretending not to see him, hobbles off, nor answers when Babyface speaks to him. Martin stands sucking his teeth for an instant and then, adopting an amiable smile, boldly approaches the policeman.

"Kinda quiet today, ain't it?" he says.

"Not with these kids around," answers the cop.

"Dat's a nice feller. Friend o' mine," says Babyface, jerking a thumb in Gimpty's direction.

"I had quite a talk with him."

"What about?"

"Oh . . . about these kids here."

"Zat all?"

"Say, that's plenty." He has put his notebook back in his pocket and gone into the Terrace. Hunk, coming to the head of the street and seeing Martin talking to the officer, stops in his tracks. The match with which he was about to light a cigarette burns his fingers.

"Jesus!" ejaculates Hunk.

"A pal of mine," laughs Babyface. "Dey don' know me . . . wid dis mug."

Hunk has brought the girl Francey. He can't see how Martin ever boddered with a cheap hustlah like her, but is quick to shut up when Babyface resents the suggestion.

Now Francey comes down the street, "an obvious whore of the lowest class, wearing her timeless profession defiantly. A pert, pretty little face still showing traces of quality and something once sweet and fine; skin an unhealthy pallor, lips a smear of rouge. Her mop of dyed red hair is lusterless, strawy, dead from too much alternate bleach and henna."

FRANCEY (*calling to* HUNK)—Hey, what ta hell's 'e idear, keepin' me standin' on a corner all day? I'm busy. I gotta git back tuh da house. Yuh want Ida tuh break my face?

MARTIN (*looks at her*)—Francey! Jesus, what's come over yuh?

FRANCEY (*turning sharply to* MARTIN)—How do yew know my name? Who are yew? (*Impatiently.*) Well, who th' hell . . . ? (*Then she recognizes him, and gasps.*) Fuh th' love a God! Marty!

MARTIN (*never taking his eyes off the girl*)—Yeah. Hunk . . .
scram! (HUNK *goes up the street, stops at the tenement stoop
and lounges there, within earshot.*)

FRANCEY (*eagerly*)—How are yuh, Marty?

MARTIN—Read duh papers!

FRANCEY—Yuh did somethin' to yuh face.

MARTIN—Yeah. Plastic, dey call it.

FRANCEY—They said yuh wuz out aroun' Coloradah—th' noos-
papuhs! Gee, I'm glad to see yuh! (MARTIN *slips his arm around
her waist and draws her tight to his body. As his lips grope for
hers,* FRANCEY *turns her face away.*) No . . . don' kiss me on a
lips! (*He tries to pull her face around. She cries furiously.*)

MARTIN (*releasing her, puzzled*)—What? What's the matter?
(*He can't believe this. He frowns.*) I ain't good enough for you
now?

FRANCEY (*quickly*)—No. It ain't dat. It ain't yew. It's me. I
got a sore on my mouth. Fuh yuhr own good, I don't want yuh
to kiss me, dat's why.

MARTIN—I ain't nevuh fuhgot da way yew kiss.

FRANCEY (*wistfully*)—I ain't neithuh. (*She laughs.*) Go on!
You wit all yer fancy dames. Where do I come off?

MARTIN—Dey don't mean nuttin'.

FRANCEY—Dat chorus goil. . . . What's 'er name?

MARTIN—Nuttin'. She ain't got nuttin' . . . no guts, no fire.
. . . But you've been boinin' in my blood . . . evuh since . . .

FRANCEY—An' yew been in mine . . . if yuh wanna know.

MARTIN—Remembuh dat foist night . . . on a roof?

FRANCEY—Yeah, I remembuh . . . da sky was full of stars,
an' I wuz full a dreamy ideas. Dat wuz me foist time. I was fourteen, goin' on fifteen.

MARTIN—Yeah. It wuz mine too. It wuz terrific. Hit me right
wheah I live . . . like my back wuz meltin'. An' I wuz so scaied
when yuh started laffin' an' cryin', crazy like. . . . (*They both
laugh, enjoying the memory, a little embarrassed by it.*)

FRANCEY—Yeah.

MARTIN—Gee, I nevuh wuz so scaied like at that time.

FRANCEY—Me too.

MARTIN (*draws her to him again, more gently*)—Come here!
Close to me!

FRANCEY (*acquiescing*)—Ony don' kiss me on a lips!

MARTIN—Closer! (*They stand there a moment, bodies close,
passionate.* MARTIN *buries his face in her hair.*)

FRANCEY (*eyes closed, whispers*)—Marty! (*And they try to re-*

capture the young past.)

MARTIN—Dose times undah da stairs . . .

FRANCEY—A couple a crazy kids we were! We wuz gonna git married. I bought a ring at da five an' dime staw.

MARTIN—Yeah. Ony we didn' have money enough fuh de license. Gee, it seems like yestiddy. We wuz talkin' about it right heah.

FRANCEY—Yestiddy! It seems like a million yeahs!

Francey is worried. Marty's gotta take care of himself; he's gotta get away and hide. But Marty is discouraged. They've got the finger on him everywhere. There are some things you can't change. Fingerprints for one. Marty has "boined his wid acid an' tings," but it ain' no good. He is ready to scram, however, if Francey will come with him. He's got money, now. They can do things.

"But I'm sick, Marty. Don't yuh see? I'm sick!"

"What's a matter wid yew?"

"What do yuh tink?"

Martin looks at her for a long minute. He sees her now. "The nostalgic dream is finished. His lips begin to curl in disgust."

"Why dincha git a job?"

"Dey don' grow on trees!"

"Why dincha starve foist?"

"Why didnchou?" And as he turns away she shouts: "Well, what ta hell did yuh expect?"

"I don' know."

Francey is clutching at a hope now. Maybe, if he has money and they get a doctor— But he knows. Yew can't git that stuff out of yuh. He has reached for a roll of bills in his inner pocket and peeled off several which he thrusts at her. Yes, it's hot money. She'd better be careful where she spends it. She can get herself somethin'. No. He won't give her any more—not for some guy she probably has up in her room. She can beat it, now. Francey starts and then turns back. For old times' sake—will he kiss her—on the cheek? He does, scowling. She laughs—"at his obvious disrelish."

"Tanks!" calls Francey, as she disappears up the street. "Martin spits and wipes the kiss off his lips with a groan of distaste."

"See? Twicet in one day," observes Hunk. "I toldja we shouldn' a come back. But you wouldn' listen a me. Yuh nevuh listen a me."

Hunk is all for getting back to St. Louis. There's dames there waitin' for Marty. Martin isn't interested. He has just seen a little girl bouncing a rubber ball through the gate of the Terrace. An idea is born. There are a lota rich kids aroun' there. Why not a snatch—

Hunk is agin' it. Kids ain't their game. But Martin will not give up the idea. They'll get in touch with Whitey. Whitey'll know. . . .

The ominous tap of Gimpty's cane is heard. A second later, Gimpty, "tight-lipped, pale, grim," comes down the street. Martin smiles at him and speaks. Gimpty does not answer. A man who has been walking about the Terrace reappears. He catches Gimpty's eye. Gimpty points his cane at Martin. Martin wheels and faces Gimpty. "What's eatin' yuh, wise guy?" he says.

The man from the Terrace comes through the gate with revolver drawn. He steps quickly back of Martin and digs the gun into his back.

"Get 'em up, Martin! The Department of Justice wants you!"

"What ta hell . . ."

"Come on, get 'em up!"

"I ain' Martin. My name's Johnson. Wanna see my license?"

Martin slides his hand into his breast pocket, wheels around, draws his gun and fires on one motion. The G-Man drops his gun, crumples onto the sidewalk. Martin turns to face Gimpty, who has backed away. "From behind the hopper and the tenement doorway guns explode. Two other G-Men appear and descend on Martin, firing as they come. Martin groans, wheels and falls, his face in the gutter, his fingers clawing the sidewalk. One of the G-Men goes to aid his wounded comrade. The other G-Man stands over Martin's body, pumping bullet after bullet into him, literally nailing him to the ground. The G-Man kicks him to make sure he's dead. No twitch! . . . Martin lies there flat. The G-Man takes out a handkerchief, picks up Martin's gun gingerly, wraps it in the handkerchief, puts it in his pocket."

A crowd gathers. Windows go up and tenement dwellers lean out of them, faces tense with excitement. The Policeman who was looking for Tommy comes charging through the crowd. He is completely flabbergasted when he realizes it was Babyface Martin he had been talking to a few minutes before. A police ambulance is summoned. The officers push back the crowd.

"You'll get cited for this," his pals tell the wounded man.

"That's dandy! That's just dandy!" he whispers, hoarsely. "Give the medal to my old lady for the kids to play with . . . an' remember, they once had an old man who was a . . . hero."

The Doorman has spotted Spit in the crowd, and tells the officer that he is one of the gang. They grab Spit and hold him against his protests that he never done nuttin'. The ambulance men arrive and take the wounded G-Man away. They leave Baby-face, "with nothing left to look at except chopped meat," as the interne says, to wait for the wagon to trundle his body to the morgue. The Medical Examiner has marked it D.O.A. "Dead on arrival."

Now they turn back to Spit and his captor. "Officer! What did this boy have to do with it? Why are you holding him?" demands a woman in the crowd.

"Never mind! Stand back!" shouts the officer.

"Lemme go! I didn't do nuttin'. Whadda yuh want?" wails Spit.

"You're one of the gang who beat up a boy here today and stabbed his father, ain't you?"

"No, I yain't. I didn't have nuttin' tuh do wid it. It wuz a kid named Tommy McGrath."

"Tommy McGrath! Where does he live?"

"On Foist Avenya between Fifty-toid and Fifty-faught."

"Sure?"

"Yeah."

"Take this kid around there, will yuh? Get ahold a Tommy McGrath. He's wanted for stabbin' some guy. I got to wait for the morgue wagon."

A second officer is taking Spit through the crowd, promising to let him go if he shows them where Tommy lives. A G-Man crosses to Gimpty, who is leaning against the sand hopper, white and shaking.

"Good work, Mac," the G-Man says to Gimpty. "Come over to the office and pick up your check."

The Doorman has brought a coat belonging to one of his discarded uniforms. They lay it over Martin's body. "The murmur of the crowd rises high. A boat horn in the river bellows hoarsely and dies away."

The curtain falls.

ACT III

It is a very dark night. The gang has built a fire in an old iron ashcan and is roasting potatoes. From the floating dock below come the sounds of a gay party. The ship's lanterns at the gates of the Terrace shine brightly through the gloom. The lights in the windows of the tenement are dull and yellow and glum. The street lamp at the corner burns faintly.

The talk is still of the shooting of Babyface Martin. There is a good deal of disputing as to who first heard the shots and who saw the most of what happened. The gang is greatly impressed with what it has seen and heard.

"Da papuhs said dey found twenty gran' in 'is pockets," reports T. B. awesomely.

"Twenty G's! Boy, 'at's a lota dough!" agrees Angel.

"Boy, he mus' 'a' bin a putty smaht guy," says Spit.

"Babyface? Sure! He wuz a tops!" boasts T. B. "Public Enemy Numbuh One. Boy, he had guts. He wasn'a scared a nobody. Boy, he could knock 'em all off like dat . . . like anyt'ing! Boy, like nuttin'!"

Dippy has taken a stick from the can and is pretending it is a machine gun. "Bang! Bang!" Dippy has mowed them down, but Angel, using his kazoo as a revolver, wipes out Dippy with a single well-aimed shot. Nor can Dippy get any further action with his machine gun. So far as Angel is concerned he is dead.

Milty has rushed in from the street breathless with excitement. The cops are wise to Tommy, Milty reports, and the search is hot. The cops were at Tommy's house, but Tommy got out the fire escape, into the yard, over the fence, through the cellar and away before they knew what was happening. "Dey don' ketch Tommy so quick," promises Milton.

When they do get him they'll send him to refawm school. T. B. is sure of that. They sent T. B. to reform school "fuh jest swipin' a bunch a bananas. An' 'ey wuz all rotten, too, most a dem."

"Gese, poor Tommy!" laments Angel, dipping the potato he has found too hard back into the fire. "If dey ketch 'im, he don' git no maw mickeys like dis fer a long time."

"Dey git mickeys in refawm school, don' dey?" Dippy wants to know.

"Slop dey git—slop . . . unless dey git some dough tuh smeah da jailies wid," says T. B.

"Aw, shat up!" Spit is the disgusted one. "All a time yuh shoot yuh mout' off about refawm school . . . like yew wuz 'e ony one who evuh went."

"Yeah. Yew wuz on'y deah six mont's."

"Tommy'll git two yeahs."

"Tree, maybe, I bet."

"Gese, dat's lousy."

"Ah, shat ap, will yuh?"

"Yeah, nevuh mind. Yuh loin a barrel o' good tings in refawm school," insists T. B.

The Doorman has come to try to chase them away, but he meets with no success and a barrage of insults. Lettim calla cop. Dey'll mobilize 'im! . . .

Now Drina, frightened and desperate, has come looking for her brother. No one knows where Tommy is—no one except Milty, according to Spit, and Milty won't tell. Tommy said not tuh. Nor do Spit's threats to mobilize him nor Drina's earnest pleading move Milty until she is able to convince him that she must know where Tommy is for his own good. Then Milty agrees to show Drina.

They have no sooner started than Spit sends all the boys except Angel out to rustle wood for the fire. With them gone he leaves Angel to guard the mickeys while he trails Milty and Drina. He wants to find out where Tommy is himself.

A moment later Tommy has come from back of the sand hopper timbers. He's gonna get away where the bulls won't find him, he tells Angel. But first he's got something to do. He's gotta find the guy that snitched on him. He thinks it's Spit. But to make sure he wants Angel to tell Spit, when he comes back, that the guy what was stabbed was there askin' for Spit, so's he could give him five dolluhs fer tellin'. Tommy'll be watchin' from the sand hopper, and if Spit's caught he'll come out and put the "mahk a de squealuh" on him, a mahk, he pantomimes, that runs diagonally across the cheek. . . .

Kay has come from the Terrace in answer to a note from Gimpty. Gimpty is waiting for her. There is something he wants to tell her about the shooting of Babyface Martin. It was quite horrible to Gimpty. Even now he finds it difficult to talk about it. Seeing that he is emotionally upset Kay leads Gimpty to the edge of the wharf to find a place where they can sit down. A gay quartet in evening clothes comes from the Terrace, laughing merrily and a little foolishly. The yacht party, Kay remarks, is turning into something of a brawl.

A sailor has come with the Doorman to tell Miss Mitchell that Mr. Hilton is ready to cast off and they are waiting. Kay sends him back with word that she will be there in a minute.

"Kay, there's still time," pleads Gimpty, recovering control of his nerves. "You don't have to go."

"I'm afraid I do."

GIMPTY—Listen . . . I knew where Martin was. And I told the police.

KAY—You? How did you recognize him?

GIMPTY—I used to know him when I was a kid.

KAY—Oh!

GIMPTY—I know it was a stinkin' thing to do.

KAY—No. It had to be done.

GIMPTY—There was a reward.

KAY—Yes, I know. I read about it. That's a break for you, Pete. You can help your mother now. And you can live decently.

GIMPTY—How about you?

KAY—This isn't the miracle we were looking for.

GIMPTY—No. I guess you're right.

KAY—How long would it last us? Perhaps a year, then what? I've been through all that. I couldn't go through it again.

GIMPTY—I guess it is asking too much.

KAY (*softly, trying to make him see the picture realistically, reasonably*)—It's not all selfishness, Pete. I'm thinking of you too. I could do this. I could go and live with you and be happy (*and she means it*) . . . and then when poverty comes . . . and we begin to torture each other, what would happen? I'd leave you and go back to Jack. He needs me too, you see. I'm pretty certain of him. But what would become of you then? That sounds pretty bitchy, I suppose.

GIMPTY—No . . . no, it's quite right. I didn't see things as clearly as you did. It's just that I've been . . . such a dope.

KAY—No! It's just that we can't have everything . . . ever.

GIMPTY—Of course.

KAY (*rising*)—Good-by, darling.

GIMPTY (*rises*)—Good-by, Kay. Have a pleasant trip.

KAY (*one sob escapes her*)—Oh, Pete, forgive me if I've hurt you. Please forgive me!

GIMPTY—Don't be foolish. You haven't hurt me. It's funny, but you know, I never honestly expected anything. I didn't. It was really just a . . . whimsy I played on myself.

KAY—Pete.

GIMPTY—Yes?

KAY—Will you stay here and wave good-by to me when the boat goes?

GIMPTY—Naturally. I expected to.

KAY—Thanks. (*She kisses him.*) Take care of yourself!

Spit is back to report that Milt couldn't find Tommy. Milt's a lot of bushwa. T. B. has dragged in an empty fruit crate for the fire, which the gang proceeds to demolish by jumping on it. Dippy, the dope, has brought the remains of an automobile seat. He t'inks it'll boin. But Spit t'inks it will stink, and that's out.

The band on the boat is playing "Anchors Aweigh" and there is much laughter and shouting from the dock, a blowing of whistles and ringing of bells. There's a dame on the boat wavin'. Angel thinks it may be him she's wavin' at, but T. B. knows it's Gimpty. Gimpty stares dreamily after the yacht. . . .

"Hey, Spit," calls Angel, when the mickeys have been salvaged from the fire and the banquet is on, "dey wuz a guy heah . . . yuh know da guy what Tommy stabbed? . . . well, he wuz heah."

"What fuh?"

"He wuz lookin' fuh yew."

"Fuh me?"

"Yeah."

"What faw?"

"He said he wuz gonna give yuh five bucks fuh snitchin' on who done it."

"Wheah izzee? Wheah'd he go?"

"Did yew snitch on Tommy?"

"Sure. Sure I did."

A chorus of disapproval greets the confession, bringing Spit to his feet and on the defensive, if any of them want to make anything of it.

"Yew snitched on Tommy! Gese!" mutters T. B.

"Aw, shat ap, or I'll give yuh yuhr lumps," threatens Spit. "Wheah'd he go? Which way? I want dat five bucks."

Tommy has rushed from his hiding place, leaped on Spit's back and borne him to the ground, his knees pinning Spit's arms to the ground.

"Yuh'll git it, yuh stool pigeon! In a pig's kapooch yuh will! . . . Ah'll give yuh sump'n' yuh won't fuhgit so easy. Say yuh prayuhs, yuh louse!"

"Lemme go! Lemme go!" screams Spit. "Aw, Tommy, I didn't mean tuh! Dey had me! Duh cops had me! What could I do?"

"Yuh know whatcha gonna git fuh it?" Tommy has taken out his knife. As Spit squeals with terror Tommy slaps his hand over his victim's mouth with a muttered: "Shat ap!"

The gang circles the two muttering fearfully of what Tommy is going to do. Spit has begun to cry.

"Tommy, don't, will yuh? I'll give yuh dose bike wheels I swiped. I'll give yuh me stamps. I'll give yuh me immies. I'll give yuh dat five bucks. Ony lemme go, will yuh?"

"Dis time yuh don' git away wid it so easy, see?"

"Hey, felluhs! Hey, Gimpty! He's got a knife!"

Gimpty notices for the first time what is happening. He has rushed over now to plead with Tommy to stop being a crazy kid. But Tommy is not in a mood to listen. If Gimpty interferes he'll get his, too. Gimpty continues to plead soberly with Tommy. If he won't give up the knife, will he sell it? no.

"What's the matter? You a yellow belly, Tommy?"

"Who's a yaller belly?"

"Only a yellow-belly uses a knife, Tommy. You'll be sorry for this."

"Well, he squealed on me."

It is Drina who saves Spit. She and Milty are back after looking for Tommy and rush to him now. Drina is not afraid of the knife.

"Tommy!" screams Drina. "Give me that knife. . . . What's the matter with you? Aren't you in enough hot water now? Don't you understand what you're doing? Give me that knife!"

Tommy hesitates, but finally he hands over the knife and lets Spit up. With one solid kick he speeds the squealer on his way.

"I wuz ony gonna scare 'im," says Tommy.

DRINA (*grabbing* TOMMY *by the shoulders and shaking him*)— Listen to me! The cops came up the house ten minutes ago. They were lookin' for you. You stabbed some man! Why! Why! (TOMMY *turns away.*) Don't you see what you're doing? They'll send you to jail, Tommy!

TOMMY (*all the fight gone*)—No, dey won't. Dey gotta ketch me foist.

DRINA—What do you mean?

TOMMY—I'm gonna run away.

DRINA—Run away? Where to?

TOMMY—I dunno.

DRINA—Where?

TOMMY—Dere a plenty a places I kin hitch tuh. Lots a guys do.

DRINA—And what are you gonna eat? Where you gonna sleep?

TOMMY—I'll git along.

DRINA—How?

TOMMY—I dunno. Some way. I'll snitch stuff. I dunno. (*Belabored and uncertain.*) Aw, lemme alone!

DRINA—I can see what's gonna happen to you. (*Fiercely.*) You'll become a bum!

Tommy—Aw right! I'll become a bum, den!

Drina (*hurls the knife onto the sidewalk, and screams*)—That's fine! That's what Mamma worked her life away for! That's what I've worked since I was a kid for! So you could become a bum! That's great!

Tommy (*shouting back*)—Aw right! It's great! Well, gese, whadda yuh want me tuh do? Let da cops git me an' sen' me up the rivuh, Drina? I don' wanna be locked up till I'm twenty-one. Izzat what yuh want me tuh do?

Drina (*suddenly very soft and tender, maternally*)—No, darling, no. I won't let that happen. I won't let them touch you, Tommy. Don't worry.

Tommy—Well, what else kin we do?

Drina—I'll run away with you, Tommy. We'll go away, together, some place.

Tommy—No, Drina, yuh couldn't do dat. Yer a goil. (*Pause.*) Yuh know what? Maybe, if I gi' myself up an' tell 'em I didn' mean tuh do it, an' if I swear on da Bible I'll nevuh do it again, maybe dey'll let me go.

Drina—No, Tommy, I'm not gonna let you give yourself up. No!

But Tommy has made up his mind. When the Policeman has scattered the gang he gets away from Drina and goes to the officer. "I'm Tommy McGrath," he says. "I'm da kid dat stabbed dat man today. . . . Yeah, he wuz chokin' me an' breakin' mu ahm . . . so I did it."

Drina is hysterical and pleading with the officer. The Doorman is shouting an identification of Tommy. They have sent for Mr. Griswald to make sure. T. B. has sidled over to give Tommy a little advice about the refawm school. Let 'im look up a guy named—

Gimpty has succeeded in quieting Drina when Mr. Griswald comes, but she turns from pleading with the officer to him. Can't he give her brother another chance? He is such a baby. He didn't know what he was doing. Tommy adds his pleas to hers. And his promises never to do it again.

Griswald is obdurate. He can see no good in turning Tommy loose to attack others. Perhaps to kill next time. He will be better off where the law will send him. They'll teach him a trade. Let the officer take the boy away. He will be down in the morning to make the complaint.

Griswald is turning away when Gimpty stops him. Gimpty

would like to talk to him a moment, even though Griswald insists there is no use. With a reluctant "Well, what is it?" he turns to listen.

GIMPTY—You know what happened here today? A man was shot . . . killed.

GRISWALD—You mean that gangster?

GIMPTY—Yes.

GRISWALD—What about it?

GIMPTY—I killed him.

GRISWALD—You what?

MULLIGAN—He's crazy. (*To* GIMPTY.) What are you trying to do?

GIMPTY—It was I who told them where to find him.

GRISWALD—Well, that may be so. Then you were doing your duty. It's simple enough. And I'm doing mine.

DRINA (*hysterically*)—No! It ain't the same! Martin was a butcher, he was like a mad dog, he deserved to die. But Tommy's a baby. . . .

GIMPTY—Please! That's not the point!

DRINA—It is!

MULLIGAN (*to* ANGEL *and* MILTY, *who are back again*)—How many times have I gotta tell you . . . ! (*They retreat.*)

GIMPTY—Yes, maybe it is. Anyway, I turned him over for my own selfish reasons. And yet the thing I did, Griswald, was nothing compared to what you're doing. . . . Yeah. . . . Martin was a killer, he was bad, he deserved to die, true! But I knew him when we were kids. He had a lot of fine stuff. He was strong. He had courage. He was a born leader. He even had a sense of fair play. But living in the streets kept making him bad. . . . Then he was sent to reform school. Well, they reformed him all right! They taught him the ropes. He came out tough and hard and mean, with all the tricks of the trade.

GRISWALD—But I don't see what you're driving at.

GIMPTY—I'm telling you! That's what you're sending this kid to.

GRISWALD—I'm afraid there's no alternative.

DRINA—Are you so perfect? Didn't you ever do anything you were sorry for later? (*Screams.*) God! Didn't anybody ever forgive you for anything?

GRISWALD (*looks at her in silence for a moment. Then gently, and sympathetically*)—Of course. I'm sorry. I'm very sorry. Believe me, I'm not being vindictive. I'm not punishing him for hurting me. As far as this goes (*touches his bandaged wrist*) I would forgive him gladly. But you must remember that I'm a father . . . that today he, unprovoked, beat my boy with a stick and stole his watch. There are other boys like mine. They've got to be protected, too. I feel awfully sorry for you, but your brother belongs in a reformatory. (*To* MULLIGAN.) All right, officer!

Officer Mulligan has taken Tommy away now, Drina smiling bravely as her brother calls back that he is not worried. T. B. has followed after for a ways and then, not being able to get his information across to Tommy, he comes excitedly back. There's a guy in refawm school named Smokey that T. B. is eager Tommy should be nice to, because Smokey knows a lotta rackets fuh Tommy when he gets out.

"Oh, Mom, why did you leave us?" sobs Drina, scared and helpless. "I don't know what to do, Mom. I don't know where to turn. I wish I was dead and buried with you."

It is Gimpty who takes charge now. He has sent T. B. away and gone to Drina, putting a protective arm about her shoulders, and urging her to quiet her sobs—

GIMPTY—Now you stop crying and listen to me. Tomorrow morning you meet me right here at half-past nine. We're going down town. We're going to get the best lawyer in this city, and we'll get Tommy free.

DRINA—But that'll cost so much!

GIMPTY—Don't worry about that. We'll get him out.

DRINA—Do you really think so?

GIMPTY—I know so.

DRINA—Oh, God bless you . . . you're so . . . (*Breaks into sobs again.*)

GIMPTY—Now, now. You go along now and stick by Tommy.

DRINA (*controlling herself*)—You've been so awfully good to us, I . . . I hate to ask for anything else, but . . .

GIMPTY—Sure, what is it?

DRINA—I wish you'd come along with us now. I know if you're there . . . they wouldn't dare touch . . . (*Her voice catches.*) Tommy!

GIMPTY—Me? I'm nobody. I can't . . .

DRINA—I wish you would. Please?

GIMPTY (*softly*)—All right. (*They go up the street, his arm still around her, his cane clicking on the sidewalk even after they've disappeared from sight.*) (*Awed by the scene the kids*

gather about the fire again.)
ANGEL—Gese, whadda yuh t'ink'll happen tuh Tommy?
MILTY—Dey'll git 'im off. Dey'll git 'im off. Yuh'll see.
T. B.—Even if dey don't, yuh loin a barrel a good t'ings at refawm school. Smokey oncet loined me how tuh open a lock wid a hair pin. Boy! It's easy! It's a cinch! I loined one-two-tree, but now I fuhgit. . . .

The Doorman has appeared with a garden hose. He thrusts the nozzle into the ashcan and turns on the water. "The fire hisses, spits and dies. A thick pillar of smoke ascends skyward out of the can. It catches the gang's imagination.

ANGEL (*looking upwards, entranced*)—Holy smokes!
DIPPY—Whee!
ANGEL—Look a' dat!
T. B.—Boy! Right up tuh duh sky!
ANGEL—Right up tuh duh stahs!
DIPPY—How high ah dey? How high ah duh stahs?
DOORMAN (*turning back at the gate*)—And you rats better not start any more trouble if you know what's good for you! (*He goes in. The boys wait till he is out of earshot, then they hurl a chorus of abuse.*)
MILTY—Gay cock of'm yam!
ANGEL—Fongoola!
DIPPY—Nuts ta yew!
T. B.—In yuhr hat!

"Angel plays a mocking tune on his kazoo. T. B. sings the lyrics. 'Te-da-da-da-da bushwa. Te-da-da-da bushwa.' "

ANGEL—Ah'll goul him!
DIPPY (*laughs*)—Yeah. (*After this outburst there is a long pause. They watch the smoke coiling upward.*)
MILTY (*softly*)—Gee! Looka dat smoke!
T. B.—Dat reminds me—all a time at refawm school Smokey usta sing a song about Angels—"If I had duh wings of a Angel." (*They laugh.*)
MILTY—Angel ain't got no wings.
DIPPY—Real ones got wings. I saw it in a pitcha oncet. (ANGEL *starts playing "If I had the wings of an Angel" on his kazoo.*)
T. B.—Dat's right. Dat's it! (*In a quavery voice he accompanies* ANGEL.) "If I had duh wings of a Angel. Ovuh dese prison

walls I wud fly. . . . (*The others join in, swelling the song.*)
Straight tuh dee yahms a my muddah. Ta da da, da da. . . . (*A
passing tramp steamer hoots mournfully. The smoke continues to
roll out of the can, as their cacophony draws out to a funereal
end.*) Da . . . da . . . da . . . dum."

THE CURTAIN FALLS

CALL IT A DAY

A Comedy in Three Acts

By Dodie Smith

IN late September Philip Merivale, who had enjoyed a successful season the Winter before playing Bothwell to Helen Hayes'
Mary of Scotland, and Gladys Cooper, the English actress who
had been happily cast in Keith Winter's "The Shining Hour,"
combined forces and began a co-starring engagement in two
Shakespearean revivals under the direction of Crosby Gaige.
They opened September 27 with "Othello." After ten disappointing days of this they tried "Macbeth." A week of this and they
were through. There was little audience response to either tragedy.
It may have been too early in the season, though Shakespeare is
none too popular on Broadway at any time of year, or it may
have been that the handsome settings, in which expensive drapes
figured conspicuously, serving to enhance rather than minimize
the artificiality of the action, were a disappointment to playgoers. In any event the Merivale-Cooper Shakespearean venture,
begun with high hopes, was soon numbered with the season's
failures.

A few weeks later word came from London of the success there
of a new comedy written by the Dodie Smith who, under the
pen name of C. L. Anthony, had done so well with "Autumn
Crocus" the year before. This new play was entitled "Call It a
Day," and the American rights had been acquired by a London
producer named Lee Ephraim. Mr. Ephraim, bringing his contract
to America, sought a partner and found one in the New York
Theatre Guild, just then seeking a fourth play for its subscription season. This assured "Call It a Day" a Guild production plus
Guild prestige.

The result, as might reasonably have been predicted, was a complete success for both players and producers. Nothing more anti-
thetical to the classic repertory than this simple tale of a middle
class English family's adventures through the sixteen waking
hours of a single day could readily be imagined. But while these
were simple adventures, as reasonable and as wholesome as they
well could be, there was also a holding suspense in the potential

277

tragedies that might have happened. The comedy bounded immediately into a favor that held until it was withdrawn in early July.

It is eight o'clock in the morning of a day in Spring as "Call It a Day" begins. Dorothy and Roger Hilton are still asleep in twin beds in their house in St. John's Wood, a London suburb. The bedroom is pleasantly furnished, the decorations and furniture suggesting "the taste of people who have been married twenty years." Roger Hilton, in the right-hand bed, "is represented by a mound of clothes and a disheveled lock of hair." Dorothy, "lying with unruffled bedclothes and wearing a net bonnet to keep her wave in place," reveals "the gift of sleeping prettily—there is something a little child-like in the gentle relaxing of her features." Later the full light of day will show Dorothy as a little past forty, but at the moment the drawn curtains are kind.

Dorothy is the first to be awakened. It may be she hears the church clock strike eight. More likely she is waiting for a knock at the door that announces Vera, the maid, a pleasant young woman who comes now to bring a tray of morning tea and a copy of the *Times*. Vera already has had the Hilton terrier for a run and found the day very warm and pleasant, the first real Spring day they've had. . . .

It now becomes Vera's job to shake Roger Hilton into wakefulness. That is always a maid's job in the Hilton house. Vera, being new, goes about the task timidly, but manages it finally, Roger starting up with a grunt of protest. Vera's technique of shaking is strange to Roger. Not at all like her predecessor's. In fact, it is Roger's opinion that Dorothy should take on the shaking job herself. "It's very disconcerting to have strange females dashing at one in the early morning," he protests, when Vera goes to draw his bath.

Slowly the Hiltons take on the activities of the morning routine. Roger has moved into his dressing gown, protesting that he really should have been called earlier on so fine a morning. That would have given him a romp in the park with his dog, which, Dorothy agrees, would have been good for him, seeing that he obviously is putting on weight.

"You know, you women with this skinny complex are laying up a wretched old age for yourselves," prophesies Roger. "Stringy, that's what you'll be. Stringy and desiccated."

"Well, that's better than having two double chins and three double stomachs," counters Dorothy. . . .

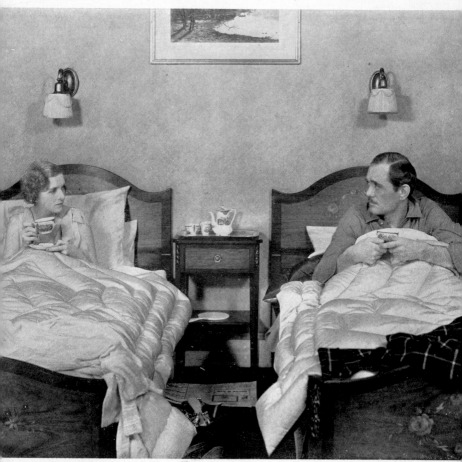

"CALL IT A DAY"

Roger, having been shaken into wakefulness by Vera, the new maid, voices a protest. He thinks rothy should take on the shaking job herself. "It's very disconcerting to have strange females hing at one in the early morning," declares Roger.

(Gladys Cooper, Philip Merivale)

Dorothy has adjusted horn-rimmed spectacles and settled down to reading the *Times* in bed when Ann Hilton appears. Ann is fifteen, a pretty girl and with an unusually intelligent little face. She has come to protest her sister Catherine taking the bathroom first and taking her time with it. It is particularly important that Ann should get an early start for school. She is worried about her algebra. Ann can't see where algebra can possibly have any use in her after-life—her after-school life. She would give it up, if her mother would let her, as she already has given up her science —so she would have more time to devote to really important things—like poetry. Ann is reading Rossetti at the moment, and is thrilled, particularly with the more difficult Rossetti poems, like "The Stream's Secret"—"I don't quite understand it yet," she admits, "but you can feel it without understanding it. It's lovely to read aloud."

Roger, in the bathroom, is singing noisily. His good humor suggests to Ann that he might be willing to shave in the dressing-room and let her have his bathroom. She manages the trade finally, but not before her mother has had a chance to take her to task, first for the condition of her nails, and second, for a recently developed tendency that verges on morbidity.

"I suppose a lot of great people have been morbid," muses Ann, having surveyed her features carefully in the mirror and decided that, like most young girls of her age, she is probably like a sensitive plant. "Rossetti buried his poems in his wife's coffin. But then he dug them up. Mummy, if I die I'd rather you didn't cremate me."

"Ann—you're not to talk like that. It's not a bit clever to be morbid. . . ."

Dorothy has returned to the *Times*. She is trying to retrieve parts of it a draught has scattered when her son, Martin, appears. Martin is a pleasant-looking boy of seventeen and he, too, is looking for a vacant bathroom. Cath is still occupying the second one, and is likely to be there a long time—

"When Cath's using bath salts she thinks anything under an hour's wasteful," declares Martin. It may be Cath's even fainted. She's been so "soppy" lately she might do anything.

While he waits, Martin would like to find out what his father's reaction has been to his going away with a young man named Alistair at Easter. Dorothy is convinced that Mr. Hilton will not agree. He doesn't like Alistair. But Martin thinks he will go any-way, with or without his father's consent. Now he has moved over to the window and is sitting on the sill when suddenly his eye is attracted. "Dear, dear, something very nifty has broken out in the next-door garden," he announces, smiling wisely.

"Yes, she's pretty," agrees Dorothy.

"Well, well. Frisking about like a young antelope. Girls are rather tripe, really.—Well, I'm damned! There's Cath sitting at the bathroom window."

"What's she doing?"

"Nothing whatever. Just looking completely blah. (*Calling.*) Hi, there! Come out of it, you batty-looking hag— (*Breaks off and draws back.*) Oh, my Lord—the vision next door thinks I mean her."

"Martin—really."

"My dear—she's glaring like old boots—not at all a bad-looking gawk, really. What a lark. . . ."

Catherine has finally come from the bathroom. Catherine "is just under nineteen, a really beautiful girl of unusual type, dark and intense and, at present, rather sullen."

"Of all the selfish, greedy—" Martin begins, with considerable vehemence.

"I'm not talking to you," snaps Catherine.

"But I'm talking to you. What do you think the rest of us are doing while you get stuck in a trance at the bathroom window? I suppose you think you looked like that Rossetti picture Ann's got over her bed."

"I don't look at Ann's pictures and I wish she'd clear the rotten things out. I'm sick of sharing a bedroom. There's no privacy anywhere in this house."

"So you thought you'd have a little privacy in the bathroom while two of us waited?"

"Oh, shut up. It's bad enough having you about the house without listening to you. One minute you're just a grubby little schoolboy and the next minute you're trying to be Noel Coward, and both ways you're equally disgusting."

"*Good* morning. There, you see, mother—loopy. You know what'll happen to you, my girl. They'll come for you in a van."

"Go and have your bath, dear."

"Right you are. Call father if she gets dangerous. (*As he passes behind* CATHERINE.) Dear, dear—all that time in the bath and her neck's still dirty."

Somebody should speak to Martin, Catherine is convinced. As for herself, she sees nothing wrong in her taking a few extra minutes in the bathroom. "My God, anyone would think we were at boarding school," protests Catherine. And she will not promise

not to say "My God!" again, either. Not unless her mother is
willing to make a trade with her. If Catherine can have the spare
room for her own, then she will give up the expression. She is
tired of rooming with Ann—tired of Ann's early morning reading
and her early evening prayers as well.

"No, Cath. I'm sorry, dear, but—"

"You're not a bit sorry," answers Cath sharply. "You're the
most un-understanding mother I've ever met. How can anyone
be so beastly on a lovely day when everything—everything—
Oh, God, how I hate this whole rotten house!"

Catherine has rushed from the room, slamming the door behind
her. Nor does she heed her mother's calls. Dorothy is troubled.
She admits as much to the shaved and dressed Roger when he
reappears.

"Really, there must be something wrong with her," Dorothy
is saying, still gazing in the direction in which Catherine has fled.

ROGER—Oh, rot. I tell you it's just a phase.

DOROTHY—It's not Ann now—it's Cath. I never heard such
an outburst. Just because I won't give her the spare bedroom.
(ANN *enters from the bathroom.*) Ann, have you noticed anything wrong with Cath?

ANN (*after a second's pause*)—No, darling. I think she's quite
all right.

DOROTHY—Is she sleeping well?

ANN—I—I think so. Skuse me, darling. I'm frabjously late.
(*She scuttles out.*)

DOROTHY—Roger, that child was hiding something.

ROGER—Rubbish. You fuss over them too much.

DOROTHY—But if you'd heard Cath.

ROGER—She's always had a bit of a temper. Why not let her
have the spare room?

DOROTHY—And what about your mother and your sisters?

ROGER—Let them go to a hotel.

DOROTHY—I'd like to see your face if I suggested it. What are
you doing in that drawer?

ROGER—Thought perhaps some of my linen handkerchiefs had
got in by mistake.

DOROTHY—Of course they haven't. (*As he takes one.*) Now,
Roger—that's one of the large ones I keep for my colds.

ROGER—Well, you haven't got a cold now, have you, old lady?
(*He grins and pockets handkerchief.*)

DOROTHY—What on earth you do with your handkerchiefs—

No, it's no use. I'm sure I oughtn't to give in to her. It's not natural—this longing to be alone.

ROGER—Oh, yes, it is—everyone feels it sometimes. (*He gazes out of the window.*) Well, I'm going to have fine minutes' run.

DOROTHY—Now, for goodness' sake, don't keep breakfast waiting on Vera's first morning.

ROGER—All right—all right. I'm only going in the garden.

DOROTHY—Did you try those scales? (ROGER *hums.*) I said, did you try those scales?

ROGER—What?—Oh, yes. The rotten things never were correct. (*He catches sight of the disheveled* Times.) My God, look at that paper.

DOROTHY—Oh, don't fuss. I'll put it straight.

ROGER—Like hell you will. No woman ought to be trusted alone with the *Times*.

DOROTHY (*battling with the fallen sheets*)—I should think very few women would want to be. Oh, run along and don't be late.

ROGER—You're in a very bossy mood. Look at the weather, woman, and relax—relax. (*He goes out.*)

MARTIN (*puts his head round the door*)—It may interest you to know that my bath was stone cold.

DOROTHY—If anyone else mentions the word bath I shall go raving mad.

MARTIN—Sorry, lady, but facts is facts. (*He closes door and disappears.*)

Dorothy crosses to the dressing table and looks in the glass. She finds the sunlight very revealing and gives a little sigh as she examines her face and strokes her throat. She takes her shingle net off. Suddenly she sees a gray hair, concentrates, pulls it out. Then in a matter-of-fact way, takes a towel and some grease. She is about to do her face when the curtain falls.

The Hiltons' kitchen, once Victorian, has been greatly modernized. The walls are painted white and there is a good deal of blue and white in the decorations. An old-fashioned range takes up a good part of the back of the room, a modern electric stove and kitchen dresser are at one side.

At the moment Cook, buxom and middle-aged, is getting breakfast ready. Vera is helping by minding the toast. Egg-cups are ready on a tray to be taken upstairs.

Cook is having trouble. Vera, being new, has set the clock up straight, not knowing that it will run only on its side, and Cook is late. Neither is Vera as much help as she would be if she were better informed as to where things are kept. She has some difficulty locating the "Sugar" canister for example. "Sugar's in 'Sago,'" Cook explains. "Sago's in that little old tin of Cadbury's cocoa."

Vera is cheerful about it. "I'll soon remember," she chirps. "At Mrs. Cardew's sago was in 'Mixed Herbs.'"

Vera has taken the eggs and bacon, the toast and milk upstairs now, and Cook is welcoming Mrs. Milsom, "a small, bird-like charwoman, whose invariably gloomy sentiments are delivered with a surprising briskness."

"Morning, Mrs. Hawkins," calls Mrs. Milsom, taking off her coat. "Treacherous sort of day."

"Looks all right to me," answers Cook, with some spirit.

MRS. MILSOM (*hanging her coat behind the door*)—Yes. It looks all right. That's what's wrong with it. It tempts people. They go leaving things off. There'll be some pewmonia about next week.

COOK—How's your husband? (*Getting bacon from oven.*)

MRS. MILSOM—Bad. He looks better and he says he feels better. But I *know*. Gone back to work, he has.

COOK—Well, that's a good job.

MRS. MILSOM—So you might think. But like as not he'll have to come home in a cab—if not something worse.

COOK—How do you mean worse? (*She brings the bacon to the table.*)

MRS. MILSOM—I said to him before he went, "One of these days you'll come home feet first." Is that a bit of bacon?

COOK—Yes. Want to make yourself some toast?

MRS. MILSOM—No, bread'll do. (*She settles to the table.*) I like a bit of bacon. Though I sometimes wonder at you eating it.

COOK—Why?

MRS. MILSOM—Blood pressure.

COOK—What do you mean, blood pressure?

MRS. MILSOM—You've got it, haven't you?

COOK—First I've heard of it.

MRS. MILSOM—You're just the right build for it. My sister-in-law's had it something shocking. Doctor told her if she touched a bit of bacon she might drop down dead.

COOK—Bacon's never done me any harm. (*She is about to help herself; then stops.*) What's the blood press on?

MRS. MILSOM—Everything. All the time. Do you get noises in your head?

COOK—No.

MRS. MILSOM—Well, you can have blood pressure without that. Do your legs swell?

COOK—A bit. But they always did.

MRS. MILSOM—P'raps you always had it. Lots of people never know anything about it till they has a stroke.

COOK—Well, you are a nice cup of tea. How do they cure it?

MRS. MILSOM—Knocks you off things.

COOK—What things?

MRS. MILSOM—Most things. Gets you down to skin and bone. They got my sister-in-law down to six stone two. Completely cured, she was. She's got anaemia now. You eating that bit of bacon?

COOK—I don't know that I am. But there's Vera yet. Oh, well, she can do herself some more. (MRS. MILSOM *helps herself.*) My legs have been bad this last month. Do you think I ought to see a doctor?

MRS. MILSOM—Doctors can't always tell. But you might as well. If he doesn't find that he may find something else.

Vera is back with reports of the way breakfast is going above stairs. A favorable report, save that Master would select the one burned piece of toast. And there was a slight outburst from Miss Catherine who, when her father was going on about his eggs, suddenly came forward with an "Oh, for God's sake, take mine! What does the beastly egg matter?" and went flouncing out the door.

Catherine's mother was greatly upset, but the Master quieted her in the cause of a little peace.

"If you ask me, Miss Cath's head's been getting a bit turned, having her portrait painted and what not," volunteers Cook.

"Anyone can have their portrait painted," suggests Vera.

"If they pay for it. But they're doing her for nothing. This man wrote to the Master and said he'd like to have the privilege of painting his daughter because she was the most beautiful English girl he'd seen for years. Susan happened to catch sight of the letter."

"Well, she's not my idea of beauty."

"He's a famous artist. The missus says it'll probably be bought for the nation."

"Do you mean she won't have any clothes on?"

"Course she'll have her clothes on."

"Well, lots of national pictures haven't."

"You're right there," confirms Mrs. Milsom. "I'm surprised at Mrs. Hilton letting Miss Cath sit for an artist. I cleaned for a couple of them once."

"Was it awful?"

"Well, it was and it wasn't. I'll say this for them. They wasn't fussy about the cleaning."

"This Paul Francis was at school with the Master. So Miss Cath won't come to much harm."

"What, because he was at school with her father? I don't see how you make that out."

Before the things are cleared Vera learns more of the Hiltons from Cook. The Master is an accountant—a charted accountant, which is different. And Martin just now is in the midst of his exams. Martin's going into his father's office after Easter.

The bell has called Vera to come and clear. Rings rather furiously before she makes headway toward answering it. "Gracious, what's wrong with them?" wonders Vera, petulantly.

"Fire engines, that's what they think we are," suggests Mrs. Milsom, sitting immovable at the table.

Cook drops a plate in the sink and philosophically slithers the broken pieces into the dust-bin. She is singing "I'm forever blowing bubbles" in opposition to the noise of the dishes as the curtain falls.

In the dining-room, which is pleasantly conventional, the Hiltons are at breakfast. Roger is reading the *Times*. Dorothy has a draper's catalogue in her lap. Martin is busy with a large pile of motor catalogues. Ann, having mislaid her algebra exercise book, is ringing the bell. Perhaps Vera has seen the algebra.

Vera hasn't seen any book. Ann's hunt goes on, growing more hysterical by the minute. Finally the algebra is uncovered in one of Martin's catalogues, and a fight threatens. Now the excitement turns to Ann's getting to school. She is late; she can't take time to eat anything more than a slice of bread and marmalade and the marmalade drips on the book.

Dorothy has managed to sponge off the algebra, and Roger has agreed to stop fussing about Ann's taking a taxi by taking her with him in the car, which, in Ann's opinion, makes Daddy an angel lamb.

"Roger! You never use the car in the morning," Dorothy protests.

"I feel like it today," calmly answers Roger. "Might drive back through the park. You don't want it, do you?"

DOROTHY—Oh, no. I'm spending the day with Muriel Weston.

ROGER—Rather you than me. Lord, how that woman talks.

DOROTHY—We're going to shop this morning and to a matinee this afternoon. And then we're going to tea at her brother's rooms.

ROGER—Didn't know she had a brother.

DOROTHY—He's been rubber planting for years.

ROGER—What matinee are you going to?

DOROTHY—A special show Fawcett's putting on. I want to see this new girl he's discovered.

ROGER—What, Beatrice Gwynne? Are you sure there's a matinee today?

DOROTHY—Why shouldn't there be?

ROGER—She's coming to see us about her income tax. But her appointment's pretty late. I suppose the matinée will be over.

DOROTHY—Rather small fry for you, isn't she?

ROGER—Fawcett asked us to look after her. She's got herself into some jam over her American earnings. (*He has been searching the* Times *as he talks.*) Oh, my Lord, Dorothy, this is a jig-saw puzzle, not a morning paper. Where's the financial page?

DOROTHY—It just may have gone under my bed. I'll get it.

ROGER—No, thanks. (*He rises.*) Cut along, infant, and get your things on.

ANN—Right, darling one. (*She goes out.*)

ROGER (*to* MARTIN, *who is immersed in catalogues*)—I should get a Rolls-Royce, if I were you. Why you should burden the postman—

MARTIN (*loftily*)—If you want to know, Alistair's mother has asked my advice about her new car. He's coming over to discuss it this afternoon. She may quite possibly get a Rolls.

ROGER—Well, if you could bring yourself down to our lowly state of life, perhaps you'd go and start the Morris.

MARTIN (*with dignity*)—Certainly. (*He goes out.*)

ROGER—I say, Dorothy, can't you do something about this Alistair business?

DOROTHY—But what can I do? He's a charming boy.

ROGER—Like hell he is.

DOROTHY—I really do think you're most unjust about him. His mother's one of my oldest friends.

ROGER—Now, look here, you know exactly what I think of Alistair—

DOROTHY—Stuff and nonsense. Just because the boy isn't rough and wild! He's an excellent influence for Martin. If you want to know, it's Cath I'm worried about. Roger, are you sure Paul Francis is all right?

ROGER—He's one of the best artists living, if that's what you mean.

DOROTHY—It certainly isn't. I mean—well, you know what his reputation is.

ROGER—Grossly exaggerated. You've met his wife—they're perfectly happy. You surely don't imagine—

DOROTHY—Well, Cath's behaving so queerly. If he were making love to her—

ROGER—My dear old girl, you're crazy. Even if he is a bit of a lad she'd be as safe as houses with him. I've known him thirty years. I was at school with him.

DOROTHY—Well, I was at school with Alistair's mother.

ROGER—That's neither here nor there.—You're just a fussy old lady. There's nothing wrong with the girl but a bit of temperament.

ANN (*entering the room*)—Car's waiting, Daddy.

ROGER—Right.

ANN—Do you know it's the most marvelous day. I feel as if something terribly exciting was going to happen. I'm psychic, you know.

ROGER (*gives a chuckle and then turns to* DOROTHY)— Good-by, darling, don't fuss. Enjoy your matinee. I wonder if that Gwynne girl will keep her appointment?

DOROTHY—Don't forget your paper.

ROGER—No, thanks. I'll get one that hasn't been woman-handled.

Catherine's back. The tea's cold. Could she have some fresh? Her mother thinks not. Breakfast's over. The maids have their work to do. Dorothy would like to know what's wrong with Catherine. Something must be wrong to make her so restless and discontented. It isn't Mr. Francis, the artist, is it? Sometimes married men—

"Mother, how can you? I think you've got a thoroughly nasty mind. If you want to know, Mrs. Francis is there nearly all the time."

"Oh, well, I'm sorry. But really—"

Vera has come to clear away the dishes. Catherine has dashed from the room, followed by her mother. Mrs. Milsom has brought in the Hoover. Vera is at the window.

"My word, it is a lovely day. Makes you feel quite different, doesn't it?" ventures Vera.

"There'll be a lot of folk feel differently before it's over," predicts Mrs. Milsom, with conviction.

"Oh, get along with you. A day like this does everyone good. Makes you feel you could do anything."

"That's just it. Puts ideas into people's heads:

"   'The first Spring day
        Is in the Devil's pay.'

You never heard that?" (*A bell rings.*)

"That'll be Mrs. Weston," mutters Vera, hastening out. Mrs. Milsom plugs in the Hoover and starts pushing it across the floor as the curtain falls.

ACT II

At 4.45 that afternoon Paul Francis, Ethel Francis and Catherine Hilton are in Paul's studio in Holland Park. The room, originally the studio of Paul's father, "still retains a rich Victorian atmosphere. . . . There are books, flowers, draperies—a varied and colorful medley, where two utterly diverging schools of painting have met and grown accustomed to each other."

Paul, "a handsome, florid man of forty-five," is at his easel. Ethel, his wife, sits knitting in one corner of the room. "She might be an old thirty or a young fifty." . . . "A close scrutiny would reveal that she is no fool." Catherine is seated on the model's throne, wearing a wine-colored silk dress with tight bodice and full skirt. "A very old olive-green shawl is draped across her shoulders. A book lies open in her lap."

Catherine is gazing intently at Paul as he works. She drops her eyes whenever he looks at her. He is conscious of this and cautions her against it. Each time she looks up it takes half a minute for her to get her face into repose again. He would have her read the book.

Catherine is tired of reading. She is, thinks Ethel, also tired of posing, although, as Paul points out, she just had a rest five minutes ago. Finally, in exasperation, Paul decides he will paint the shawl and let the face go. This is even more annoying to Catherine. She hates the shawl. It's old and dirty. She is not used to wearing things out of second-hand clothes shops. To Paul it is a marvelous shawl, and of great help to him in bringing out the exact sallowness of Catherine's skin—

"I'm not sallow," snaps Catherine. "It's just this filthy color near my face—"

"You're going to be sallow, my girl," answers Paul with conviction. "What do you think this is? Something for the window at Maison Lyons?"

Ethel has a look at the picture and approves it. She does not agree with Paul, however, that there is an expression in it that recalls a certain Tilly Marchmont. Paul had forgotten all about Tilly until he noted that expression—

"Wonder if she's dead?" he muses, as he works. "She was a violent sort of girl. Yes, I bet she's dead all right. God, wasn't she beautiful that first year—before she went and got herself sunburnt? Shall I ever forget it! Coming into the studio with her arms and legs dark brown and her body pale pink. The most indecent sight. (*He laughs noisily.*) Do you remember?"

ETHEL—I wasn't in that afternoon.

PAUL (*remembering*)—No. So you weren't. Lord, I was mad with her—at first. (*He pauses for a second.*) After that she tried to get herself brown all over and nearly got run in by the police.

ETHEL (*laughing*)—Poor Tilly.

PAUL—She wasn't poor. She was damn well off. She gave me a gold cigarette-case. Ethel, what happened to that cigarette-case?

ETHEL—I don't know, dear. I'll look for it.

PAUL—Tilly Marchmont. (*He gazes at* CATHERINE.) I'm getting it again now. Only the head, though. Cath's figure isn't a patch on hers.

ETHEL—I'm sure Cath's got a very nice figure.

PAUL—Don't be an ass, Ethel. You know perfectly well that these girls with slim modern figures look like the wrath of God in the nude. (*Remembering again.*) Tilly had damn near the best body I ever saw. I'd like to paint her again.

ETHEL—Do you want me to find her?

PAUL—No. She'll be past her best now—look like one of Renoir's boiled ladies. I wonder what happened to her. She *was* a violent girl. I bet she's dead. (*Suddenly.*) Hey, I've got an idea. Catherine, put that shawl right over your head—cover all your hair up.

CATHERINE—I won't.

PAUL—What do you mean, you won't?

CATHERINE—The thing's filthy. I won't put it on my head. I won't have it near me any longer. (*She throws the shawl down and kicks it away.*) There!

PAUL—Hey—you'll damage it. It's dropping to pieces already.
(*He picks it up, smooths it and goes towards* CATHERINE.) Now
look here, young woman—

CATHERINE—Don't you come near me with that thing. Don't
you dare— (PAUL *is about to put the shawl round her.*)

ETHEL—Paul!

CATHERINE—You're not paying me for these sittings—

PAUL—Paying you! I only pay people who know their job.

CATHERINE—I'm sorry I can't offer you gold cigarette-cases—

PAUL—Damn you, Catherine!

CATHERINE (*suddenly snatching the shawl and tearing it
fiercely*)—There! (*She flings it away.*) I'm going home. (PAUL
rushes to examine the damage. ETHEL *rises and crosses to* CATH-
ERINE, *putting her arm round her.*)

ETHEL (*very kindly*)—Oh, no, dear, you can't go like that.

CATHERINE—Yes, I can. (*She pulls herself away.*) Let me go,
please.

ETHEL—You've got to change your dress anyhow. And I'm
going to make some tea.

CATHERINE—No, thank you, really. (*Suddenly.*) Oh, I'm terribly sorry.

ETHEL—Nothing to be sorry about. Paul was very annoying.
Do sit down, dear. (*She persuades* CATHERINE *to sit again and
then turns to* PAUL *who is engrossed with his damaged treasure.*)
It's no use fussing about that. I'll get it mended.

Ethel again insists on going for tea, though Paul's protest is
ever so pointed. She has gone now, and taken the shawl with her.
She will have no more nonsense about that. For a little Catherine
sits quietly listening to Paul lament the loss of his lovely shawl.
Then she would stop his romantic imaginings about the shawl
and turn his attention to her. She is crushed now, and of a mind
to go home. She has started for the door when she turns for a
final plea:

"Paul, what *is* it? What have I done? I'm terribly sorry about
the shawl, but you changed to me last week—before you bought
it. What is it, *please?* I'll go mad if you don't tell me."

PAUL (*irritably*)—My dear child—

CATHERINE—Have I done something? I've thought and thought
—right through the nights. Oh, it's been so awful—I can't even
cry because of Ann hearing. Is it just that you're tired of me—

just in a few weeks?

PAUL—For the Lord's sake, shut up, Catherine. You're talking as if—as if something— Damn it, I haven't even kissed you. Or have I?

CATHERINE—No. You were going to when that wretched old tramp came along.

PAUL—God bless him!

CATHERINE—Paul—that morning on Primrose Hill, when it was all beginning—

PAUL—"It was all beginning"? Well, it isn't going to begin, Catherine. It isn't going on, anyhow.

CATHERINE—But *why?* What's gone wrong? It's not knowing that that's so—

PAUL—Good Lord, child, it's pretty obvious. Your father—

CATHERINE—So that's it. Just because you know father.

PAUL—It isn't all of it. I'm twenty years older—more than twenty years. And—though I hate to stress the fact—I really am married.

CATHERINE—I'm sorry about your wife. But she must be used to it by now. There have been lots of Tilly Marchmonts.

PAUL (*instantly reminiscent*)—Tilly Marchmont. She *was* a girl. She—

CATHERINE—Oh, don't keep talking about her.

PAUL—But, my dear child, if you feel like that—

CATHERINE—I don't know how I feel. I know you make love to dozens of people. It's hateful—but it doesn't seem to make any difference.

PAUL (*amused*)—I was afraid it mightn't.

CATHERINE—Don't you care for me at all?

PAUL (*overdoing determination*)—No.

CATHERINE—I don't believe you. You're just trying to cure me. That day on Primrose Hill—

PAUL—In my whole life I have only once been on Primrose Hill at seven in the morning and you had to be there.

CATHERINE (*intensely*)—Don't you think that was Fate?

PAUL—I do not. I think it was the after-effects of a studio party in Camden Town.

CATHERINE—Do you mean you were drunk?

PAUL—Certainly not. I am never drunk.—You see, someone at the party said that you could see the Crystal Palace from Primrose Hill—or you couldn't see it—I forget which. So on the way home I thought I'd go and find out. It now seems to me a very exaggerated interest to have taken.

CATHERINE—Oh, don't keep spoiling it. It was so marvelous. Do you remember—

PAUL—If you want to know, Catherine, I remember remarkably little about it. I don't even remember if you could see the Crystal Palace.

CATHERINE—Oh, do stop about the wretched Crystal Palace! —I'd been in love with you for weeks—but I wouldn't have said anything ever—I knew I'd got to fight it—and then, suddenly, just when I was thinking of you— (*She stops; a light comes into her eyes.*) Paul, you're just pretending. You couldn't have said those things if you didn't mean them. You're just trying to put me off for my own good—

PAUL—Catherine—for heaven's sake—

CATHERINE—It's wonderful of you, but it's no good. I can fight now I know I've got something to fight for! Paul, look at me. (*She goes close to him and looks in his eyes.*)

PAUL (*backing*)—You go away.

CATHERINE (*putting her hands on his shoulders and looking in his face*)—I'll never go away.

PAUL—Oh, my sweet child— (*His arms go round her. The door-bell rings. PAUL breaks away.*) Thank God! (*He mops his forehead.*)

CATHERINE—It was only the door-bell.

PAUL—It spoke with the tongue of men and angels. (*Seeing that she is advancing towards him, he waves his hands at her as if scaring her off.*) Tch, tch, tch—Ethel will be back in a minute.

Catherine is not easily convinced. She is quite willing they should tell Ethel all. Catherine can be violent, too, as Tilly Marchmont was, if that is necessary to get what she wants. Catherine is still playing the pursuer when Ethel's voice is heard on the landing. There is someone with her now, and the someone is sister Ann. Ann, knowing Catherine is there, has come to borrow a little money. She has just found a heavenly Rossetti print that she must have. Paul is interested in that. It must be a great bargain at four-and-six—though he doesn't remember a Rossetti "Woman with a hair-brush and a jewel-box and a monkey and a little glass house and the back view of a peacock," which Ann describes.

Ethel would have Catherine go home with Ann, now the sitting is finished. But Catherine is feeling much better and eager to go on. Paul finally declares the shop to be closed for the day. He isn't sure he will go on with the portrait at all. He may paint

Ann instead.—

Catherine and Ethel have gone and Ann has a chance to peek at Catherine's portrait. She likes it—rather. "I don't understand it very well," Ann admits; "all those little dabs. It looks as if—as if you were angry with it."

"Ha! Come away from it, you horribly perspicacious child," laughs Paul.

Ann is wandering about the studio, fascinated by the things she finds and quite overcome with joy when she comes upon a Rossetti sketch that Paul had forgotten was there. Rossetti had given it to his father, and now Paul would give it to Ann. She is quite thrilled at the thought of having something that Rossetti has touched, but this is too valuable for her to accept. Catherine thinks so, too, when she comes back, but Paul will not listen to their objections. He will explain to Mrs. Hilton—and the Rossetti is Ann's. . . .

Ethel and Ann have gone into the hall and Catherine has lingered. She would have a final assurance from Paul that all is well. He takes her good-naturedly but firmly by the shoulders and puts her through the door, and sighs with relief when the door is closed.

Now he would take his wife to task for insisting on leaving the studio to make the tea. Nor is he satisfied with her explanation that she thought Catherine was entitled to a few minutes with him. He will, he must know, have to cope with her sooner or later. And when he calls her irritating she demands to know what he would have her do? Have hysterics? She had used those up the first year they were married.

Suddenly Catherine reappears. They had forgotten to arrange about a next sitting. When Paul tells her that he has decided not to do any painting for a day or two she remembers that she must have left her handkerchief and starts looking for that. No handkerchief being found, Ethel goes to find a clean one, accompanied again by Paul's swift, dark glances of protest. Now, alone with Catherine, Paul turns his back on her and goes to the window. But she is not to be put off—

"Paul, please—oh, please listen," she pleads. "I don't want to be a nuisance. I know you're doing everything for the best, but— if you could just make me understand—if you'd talk to me quietly— It's so terrible not being able to see you alone."

"I don't want to see you alone," he shouts, furiously. And then, at sight of her face, his anger is softened and he would explain. He cannot meet her again on Primrose Hill, nor anywhere else. Not even the Zoo. A moment later he has weakened and promised to be at the Park Villages at 9. He would immediately withdraw the suggestion if he could, but Ethel's return prevents that. Catherine has dashed away in great good spirits, his promise ringing in her ears.

"I'm so happy I could die," shouts Catherine, running to the window. "Look at that lovely, lovely tree!—I'll go now—I won't wait for the handkerchief—"

But Ethel meets her at the door and hands her the handkerchief as she rushes madly past, calling back as she goes—

"Oh, thank you. I'll rush now. Ring me up when you want me. Good-by! Good-by—Mr. Francis."

Ethel, conscious of "the rather histrionic 'Mr. Francis'" and Catherine's exalted manner, goes quietly about straightening up the studio. Paul returns to his brushes to sort them and put them away, trying to whistle unconcernedly as he works. For a moment they continue with their work. Then Ethel asks quietly:

"Are you going to seduce that girl?"

"Really, Ethel!"

ETHEL—Because I don't think her parents will like it.

PAUL (*furiously*)—Then why don't they look after her? Why don't you look after her? Dashing out of the room—

ETHEL—What happened?

PAUL (*his expression both impish and mulish*)—You can mind your own business.

ETHEL—I see. It's like that. I was afraid it would be, sooner or later. (PAUL *moves round the studio*.) She's not nineteen yet. Only four years older than the child you gave the picture to.

PAUL—Damn it, I'm only going to have a talk to her.

ETHEL—I wonder if Roger Hilton will find out. I should think she's too excitable to be discreet.

PAUL—Of all the infuriating women—

ETHEL (*suddenly*)—Paul—

PAUL—What?

ETHEL—I saw Tilly Marchmont last week.

PAUL—You said she was dead.

ETHEL—No, I didn't—you did. She's not dead at all. She's lovelier than ever.

PAUL—Thinner or fatter?

ETHEL—Thinner.

PAUL—That's queer. I thought she'd get fat.

ETHEL—She's improved a lot. She was just going out to

Majorca. We've never been there.

PAUL—Fancy old Tilly getting thinner.—Same lovely pudding-face?

ETHEL—She's got more expression. (*There is a pause, while she knits.*) The Edgar Smithsons were in Majorca last year. We could go and talk to them about it this evening.

PAUL—No, not this evening. (*He rearranges a picture.*) At least— (ETHEL *raises her eyes and meets his glance.*) I'll let you know. (*He sits on the window-sill.*) Think you're clever, don't you?

ETHEL (*knitting again*)—I wonder if Cath will let me have that handkerchief back. It was rather a nice one.

The curtain falls.

It is 5.15 in the afternoon. Muriel Weston, "a pretty but over-plump woman of about forty," is just coming into the sitting room of Frank Haines' house in Jermyn Street. It is "a pleasant, rather attic-like little room," with growing daffodils in the window boxes, a comfortable sofa and a table set for afternoon tea. The furniture is semi-antique. Mrs. Weston's arms are filled with parcels. She is shortly followed by Dorothy Hilton, also loaded down with "the trophies of a day's shopping." Both women are relieved to have finished the climb up the stairs and ready for the tea that Haines, Mrs. Weston's brother, is to give them.

Haines, just back in London after five years on a rubber planta-tion, had rushed out for more cakes as soon as Muriel had tele-phoned, his housekeeper reports, and has not returned. Muriel and Dorothy have time to go over the day's adventures while they wait. The matinee they had seen was satisfactory, if not thrilling. The leading actress, a girl named Gwynne, was rather pretty and attractive. She is the one for whom Roger Hilton is doing some income tax work. Which, thinks Muriel, is probably all right, seeing that Roger is the "blinking marvel" he is, though she wouldn't trust *her* husband, who is subject to tropical reactions, in the same theatre with Miss Gwynne. Muriel has often won-dered if Roger can be as respectable as he seems.

Muriel has stretched out on the sofa, loosened her shoes, and taken to the sandwiches. Fortunately she is on a perfectly mar-velous diet. She eats as much as she can between meals, and then never really wants a big meal. Dorothy, shaking her hand to get the blood back into the fingers with which she has been carrying her packages, is suddenly aware that she has shaken off her wedding ring. Indicating that if she would save herself from losing it, which is terribly unlucky, she will have to have it reduced at once. To be sure that she does, Muriel, who has an errand at the jeweler's, takes the ring and promises to deliver it.

Now they have found an old photograph of Muriel on her brother's dresser. It was taken before she was married, when she had a waistline and wore hobble skirts. That takes them back a bit. There is also a picture of brother Frank. He is still ridiculously the same.

"He looks nice," decides Dorothy.

"He's a good old thing," agrees Muriel. "We used to be terribly fond of each other when we were kids. But somehow— I suppose it's because he and George are so unlike.

DOROTHY—Aren't Frank's reactions tropical?

MURIEL—Good Lord, no. Old Frank's the backbone of the Empire—dresses for dinner each night in his lonely bungalow and thinks women are on a higher plane.

DOROTHY—It must be dreadfully lonely for him out there. Why doesn't he marry?

MURIEL—He's going to, my dear—if I have to drag him to the altar. I'm going to get him all fixed up this leave.

DOROTHY—Does he know?

MURIEL—As a matter of fact, he's been a good deal more sensible than I expected. I've been paving the way in my letters for weeks. I *think* I shall bring it off.

DOROTHY—Who's the girl?

MURIEL—Dolly Walton.

DOROTHY—Oh. No one I know.

MURIEL—Of course you know her. She sat next to Roger last time you came to dinner. Fairish—a bit heavy.

DOROTHY—Oh. I remember. Not very exciting, is she?

MURIEL—Well, rubber planters can't be choosers. Dolly's not a bad old thing. Of course, she's a bit short in the wind and long in the tooth—but she's still got most of her faculties.

DOROTHY (*laughing*)—Muriel, you are revolting.

MURIEL—But, my dear—

DOROTHY—I could understand it if it was some charming young girl you'd found for him—

MURIEL—Good Lord, how am I to get him a charming young girl—sandbag her? He isn't even well-off any more. Besides, he'd be miserable with a young girl. He and Dolly will rub along splendidly.

DOROTHY—Oh, well—if they both really like each other.

MURIEL—Don't be funny—they haven't met yet.

DOROTHY—Oh, good heavens—then the whole thing's just in the air.

MURIEL—It certainly is not. The whole point is that they haven't met. I've fixed up three girls like this. As a matter of fact I've never had a failure.

DOROTHY—What do you mean?

MURIEL—The point is to get the thing so settled in their minds before they meet that neither of them likes to back out. Not that Dolly will be doing any backing out. She's had a new perm and a course of face massage. The old war-horse is going right into battle.

DOROTHY—I never heard anything so cold-blooded. Trying to force your own brother—

MURIEL—Dorothy, don't be such an idiot. It's just a matter of common sense—Frank needs a wife and old Dolly needs a husband—and how she needs one! She'll be thanking God on her knees—if she can still get down on them.

DOROTHY (*laughing*)—Muriel, you really are disgusting. I hope he jolly well picks someone for himself.

MURIEL—He won't, my dear. He'll never let old Dolly down. They're both coming to stay at Easter. I'll bet you I get their engagement announced within a week.

Suddenly Muriel is aware of the hour and her jeweler's appointment before six. She will have to rush. She is bustling into her things and collecting her parcels, but she has time for a little friendly advice for Dorothy, who, during the day, has confessed to a good deal of worrying—about Catherine, about Martin's going into the office with Roger—

"What you want's something really to worry about," insists Muriel. "It would do you good if Roger was to break out. Though I suppose it would do you more good if you were to break out yourself."

"What do you mean?"

"Have you ever thought of kicking over the traces?"

"No. Have you?"

"Have I what, thought or kicked? As a matter of fact, I've done both."

"Muriel! Don't you feel awful about it?"

"I feel damned pleased, when I think of how George goes on. But it's made me understand him better. People make a hell of a fuss over that sort of thing. But it doesn't really mean much."

"I couldn't ever feel like that."

"I believe you're shocked."

"Rubbish. But it's rather flabbergasting. Somehow it makes you quite different."

"It doesn't really. You try it and see.—I say, I'll have to go." (*She rises and begins to collect herself.*)

"I wish you hadn't told me just as you're dashing off. I'd have liked to have talked about it."

"We'll take our back hair down on it one of these days. It's all very ancient history."

Muriel has grabbed her parcels, and her hat, and is just rushing through the door when Frank Haines arrives, also with an armful of things. "He is a pleasant-looking man, a little over forty, with a shy, rather boyish manner." There is barely time for Frank to explain that his taxi got stuck in Bond Street, forcing him to walk, and for Muriel to shout back that she knows she does not have to introduce him to Dorothy, before Muriel has rushed down the stairs and the door has closed after her.

A moment later, as she pours tea and tries her best to put her host at his ease, Dorothy finds herself confessing that she feels they must have met before, because she has a feeling that she knows him. Frank feels the same, but is sure they never have met before. Certainly he would not have forgotten her.

"Of course," Frank is saying, "Muriel's a wonderful woman, but she's—well, not very imaginative. Just throwing us together like this—it might have been so awkward."

"Might it? Why?"

FRANK—We mightn't have liked each other.

DOROTHY—Well, that wouldn't have been very serious.

FRANK—It would to me. I say, have another cake.

DOROTHY—No, really—I couldn't. I shall have to go soon.

FRANK—Oh, please don't. I was wondering—are you fond of theatres?

DOROTHY—Very. Muriel and I have just done a matinee—a play called "Swift Contact."

FRANK—Was it good?

DOROTHY—Oh, middling. Not very convincing—two people meeting for the first time and rushing into violent love. It never happens, really.

FRANK—I think it might in certain circumstances.

DOROTHY—They'd have to be very queer ones. More tea?

FRANK—No, thanks. I say—I don't suppose you feel like another theatre but—couldn't we have dinner?

DOROTHY—That's awfully nice of you, but I've got to get back.

FRANK—Oh—I'm sorry.

DOROTHY—I expect you're finding it a bit lonely until you go down to Muriel. I wish you'd come along and see us.

FRANK—I'd love to. I'd no idea you were staying in Town. (*He knocks his cake on the floor and picks it up.*) I'm making an awful fool of myself. I'm not always like this. I—I think it must be relief.

DOROTHY—What on earth do you mean?

FRANK—I suppose I'd better make a clean breast of it. When old Muriel rang me up after lunch I—I almost felt like dashing under a bus— I say, you didn't loathe me on sight, did you?

DOROTHY—Good heavens, no.

FRANK—Of course, it's too much to hope you feel like I do— as relieved, I mean. But then perhaps you weren't feeling so bad. And then it's so easy for a woman—you can always back out.

DOROTHY—Back out?

FRANK—Oh, for God's sake don't think *I* want to back out. The minute I saw you— Don't quell me. I think I've gone a little mad.

DOROTHY (*flabbergasted but laughing*)—I think you have.

FRANK—It's the relief, I tell you. All afternoon you've been getting fatter and fatter and older and older—and, damn it, you're the prettiest woman I've ever seen in my life. Let's shake hands, shall we? We haven't yet. (*He takes her hand.*)

DOROTHY (*protesting*)—Mr. Haines—

FRANK—Oh, come— (*He is shaking her hand violently.*)

DOROTHY—Well, Frank, then—please—

FRANK—Am I allowed to call you Dolly yet?

DOROTHY—No one ever calls me Dolly.

FRANK—Muriel does.

DOROTHY—No—Dot or Dorothy. Oh! (*She suddenly realizes what has happened.*)

FRANK—Well, I shall call you Dolly. I say, you're looking terribly frigid. You probably think I'm taking a hell of a lot for granted. I'm not—I know I can't expect you to feel like I do— not yet. But surely you see it's a compliment if I put all my cards on the table—now, at the beginning?

DOROTHY—Oh, please don't go on.

FRANK—I'm sorry. I won't try to rush you any more. I sup-

pose you wanted us to meet just as casual acquaintances, but
somehow—well, it seems so damn hypocritical after Muriel's
letters—and I wanted us to be friends as soon as possible. Have
I offended you?

DOROTHY (*terribly distressed*)—Oh, it isn't that.

FRANK—I've been all sorts of a damn fool. You're sensitive
about the whole thing. I'll tell you what—let's drop it now and
tomorrow I'll hire a car—we'll go out in the country. I'm sure
we can get it straight if—

DOROTHY—Oh, stop—stop! I'm Dorothy Hilton—not Dolly
Walton.

FRANK (*quietly*)—Oh, my God.

DOROTHY—I've got a husband and grown-up children.—I kept
trying to stop you. (FRANK *turns away and goes to the window.
She watches him. There is a moment's dead silence. Then he
turns to her.*) I'm so terribly sorry.

FRANK—I can't even start to apologize.

DOROTHY—It's my fault. I was so slow. It was quite a natural
mistake—Dot Hilton, Dolly Walton—on the telephone—

FRANK—Yes. Please don't let it worry you.

Dorothy would, if she could, pass the mistake off quite casually. But it isn't possible for Frank to be casual. He is too hard
hit. He must go on with his confession. He's in love with Dorothy.
Nothing like this has ever happened to him before and he does
not know just what to do about it.

Dorothy is sure he is exaggerating. It is just because he has
been planning to fall in love, and because he is lonely. Does she
like him at all? Of course she likes him. He's Muriel's brother—
and, well, yes, she likes him anyhow. She is sure they could
have been friends. As it happens she is happily married—

"All right. I'll come and see you," he interrupts, earnestly.
"I won't be a nuisance. Half a loaf, you know."

"But there isn't even half a loaf."

"Then crumbs, my dear. I'll be grateful for anything I can get.
When can I come?"

With a little effort Dorothy pulls herself together. "This is insane," she mutters, worriedly. "Of course you can't come. You
must go down to Muriel's and meet Dolly."

Dolly! Frank has a mental picture of Dolly! He has seen a
snapshot. Dolly's fat, and probably has a face like the back of a
cab. He is not interested in Dolly. He wants to know when he
can come to see Dorothy—and the children—and the happy hus-

band, damn him! Frank is not normal. He admits it. He might insist on kissing Dorothy but she has gathered up her parcels and held them in front of her to fend him off.

"I know what it is," says Dorothy, a touch of excitement in her voice. "You're like Muriel's husband—your reactions are still tropical."

FRANK—I tell you I never *had* any reactions before. You've got a boy to cope with.

DOROTHY—I've got a lunatic to cope with. (*Her manner suddenly changes.*) Look here, are you talking all this nonsense to put me at my ease—to make me feel that this wretched mistake—that you don't mind?

FRANK—But I mind like hell.

DOROTHY—I'm desperately sorry—but what can I do?

FRANK—Let me come and see you—let me work this thing out my own way. Where do you live?

DOROTHY—Forty-six Beech Tree Road—it's off St. John's Wood Road. Oh, but you mustn't—anyhow, not till you've seen Dolly.

FRANK—To hell with Dolly! The whole thing was insane.

DOROTHY—Oh, poor Dolly! She had a new perm. (*She starts to laugh.*)

FRANK—A what?

DOROTHY (*through her laughter*)—A permanent wave. (FRANK *also starts to laugh.*) I know it's awful but I can't stop laughing.

FRANK—Just two lunatics. (*Still laughing, he has strolled round by the windows. His eye falls on the window boxes.*) Damn it, you *shall* have some flowers. (*He opens a window and plucks the daffodils.*)

DOROTHY—Oh, no—not your daffodils—oh, please don't. (*Through the open window comes the sound of a clock striking six.*) There's six o'clock striking. I'm going. (*She collects her parcels feverishly.*)

FRANK—There. (*He places the flowers on her arm.*) I'm coming this evening.

DOROTHY—No—really—oh, where's my hat— (FRANK *finds the hat and puts it on her head, where it looks ridiculous.*) We've both gone crazy.—I'll think about it—I'll write to you— (*For a second she looks at him, then crushes her hat on somehow and, clutching parcels and flowers, dashes from the room.*)

FRANK (*following her to the door and calling*)—Forty-six Beech Tree Road—this evening. At nine o'clock.

The curtain falls.

It lacked five minutes of six when Roger Hilton, in his office in the Temple—a large, somber room lined with deed-boxes—"a room that has been an office for generations but still retains a certain charm"—takes the last batch of letters from Elsie Lester, his secretary, "a neat, anemic girl of twenty-seven," and prepares to sign them. There is one more appointment on his schedule, that with Beatrice Gwynne, the actress, but the lateness of the hour would indicate that Miss Gwynne has forgotten it.

Roger is in a lightly restless mood. Spring's in the air and his partner is in Paris, where the chestnuts are out. Roger wishes he might be in Paris, but Miss Lester would remind him that there are also chestnuts in Regent's Park, though they are not out yet. . . .

The letters are signed, the day's work is over. There is still a matter of Mr. Hilton's aunts—he has promised, Miss Lester reminds him, to let them know about their investments. He has appointments all through the next day, and Miss Lester thinks if he would stay tonight until she got all the reports together for him to see he could have the next day clear. Miss Lester doesn't mind working late. She doesn't care much for pictures.

"All right," agrees Roger. "Look—we'll give ourselves till seven and then I'll run you home in my car. It's on my way."

The prospect is thrilling to Miss Lester. The next moment the desk buzzer has announced the arrival of Miss Gwynne. That's cheek, Miss Lester thinks. To come as late as this—

"Must I get her some tea?" she inquires.

"No—she'll gossip if she gets tea," decides Roger. "Come in with that letter when it's finished. It'll help to hurry her."

Now Miss Gwynne has arrived. "She is a very handsome young woman in the early twenties. Not at all a typical actress, she is more the accepted idea of an art student. She wears a black felt hat, a black cloak, and a bright blue dress."

Miss Gwynne's greetings are formal and pleasant, though she confesses to being in a bad temper. Her matinee has not gone well, and this matter of income taxes is none too soothing. It appears that Beatrice had, two years before, earned considerable money in the United States. She had paid a tax to the American government, and now she is expected to pay more to her own government. How can she? She has spent the money.

Roger decides that, considering her nervous state, Miss Gwynne should have tea and tells Miss Lester. While they wait for tea he lets his client tell him of her experiences playing leads to Sir Harold, who insists on doing nothing but his everlasting drawing-room comedies. Beatrice wants to play something real. This play she is in is real, but it is not going to last.

"I've never played a big love scene before. It's the most extraordinary feeling—almost larger than life. And then, suddenly, when Harold went all wooden, it was like a smack in the face."

"You'll get other chances, you know."

"I wonder."

"I'm sure. We get a good many actresses here. You're right out of the usual run."

"Did you think I was going to be all peroxide and ruffles—talking about the 'dreful income-tax man'?"

"Not exactly. But you're not like any actress I've ever met. I think you'll go a long way."

Getting back to Beatrice's affairs, it is Roger's advice to her that she sign the new contract Sir Harold has offered her, because sooner or later she will have to settle with the government and to assign a part of her salary to that obligation is the best way to clear it. Beatrice is still rebellious, however. She is fed up with Sir Harold. The fact that he is in love with her does not help, and makes Sir Harold look rather a fool. . . .

They have had tea. Beatrice is wandering about the room, liking it a good deal and finding much to surprise her. She is kneeling on the window seat looking into the court when Roger joins her. "I like it here, Beatrice admits. "You're not a bit my idea of an accountant."

"What is your idea?"

BEATRICE—Old and doddery, like a solicitor.

ROGER (*laughing*)—You mean a stage solicitor.

BEATRICE—Do I? Perhaps I do. (*She smiles up into his face. For a moment he is completely fascinated by her. He looks directly into her eyes.*) What exactly *is* an accountant?

ROGER (*pulling himself together*)—You come and find out. (*He goes back to his desk.*) Now, let's get down to these expenses. In New York: I suppose you lived in an hotel?

BEATRICE (*leaving her cup on the window-seat, she crosses and ledges on the side of the desk*)—Only for a bit. I was in a studio most of the time.

ROGER—What was the rent?

BEATRICE—I don't know. I didn't pay it. I wanted to share it but my young man wouldn't let me.

ROGER—What young man?

BEATRICE—The young man I was living with.

ROGER—Hm. (*Fully aware that she is watching him, he exhibits no surprise whatever.*) Well, I think we'll tell the Inspector you paid the rent.

BEATRICE—Oh, please don't bother to whitewash me.

ROGER—My good girl—

BEATRICE—Don't call me your good girl.

ROGER—Not suitable? (*He catches her eyes and chuckles.*) Now look here, Miss Beatrice Gwynne with the flowers in your hat. The Inspector doesn't give two hoots who you lived with in America, and neither do I, so you can just stop trying to shock me. The Inspector wants your money and I want to save it for you, so let's get down to brass tacks and think up some expenses.

BEATRICE (*holding up her hat with the flowers in it*)—Looks nice, doesn't it?

ROGER—Charming. My secretary will be delighted.

BEATRICE—Oh, yes—I'd forgotten her. (*She twiddles the hat on her finger, then puts it on comically.*) Do you like me?

ROGER—Yes.

BEATRICE—Good. I like you. (*She takes the hat off again.*) I say, I don't feel awfully like concentrating on this stuff.

ROGER—So I've noticed.

BEATRICE—Why not bring all the papers up to my flat this evening?

ROGER—Am I being invited to come up and see you some time?

BEATRICE (*a moment's pause and then she looks straight at him*)—Yes.

ROGER—Are you trying to make a fool of me?

BEATRICE—No. I mean it.

ROGER—Do you know it's exactly ten minutes since we met?

BEATRICE—That's got nothing to do with it. I knew after five minutes—less than that.

ROGER—What exactly did you know?

BEATRICE—Do I have to put it into words?

ROGER—No—I don't think you'd better.

In an attempt to recover his professional dignity Roger announces that he shall immediately turn her case over to one of his older partners, a dear old gentleman with white whiskers. But when he phones the older partner he has gone. Beatrice doesn't think Roger is playing quite fair. He has let her see that he is interested. He should have snubbed her before that happened. Is he really going to snub her now?

Roger doesn't know. However common such an experience may be for her nothing remotely like it has ever happened to him before. "Oh, my child—do you realize I'm just a stodgy, middle-aged, married man?" Roger asks.

"I don't mind your being married," answers Beatrice.

"That's extremely magnanimous of you—but—no, my dear, it won't do. I'll tell you why—"

Miss Lester is in with a letter to be signed. It is quite evident she is not at all pleased with the development of the situation, but she quickly retires.

"You were about to tell me why it—us—my kind invitation —wouldn't do," prompts Beatrice.

"Was I?" Roger is helping her with her coat.

"Well, go on. Why won't it do?"

"I've forgotten."

"Are you coming to see me tonight?"

"Yes, damn it, I am. (*He is holding her shoulders.*) And I'll make you give me those figures if I have to shake them out of you."

"All right. There won't be any secretaries barging in."

Nine o'clock is to be the hour. Roger is still worried. He thinks of his own daughter, almost as old as Beatrice. He never could think of her—

"Throwing herself at a man?" prompts Beatrice when he hesitates. "Don't you be too sure. You're behind the times, you know. Nine o'clock?"

And when Miss Lester is back again Beatrice cheerily gives her the address. "Forty-four Glenster Grove House—it's just off Cheyne Walk." She turns to Roger. "I always think forty-four such a nice easy number to remember, don't you?"

"Yes," answers the flurried Roger.

Elsie Lester is outraged. She has noticed that the nosegay on Miss Gwynne's hat was made from the scilla flowers she had that morning put on Mr. Hilton's desk. "Fancy walking into anyone's office and grabbing the first thing that takes your fancy," fumes Elsie.

"Very reprehensible character," agrees Roger. "There. Now run along and get some air."

"But your aunts' investments—"

"Oh, bother my aunts—why don't they go to a broker? I'll do them some time or other."

"But you said—"

"Oh, Lord—I was going to drive you home, wasn't I? Look here—get yourself a taxi out of the petty cash, will you? I've got to get home early—something I'd forgotten. An appointment."

"An appointment? Oh, I see—for this evening."

"Yes. An appointment for this evening. Good night. Get yourself that taxi."

Roger has left, and in very high spirits. Elsie, looking disconsolately after him, has gone to the window. She stands there pensively a moment—then she begins straightening up the office. There are tears in her eyes and she has taken out her handkerchief to wipe them away as she goes out of the room.

The curtain falls.

ACT III

The Hiltons' back garden is furnished with deck chairs, and there is a scattering of flowers, though the beds are not formally arranged. Now in a sort of pearl-gray twilight, the shadows are appealing. There is a high wall at the side, separating the garden from the "next doors."

In the deck chairs Alistair Brown and Martin Hilton are sitting, Martin poring over automobile catalogues, Alistair resting lazily, a pile of discarded magazines and text books by his side. There is some talk of their selecting a car for Alistair's mother. Martin's selections, naturally, are a bit skittish for mother, but Alistair hints vaguely that perhaps something can be done about that. Alistair is greatly interested in Martin, and a little anxious at the moment about his going into his father's office. Alistair thinks perhaps they might go into something together, he and Martin—interior decorating, for example. Alistair to take care of the artistic side and Martin to handle the business part. Alistair is sure his mother would "stump up the capital." The idea is interesting to Martin, though he had hoped he might get into something that has to do with driving cars.

In the house Ann Hilton is playing her concert piece, Henselt's "Si oiseau j'étais." Alistair is impressed.

"Queer how some moments crystallize themselves for one," he murmurs. "I believe when I'm an old man I shall remember this garden and that tune. . . . She's stopped. I'm going. Would you like to come out tonight? There's a marvelous film at the Curzon."

"The Curzon's a bit expensive, isn't it?"

"This is my party. And, Martin, if your parents are huffy about Easter you can count on me for expenses. Then you can snap your fingers at them."

Martin thinks he could not allow anything like that, but he might borrow from Alistair and pay him back when he is earning a salary. . . . Alistair gone, Martin is studying the catalogues when suddenly the head and shoulders of an attractive young girl appear above the side wall. "She is Joan Collett, eighteen and enchantingly pretty."

Joan has heard voices, and though she had intended coming in the front way, this will do. It is really Martin's father she wants to speak with. She had heard him setting his dog on the Colletts' cat that morning and she wanted to ask him to be a little more considerate. The cat is about to have a family of kittens and a shock just now might prove fatal to her. "You'd think a man of his age would have more sense," says Joan, adding, "It must be funny having a parent like that. Mine are both elderly—fat and tractable."

"Are they? Funny. I haven't seen them yet. If they're elderly I suppose that isn't their Singer sports that stands outside your house sometimes?"

JOAN—Oh, that's mine.

MARTIN—Good Lord!

JOAN—Father gave it to me.

MARTIN—How perfectly marvelous.

JOAN—I suppose it is in a way. And yet, you know, life can be very ironic.

MARTIN—How do you mean?

JOAN—Now I've got it, I don't really like driving it. It's almost unbelievable, isn't it?

MARTIN (*fervently*)—Quite unbelievable.

JOAN—You have to concentrate so hard. And you can't look at things.

MARTIN—Good Lord. I say—I mean, don't think it's the most frightful cheek, but—well, if you really feel like that—

JOAN—Do you drive a car?

MARTIN—Well, I drive our glossy new perambulator. As a matter of fact I did once drive a Singer sports.

JOAN—Would you like to try mine?

MARTIN—Well, of course I would. Wouldn't your people mind?

JOAN—Heavens, no.

MARTIN—I say, do come down this side, won't you? I'll find a ladder.

JOAN—I can manage if you give me a hand. (*He helps her and she jumps.*) Goodness, that was further than I thought. (*She flops into a deck-chair.*) I say, who was that frightfully good-looking boy sitting here with you just now?

MARTIN—Alistair Brown. He's my best friend. Would you like to meet him?

JOAN—I don't think so. I'm not keen on handsome men. There's always a catch about them.

MARTIN—Alistair's a marvelous chap. Frightfully brainy. I should think girls would find him fascinating.

JOAN—I shouldn't.—What are your sisters' names?

MARTIN—Catherine and Ann.

JOAN—Is Catherine the eldest?

MARTIN—Yes.

JOAN—I should think she's a bit haughty.

MARTIN—She's got a foul temper.

JOAN—I'll tell you something. I've been wanting to know you all most awfully.

MARTIN—Have you really?

JOAN—This is the first time we've lived in London. We don't seem to know anyone.

MARTIN—How rotten for you.

JOAN—I've been kicking about by myself all this lovely day. And just now, when I heard voices—well, I thought I'd pop over. Your dog chasing Silky was—well, a bit of an excuse. Do you think I'm awfully pushing?

MARTIN—Rather not.

JOAN—We used to have such loads of friends up North. It feels all wrong down here. I wonder if Cath would be too haughty to come to tea.

MARTIN—I'll jolly well see she isn't.

JOAN—I thought she looked awfully interesting when she was sitting at the bathroom window this morning.

MARTIN—Oh, good Lord—I say, when I was shouting at her— you didn't really think I was—

JOAN—Shouting at me? Just for a minute. But I soon saw. I was jolly disappointed because I was going to shout back, and then we'd have known each other.

MARTIN—Well, we know each other now.

Ann is back at *"Si oiseau j'étais."* Joan recognizes it. She put
in a whole term on that piece, too. And it is a lucky piece for her.
Not a thing went wrong the term she was learning it. That's the
time her father gave her the car. Martin is about to help Joan
back over the wall when she suddenly remembers that they, the
Colletts, are going to the theatre that night—to see the new
Cochran piece. As it happens, there is an extra seat. Her father
won't be home. Would Martin care to come? Would he? Martin
certainly would like to come. He'll call up Alistair and fix it about
the movie.

"Do you know, I'm glad she's playing that tune," says Joan.
"I shall remember it as long as I live."

"Why?"

"I told you it's lucky for me. Call for us at eight, will you?
It's an eight-thirty show."

"I say, are you sure your mother won't mind?"

"Mother's so jolly lonely she wouldn't mind if I brought the
dustman home. See you later," calls Joan, dropping down on her
side of the wall. . . .

Cook has come out with a pan of potatoes to be peeled. Cook
does not approve of this new acquaintance with the next-doors.
Certain to lead to borrowing and all that. They'll always be popping in and popping out, and Mrs. Hilton is not one to be popped
in on. . . .

Martin has dashed into the house to confirm an awful suspicion that he hasn't a clean dress shirt. Vera, having been out
with the dog, is back and full of tales of adventure with the bulldog up the street. Quite a nice lady bulldog it is. The Hiltons'
terrier has taken quite a fancy to her. . . .

Catherine, nervous and impatient, has come to suggest
Cook's hurrying dinner. She has a headache and she is planning
to go for a walk. Ann would go with her, if Catherine would let
her, but Cath prefers to walk alone. She prefers to be alone right
now, too, but Ann is of no mind to leave her.

Now Dorothy Hilton has come into the garden and Catherine
has gone quickly back into the house. Dorothy is in a most gentle
mood. She cannot even remember that Ann had been cross in the
morning. They are sitting in the deck chairs exchanging adventures of the day. Dorothy has been to the matinee and then to
tea with Muriel Weston's brother. He's coming to call this evening,

which will mean that Ann will have to do her studying in the dining-room, whether she enjoys that or not.

Ann, too, has had an exciting day. Her algebra was foul, but nothing could have been more exciting than her visit to the Francis studio. "I saw a picture and I didn't have enough money," recounts Ann; "so I went to Cath, and before I could borrow it they gave me tea and we talked, and Mr. Francis found I was crazy about Rossetti and he gave me a sketch—not a print—a real, original sketch."

"Mr. Francis gave you one of his sketches?"

"Not his—at least, it was his but he hadn't done it. Rossetti had. He knew his father—I mean Rossetti did. And—oh, Mummy, I can keep it, can't I?"

"Is it very valuable?"

"Only to me. At least—well, it may be a little bit valuable. But Mr. Francis said it would be all right. And Mrs. Francis said she'd talk to you. They promised me you wouldn't mind."

"Oh, well, I can't very well be ungracious to them. It's terribly kind of them."

"Then it's all right?"

"Yes, I suppose so."

"Phew! That was easier than I expected. You must be jolly tired."

Ann and her mother have a quiet few minutes—as quiet, at least, as Ann's chatter permits—and then Ann excuses herself. "I'm just going to write a poem before dinner," she explains. . . .

Roger Hilton is home, but he will have to be going back after dinner. "That girl—Miss Gwynne—her affairs are in an unholy muddle," Roger explains. "I've got to straighten them out."

"Do you mean you're going back to the office?"

ROGER (after a second's pause)—No—I'm going to see her. She was tired with the matinee today—she wasn't up to much. (He feels self-conscious.) By the way, you saw her, didn't you? Is she any good?

DOROTHY—Yes, she's rather remarkable. Queer and spasmodic, but full of feeling. Did you like her?

ROGER—Oh, so-so. Yes, she seemed all right.

DOROTHY—Funny. I should have thought she was a girl one would have very definite opinions about. Must you go and see her tonight? Frank Haines is coming over.

ROGER—Who is Frank Haines?

DOROTHY—You know who he is. Muriel's brother. We had tea

with him today.

ROGER—What on earth made you ask him tonight?

DOROTHY—Well—he rather asked himself. I think he's lonely. Roger— (*She stops.*)

ROGER—Yes?

DOROTHY—I'd like you to be in if you could.

ROGER—But I can't, I tell you. This girl's business is urgent.

DOROTHY—Surely tomorrow would—

ROGER—I can't put her off now—perhaps she can't manage tomorrow. She may be playing or rehearsing or something.

DOROTHY—I shouldn't think so. She's not in any regular run. Roger, I do particularly want you to be in.

ROGER—My dear girl, isn't that damned unreasonable? This chap can't possibly want to meet me, and if he's anything like Muriel I shall be jolly glad to miss him.

DOROTHY—It's so odd you going out like this. You never have before. I can always count on you in the evenings.

ROGER—Well, you counted on me once too often, didn't you, old lady?—Look here, ring up and put Haines off till tomorrow.

DOROTHY—No. I don't think I can do that.—Oh, well, I suppose the children will be in.

Martin hasn't found the shirt he needs and has come now to try to borrow one from his father. Martin would borrow the shirt in a whisper, from the balcony, fearing his voice may carry across the wall. But Roger has no idea of whispering and must know a good deal about where it is Martin is going and why. Dorothy, too, would know more of this quick new friendship that has leaped the garden wall. It is all quite embarrassing for Martin, but he manages it finally, and is off with a rush to continue his dressing.

"Roger, you'd no right—" protests Dorothy.

"Hey, hey, old lady—he's grown-up. You can't stop him making his own friends."

"You're always trying to stop his friendship with Alistair."

"Hm. (*Very pleased.*) Well, I'm not trying to stop his friendship with the young woman next door. She's damn pretty. (*He sits down, then half rises.*) Good Lord, I hope he's not taking one of my new shirts."

"I'll see to it. I'm going up. (*She turns on the steps.*) Roger."

"Yes?"

"*Must* you go out to see this Gwynne girl tonight?"

"Good Lord, Dot—what's the matter with you?" demands

Roger, irritably. "Do you think I'm smitten with her or something?"

"No. I hadn't thought of that." (*But she has now.*)

Mrs. Milsom has come from the kitchen. She is on her way home with a parcel awkwardly tied. Now the string around it has broken and an assortment of foodstuffs roll out on the ground. Roger would help her get them together, somewhat to the charwoman's embarrassment. They're just a few things Cook had left over. They'd gone to the dustbin if she hadn't taken them. That is Mrs. Milsom's explanation.

"Of course they're not fit for human consumption," she admits. "But I thought they might do for my husband."

She has gone now, muttering about the day she has had, what with the white paint started and not finished because of her back—

"A day like this lets you in for things," says Mrs. Milsom. And as she disappears she calls: "Cook's been rushing it, as you've all got fish to fry. Good night, sir."

"Good night."

The light behind the drawn curtains of the dining room goes on. A gong sounds within the house. Roger runs up the iron steps as the curtain falls.

Lights are out and presumably both Ann and Catherine Hilton are asleep in the pretty bedroom they share. It is 11.30 that night. "The furniture is simple, painted and rather childish." The beds are in different angles of the room. "Catherine's part of the room is bare of pictures and books. . . . Ann's has several little bookcases and the wall above her bed is crowded with pictures. These include several Rossetti reproductions and portraits of Rossetti, Browning, Shelley, Charles II and Napoleon and one of Leslie Howard detached from the others.

There is a sound of stifled sobbing. Presently Catherine sits up in bed, searching for a handkerchief. She is out of bed and by the window, her head bowed against the pane, when Ann sits up. Ann has heard the weeping and would comfort Catherine, but Catherine wants only to be left alone. Ann has also guessed the truth—Catherine's in love with Mr. Francis—and all Catherine's denying it has no effect. Neither is Ann impressed when Catherine calls her attention to the fact of Mr. Francis being married.

"That doesn't make any difference," says Ann. "People often fall in love with someone who's married. Lots of great people have done it. Perhaps you're going to be great, though I can't think what at. He likes you awfully, doesn't he?"

"Did you think that?"

"Wait a minute. I'll come over." Ann has wrapped the eider-down around her, scuttled across the room and jumped into Catherine's bed. "I think it's terribly romantic."

"Aren't you shocked?"

"You can't shock a person whose favorite king is Charles the Second," announces Ann, with conviction.

Catherine isn't sure whether or not she wants Mr. Francis to leave his wife and marry her. Catherine isn't very sure about any-thing except her own misery. She remembers the morning she met the artist on Primrose Hill and he said so many wonderful things to her. He would have kissed her that morning, if a beastly old tramp hadn't come along. Ann is awfully sympathetic, but there is nothing she can do. Unless perhaps Catherine would like her to write a poem about Primrose Hill. Poetry is such a help.

Catherine doesn't want any poems. Tonight Francis was to have met her and he never came. For two hours Catherine waited and waited. Ann thinks she should have called up to ask what happened. Surely, if Mrs. Francis knows about it, calling up wouldn't matter—

Dorothy Hilton has come, in nightgown and dressing-gown, to find out what on earth her children are chattering about. Quickly Ann jumps out of bed and gets between her mother and Cath-erine. She and Catherine have been looking at the moon, Ann explains, while Catherine industriously mops her eyes.

Dorothy shepherds Ann back into her bed and tucks her in. She has been wondering why neither of her girls had come to speak to Mr. Haines when he called. "Muriel's brother will think I've got no family at all," she says. There was also a telephone message for Catherine, which she missed. A message from Mrs. Francis—

"They're going abroad tomorrow—quite suddenly—joining friends in Majorca," reports Dorothy.

There is an involuntary gasp from Catherine, which the pro-tective Ann is quick to cover by distracting her mother's atten-tion to the Rossetti sketch, looking marvelous in the moonlight. Now Dorothy has tucked Ann in a second time and is going back to her own room. "Do you mind very much about the picture?" she calls to Catherine from the doorway.

"Oh, no—the sittings were rather a bore," answers Catherine, with an effort.

"We'll think of something for you to do, now they're off your mind. Heavens, that moon *is* strong. Now, no more talking." And she has gone.

There are fresh sobs from Catherine. And fresh offers of sympathy from the troubled Ann. It is a compliment, in a way, thinks Ann—Francis going away like that. It's his conscience!

"I haven't anything left—not even a letter from him," wails Catherine.

"Oh, goodness—I wish I could help," sighs Ann. Suddenly she remembers her Rossetti. Perhaps Catherine would like that. At least it is something Francis has touched. She is out of bed and has taken the Rossetti over to Catherine and found a nail for it above the bed. "You can touch the frame in the night if you want to," she explains to Cath. As for the vacant spot on her own wall—she'll just put Leslie Howard back in that.

"Oh, what am I going to do?" sobs Catherine.

"He's bound to come back some time," comforts Ann. "And he'll want to finish that portrait. Great artists never let anything get in the way of their work."

"But to go off like that—to get his wife to ring up. I'd have been content with so little—just to see him sometimes."

Now Ann has found a comforting poem, which she would read to Catherine to help her sleep—a poem by Alice Meynell—beginning, "I must not think of thee"—but it makes Catherine feel even worse.

Now there is a knocking on the wall and Ann has scuttled back to her own bed. There she listens for a moment.

"She's not coming," reports Ann, relievedly. "Wouldn't it be frightful if she found out? Cath, mustn't it be queer to be old like that and know nothing exciting can ever happen to you?"

"It must be jolly peaceful," thinks Catherine. "They haven't a worry in the world."

"Cath, if my Rossetti isn't any *real* help to you, I think perhaps I'll have it back tomorrow."

The knocking is heard again. Catherine drops the book of Meynell poems. Ann dives under the bedclothes. The curtain falls.

Dorothy has returned to the Hiltons' bedroom just as Roger emerges from the bathroom in pajamas and dressing-gown. Following a customary routine he picks up his watch from his bedside table and winds it; takes a cigarette from his case and lights it, moving about restlessly.

Dorothy, having taken the setting lotion from the bathroom,

is at her dressing table doing what she can with her hair. She
has some hope of making the set last a week.

The talk is desultory. Catherine doesn't seem at all upset about
Francis leaving her portrait unfinished, which, thinks Roger,
knocks on the head Dorothy's idea that he had been making love
to Cath.

"I never said any such thing," protests Dorothy, with spirit.
"The idea only passed through my head. But I should have known
if there'd been anything like that really—one can always tell.
I wish Martin would come in."

Martin has probably gone out to supper, Roger thinks, and
Dorothy is a fathead to worry about it. Which reminds him that
Muriel's brother had made a pretty late stay of his visit. Was he
very boring? No, he wasn't at all boring, Dorothy insists. And
she thinks Roger might have stopped in a minute when he came
home. Roger didn't feel like stopping.

"Tell me about Beatrice Gwynne," suggests Dorothy.

"Oh, good Lord—"

"What's the matter?"

"Can't you let the girl drop?"

"What on earth do you mean? I'm simply taking a normal
interest in—"

"Normal my foot. You've been one mass of suspicion ever
since I first mentioned her."

"Well, I'm damned. Of all the idiots. If you want to put
thoughts into my mind—"

"Can you honestly tell me you haven't had your teeth into
Beatrice Gwynne since the first minute you knew I was going to
see her?"

"Certainly I can."

"Then you're not even a very good liar."

"Roger!—Look here, this is getting rather ridiculous, isn't it?
Let's not shout. I'll be perfectly honest with you. I did think it
was a bit queer when you absolutely refused to cancel your appointment with her—"

"You did?"

"But I wasn't suspicious—not really suspicious. I'm sorry if I
gave you that impression."

"Oh, don't apologize."

"Though I'm damned if I know why you should get savage
about it unless—"

"Unless there was something in it. Go on, say it."

"Stop putting words into my mouth. What's the matter with

you? I've told you I'm sorry if I seemed suspicious. I've never been suspicious before."

Dorothy has gone back to her dressing table. Roger, quite unhappy, continues to pace the room and try to explain. He is not very good at that sort of thing, he confesses. He may improve with practice, thinks Dorothy. Of course he knows, she says, that Miss Gwynne is young enough to be his daughter. Probably he agrees a man is as old as he feels, and he felt jolly young.

If he did, he feels damned old now, Roger admits. He is also convinced that Miss Gwynne is different. Theirs was not a flirtation—

Dorothy has her own ideas as to that. She also thinks it pretty beastly of Roger standing there trying to justify such a girl.

"Roger, will you tell me at once what happened?" Dorothy demands, finally.

"Nothing happened. But it wasn't a flirtation."

DOROTHY—Then what was it?

ROGER—I don't know. She's not a girl you can flirt with. There's something ruthless about her. I think she'll be a great actress one day.

DOROTHY—What on earth's that got to do with it? You say nothing happened—

ROGER—As a matter of fact Harold Fawcett turned up about ten o'clock.

DOROTHY—And if he hadn't?

ROGER—I don't know.

DOROTHY (*returning to her hair savagely*)—Well, you can find out. There'll be plenty of other evenings.

ROGER—Dot—

DOROTHY—Why are you telling me all this? Are you getting some sort of kick out of it?

ROGER—Oh, good Lord! I'm sorry. You asked me to tell you.

DOROTHY—You seemed to want to. I didn't know you were just wanting to justify yourself—just gloating over the whole thing.

ROGER—Oh, hell—do I look as if I'm gloating? You're taking it all too seriously.

DOROTHY—I see. You just wanted me to pat you on the back. You'd like me to be the sort of wife who was amused at her husband having affairs—who had affairs herself. (*Turning round to him suddenly.*) Well, if you would—

ROGER—What the hell do you mean?

DOROTHY—If you want to know—I've had an offer, too.

ROGER—A what?

DOROTHY—An offer. There's someone who—well, someone who—

ROGER (*bursting into laughter*)—Great jumping Jehoshaphat—has this what's-his-name been holding your hand all evening.

DOROTHY—There's nothing whatever to laugh at. It's a very serious matter.

ROGER—Fell in love with you at first sight I suppose?

DOROTHY—It was an accident.

ROGER (*laughing*)—Ha.

DOROTHY—He mistook me for someone else. It's a long and very sad story and I haven't the slightest intention of telling you about it.

ROGER—Thank you very much. Am I to understand that this —oh, what the hell is his name?

DOROTHY—Frank Haines.

ROGER—What a damn ridiculous name. Is this Haines proposing you should help him to enjoy his leave?

DOROTHY—It's nothing like that at all. He wants to marry me. The whole thing's on a different level from your beastly little intrigue.

ROGER—Oh, quite, quite. Ever so high-minded. Just proposing to break up a man's home.

DOROTHY—He's not, I tell you. The whole thing's terribly sad. I sent him away—

ROGER—But you could whistle him back. Let me tell you that if he ever sets foot in this house—

DOROTHY—He's setting foot in it next Saturday. He's coming to dinner.

ROGER—My God, of all the outrageous women! What would you say if I asked Beatrice Gwynne here? What would anyone say of a man who brought his lady friend into the house—

DOROTHY—But Frank isn't my lady friend—I mean he's not my gentleman friend— (ROGER *roars with laughter*.) Oh, yes, you can laugh. I've done nothing I'm ashamed of. The thing's a tragedy for Frank and I'm going to do everything I can to help him. I want him to meet the children.

ROGER—Well, for utter indecency, give me the high-minded.

Thoroughly enraged, Dorothy has jerked the bottle of setting lotion in Roger's direction. Suddenly he claps a hand over his eye and snorts with pain. Immediately she is solicitous, but in an

effort to have a look at the eye she, still clutching the setting
lotion, dashes some in Roger's other eye. Now there *is* excitement. In the midst of which young Martin bursts into the room.

Roger and Dorothy are able to compose themselves at sight of
their son, who reports a marvelous evening and is prepared to
announce to his father that he has decided to stay at home Easter.
Old Alistair will probably be pretty sick over it, but Martin will
be staying around to drive Joan's car.

Now Martin has dashed off to bed and Roger and Dorothy
return to their discussion. But the lash and sting have gone out
of it. Dorothy is near tears as she tries to complete the application of the setting lotion. Roger hovers about uncertainly, not
knowing just how to go on—

"Dot!" he begins.

"It's all so damned silly," Dorothy interrupts. "You can do
what you like about the Gwynne girl. I shall just call on the
neighbors and preside over the family picnics."

ROGER—Oh, my dear. (*He goes to her, sees she is still holding
the setting lotion, and takes it firmly away.*) I don't want to do
anything about the damn girl. I started by telling you I'd made
a fool of myself.

DOROTHY—If you want to go on with it—

ROGER—Do you seriously think I should have told you about
it if I'd been going on?

DOROTHY—You might. We do tell each other things. It's no
use just forcing yourself to give her up.

ROGER—There's no forcing. I don't see myself looking the kind
of fool old Fawcett looked. You know, it's queer, Dot, she *is*
interesting and unusual—this afternoon I felt as if I must get to
know her better. I could have sworn there was something to know.
But—I knew everything essential about her in that first ten
minutes.

DOROTHY—How do you mean?

ROGER—She'll never give anyone anything, unless it's through
her art. One can watch that. (*There is a shade of wistfulness in
his tone.*)

DOROTHY—Let's go to bed, shall we? I still feel a bit feminine
and idiotic about her. (*She is putting on her little net bonnet.*)

ROGER—And how about your Frank Haines?

DOROTHY—That's different. I knew all the time he never really
threatened you.

ROGER—And you think this girl really threatened you?

DOROTHY—I don't want to think about it. Is your eye better?

ROGER—Yes. Both of them.

DOROTHY—Are you ready for bed? (*She puts the main light out, leaving only the bedside light.*)

ROGER—You're a queer woman. Don't you want to have it all out?

DOROTHY—Some time perhaps. Not now. I just want to think. Is the window open?

ROGER (*crosses to the window*)—Good Lord! There's that new girl of ours. She's got Terry out.

DOROTHY—At this time of night? (*She joins him at the window.*)

ROGER—She's talking to someone.

DOROTHY—It's that manservant at the corner house.

ROGER—Shall I shout? Terry's shivering. It's turned damned cold.

DOROTHY—She's coming now. Oh, dear, I shall have to speak to her in the morning. I don't believe she'll do. (*She gets into bed.*)

ROGER (*leaving the curtains undrawn and crossing to his bed*)—I say, something's struck me. We've been married twenty years, haven't we?

DOROTHY—Yes.

ROGER—And this is the first time either of us has—how did you put it?—had an offer.

DOROTHY—As far as I know.

ROGER—And we've both handed it to each other on a plate within ten minutes of being alone. We shan't do very well as a dashing, modern couple. (*He sees that* DOROTHY *is lying back in bed, quietly crying.*) Hi, Dot.

DOROTHY—It's nothing. I'm just tired. I'll tell Frank I can't see him again. It'll be kinder in the end. I believe you'd have liked him.

ROGER—Like hell, I should. (*He gets into bed, throwing the eiderdown off.*)

DOROTHY—Those children are talking again. Thump, will you?

ROGER (*thumps on the wall*)—Funny kids.

DOROTHY—Thank goodness we've made a happy life for them. They've no problems or difficulties. (*She suddenly sits up in bed.*) Roger, I've a feeling I would like to talk this out—to get it all straight between us.

ROGER—All right, old lady. We'll have it all out on the mat. But not now. Let's chuck it for tonight. All right?

Dorothy—All right. (Roger *turns the bedside light out, then lies down. There is a faint light from the window.*)

Roger—Where's that damned eiderdown?

Dorothy—Funny turning so cold after such a lovely day.

Roger (*pulling the eiderdown on*)—It was just a fluke. We shall be back to normal again tomorrow. Good night. (*He lies down.*)

Dorothy—Good night.

(Roger *suddenly stretches his hand across to* Dorothy. *She takes it. He gives her hand a little squeeze and relinquishes it quickly. Outside, a clock begins to strike midnight.*)

THE CURTAIN FALLS

ETHAN FROME

A Drama in Three Acts

BY OWEN DAVIS AND DONALD DAVIS

(Suggested by a previous dramatization by Lowell Barrington)

A PLAY version of Edith Wharton's story of the north of New England, "Ethan Frome," was made some years back by Lowell Barrington and frequently threatened with production by Jed Harris. Its production was many times delayed and finally abandoned. Owen Davis took over the play from Mr. Harris, drafted his son Donald as a collaborator, and completed a new version which was later acquired by Max Gordon.

The Davis version, handicapped by the suspicions of those theatre experts who are quick to insist that no novel can ever be brought to the stage with complete success, was produced in January and immediately put its critics on the defensive by becoming one of the season's plays most enthusiastically received by its first audiences in both Philadelphia and New York.

The Davises have not hesitated to transfer the whole somewhat depressing and tragic atmosphere of "Ethan Frome" to the stage. Boldly they have begun their play with a prologue that, in effect, forecasts the story's conclusion, technically a risky thing to do. But so genuine is their feeling for both story and characters, and so absorbing the fidelity with which the tragic tale has been translated in stage terms, that audience reaction has been consistently favorable. The play is an expansion rather than a contraction of the novel, the Davises being compelled to supply a good deal, particularly in the matter of dialogue and the filling in of suggested situations, that Mrs. Wharton left to the imaginations of her story's devoted readers.

Analyzing the three characters chiefly concerned with the tragedy, Ethan and Zenobia Frome and Mattie Silver, Zenobia's poor relation, Brooks Atkinson has written: "They lived out the Winter with the grave resignation of animals. They hibernated within themselves and concealed their thoughts under chilly exteriors. They were not a community of jolly comrades; the cold air, like a sculptor's chisel, cut them into wind-bitten individuals,

321

tight-lipped, gaunt and solitary."

Only a fine feeling for human drama, backed by an exceptional setting, could have achieved the success which followed the production of "Ethan Frome." Jo Mielziner designed the scenery, bringing the realities of a northern New England Winter so vividly to the audience that there was but little strain upon its imagination.

It is dusk of a Winter evening as the play opens. The scene is the bleak, cold, shabby exterior of the Frome farm house near Starkville in Northern New England. The house stands in deep shadow. The pale yellow light of a coal-oil lamp inside the house outlines window and closed doorway. The dooryard is barren and snow-covered, and in one corner the headstones of the private Frome burial ground can be seen reaching above the drifts.

Presently two men appear around the corner of the house. One is Herman Gow, neighbor. The other, a younger man, is a stranger. They have come, at Gow's suggestion, to ask Ethan to drive the stranger over to the railway station at Corbury. It seems reasonable to Gow that Ethan will be glad to take on the chore, if there's a dollar to be earned.

"Don't be surprised if Ethan don't ask you in," warns Gow. "He don't's a rule. He don't mean anythin' by it. It's just his way. Things ain't gone any too well with them in there, you know—an' I guess Ethan likes to keep his troubles pretty well to himself."

Ethan comes to the door in answer to their knock. "He is not much over fifty . . . the ruin of a once powerful man, though still a striking figure. His face is scarred, there is a huge deep gash across his forehead, and his right side is so warped that each step he takes costs him a visible effort. There is something terribly bleak and unapproachable in his face . . . and he is so stiffened and grizzled that he might easily be taken for a much older man. He moves away from the doorway, his lameness checking each step he takes."

The stranger has explained his errand and his hope that Ethan will drive him to Corbury. Ethan is not greatly interested—thinks they'd better try Eady's livery—until he hears the young man say he expects to pay, probably a dollar for the round trip. Then he decides to do it.

Ethan has gone for his coat. Gow and the young man are moving toward the barn to start hitchin' up the sleigh. "This place never was wuth much," Gow is saying, "but before anythin' happened to Ethan he kind've choked a livin' out of it somehow . . .

I don't just see how he gets along now."

"What happened to him?"

"Don't know much about it." The Gow tone is short.

"After I'd seen him yesterday . . . I asked the people around the post-office," continues the young man, a note of exasperation creeping into his voice. "Everybody knew who he was all right . . . but nobody would tell me anything about it."

"A-yeah . . . Well, it was more'n twenty years ago . . . an' I remember at the time . . . old Mrs. Hale tryin' to find out about it from Zeena . . . but she didn't get very far, an' Zeena's Ethan's wife! An' Ethan . . . well . . . he knows all right. (*He adds abruptly.*) But I wouldn't never ask him . . . an' from that day to this he ain't's much's mentioned it."

They have disappeared. Shortly Ethan comes from the house, bundled in hat and coat and carrying a lighted lantern. As he shuffles across the yard there is the sound of the door bolt being thrust back into place inside the house. The lights fade gradually as the curtain falls.

ACT I

The time is twenty years before the close of the prologue. The scene is the kitchen of the Frome house, "a bleak and cold-looking place with an atmosphere of sordid poverty."

There are two stoves in the room, a square wood-burning stove for cooking and a "Fancy Hero" wood-burning stove to help keep the house warm in Winter. An unpainted dish cupboard, a kitchen table and chairs, a rocker and a geranium plant or two by way of decoration.

Ethan Frome, now a slim, powerfully-built New Englander of twenty-eight or thereabouts, comes shortly from the yard with an armful of fire logs. Carrying these to the stove he proceeds to split them into kindling and toss them into the woodbin.

Presently Zeena Frome comes down the stairway into the room. Zeena is wearing a shapeless, nondescript calico dress. "She could obviously never have been anything but a rather drab, humorless woman . . . but long years of many indescribable maladies . . . or of chronic hyperchondria . . . or possibly both . . . and we find Zeena tired, sickly, and seemingly ageless . . . at thirty-two."

Zeena pays not the slightest attention to Ethan. She moves toward the rocker with some effort, and when she is settled speaks in a whining monotone. Her complaint is against Ethan for not having fixed a window in the spare room, though she's spoken about it perhaps a dozen times. Zeena would fix it herself if she had the stren'th, but—

With a slightly savage toss of the last stick of kindling into the bin Ethan has run upstairs and is presently heard tampering with the window. Zeena stops rocking, moves over to the cupboard, selects one from a long row of medicine bottles and pours herself a dose of brown liquid. By the time Ethan comes down she is sipping a cup of hot water and reading a mail-order catalogue.

An Energex Vibrator interests Zeena most in the catalogue. It is "beneficial in the treatment of inflammatory conditions . . . and all deep-seated complaints," she reads, and can be had for twenty-two ninety-five. Zeena has been "awful set on easin' her pains a mite with one of them things," but Ethan isn't paying any attention to her complaint.

"I was sayin' I only wisht you'd get me one of them Energex Vibrators," Zeena repeats. "You could get it all right, Ethan, if you was a mind to . . . and if my complaints ain't deep-seated . . . I don't know what is!"

"How'd I pay for it?" demands Ethan, sharply.

Zeena is slow in replying, but she evidently has her own ideas of what could be done. There's the cow—Ethan is quick enough to squelch that suggestion. He won't sell the cow, if that is what she's driving at. And, though Zeena goes on with a further suggestion that with a little feedin' the cow could probably fetch as much as thirty or forty dollars, Ethan refuses to listen.

Ethan has gone back to his wood when Zeena has another idea. It is about the doctor. The doctor doesn't believe she can live long unless Ethan gets someone to help her with the housework. "Doctor Harmon says to me, 'Mrs. Frome,' he says, 'you see't Ethan gets you a hired girl. . . . I don't want you should wear yourself out workin' around that house—you just can't stand it,' he says!"

Still Ethan pays but little attention. Not until Zeena suddenly announces: "Mattie Silver's comin'!"

"No, she ain't!" answers Ethan, throwing down his hatchet and facing Zeena. "If I told you once I told you fifty times I won't have her here—I won't have nobody here! And I won't have you whinin' and moanin' for doctorin' and Energex Vibrators and hired girls with my cattle out there starvin' to death!"

"She's only comin' to try and help me out."

"I got cows in that barn starvin' because I can't buy feed—I ain't paid Jotham in months—we ain't had enough to feed our-

selves . . . Zeena, there ain't no use talkin'—we can't do it—
we just can't have no hired girls!"

"Now, Ethan—Mattie ain't a hired girl—she's my cousin.
She's comin' all the way up here just to help me in my last
sickness—(*She sighs pathetically*.) Besides the poor girl ain't got
any place else to go—you can't turn her out, Ethan—my own
flesh and blood . . . (*Then she adds practically*.) And bein' my
cousin—course we won't have to pay her wages."

"I can't do it—and I won't!"

"Well—she's comin' just the same, Ethan."

The sound of horse and cart in the dooryard suggests that
Mattie has already arrived, but it is only Denis Eady, the grocer's
son, bringing her trunk. Denis might as well take the trunk right
back where he got it, Ethan suggests, but Denis couldn't think
of doing that—not for nothin'. That settles the argument. The
trunk stays.

Denis, who is one of Starkfield's younger set and might readily
be classed as a "snappy dresser," reports seeing the Fromes' expected hired girl standing on the station platform while he was
helping Jotham get her trunk off the train. She didn't look so
much to Denis.

"All this time you ain't said a word about her comin' here,"
explodes Ethan, as soon as Denis has left. "You been writin'
Aunt Prudence down to Bettsbridge—plannin' and arrangin' and
most likely sending my money so's to get that girl here—knowin'
as well as I do I ain't even able to feed her!"

ZEENA—Ethan, the doctor says I just got to have somebody
here—(ETHAN *turns away abruptly*.) All right, Ethan . . . so
be it . . . if you won't sell the cow to get me a Energex Vibrator
to relieve my sufferin' a mite and you won't let Mattie Silver
. . . my own flesh and blood . . . come here to care for me in
my last sickness . . . all right! (ETHAN *drops his hatchet*. . . .
She is pleased to see he is weakening.) I won't be a burden to you
much longer—all I ask is you should remember I ain't got a
stitch to my name except that old brown merino dress I was
married in. It ain't fit to wear, Ethan—so the least you c'n do
is to get me somethin' decent to die in! (ETHAN *gets up abruptly,
goes to the window*.) You'll be sorry when I die! (ETHAN *doesn't
move . . . nor seem to pay any attention*.) Ethan, you c'n let
Mattie stay and do the housework without it costin' you anythin' . . . just the spare room'n three meals a day. . . . Well—
the way I'm feelin' now . . . I can't eat anythin' myself to speak

of . . . so what she gets'll be the same as my share if I was able
to eat proper! Don't fret, Ethan—I'll see that's all she gets!
And I'll see't she earns it! Mattie's a real bargain, Ethan . . .
course I don't say she's worth anythin' . . . but then she don't
cost anythin'!

Zeena is still reporting what Aunt Prudence has said of Mattie
—that she's willin' enough but not very handy—and that she
had worked in the shoe mills and in a big department store at
Willimantic until her health kept breakin' down—when Mattie
and Jotham arrive.

Mattie is twenty. To an urban eye she is a rather drab-
looking small-town girl . . . pretty . . . but certainly not beautiful . . . nondescript except for her youthful exuberance . . .
which has not been dulled by a rather hopeless existence. She
wears a drab coat and a dress that is shabby enough but is gay
. . . and even perhaps a bit too dressy. She carries a battered
carpet bag. Mattie brings an eagerness into the room . . . which
is immediately and obviously resented by Zeena, and, automatic-
ally, repelled by Ethan. She stands looking from one to the other
for a second. "You must be Ethan," she ventures, but Ethan is
too busy telling Jotham what to do with the sorrel to acknowl-
edge his identity more than briefly.

"So you're Mattie?" continues Zeena, a light tone of wonder
in her voice.

"How are you, Zeena?" answers Mattie, smiling a friendly
smile and looking brightly about the room and through the window. "My . . . thk. . . . Just look at all them trees and all!
My, it's real pleasant!" And then to Zeena: "How'd you say you
was feelin', Zeena?"

ZEENA—How do I look like I was feelin'?

MATTIE (*innocently and cheerfully*)—Well, of course I don't
know how you're used to lookin', Zeena! And from the way you
went on about it in your letters . . . well . . . (*She laughs.*) I
just don't know what all I expected! So I guess you ain't's bad
off's you might be! (*She takes a small package from under her
arm.*) Look . . . I brought you somethin'—(ZEENA *seizes the
package.*) I made it myself . . . it's molasses . . . (ZEENA *puts
the package aside without comment.*) I guess it ain't so very good.

ZEENA—Well . . . Mattie . . .

MATTIE—I'm awful glad to see you, Zeena!

ZEENA—You look sort of foolish hangin' on to that carpet bag.

"ETHAN FROME"

ena: I was sayin' I only wisht you'd get me one of them Energex Vibrators. You could get it ight, Ethan, if you was a mind to . . . and if my complaints ain't deep-seated . . . I don't w what is!

han: How'd I pay for it?

(Raymond Massey, Pauline Lord)

MATTIE—Don't I just! (*She chuckles.*) You know I was in the ladies' waitin' room down to Worcester where I changed to the branch line . . . and I got one look at myself . . . and, well . . . I thought I'd die laughin' . . . (ZEENA *looks at her without comment.*) And I says to myself . . . I says . . . Mattie Silver . . . you look awful foolish standin' there holdin' on to that suitcase . . . ! (*She sets it down abruptly . . . then picks it up again.*) That ain't where to put it . . . is it, Zeena?

ZEENA—No . . . it ain't. . . . Never mind it now, Mattie. . . . You can take it upstairs after supper . . . (ETHAN *and* JOTHAM, *the occasionally hired man, a dour-faced old fellow, enter from the porch.* ZEENA *continues firmly to* MATTIE . . . *as* ETHAN *and* JOTHAM *pause in the doorway.*) You'll have to start right in, Mattie. . . . I got that shootin' pain so bad I won't be able to help you much this evenin' . . .

MATTIE (*going to stove*)—Oh, I ain't a bit tired!

ZEENA—Jotham . . . you see't that trunk gets upstairs to the spare room . . . if you ain't too helpless . . . Ethan might help you . . . 'stead of standing there . . . (*Then to* MATTIE.) You can put supper right on . . . soon's it's ready, Mattie. (ZEENA *is having herself a fine time issuing orders.*)

ETHAN (*to* MATTIE)—If I was you . . . I'd take my coat off first.

MATTIE—I forgot! I've been in it so long . . . I forgot I had it on! (*She slips out of her coat, drops it on a chair.*)

ETHAN (*drily*)—There's pegs to hang it up on.

ZEENA—You'll have to learn not to clutter up the whole place with your things, Mattie.

Nothing that Mattie does is at all pleasing to Zeena. Nor does Zeena like the dress Mattie wears. It looks kind of like a pair of "porteers," if you ask Zeena, but to Mattie it is her one and only. Once she had a calico wrapper at the shoe mill, but when she got sick they wouldn't let her keep it because she had only been workin' there three months.

Nor does Zeena take kindly to Jotham's naïve suggestion that he should be entitled to something to eat, after his drive to the Flats and back. There ain't enough for Jotham, whatever anybody thinks, decides Mattie. Jotham is content. Even cheerful. But he has to laugh. He has to laugh at something Mattie said when she got off the train. "She says to me she just can't wait to get here!" says Jotham, gaily, moving toward the door. "Have to laugh every time I think of it." He's gone.

Zeena is furious. "You're forgettin' I'm a very sick woman," she snaps. "You'll have to learn about holdin' your tongue, Mattie, if you want to stay."

"I'm terribly sorry, Zeena."

"Well, we'll see how you get along. . . . But you might's well know right from the start . . . you come here to work . . . same's a hired girl . . . except of course we can't afford to pay you anythin' . . . but seein's you're my blood cousin . . . we'll treat you right's long as you behave yourself. And I'll see't Ethan takes you and fetches you from the church sociables once a month and of course you'll live here and eat the same's us."

"I'm beholdin' to you, Zeena. . . . I want you should tell me just everythin' you want me to do!"

"You might get supper! . . ."

The supper, consisting of a pot of stew, is nervously and awkwardly dished up by the frightened Mattie. Ethan reluctantly helps when necessary, but Zeena sticks to her chair. Zeena ain't up to movin' a muscle, though she is not at all pleased with the way Mattie is going about things.

"You don't look so good to me, Mattie," she says, finally.

"I'll be all right . . . when I kind of get the hang of things a bit. Honest I will, Zeena!"

Zeena is still doubtful. Of course she and Ethan can't look a gift horse in the face, but—"What do you think, Ethan? She don't look much on housework."

Ethan hesitates before he answers. Glances quickly at Mattie and thaws a little. There is the suspicion of a smile about his mouth as he concedes—

"Well, she ain't a fretter, anyhow."

Mattie smiles gratefully. They are starting to eat their stew as the curtain falls.

Outside the storm door of the Starkfield Congregational Church vestry a Winter evening a year later the snow has piled in drifts against the trees and the church building. Inside what the natives call the "Social Hall" a dance is in progress. The sounds of a fiddle and a harmonium can be heard.

Presently Ethan Frome shuffles in through the snow and half conceals himself in an angle of the building. He waits there until the dance is finished and then moves deeper into the shadow. Presently some of the crowd appear, bundled against the cold, starting home. They recognize Ethan and speak to him curtly. He answers them in kind. Occasionally one asks about Zeenie.

Presently Ed Varnum arrives. He has come to fetch his daughter. It is Ed Varnum who bought a cow from Ethan. Now the money's been spent for Zenobia's Energex Vibrator and Ethan would like to sell Ed some spruce. But Ed doesn't want any spruce—

More of the crowd start home. They report to Ethan that Mattie is dancin' with Denis Eady. Looks a little like Mattie's taken a fancy to Denis. Now Mattie herself has come to the door to look for Ethan, followed by Denis. They were wonderin' if Ethan'd mind if they had another dance. He might come in where it's warm and wait. Ethan does not answer them. The fiddler comes to urge Mattie and Denis to come back. They are to lead the square dance. Mattie goes back—but not until she has called to Ethan to wait for her. . . .

The dance is over. The crowd is leaving. Presently Denis has come with Mattie. If Ethe doesn't mind Denis would like to take Mattie home. He has got the old man's cutter waitin'. He thought maybe Mattie would like a little ride.

Ethan doesn't want Mattie to go, and he doesn't want to go himself. They'll walk, as they always do. Still, when Mattie joins them, Ethan says he is willin' she should go with Denis— if she wants to. It's gettin' late, but it's up to her. Mattie makes the decision. She'll walk with Ethan. And she wouldn't have waited for that last dance if she'd knowed he was goin' to be put out about it.

"I ain't put out," insists Ethan. "Come on, if you're comin'."

They have walked over to where the path divides. "Let's go this way, Ethan—it's easier walkin'," suggests Mattie. "I'm goin' this way—it's shorter," snaps Ethan.

"You're as stubborn's a mule, Ethan—"

"I ain't near's stubborn's you are! This way—if you're goin' with me."

"Oh, Ethan—come on this way, huh?"

They stand looking at each other for a second. Then Mattie dashes over to Ethan, touches him quickly on the sleeve and runs off calling merrily: "Last touch!" Ethan looks after her for a moment then turns deliberately and takes the other path as the curtain falls.

There are two paths converging at the crest of a hill lying between the Social Hall in Starkfield and the Frome farm. Just over the crest the ground slopes away abruptly. It is the starting place of the village bob-sled ride. There is a sled standing up in the snow, deep in the drifts, as though it had not been used for a long time. A fallen tree near the sled provides a rough sort of bench for the sledders.

Shortly Ethan appears trudging up one of the paths from Starkville. He stands for a moment and then Mattie, coming up the other path, joins him. Ethan is for going on toward the farm, but Mattie pulls his sleeve. After all it is a lovely night. Why should they be acting stubborn any longer?

Ethan's willing not to be stubborn, but, for that matter, it was all right for Matt to go home with Denis if she wanted to. But Mattie didn't want to. Makes her kinda mad to think Ethan thinks she did. Matt was awful glad to see Ethan at the Social Hall, seein' how long a walk it is from the farm and all. But Ethan doesn't mind the walk. Gettin' so he kinda likes it, in fact. It gets kinda lonesome at the farm.

"Zeena ain't a whole lot of company . . . when she's feelin' low," says Ethan.

"No . . . she ain't," agrees Mattie.

"Not that I blame her!"

"Oh, no, Ethan!"

"Well—it's a great night out tonight, all right," Ethan admits, with some difficulty.

"Ain't it—just?" Ethan is looking a little helplessly at Mattie, as she adds, quickly, "I ain't a mite cold . . . are you, Ethan?"

"Me? No!"

Mattie can't see as there'd be much harm in their settin' awhile. Nor can Ethan. It is interestin' talkin' sometimes. And they don't get much chance at home. Ethan hasn't talked so much since he was married. . . . Mattie was awful glad to see Ethan waitin' outside the hall. She was a little afraid he wouldn't be able to come for her. Zeena hadn't been feelin' any too well—

"I had an awful funny dream last night," reports Mattie. "You know what I dreamed? I dreamed Zeena come downstairs sayin' she was feelin' better and for a while this mornin' I didn't know if it was a dream or not . . . till I heard her!"

"Feelin' better?" echoes Ethan. "Well, that's one thing I ain't never heard her complain about!"

They sit silently for a moment. Then Mattie, peering over the crest of the hill and drawing away with a shudder, is suddenly conscious of the coastin' and its dangers. Mattie has never coasted, never once in her life, but she has watched the others. Ethan thinks they might try it some night. Tomorrow night they might try it. The thought is exciting to Mattie. Still she remembers seeing Ned Hale and Ruth Varnum nearly get killed the night they just barely missed the big elm at the bend.

"Ned ain't much on steerin'," says Ethan. "I guess I could take you down all right."

"Could you, Ethan? Right past the big elm? . . . It's awful dangerous-lookin'."

"I guess you wouldn't have to be afraid with me."

He is looking at her so intently she turns quickly away. "No," she says, with careful indifference, "I don't guess I would!"

Suddenly Ethan has discovered the sled standing in the snow. It's Sam Colt's and Sam never uses it. They might borrow that and— But it *is* getting pretty late. And it is a long walk back. They'd better wait.

They have gone back to surveying the stars and reveling in their magnificence. Ethan knows quite a lot about the stars—about Aldebaran and Orion, and the Pleiades and all. Ethan had pretty near a year at the technological college at Worcester—

ETHAN—A-yeah. But 'bout the time I got acclimated . . . the old man died and I had to come back and take care of the farm. So I didn't get to learn much to speak of . . . just enough to get me wonderin' about things once in a while.

MATTIE—You know. I get to wonderin' once in a while myself . . . about things . . . and places . . . nice warm places mostly . . . like take down South!

ETHAN—Ever seen any pictures of them palm trees they have down there? (*She nods eagerly.*) Mighty pretty.

MATTIE—I can just imagine!

ETHAN (*drily*)—A-yeah. Well, for a good while there I could call up the sight of them pictures easy . . . but these last couple of winters the recollection's been gettin' kind of snowed under!

MATTIE (*sighing*)—Oh, my . . . it must be real nice to travel places . . .

ETHAN—A-yeah.

MATTIE—I got's far down as Hartford once . . . Guess that's 'bout's far's I ever will get.

ETHAN—Hartford's quite a ways at that.

MATTIE—Yes . . . 'tis.

ETHAN—Most to New York.

MATTIE—Can you picture it? And I didn't get tired travelin' at all. . . . I could've kept right on goin' an' goin' an' goin' . . . (*She sighs longingly.*) Oh, dear!—

ETHAN—Glad you didn't.

MATTIE—It's awful interestin' to talk about things like that though, ain't it? I still ain't a mite cold . . . are you?

ETHAN—Me? No . . . 'course not! (*She crosses back to the log and he follows.*)

MATTIE—I was thinkin' we might set a while longer. (*They sit.*) Ain't it funny the way things go now when you just stop to think about 'em? Just supposin' my father hadn't've married Zeena's cousin . . . why, I most probably wouldn't've been born at all! (*Then thoughtfully.*) Still'n all . . . I don't know's I'd mind that!

ETHAN—Some people might.

MATTIE—Well . . . anyhow . . . bein' me I'm glad he did.

ETHAN—A-yeah . . . well . . . I'm kind of glad myself . . . bein's that's why you're here.

MATTIE—Ain't it just the luckiest thing! Why, I'm just so glad to be here . . . 'stead of down there in them big towns! You know, I never did take to workin' in the mills . . . first off I ain't got the stren'th . . . and then them foremen used to get me so flustered . . . why, the harder I tried the more flustered I'd get and the sooner I'd get fired . . . and then first thing you know . . . I got fired so much . . . there wasn't any more jobs . . . (*She sighs contentedly.*) An' my health's better here an' everything and I don't have to fuss about a place to sleep and somethin' to eat . . . ! Oh, yes . . . bein' here's been real pleasant.

Still Ethan is troubled. Folks have been talkin'. Folks have been sayin' that she'll be leavin' them soon—

Mattie is quite excited by that suggestion. Could it be that Zeena has said something? Could it be Zeena isn't satisfied? Mattie knows she isn't very good as a hired girl, because she ain't got the stren'th, but if Ethan would tell her what Zeena wants her to do Mattie could learn. He ought to tell her—unless he wants her to go himself—

Even the thought of such a catastrophe is a little too much for Ethan. With an effort he controls his feelings. If Matt doesn't want to go of her own accord she doesn't have to go. Only, of course, she might be wantin' to leave to get married— That'd be natural. Folks do get married—

Mattie can't think of anybody who'd think of marryin' her. The thought is embarrassing. She gets up abruptly and starts down the path. Ethan follows quickly after her.

"Why, Matt—lot's o' folks'd want to marry you—" he ventures, comfortingly.

"I ain't noticed any great rush so far."

"Well . . . take now . . . I would . . . if I could."

"That's interestin', ain't it?" she says, stopping and looking at him. "Maybe you would, Ethan . . . but nobody else . . . anyhow you couldn't."

"No, I don't guess I could . . . but, I mean, if I could . . . I would."

"Oh, well, sayin' that don't mean anythin'!" She looks up at him and smiles. "Still'n all . . . it's real nice of you to say it!"

They are continuing on down the path as the curtain falls.

A moment later Ethan and Mattie walk into the dooryard of the Frome farm. The house is dark and forbidding in the starry night. For a moment neither Ethan nor Mattie notices the house. They are too interested in the heavens. Ethan is trying to help Mattie find the constellation of the Big Dipper and show her how she can find the North Star by first locating the pourin' end of the Dipper.

Now, suddenly, they are aware of the house and the darkness, and move away from it. Mattie would read some of the inscriptions on the Frome tombstones. "Sacred to . . . the memory . . . of Ethan Frome . . . and Endurance . . . his wife . . . who . . . dwelled together . . . in peace . . . for fifty years." Fifty years! That's an awful long time. Zeena and Ethan have been married only seven years—since the Winter Ethan's mother died. . . . The house had been pretty lonesome even with the elder Mrs. Frome alive, seein' she hardly ever said anything, Ethan explains. After she died he felt he could not go on without someone to talk to. Zeena, always a great hand for sickness and doctorin', had helped take care of Mrs. Frome. When Ethan asked her to marry him and stay on she agreed.

They can hear a dog howling in the distance. That means something as Mattie remembers it. Means death. But Ethan has a less frightening superstition. A dog's howling doesn't mean anything unless you hear it twice, and even then it isn't sure.

"Maybe it won't be fifty years, Ethan," says Mattie, with a nervous laugh. The next minute she is startled by suddenly realizing the complete darkness of the house. For the first time Zeena hasn't left a light. Ethan thinks it's foolish to be scared by a thing like that. He'll get the key. But, though he searches thoroughly under the mat, where Zeena usually puts the key, Ethan can't find it. Now Mattie *is* frightened. The key just must be there. Zeena has always left a light and the key before. And it's terrible late tonight.

Together they make one more frantic search. Ethan lights his last match and they search carefully in the light of its short flare. There is no key. They are facing each other in despair when a vague light appears suddenly shining through the cracks of the house. They stand tensely waiting as the light approaches the door. Then the door opens and Zeena is standing there, a lamp in one hand, the other pulling a quilted counterpane about her shoulders. She stares at them briefly, conscious of their uneasiness.

"I felt so mean't I couldn't sleep," she explains.

They move forward slowly through the door into the kitchen. Without another word Zeena slowly closes the door as the curtain falls.

ACT II

It is five-thirty the following morning. In Ethan's and Zeena's bedroom, close under the slanting eaves of the house, Ethan is shaving by the light of a frosty window and a sputtering tallow candle.

It is a bare room, with a curtain hung across the corner to serve as a clothes closet. In the bed, cramped under the slanting roof, Zeena sits with her knees drawn up under her chin shivering with the cold, coughing, sputtering and trying to make a selection of medicine from an array of pharmaceutical bottles and boxes on a rackety table by the side of the bed.

Zeena, wearing a flannel wrapper over her corsets, has managed to get her second stocking under the covers and pulled on. Ethan, staring into a piece of mirror nailed to the wall, goes on with his shaving, apparently unconscious of Zeena. He is even quite gay, humming a tune he had heard at the church social.

"Gettin' a bit light-headed lately, ain't you, Ethan?" ventures Zeena, resentfully. "That's the third time't you've shaved this week."

"A-yeah," mutters Ethan, unconcernedly. "Sort of nippy, ain't it?"

Zeena pulls herself together courageously, swings out of bed, grabs her petticoat, drops it over her head and wiggles her way through. Now she has recovered her wrapper and climbed into bed again, shivering and sputtering with the cold.

"You know what, Zeenie . . . I'd stay right under them blankets today . . . if I was you! I wouldn't get up out of bed at all." Ethan is just finishing his shaving. "A-yeah—just stay right there and I'll have Mattie fetch the hot-water bottle."

"If I had someone to take care of things proper maybe I could stay in bed," snaps Zeena. "Have to work twice as hard now's I ever did before—that's what's ailin' me . . . followin' her around . . . showin' her . . . watchin' over her . . ."

ETHAN—Well—Mattie's willin' enough . . . that's one sure thing!

ZEENA (*continuing in the same tone . . . as though he hadn't interrupted*)—'Tain't right't I sh'd have to keep on doin' everythin' myself . . . (*She blows her nose sharply.*) I'm beginnin' to wonder if she's wuth it!

ETHAN (*has finished shaving and now he plunges his face into the water*)—Oh, you're just frettin' yourself, Zeenie!

ZEENA (*in tears . . . whimpering and shuddering with the cold*)—She can't cook—she can't clean—she can't even scrub proper— (*She stops and blows her nose again and gasps as she wipes the tears from her eyes.*)

ETHAN (*straightens up from the washbowl—reaches out blindly for the towel*)—Well . . . just as long's she keeps on tryin'! (*There is a pause . . . he finds the towel.*)

ZEENA—Well . . . (*She sniffles.*) I won't be sorry to see her go. (ETHAN *stops abruptly.*) Course she will go . . . sooner or later . . . (*She dries her eyes.*) I wouldn't want it said't I'd stood in her way!

ETHAN—Oh, that's just fool talk! (*He goes on drying his face.*)

ZEENA—Well . . . a poor girl like Mattie Silver . . . it wouldn't be right to stop her leavin' . . . if she got a chance to get married!

ETHAN (*easily*)—Well, 'tain't very likely! (*He picks up his shirt from the chair.*)

ZEENA—Don't you go and be too sure now, Ethan! (*Significantly.*) Anyway—whatever happens—I ain't goin' to be left alone—without anybody to do for me—you know what the doctor said—! You know he warned me—

ETHAN (*interrupts*)—What's got into you this morning, Zeena! You must be gone queer in the head!

ZEENA (*violently*)—No, I ain't! And don't you never say a thing like that to me again! You hear!

Mattie has called from the kitchen for Ethan to come to his breakfast. She comes for him herself finally, quite gaily, but all

the spirit goes out of her voice the moment she sees Zeena. Mattie
is eager to help. Goes for the hot-water bottle. Sympathizes with
her for the chill Zeena insists she took on because she had to get
out of a warm bed to let them in the night before.

Both Ethan and Mattie have explanations for being late home
from the social. Ethan has said it was because he got to talkin'
business with Ed Varnum and was late callin' for Mattie. Now
Mattie explains that it was because she insisted on dancing a
last dance with Denis Eady and made Ethan wait. Zeena draws
her own conclusions and smiles wisely.

Now Ethan has gone about his business and Mattie and Zeena
are alone. Zeena finds it a good time for further correction. There
are many things Mattie is continuing to neglect, even after she's
been told time and time again. It is a good time for giving advice, too. If it should happen that Denis Eady should be interested in Mattie, Zeena says, she is anxious that nothing should
be put in the way of his interest. Denis might propose if he was
given a chance. Mattie is sure he never would. Besides, she
doesn't like Denis.

"Paupers can't be choosey, Mattie," warns Zeena.

"Oh, I'm not choosey . . . Zeena . . . honest I'm not," insists Mattie. "Like I was sayin' to Ethan only last night . . . I
says nobody ain't never asked me yet, I said, and he said if he
wasn't married he might ask me himself . . . so 'course I said,
sayin' that don't mean anythin' . . . 'But still'n all,' I says,
'it's real nice of you to say it' . . . and it was, too, wasn't it?"

Zeena is sitting rigidly upright in bed now. Mattie, glancing
at her, is terrified. Quickly Mattie reaches for the breakfast tray
she has brought up. Zeena, making an effort to get away from
Mattie, upsets a cup of coffee on the blanket. Mattie is frightened
white. Zeena is silent and still rigid, ominously accusing.

"Oh, Zeena! Oh, my . . . if I'd only been thinkin' what I was
doin' . . . oh, them blankets is just ruint—simply ruint!" wails
the unhappy Mattie. "Thk—I only wish I c'd pay you somethin'
for the damage and if I c'd I would . . . right off . . . but take
the way things are . . . I ain't complainin' . . . but without
your payin' me anythin' . . . I don't see what I c'd do. (*She
sighs—unconsciously adopting* ZEENA's *perpetually worried domestic manner.*) I got an awful lot needs tendin' to up here today.
. . . Them floors to scrub and the windows want washin' real
bad an' them blankets'll have to be washed out an' I don't know
how I'll ever get things to dry this weather . . . thk-thk."

Zeena is out of bed. Disdaining help from Mattie she has gone to the closet and climbed on a chair, the better to get at things on the shelf. Now she has found and nervously dropped her best bonnet, and is ready to strangle Mattie when she picks it up.

"Don't you never touch none of my things!" snaps Zeena, shrilly. "You hear me! You keep your hands off my things. And don't forget that as long as you live!"

This burst of anger is too much for Zeena. She catches at her side and reaches the bed with an effort. Still she will have no help from Mattie. Now she is able to get back to the closet and sends Mattie downstairs. Zeena has got out her brown merino dress and is smoothing out the wrinkles between sighs of distress as the curtain falls.

In the kitchen below Ethan is seated at the table eating his breakfast. It is rapidly growing lighter outside, but an oil lamp is still burning on the table. Presently Mattie, carrying the stained blankets, comes hurriedly down the stairs. She is still distraught. She does not hear Ethan ask for more coffee. Not until he speaks a second time. She has found a place for the blankets by then and got a tin washtub in the sink, under the water spout.

"What's she said to you, Matt?" demands Ethan, conscious that something is wrong. Then he adds, comfortingly—"I wouldn't take too much notice—you know how she is these cold mornin's—"

Now Ethan has noticed the blankets and she has told him, excitedly and anxiously, what has happened. Nor is she comforted by his conclusion that what she has done isn't exactly a crime. She is still excited and frightened as she hurries about building up the fire. Ethan awkwardly tries to help, and to explain—

"I guess she don't mean more'n half of anythin' she says," he ventures. "You know well's I do—how she don't say so much as a word—for days and days—and all the time them little things that don't amount to a hill of beans keeps poisonin' her till sooner or later she's just got to bust loose!"

There is a noise at the head of the stairs. Presently Zeena is seen coming down. She is wearing her brown merino and her high bonnet. They do not see her at first. She stops for a minute and smiles faintly at Ethan's domestic activities. She is carrying an old carpet bag. She is near the foot of the stairs when Ethan and Mattie turn a little consciously to stare at her.

Ethan would know where Zeena is going. She makes no reply to his inquiry. When she has put her coat and her bag down she takes her place at the breakfast table and calls to Mattie to wait

on her. Zeena is surprised a little at finding Ethan there, seein'
he has so much spruce to haul. Nor is she diverted by his insisting that in his opinion she should not have tried to get up, feelin'
the way she does. She should have stayed right under those
blankets—

"While I'm gone, Ethan . . . if you c'n spare a minute from
all that there haulin't you're doin' today," calmly instructs
Zeena, "you'd better be sure't this girl gets them blankets washed
out and dried before night . . . or you'll have to sleep down
here in the kitchen! (*She finishes her potato . . . takes another
gulp of coffee.*) Get out to the barn there, Mattie . . . like a
good girl . . . and find Jotham right off . . . and tell him't I
said he sh'd hitch up the sorrel."

For a second Mattie stands motionless, and then glances questioningly at Ethan. Zeena notices that glance, but is not disturbed.
Surely Ethan ain't got anythin' to say against Jotham hitchin'
up the sorrel. If he has she might find stren'th enough to plow
through the snow as far as Starkfield, where she could get Denis
Eady to drive her the rest of the way.

What's she goin' for? She's goin' to catch the train for Bettsbridge and she's goin' to see that new doctor—

"But you can't do that now, Zeena!" Ethan protests, his suspicions aroused and his apprehension growing. "You know we
just ain't got the money to lay out for any new doctors any
more'n we had for that new-fangled vibratin' machine there—
that you don't even know what it's for!"

"I know," sighs Zeena, staring fixedly at Ethan. "I know I'm
just a burden to you! . . . Right this minute I got pains way
down to my ankles and shootin' back up through me . . . like I
was bein' stabbed!"

ETHAN—I heard enough about that chill you got—but you
didn't say nothin' about any pains this mornin'! (*Then urgently.*)
Zeena . . . how're we goin' to pay the doctor anyway!

ZEENA (*easily*)—Well . . . I got what's left of the cow money
. . . 'tain't much . . . but it'll have to do, I s'pose.

ETHAN—That's every cent we got in the world! You can't take
that money, Zeena . . . you just can't!

ZEENA—Nonsense! Why, course I can, Ethan . . . you ain't
that mean! (*She gets up . . . reaches for her coat.*) As I was
sayin'—I hate to put you out any but I guess I just ain't got
the stren'th to walk . . . somebody'll have to drive me over's

far's the Flats.

ETHAN (*frantically*)—I don't aim to be mean but I can't do it . . . I just ain't got the time . . . I got to see Andrew Hale and try an' get cash enough out of him to buy feed for the stock . . . or all them critters'll die on us . . .

ZEENA (*shrewdly*)—I thought Andrew Hale didn't never pay under three months!

ETHAN—He don't's a rule . . . but I need it bad . . . I just got to get enough for the feed anyhow!

ZEENA—If Andrew Hale's payin' cash down for all that spruce . . . that'd pay for feed and we c'd still afford the little bit I'm costin' you . . . and some to spare— (*Then thoughtfully.*) There's an awful lot of medicines I been needin' real bad.

ETHAN—I said I ain't got no reason to s'pose he will pay cash! He ain't never done it before!

ZEENA—I know! That's just what I was thinkin'! (*She sighs and shakes her head.*) Well . . . it's all right, Ethan. . . . If you don't want to bother to drive me over . . . Jotham will . . . I wouldn't want to trouble you none . . .

Mattie has reported the sorrel hitched. Zeena is ready to start. She pauses to explain carefully that she will spend the night with Aunt Martha Pierce—and will probably not be back before the next night, if then. Ethan and Mattie are visibly embarrassed, and that interests Zeena.

"Not't I'll be missed," she adds, significantly. "I guess you c'n get along fine without me."

Zeena has taken her carpet bag and gone into the yard. For a moment Ethan and Mattie stand staring awkwardly and embarrassedly at each other. Finally Ethan finds voice to say that he will be down at the wood lot most of the day, if Mattie should need him. Mattie is thoroughly frightened now. Ethan has started for the door when she runs after him.

"Oh, Ethan, Ethan—what's she goin' to do," she cries.

"I don't know . . . Matt," he answers, bewilderedly.

"Oh, Ethan—I'm scared . . . Why can't she never say what she's goin' to do. Why can't she never say it right out?"

"Well, I guess there's no use frettin' about it now . . . anyhow."

"Guess not . . . Ethan." Awkwardly he moves toward the door. "Well . . . I'll be gettin' along," he says.

Mattie is smiling faintly at him as he goes through the door.

The smile vanishes and she goes back to work. She is working breathlessly and in a moment the smile again appears. She is humming a little as the curtain falls.

At supper time that night Mattie is hustling happily with preparations for the evening meal. It is getting dark outside, but she has not yet lighted the lamp. The table has an almost gay appearance and Mattie is wearing her "other" dress.

From upstairs Ethan calls cheerfully from time to time to learn how Matt is getting on with the supper. Ethan is starved. Mattie, hurrying with the last touches, has an exciting idea. Getting on a chair she fumbles among the dishes and medicine bottles on the top shelf until she finds Zeena's red pickle dish. Carefully, almost tenderly, she takes it down. She is at the sink washing it when Jotham appears. He has come to get thawed a bit before he goes on home. Being thawed, he is vastly interested in the food cooking on the stove.

Now Ethan has come down stairs, relieved to find the visitor to be Jotham and a little excited by what Jotham has brought: a jug of sweet cider! Mrs. Andrew Hale had given it to Ethan and it ain't gone hard or nothin'.

Jotham, still sniffing around the stove, has a feeling that he is in the way, but he makes no move to go. Presently Mattie suggests that he sit up to the table. She had fixed a place for him special. And Jotham is not slow to accept. He will, however, certainly get out the minute he ain't wanted.

Ethan is standing by the stove, grinning broadly. Something has happened. Mattie knows that. But what? It's about Ethan's visit to Mr. Hale. Ethan has made Hale give him twenty dollars worth of food for the livestock and it's in the barn right now!

That's pretty thrilling news to Mattie. That's enough feed to last the cattle right up to pasturin' time. She certainly is glad that she fixed supper special! With enough coffee so's they can have three cups apiece!

Now she gaily draws attention to the pickles. And the pickle dish. Ethan ain't never seen that before. Because, as Mattie explains, it ain't never been used before.

"Don't she like pickles?" asks Jotham.

The suggestion sets them giggling. Ethan and Mattie exchange glances and then go back to their eating.

"S'pose that new doctorin' will do her any good, Ethan?" Jotham asks. Getting no reply he adds: "Hope so. Them pains of hers has been gettin' a bit tryin'."

It is hard for Ethan and Mattie not to laugh at Jotham, but

they manage to keep their faces straight. . . .

They have all finished now. From the window Ethan notices that the snow is still driftin', which suggests to Jotham, "completely unaware of their embarrassment," that the driftin' on the Flats might tie up the trains for fair. Mattie quickly changes the subject back to the dinner. Maybe Jotham would like some more —if there was any more! Jotham is quite satisfied, but he could stand a swallow of cider—

They had forgotten all about the cider. Now they drink it with gusto and find it great.

"I guess you more'n earned that all right, Jotham, drivin' away over to the Flats," suggests Ethan.

"Well, you can just bet your boots I did," answers Jotham, thoughtfully. "A-yeah—train was late—'count of snow up the line . . . course Zeena got the notion it was my fault or somethin' . . . I ain't figured out yet how that could be . . . all's I know is . . . we sat and waited 'bout an hour and a half . . . and she was still goin' strong. . . . (*He sits there remembering painfully, then he sighs and shakes his head.*) Guess I'd ought to be glad it wasn't any longer."

Jotham has decided finally to go, before he wears out his welcome. Nor can they induce him to stay, even for another glass of cider. He is in his coat and standing at the window when he turns to suggest—

"Cozy in here tonight—if I was you two—I'd just sit right up into that there 'Fancy Hero' stove. 'Night," he calls back from the door; "obliged to you both."

" 'Night," calls Ethan. " 'Night, Jotham," echoes Mattie.

Mattie and Ethan are alone now and terribly self-conscious. Mattie quickly remembers the dishes. Ethan wanders aimlessly about the room.

"Well . . . !" says Ethan, finally. "Mighty fine supper, Matt!"

"Oh, I guess it wasn't so much," answers Mattie, chortling with pleasure and pride. "I c'd do even better than that another time."

ETHAN (*after a moment, turns to the window, then glances at her*)—Say, Matt!

MATTIE—Hhm?

ETHAN—Bet you don't never see snow like this down there to Willimantic.

MATTIE—No, sir, I ain't never seen nothin' like . . . nowheres near!

ETHAN—By Jimminy, you know, it's kind of pretty at that!

A-yeah . . . don't seem to mind it at all tonight! . . . Stove's drawin' like a house a-fire. Say . . . ain't this the night we was goin' coastin'?

MATTIE—I guess you must've forgot all about it, Ethan.

ETHAN (*after a pause*)—No, no, I didn't exactly forget, Mattie . . . Only thing is . . . I guess it's . . . sort of dark out.

MATTIE—Let's see . . . (*glancing out the window.*) Oh, my, yes . . . isn't it though! My goodness! It's dark as Egypt out!

ETHAN—Course if you really want to go . . .

MATTIE—Do you?

ETHAN (*doubtfully*)—Well . . . it's kind of dark, but . . . I'll go . . . if you say so . . . (*Yawning.*) Nice and warm in here tonight, ain't it?

MATTIE—Maybe it is too dark out, huh, Ethan!

ETHAN (*with relief*)—A-yeah. Maybe it is . . . we c'd wait an' go tomorrow if there's a moon.

MATTIE (*eagerly*)—Oh, that'd be just wonderful.

ETHAN—A-yeah. Well, we'll go tomorrow . . . I'd be afraid to go down that Corbury road tonight!

MATTIE (*laughingly*)—Yes, you would! Still'n all, it would be awful dangerous, bein' it's so dark out and all!

ETHAN—A-yeah.

MATTIE—I guess we're well enough here tonight, Ethan!

ETHAN (*getting his pipe filled*)—A-yeah. Couldn't ask no better. Say, Matt . . . I c'd give you a hand there, with them dishes . . . if you say so.

MATTIE—You just set, Ethan.

ETHAN—A-yeah . . . it's all right.

MATTIE—Hhm? What's all right, Ethan?

ETHAN—Sittin'.

MATTIE—I'll just bet!

ETHAN—A-yeah . . . You know . . . (*His speech is lost in a luxurious yawn.*)

MATTIE—What was you just too lazy to say, Ethan?

ETHAN—Oh . . . I don't know . . . Mighty peaceful tonight, ain't it, Mattie?

MATTIE—Hhm! Ain't it, though!

ETHAN—A-yeah. Hurry up and set, Matt . . .

MATTIE—Soon's I put the dishes away!

Ethan is tugging at one of his boots. Mattie quickly stops what she is doing and fetches his slippers. She is kneeling before him trying to put the slipper on when he suddenly becomes acutely

conscious of her nearness. When she would help him with the
second boot he draws a little roughly away from her. Mattie is
both surprised and hurt. She says nothing, but gets up quickly
and goes back to her work. Ethan, having adjusted the second
slipper, shuffles over to her. He finds explanation difficult, but
necessary.

"Matt! Matt! . . . that was real nice of you . . . an' I didn't
mean to complain. I guess I ain't used to . . . anyone . . . doin'
for me . . . an' . . ."

They are standing close together and Mattie is smiling gratefully. He suddenly realizes that in another moment they will be
in each other's arms. He moves away slightly, and quickly offers
to help with the dishes. She would have him return to his settin',
but he insists on helping. They are both reaching for Zeena's
prized pickle dish when it suddenly crashes to the floor and
breaks!

Mattie is aghast at this tragedy. She stares at the broken dish,
frantic with fear. Ethan would comfort her. After all it is something she couldn't help, and he'll get another pickle dish at Starkfield next day. But Mattie is not to be comforted. She knows what
store Zeena sets by the dish and she had been told never to touch
any of Zeena's things. "She hates me, Ethan . . . and I'm scared
of her!" wails Mattie.

Ethan stands close to her, conscious of a new danger. His arms
swing helplessly at his sides. He would have Mattie sit down
while he gathers the pieces together and puts them back on the
shelf. Nobody could tell, less they looked right close. Tomorrow
he will get glue and stick the pieces together and the first time
he's at Shadd's Falls or Bettsbridge he'll get a new dish.

Mattie is calmed a bit by Ethan's reasoning. Anyway Zeena
won't be back until the next night and there ain't no use worryin'
tonight. Ethan agrees to that.

". . . I been lookin' forward a lot . . . all day, I ain't been
thinkin' about a thing . . . but this evenin'," says Ethan.

"Me neither, Ethan. I been most of the day fixin' my 'one
and only.' It doesn't look so bad now . . . does it, Ethan . . .
I mean considerin'. Oh, Ethan . . . what'd she say to you up
there this mornin' before I came up?"

"We wasn't goin' to talk about it . . . She'll be back here
. . . this time tomorrow . . . rockin' away . . . creakin' and
whinin' . . ."

"Ethan . . . I promise . . . I ain't goin' to even think about
it once more tonight!"

Suddenly Mattie is conscious that it is almost nine o'clock—which goes to show just how time flies. She thinks she better be goin' to bed, but Ethan pleads with her not to go—not right away. It's so warm and comfortable— Again he is gazing at her, helplessly inarticulate. Mattie turns away to fix the fire.

It's been a wonderful evenin'. They're both agreed on that. There is something more that Ethan would say—if he could find words. He is standing with his hands gripping the back of Zeena's rocker convulsively. Mattie has blown out the flame of the oil lamp and lighted her candle. She is standing at the foot of the stairs as he calls, intensely—

"Good night, Matt!"

"Good night, Ethan!"

Slowly Mattie moves up the stairs, Ethan staring after her. As she disappears he loosens his hold of Zeena's chair, which rocks back and forth in front of him, creaking ominously. He stares at it as the curtain falls.

ACT III

In the early evening of the following day Mattie can be heard in her own room across the hall from Zeena's and Ethan's bedroom, working and humming gaily to herself. A moment later Ethan has burst into the kitchen below, bounded eagerly up the stairs to his bedroom, and demanded again the state of supper preparations. Ethan has been over to the Widow Homan's and brought home two small, mysterious packages. One, it transpires, is the glue to fix the pickle dish. The other is a pink, silk-covered pin cushion. That's for Matt. It's for pins, he announces solemnly, and she is properly impressed.

Ethan has filled the bowl with water and is washing his face vigorously. "Well," he sputters, gaily, "looks like we might have one more evenin', hey?"

But the smile vanishes suddenly from his face. Mattie, coming back from taking the pin cushion to her room, stands in the door. Her face is white. He knows the worst before she speaks.

"Oh, Ethan—Zeena's come! I seen her and Jotham from my window just now . . . as they was makin' the turn in. Oh, Ethan—what're we goin' to do . . . the pickle dish ain't fixed and . . ."

"Don't fret, Matt."

A moment later Zeena has come through the kitchen and up the stairs. She still has her coat and hat on. She speaks no word until she finds a place on the window seat. Zeena is a sick woman. A lot sicker than they think, she says. She's got complications now, and complications is nearly always fatal. She wants Ethan to know that it ain't no time for him to set himself against her.

The new doctor has told Zeena about the complications. He's a great doctor with an office on Worcester's main street. He comes only once a fortnight to Bettsbridge. Zeena plans to do everything he says. First of all the doctor was awfully surprised that she had stood the slavin' she's been doin' as long as she has. Now she must have a regular hired girl. Not to waste any time, Zeena had got Aunt Martha Pierce to hire her one right off.

This is bad news for Ethan. Maybe the doctor also told her how he was goin' to pay a hired girl. Ethan just can't do that. Which appeals to Zeena as being pretty mean, seein' she had lost her health nursin' his mother—

Ethan is trembling with fury at the charge. He starts menacingly toward Zeena, but is able to control himself. . . . They return to the discussion of the hired girl. There is, suggests Zeena, the money Ethan is goin' to get from Andrew Hale for the spruce. But Ethan didn't get that money. He took feed instead—

"So . . . seein's I ain't got a cent in the world . . . and ain't goin' to see a cent for three months anyhow and nothin' then to speak of . . . I guess you'll just have to do without the hired girl . . . You're a poor man's wife all right, Zeena . . . I'd like to do what I can for you . . . but I guess you'll have to send that there new girl right back where she's comin' from."

ZEENA—Oh, I figured I wouldn't take no chances countin' on you . . . so 'stead of buyin' myself a lot of medicines I been needin' real bad . . . I paid the girl a half a month in advance out of the cow money and give her a dollar extry like I said.

ETHAN (*furiously*)—You get that money back from her . . . and send her packin' just as soon's she comes! I can't afford it.

ZEENA—Oh, I guess we'll make out all right. There'll be Mattie's board less anyhow. (ETHAN *looks at her quickly and speechlessly . . . he has feared this from the first . . . and avoided it.*) Why, Ethan Frome . . . you didn't suppose I wanted you should keep two hired girls . . . did you! (*She laughs out loud.*) No wonder you was so upset about the expense!

ETHAN—Mattie Silver ain't a hired girl . . . she's your own blood relation.

ZEENA (*casually*)—Oh, she ain't nothin' to me . . . 'cept a pauper like her no-good father before her . . . and just 'cause she can't take care of herself's no reason we should keep her . . . it's somebody else's turn now.

ETHAN—You know there ain't anybody else!

ZEENA—That ain't my fault!

ETHAN (*violently*)—You ain't goin' to do it, Zeena . . . You ain't goin' to send Mattie away! I ain't goin' to let you do it! (*He stops abruptly . . . they are both acutely aware that his passionate words and tone have betrayed him.*) You can't do it, Zeena . . . where'd she go if you send her away? Why, even if she could get a job down there to Willimantic . . . she couldn't keep it . . . what with the work bein' too heavy and all . . . you know she was as sick's you was when she first come here . . . She's got no place to go, Zeena! Why, Zeena—you just got to think of what'd happen if you was ever to drive Mattie away . . . think what Emma and Abigail Varnum and Mrs. Hale and even your own Aunt Martha Pierce . . . think what they'd go and say of you!

ZEENA—I know too well what folks is sayin' now . . . of my havin' kep' her here's long's I have!

With that thrust Zeena has gone to the door and called Mattie. A moment later she goes in search of some stomach pills and leaves Ethan to tell Mattie what has happened.

Ethan stands for minutes dully trying to speak. Mattie, wild with apprehension, would remind him that his dinner is getting cold—though of course there ain't no reason for him to eat unless he wants to.

They are drawn together by their mutual misery. Still Ethan cannot speak. Finally, standing close beside Mattie, hearing her piteous pleas to be told what has happened, Ethan begins awkwardly—

"You see this here new doctor he's got her so scared about herself . . . you know how she is . . . believes everything they tell her . . . and he says . . ."

He can go no farther. Suddenly he takes Mattie in his arms. They cling together passionately for a moment in this first embrace.

"I can't let you go, Matt! I don't care what she says . . . I can't let you go now."

"Must—I—go?"

"Mattie!" Zeena is calling from below.

"Ethan . . . must I go?"

"Well . . . that's what she says tonight."

"If she says it tonight . . . she'll say it tomorrow."

"Mattie . . . I been calling you!" Zeena's voice takes on an added sharpness.

"Ethan . . . don't trouble—"

Mattie has gathered up the tray of dishes and started down the stairs as the curtain falls.

The following afternoon Mattie stands at the kitchen window anxiously watching for someone. A step on the porch excites her, but it is only Jotham. Jotham has come for Mattie's trunk. He hasn't seen anything of Ethan since Ethan said he had some business or something over to Starkfield. The fact that Mattie's leavin' is no surprise to Jotham. Leavin' is about the smartest thing she could do.

Jotham has gone upstairs to get the trunk when the door opens suddenly and Ethan comes in. Mattie rushes excitedly to him.

MATTIE—Oh, Ethan! I thought I wasn't never goin' to see you again!

ETHAN—Why, Matt! What'd ever make you go and think that!

MATTIE (*still a little breathless—and frantic*)—You wasn't here for breakfast . . . and I was scared . . . and then when Jotham come and told me you said you was goin' to town and we wasn't to wait dinner for you . . . Oh, Ethan, I thought for sure . . .

ETHAN—Oh, no, Matt!

MATTIE (*worriedly*)—Oh, Ethan . . . you must be just froze and starved . . . you was down here all night, wasn't you?

ETHAN—How'd you ever know that, Matt?

MATTIE—I heard you go downstairs again after I went to bed and I lay there listenin' all night . . . and you didn't never come back up . . . (*She stops abruptly . . . and then moves toward him.*) Don't be too sorry, Ethan . . . I don't want you should trouble!

ETHAN—I don't want you should trouble either.

MATTIE (*in a low voice*)—No, Ethan . . . I ain't goin' to trouble.

ETHAN—Matt! (*He adds quickly.*) Things might straighten out— All night and all day I been figurin' and plannin' and tryin' and strivin' . . . (*She looks up at him impulsively and he is forced to add.*) Maybe things'll be straightenin' out! (*She doesn't answer . . . they look at each other for a moment . . . then he nods toward the stairway.*) She said anythin' more?

MATTIE (*shaking her head*)—She ain't said anythin' at all!
I ain't so much's seen her. She's upstairs there and ain't been out
of her room all day . . . I knocked on the door there onc't and
said to her, I said . . . "Zeena, what should I do, should I bring
down my trunk or what?" And she said she had them inside
pains again and didn't want to be troubled.

ETHAN (*drily*)—She don't trouble easy.

MATTIE—No, she don't and that's a fact, Ethan . . . not
when she ain't a mind to.

ETHAN (*terribly confused*)—Mattie . . . I don't know yet
how . . . but some way . . . things'll turn out all right . . .
they're bound to, Mattie . . . now don't you go and give up
hope.

MATTIE—No, Ethan. . . . I know there ain't anythin' you
wouldn't do . . . if you could.

ETHAN—It ain't that bad now . . . you wait and see . . .
I'm goin' to do somethin'. I'll speak to her again . . . or somethin' . . . I been thinkin' about it all night and all day an' . . .
it's bound to come out all right . . . I'll speak to her and she's
bound to see things different today.

Jotham is down with the trunk and Ethan would stop him from
moving it. Ethan hasn't said anythin' about the trunk's goin'.
Still, Jotham has his reasons. Besides Mis' Frome is expectin' the
new girl to be met at the Flats at 5—an hour before Mattie takes
the train for Willimantic, or wherever she's goin'.

Ethan stands firm. Even against Zeena, who would take a hand
in settling the matter. But first there are a few other things
Zeena would like to take up with Mattie. There's a huckabuck
towel missing' for one thing. And a match safe for another. And
there's Aunt Martha's geranium that's been left to die—

Mattie flares up at that. She is sorry about the towel and the
match safe and will surely find them. But the geranium—she's
nursed that there geranium like it was her own and she won't let
no one say she hasn't. She is in tears now, and running up the
stairs.

Ethan still stands motionless in the center of the room, too
stunned to speak. Nor does he pay the least attention when Zeena
calls to him to help Jotham with the trunk. Jotham finally gives
up and moves out to the porch to wait to see whose orders he is
to take—Zeena's or Ethan's.

"Zeena—Mattie's always done her level best for you, and you

know it!" Ethan suddenly bursts out.

"Well—'tain't enough!" Zeena answers, shortly.

ETHAN—But she's tried . . . you know that . . . she's tried awful hard and you can't go and drive her out of the house like she's a thief!

ZEENA—Fiddlesticks!

ETHAN—She's got no place to go, Zeena . . . what'll she do . . . you can't drive her out!

ZEENA—Rubbish! First you deviled me and nagged because you wouldn't have her here . . . and now . . . Stuff'n nonsense! If she can't take care of herself like you say—how's she goin' to take care of a woman's sick as I am . . . let alone take care of this house?

ETHAN—Zeena . . . you won't have to raise a hand in this house . . . you won't have to do a stick of work around here . . . I promise you . . . I'll do it all myself . . . I'll do every bit of it!

ZEENA—A-yeah! I been noticin' how you been neglectin' the farm lately . . . hangin' around here helpin' Mattie sweepin' and scrubbin' floors . . . gettin' to be a regular old woman . . . ain't you, Ethan? Hm? . . . And you been cryin' over every mouthful we've et and complainin' how poor you are . . . Well . . . I only hope't you'll get a little work done once the new girl gets settled.

ETHAN—It just ain't no use, Zeena . . . for seven years now I done all I could for you . . . and it just ain't no use and I want you to listen to me now! I ain't blamin' you at all, Zeena, but I got to do somethin'. I been tied hand and foot to this farm all my life, Zeena. I been wearin' out my years one right after the other . . . and what's it got either of us? . . . Zeena, I can't go on! I ain't never had a chance here. . . . I mean like now take the opportunities they is out there in the West. If ever I c'd get out there . . . I'd be sure of pickin' up work. Why, that year I put in down to the technological school in Worcester—the same year my father died . . . Well, now, I ain't sayin' I learned much to speak of—but maybe—it was enough so's if ever I got the chance somewheres like out West—why, I might be able to make's much of my life's the next fellow! I want a chance to make a new start—I want to get away and go out West an' make a fresh start, Zeena!

ZEENA (*practically*)—What'd I do?

ETHAN (*quickly and eagerly*)—I'll give you the farm and the mill, Zeena! For your own—I'll make 'em right over to you!

ZEENA—What'd I do with 'em?

ETHAN (*with less certainty*)—If you couldn't get somebody like now Jotham, he's a good man . . . or somebody to run 'em and make 'em pay—you could sell them— (*And he adds emphatically.*) and keep the money! You c'd sell 'em both and keep the money, Zeena . . . all for yourself!

Zeena is not impressed. Who'd she sell to? She knows that is a poser. Ethan knows it, too. But, suggests Ethan, maybe if she couldn't sell right away—maybe out West he could get a fresh start and send her her board! How'd she eat till then, Zeena wants to know. On borrowed money! Ethan would borrow money from Andrew Hale! Money to help him run off and desert his poor sick wife, who ain't hardly able to stand up? . . .

"A woman who's worked and slaved for you, an' your mother before you? Andrew Hale, a man who's a deacon in the church and I don't know what all!—Now, would he do a thing like that? Would he, Ethan? If you got any sense at all—you'll buckle down and tend to your business and stop all this stuff'n non-sense!"

Zeena is up from her rocker now, calling Mattie, ordering Ethan to get the trunk out. She can hear Denis Eady coming. A moment later Denis arrives, Mrs. Hale with him.

"Howdy, Zenobia!" Mrs. Hale calls from outside. "Denis was just now tellin' me you was over to Bettsbridge. . . . How're all the folks and what's the new doctor like? Had any more trouble passin' your food? (*She appears in the doorway.*) How-do—Ethan—awful glad you been able to get Zenobia a new hired girl like the doctor said. My, I only wish't Andrew c'd afford to get me one—well, I always said I don't know what poor Zeena'd 'a' done without she had you to take care of her all these years—Hope't you'll be feelin' fit afore time for the next meetin', Zenobia . . . I'll remember you to the Eastern Star girls! Well—g'by, Ethan. . . . Zenobia!"

Denis and Mis' Hale have gone with the trunk. Jotham has hitched the sorrel and is waiting for Mattie. But Ethan has de-cided to drive Mattie over himself. Nor does Zeena's rather peremptory demand that he stay at home change his mind. He has decided that he will drive Mattie as far as the Flats and there ain't no one goin' to stop him.

Now Zeena is suddenly threatened with an attack. She gasps and holds her hand against her heart. She leans heavily against the cupboard. Now she knows she should have taken her stomach powders last night. She has dragged a chair over to the cupboard and clambers up on it as Ethan and Mattie stand staring at her, fascinated by her every move.

Zeena is fumbling about on the top shelf for her stomach bitters when her hand suddenly comes in contact with the broken pickle dish. One piece falls to the floor. Slowly, reverently, Zeena gathers the other pieces in her hands and gets down from the chair, staring blankly at the broken dish.

"I want to know who done this?" she demands. They do not answer. "I want to know who done this?" she repeats. "Why, Ethan . . . there I was up there gettin' at them stomach powders . . . I'd put away in Father's old spectacle case . . . away up there on the top shelf where I keep all the things I set most store by . . . just so's folks shan't meddle with them. (*She stops abruptly. . . . Her voice breaks. . . . She is more bewildered than angry.*) Why, you seen where I was . . . it took me the kitchen chair and a good long reach to get away up there to Aunt Philura Maple's best pickle dish. I put it up there o' purpose when we was married . . . and it ain't been down once since . . . not once . . . exceptin' only come spring cleanin' time and I lifted it down myself . . . each year . . . with my own two hands . . . so's it shouldn't never get broke . . . I want to know who could've done it."

It might have been the cat, Ethan suggests. The cat couldn't have put the pieces back again, Zeena answers.

"It ain't Ethan's fault, Zeena," speaks up Mattie. "I got it down from the top shelf and I'm the only one to blame for it's getting broke."

"I don't see why you done it . . . I don't see how anybody c'd of went and done a mean thing like that . . ."

"I wanted to make the table look pretty."

"If I'd only listened to what folks is sayin' . . . you'd 'a' gone long before now . . . and this'd never, never've happened! (*She is crying openly now for the first time in her life.*) You're a no-good girl, Mattie Silver, and I've always knowed it . . . I was warned against you when I took you in here out of the kindness of my heart . . . and . . . I tried to keep my nice things where you couldn't get at 'em . . . and now you've went and broke the one thing I cared for most of all!"

She turns away and, carefully carrying the bits of pickle dish, goes up the stairs . . . Ethan and Mattie stand watching her . . . guilty and embarrassed. Then abruptly Ethan stoops over

. . . picks up Mattie's carpet bag and strides forward toward the door. He hesitates there . . . a bit impatiently. Mattie is following slowly . . . looking around. She exits after him.

The curtain falls.

A half hour later Ethan and Mattie arrive at the crest of the hill. They have stopped their sleigh a little distance away and come for a last visit at a spot dear to them. Mattie is nervously apprehensive. They should be going on. But Ethan wanted they should stand there a minute—

"Down there's where we sat at the church picnic last summer," Ethan recalls, pointing over the slope at the back. "I remember findin' your locket for you when you went and lost it. . . . You know you was awful pretty in that pink hat."

"Aw—I wouldn't go's far as that—I guess it was just the hat," protests Mattie.

They wonder where Mattie will go and what she will do. She is near to tears as she supposes she will go back to the mills, and Ethan near to breaking as he protests that she is not strong enough for that work. Still, there is nothing else for her to think of doing, and no relatives she'd ask to help her. Ethan would go with her if he could. Go anywhere. She must know that. Would Mattie have gone with him? "Tell me, Matt! Tell me!" he pleads.

For a moment Mattie cannot control her tears. When she does she answers him quite calmly.

MATTIE—I used to think of it sometimes, summer nights when the moon was shinin' in my window so bright't I couldn't sleep.

ETHAN (*amazed*)—As long ago as that?

MATTIE (*very honestly*)—The first time was right down there . . . at the picnic in the beginning of summer. . . . Still'n all . . . I guess we didn't get to be what you might call friends for a long while after that . . . did we?

ETHAN—I guess I was thinkin' a lot about you . . . right from the first, Matt.

MATTIE—You was! My, you'd never've knowed it!

ETHAN (*with difficulty*)—I guess I didn't get to know it myself . . . right up till we was here . . . the other night. . . . I'm tied hand and foot, Matt . . . there just ain't anythin' that I c'n do!

MATTIE—You c'n write me sometimes—

ETHAN—What good'll writin' do? I want to do for you and care for you like you need! I want to put out my hand and touch you . . . I want to be there if you're sick and when you're lonesome!

MATTIE (*trying hard to convince him*)—Oh, you mustn't think but what I'll be all right, Ethan! (*Then suddenly terribly afraid.*) Oh, I wish't I was dead! I wish't I was!

ETHAN—Matt! Don't you say it!

MATTIE—Why shouldn't I when it's true and I ain't ashamed, and I been thinkin' it all night and all day!

ETHAN—Matt!

MATTIE—It's so and I want to be dead!

ETHAN—You be quiet, Matt, and don't you even think it!

MATTIE—There's never nobody been good to me but you!

ETHAN (*sharply*)—Don't go and say that neither 'cause I can't so much's lift my hand for you!

MATTIE—But it's true all the same!

Ethan has moved abruptly away to the crest of the hill. Mattie follows and takes hold of his arm. From across the valley comes the faint sound of children's laughter. That reminds them that this was the evening they were going coasting. They can still go, Ethan decides quickly. They can and will! Over Mattie's protests he has taken Sam Colt's sled and has carried it to the top of the hill.

"Come on, Matt—hop on," he shouts, joyfully. "It's the last chance we'll get! You ain't a-scared, are you?"

"I told you I ain't the kind to be scared," she says. But suddenly she is scared. "Oh, Ethan . . . Ethan!" she cries, burying her face in his coat; throwing her arms about his neck; pulling his face down to hers and kissing him. "Good-by . . . good-by, Ethan!"

"I can't let you go now! I can't!"

"Oh, I can't go, either."

Helplessly they stare at each other, and from their misery an idea is born in Mattie's mind.

"Ethan! Ethan! We're goin'!"

"But where, Matt!"

"I want you sh'd take me down with you!"

"Down where?"

"Down the coast right off!"

"What?"

"Down the coast so't we'll never, never come up again . . . never!"

"What do you mean?"

"Right into that elm down there . . . you c'd do it . . . you c'd, Ethan . . . so't we'd never have to leave each other any more!"

"What're you sayin' . . . what're you sayin' . . . Oh, Matt . . . Matt . . ."

"Ethan, where'll I go if I leave you?" Matt is breathless, her fevered enthusiasm sweeping Ethan along with her. "I don't know how I'd get along alone . . . you said so yourself . . . you said I couldn't never do it . . . an' I don't want to an' there'll be that strange girl in the house, an' she'll sleep in my bed where I used to lay nights and listen to hear you come up the stairs . . ."

"I can't go back there . . . I can't go back to that place, never again," says Ethan.

Ethan is as breathless as Mattie, now. He has drawn up the sled. She seats herself on the front of it, but that is not the way Ethan would arrange it. "We're goin' down headfirst and together . . . holdin' each other tight," he orders.

He has spun Mattie around and seated himself on the sled ready to lie down beside her.

"Don't be a-scared, Matt . . . it ain't goin' to hurt . . . it ain't goin' to hurt at all . . . we're goin' to fetch that elm so hard we won't feel anything at all . . . exceptin' only each other."

He has lain down. Their arms are about each other. Ethan pushes the sled forward. It hangs momentarily over the crest.

"Hold me . . . hold me tight, Ethan!"

The sled has plunged over the drop. The lights fade out. There is the sound of the sled rushing down the hill as the scene fades from view.

With the raising of the lights we are back in the kitchen of the Frome farmhouse the night of the prologue. Zeena, her gray hair thinned at fifty-five, wearing a slatternly and shapeless calico dress, is dozing in her rocker by the stove, a mail-order catalogue in her lap.

From outside the jingle of sleighbells is faintly heard. Presently Ethan enters, carrying a lantern. He walks slowly, dragging one leg. His face is drawn and sunken and old. Zeena helps him get his overcoat off his hunched shoulders. He lurches awkwardly toward a chair at the table.

"Did you get that dollar?" Zeena wants to know.

"That's what I went for—ain't it?" snaps Ethan.

"Well—a dollar's a dollar, Ethan—but it ain't a whole lot for drivin' all the way over to Corbury an' back this weather—I don't know's I'd do it again in the mornin'—for that price."

"Another dollar'll come handy, won't it?"

A querulous whining call comes from the parlor. "Zeenie! Zeenie!" A moment later Zeena has shuffled into the parlor and reappeared pushing a crude home-made wheel chair. In the chair sits Mattie Silver, her thin, gray hair unkempt, her face bloodless and drawn. "In her eyes is that vacant stare not uncommon among people who have suffered a paralysis of the spine." The chair tips a bit as Zeena pushes it across the door jamb. "Oh, Zeenie! You hurt! You did that on purpose!" whines Mattie.

"No—now don't say that, Mattie. You can't say that when I've been doin' what I can for you for twenty years."

"I wish you hadn't—I wish you'd let me die. Why didn't you let me die that night they carried Ethan an' me in here!"

Zeena has filled a cup with warm milk from the stove and held it to Mattie's lips. She calls to Ethan to get a blanket and put it around Mattie. But Mattie will have none of Ethan's help.

"No! Don't you touch me!" she whines, as Ethan lurches forward with the blanket. "Zeenie, you do it. He's so clumsy—he always hurts me . . . I can't stand havin' him touch me . . . Ain't you ever goin' to die, Ethan Frome?"

Ethan has shuffled back to his chair. He sits motionless facing Mattie.

"The Fromes're tough, I guess," he says. "The doctor was sayin' to me only the other day—'Frome,' he says, 'you'll likely touch a hundred.' " Slowly—

THE CURTAIN FALLS

PRIDE AND PREJUDICE
A Comedy in Three Acts

By Helen Jerome

(From the Novel of Jane Austen)

ONE of the major surprises of a surprising season was the immediate and continued success of Helen Jerome's Jane Austen dramatization, the sentimental comedy called "Pride and Prejudice," after the novel from which it was made.

It was counted a little incredible that any hard-bitten Broadway manager would consider the production of so frankly artificial a period drama as this, and equally incredible that New York playgoers in any considerable numbers would support it if it were produced. After all, there has been a definite tendency on the part of producers to favor the drama of bite and sting, written in dialogue that sears as frequently as it blisters; a drama infrequently credited with anything resembling charm, either in its character types or its pictured scene. And this modern drama has been generally accepted as fixing the style of the current theatre.

"Pride and Prejudice" did, as a matter of record, wait a year or more for production, due to managerial reluctance to take the necessary chance. Arthur Hopkins held an option on the play a year ago, hoping to bring Katharine Hepburn back from pictures for another try at the acted drama. When Miss Hepburn was not available he gave up the enterprise. The play fell to Max Gordon and he, having the backing of certain motion picture interests, which served reasonably to strengthen his normal gambling instinct, decided it could be done with a proper cast. He sent to England for his leading players, Adrianne Allen and Colin Keith-Johnston, made a most careful and wise selection of other players for the supporting roles and was rewarded with the success noted.

"Pride and Prejudice" is a restored daguerreotype. That it should preserve and perhaps sharpen the Jane Austen wit was a complete surprise to its critics and largely responsible for their expressed joy in the dramatization. "I had felt that the glorious and abundant subtleties of Miss Austen's text . . . would be obscured when transferred to the more obvious medium of the

theatre," wrote John Mason Brown. ". . . Amazingly enough the
same quiet technique which is so winning in the novel is effectively maintained in the performance."

It was, however, generally admitted by the play reviewers that
the comedy does demand a superior type of casting if its flavor
is to be properly enjoyed. It could, shabbily done, doubtless
prove quite terrible.

Miss Jerome, who has taken surprisingly few liberties with
the text, her chief condensation reducing the number of Bennet
girls from five to three, opens her play in the Bennet living room
at Longbourn, "a large, deep, comfortable room, shabby and
used." There is a large family portrait of a man with side whiskers
over the fireplace, and through colored French windows at the
back a view may be had of the conservatory. There are large
double doors, also at the back, leading to the principal hall of
the house. "The furniture is not of one style or period, but gives
the impression of having been accumulated over a space of years."
It is a frosty Winter afternoon. Mr. Bennet is huddled in an
easy chair before the fire with a book and his pipe, apparently
greatly enjoying a comfort that is shortly disturbed by the appearance of Mrs. Bennet in a state of some excitement and fairly
bursting with news. Netherfield Park, she is eager to report, has
been rented at last; taken by a young man of large fortune from
the north of England who has already installed a retinue of
servants.

The name of the new tenant is Bingley. He is single and his
fortune must run to four or five thousand a year. It is quite possible, Mrs. Bennet is convinced, that Mr. Bingley may fall in
love with one of her daughters, and it is therefore imperative
that Mr. Bennet should call upon him at the earliest possible
moment.

Mr. Bennet successfully resists Mrs. Bennet's excitement. He
sees no reason for such a call upon the new neighbor. If she likes,
Mrs. Bennet may take the girls over, or send them by themselves. Mr. Bennet is not particularly interested. Even when Mrs.
Bennet would stir him to competitive action by reporting that
Sir William and Lady Lucas are already thinking of such a visit,
he refuses to respond with more enthusiasm than to suggest that
he might write Mr. Bingley assuring him of his (their father's)
consent to whichever of his daughters he desires to marry, and
put in an especially good word for little Lizzy.

"I hope you'll do no such thing," indignantly replies Mrs.
Bennet. "And Lizzy is not a bit better than either of the others:

she's not as beautiful as Jane, nor as good-humored as Lydia. (*Resentfully.*) But you always *did* give her the preference."

"Well, they have none of them much to recommend them. They're just as silly and ignorant as most girls, though Lizzy has *some* glimmerings of sense."

"Mr. Bennet, how can you abuse your own children? You take delight in vexing me! You have no compassion on my nerves."

"You are mistaken, my dear. I have a high respect for your nerves. I have heard you mention them with consideration for these last twenty years."

By this time Mrs. Bennet is on the verge of tears and Mr. Bennet has decided to take a ride before tea.

A moment later Lady Lucas and Miss Lucas have arrived. Mrs. Lucas swoops in fussily and Charlotte, her daughter, follows with a certain demureness that in no way detracts from her natural poise. Lady Lucas is also quite full of the news of the new neighbor. The Lucases have met the young man and Charlotte is, in her mother's estimation, already quite smitten. Now, if they can only keep pretty Jane Bennet out of the way—

Jane and her younger sister Lydia come bounding into the room at this juncture, followed the next moment by Elizabeth. Jane, it may be, is the prettiest as well as physically the frailest of the trio. Lydia is the more sturdy, self-reliant type, and Elizabeth a composed and prettily dignified third.

The news is that Mr. Bingley has just returned to London, thereby missing a dinner at the Lucases to which Charlotte, her mother is sure, had been looking forward with great interest. He is to return shortly, however, and is to give a ball at Michaelmas. Mr. Bingley is also bringing his sister Caroline back with him to keep his house, and is to have a Mr. Darcy down. Darcy is the squire of Pemberly, and is even wealthier than Mr. Bingley, as well as his inseparable friend. It is reported also that Mr. Darcy is engaged to the daughter of the Lady Catherine de Bourgh, and that he is a high and mighty young man who would not look at anyone under a peer's daughter—

"Then Charlotte is not in the running, either," observes Mrs. Bennet, with considerable satisfaction.

"You forget, dear Mrs. Bennet, that since Sir William was knighted by His Majesty, Charlotte has been presented at Court."

"Mr. Bennet was *born* a gentleman, dear Mrs. Lucas," counters Mrs. Bennet, with added sweetness; ". . . isn't it fortunate for us? My girls don't need to be presented. It saves so much expense."

Run.

granola bars

fruit

"PRIDE AND PREJUDICE"

r. Wickham repeats the story that Darcy had injured and ruined him. . . . "I have never d Mr. Darcy," admits Elizabeth, slowly, "but I did not believe him dishonest."

(Adrianne Allen, John D. Seymour)

The Lucases, ready to go, pause at the door. Lady Lucas has a parting compliment for Jane. "Yes, child, I wish Charlotte had been endowed with a quarter of your good looks. . . . You'll certainly be the belle of the Bingley ball—though it is true that sometimes—men prefer character. Good-by, my dears, thank you for the delightful tea . . . good-by, Mrs. Bennet."

Mrs. Bennet is properly incensed at her ladyship's catty farewell thrust, but the girls are not hurt. Jane doesn't care whether she has character or not, so long as they all love her, and Elizabeth is convinced that her sister has the loveliest character in the world.

Now the female Bennets are thrown into a further state of excitement by the sudden and unexpected appearance of Mr. Bennet with two young gentlemen. These turn out to be none other than the new neighbors, Mr. Bingley and Mr. Darcy, the former a friendly, unaffected young man, the latter a rather bored, superior sort. Mr. Bennet had been riding to Netherfield to call on Mr. Bingley and his friend when he met them en route to the village.

Introductions having now been attended to, it is Mrs. Bennet who, with gushing enthusiasm, would welcome the newcomers to Maryton.

"It *is* so nice to have some eligible young men in the neighborhood at last, Mr. Bingley," she is saying. "I hope we shall see you very often this winter?"

"I think I can promise that, ma'am," replies Bingley, his eyes on Jane, to whom he has been paying as much direct attention as circumstances permit.

"I hope you are finding our part of the country to your liking, Mr. Darcy," ventures Elizabeth, seeking to entertain the haughty and unresponsive friend.

"I do not care for the country, Miss Bennet," replies Darcy, with a stiff bow.

"What a pity! Then it must irk you to be compelled to live in it. . . ."

The bored Darcy makes no response. There is a puzzled look in Elizabeth's eyes, but she does not pursue the subject further. Tea is served and the conversation becomes more general. Lydia, quite obviously bored, slips out, leaving the field to her sisters. An exchange of compliments between Elizabeth and Mr. Bingley moves Mr. Darcy to suggest that Elizabeth must be a student of character and she admits that at times she is.

"But you must have little use for your gift here?" Darcy continues.

"On the contrary, sir. I find that the people who live where they can see the sky are scarcely less interesting than those who prefer noise and close proximity to others."

"I am of the opinion that those who live in the country . . . belong to the country."

Darcy's supercilious implication has not eluded either Elizabeth or her father. It is Bingley who clears the situation. "Well, as for me, I like 'em both," he admits, moving closer to Jane and pretending to need another cup of tea. "Give me a horse, a long road, a whiff of hay . . . (*in a tone only meant for* JANE's *reddening ears*) and a country rose!"

It is embarrassing to Jane suddenly to hear her mother again extolling her beauty. She has shyly made room for Mr. Bingley on the couch beside her, and the others are not unmindful of the frank avowal of interest the young people are showing in each other.

"Why, when Jane was only fifteen," Mrs. Bennet is saying, "there was a gentleman at my brother's at Cheapside, London—"

Mr. Darcy shudders. "Cheapside is not mentioned in polite society, Mother," interposes Elizabeth, noting the shudder.

MRS. BENNET—Nonsense, Lizzy. . . . (*Continues to* BINGLEY.) He was so much in love with her that my sister-in-law was certain he would make her an offer before we left.

DARCY (*dryly*)—And did he?

MRS. BENNET (*defiantly*)—I'm sure he thought her too young. (*Brightly.*) But he wrote some verses on her . . . very pretty they were too.

ELIZABETH—And so ended his affection. Poetry can often do that. (*Smiling.*) Love has to be pretty strong to survive a bad sonnet.

BENNET—Even a good one might be enough to finish it.

DARCY (*to* ELIZABETH)—I thought that poetry was the food of love?

ELIZABETH (*smiling politely*)—I could not imagine you ever thought about either, Mr. Darcy.

DARCY—Is this an example of your gift, Miss Bennet?

ELIZABETH—Oh, no, sir, I only study those characters that interest me.

BENNET (*rising*)—What about releasing the gentlemen to come to the library for a glass of Madeira wine, my dear? (*To* MRS. BENNET.) That homicidal feeling is creeping over me that invariably attacks me at tea parties.

BINGLEY—That is very good in you, sir, but we must be getting back to Netherfield. My sister is alone.

MRS. BENNET (*giggling affectedly*)—You mustn't believe that Mr. Bennet really wishes to murder my guests, sir. He is not such a bear as he pretends. (*Shaking a finger at* BENNET.) If you continue to say things like that the gentlemen will begin to pity me.

DARCY (*bowing stiffly before her*)—Indeed, ma'am, we should never dream of pitying you. (*The slightest emphasis on the "you."*)

BINGLEY (*bowing over* MRS. BENNET's *hand*)—Your servant, ma'am. I trust we may look forward to your visit to Netherfield very soon . . . (*a glance at* JANE *and a smile at* ELIZABETH) . . . with your daughters? My sister is impatient to receive you.

MRS. BENNET (*ecstatically*)—Tell Miss Bingley we shall call tomorrow. Indeed, we should have done so earlier but understood . . . that . . . you were both in town . . . Lady Lucas . . .

A warning look from Elizabeth stops her mother. Mr. Bennet at the door has soon ushered the visitors into the hall. Now the Bennet women are agreed that Mr. Bingley is a darling, but that Mr. Darcy is quite beyond words, being no less than a stuck-up prig. Even Lydia, rejoining the group, had seen enough of Darcy to disapprove of him violently. On the other hand, the impression that Jane had unquestionably made upon Mr. Bingley is decidedly encouraging.

Mr. Bennet, returned from seeing his guests depart, is forced to a confession. A letter had come for him a week before about which he several times had tried to tell them, but each time had been interrupted. The letter brought news that Mr. Bennet's cousin, Mr. William Collins, would be with them for dinner this evening and prepared to stay some time as their guest.

This is startling news, particularly to Mrs. Bennet, who loathes Mr. Collins as the odious creature to whom the Bennet estate is entailed, and who will inherit it upon the death of Mr. Bennet—

"Well, you can all laugh, but I simply can't bear to think of Collins coming and taking my home when you die," declares Mrs. Bennet, with tears in her voice. "If it were not for the entail I shouldn't mind it."

"What should you not mind, Mrs. Bennet?" asks her husband.

"I shouldn't mind anything at all."

"Let us be thankful then that you are preserved from such a

state of complete insensibility."

"I can never be thankful, Mr. Bennet, for anything about the entail. How you could have the conscience to entail an estate away from your own daughters, I shall *never* understand, and all for the sake of Mr. Collins. Why should *he* have it any more than anyone else?"

"I can only leave that . . . for you to determine, my dear. It certainly *is* a most iniquitous affair, and nothing can clear Mr. Collins from the guilt of inheriting it, but if you will listen a moment . . . I shall tell you his reason for inviting himself . . . your heart may be softened."

"Indeed, I will not. I think it very impertinent of him to invite himself—and very hypocritical—and I shall be very reserved with him—very reserved indeed!"

In his letter it appears that Mr. Collins has hinted that one object of his visit will be to look over the Bennet daughters with the idea of choosing one for a wife, "so that he can partly atone for the guilt of inheriting our estate," as Mr. Bennet explains.

This admission indicates to Mrs. Bennet that it is possible that Mr. Collins *has* some proper feeling, and likewise changes to some extent the attitude of the girls. They are now inclined to agree with Lydia that such a man must be a bit of an ass, and to laugh at their mother for defending him.

Now it is discovered through the butler that Mr. Collins has already arrived and been taken to his room. A moment later Collins has entered the living room with "a grave, stately air and ridiculously formal manners." In his greetings he bows himself almost double and it is as much as Lydia can do to suppress her mirth. There are compliments following the introductions, and it is not long before Mrs. Bennet has referred not too delicately to the matter of the entailed estate—not, of course, that she blames Mr. Collins—who is duly aware of the unpopularity of his position.

"Indeed," admits that lightly embarrassed cleric. "I am very sensible of the hardship to my fair cousins." He bows low, and smiles roguishly. "But I have come with a plan." He surveys the girls, "not without a slightly carnal look in the corner of his pious eye." . . . "Perhaps, when we are better acquainted . . ."

"Oh, Mr. Collins, sir. You must excuse me. I must go see that Hill is getting out some of Mr. Bennet's better port—we don't usually serve it except for special guests—"

"You are hospitality itself, dear Mrs. Bennet."

Lydia gives a stifled explosion and moves nearer the door as

Mr. Bennet, not entirely in control of an impulse to sympathize with his daughter, takes up the conversation. Mr. Bennet has been pleased to note, through Mr. Collins' letters, the latter's good fortune in his patroness, the Lady Catherine de Bourgh, and Mr. Collins is pleased to suggest that it will be quite possible for them all to meet her ladyship. Lady Catherine is a most kindly person of rank, and has twice invited him to dine at Rosings, which is her mansion, and once to make up her poole at quadrille.

The Bennets are duly, though lightly, impressed, and Mr. Collins continues with an account of certain subtle flatteries by which he has pleased her ladyship.

"You certainly have a high sense of duty," ventures Mr. Bennet. Mr. Collins bows with proper humility. "How lucky that you possess such a delicate talent for flattery! (*In a tone of awe.*) May I ask whether it comes naturally or do you think it out?"

COLLINS (*with a deprecating air*)—No, it is quite natural with me, sir. I try to find the compliment to fit the occasion as elegantly as I can. (*A chime comes from the hall.*)

JANE—Ah, the dressing bell! We dine at seven-thirty, Mr. Collins.

COLLINS—After dinner, my dear cousins, if you care for it—I am considered a tolerable reader—I will gladly read aloud to you as we gather round the fire. (*They turn back before going out.*)

LYDIA—Oh, that will be entrancing! (*Mischievously.*) We have a vast deal of novels from the lending library at Meryton. Some truly delightful—

COLLINS (*breaks in here too horrified to listen to more*)—Novels! Oh, my dear cousin! I never read such works! (*Brightly.*) But I have brought with me an excellent volume of Fordyce's Sermons. . . .

The sisters gasp and chuckle as they exit and the curtain falls.

Some weeks later the Bennets are giving an assembly. The living room is brightly lighted and from the ballroom the sound of dance music can be heard. On a long side table there is a punchbowl and presently couples begin drifting into the room and toward the punch.

At the moment the assembly is breaking up. Mrs. Bennet and Lady Lucas have sought the living room for a few moments' rest and a few moments' exchange of observations as well. Mrs. Bennet has been agreeably impressed with the manners and appearance of the group now drawing away from the punch and saying their good nights.

"Ah, me! To be young again! . . . and have nice young gentlemen wanting to protect one," sighs Mrs. Bennet. "Mr. Bennet is not a bit romantic. Don't you think our husbands could learn the art of pretty speeches from that gallant young Wickham?"

"Pretty speeches are more difficult *after* marriage, my dear Mrs. Bennet."

Elizabeth Bennet and Charlotte Lucas, coming into the room at this moment, overhear Lady Lucas. Elizabeth would protest such a statement. It is shattering to her dreams, and, she feels sure, to those of Charlotte as well.

But Charlotte has neither dreams nor illusions. "I was disillusioned when I was ten," says she. "I read the life of Henry the Eighth."

"That's not nice reading for young ladies, my love," protests Mrs. Bennet. "Wasn't he that very fickle gentleman? I hear he was quite rude to his wives, too."

"Oh, no . . . he only had their heads chopped off when they annoyed him . . . not altogether a bad idea," suggests Charlotte.

Mrs. Bennet, dragging Lady Lucas with her, has gone to speed the remaining guests. Elizabeth and Charlotte are alone.

ELIZABETH—Isn't it a relief to get away from all those dancing dervishers? Will you have some of this shrub, Charlotte?

CHARLOTTE (*accepting*)—Mr. Bingley was saying what a good idea it was to have this away from the supper room "where a fellow could have his tipple in peace." Nice young gentleman, isn't he?

ELIZABETH—Quite charming. Jane seems to think so too. How lovely the darling looks tonight. Her eyes are like stars. I wonder if her shyness is such an asset, though?

CHARLOTTE—You fear Bingley might need encouragement?

ELIZABETH—Few men possess enough heart to be really in love without it.

CHARLOTTE—Yes, but if you and I can see her preference for him, he must be a simpleton indeed not to discover it.

ELIZABETH—Ah, but remember, he doesn't know Jane's disposition as we do. (*Thoughtfully.*) I wonder if she is sure of her own feelings. . . . With Jane . . . one can't be sure . . . she is so reserved. . . .

CHARLOTTE—Well, I should think she has as good a chance of happiness if she married him now as if she had been studying his character a twelvemonth. Happiness in marriage is entirely a matter of chance. It's better to know as little as possible of the defects of anyone. (*Both pause and exchange rather wise smiles.*)

ELIZABETH—Be careful, that punch is potent. Father mixed it himself before he went off and locked himself in his study. (*Chuckles.*) He said that we should need a good stimulant to bear this menagerie we had collected for tonight. He hates all this sort of thing. . . . I don't think it so very amusing myself . . . do you, Charlotte?

CHARLOTTE—It's a means to an end . . . and surely Miss Bingley is warning enough against spinsterhood.

ELIZABETH (*laughing*)—Is a warning needed?

CHARLOTTE—Did you notice the fair young Lydia's triumphant progress in the ballroom? Right under the maternal nose too, and your mother just beamed on her.

ELIZABETH—Yes, Mamma is rather astonishing at times. Shocked if a gentleman glimpses our ankles, but to let him understand that he may attain complete possession is perfectly proper.

The name of a Mr. Wickham has come into the conversation. He is a new man, brought by Lydia's Captain Denny. Very attractive, Elizabeth thinks. But Charlotte is not so sure. There is something not just "right" about Mr. Wickham, she feels.

"Don't waste your time, dear. Concentrate on Darcy . . . rich . . . aristocratic—"

"—priggish and snobbish," counters Elizabeth.

"Yes, but when do we ever meet the knights of our dreams? Men were put into the world to teach women the laws of compromise."

"Don't be ridiculous, Charlotte."

Elizabeth and Charlotte have gone into the conservatory. They are there when Captain Denny and Lydia come for a glass of punch—which Lydia has been forbidden, but of which she is excessively fond. It has been a great night for Lydia, with not a dance missed nor an officer overlooked.

Elizabeth and Charlotte are still in the conservatory when Darcy drifts into the living room. He is gazing moodily into the fire when Bingley comes anxiously in search of him. Elizabeth and Charlotte are at the door listening when Bingley frankly upbraids his friend for not taking a more active part in the dancing.

"I certainly will not dance," they hear Darcy say. "You know how I detest it unless I am particularly acquainted with my partner. At such an assembly as this it would be insupportable." (*The girls show various reactions to this.*)

"But—"

DARCY (*interrupting*)—Your sister is engaged for most of the dances, and there is not another woman in the room with whom it would not be a punishment to stand up. (*The girls drop him an ironical curtsey.*)

BINGLEY—Darcy, I wouldn't be as fastidious as you for a kingdom. Upon my honor, I've met never with so many pleasant girls in my life as I have this evening, and some of them are uncommonly pretty.

DARCY—You've been dancing with the only pretty girl most of the evening. (*Girls prick up their ears comically.*)

BINGLEY (*rapturously*)—Isn't she exquisite? The loveliest creature I ever beheld. But what about her sister? She's quite pretty and I daresay just as charming.

DARCY (*boredly*)—Miss Elizabeth? Thank you!

BINGLEY—But really, she is most agreeable.

DARCY—Tolerable—just tolerable. Not handsome enough to tempt *me*.

BINGLEY—But she is the daughter of the house. It's scandalous to allow her to sit out any dances . . . she has missed two or three . . .

DARCY (*amused*)—I am in no humor to give consequence to young ladies who are slighted by other men.

BINGLEY (*banteringly*)—Shame on you, Darcy. She is a delightful girl. Come and find out for yourself.

DARCY (*submitting*)—Oh, very well . . . for your sake. But I'll only stand up with her once. (*Exit to ballroom.*)

ELIZABETH (*coming in with* CHARLOTTE)—Why do we tolerate that man?

CHARLOTTE—No doubt because he is of the very rich. Those who do not envy the tribe, adore it.

ELIZABETH—Well, I shall see that he does not come here again.

CHARLOTTE—You forget, dear, that he is the bosom friend of Bingley and may influence him against Jane.

Mr. Wickham has come from the ballroom in a state of agitation. Something very unpleasant has happened. Mrs. Bennet had introduced him to Darcy and Darcy had turned his back and walked away. Mr. Wickham is greatly insulted!

Elizabeth is at a loss to understand why Mr. Darcy should

object to Mr. Wickham, seeing that they had never met—
But it appears that they had met. In fact they know each other
very well. Mr. Wickham's father, it seems, had been manager of
the Darcy estates in Derbyshire.

"My father managed the estate so well, in fact," relates Mr.
Wickham, "that before the elder Darcy died he instructed his son
to pay me a sum of money and to bestow on me the clerical living
in his gift at Pemberley. But I bore you . . . with all this . . .
I'll say good night." (*Turns to bow, also to* CHARLOTTE.)

"No, wait. Sit down, Mr. Wickham. . . . I want to hear this,"
Elizabeth protests. "I am more interested than you think."

Mr. Wickham is not eager to stay; he would not meet Darcy
again and he continues to watch the door anxiously. He repeats
the story that Darcy had injured and ruined him and had, in fact,
forced him to enter the army, a life which he detests—

"I have never liked Mr. Darcy," admits Elizabeth, slowly,
"but I did not believe him dishonest."

"Thank you for your sympathy. It is very precious to me."
Mr. Wickham is edging nervously toward the door. "Convey my
thanks and regrets to your mother. . . . Good night, Miss Elizabeth. Good night, Miss Lucas. I'll go out this way—" He has
disappeared through the conservatory.

"There's a sample of Darcy for you," snaps Elizabeth. Nor
will she accept Charlotte's suggestion that there must be two
sides to the story. . . .

Darcy comes from the vestibule. He is searching for Miss Elizabeth to ask her to dance the last extra with him. Elizabeth is
too tired to dance any more. Besides she feels the honor would be
more than she could bear.

DARCY—Have I had the misfortune to offend you?

ELIZABETH—It is rather Mr. Wickham whom you have
offended, sir . . . one of my mother's guests.

DARCY—It is too great an honor for him, ma'am.

ELIZABETH—I beg your pardon. I found him very charming
. . . and I am sure my mother did.

DARCY—He is blessed with the charm that makes new friend-
ships. I doubt if he possesses the quality to retain them.

ELIZABETH (*moving away indifferently*)—He certainly lacked
the talent to retain yours. (*They stand facing each other, neither
speaks. There is a rather funny silence.*) Did you enjoy the
music, Mr. Darcy?

DARCY—Very much, thank you.

ELIZABETH (*ironically*)—It's your turn to make a remark now.

DARCY—Whatever you wish me to say, you may consider said.

ELIZABETH—Very well. I daresay there are times when perhaps it is better to limit conversation to yes or no.

DARCY (*quietly*)—Are you consulting your own feelings . . . or do you imagine that you are gratifying mine?

ELIZABETH (*defiantly*)—Both. . . . I recognize our similarity. We are each unsociable and taciturn . . . reluctant to speak unless we can say something that will astonish the whole room or be handed down to posterity.

DARCY—I hardly think that describes your character, Miss Bennet . . . you are probably describing mine and include yourself out of pity for my wounded feelings.

ELIZABETH—Have you any, Mr. Darcy?

DARCY—Evidently you have decided about that. . . .

ELIZABETH—I hear such different accounts of you . . . I am puzzled. . . . When you are present some of the reports seem . . . difficult to believe.

DARCY (*haughtily*)—Why bother to try to solve the puzzle? It's much easier to—

Miss Bingley has come in search of Mr. Darcy. She is tall, definitely spinsterish and of rather commanding presence. She, too, is interested in Mr. Wickham's appearance at the Bennets', and particularly interested in noticing that Elizabeth had been noticeably attentive. She has heard, too, of the romantic tales with which Mr. Wickham had been entertaining Elizabeth.

"Did he happen to remember to tell you that his father was merely a steward on the Darcy estate . . . a sort of servant?" inquires Miss Bingley, as Darcy, obviously displeased with the trend the conversation is taking, turns away. "No doubt he told you that Mr. Darcy had injured him?"

"He did."

"Do let me caution you not to give too much credence to his tales. The truth happens to be just the contrary. . . . I am sorry you must be disillusioned. . . . But what can you expect, considering his origin?"

"That seems to be his chief fault in your eyes, Miss Bingley. People don't arrange their origins in advance . . . nor have I observed that the well born are invariably the well bred. (*Slowly and meaningly.*) I think perhaps you attach too much importance to the accident of birth."

"Accident? Really, Miss Bennet!"

"Didn't you ever learn any biology?"

"I hope I was never so unfeminine (*with distaste*). I'm told you are clever . . . and read books on subjects that only belong to gentlemen. . . . Well, it won't get you very far. Men detest clever women."

"They make them feel uncomfortable, no doubt. When you speak of 'getting far,' I suppose you refer to marriage with one of them?"

"Certainly. And you are going the wrong way about that, I assure you."

"Well," interposes Charlotte, with a drawl, "why did you let them discover how clever you are, Miss Bingley?"

Elizabeth has quickly excused herself to see Charlotte to the door. It is a relief to Miss Bingley to have her go. Miss Bingley can hardly wait to get back to Netherfield to hear Mr. Darcy's opinion of this ill-bred young woman. Mr. Darcy, on the other hand, seems slightly amused. Far from holding an unpleasant thought about Elizabeth, he has been thinking of what "beautiful eyes can do in the face of a pretty woman."

Miss Bingley is a little shocked and resentful. Mr. Darcy must know that the Bennet family is really quite impossible. The fact that her brother Charles seems to be falling in love with Jane Bennet is becoming a source of great worry to Miss Bingley. She does not dislike Jane, but her brother's interests must come first. She thinks perhaps Charles should be induced to return to London for a while, that his mind may be diverted by a little play-going and other excitement. Mr. Darcy is quite willing to help Miss Bingley with this conspiracy. . . .

Mr. Collins has joined Miss Bingley and Mr. Darcy. He is quite twittery about a recent discovery that Mr. Darcy is the nephew of Lady Catherine de Bourgh. He is pleased to bring Mr. Darcy news that her ladyship is enjoying robust health and is quite interested in his (Collins') wooing. It is Miss Elizabeth, Collins coyly admits, whom he has chosen to be the mistress of his parsonage. He has not spoken, but his attentions must surely have plainly indicated his desires.

"May I congratulate you, Mr. Collins?" asks Miss Bingley, with considerable enthusiasm. "A most suitable marriage! I don't imagine you will be refused. It is no easy matter for girls without connections *or* wealth to find suitable husbands, especially when they are hampered with an over supply of intelligence."

"Oh, you do her an injustice, Miss Bingley," Mr. Collins is quick to answer. "I'm sure my dear cousin is not unsexed with too much brain. I shouldn't like that at all, you know. . . ."

Mr. Collins has gone and Charles Bingley has arrived. Charles is ready for the drive home, but reluctant to leave. He has had such a good evening. And he has found out all about Jane Bennet's uncle.

"I dislike speaking badly of a man I've never met," Charles admits. "She told me he is an attorney! . . ."

"Good heavens!" This from Darcy.

"And lives at Cheapside!" An echo from Miss Bingley.

"Well, if Jane and Elizabeth have enough uncles to fill all Cheapside, it doesn't make them one bit less lovable and charming," answers Charles, with spirit.

"True, but it does materially lessen their chances of marriage with men of any consideration in the world," says Darcy.

They have all gone now. Elizabeth and Jane have come to see that the room is straightened up and the fire safely out.

"Well, darling? You've had a happy time? I've noticed you." Elizabeth is proud of Jane.

"Lizzy . . . I'm too happy! It frightens me!"

"My darling . . . happiness belongs to you . . . you are so sweet and good. . . . Is it Charles?" And, as Jane shyly nods, she asks: "Has he made you an offer, dearest?"

"Oh, no, Lizzy, you know he will ask my father first . . . but I know he will . . . oh, I know. . . ."

"One can't always be sure . . . in these matters. . . . What makes you so sure?"

And Jane, suddenly suffused with blushes and clinging tightly to her sister, confesses: "He . . . *kissed* . . . me, Lizzy!"

Jane and Elizabeth "cling together in the emotion of two innocent and tender souls to whom a kiss meant love and love the whole meaning of life. They shed a few trembling tears and wipe them from each other's cheeks with their doll-like handkerchiefs."

"Well then, darling, you're as good as married," prophesies Elizabeth. They are contemplating each other with wet, shining eyes as the curtain falls.

ACT II

A week later, on a cold, damp, typically English morning, the Bennets are gathering one by one in the living room following a typically detached English breakfast. The first to arrive is Lydia. The youngest Bennet bounds in and goes straight for the *Times*, which Hill has carefully placed on a small table by the master's favorite seat before the fireplace. Miss Lydia is no respecter of her father's crankiness about his morning paper, nor one to listen to the protesting Hill, who knows that he will bear the brunt of the Bennet anger if the paper is disturbed.

Miss Lydia is eager to discover where Captain Denny's regiment is stationed, and she clings to the paper till the last minute. Then, aware of her father's approach, she reluctantly puts the *Times* down just before he reaches his chair.

It is Mrs. Bennet's opinion that Lydia is wasting her time with penniless fellows in uniforms, but Lydia is deeply impressed with the way a uniform shows off a dashing figure, in addition to being extremely genteel, a statement that is a little too much for Mr. Bennet, who comes out from behind his *Times* to remark with asperity—

"Upon my word, I think you must be quite the silliest creature in the country. I've suspected it for some time. But now I am convinced."

"I am astonished, my dear Mr. Bennet, that you should be so ready to think your own daughter silly. If I wished to think that way of anybody's child, it would never be my own."

"If my children *are* idiots I hope I am intelligent enough to know it," hopes Mr. Bennet.

Elizabeth and Jane have joined the group, and likewise the argument. It is Mrs. Bennet's asserted belief that Lydia is no more interested in officers than her mother was at her age, and it is Elizabeth's conviction, which she is pleased to state to her father, that he is using the wrong tactics with Lydia. Jane is of a similar mind—

"She's only a baby yet," insists Jane, "soldiers are romantic to her."

Mr. Bennet is still pretty angry about Lydia's attitude toward the military and hopeful that she will gain more sense as she grows older—though as to that he is doubtful if sense ever comes if it isn't born in a female. Now he has gone to his room, where he hopes to read his paper in peace. . . .

Mr. Collins, who has been working on his sermons, has come in search of Mrs. Bennet. Elizabeth and Jane immediately take advantage of that fact to slip out of the room. This saves Mr. Collins some little embarrassment. He has come to ask Mrs. Bennet, and Mr. Bennet, of course, if he may have their permission to pay his addresses to Miss Elizabeth. If possible he should like an interview with Elizabeth this morning—

Mrs. Bennet is quite pleasurably excited and, after some little difficulty, succeeds in bringing Elizabeth back into the room, and, finally, in leaving her there, alone with her suitor. With a sigh of resignation Elizabeth seats herself and listens as Mr. Collins begins—

"You can hardly be in doubt as to what I am about to propose, my dear and lovely Elizabeth! Your natural delicacy may lead you to dissemble . . . but I flatter myself my attentions have been too marked to be mistaken."

With increasing assurance Mr. Collins would enumerate his reasons for having selected Elizabeth as the companion of his future years. For one, his noble patroness has advised his marriage and has even gone so far as to promise to visit the lady he chooses. For another, he is to inherit the Bennet estates eventually and he would like if possible to keep the property in the family—

"I know that one thousand pounds in the four per cents is all you will have as dowry . . . and . . . (*a little ruefully*) even *that* you will not receive until your mother's death . . . (*pauses, then reassures her, delicately.*) but you can rest assured that on *that* score no ungenerous reproach shall ever pass my lips after we are married."

"Aren't you a little hasty, sir?" Elizabeth demands, speaking slowly and with deliberation. "You seem to forget that I have made no answer to this dazzling offer! I appreciate the honor you seem to feel you have done me . . . and I decline it with thanks."

She would thus end the interview, but Mr. Collins will not permit that. He understands perfectly. He knows it to be a charming and delicate custom for a young lady of breeding to say No when she means Yes—

"Upon my word, sir, you are difficult to discourage," continues Elizabeth, with a show of exasperation. "I assure you I am *not* one of those idiotic young ladies you describe, if indeed they exist outside of novels. Difficult as it seems for you to believe it . . . I will *not* marry you. You could not make *me* happy, and I certainly could not make *you* . . . (*moves further away*) and I have no ambition at all to try."

Still Mr. Collins persists. Nor is his confidence in any way affected by her suggestion that he return to the Lady Catherine de Bourgh and permit her to select for him a young woman with a humbler and more contrite heart—

"I am too well aware, dear cousin, that it is by no means certain that any other gentleman will ever make you an offer," and Mr.

Collins smiles forgivingly; "so I naturally understand that your rejection of my suit is according to the usual practice of elegant females."

"I see! Well, if you can, you'd better stop thinking of me as an elegant female. Just picture me as a rational creature, with a most inelegant habit of speaking the truth."

"Ah, you are quite adorable! I am certain now that when my proposal is formally sanctioned by your excellent parents, you will plainly say yes."

Elizabeth has swept out of the room, and Mr. Collins is pirouetting with every sign of satisfaction in an ultimate conquest when Mrs. Bennet returns to wish him joy as her future son-in-law. She is quite alarmed to hear of Elizabeth's decision, despite Mr. Collins' confidence, and quick with a promise to make her headstrong daughter change her mind. Mr. Bennet will see that Elizabeth is brought to reason—

Mr. Collins has suddenly remembered an engagement at the Lucases. Mrs. Bennet is nearly in tears by the time Mr. Bennet is told of what Elizabeth has done to blight the family prospects. Mr. Bennet alone remains unmoved. But when Elizabeth comes he puts the question to her directly—

"I understand that Mr. Collins has made you an offer . . . and that you have refused it."

"I have, Papa."

"Very well, let's come to the point. Your mother insists on your accepting him. Isn't that so, Mrs. Bennet?"

"Or else I shall never speak to her again." Mrs. Bennet is sniffling.

"Then it seems that an unhappy alternative awaits you, Lizzy. (*Balances his glasses in his hand.*) From this day forth you must be a stranger to one of your parents. Your mother will never speak to you again if you do *not* marry Mr. Collins . . . and I . . . will never speak to you again if you *do.*"

Elizabeth has burst into laughter and thrown herself into her father's arms, as Lydia comes to report Mr. Collins on the way to the Lucases'. Now Mrs. Bennet suffers further distress at the thought that Mr. Collins is quite sure that Charlotte Lucas, "the plain-faced, scheming little cat," will get him. This worry is no more than firmly seated in her mind than unhappy Jane appears, traces of tears on her face, to admit having had a distressing letter from Caroline Bingley from London. The Bingleys have left Netherfield.

Poor Jane is in tears and only Elizabeth is there to comfort her when the others diplomatically leave. It is Elizabeth's idea that Jane should not grieve. Mr. Bingley is sure to come back—

JANE (*through her tears*)—But, Lizzy, he hasn't sent one word —not one! I can't understand it. Caroline merely tells me they are not coming back until the spring . . . perhaps not then. It's all over . . . he doesn't care . . . I only imagined it.

ELIZABETH—Nonsense, you'll see, he will be here to see Papa before the week is out. Don't you *know* he loves you? One *knows* these things.

JANE (*in a low voice*)—He *kissed* me . . . that *must* mean he loves me . . . mustn't it, Lizzy?

ELIZABETH—Of course. . . . What more proof do you want? (*A pause.*) Only, darling, don't trust Caroline. She's fond of you, I know, but she doesn't want you as her brother's wife. We are not grand nor rich enough.

JANE—Oh, no, Lizzy, Caroline has been so sweet to me . . . think how often she has invited me over there. Oh, no . . . She is incapable of deceit!

ELIZABETH (*tenderly*)—All right, my sweet, whitewash her, as you do everyone. Now, you've done your duty. One comfort— even *she* can't persuade Charles that he doesn't love you.

JANE—But how can I marry him if his sister is against it?

ELIZABETH—*That* you must decide for yourself, my dearest little saint. If . . . you decide that the anguish of disobliging his cat of a sister is more than equal to the joy of marrying him, then I advise you to refuse him.

JANE (*laughing through her tears*)—You naughty girl, Lizzy. You know very well that I should marry him if it vexed every relative he has. . . . But if he doesn't come back . . . Lizzy, Lizzy . . . I couldn't bear it. (*Wistfully.*) I think I should die.

ELIZABETH—He *must* come back . . . he won't be able not to. . . . Jane, Jane, any man who once knew your sweetness wouldn't be *able* to give it up.

MRS. BENNET (*re-entering*)—Jane dear, your father and I have decided to let you accept your Aunt Gardiner's invitation . . . to spend a few months with her and my brother in London.

JANE—But, Mamma . . . I didn't know my aunt had invited me.

MRS. BENNET—Never mind about that, my love. . . . My letter will be on the way to London tomorrow, and your father is willing to take you up there as soon as you can make ready. (JANE *seizes her mother and hugs her.*)

ELIZABETH (*admiringly*)—Well, Mrs. Bennet . . . *you* certainly don't believe that marriages are made in Heaven.

MRS. BENNET (*dryly*)—From what I know of men, my dear, if we left it to them and Heaven . . . we should all be old maids!

Elizabeth bursts into laughter and hugs her mother as the curtain falls.

A month later, in Jane Bennet's Aunt Gardiner's home, Cheapside, London, fairly elaborate preparations are being made for a tea which Mrs. Gardiner is giving in Jane's honor. Jane has been ill for some days and is a pale, frail child as she comes now to look over the preparations. The chief guest is to be Caroline Bingley, and there is a vague hope that Miss Bingley will bring someone else with her. Whether she does or not, Jane, her aunt points out, will be expected to return the call and then she will again meet Charles and possibly discover what has happened that he should have so long neglected one of whom he gave every evidence of being very fond.

Caroline Bingley, however, is not the first guest. Elizabeth Bennet achieves that distinction by arriving quite unexpectedly by mail coach. Elizabeth is on her way to Hunsford, of all places, and to visit the Rev. Mr. and Mrs. Collins. Three days after Elizabeth had refused him, the Rev. Collins had proposed to and been accepted by Charlotte Lucas.

"Mamma has refused to kiss me good night ever since," reports Elizabeth, quite gaily.

"I should think she would have thanked Heaven for your escape," ventures Mrs. Gardiner.

"Oh, no. Mamma regards *any* husband as better than *no* husband. Only Papa and I happen to think otherwise. I wish Charlotte joy of Collins . . . though she has not increased in my esteem."

Elizabeth, with Charlotte, is to spend a week with Lady de Bourgh, who is expecting her nephews—Captain Darcy and an army officer on leave from India—and is in need of entertainers.

Now Elizabeth would know of the tea for Miss Bingley and thinks well of the chances that Charles may accompany his sister. And perhaps Mr. Darcy, thinks Jane. But, to Elizabeth, there is little hope of that.

"Darcy!" she exclaims, with a nervous laugh. "He may have *heard* there is such a place as Cheapside, but I'm sure he would feel that a month's bathing would not cleanse him from the impurities of such a neighborhood. . . . I shall have to sacrifice the pleasure of meeting Miss Bingley, too. I've got to be at the London Road in time for the coach. I can't even wait for tea."

Miss Bingley drives up in style, with two horses and a coachman, before Elizabeth can escape. She greets Jane with obvious effusiveness and is friendly toward Elizabeth, though not too well pleased to see her there. Nor is she further enthused by the added information that Elizabeth is on her way to Rosings to spend a few days with her cousins.

"Rosings!" repeats the surprised Miss Bingley; "but that is the home of the Lady Catherine de Bourgh."

"Yes, isn't her ladyship fortunate to have secured two such charming young ladies as Elizabeth and Mrs. Collins to help her entertain her young gentlemen? I understand Mr. Darcy and another nephew are invited."

While Miss Bingley is growing red with anger Elizabeth recovers her wraps and is ready to start. "Good-by, Jane darling," she says, holding her sister close for a second; "I'll write you an account of all the gay doings . . . and send you some of the more brilliant quips of the Rev. Collins. (*Gaily.*) Good-afternoon, Miss Bingley, it has been such a pleasure to see you again. Do remember me kindly to your brother. Can I give any messages to Mr. Darcy?"

Mrs. Gardiner has gone to the coach with Elizabeth. Jane and Miss Bingley are left alone. Miss Bingley is full of apologies for her neglect of her friend, but she has been kept busy with social obligations which have included many affairs given by Mr. Darcy's sister, Georgiana, at the Darcy town house. Miss Georgiana is sweetness itself, according to Miss Bingley, and so very rich she is bound to be sought after by many young men. The Darcy family, of course, will see to it that she marries a young man of the highest connections and, she adds, as Jane goes white with sickening fear, there is every probability that their choice will eventually fall upon her brother Charles. Charles and dear Georgiana—

With an effort Jane is able to save herself from swooning, though the pain in her eyes causes even Miss Bingley to turn away.

"Indeed, indeed I wish them joy . . . if they truly love each other," falters Jane.

"Oh, the dear boy is so much in love . . . I tease him all the time," gushes Miss Bingley, sentimentally. "He is never home now . . . escorting Miss Darcy here, there, everywhere

. . . balls, routs, the playhouse. Mr. Darcy and I have wanted this match for ever so long. . . . Thank you for your wishes, I'll convey them to Charles. . . . Oh, I forgot in all my excitement . . . he sends you his best respects."

"Thank him for me," says Jane, weakly.

Mrs. Gardiner has brought in the tea and taken up the social issue in Jane's favor. The poor child is overtired, she explains to Miss Bingley. She has been going far too much. Jane would protest such overstatement, but Miss Bingley has no sooner gone than she collapses into her aunt's arms.

"There, there, my darling, I know . . . it's the disillusionment that cuts the very heart." Mrs. Gardiner is all sympathy.

"But to abandon me—without a word!" weeps Jane. "What could I have done to him? He loved me, Auntie . . . he did, he did! He *kissed* me . . . once . . . and . . . (*shamefacedly*) I kissed him. (*Anxiously*.) You believe—don't you—that I should never have done *that* if I hadn't been sure he wanted to make me an offer . . . don't you, Auntie?"

"Of course I do, my lamb!"

"And do you suppose *he* understands that too? I wouldn't have him think badly of me."

"It's all a mystery to me," admits Mrs. Gardiner, quite astounded by such innocence. "When I met him at Longbourn he seemed such a properly sweet young gentleman."

"Oh, he *is* . . . I do assure you, Auntie . . . he *is* . . . and now it's all over. I can't bear it, I can't, I can't. . . ."

Jane with her head on her aunt's breast is weeping in low, broken sobs as the curtain falls.

It is morning a few days later. Lady Catherine de Bourgh's drawing room at Rosings Park, Hunsford, Kent, is bright with the sunlight that pours through a window before which Elizabeth Bennet is seated writing a letter. Presently Mr. Darcy appears at the door, sees Elizabeth, hesitates, and then would engage her in conversation.

Elizabeth's replies to Darcy's cheery good morning are frigidly polite. Though he persists in the interruption, she makes it quite apparent that she would prefer to continue with her writing. If it is conversation that Mr. Darcy is seeking Elizabeth is sure his aunt will be glad to supply it.

Lady de Bourgh, followed by the attentive Collins, arrives before Darcy accepts his dismissal. She, too, would lure Elizabeth away from her writing. Lady de Bourgh prefers to visit. She would know more of Elizabeth's sisters and their prospects of marriage. She would know more of Elizabeth and is quite upset by her frankness. Particularly when Elizabeth admits the irritation she feels whenever she recalls how badly Darcy had acted while he was in Hertfordshire. Her criticism is so marked that Darcy finally stalks from the room under its subtle sting.

Lady Catherine and the Collinses have gone to do Charlotte's shopping, which her ladyship insists on overseeing, and to visit the cottagers, who, it is reported, are complaining again.

"I have told them so often the duty of counting their blessings, your ladyship," Mr. Collins is at pains to report.

"You wouldn't believe how discontented some of those foolish people are with their nice little two-roomed cottages," adds Charlotte, exchanging glances with the receptive Elizabeth; "but Lady Catherine settles all their differences and silences their complaints."

"I can well imagine it."

"Now, I will really listen to no more compliments for today, my dears," protests Lady Catherine. "Come, Collins. . . . We must go to your parsonage first, Mrs. Collins. I must carefully examine that lace you have bought to trim your new curtains. I am afraid it is a little too elaborate for a small house like yours. One must always keep within one's position, my dear. You and Mr. Collins may walk across . . . (*to* COLLINS) and I will drive over in the phaeton and join you. . . . Good morning, Miss Bennet. . . .

The Hon. Guy Fitzwilliam would also take Elizabeth away from the house for a walk in the open.

"I say, why don't you come for a walk with me, Miss Bennet?" demands Fitzwilliam. "You can write your dashed old letter later."

ELIZABETH (*looking out*)—It *is* tempting out there . . . in that dew-drenched world . . . it's all so green and wet and shining. No, I shall be firm. . . . But I will promise to meet you on your way back, though I shall have to do it by stealth.

FITZWILLIAM—Good! By Jove, it must be dull being a young lady. . . . I have often thought about it . . . never going anywhere alone, sitting knitting or netting—whatever it is you call it—purses and things . . . waiting for some chap to make you an offer. . . . Egad! How does a girl like you put up with it?

ELIZABETH—Well, for one thing, I don't net purses, and I'm not waiting for any offers, and I actually came to Hunsford alone in the mail coach. Now, what do you think of that?

FITZWILLIAM—You are too intelligent for a girl . . . that's your trouble.

ELIZABETH—. . . And for most of the young gentlemen I meet as well.

FITZWILLIAM—No chance for me, then?

ELIZABETH—Oh, come now, be careful . . . I might take you seriously.

FITZWILLIAM—Well, you know how it is with younger sons— we must become used to self-denial (*gloomily, looking at her with unmistakable covetousness*).

ELIZABETH—Are you asking for sympathy? (*Banteringly.*) I don't think the younger son of an earl is much of an object for it. When have you had to deny yourself?

FITZWILLIAM—Well, I'm doing it now. . . . (*Meaningly.*) Younger sons can't marry where they want to . . . we're brought up in a luxurious way of living, and rank makes money necessary.

ELIZABETH—And pray, just for information, what *is* the usual price of an earl's younger son? Would fifty thousand pounds be a fair offer?

FITZWILLIAM—Oh, isn't that hitting below the belt rather? (*Wants to change the subject.*) I'll be off . . . I say . . . Miss Bennet?

ELIZABETH—Well, what now?

FITZWILLIAM—Do you mind if I ask you something?

ELIZABETH—As long as I don't have to answer.

FITZWILLIAM—It's about Darcy. . . . You hurt him just now! I'm fond of the old solemn owl. Why are you so prejudiced against him?

ELIZABETH—Prejudiced? . . . I didn't know I was *that*. But frankly I dislike him. It isn't very polite to show it . . . I hoped I didn't. I have really very good reasons for my . . . prejudice. . . . As to that, you might with just as much reason ask *him* why he adopts such a superior attitude.

FITZWILLIAM—It's that confounded pride of his—it's always mistaken for conceit. But when you really know him, he's—

ELIZABETH—Is there really much to know, beyond a supreme self-assurance and a disdain for anyone under a peer? Such snobbery in a well-born man is incomprehensible to me. I always thought only inferior people were snobs.

FITZWILLIAM—Well, it's surprising how many well-born people are like that. It's taught them by nursemaids and governesses when they are youngsters. But Darcy has an awfully decent character underneath all that nonsense. He has a heart, and a mind too, if you can get him to open up.

ELIZABETH—I shouldn't bother to try.

FITZWILLIAM (*wistfully*)—I'd really like to change your opinion about the old sobersides. . . . I'm such a stupid ass, I have no vocabulary . . . when I want to convince. . . .

ELIZABETH—You're a loyal friend, and I like you for it.

Elizabeth might change her opinion of Darcy, she admits, if Colonel Fitzwilliam could recall even one kind action which Darcy had performed. And that Fitzwilliam can do. He recalls that all last Winter Darcy had sacrificed himself for a friend by staying in London to keep the friend away from the temptation of making a disastrous marriage. Darcy had not mentioned the sacrifice to Fitzwilliam, but he had admitted that the mother of the girl in whom his friend was interested was rather impossible—

Elizabeth receives the innocently delivered blow with something like a gasp, but is able a moment later to overcome the pain, humiliation and anger that Fitzwilliam is startled to note in her expression by a forced lightness with which she dismisses him and returns to her letter.

Now Darcy has returned to the drawing room to make a second determined effort to talk with Elizabeth. This time he refuses to be put off. With some embarrassment Darcy finally manages to say that he has come back because he could not stay away. He could not stay away because he had to tell Elizabeth how ardently he admires and loves her.

"I have fought with myself all these months," Darcy is saying, as Elizabeth leaves her chair and stands staring at him expectantly. "You may think I am speaking without due thought . . . that my feelings for you outweigh my common sense . . . that this love for you that consumes me . . . (*slowly and passionately*) is a thing that will pass when I stop to realize the unsuitability of a marriage with you."

"Mr. Darcy!" protests Elizabeth, white with anger.

DARCY—I have tried to drive you from my heart, but I cannot. I have told myself that your family connections are inferior . . . Elizabeth, I love you.

ELIZABETH—Do you really expect me to take you seriously, sir? What am I supposed to reply to this extraordinary harangue? One can scarcely call it an offer of marriage. . . . (*Her tone is full of wounded pride.*) You do not, I suppose, expect me to feel flattered?

DARCY—But do you expect *me* to be glad that your family is inferior to mine? Or blame me for being honest and sincere when making the momentous decision of my life?

ELIZABETH—*Decision? (Her voice is like ice.)*

DARCY—Yes, my dearest. I have decided to . . . ask you to marry me.

ELIZABETH *(facing him)*—I suppose I should be overwhelmed at this honor?

DARCY—But . . .

ELIZABETH—I ought to congratulate you on overcoming the battle between your unwilling affection and my unworthiness . . . *(laughs with a sob under it)* but you see I happen to be quite uninterested in your problems.

DARCY—Elizabeth . . .

ELIZABETH—You astonish me.

DARCY—I astonish myself. . . .

ELIZABETH—If you were not so lacking in perception, sir, you might have spared yourself my refusal. . . .

DARCY *(dumbfounded)*—You refuse me?

ELIZABETH *(quietly)*—You might have noticed the fact long ago. . . . I have never hidden it. . . . I neither aspire to nor could I ever return your affection. *(Cuttingly.)* As for your scruples about marrying into my family . . . don't let that ever concern you again.

DARCY *(white with shock and humiliation)*—Is that all the reply I am to be honored with? I might perhaps deserve to be told *why* I have been rejected . . . *(resentfully)* and with so little civility.

ELIZABETH—I also might deserve to know why you consider my feelings so little while expressing your own. It is scarcely a compliment that you care for me against your better judgment, Mr. Darcy.

It is not the manner of Mr. Darcy's proposal only that has caused her incivility, Elizabeth explains, but his cruel and selfish treatment of Mr. Wickham. Mr. Wickham, Darcy replies with spirit, is no better than a cad and one of whom he would advise Miss Bennet to be wary. In addition to the Wickham matter, Elizabeth continues, there is Mr. Darcy's confession that he had deliberately come between Jane Bennet and Charles Bingley.

"I did everything in my power to separate my friend from your sister," Darcy admits. "Towards him I have been wiser than towards myself."

"They loved each other, she and Charles. Jane is of those who only love once. You talk to me of love! You who have trodden on a heart!"

"You wish to think badly of me."

"I have no choice."

"I have made the mistake of being honest with you."

"Honesty is a very overrated virtue. Tact and taste are more agreeable ones."

"My scruples with regard to your family were natural."

"And should have been kept to yourself. Let us end this distasteful subject. You could not have made your offer in any way that would have tempted me to accept it. (*She turns and looks straight at him, intent to hurt in her every line.*) You are the last man in the world whom I could ever be prevailed upon to marry."

"Forgive me . . . for having taken up your time," concludes Darcy, pride and pain in his voice. "I wish you every happiness."

Elizabeth has sunk into a chair and is in tears as the curtain falls.

ACT III

A week later Jane Bennet's illness has brought Elizabeth back to Longbourn from London. She finds the family still greatly worried. Jane, suffering from nothing more tangible than a complete disinterest in living, spends most of her time in the conservatory, watched over by Mrs. Lake, a nurse, and her mother. At Mrs. Lake's suggestion Elizabeth conspires to keep Mrs. Bennet away as much as possible. Mrs. Bennet's frequent references to the responsibility of Charles Bingley for her daughter's decline is bad for Jane.

Lydia Bennet, it transpires, is now at Brighton, and recent reports of her are that she has been having a gay time with Mr. Wickham and other officers dancing attendance upon her. Mrs. Bennet is quite sure that Lydia can take care of herself, but Mr. Bennet is plainly worried.

Presently Lady Catherine de Bourgh is announced. She has come, her ladyship admits, to talk with Elizabeth alone, and Mrs. Bennet, duly impressed with any excuse that brings Lady Catherine to Longbourn, is quick to make such an interview possible.

Lady Catherine suspects that Elizabeth knows very well why she is there, nor is she satisfied with Elizabeth's denial of that charge. Lady Catherine has been put in possession of the report that Elizabeth has dared to entertain a hope of marrying her nephew, Mr. Darcy, and she has made this special trip to assure her that such a marriage will never, never take place.

". . . Has my nephew made you an offer of marriage?" demands Lady Catherine, made furious by Elizabeth's thinly veiled contempt.

"But your ladyship has already declared that to be impossible," answers Elizabeth, quietly.

LADY CATHERINE—It certainly *should* be. But your arts may have entangled him into forgetting what he owes to his family.

ELIZABETH—Then surely I should be the last to admit it. (*Laughs.*)

LADY CATHERINE (*furiously*)—Miss Bennet, do you know *who* I am? I have not been accustomed . . . (*Pauses, almost in a fit.*) I am the nearest relative he has and entitled to know his dearest concerns.

ELIZABETH (*calmly*)—Then question *him*. You certainly are not entitled to know *mine*.

LADY CATHERINE—This marriage to which you have the effrontery to aspire . . . will *never* take place. *Never!* Mr. Darcy is engaged to *my daughter*. Now what have you to say?

ELIZABETH—Only that if this is true, why are you worrying? How could he make an offer to me? . . . Or has he a case of bigamy in view? (*Smiles.*) It is still a crime in England, you know.

LADY CATHERINE (*hesitatingly*)—Well, they were intended for each other since infancy . . . my sister, the Lady Anne . . . hoped it with her last breath. . . . Didn't you hear me say at Rosings, before the gentlemen came in after dinner, that I wish him to marry my daughter?

ELIZABETH (*placidly*)—Certainly. You gave expression to that wish several times. But if there were no *other* objections to my marriage with Mr. Darcy . . . your *wish* certainly would carry little weight.

LADY CATHERINE (*threateningly*)—Very well. If you persist. Don't expect to be received by his family . . . *or* his friends . . . *or* . . . *me! Your name will never be mentioned by any of us!*

ELIZABETH—I must confess to your ladyship that this will not give me a moment's concern.

LADY CATHERINE (*in a rage*)—I am *ashamed* of you. Is *this* your gratitude for my hospitality?

ELIZABETH—Gratitude! But, Lady Catherine, I regard hospitality as a mutual grace, and by no means consider myself as an object for charity.

LADY CATHERINE (*puffing about like a war horse*)—Understand, my girl, I came here determined . . . I am not used to submitting to any person's whims nor brooking disappointments.

ELIZABETH (*demurely*)—That is unfortunate. It is rather late in life for your ladyship to be receiving your first taste of it. . . .

LADY CATHERINE—Be silent. The idea of you wanting to marry out of your own sphere!

ELIZABETH (*smiling*)—Oh, I should not consider it so. Mr. Darcy is a gentleman. I am the daughter of one.

LADY CATHERINE (*with incredible vulgarity*)—And pray what was your mother? A lady? (*Laughs scornfully.*) The daughter of a shop-keeper, with a brother . . . an attorney!! You see I am not deceived by your airs and graces.

ELIZABETH—And you, Lady Catherine, the daughter of a peer! It's strange how little birth seems to affect questions of taste . . . or gentleness of heart.

LADY CATHERINE—As if you could possibly know anything about such things. . . . Answer me once and for all, *Are you engaged to my nephew?*

ELIZABETH—I must ask you to speak in a lower key . . . my sister is asleep out there. (*Indicates conservatory.*) No, I am not engaged to anyone.

LADY CATHERINE—And will you promise me you never will be?

ELIZABETH (*quietly*)—I will not.

Lady Catherine is of a mind to refuse to leave the Bennet home until she has Elizabeth's promise never to permit herself to become engaged, but she agrees to leave under protest when Elizabeth calmly orders her coach. . . .

The next excitement in the Bennet family is caused by Mr. Bennet's receipt of a letter from Colonel Forster informing him that Lydia has run away with Mr. Wickham. This is a serious business, inasmuch as no mention is made of a marriage ceremony having been performed. For that matter Mrs. Bennet does not see how it would have been possible for Lydia to have married, seeing she has no wedding clothes.

Mr. Bennet is preparing to take matters in his own hands, and go at once in pursuit of Mr. Wickham when Mrs. Bennet is threatened with hysterics and a heart attack. The very thought of such a meeting unnerves her and she has to be helped upstairs.

It is decided that Mr. Bennet shall start for London at once. He will, pleads Elizabeth, concentrate only on seeing that Mr. Wickham marries Lydia, and let the punishment of that young man go for the present. Elizabeth believes that neither she nor her father is entirely blameless in the matter, shameless as Lydia's action may have been. Mr. Bennet has been too easygoing, and she, though warned as to Mr. Wickham's true character, had not taken the warning with such seriousness as should have prompted her to protect her sister.

Mr. Bennet is packed and ready for the pursuit of the runaway pair when Mr. Darcy appears suddenly on the scene. He has come, he explains to Elizabeth after her father has left, to set her right about certain things.

"You can't expect me to feel very interested in anything you might now say," says Elizabeth, quite coldly. "You sympathize with my trouble over my sister, yet you are the cause of it."

DARCY (*earnestly*)—I swear to you on my honor as a gentleman that I had no idea that Miss Jane cared seriously for Charles. He knew as little of it as I. Miss Bingley assured us that your sister had only a passing interest in him.

ELIZABETH—Miss Bingley *knew* that was untrue. She "confided" to Jane in London that Mr. Bingley was almost engaged to your sister. . . . When you consider that he and Jane . . . (*Stammers, blushes, thinking of the kiss to which Jane had confessed.*) Well, Jane regarded herself as betrothed . . . as any girl would . . . and then you took him away to London, and she never heard from him again.

DARCY (*shocked*)—I had no idea! No wonder you hated me! I am astonished at Miss Bingley.

ELIZABETH (*coldly*)—Are you? In any case, you took a great deal upon yourself to assume anything about Jane's feelings.

DARCY (*bows his head*)—But as for Wickham . . . there at least I have not been in the wrong. (ELIZABETH *is alert.*) It's true my father *did* leave him a sum of money, and the promise of the clerical living at Pemberley. I was ready, anxious to fulfill it, but on my father's death, Wickham informed me that he had no vocation for the church and preferred to study law and suggested I should augment the sum my father had bequeathed to him. I sent him three thousand pounds (*She gasps.*) and expected he would use it to obtain his degree. Instead, at the end of two years, he wrote me that the money was gone and that he did not find the legal profession congenial, and would like to receive the clerical post. I naturally refused. (*He looks at her for approval. She nods.*) I did not regard him as a man who should be ordained. You will scarcely blame me?

ELIZABETH (*in a low voice*)—No.

DARCY—Miss Elizabeth, I am going to confide something to you that I have never told anyone. (*Pauses, under a strain.*) My sister, who lives at our home at Pemberley with our aunt, went to Ramsgate a year ago on a visit. Mr. Wickham followed her there. (ELIZABETH *starts in alarm. Her voice is choked with anger.*)

ELIZABETH—Wickham! And *your* sister?

DARCY—He convinced that child of fifteen that she was in love with him and persuaded her to promise to elope at a date set. Thank God, I arrived unexpectedly and spoiled the plan. (*For a moment he cannot continue.*) My sister confessed to me . . . you can understand now with what feelings of hatred and contempt I regard that scoundrel, who, of course, fled the moment I had arrived. (ELIZABETH *covers her eyes an instant.*) Surely . . . you do not . . . care for him?

ELIZABETH—No . . . no . . . of course not . . . it's Lydia . . . poor little Lydia!

DARCY (*stunned*)—Lydia!

ELIZABETH (*in a monotonous exhausted voice*)—She was staying at Brighton with the Forsters . . . the corps is quartered there. She and Wickham eloped. That's why my father has just gone up to London and my mother is ill upstairs. (*Against her will she breaks down, rises, goes to mantel, leans her head in her arms. He stands, his face grave, thinking. Getting hold of herself, facing him.*) You were right. You warned me about Wickham. I might have saved Lydia! (*Her voice breaks. He looks at her tenderly, but is silent.*) He will never marry her. She has no money, no connections, nothing to tempt him! (*Throws herself in a chair.*) Lydia is done for.

DARCY (*quietly*)—No, you must not despair.

ELIZABETH (*bitterly*)—You see, my family is not only inferior . . . but disgraced now. You should be grateful to me. (*Ironically.*)

DARCY (*gives her a strange poignant look, crosses to her, bows.*)—I will not intrude any longer. . . . I only beg you not to lose hope.

Mr. Darcy is about to withdraw, with a suddenness that hurts Elizabeth, when Charles Bingley is announced. Charles, having heard from Darcy of Jane's illness, has come to explain that previously he had not known and is now most anxious, if such a thing is possible, to see Jane. He is quite sincerely miserable and Elizabeth, after some little hesitancy, sends him into the conservatory as the curtain falls.

Two weeks later, on a beautiful May morning, Jane is propped up on a couch in the living room "radiant with happiness and returning health." Near by Mrs. Bennet is sewing on a trousseau for her daughter's approaching marriage to Charles Bingley. There is considerable mutual rejoicing over the prospect.

"Two sons-in-law!" murmurs Mrs. Bennet, ecstastically. "Both my daughters to be married women! How proud I feel to be sure! Lydia already married to that naughty Mr. Wickham! Your father certainly managed all that business very well. If it were not for Lizzy! I certainly cannot bear her to turn out to be an old maid. If only she had not been so uppish with that young Collins!"

Even Mr. Bennet, joining the two, is touched with the joy of the moment. Mr. Wickham, he is now willing to assert, though with a slightly ironical smile, is a fine fellow who has taken to making love to them all, and Charles is completely redeemed. It is interesting to Mr. Bennet to learn that it was Darcy who had told Charles of Jane's illness, and thus brought him back to Longbourn; that it was Elizabeth who had told Darcy and that it was Miss Bingley who had caused the misunderstanding by taking it upon herself to inform her brother that he enjoyed no part of Jane's affections. . . .

Elizabeth comes from the conservatory with her arms full of flowers. She too reflects the general radiance, though her mother is still distressed by the thought that she is the only daughter remaining unwed. If Elizabeth only had been wiser in the Collins matter! Elizabeth, however, is content. Still, there is one item that troubles her. Somewhere Mr. Bennet had found ten thousand pounds to supply Lydia with a dowry. It was because of the dowry that she was able to bring Mr. Wickham to the altar. Mrs. Bennet intimates that it was her brother, Uncle Gardiner, who produced the money, but Elizabeth is not altogether satisfied with that explanation—

"Well, it is none of your business, Lizzy," snaps Mrs. Bennet. "Lydia is married and secured. That is all that matters."

Elizabeth stands for a moment contemplating her mother. "Cannibals and brigands are *gentle*—in comparison," she muses.

"In comparison? With what?"

"Mothers," answers Elizabeth, laughingly.

And then the mystery is effectively cleared by Mr. Bennet, who observes, quietly and casually, "as though he were not dropping a bombshell"—

"Ah! Did I mention that it was through Mr. Darcy's efforts we found the pair, and— (*Pretends not to observe* ELIZABETH's *start.*) that he obtained the money for us—to buy back Lydia's —respectability?"

Elizabeth "cowers in humiliation" at this revelation. Mrs. Bennet is more puzzled than before. She would greatly have preferred that Lydia's dowry had come from the family.

Now Mr. Bennet casually drops another exciting bit of news: Lydia and her new husband are shortly to visit Longbourn on their way to rejoin Mr. Wickham's regiment. They are due, in fact, to arrive today, a statement that throws Mrs. Bennet into a flurry at the thought of how to receive the visitors. She is, however, completely happy at the prospect. . . .

Charles Bingley has arrived, bringing his sister's greetings from Netherfield, and hoping he is to receive Mr. Bennet's formal consent to his engagement to Jane, previously agreed to by correspondence.

"My boy, you are the first suitor for any of my daughters who has met with my approval," beams Mr. Bennet, shaking hands with the happy Bingley. "With all my heart, sir!"

"I have not a single doubt about the success of this marriage," Mr. Bennet adds. "You are too much alike not to agree. You are both so sweet-tempered that your servants will always impose on you. (*Laughs, as they do also.*) And so generous that you will always exceed your income. Bless you, my children."

A few minutes later Lydia and Wickham have arrived. Quite unabashed, they cheerfully present themselves for the congratulatory greetings of those assembled: "Wickham debonair and handsome in uniform; Lydia gay and proud of her accomplishment."

The greetings are for the most part formal and strained. Only Mrs. Bennet is emotionally moved. Lydia bubbles with gaiety and pride and is quite eager that everyone should realize that she is not only a married woman, but the first of the Bennet sisters to achieve that honor. She knows that Elizabeth and Jane must be jealous of her. They must both go to Brighton, that's the place to find husbands. Or the next Winter they must visit her at Newcastle and she will guarantee to find husbands for them—

"Thank you for your kind intentions, but I don't particularly care for your way of getting husbands," quietly remarks Elizabeth, as she leaves the room. . . .

The Wickhams have gone upstairs to prepare for luncheon, and Charles is about to take his adoring Jane into the garden, when Mr. Bennet returns with Mr. Darcy. Jane disentangles herself from Charles' arms a little embarrassedly to greet Darcy with enthusiasm.

"Mr. Darcy . . . please wish me joy . . . it's your doing, you know."

"Words wouldn't do it for me, my dear Miss Jane. . . . I wish you both every kind of happiness."

Mr. Bennet has gently pushed them into the garden and as gently taken Mrs. Bennet by the shoulders, when she would come back into the room, and propelled her with a whispered warning through a door, following her as she goes. Darcy, walking toward the library with his back turned, is not aware of what is taking place in back of him. He hesitates a second and then knocks firmly upon the door. Elizabeth responds to the knock, appearing "astonished, bewildered and on the defensive."

"You? I did not expect—" Her voice is trembling in spite of her effort to control it.

DARCY—I hope I am not altogether unwelcome?

ELIZABETH (*trying to sound aloof*)—I am glad of the opportunity . . . (*He starts, hopefully.*) of expressing my gratitude for all you have done . . . for my sisters. (*Her voice trembles.*) Indeed, indeed I *must* thank you.

DARCY—Then let it be for yourself alone . . . (*passionately*) for whatever I did . . . I thought only of you.

ELIZABETH—Of *me?* . . . After all I . . .

DARCY (*humbly*)—Miss Elizabeth, you are too generous to trifle with me. (*She looks surprised.*) I came to ask you if you continue to feel towards me as you did at Rosings?

ELIZABETH (*trying to be cold and distant, but inwardly excited*)—I could not imagine that such matters still concerned you, sir.

DARCY (*with grave simplicity*)—*That* matter . . . will always concern me, Elizabeth.

ELIZABETH (*bitterly*)—I was so clever; I knew everything! I criticized you about Wickham. . . . (*With passionate self-accusation.*) I never spoke to you without wanting to hurt you.

DARCY—I well deserved it. (*She shakes her head. He comes closer.*) Can you ever forgive my past arrogance?

ELIZABETH (*smiling a little tearfully*)—Surely in such a case a good memory would be unpardonable?

DARCY (*smiles at this flash of the old* ELIZABETH. *They suddenly look a little tremulously at each other*)—Elizabeth! . . . does that mean . . . ?

ELIZABETH—It means . . . that . . . I am ashamed. (*Her head down. A tear glistens on her cheek. The sight fills him with tenderness.*) If you had not been noble and just you would have hated me. No . . . I was the stupid one . . . the foolishly proud one.

DARCY (*tenderly*)—No, my dearest . . . only the prejudiced one.

ELIZABETH—When I think of the way you requited my incivility . . . my cruelty . . . (*Brokenly.*) oh . . . I cannot bear your kindness.

DARCY—But if all these things you so exaggerate had been done by your husband?

ELIZABETH—Enjoy your triumph! (*With bowed head.*) I am abased! (*A final flash.*) I never wanted to see you again!

DARCY—Do you mean that?

ELIZABETH (*passionately*)—Yes! (*More softly.*) No.

DARCY—Dare I ask you . . . again?

ELIZABETH (*smiles up at him through her tears*)—My father says you are the sort of gentleman whom one would not dare refuse anything he condescended to ask.

DARCY (*takes her in his arms*)—My cruel . . . my kind . . . oh, my lovely Elizabeth! (*Folds her close, his lips on hers.*)

THE CURTAIN FALLS

THE PLAYS AND THEIR AUTHORS

"Winterset." A drama in three acts by Maxwell Anderson. Copyright, 1935, by the author. Copyright and published, 1935, by Anderson House, Washington, D. C.

The author of "Winterset" has appeared in four previous volumes of "Best Plays" and is therefore well known to readers of these year books. Other Anderson contributions have been "What Price Glory?" (with Laurence Stallings), "Elizabeth the Queen," "Mary of Scotland" and "Both Your Houses," the Pulitzer prize winning play of 1932-33. He is the son of a minister, was born in Atlantic, Pa., and was an editorial writer in both San Francisco and New York before taking up playwriting. His first years out of college he spent teaching.

"Idiot's Delight." A drama in three acts by Robert E. Sherwood. Copyright, 1935, by the author. Copyright and published, 1936, by Charles Scribner's Sons, New York.

Robert Sherwood's first appearance in this series of selected plays was in 1931-32, when he wrote "Reunion in Vienna." He appeared again last year with "The Petrified Forest." This year his "Idiot's Delight" was the runner up for the newly created New York Drama Critics' Circle award and the winner of the Pulitzer committee's award. He is a native of New Rochelle, New York, left Harvard to go to war in 1918, and has been a magazine editor and motion picture reviewer.

"First Lady." A comedy in three acts by Katharine Dayton and George Kaufman. Copyright, 1935, by the authors. Copyright and published, 1935-36, by Random House, New York.

Katharine Dayton was born in Philadelphia, but, as she says, "realized after two years that this would never do and moved to Glen Ridge, N. J." From New Jersey it was an easy ferry jump to New York, though she did not make it as a permanent arrangement until after she had "staggered through Glen Ridge Grammar

School." It was first year Latin and Algebra that finally got the future playwright down, and she was permitted to substitute "illustration, music and practically any old art that came along, except toe-dancing and burnt-wood book ends." Her father, James C. Dayton, was for fifteen years publisher of Mr. Hearst's New York *Evening Journal,* which accounts for her interest in writing. She sold her first important story to Frank Crowninshield for *Vanity Fair,* her second to George Lorimer for the *Saturday Evening Post* and then went to Washington to write pieces for David Lawrence's Consolidated Press Service. Two years of this and she began a series of short playlets entitled "Mrs. Democratic and Mrs. Republican" in the *Post,* in which she waxed sarcastic, or at least was pretty hard on the New Deal and most of its works. These articles are still a feature of the campaign. A collection of Miss Dayton's earlier writings has been published by Doubleday under the title of "Loose Leaves." Her collaboration with Mr. Kaufman on "First Lady" is her first playwriting experience.

George Kaufman is a hardy annual so far as the year books are concerned, having contributed to no less than ten of the sixteen volumes, and to all but three of the thirteen volumes issued since he began writing plays and made his first "Best Play" appearance as co-author with Marc Connelly of "Dulcy" in 1921-22. He has, however, frequently changed collaborators, having worked previously with Marc Connelly, Edna Ferber, Ring Lardner, Morrie Ryskind and Moss Hart. Mr. Kaufman was born in Pittsburgh, entered newspaper work as a columnist, became a drama editor for the New York *Times* and gave that up to devote all his time to playwriting, scenario writing and bridge.

"End of Summer." A comedy in three acts by S. N. Behrman. Copyright, 1935, by the author. Copyright and published, 1936, by Random House, New York.

Mr. Behrman also wrote "Biography," which was a featured best play in the 1932-33 issue of this series. Likewise the "Brief Moment" that appeared in 1931-32. "End of Summer" this season tops both the others, and is considered by many the best Behrman play to date. This author, who was born in Worcester, Mass., and has degrees from three universities, has given a good deal of time to writing scenarios for the motion pictures, but is never quite happy unless he has a "real" play in preparation for the living theatre. "The Second Man," "Meteor," "Rain from Heaven" and "Serena Blandish" are others of his works.

"Victoria Regina." An historical drama in three acts by Laurence Housman. Copyright, 1935, by the author. Copyright and published, 1936, by Charles Scribner's Sons, New York.

Laurence Housman, born in London in July, 1867, has the unique distinction of being the writer of the "cleanest" plays in England and being at the same time the most frequently censored of English dramatists. No fewer than thirty-two of his dramas, long and short, have been banned by the Lord Chamberlain because they have dealt either too intimately with English royalty or too frankly with religion. His "Victoria Regina" has never been shown in England save at a few private performances. On these occasions, incidentally, Mr. Housman, who has a fondness for acting, frequently reads the part of Lord Beaconsfield. Other plays written by this poet dramatist include "Prunella" (with H. Granville Barker), produced by Winthrop Ames at the Little Theatre in New York in 1913; an adaptation of "Lysistrata," "Bethlehem," "Pain and Penalties," relating the matrimonial adventures of George IV, and "The Little Plays of St. Francis." "Victoria Regina" in book form consists of thirty episodes from the life of England's favorite Queen, from which ten were selected for use in the play.

"Boy Meets Girl." A comedy in three acts by Sam and Bella Spewack. Copyright, 1936, by the authors. Copyright and published, 1936, by Random House, New York.

For Samuel and Bella (Cohen) Spewack America has proved such a land of opportunity as has frequently been referred to in biographical fiction. Samuel is Russia born, Bella Hungary born. They were both brought up on the East Side of New York. They were both radicals, Bella probably the more radical of the two, before they made the Park Avenue grade, and still are radicals to what may be classified as a liberal extent. When they came back from Hollywood recently, for example, they were particular to hunt out a hotel that had done fairly by its help in a recent strike. They were both newspaper reporters when they met, doing their best work finally for the old *Morning World,* for which Sam served as foreign correspondent, winding up in Russia. The Spewacks lived for some time in Moscow and do not think much of communists. Communists, Bella has been quoted as saying, are smug—smug fanatics. Bella was a short story writer (making the O'Brien collection one year), and they had a hankering to do plays, both before and after they went to Hollywood in the early depression years, to write scenarios at a pretty salary. Their first Broadway piece was a satircial comedy called "Clear All Wires," a bit too extravagant for wide popularity, being the story of a wild newspaper genius whom the lay public could not quite accept as a credible character. At that, "Clear All Wires" was more of a success than their "Spring Song," a sentimental comedy Francine Larrimore played in 1934. It was not until their appearance this season with "Boy Meets Girl" that they literally took Broadway captive. They are back at the scenario business, but with other living plays up their kimono sleeves.

"Dead End." A drama in three acts by Sidney Kingsley. Copyright, 1935, by the author. Copyright and published, 1936, by Random House, New York.

Sidney Kingsley, whose "Men in White" won the Pulitzer award two years back, came out of Cornell with an ambition fixed on playwriting and play production. He did a bit of professional acting, with a stock company in the Bronx and in the production of "Subway Express" on Broadway, before he sold "Men in White," which he first called "Crisis." He is still under thirty and is therefore not obliged to hurry his career. He fussed two years with "Dead End" before he was satisfied with it. He has won two Theatre Club medals with his two produced plays, one Pulitzer prize and been a runner-up in innumerable other best play voting contests. He was a leader in the dramatic club activities of both high school and college.

"Call It a Day." A comedy in three acts by Dodie Smith. Copyright, 1935, by the author. Copyright and published, 1936, by Samuel French, New York and London.

When Dodie Smith, writing then under the nom de plume of C. L. Anthony, scored a success with her first produced play, "Autumn Crocus," the London journalists wrote quite freely about her as a modest little girl working behind a counter at a prominent draper's, which would be a London department store to us. As a matter of provable fact she was employed by the London firm of Heal & Sons, but not behind the counter. She was, and may be still, a buyer of toys and pictures for them. Neither was she without experience in the theatre. Miss Smith is the daughter of a Lancashire family that has got on very well. She was born in the village of Whitefield, near Manchester, and educated at St. Paul's School for Girls in London. She studied at the Royal Academy of Dramatic Art, played several parts in London and toured the provinces; decided she was a bad actress and left the stage to go into trade. She did some writing for amateur groups. Her plays for the professional stage include the two America has seen, another called "Service" that was a London success and one called "Touch Wood."

"Ethan Frome." A drama in three acts, dramatized by Owen Davis and Donald Davis from the novel of Edith Wharton, suggested by a previous dramatization made by Lowell Barrington. Copyright, 1935, by the authors. Copyright and published, 1911-22-36, by Charles Scribner's Sons, New York.

The career of Owen Davis as a playwright divides itself easily into two periods: That of his youth, when he wrote a series of popular-priced melodramas of the "Confessions of a Wife" and "Bertha the Sewing Machine Girl" type, and that of his middle years, when, in 1910, he moved uptown to Broadway and began writing plays for the better theatre, beginning with "The Wedding Ring" for Marguerite Clark and "Lola" for Laurette Taylor. He continued through "The Family Cupboard" and "Sinners" to "The Detour," "The Nervous Wreck" and "Icebound," with which he won the 1922-23 Pulitzer award, to "The Great Gatsby," "The Ninth Guest," "The Good Earth," etc. Mr. Davis attended the University of Tennessee two years and was graduated from Harvard in 1923, having gained a college reputation as a fair student and a darned good runner.

Donald Davis, collaborator, born in New York, is Mr. Davis' elder son. Owen Davis, Jr., the younger brother, took to acting rather than writing, though he served a term with George Pierce Baker at Yale and is now "in pictures," as they say. Donald's early years were devoted to the sea. He was appointed a cadet at Annapolis and, after he left the Naval Academy, he went sea-roaming for several years. He came back to take courses in philosophy, sociology and marine engineering at Columbia, and then settled down to writing plays. Proving, as the biographers say, that blood is thicker than water. He had five years' experience doing scripts for Paramount and did a play called "The Promised

Land" with a Hollywood background which Brock Pemberton would have produced if George Kaufman's and Moss Hart's "Once in a Lifetime" had not beaten him to the Broadway tape. Donald also did something called "Haunch, Paunch and Jowl" which was never produced in English, but which he was surprised to discover in the repertory of a Yiddish theatre some months ago. His first major achievement was his collaboration with his father on the dramatization of Pearl Buck's "The Good Earth." "Ethan Frome" followed, most of the dialogue of which was supplied by the son rather than the father.

"Pride and Prejudice." A comedy in three acts by Helen Jerome, dramatized from the novel of Jane Austen. Copyright, 1935, by the author. Copyright and published, 1935, by Double-day, Doran & Co., Garden City, N. Y.

Helen Jerome was born in Australia and her early literary life found expression when she became a contributor of short stories and poems to the newspapers and magazines of Sydney. At one time she wrote dramatic criticisms for the Melbourne *Dramatic News*. She has had two books published in Australia, one a book of poems, "Petals in the Wind," the other "Japan of Today," and she has had one book published by Liveright in America, "The Secret of Woman." Her "Pride and Prejudice" brought her prominence as a playwright. Following its success she has sold a first play, "Charlotte Corday," to Alex Yokel, who is scheduled to produce it first in London in association with Sydney Carroll. Next season she will be represented by "Jane Eyre," which Kath-arine Hepburn is coming back from Hollywood to play for the Theatre Guild in New York. Miss Jerome, the wife of George Ali, a retired Standard Oil executive, took a house in Mt. Kisco, New York, for the summer.

PLAYS PRODUCED IN NEW YORK

June 16, 1935—June 15, 1936

(Plays marked with asterisk were still playing June 15, 1936)

GRAND GUIGNOL HORROR PLAYS

(12 performances)

Three one-act plays. Produced by George K. Arthur and presented by the International Players at the Chanin Auditorium, New York, July 11, 1935.

SOMETHING MORE IMPORTANT

By H. F. Maltby

Cast of characters—

The Man	Leo Kennedy
The Woman	Doris Packer
The Boy	Robert Johnson
The Inspector	Herbert Warren
The Detective	Jack MacLennon
The Constable	Jerome Sheldon

Scene—A Room in Seven Dials, London.
Staged by George Arthur; setting by Jack MacLennon.

THE OLD WOMEN

By André de Lorde

Cast of characters—

The Sister	Doris Packer
Louise	Virginia Milne
The Doctor	Herbert Warren
Madame Robin	Valerie Bergere
The Woman	Florence Auer
The Hunchback	Virginia Gregori
The House Physician	Robert Johnson

Scene—Dormitory in an Asylum.
Staged by George K. Arthur; setting by Jack MacLennon.

"E & O E"

By Eliot Crawshay

Cast of characters—

James Smith	Leo Kennedy
Mary Smith	Virginia Milne
Jane Macintosh	Florence Auer

Charles Crosby..................................Jerome Sheldon
Henry Stone.....................................Herbert Warren
Scene—A Bedroom in the Smith Home, London.
Staged by George K. Arthur; setting by Jack MacLennon.

CIVIC LIGHT OPERA COMPANY SEASON

A season of Gilbert and Sullivan operettas revived by Lodewick Vroom at the Adelphi Theatre, New York, July 15, 1935, to September 7, 1935.

THE MIKADO

(16 performances)

Cast of characters—

The Mikado of Japan...........................William Danforth
Nanki-Poo......................................Howard Marsh
Ko-Ko..Frank Moulan
Pooh-Bah.......................................Herbert Waterous
Go-To..John Cosby
Pish-Tush......................................Bertram Peacock
Yum-Yum..Margaret Daum
Pitti-Sing.....................................Vivian Hart
Peep-Bo..Nina Dean
Katisha..Vera Ross
Act I.—Courtyard of Ko-Ko's Official Residence. Act II.—Ko-Ko's Garden.

PIRATES OF PENZANCE

(July 22, 1935)

(12 performances)

Cast of characters—

Richard..Herbert Waterous
Samuel...Bertram Peacock
Frederick......................................Howard Marsh
Major General Stanley..........................Frank Moulan
Edward...William Danforth
Mabel..Vivian Hart
Kate...Nina Dean
Edith..Margaret Daum
Isabel...Frances Baviello
Ruth...Vera Ross
General Stanley's Daughters, Pirates, Policemen, etc.
Act I.—Rocky Shore Off Cornwall. Act II.—Ruined Abbey.

YEOMEN OF THE GUARD

(July 29, 1935)

(12 performances)

Cast of characters—

Sir Richard Cholmondeley.......................Bertram Peacock
Colonel Fairfax................................Howard Marsh

Sergeant Meryll..............................Herbert Waterous
Leonard..George Rogers
Jack Point.......................................Frank Moulan
Wilfred Shadbolt............................William Danforth
Elsie Maynard..................................Margaret Daum
Phoebe..Vivian Hart
Dame Carruthers......................................Vera Ross
Kate............................Eleanor Gilmore and Nina Dean
First Yeoman.....................................George Ebert
Second Yeoman...................William Venturo and Solon West
First Citizen.......................................Alfred Drake
Headsman...John Cosby
    Scenes 1 and 2—Tower Green, London.

THE GONDOLIERS

(August 5, 1935)

(12 performances)

Cast of characters—

The Duke of Plaza-Toro...........................Frank Moulan
Luiz..Walter Andrews
Don Alhambra Del Bolero......................William Danforth
Marco Palmieri....................................Howard Marsh
Giuseppe Palmieri..............................Bertram Peacock
Antonio...George Rogers
Francesco.......................................William Ventura
Giorgio..John Cosby
Annibale..Solon West
The Duchess of Plaza-Toro...........................Vera Ross
Casilda..Margaret Daum
Gianetta...Vivian Hart
Tessa..Peggy Strickland
Fiametta..Frances Baviello
Vittoria..Edith Gibson
Giulia..Eleanor Gilmore
Inez...Ione Haals
    Act I.—Venice. Act II.—Pavilion in Palace of Barataria.

TRIAL BY JURY

(August 12, 1935)

(12 performances)

Cast of characters—

The Learned Judge...............................Frank Moulan
Foreman of the Jury............................Herbert Waterous
Defendant...Howard Marsh
Counsel for the Defense........................Bertram Peacock
Usher...William Danforth
Counsel for Plaintiff.............................George Rogers
Plaintiff...Margaret Daum
    Scene—Court of Exchequer.

H.M.S. PINAFORE

(August 12, 1935)

(12 performances)

Cast of characters—

The Right Hon. Sir Joseph Porter, K.C.B.	Frank Moulan
Captain Corcoran	Bertram Peacock
Ralph Rackstraw	Howard Marsh
Dick Deadeye	William Danforth
Bill Bobstay	Herbert Waterous
Josephine	Margaret Daum
Little Buttercup (Mrs. Cripps)	Vera Ross
Hebe	Peggy Strickland
Midshipmen	Royce Perez, Ramon Perez
Bob Becket	John Cosby
Sergeant of Marines	George Stevens

Scene—Deck of "H.M.S. Pinafore" off Portsmouth, England.

All operas staged by R. H. Burnside; settings by Eugene Dunkel.

"The Mikado" was repeated for half-week runs August 19 and September 5; "Pirates of Penzance," August 22; "Yeomen of the Guard," August 26; "The Gondoliers," August 29; "Trial by Jury" and "H.M.S. Pinafore," September 2.

THE GREAT WALTZ

(Return engagement 49 performances)

Operetta in two acts by Moss Hart; lyrics by Desmond Carter; music by Johann Strauss, father and son. Returned by Max Gordon to the Center Theatre, New York, August 5, 1935.

Cast of characters—

Greta	Jessie Busley
Ebeseder	Dudley Clements
Leopold (Poldi)	Dennis Noble
Therese (Resi)	Lee Whitney
Johann Strauss, Jr. (Schani)	Guy Robertson
Augustina	Virginia Watkins
Lottie	Patti Heaton
Hans Heindrich	Bruce Barclay
Paul Heindrich	Donald Lee
Countess Olga Baranskaja	Marie Burke
Wilhelm	Richard Lambart
Lili	Wilma Kaye
Franzi	Tanya Sanina
Tini	Diana Walker
Mali	Ruth Vollmer
Sini	Rosalynd Hutner
Mitzi	Nina Dean
Nini	Ruth Clayton
Betti	Dorothy Forsyth
Karl Hirsch	Stanley Harrison
Johann Strauss, Sr.	H. Reeves-Smith
Kathi Lanner	Vivien Fay
Dommayer	Solly Ward

Captain Boris Androff..........................Ralph Magelssen
Dreschler...................................Robert C. Fischer
Hartkopf...Richie Ling
Franz Ludwig..................................Charles Romano
Gretchen Ludwig....................................Aphie James
Lieutenant Carl Boch............................Ralph Glover
Captain Hal Fredrich..........................Charles Brokaw
Lieutenant Ferdinand Holmann.....................Albert Amato
        Act I.—Scene 1—Outside Ebeseder's Pastry Shop. 2 and 4—The
Little Garden. 3 and 5—The Big Garden. 6—The Sitting Room.
Act II.—Scene 1—The Ballet. 2—The Pavilion. 3 and 4—The
Gardens. 5—The Ballroom.
        Staged by Hassard Short; dances and ballet by Albertina Rasch;
settings by Albert Johnson.

"The Great Waltz" was first produced at the Center Theatre
September 22, 1934, and continued there until June 8, 1935,
298 performances.

SMILE AT ME

(27 performances)

A revue in two acts by Edward J. Lambert; music by Gerald
Dolin. Produced by Harold Berg at the Fulton Theatre, New
York, August 23, 1935.

Principals engaged—

Jack Osterman	Ruth Edell
Edward J. Lambert	Avis Andrews
Hal Thompson	Dorothy Morrison
Jesse Wolk	Gene Fontaine
Ivan Bankoff	Beth Cannon
Dean Wheeler	Dorothy Davis
Eddie Bruce	Betty Fontaine
Paul Mears	Poppy Mears
Georges Vito	Irene Piri

        Staged by Frank Merlin; settings by Karl Amend; dances by Paul
Florenz; costumes by Dorothy Van Winkle.

MOON OVER MULBERRY STREET

(303 performances)

A comedy in three acts by Nicholas Cosentino. Produced by
Standish O'Neill and Paul de Maria at the Lyceum Theatre,
September 4, 1935.

Cast of characters—

Piccino Morello..............................William Edmunds
Lucia Morello..................................Valerie Bergere
Angelo Baccolini..............................Mische Ferenzo
Nina Baccolini...................................Olga Druce
Marie Morello...................................Phebe Root
George Bowman..................................Edward Marr
Fillipo Morello..................................Cornel Wilde
Carmella Baccolini..........................Adelina Roattino
Giovanna Baccolini............................Betty Kashman
Helen Richards................................Gladys Shelley

Grant Whitmore.....................................James Metcalf
     Acts I, II and III.—Morello Basement Flat on Mulberry Street,
New York's Little Italy.
     Staged by William Muir; setting by Louis Kennel.

Fillipo Morello, son of an Italian janitor in Mulberry street, is being helped through law school by an uptown attorney named Richards. Fillipo falls in love with Richards' daughter Helen, but Helen thinks it were better if she remained true to caste. She is prepared to marry, however, in Park avenue and love in Mulberry street, an arrangement Fillipo will not accept. He turns finally to Nina Baccolini, an apartment neighbor who has loved him all the time.

"Moon Over Mulberry Street" closed January 4 and re-opened January 13, 1935.

AWAKE AND SING

(First engagement 185 performances; return 24. Total 209)

A play in three acts by Clifford Odets. Returned by the Group Theatre, Inc., to the Belasco Theatre, New York, September 9, 1935.

Cast of characters—

Myron Berger...Art Smith
Bessie Berger...Stella Adler
Jacob..Morris Carnovsky
Hennie Berger.......................................Phoebe Brand
Ralph Berger...Jules Garfield
Schlosser..Roman Bohnen
Moe Axelrod..Luther Adler
Uncle Morty..J. E. Bromberg
Sam Feinschreiber...............................Sanford Meisner
Tootsie...Tootsie Miller
     Acts I, II and III.—Apartment in the Bronx.
     Staged by Harold Clurman; setting by Boris Aronson.

"Awake and Sing" was first produced February 19, 1935, at the Belasco Theatre, continuing for 185 performances. "Best Plays of 1934-35."

WAITING FOR LEFTY

(First engagement 144 performances; return 24. Total 168)

A one-act play by Clifford Odets. Transferred by the Group Theatre, Inc., to the Belasco Theatre, New York, September 9, 1935.

Cast of characters—

Fatt...Russell Collins
Joe...Lewis Leverett

```
Edna................................................Ruth  Nelson
Miller..............................................Tony  Kraber
Fayette.............................................Grover  Burgess
Irv.................................................Walter  Coy
Florrie.............................................Paula  Miller
Sid.................................................Herbert  Ratner
Clayton..........................................William  Challee
Agate  Keller.......................................Elia  Kazan
Henchman............................................Art  Smith
Second  Henchman...............................Sanford  Meisner
Dr.  Barnes.........................................Roman  Bohnen
Dr.  Benjamin.......................................Luther  Adler
     Scene—A  Strike  Meeting  Hall.
```

"Waiting for Lefty" was first coupled with a second one-act play by Mr. Odets called "Till the Day I Die." As a double bill these plays were given for 136 performances at the Longacre Theatre, beginning March 26, 1935. "Best Plays of 1934-35." "Till the Day I Die" discontinued when "Waiting for Lefty" was transferred to the Belasco Theatre where it ran with "Awake and Sing" for one week, closing July 27 and re-opening September 9, 1935.

KIND LADY

(First engagement 82 performances; return 20. Total 102)

A play in three acts by Edward Chodorov, adapted from a story by Hugh Walpole. Returned by Potter and Haight to the Longacre Theatre, New York, September 9, 1935.

Cast of characters—

```
Mr.  Foster.........................................Francis  Compton
Mary  Herries.......................................Grace  George
Lucy  Weston........................................Irby  Marshal
Rose................................................Marie  Paxton
Phyllis  Glenning...................................Florence  Britton
Peter  Santard......................................Alan  Bunce
Henry  Abbott.......................................Henry  Daniell
Ada.................................................Justine  Chase
Doctor..............................................Ralph  Urmy
Mr.  Edwards........................................Ralph  Theadore
Mrs.  Edwards.......................................Elfrida  Derwent
Aggie  Edwards......................................Barbara  Shields
Gustav  Rosenberg...................................Jules  Epailly
     Prologue,  Acts  I,  II  and  III  and  Epilogue.—Living  Room  of  Mary
Herries'  Home  in  Montague  Square,  London.
     Staged  by  H.  C.  Potter;  settings  by  Jo  Mielziner.
```

The original engagement started April 23, 1935, and suspended June 29, 1935. "Best Plays of 1934-35."

A SLIGHT CASE OF MURDER

(69 performances)

A comedy in two acts by Damon Runyon and Howard Lindsay. Produced by Howard Lindsay at the 48th Street Theatre, New York, September 11, 1935.

Cast of characters—

Lefty	James La Curto
Giuseppe	Clyde Veaux
Innocence	F. H. Day
Mike	Joseph Sweeney
Douglas F. Rosenbloom	Roy Le May
Chancellor Whitelaw	John Griggs
The Singin' Kid	Frankie Wheeler
Sad Sam	Harry Levian
Remy Marco	John Harrington
Commissioner Mahoney	Percy Moore
Gammon Smith	Sydney Booth
Mary Marco	Phyllis Welch
Nora Marco	Georgia Caine
Telegraph Boy	Nick Dennis
Theodore Whitelaw	Lawrence Grossmith
Ex-Jockey Kirk	Richard Taber
Mrs. Ryerson	Beth Franklyn
Loretta Paige	Eleanor Brent
Pete Ryan	Paul E. Burns
The Champ	Ray Devlin
Mrs. Ritter	Joy Hathaway
Calvin Ritter	John M. Kline
George Hatch	Charles Wellesley
Clyde Post	Malcolm Duncan
Colonel Jake Schultz	George Christie
Taxi Driver	Walter Wagner
1st Policeman	Clyde Franklin
2nd Policeman	Jose Ferrer

Passers-by: Geoffrey Lind, Richard Courtney, R. Norvak, M. Miltos, James Kearns, J. Fitzgerald, E. Molenedyk, Marga Barbet, Winton Sears, T. Lynn Kearse, Irja Koski, Marion Frederic, Frances Levian, Annette Le May, Fred Steinway, Ted Levey, Eleanor Healy, Alice Frey, Dan Malloy, Mrs. Fralick.

Acts I and II.—A House in Saratoga Springs, New York.
Staged by the authors; setting by Kate Drain Lawson.

Remy Marco, once a beer racketeer, now a respectable brewer, takes a house at Saratoga Springs for the racing season. Moving in with certain of his old gang and his socially hopeful wife and daughter, Remy discovers the corpses of four hijackers sitting stiff and cold around a poker table on the third floor. They had robbed a truck of a fortune in bookmakers' money and were preparing to get even with Remy for an old grudge when they were knocked off. Remy decides to scatter the cadavers around the neighborhood. No sooner done than he discovers the government has offered a reward of $10,000 for each of them dead or alive. He manages to gather them in again, induces a novice State Trooper to shoot them all over and present them for the reward. For himself he keeps the recovered bookmakers' boodle.

NIGHT OF JANUARY 16

(235 performances)

A melodrama in three acts by Ayn Rand. Produced by A. H. Woods, Ltd., at the Ambassador Theatre, New York, September 16, 1935.

Cast of characters—

Court Stenographer..............................Richard French
Bailiff...Donald Oliver
Judge Heath.................................J. Arthur Young
District Attorney Flint..........................Edmund Breese
Defense Attorney Stevens......................Robert Shayne
Clerk of Court................................George Anderson
Karen Andre.......................................Doris Nolan
Dr. Kirkland.......................................Edward Wing
John Hutchins....................................Calvin Thomas
Homer Van Fleet..................................Harry Short
Elmer Sweeney....................................Leo Kennedy
Nancy Lee Faulkner...............................Verna Hillie
Magda Svenson...................................Sarah Padden
John Graham Whitfield............................Clyde Fillmore
James Chandler..................................Maurice Morris
Siegurd Jungquist................................Arthur Pierson
"Guts" Regan....................................Walter Pidgeon
Roberta Van Renssalear..........................Marcella Swanson
      Acts I, II and III.—New York Courtroom.
      Staged by John Hayden; setting by Herbert Moore.

Karen Andre is being tried for the murder of Bjorne Faulkner, in whose employ she had worked as secretary and later as mistress. A jury is impaneled from the audience and the trial proceeds. Faulkner, after being shot, had fallen or been pushed from the parapet of a penthouse. The prosecution claims Miss Andre inspired the plan to put him out of the way. The defense insists the evidence supports the theory that Faulkner, financially involved to the extent of millions, was a suicide. During the trial it is revealed that the body supposed to have been that of Faulkner was a substitution. Faulkner had escaped but later had crashed in an airplane. Miss Andre admits having been a party to this conspiracy. She was to have joined Faulkner later in South America. The jury must decide which story to believe. There are two endings, making it possible to fit any jury's verdict.

FEW ARE CHOSEN

(15 performances)

A play in three acts by Nora Lawlor. Produced by the author at the 58th Street Theatre, New York, September 17, 1935.

Cast of characters—

Mother Mercy....................................Alma Kruger
Sister Pius..Lida Kane
Sister Celestine..................................Sylvia Leigh
Sister Ernestine...................................Alney Alba
Sister Madonna..................................Norma Downey
Sister Geraldine................................Charlotte Gloer
Sister Pauline..................................Louise Kirtland
Sister Emily......................................Mary Hone
Sister Olivera.....................................Ara Gerald
Sister Ignatius...............................Gertrude Maitland
Sister Loretta...................................Mary Drayton

Mrs. Manville.......................................Madeline Grey
Ralph Hughes.......................................Coburn Goodwin
Marianne...Janet Pearsall
        Act I.—Scene 1—Chapel in a Convent. 2—Community Room.
    Act II.—Scene 1—Sister Madonna's Room. 2—Community Room.
    Act III.—Community Room.
        Staged by Gregory Deane; settings by Alfred Bauer; costumes by
    Greta Baum.

Sister Olivera is one of a class of seven novitiates entering a
convent for preliminary study preparatory to becoming nuns.
She and four of the others have difficulty in sticking to their
resolutions respecting the cloistered life. Sister Olivera is pur-
sued by a memory of the lover she left roaming the world; Sister
Madonna is beset with a hunger for motherhood; Sister Emily
loses her mind when she would embrace sainthood; Sister
Geraldine, stricken with tuberculosis, confesses an unsettled faith
in the gratitude of the Lord. Of the seven who were called but
two are chosen in the end.

AT HOME ABROAD

(198 performances)

A revue in two acts by Howard Dietz and Arthur Schwartz.
Produced by the Messrs. Shubert at the Winter Garden, New
York, September 19, 1935.

Principals engaged—

Paul Haakon	The Continentals
Herb Williams	Beatrice Lillie
Eddie Foy, Jr.	Eleanor Powell
James McColl	Ethel Waters
Reginald Gardiner	Nina Whitney
Andre Charise	Vera Allen
Woods Miller	Julie Jenner
Sue Hastings' Marionettes	Gene Martel
Six Spirits of Rhythm	

        Staged by Vincente Minnelli; dances by Gene Snyder and Harry
Losee; dialogue by Thomas Mitchell; sets by Minnelli.

LIFE'S TOO SHORT

(10 performances)

A comedy in three acts by John Whedon and Arthur Caplan.
Produced by Jed Harris at the Broadhurst Theatre, September
20, 1935.

Cast of characters—

Hannah Priest.....................................Katherine Squire
Alfred..Edward Bracken
Irene Regan.......................................Gerrie Worthing
Ethel Rosenberg...................................Janet Fox

Edward Fowler..John B. Litel
Ruth Fogarty...Evelyn Varden
J. M. Babcock..Priestly Morrison
James Collins...Leslie Adams
Helen Fowler..Doris Dalton
Mrs. Remson..Ethel Wilson
Waiter..Joseph de Villarde
Mrs. Collins...Lea Penman
    Act I.—Scene 1—Office of Elite Food Corp. 2—The Fowlers'
Apartment. Act II.—Scenes 1 and 3—The Fowlers' Apartment.
2—Restaurant. Act III.—Scene 1—Collins' Office. 2—Office of Elite
Food Corp.
    Staged by Jed Harris; settings by Raymond Sovey.

Edward Fowler has been working for the Elite Food Corporation for seventeen years. For seven years he has been happily married to Helen Fowler, who formerly had been secretary (and mistress) to James Collins, Elite executive. In the depression Fowler loses his job. After seven months' idleness his savings are gone and his nerves are shattered. Hearing that Helen has asked Collins to help get her husband's job back, Fowler grows fiendishly suspicious and practically drives her from the house. Helen, disgusted, returns to Collins. Fowler takes his old job and concludes that life is too short to let things like that whip you.

A TOUCH OF BRIMSTONE

(98 performances)

A play in three acts by Leonora Kaghan and Anita Philips. Produced by John Golden at the Golden Theatre, New York, September 22, 1935.

Cast of characters—

Janet Faber...Mary Philips
Mark Faber...Roland Young
Ben Forster...Ryder Keane
Isabel Cobb..Cora Witherspoon
Wally Cobb...Richard Sterling
Nancy McClure.......................................Hancey Castle
Larry Evans.......................................Reed Brown, Jr.
Leo Kruger..Bob Burton
Herbert...Malcolm Laing
Buddy..Jas. Dowd
Hotel Floor Clerk....................................Wm. Postance
Geoffrey Smythe....................................Wheeler Dryden
Tommy Kimball...................................William Post, Jr.
Bellows..Basil Hanbury
Featherwell......................................Reginald Carrington
    Act I.—Living Room in Home of Mark Faber, East 10th Street,
New York City. Acts II and III.—Living Room of a Suite in a
London Hotel.
    Staged by Frank Craven; settings by P. Dodd Ackerman.

Mark Faber, producer of plays and frankly an egomaniac of extravagant and annoying habits, abuses the Janet Faber who is his forgiving wife until she finds herself at the breaking point.

Taking a company to Europe, Faber seduces his ingénue en route, thereby threatening not only a break with his own wife, but the destruction of the ingénue's happiness as well. In an effort to prevent Janet from divorcing him Faber determines to leave the theatre for good. He starts by calling off his scheduled London opening. This would mean a slight to their English majesties, who were planning to attend as a compliment to a charity that is to benefit from the first performance. Faber finally agrees to let the show go on. Janet leaves him, but he is still confident of winning her back.

IF THIS BE TREASON

(40 performances)

A play in three acts by Dr. John Haynes Holmes and Reginald Lawrence. Produced by The Theatre Guild at the Music Box Theatre, New York, September 23, 1935.

Cast of characters—

Duncan	Hunter Gardner
Turner	Walter N. Greaza
Robert Gordon	John Stark
John Gordon	McKay Morris
Miss Folwell	Kathryn Givney
Mrs. Gordon	Armina Marshall
Mansfield	Robert Williams
Mrs. Bane	Kathleen Comegys
British Ambassador	Edgar Kent
French Ambassador	Marcel Journet
Bright	Donald Mackenzie
Dickinson	Boyd Davis
Fitzgerald	Leo Curley
Hill	Mitchell Harris
Smith	Lawrence M. Hurdle
Fulton	Frank Dae
Jarvis	Thomas Neal
Wilmot	Robert Lowe
Aldrich	Harland Tucker
Admiral James	James Spottswood
Brainard	Thomas Chalmers
Todu	Bacouren Yoshiwara
General Nogatu	Edgar Kent
Dr. Fujimoto	Takashi Ohta
Lord Carrington	Charles Bryant
Yato	Tom Powers
Baron Ishiwara	George Hiroshe
Koye	Arthur Hughes

Acts I and II.—The White House. Act III.—Scene 1—Anteroom in Hotel, Tokio, Japan. 2—Conference Chamber, Tokio.
Staged by Harry Wagstaff Gribble; settings by John Root.

John Gordon, elected to the presidency of the United States on a pacifist platform, finds himself soon faced with a threat of war. Japan, smarting under an ultimatum issued by Gordon's immediate predecessor, seizes Manila. Gordon, in place of meeting the threat with a declaration of war, recalls the navy, holds the army at home and goes personally to Japan to talk the situation over with the Premier. In Japan he discovers a crusading pacifist named Koye has so aroused the people they are ready to join with the people of the United States in outlawing war.

BLIND ALLEY

(119 performances)

A play in three acts by James Warwick. Produced by James R. Ullman at the Booth Theatre, New York, September 24, 1935.

Cast of characters—

Doris Shelby	Katharine Warren
Fred Landis	James Truex
Dr. Anthony Shelby	George Coulouris
Agnes	Edna Ramsey
Teddy	Lloyd Barry
Nora	Mabel Montgomery
Hal Wilson	Roy Hargrave
Mazie Stoner	Ruth Fallows
Buck	Jay Adler
Nick	James Brooks
Officer Thorne	Albert G. West

Acts I, II and III.—Living Room of Dr. Shelby's Home.
Staged by Worthington Miner; settings by S. Syrjala.

Dr. Anthony Shelby, professor of psychology, is living with his wife in a suburb near the water. Hal Wilson, a minor Dillinger, escaping the police and expecting to meet a boat near the Shelby place, takes over the Shelby bungalow by force of arms and announces that he and his mob will hold it until the arrival of the boat. Dr. Shelby, his professional curiosity aroused, manages to engage Wilson in conversation. He succeeds finally in so entangling and exposing the mental weaknesses of the gunman's defense that Wilson prefers to make way with himself rather than to continue his war against society. Meantime there have been several murders and other excitements.

REMEMBER THE DAY

(122 performances)

A play in three acts by Philip Dunning and Philo Higley. Produced by Philip Dunning at the National Theatre, New York, September 25, 1935.

Cast of characters—

1st Bellboy	John Drew Devereaux
Nora Trinell	Francesca Bruning

```
Flower Girl.....................................Virginia Dunning
2nd Bellboy.........................................Peter Johnston
Reporter............................................Keenan Wynn
Dewey Roberts................................Frankie Thomas
Kate Hill..........................................Mary McQuade
Tom.................................................Robert Mayors
Steve Hill...........................................Joe Brown, Jr.
Ellen Talbot.........................................Charita Bauer
Miss Price........................................Kathleen Kidder
Dan Hopkins.......................................Russell Hardie
Mr. Steel.......................................J. Hammond Dailey
Edith Phelps........................................Martha Hodge
Mrs. Roberts........................................Jane Seymour
Charlie...........................................Clifford Stallings
Dorothy..............................................Edna Hagan
Mr. Roberts...................................Frank Thomas, Sr.
Mr. Phelps........................................Charles Walton
Miss Kline.......................................Katherine Bauer
Anna...........................................Jessamine Newcombe
D. R. Roberts.........................................Grant Mills
```
      Prologue and Epilogue.—Alcove in Hotel Lobby, Washington,
   D. C. Act I.—Scene 1—Schoolroom in Middle Wesfern Suburb.
   2—Living Room in Dewey's Home. Act II.—Scene 1—School Corridor. 2—Dewey's Home. Act III.—Dewey's Home.
      Staged by Melville Burke; settings by Syrjala.

Dewey Roberts, 14, taking 7B from Nora Trinell, falls in love
with teacher. Dewey manages to be pretty happy about it until
the day he is going back to apologize to Miss Trinell for having
been rude to her. Then he sees his goddess kissing the athletic
coach, Dan Hopkins, and things swim before Dewey's eyes. He
is miserable for weeks, and his parents send him away to boarding school for the good of the change. Years after Dewey, grown
famous, met Miss Trinell, grown old, in the lobby of a Washington hotel. He barely remembers her.

WINTERSET

(First engagement 179 performances; return 16. Total 195)

A play in three acts by Maxwell Anderson. Produced by
Guthrie McClintic at the Martin Beck Theatre, New York,
September 25, 1935.

Cast of characters—

```
Trock............................................Eduardo Ciannelli
Shadow............................................Harold Johnsrud
Lucio...........................................Morton L. Stevens
Piny.............................................Fernanda Eliscu
Miriamne ................................................Margo
Garth............................................Theodore Hecht
Esdras........................................Anatole Winogradoff
1st Girl............................................Eva Langbord
2nd Girl...........................................Ruth Hammond
Hobo..............................................John Philliber
Judge Gaunt....................................Richard Bennett
Carr..............................................Billy Quinn
Mio...........................................Burgess Meredith
Sailor..........................................St. John Terrell
Radical...........................................Abner Biberman
```

Policeman...Anthony Blair
Sergeant..Harold Martin
Two Young Men...................Stanley Gould, Walter Holbrook
    Act I.—Scenes 1 and 3—Under a Bridge. 2—In a Tenement.
Act II.—In a Tenement. Act III.—Under the Bridge.
    Staged by Guthrie McClintic; settings by Jo Mielziner.

See page 32.

PATHS OF GLORY

(23 performances)

A tragedy in sixteen scenes by Sidney Howard, adapted from a novel by Humphrey Cobb. Produced by Arthur Hopkins at the Plymouth Theatre, New York, September 26, 1935.

Cast of characters—

The Proprietress of the Café du Carrefour...............Ann Dere
Langlois......................................Myron McCormick
Didier...William Harrigan
Colonel Dax.......................................Lee Baker
Captain Renouart.................................Edgar Barrier
Lieutenant Roget....................................Roland Drew
General de Guerville..............................Cyril Scott
General Assolant.................................Jack Roseleigh
Lieutenant Saint-Auben.........................Nicholas Harlow
Colonel Labouchere.............................Ranney Compton
Captain Nicholas...............................Leonard Penn
Ferol...Jerome Cowan
Meyer...George Tobias
Perdreau..Jack Daniels
Dufour..Roger Quinlan
Rothier.......................................Herschel Cropper
Constant..David Leonard
Lieutenant Arnaud..............................Norman Stuart
Captain Herbillion..............................Jack Davis
Captain Charpentier...............................Guy Repp
Captain Sancy...................................E. J. Ballantine
Sergeant Gounod.................................Dick Purcell
Sergeant-Chaplain Picard.......................Perry Ivins
Corporal Riviere.................................John Bohn
Duval...Milo Boulton
LeJeune...Stephen Crane
Clermont..Richard Ross
Durand..Paul Alberts
Beyle..Bernard Fabrizi
Jouvet..Robert Adams
Tessier..Ted Erwin
An Observer......................................Jerry Sloane
Nolet..Bernard Kisner
Sergeant Jonnart.................................Harold Moffet
Sergeant Darde.................................George W. Smith
Lalance.......................................Wardell Jennings
Richet...Philip Robinson
Sarcy..Sanford Bickart
Poujade..Clem Wilenchick
Fasquelle...Paul Stiller
Thionville.....................................Arthur Marlowe
Captain Etienne....................................Carl Frank
Captain Ibels......................................John Seager
Captain Tanon....................................George Ryan
A Regimental Doctor.......................Benedict MacQuarrie
    Scene 1—Café du Carrefour, Army Zone in France, 1915. 2, 5 and 10—The Road. 3 and 11—Division Headquarters. 4—4th Co. Bar-

racks. 6—2nd Co. Barracks. 7—The Trenches. 8—3rd Co. Dugout.
9—Observation Post. 12—Regimental Headquarters. 13—4th Co.
Headquarters. 14—3rd Co. Barracks. 15—Château de l'Aigle. 16—
Stables.
Staged by Arthur Hopkins; settings by Henry Dreyfuss.

The vanity of General de Guerville and the ruthless ambition
of General Assolant send a regiment of French troops, recently
returned from the line, back to the front to stage an assault upon
a practically impregnable German position. When the assault
fails Assolant orders the execution of representatives from every
company of the First Battalion on a charge of cowardice as an
example to the rest of the regiment. Three men, though heroes
in their own right, are condemned by a framed court-martial and
shot.

OTHELLO

(11 performances)

A tragedy by William Shakespeare. Revived by Crosby Gaige,
Inc., at the Ethel Barrymore Theatre, New York, September 27,
1935.

Cast of characters—

Duke of Venice	Henry Morrell
Brabantio	Harold Gould
Gratiano	Hannam Clark
Lodovico	Charles Francis
Othello	Philip Merivale
Cassio	Kenneth Hunter
Iago	Kenneth MacKenna
Roderigo	Roland Bottomley
Montano	Jerome Lawler
First Gentleman	Joseph Holland
Second Gentleman	Staats Cotsworth
Third Gentleman	Bram Nossen
A Sailor	Edward Broadley
An Officer	Ralph Nelson
A Messenger	Maurice Manson
Desdemona	Gladys Cooper
Emilia	Alexandra Carlisle
Bianca	Betty Bourjaily
Cyprian Women	Connie Lent / Constance Pelissier / Margaret English

Part I.—Scenes 1, 2 and 6—Street in Venice. 3—Council Chamber. 4—Lobby. 5—Seaport in Cyprus. 7—Hall in Castle. Part II.—
Scene 1—Terrace of the Castle. 2 and 4—Before the Castle. 3, 5 and
7—Bed-Chamber. 6—Street.
Staged by Henry Herbert; settings by P. Dodd Ackerman; costumes by C. B. Falls.

"Othello" has figured prominently in the repertories of all outstanding Shakespearean stars from the beginning of recorded
stage history. An actor named Robert Upton was the first
Othello in New York, playing the role at the Nassau St. theatre

in 1751. Booth and Barrett alternated the roles of the Moor and
Iago. Edwin Forrest, E. L. Davenport, and John McCullough
were successful in the part. The role marked Booth's return to
the stage following the Lincoln tragedy. Tomasso Salvini played
Othello to the Iago of Booth. Robert B. Mantell, Louis James,
Johnstone Forbes-Robertson, William Faversham and Walter
Hampden have been comparatively recent Othellos.

THE TAMING OF THE SHREW

(129 performances)

A comedy in two parts by William Shakespeare. Produced by
The Theatre Guild, Inc., at the Guild Theatre, New York, September 30, 1935.

Cast of characters—

IN THE INDUCTION

Christopher Sly	Richard Whorf
A Lord	Lowell Gilmore
First Huntsman	John Balmer
Second Huntsman	Gilmore Bush
Third Huntsman	Winston Ross
Bartholomew	William Clifford

IN THE PLAY

Lucentio	Alan Hewitt
Tranio	Bretaigne Windust
Two Townswomen	Jacqueline De Witt / Ernestine De Becker
Pantaloon	LeRoi Operti
Baptista	Sydney Greenstreet
Gremio	George Graham
Hortensio	Barry Thomson
Bianca	Dorothy Mathews
Biondello	George Meader
Petruchio	Alfred Lunt
Grumio	Horace Sinclair
Widow	Doris Rich
Maid	Jacqueline De Witt
Katherine	Lynn Fontanne
Curtis	Alice Belmore Cliffe
Nathaniel	Gilmore Bush
Joseph	Thomas Coley
Gregory	William Gray
Philip	Winston Ross
Cook	Stephen Sandes
Haberdasher	S. Thomas Gomez
Tailor	LeRoi Operti
A Pedant	Robert Vivian
Vincentio	David Glassford
Officer	S. Thomas Gomez
A Prisoner	Stephen Sandes
Horses	Harry Be Gar / Arthur Chester

Acrobats: Roy Rognan, George Snare, Stuart Barlow.
Dwarfs: John Ballas, Freddie Goodrow, Ray Holgate, Ray Schultz.
Parts I and II.—House of a Noble Lord.
Staged by Harry Wagstaff Gribble; settings by Carolyn Hancock;
costumes by Claggett Wilson.

There have been several notable revivals of "The Taming of the Shrew" in New York. It was first given by Lewis Hallam and Margaret Cheer in 1768, and again in 1785. An 1887 revival by Augustin Daly, with John Drew and Ada Rehan, was a talked-of event and a great help to Mr. Drew's reputation as an actor. Otis Skinner and Ada Rehan toured in the comedy in 1902, and Charles Richman and Miss Rehan in 1905. It was long a feature of the Sothern-Marlowe repertory. In 1927 Basil Sydney and Mary Ellis played it in modern dress with considerable success.

MOST OF THE GAME

(23 performances)

A comedy in three acts by John Van Druten. Produced by Dwight Deere Wiman and Auriol Lee at the Cort Theatre, New York, October 1, 1935.

Cast of characters—

```
Al Sessums..........................................James Bell
Hugh Collimore....................................Robert Douglas
Joanna Dulcken....................................Dorothy Hyson
Sir Henry Dulcken.................................Lionel Hogarth
Lady Nona Collimore..............................Diana Campbell
Rex Musgrave......................................Robert Wallsten
A Waiter...........................................Joshua Logan
```
Acts I, II and III.—Sitting Room of Private Suite in New York Hotel.

Staged by Auriol Lee; settings by Raymond Sovey.

Hugh Collimore, English novelist, playwright and lecturer, hounded by celebrity head hunters in Hollywood, engages Al Sessums, American newspaper man, as secretary and social protector. Al, learning in confidences that Collimore does not love Mrs. Collimore, but is strongly drawn to Joanna Dulcken, and that Mrs. Collimore greatly prefers Rex Musgrave, movie hero, to her husband, unknowingly reveals the truth when he is under the influence of liquor. The four interested parties thereupon rearrange their affairs, being most grateful to Al for his unwitting exposures.

SQUARING THE CIRCLE

(108 performances)

A comedy in three acts by Valentine Katayev adapted by Dmitri Ostrov from a translation by Charles Malamuth and Eugene Lyons. Produced by the Tri-Art at the Lyceum Theatre, New York, October 3, 1935.

Cast of characters—

Vasya	David Morris
Ludmilla	Beatrice de Neergaard
Tonya Kuznetzova	Fraye Gilbert
Abram	Eric Dressler
Sashka	Sashka
Rabinovitch	George Heller
Emilian Tonkonogov	Albert Van Dekker
Boris Novikov	Aristides de Leoni

Members of the Communist League of Youth:

Bassova	Stella Reynolds
Nikonorov	Joe Bates Smith
Martova	Mildred Todd
Stchepkina	Cyrilla Dorne

Acts I, II and III.—A Municipalized Apartment Building in Moscow under the Soviet Regime.

Staged by Dmitri Ostrov and Edward Mendelsohn.

Vasya and Abram are fellow lodgers in Moscow during the early experiments with the Five-year plan. Unknown to each other both register the same day at the marriage bureau and both bring their brides to live in their one room, borrowed from Emilian. Vasya and Ludmilla, Abram and Tonya, divide the room and set up housekeeping. Emilian returns unexpectedly and complicates matters. Within a short time Vasya discovers that it is Tonya he really loves and Abram is smitten with the simple Ludmilla. Emilian, shocked by these liberties with the ethics of the revolution, calls for a judicial decision from a party officer, who approves the transfer of wives.

MACBETH

(8 performances)

A tragedy by William Shakespeare. Revived by Crosby Gaige, Inc., at the Ethel Barrymore Theatre, New York, October 7, 1935.

Cast of characters—

Duncan (King of Scotland)	Henry Morrell
Malcolm	Jerome Lawler
Donalbain	Staats Cotsworth
Macbeth	Philip Merivale
Banquo	Charles Francis
Macduff	Kenneth MacKenna
Lennox	Joseph Holland
Ross	Kenneth Hunter
Angus	Roland Bottomley
Fleance	Connie Lent
Siward (Earl of Northumberland)	Harold Gould
Young Siward	Ralph Nelson
Seton	Maurice F. Manson
Boy	Margaret English
A Doctor	Henry Morrell
A Captain	Bram Nossen
A Porter	Hannan Clark
An Old Man	Edward Broadley

```
A Messenger.....................................Staats Cotsworth
A Servant............................................Thomas Bate
First Murderer.....................................Bran Nossen
Second Murderer...............................Edward Oldfield
First Witch.......................................Harold Gould
Second Witch.....................................Hannan Clark
Third Witch....................................Edward Broadley
Lady Macbeth....................................Gladys Cooper
Lady Macduff..................................Alexandra Carlisle
Gentlewoman .................................Constance Pelissier
Court Ladies ................................. { Betty Bourjaily
                                               { Catherine Cale
```

Staged by Henry Herbert; settings by P. Dodd Ackerman; costumes by C. B. Falls.

Recent important revivals of "Macbeth" have included that made by Arthur Hopkins for Lionel Barrymore in 1921, with Julia Arthur playing Lady Macbeth; and the George C. Tyler revival in 1928, with Lyn Harding the Macbeth and Florence Reed his lady. The tragedy has long been included in the repertories of Walter Hampden and Fritz Leiber and was given twenty-seven performances by the Shakespeare Theatre company in New York the season of 1932-33.

PORGY AND BESS

(124 performances)

An American folk opera in three acts adapted by DuBose Heyward and Ira Gershwin from a play by DuBose and Dorothy Heyward; music by George Gershwin. Produced by the Theatre Guild at the Alvin Theatre, New York, October 10, 1935.

Cast of characters—

```
Mingo..............................................Ford L. Buck
Clara .............................................Abbie Mitchell
Sportin' Life....................................John W. Bubbles
Jake ...........................................Edward Matthews
Maria ..........................................Georgette Harvey
Annie ..............................................Olive Ball
Lily................................................Helen Dowdy
Serena...............................................Ruby Elzy
Robbins............................................ Henry Davis
Jim..................................................Jack Carr
Peter..............................................Gus Simons
Porgy............................................. Todd Duncan
Crown......................................... Warren Coleman
Bess.........................................Anne Wiggins Brown
Detective....................................Alexander Campbell
Two Policemen....................Harold Woolf, Burton McEvilly
Undertaker.........................................John Garth
Frazier.......................................J. Rosamond Johnson
Mr. Archdale.................................... George Lessey
Nelson..............................................Ray Yeates
Strawberry Woman...............................Helen Dowdy
Crab Man...........................................Ray Yeates
Coroner..........................................George Carleton
```

Act I.—Scene 1—Catfish Row, Charleston, S. C. 2—Serena's Room. Act II.—Scenes 1 and 3—Catfish Row. 2—A Palmetto Jungle. 4—Serena's Room. Act III.—Catfish Row.

Staged by Rouben Mamoulian; settings by Sergei Soudeikine; orchestra directed by Alexander Smallens; chorus by Eva Jessye.

The operatic version of "Porgy" closely follows the story of the play, produced by the Theatre Guild October 10, 1927. It begins with the awakening of Catfish Row and includes the crapgame that ends in the murder of Robbins by Crown; the appeal of Bess, Crown's girl, to the crippled Porgy for protection; the Robbins wake and saucer funeral; the picnic at which Crown takes Bess back; the hurricane; Porgy's killing of Crown; Bess' elopement with Sportin' Life and Porgy's following year. A digest of the original is given in "The Best Plays of 1927-28."

SWEET MYSTERY OF LIFE

(11 performances)

A comedy in three acts by Richard Maibaum, Michael Wallach and George Haight. Produced by Herman Shumlin at the Shubert Theatre, New York, October 11, 1935.

Cast of characters—

Andy Flannigan	Edward Butler
Rosmer Peek	Hobart Cavanaugh
Boop Oglethorpe	Broderick Crawford
Norma	Mady Correll
Lucille Bailey	Kathryn March
Loretti	Louis Polan
Wethered	Franklyn Fox
Steiner	Herbert Warren
Herring	William David
Samuel L. Blauker	Gene Lockhart
Doctor MacDuffy	Joseph Eggenton
Doctor Warren	Erskine Sanford
Doctor Bell	Thomas F. Tracey
Doctor Worshofsky	Curtis Karpe
Cigarette Girl	Virginia Shields
Genevieve	Evelyn Allen
Mrs. Minninger	Virginia Tracy
J. C. Nichol	Pass Le Noir

Staged by Herman Shumlin; settings by Donald Oenslager.

Samuel L. Blauker, fifty-eight years old and victim of imaginary ills, is the subject of his business partners' grave concern. When he proposes turning his chain stores over to his employees they propose as a counter move that he first insure his life for $5,000,000 and make the business the beneficiary. Blauker, suspicious but curious, submits to a medical examination and is passed by four insurance companies. Rosmer Peek, the surprised agent selling the policy, all but dies of shock. With the signing of the policy it becomes the insurance company's business to keep Blauker alive. Peek is appointed his guardian. Together they take up the sane life and go excursioning. Blauker grows stronger by the minute. The conspiring partners hopefully introduce him to an adventuress. Blauker not only embraces the adventuress, but marries her. The conspiracy fails.

JUBILEE

(169 performances)

A musical comedy in two acts by Moss Hart; music and lyrics by Cole Porter. Produced by Sam H. Harris and Max Gordon at the Imperial Theatre, New York, October 12, 1935.

Cast of characters—

The King	Melville Cooper
The Queen	Mary Boland
Prince James	Charles Walters
Princess Diana	Margaret Adams
Prince Peter	Montgomery Clift
Prince Rudolph	Jackie Kelk
Lord Wyndham	Richie Ling
Eric Dare	Derek Williams
Karen O'Kane	June Knight
Eva Standing	May Boley
Charles Rausmiller (Mowgli)	Mark Plant
Mrs. Watkins	Jane Evans
Laura Fitzgerald	Olive Reeves-Smith
A Sandwich Man	Charles Brokaw
Professor Rexford	Ralph Sumpter
The Beach Widow	Dorothy Fox
Cabinet Minister	Leo Chalzell
Cabinet Minister	Charles Brokaw
Lifeguard	Don Douglas
Announcer	Albert Amato
Master of Ceremonies	Harold Murray
The Drunk	Jack Edwards
The Usher	Ted Fetter
Keeper of Zoo	Leo Chalzell

The Satellites, The Pages, The Martinique Orchestra

Act I.—Scene 1—The Throne Room of the Palace. 2—Ante Room in the Palace. 3—Nicodemus Bar. 4—The Municipal Park. 5—Street Scene. 6—The Acme Motion Picture Theatre. 7—The Stage Door. 8—Café Martinique. 9—Prime Minister's Library. 10—Eva's Sitting Room. 11—Karen's Boudoir. 12—The Hall of Eva's House. 13—The Ballroom of Eva's House. Act II.—Scene 1—Breakfast Room at Feathermore. 2—The Beach Wagons at Rockwell Beach. 3—The Beach. 4—Along the Cliffs. 5—The Zoo. 6—The Zoo Garden. 7—Ante Room in the Palace. 8—The Throne Room of the Palace.

Staged by Hassard Short; dialogue directed by Monty Woolley; orchestra directed by Frank Tours; dances by Albertina Rasch; settings by Jo Mielziner; costumes by Irene Sharaff and Connie de Pinna.

The King, the Queen, Prince James and Princess Diana are terribly fed up with court life. When a mischievous nephew throws a stone through the palace window threatening an uprising of radicals the royal quartet are ordered to a distant and gloomy castle. They rebel and escape, going incognito to town and having a grand time. The King is able to develop his parlor tricks. The Queen meets Mowgli, the ape man of the movies, in the flesh. Prince James takes on a dancer in a night club and Princess Diana achieves her heart's desire singing duets with Eric Dare, novelist and playwright. A few days' holiday, then reluctantly back to court for the jubilee.

ACHILLES HAD A HEEL

(8 performances)

A play in ten episodes by Martin Flavin. Produced by Walter Hampden at the 44th Street Theatre, New York, October 13, 1935.

Cast of characters—

```
Keeper of the Elephant..........................Walter Hampden
Slats ......................................................John Wray
Director.............................................Alfred Kappeler
Doctor ...........................................Arthur Donaldson
Tramp .............................................Harry Mestayer
Pickpocket.............................................Jack Harling
Jake ...................................................Royal Beal
Momba ...................................Howland Chamberlain
Lou .....................................................Sylvia Field
Little Girl...........................................Clarice Cornell
Little Boy..........................................Charles Bellin
Governess ............................................. Anita Rothe
School Girl...............................................June White
School Boy............................................Edwin Mills
Gentleman ......................................Mortimer Weldon
Policeman ......................................... Eddie Garvie
Nursemaid .......................................Harriet Ramsey
Woman ...............................................Sara Floyd
G.A.R. ....................................Jas. Francis-Robertson
Rubbish Man.....................................Meyer Berenson
Ragamuffin .......................................Harris Berger
Peanut Vendor..................................Edwin Cushman
Tacky Girl.......................................Elizabeth Dewing
Sporty Girl........................................Linda Lee Hill
Lady ...................................................Mabel Moore
Minerva ...........................................Shirley Poirier
Moses ..............................................Buddy Buehler
```

Monkeys and Members of Society: Virginia Grey, Jane Archer, Mary Martin, Mildred Starkweather, Herbert Vigran, Trueman Quevli, Marshall Wray, Roland Kibbee, Norman Williams, Sandy Strouse, Clarence James, Peter Horton, James Danehey, Fred Trench and others.

The action takes place in a Zoo.

Staged by Walter Hampden, Martin Flavin and Howard Lindsay; settings by Claude Bragdon.

A colored war hero finds himself the keeper of an elephant in a zoo. There is a strong attachment between the two. Across the way Slats, who was the Negro's white captain in the war, is now the keeper of the monkeys and resentful. Slats would be revenged upon the Negro. Every plan he tries fails until he introduces a mulatto prostitute name Lou to his rival. Lou debauches the Negro. He loses his job and is demoted to the monkey house. Slats is put in charge of the elephant. The elephant kills Slats. The Negro is recalled and manages to quiet his old friend. The mulatto finds herself locked in with the other monkeys.

TRIUMPH

(8 performances)

A comedy in three acts by George Austin. Produced by Elizabeth Miele at the Fulton Theatre, New York, October 14, 1935.

Cast of characters—

Thomas Mackay	Douglas Gregory
A Waiter	Paul Foley
Major James A. Edwards	Clifford Stork
Gloria Kendall	Ruth Matteson
James Dowling	Howard Miller
Grace Lindley	Lucia Laska
Ruth Thompson	Gladis Griswold
Dan Thompson	Howard St. John
Nick Martine	Louis Tanno
Sam Todd	John Raby
Mrs. Ellen Pomeroy	Leslie Bingham
Mrs. Giordana	Zamah Cunningham
Melville Kendall	Lyster Chambers
Angelo Spinelli	Carlo Conti
Tillie Martin	Emily Winston

Act I.—Scene 1—The King's Café, Downtown New York. 2—Gloria Kendall's Law Offices. Act II.—Gloria's Law Offices. Act III.—Scene 1—King's Café. 2 and 3—Gloria's Law Offices.

Staged by Priestly Morrison; settings by Philip Gelb.

Gloria Kendall, lawyer, is engaged to marry Thomas Mackay, an assistant district attorney, who previously had been sweet on Gloria's partner, Ruth Thompson. Ruth conspires to make it appear to the jealous Mackay that Ruth is cheating him. Mackay leaves Gloria and marries Ruth, living to rue the day. Ruth, appointed to the bench, acquires such influence and such knowledge of shady bank deals in which Mackay becomes involved that she is able to bring practically everybody to their knees before her begging for help.

BRIGHT STAR

(7 performances)

A play in three acts by Philip Barry. Produced by Arthur Hopkins at the Empire Theatre, New York, October 15, 1935.

Cast of characters—

Kate Hastings	Jean Dixon
Emily Updike	Katherine Grey
Sam Riddle	Louis Jean Heydt
Quin Hanna	Lee Tracy
Hope Blake	Julie Haydon
Paul Herrick	Damian O'Flynn
Stella	Mae Castle
Libby Eldrege	Rosalie Norman

Acts I, II and III.—Living Room of the Old Blake House in a Small City in a Small New England State.

Staged by Arthur Hopkins; settings by Raymond Sovey.

Quin Hanna, returned to the New England home of his youth, which he hated as a boy, determines to stay on and work for the town's redemption. Hope Blake, the town's richest girl, falls desperately in love with Quin. Without loving her Quin marries Hope and accepts the town's newspaper as a wedding gift from his bride. Three years of Hope's devotion and the strain of domesticity, coupled with his awakening disgust of himself in not having played fair with Hope, determines Quin to take himself out of the picture. Hope senses his desertion but bids him farewell with a smile. A few moments later she is dead of a heart attack.

STRIP GIRL

(33 performances)

A comedy in three acts by Henry Rosendahl; music by Harry Archer; lyrics by Jill Rainsford. Produced by L. Lawrence Weber at the Longacre Theatre, New York, October 19, 1935.

Cast of characters—

Satchel Pants	C. Norman Hammond
Straight Man	Paul Morton
Dixie Potter	Mayo Jane Methot
Stage Manager	Edwin Redding
Peaches Moran	Doris Packer
Leonard Potter	Dick Wallace
Bellhop	Seymour Gross
Wells Carter	Walter Gilbert
Rose-Marie	Julia Steger
First Detective	Howard Sydney
Second Detective	Albert McWilliams
Third Detective	William Nugent
Magistrate	Frederick Malcolm
Court Attendant	Frederick Raymond
Doctor Griffith	Robert Le Sueur
Nurse	Helen Shields
Jail Matron	Edna West
Helen Meighen	Ruth Abbott
Larry Stevens	Frank McNellis
Schultz	Al. Raymond
Lex	Emmett Rogers
Homer	James Lewis
Peter	Dwight Goodwin
Waiter	Worthington L. Romaine
Head Waiter	George Rossum
Lex's Girl	Joan Oates
Homer's Girl	Katharine Sheridan
Peter's Girl	Elaine Blauvelt
Hotel Waiter	Franklin Heller

Act I.—Scenes 1 and 4—The stage of a Downtown Burlesque Theatre. 2 and 5—Dixie's Dressing Room. 3—Living Room in Dixie's Apartment. 6—Magistrate's Court. 7—Examining Room in Hospital. 8—Hospital Dispensary. 9—Cell in House of Detention for Women. 10—Leonard's Room in Hospital. Act II.—Scenes 11, 13, 14, 16, 18 and 20—Dixie's Living Room. 12, 15 and 19—Dixie's Dressing Room. 17—Corner in Luchow's Restaurant. Act III.—Scene 21—Dixie's Liv-

ing Room. 22—Dixie's Dressing Room. 23—Stage of Burlesque Theatre.
    Staged by Jose Ruben; settings by Cirker and Robbins; Marty Beck's orchestra conducted by Sol Bomser.

Dixie Potter, strip-tease artist of the burlesque, is sending her sickly young brother, Leonard, through school. When Leonard dies of a cancer Dixie takes to drink. Convinced she needs a new responsibility she adopts an ambitious young paper-hanger hungry for an education and spends her savings on him. The man who is keeping Dixie grows jealous of her adopted son and threatens to smash things. Dixie is able to convince him she is on the level. They are married and keep the boy.

EDEN END

(24 performances)

A comedy in three acts by J. B. Priestley. Produced by Milton Shubert at the Masque Theatre, New York, October 21, 1935.

Cast of characters—

Wilfrey Kirby.....................................Alexander Guage
Sarah ....Ruth Vivian
Lillian Kirby.......................................Louise Smith
Dr. Kirby... Edward Irwin
Stella Kirby.......................................Estelle Winwood
Geoffrey Farrant...............................Wilfred Seagram
Charles Appleby.................................Edgar Norfolk
    Acts I, II and III.—Sitting Room of Dr. Kirby's House at Eden End in the North of England.
    Staged by Auriol Lee; settings by Kate Drain Lawson.

In the early nineteen hundreds Stella Kirby ran away from her North of England home and sought a stage career. Her quest was a failure. In 1912 she returns to her home determined to again embrace its quiet and restfulness and win back, if she can, the affection of an earlier love, Geoffrey Farrant. She meets the opposition of her younger sister, Lillian, who wants Farrant for herself. Lillian, hearing Stella has been married in the profession, sends for the husband, Charles Appleby. Appleby, an expansive egotist, explodes Stella's plans and induces her to go back to the theatre and try again.

SUBSTITUTE FOR MURDER

(15 performances)

A comedy in three acts by William Jourdan Rapp and Leonardo Bercovici. Produced by William Harris, Jr., at the Ethel Barrymore Theatre, New York, October 22, 1935.

Cast of characters—

Audrey	Jessie Royce Landis
John	Francis Lister
Smittie	Ruth Gates
Dick	Myron McCormick
Cynthia	Tucker McGuire
Charles	Robert Sloane

Prologue.—Paris. Acts I, II and III.—Living Room of the Hardy Home near New York.

Staged by William Harris, Jr.; setting by John Root.

Audrey Hardy, touring Europe some years after the death of her first husband, an athletic poet, meets and loves John Lattimer, a psychologist. Bringing John to her home in America and announcing an intention of marrying him, Audrey is faced with the violent opposition of her two grown children, Dick and Cynthia. The children are ready to murder Lattimer, but compromise on getting him drunk and stowing him away in a friend's airplane which is just starting out for a non-stop record. Coming to, Lattimer forces the landing of the plane and a final showdown with Dick, Cynthia and Audrey.

CRIME MARCHES ON

(45 performances)

A farce in two acts by Bertrand Robinson and Maxwell Hawkins. Produced by George Bushar and John Tuerk at the Morosco Theatre, New York, October 23, 1935.

Cast of characters—

Nonnie Gibbons	Nonnie Edwards
Lester Gibbons	Lester Lonergan
Lenore Gibbons	Lenore Lonergan
John Gibbons	John Kreis
Martha Gibbons	Grace Mills
Bud Gibbons	R. Birrell Rawls
Hank Gibbons	F. Charles Keane
Russell Gibbons	Elisha Cook, Jr.
Milly	May Marshal
Mrs. Forsythe	Jean Shelby
Editor Fitch	Arling Alcine
Photographer	Bruce Evans
Claribel Gibbons	Claribel Bressel
J. J. Smith	Charles D. Brown
Elevator Starter	Walter Wagner
First Woman	Edith Shayne
Bus Guide	Edward Emerson
Second Woman	Minna Watts
First Husband	John M. James
Third Woman	Minnette Barrett
Fourth Woman	May Marshal
Second Husband	Frank Watts
B. Wellington Carlisle	Donald Randolph
Tenant	Foster J. Williams
Second Business Man	Karl Kohrs
Phyllis	Mary Rogers
Grace	Gay Seabrook

```
Horace P. Swan.....................................Charles Halton
Stenographer.........................................Elaine Ivans
Lieutenant Fiore.......................................Paul Huber
Dolan..........................................F. Charles Keane
Clancy.........................................Foster J. Williams
Professor Wheeler...............................Robert E. Perry
Clerk ..............................................Henry Brooks
Mrs. Finkelstein......................................Grace Mills
Radio Actor....................................John M. James
Charlie.........................................Edward Emerson
Jonathan Foster....................................Bruce Evans
Orchestra Leader...............................Edward Lissman
Page Boy......................................Lester Lonergan
Woman Visitor.................................Minnette Barrett
Freddie ............................................John Kreis
Mrs. Whetmore.....................................Jean Shelby
Magnolia ......................................... Elaine Ivans
```
Act I.—Scene 1—The Gibbons' Home in Tennessee. 2—Elevator Corridor in Empire Building, New York. 3, 4 and 6—Private Office of Horace J. Swan. Act II.—Scene 1—Back Room at 138 West 30th Street. 2—A stage. 3—Office of Horace J. Swan.

Staged by Edward Clarke Lilley; settings by John Root.

Russell Gibbons, son of lowly folk in Tennessee, wins the Pulitzer prize for poetry and is hired by J. J. Smith to go to New York and read his verse over the radio on the White Swan Soap Hour. Russell, a victim of altiphobia, faints the first time he looks out the window of the soap company on the sixty-fourth floor of the Empire State building. In his faint he dreams that he is in love with the office secretary; that he kills the boss to protect her; that he is put through the third degree by the police and helps hang an irritating radio announcer. Then he comes to. Nothing is true except his love for the secretary (played by Will Rogers' daughter, Mary).

* MULATTO

(270 performances)

A drama in two acts by Langston Hughes. Produced by Martin Jones at the Vanderbilt Theatre, New York, October 24, 1935.

Cast of characters—

```
Cora Lewis....................................Rose McClendon
William Lewis................................Morris McKenney
Colonel Thomas Norwood..........................Stuart Beebe
Sally Lewis.......................................Jeanne Greene
Talbot .............................................John Boyd
Fred Higgins......................................Frank Jaquet
Henry Richards..................................Henry Forsberg
Grace Richards................................Gertrude Bondhill
Mary Lowell...................................Connie Gilchrist
Robert Lewis.......................................Hurst Amyx
Store Keeper.........................................Clark Poth
Undertaker ......................................Howard Negley
```
Acts I and II.—Living Room of Colonel Norwood's Plantation House, Somewhere in Georgia.

Staged by Martin Jones; settings by Golden.

Cora Lewis, housekeeper on Colonel Norwood's plantation, has borne the Colonel four children. Two of them, Sally and Robert Lewis, showing their white blood unmistakably, have been sent North to be educated. Sally returns to find that she is being considered as a mistress for the brutal overseer, Talbot. Robert comes back with rebellion in his heart, determined to demand his rights as a Norwood. The Colonel would shoot Robert, but Robert chokes the life out of the Colonel. A lynching is threatened. Robert saves his last bullet for himself. Sally is seduced by the overseer. Life goes on, the mulatto's problem still unsolved.

GOOD MEN AND TRUE

(11 performances)

A drama in five scenes by Brian Marlow and Frank Merlin. Produced by Frank Merlin at the Biltmore Theatre, New York, October 25, 1935.

Cast of characters—

James Dentwood (Foreman)	Frederick Howard
Matthew Meldrum (Juror No. 2)	Joseph McInerney
Elsie G. Spencer (Juror No. 3)	Ethel Intropodi
Mary Thorpe (Juror No. 4)	Martha Sleeper
John Wilson (Juror No. 5)	Donald Foster
Watt Hayman (Juror No. 6)	Weldon Heyburn
Charles Z. Franker (Juror No. 7)	Dodson Mitchell
Mrs. Richard Nedick (Juror No. 8)	Gladys Feldman
Elizabeth Barlow (Juror No. 9)	Constance McKay
Ray Flanagan (Juror No. 10)	John Gallaudet
Annabelle Chalmers (Juror No. 11)	Vera Marshe
Nelson Trigg (Juror No. 12)	Russell Morrison
Peter Gilpin (The Alternate)	Percy Helton
Sheriff Hoffmeyer	Frank MacCormack
Ed (Deputy Sheriff)	Philip Van Zandt
Bill (Deputy Sheriff)	Richard Bartell

The action takes place in the Sitting Room of a Hotel Suite in a Middle Western Town.

Staged by Louis M. Simon; setting by Nicholas Yellenti.

Mary Thorpe and John Wilson find themselves on a mixed jury trying a man for murder in the West. During the month's deliberations of the jury they discover a mutual love. Mary insists it never can be realized because of her past. She is carrying the child of a former lover. John is willing to reason, and forget. In a fit of depression Mary throws herself off the roof to her death. The other jurors accuse John of being responsible for her murder. When, later, John holds out for the acquittal of the man on trial they threaten to kill him, too. John bargains with them: If he can prove his innocence of Mary's death will they admit the possibility of false evidence in the other case? They agree. John produces a letter from Mary revealing her suicidal intentions.

* DEAD END

(268 performances)

A drama in three acts by Sidney Kingsley. Produced by Norman Bel Geddes at the Belasco Theatre, New York, October 28, 1935.

Cast of characters—

Gimpty	Theodore Newton
T B	Gabriel Dell
Tommy	Billy Halop
Dippy	Huntz Hall
Angel	Bobby Jordan
Spit	George Cotton
Doorman	Charles R. Duncan
Old Lady	Marie R. Burke
Old Gentleman	George N. Price
Chauffeur	Charles Benjamin
"Babyface" Martin	Joseph Downing
Hunk	Martin Gabel
Philip Griswald	Charles Bellin
Governess	Sidonie Espero
Milty	Bernard Punsly
Drina	Elspeth Eric
Mr. Griswald	Carroll Ashburn
Mr. Jones	Louis Lord
Kay	Margaret Mullen
Jack Hilton	Cyril Gordon Weld
Lady With Dog	Margaret Linden
Three Small Boys	Billy Winston, Joseph Taibi, Sidney Lumet
Chauffeur	Richard Clark
Second Avenue Boys	David Gorcey, Leo Gorcey
Mrs. Martin	Marjorie Main
Patrolman Mulligan	Robert J. Mulligan
Francey	Sheila Trent
G-Men	Francis de Sales, Edward P. Goodnow, Dan Duryea
Policemen	Francis G. Cleveland, Willis Duncan
Plainclothesman	Harry Selby
Interne	Philip Bourneuf
Medical Examiner	Lewis L. Russel
Sailor	Bernard Zaneville

Inhabitants of East River Terrace, Ambulance Men, etc.: Elizabeth Wragge, Drina Hill, Blossom MacDonald, Ethel Dell, William Toubin, Marc Daniels.

Acts I, II and III.—East River Terrace, New York City.
Staged by Sidney Kingsley; setting by Norman Bel Geddes.

See page 239.

ON STAGE

(48 performances)

A comedy in two acts by B. M. Kaye. Produced by Laurence Rivers, Inc., at the Mansfield Theatre, New York, October 29, 1935.

Cast of characters—

Morgan Crawford	Osgood Perkins
Edward Gilson	Donald MacDonald

```
A Messenger Boy................................Harry Gresham
Eleanor Chanler...................................Selena Royle
Sheila Danforth..............................Claudia Morgan
Brooks Carrington............................Frederic Worlock
Jarry Harmon....................................Alan Marshal
James Sturdevant..................................Louis Hector
```
    Acts I and II.—Living Room of Morgan Crawford's Apartment in
New York.
    Staged by Robert Ross; setting by G. Bradford Ashworth.

Morgan Crawford, playwright, is drinking port wine and discussing his newest play with his friend, Edward Gilson, at the same meeting. Gilson insists the playwright's characters are not convincingly true. The playwright contends they must be true because he created them and knows them. They have, in a way, been fashioned on models he has selected from among his acquaintances. With Gilson gone, Crawford falls into a doze and dreams that he is playing his own hero and that none of the other characters in the play, for all he is their creator, will act as he dictates. The characters in fact take the drama away from him and play it their own way with dramatic and tragic results. When Crawford awakes he is only sure of one thing, that he still loves the leading woman.

THERE'S WISDOM IN WOMEN

(46 performances)

A comedy in three acts by Joseph O. Kesselring. Produced by D. A. Doran at the Cort Theatre, New York, October 30, 1935.

Cast of characters—
```
Tony Cooke.........................................Glenn Anders
Ella ..............................................Jane Bancroft
Margalo Nordoff....................................Ruth Weston
Leon Nordoff.....................................Walter Pidgeon
Irene Ploettzer...................................Frances Maddux
Carl Ploettzer.....................................Alfredo Hessé
Mrs. Carter................................Mary Horne Morrison
Hon. Paul R. Carter...............................Boyd Davis
Henri Lheureux....................................Joseph Kallini
Cecilia Wandover.................................Betty Lawford
```
    Acts I, II and III.—Duplex Apartment of Leon and Margalo Nordoff in New York.
    Staged by Harry Wagstaff Gribble; setting by John Root.

Leon Nordoff is a great pianist. Margalo, his wife, is patient and understanding, forgiving Leon most of his sins and many of his women. She balks, however, at Cecilia Wandover. Especially when Leon tells her he would like his freedom so he may marry Cecilia. Margalo knows that Leon "wants what he wants only so long as he is kept wanting." She invites Cecilia to the house, tricks her into an acquiescent state of mind, and disappears.

Cecilia, playing into the trap, becomes suddenly yielding toward
Leon. Next morning Margalo, resentful of the too complete success of her scheme, is of a mind to leave Leon. Yet, when his
great need of her again develops (he is writing a sonata she has
to help him finish) Margalo forgives Leon and resumes her mari-
tal burden.

PLAY, GENIUS, PLAY!

(5 performances)

A comedy in three acts by Judith Kandel. Produced by Lew
Cantor at the St. James Theatre, New York, October 30, 1935.

Cast of characters—

Pacci	Vaughn Godfrey
Jenny	Virginia Sale
Holliday	Stapleton Kent
Mrs. Margaret Carey	Theresa Maxwell Conover
Mr. Jay Carey	Ferdinand Gottschalk
Jorje Carey	Sam Wren
Albert Sterne	Clarence Derwent
Paul Carey	Hardie Albright
Leda Marshall	Linda Leeds
Casazza	Sydney Riggs
Diana Saunders	Judith Wood
Mr. Morgan	Butler Hixon
Aunt Nancy	Gertrude Mudge
Uncle Brian	William Fay
Cousin Doris	Barbara Brown
Uncle Richard	John T. Dwyer
Cousin Annabelle	Vera Hurst
Ambrosia	Mercedes Gilbert
Manufacturer	Maurice Freeman
First Girl	Effie Afton
Farmer	William Norton
Second Girl	Beverly Parker
Healey	Len Doyle
Third Girl	Mildred Schroeder
First Man	William Morris
Second Man	Craig Williams
Eve	Charlotte Gloer
Sascha Noodleman	Saranoff
Monty	Gavin Muir
Kelly	W. W. Shuttleworth
Proprietor	Walter Armin
Doctor	Walter Fenner

Acts I and III.—Living Room in the Carey Home, New York City.
Act II.—Scenes 1 and 3.—Diana's Apartment. 2—A Night Club.
Staged by Jo Graham; settings by Cirker and Robbins.

Paul Carey, a child prodigy, has supported his parents and
various relatives and hangers on with his violin since he was 5.
At 23 he rebels and goes on a binge, taking with him Diana
Saunders, blonde and tough. They tour the night clubs. Paul
manages to get into a fist fight and do some injury to his right
hand. The adventure is sobering in more ways than one. Next
morning Paul is through with blondes and liquor and content to
return to his fiancée and his career.

THE BODY BEAUTIFUL

(4 performances)

A comedy in three acts by Robert Rossen. Produced by Sidney Harmon at the Plymouth Theatre, New York, October 31, 1935.

Cast of characters—

Izzy Cohen	Garson Kanin
Kitty	Loretta Sayers
Boris Vassilevitch	Eugene Sigaloff
Gypsy	Claire Carlton
Charley	Leo Hoyt
Bill Farmer	Roy Roberts
Lulu Johnson	Polly Walters
Jimmy	Oliver Barbour
Magistrate	J. F. Kirk
Court Clerk	Edison Rice
Detective Gargan	Phil Sheridan
Officer	George Smith
Sue Barnes	Arlene Francis
Saunders	Frederick Clayton
Wiggins	Walter Scott Weeks
Model	Beverly Phalon
Baxter	Richard Pope
Waiter	Samuel Roland
Max Talbot	Carl Rukoff
Eddie Driggs	Richard Abert
Porter	Leslie Hunt

Act I.—Scenes 1 and 3—Dressing Room in 42nd St. Burlesque Theatre. 2—Night Court. Act II.—Scene 1—Balcony overlooking Main Floor of Midway Park Casino. 2—Lulu's Penthouse. Act III. Scene 1—The Casino. 2 and 3—The Penthouse.

Staged by Robert Rossen; settings by Boris Aronson.

Lulu Johnson, an innocent from the country with a beautiful body, gets a job in a New York burlesque theatre. Boris, the leader of the orchestra, is inspired to write a concerto for her. Lulu interprets the concerto in the nude and is a riot. Then Lulu wants to marry Jimmy, a stage hand, and Boris knows this adventure will end all. Marriage will make Lulu conscious of her body and she will not be able to give anything resembling spiritual exaltation to the concerto. The show is pinched. Jimmy is jailed for thirty days. During the thirty days Lulu advances from burlesque to a swanky night club, and from the night club is headed for a recital in Carnegie Hall. Then Jimmy gets out of jail, the honeymoon is resumed and Lulu's career is temporarily finis.

PROVINCETOWN FOLLIES

(63 performances)

A revue in two parts by Frederick Herendeen, Gwynn Langdon, Barrie Oliver, George K. Arthur; music by Sylvan Green,

Mary Schaeffer, Arthur Jones, Trevor Jones and Dave Stamper. Produced by the Greenwich Musical Guild, Inc., at the Province-town Playhouse, New York, November 3, 1935.

Principals engaged—

Barrie Oliver
Phyllis Austin
Billy Greene
Eileen Graves
Theodore Stanhope

Beatrice Kay
Cyril Smith
Wood Hawkins
Marie Alvarez
The Bernays

Staged by Lee Morrison; dances by Mary Read.

PRIDE AND PREJUDICE

(219 performances)

A comedy in three acts by Helen Jerome, dramatized from the novel by Jane Austen. Produced by Max Gordon at the Music Box, New York, November 5, 1935.

Cast of characters—

Mr. Bennet	Percy Waram
Hill	Harold Thomas
Mrs. Bennet	Lucile Watson
Lady Lucas	Frances Brandt
Charlotte Lucas	Brenda Forbes
Jane Bennet	Helen Chandler
Elizabeth Bennet	Adrianne Allen
Lydia Bennet	Joan Tompkins
Mr. Darcy	Colin Keith-Johnson
Mr. Bingley	John Halloran
Mr. Collins	Harold Scott
Amelia	Edwina Wise
Mr. Wickham	John D. Seymour
Belinda	Kathleen Moran
Amanda	Gail Bolger
A Young Man	Hugh Nevill
Captain Denny	James Jolley
Miss Bingley	Nancy Hamilton
Agatha	Jeannette Chinley
A Second Young Man	Ferdi Hoffman
A Maid	Dare Wright
Maggie	Chouteau Dyer
Mrs. Gardiner	Viola Roache
Lady Catherine de Bourgh	Alma Kruger
Colonel Guy Fitzwilliam	Stephen Appleby
Mrs. Lake	Dorothy Scott

Acts I and III.—Drawing Room of Bennet Home at Longbourn, Hertfordshire, England. Act II.—Scene 1—Bennet Drawing Room. 2—Aunt Gardiner's Home at Cheapside, London. 3—Lady Catherine de Bourgh's Drawing Room, Rosings Park, Hunsford, Kent.
Staged by Robert Sinclair; settings by Jo Mielziner.

See page 356.

BERTHA, THE SEWING MACHINE GIRL

(7 performances)

A melodrama in three acts by Charles Foster, adapted by George Damroth. Revived by Jack Stern and George Damroth at the Fifth Avenue Theatre, New York, November 5, 1935.

Cast of characters—

Bertha Bascome	Evelyn Barrows
Jasper Carter	Witcher MacMillan
Philip Hamilton	Jaron Sylvane
David Carter	George Sheldon
Jason Skinner	Theodore Tiller
Joe Skinner	John Van Zanten
Conrad Bascome	Otto Neff
Judge Fergerson	Charles Merkin
Jigwater	Lewis Ames
Lisette Graham	Diana Dowty
Jane Pinch	Edna Gordon
Hannah Williams	Mary Galin
Marty Jones	Rosmari de Salle
Marie Hutton	Zella Lenney
Officer	George Spelvin

Act I.—Scenes 1 and 3—Jason Skinner's Sweat Shop. 2—Street in New York. Act II.—Scene 1—Court Room. 2—Street in New York. 3—Bertha's Prison Cell. Act III.—Scene 1—Home of Bascome. 2—Street in New York. 3—The Wedding.

Between the acts were illustrated slides, community singing led by Miss Zella Lenney, specialties by Charles Merkin, Mary Galin and Theodore Tiller, songs of yesteryear by Edna Gordon and two screen plays of yesteryear; "Mender of the Nets" with Mary Pickford and Mabel Normand (1909) and "The Referee" with Charles Chaplin and Fatty Arbuckle (1914).

Staged by George Damroth; original settings and costumes by Ilmar and Tames.

LET FREEDOM RING

(First engagement 29 performances; return 79. Total 108)

A drama in three acts by Albert Bein based on Grace Lumpkin's novel, "To Make My Bread." Produced by Albert Bein and Jack Goldsmith at the Broadhurst Theatre, New York, November 6, 1935.

Cast of characters—

Bonnie McClure	Leslie Stafford
John McClure (As a Boy)	Eddie Ryan, Jr.
Ora McClure	Norma Chambers
Basil McClure	Robert Thomsin
Emma Martin	Paula Bauersmith
Frank Martin	Frank Tweddell
Sally Martin	Dorothy Brackett
John Kirkland (Grandpap)	Will Geer
Jim Hawkins	Lew Eckels
Jesse MacDonald	Robert Porterfield
Frazer MacDonald	Geo. Oliver Taylor
Small Hardy	Tom Ewell
Paul Randolph	Edwin Cooper

```
Bill ................................................Robert Reed
George ............................................Bigelow Sayre
Sara ............................................Lucille Strudwick
Dan ................................................Elvin Field
Sam ................................................Dean Jenks
Florrie ............................................Shirley Poirier
Lou ...............................................Patricia Barker
An Old Man.......................................Charles Kuhn
Perry.............................................W. H. Malone
An Office Boy................................Douglas Parkhurst
Victor Burnett.....................................Alvin Dexter
Tom Stevens......................................Fred Knight
Henry Brickhouse.................................Hubert Brown
Young Frank Martin (At the Age of 13)..........Norman Williams
Mill Worker's Child...............................Toni Gilman
A Millhand...................................James Clairington
Ed Allen.........................................Charles Jordan
An Interne..........................................Phil Jones
Minnie Hawkins....................................Rose Keane
John McClure (As an Adult)..................Shepperd Strudwick
Kirk McClure................................Robert B. Williams
Minnie Martin.....................................June Meier
Chester Wentworth...............................Aldrich Bowker
Young Frank Martin (At Age of 21).................Tow Ewell
Sheriff Cole......................................Charles Dingle
Deputies......................Roger Blankenship, Booth Whitfield
Mary ..............................................Herta Ware
Bessie ...........................................Isabel Bonner
Marge ............................................Mary Perry
Millhands......Richard Allen, Herbert Levin, William Triest, Eric
    Walz, Willson Tuttle, Michael Lettice, Roy Johnson.
Timothy O'Doul..............................Garland F. Smith
A Representative............................John O'Shaughnessy
Another Representative............................Eric Burroughs
```

Act I.—Scene 1—The McClure Cabin in the Carolina Mountains.
2—Receiving Office of the Wentworth Mills, Leesville. 3—Their
New Home. Act II.—Scene 1—Their New Home. 2—Outside the
Weave Room. 3—Wentworth's Office. 4—The Union Hall. Act III.—
The Union Hall.

Staged by Worthington Miner; settings by Max Gorelik.

The McClures and the Martins, kin of John Kirkland, driven
out of the Carolina mountains by the encroachments of lumber
and land syndicates, settle in Leesville and take jobs in the cotton
mills, unintentionally depriving the townsfolk of so many jobs.
Starvation wages and repellent working conditions finally breed
rebellion among the hill folk. Kirk McClure becomes a union
organizer. John McClure, his younger brother, sticks with the
millowners because of their advancement of him to a foremanship.
When the strike comes and Kirk is shot down on the picket line,
John, converted to Labor's cause, takes his brother's place as a
leader of the strikers.

NIGHT IN THE HOUSE

(12 performances)

A drama in three acts by Rodney Ackland, adapted from a
novel, "The Old Ladies," by Hugh Walpole. Produced by Helen
Arthur at the Booth Theatre, New York, November 7, 1935.

Cast of characters—

Mrs. Bloxam..Ellen Hall
May Beringer..................................Mildred Natwick
Lucy Amorest..................................Josephine Hull
Agatha Payne......................................Nance O'Neil
Boys from St. Thomas Chapel, New York. Andrew Teitjen, Master.
    Acts I, II and III.—Old House in Pontippy Square, Polchester.
    Staged by Donald Blackwell; settings by Aline Bernstein.

May Beringer, Lucy Amorest and Agatha Payne are living together in Polchester. Mrs. Amorest is a motherly soul and deeply
concerned for Miss Beringer, a nervous and apprehensive spinster.
Agatha Payne is a hateful and possessive person who manages to
keep both her fellow lodgers unhappy by preying upon their
susceptibilities. From Miss Beringer she would take her dearest
possession, a bit of carved amber. From Mrs. Amorest she filches
her peace of mind and her hope of future happiness with a roving
son. Agatha's deliberate attacks result finally in May Beringer's
collapse from a heart attack. She is preparing to focus her baleful
attentions upon Mrs. Amorest at the play's end.

PARNELL

(99 performances)

A play in three acts by Elsie Schauffler. Produced by Robinson
Smith and Frederick W. Ayer at the Ethel Barrymore Theatre,
New York, November 11, 1935.

Cast of characters—

Katharine O'Shea.............................Margaret Rawlings
Mrs. Benjamin Wood..............................Effie Shannon
Phyllis ....Ruth Yorke
Mrs. Steele.......................................Ruth Matteson
Clara Wood......................................Phyllis Connard
Captain William Henry O'Shea.......................John Emery
The O'Gorman Mahon............................Gordon Burby
Timothy Healy..................................Joseph Holland
Thomas Murphy..............................Barry Macollum
Michael Davitt............................Edward MacNamara
Montagu Harrison..............................Walter Holbrook
Parnell ....George Curzon
Gladstone ....Alexander Frank
Mr. Stanley.......................................Harry Redding
John Redmond...............................Clement O'Loghlen
1st Leader...Barry Kelly
2nd Leader......................................Charles Trexler
3rd Leader......................................Winston O'Keefe
    Act I.—Scenes 1 and 3—Katharine O'Shea's Drawing Room at
Eltham, Nine Miles from London, April, 1880. 2—Committee Room
15, House of Commons. Act II.—Drawing Room at Eltham. Act
III.—Scene 1—Gladstone's Study, 10 Downing Street. 2—Committee Room 15. 3—Drawing Room at Eltham.
    Staged by Guthrie McClintock; settings by Stewart Chaney.

Katharine O'Shea, wife of Captain William Henry O'Shea,
though estranged from her husband, agrees to assist him in the

furtherance of his political career by presiding at a series of dinners for his political associates. Among them is the leader of the
Irish party, Charles Stewart Parnell, who, at their first meeting,
falls desperately in love with Mrs. O'Shea. Later their attachment
develops into an intimate association that continues for nine
years with the full knowledge if not the connivance of Capt.
O'Shea. At the end of that time, at the peak of Parnell's success
in forcing Gladstone's support for a home rule bill for Ireland,
O'Shea files action for divorce against Mrs. O'Shea and names
Parnell co-respondent. The resulting scandal drives Parnell from
the Irish party and results eventually in his death.

MOTHER SINGS

(7 performances)

A play in prologue, five episodes, and epilogue by Hugh
Stange. Produced by William Crosby, Inc., at the 58th Street
Theatre, New York, November 12, 1935.

Cast of characters—

Mart Sullivan	Gregory Robins
Judge Purdy	John L. Kearney
Sarah Schermer	Mary Morris
Cameraman	Herbert Morrill
Rollo Floyd	Clifford Hix
Amelia Rowe	Clara Bertaud
Judge Black	E. J. Blunkall
Prosecutor Newman	Leon Stern
Ben Schermer	Wendell Phillips
Sheriff	Anthony Bassett
Eva Wilkins	Mae Shults
George Wilkins	Royal Stout
Frank Schermer	Ralph Theadore
Doctor Walton	Wilson Reynolds
Ben Schermer (the boy)	Alfred Haffner
Jenny Sykes	Virginia Runyon
Aunt Martha	Violet Hill
Bert Miller	William Nunn
Mayme Speer	Bernardine Hayes
Sergeant Joe McCaffrey, U.S.M.C.	Vincent Irolli
Dolores McCaffrey	Carol Louise

Prologue and Epilogue.—Westchester Court House, White Plains.
Episodes.—Farm House near Yorktown Heights, Westchester County,
New York.
Staged by Hugh Stange; settings by Harry Gordon Bennett.

Sarah Schermer, a mean-minded and possessive woman, married to Frank Schermer, a miserly farmer, clings with unholy
persistence to their son, Ben. After Frank dies, as Ben grows to
manhood and takes over the farm, Sarah gradually poisons his
mind concerning the normal attractions of women and keeps him
practically captive. Ben, at 42, suffers a mental degeneracy that
prompts him to butcher Mayme Speer, a summer boarder who

has proved an inflaming influence. Ben is arrested, tried and convicted of murder in the first degree. The play represents the story of Ben Schermer's life told to a newspaper reporter during an intermission of court.

JUMBO

(233 performances)

A spectacular musical comedy in two acts by Ben Hecht and Charles MacArthur; music and lyrics by Richard Rodgers and Lorenz Hart. Produced by Billy Rose at the Hippodrome, New York, November 16, 1935.

Principals engaged—

Mr. Ball..Bob Lawrence
Mr. Jellico...A. P. Kaye
First Artist..Tom Lomas
Second Artist.......................................Fred Spear
"Poodles"...Poodles Hanneford
John A. Considine...................................Arthur Sinclair
First Razorback.....................................Ray Miller
Mickey Considine....................................Gloria Grafton
Matthew Mulligan....................................W. J. McCarthy
Matt Mulligan, Jr...................................Donald Novis
Second Razorback....................................Dave Adams
United States Marshal...............................George Watts
Claudius B. Bowers..................................Jimmy Durante
Flanagan ....Henry LaMarr
Auctioneer ....Willard Dashiell
Little Girl...Sybil Elaine
Chief of Police.....................................Donald Black
Mr. Piper...Philip Wood
Sweeney ....Gene Greenlaw
McCarthy ....Walter Lewis
Reilly ....John Kuebler
Jumbo ...."Big Rosie"
                Paul Whiteman and orchestra.
Also these circus specialists, among others: A. Robins, Josie DeMotte, Grace Elizabeth Hanneford, Arthur la Fleur, Takayama, William Ferry, Barbette, Minnie LaPell, Helen Harvey and Victoria Miller, Helen Brooks, Dr. Ostermeier's "Doheos," Frances Van Ritter, Lomas Troupe, Dave Ballard, Karl Kosicsky, Tom Breen, Charles de Camo, Lenze Duo, the Nazfys, Jim Mardy, Olivette, Tyana, Harry Jackson, Sr., Mary Jackson, Harry Jackson, Jr., Arthur Sherwood, Tiny Kline, the Stonleys and the Kimris.
Staged by John Murray Anderson; book directed by George Abbott; settings by Albert Johnson; dances arranged by Allan K. Foster and Marjery Fielding; costumes by Raoul Pene du Bois and James Reynolds.

FOR VALOR

(8 performances)

A comedy in two acts by Martha Hedman and Henry Arthur House. Produced under the direction of George C. Tyler at the Empire Theatre, New York, November 18, 1935.

Cast of characters—

Mary Brown...June Walker
Robert Lake................................Thomas Coffin Cooke
Wallace I. Brown..............................Frank Craven
Postman ....George Whitson
Betsy Dale.......................................Rhea Martin
Mrs. Peter Teasdale............................Beatrice Terry
Aurelia Slater.................................Hilda Plowright
Harold Pratt......................................Charles Laite
Mr. Sims......................................Charles Dow Clark
General Von Und Zu Puppendorf.................Manart Kippen
Orderly.......................................Frederick Klein
First Officer.......................................Hans Windel
Second Officer.....................................Oscar Meyer
Third Officer......................................Karl Mueller
Fourth Officer...................................Arnold Sudman
"The Siren"......................................Lenore Sorsby
Corporal Colt.....................................Frank Coletti
Private Malinsky...................................Sam Sidman
First Landsturm.....................................Emil Hoch
Second Landsturm.............................Victor Rosenberg
Frau Fritzie Schmitt............................Frederica Going
A German Lieutenant............................John Harwood
Congressman Henry O'Day...........................Jay Wilson
A Newsreel Photographer...........................George Lewis
German Soldiers, Infantrymen, etc.
    Prologue—Inside the German Lines, Alsace, 1918. Act I.—Scenes
1 and 2—Home of Wallace and Mary Brown, Rogue River Falls.
3—German Headquarters, Alsace, October, 1918. Act II.—Scenes 1
and 3—Home of Wallace and Mary Brown. 2—Behind the German
Lines.
    Staged by Frank Craven; settings by Edward Morange.

Wallace Brown, a second lieutenant in the war, was modest
and a little dumb. Captured with two others when he led a recon-
noitering squad too far into the enemy lines he managed to escape
by stealing the clothes of an amorous hausfrau who had taken a
fancy to him. Back in Rogue River Falls, after demobilization,
Lieut. Brown married and modestly related his adventure to
Mary, his wife. Mary, being imaginative, expanded it into an act
of heroism, told her Congressman about it and had Wallace cited
for valor. The civic and war veteran societies of Rogue River insisted on making a celebration of the event and Wallace, flustered
and self-conscious, ran away to go fishing. It took a bit of squaring to re-establish the Brown family routine.

MOTHER

(36 performances)

A drama with music by Brecht based on a novel by Maxim
Gorki and translated from the German by Paul Peters; music by
Hanns Eisler. Produced by The Theatre Union, Inc., at the Civic
Repertory Theatre, New York, November 19, 1935.

Cast of characters—

```
The Mother, Pelagea Vlasova.......................Helen Henry
Pavel Vlasov...........................................John Boruff
Anton ....................................................Tony Ross
Andrei Maximovitch Nachodka.....................Herbert Rudley
Ivan Vesovchikov..............................Martin Wolfson
Masha.......................................Hester Sondergaard
A Policeman......................................Lee J. Cobb
The Inspector.................................James Macdonald
Gatekeeper ...................................Charles Niemeyer
Karpow.......................................Lester Lonergan, Jr.
Workers.........James Macdonald, Stanley G. Wood, Herbert Rudley
Smilgin.................................................Lee J. Cobb
The Teacher, Nicolai Ivanovich Vesovchikov.......Stanley G. Wood
Sostakovich...............................Lester Lonergan, Jr.
Women.......................Frances Bavier, Hester Sondergaard
A Prison Guard.......................................Tony Ross
Yegor Luchin....................................Herbert Rudley
Scab ........................................Charles Niemeyer
Butcher, Vasil Yefimovich...........................Lee J. Cobb
The Butcher's Wife...............................Frances Bavier
Lydia Antonovna.................................Frances Bavier
The Landlady, Vera Stefanovna...................Millicent Green
Another Tenant...............................Hester Sondergaard
A Doctor.....................................James Macdonald
Two Workers........................Lee J. Cobb, Herbert Rudley
An Official............................................Tony Ross
A Woman.........................................Frances Bavier
A Woman in Black............................Hester Sondergaard
A Servant Girl...................................Millicent Green
A Worker.....................................Charles Niemeyer
Other Workers: Guy Smith, Jr., Robert Miller, Bradley Louis Roberts
```

Act I.—Scenes 1, 2 and 5—Home of Palagea Vlasova, Tversk, Russia. 3—At the Gate of the Sukhlinov Works. 4—Inside the Yard of Sukhlinov Works. 6—Street. Act II.—Scenes 1, 2, 3 and 4—Home of Nicolai Ivanov Vesovchikov. 5—The Prison. 6—A Country Road. 7—The Kitchen of the Smirnoff Farms. Act III.—Scenes 1, 2 and 3—Home of Nicolai, the Teacher in Rostov. 4 and 6—The Street. 5—In Front of the Government Copper Office. 1907-17.

Staged by Victor Wolfson; settings by Mordecai Gorelik; music by Jerome Moross and Alex North.

Pelagea Vlasova, worried because of her son's activities with the radicals, undertakes to keep close to him and gradually convince him of his mistake. The closer she follows her son and her son's friends the more involved does she become as a worker. Finally she is one with the others, leading the parades, holding high the red flag and cheering the revolution. When her son is shot down the mother still carries on.

SATELLITE

(1 performance)

A farce in two acts by Kerry Shaw and Joseph Mitchell. Produced by Edward Davidow and John Cameron at the Bijou Theatre, New York, November 20, 1935.

Cast of characters—

```
Leona Wilson.......................................Joyce White
Margaret Manning...............................Barbara Weeks
```

Gene Wilson...................................George Sherwood
Bruce Taylor..................................Stanley Smith
May Manning...................................Noel Francis
Ben Bernie....................................Madame Poo
Rose Cheerful.................................Charlotte Reynolds
Jack Palmer...................................Carlyle Bennett
Emil Bierkraut................................Joseph Striker
Mr. Miller....................................Jack Soanes
Mrs. Miller...................................Rose Tapley
Lily ....Christola Williams
Liquor Man....................................Gerald Vaughn
Samuel Pokrass................................Himself
Max Goldblatz.................................Bernard Gorcey
Sunny Lane....................................Diane Tempest
    Act I.—Scenes 1 and 3—The Wilsons' Apartment in the Fifties.
2—May Manning's Dressing Room at a Broadway Theatre. Act II.—
Scenes 1 and 3—May Manning's Penthouse. 2—Tony's Bar. 4—The
Wilsons' Apartment.
    Staged by John Cameron; settings by A. W. Street.

The Manning girls, Leona, Margaret and May, are chorus girls
in New York. Leona is married to a press agent, Margaret is
working her way up in the profession and May is a gold digger.
Bruce Taylor comes from Iowa to New York with twenty thousand dollars and a large curiosity. Margaret would save him from
the temptations of Broadway. May would chisel her way into
the twenty thousand. Bruce takes to May, loses his money and is
salvaged by Margaret.

ABIDE WITH ME

(36 performances)

A drama in three acts by Clare Boothe Brokaw. Produced by
Malcolm L. Pearson and Donald Baruch in association with
A. H. Woods, Ltd., at the Ritz Theatre, New York, November 21,
1935.

Cast of characters—

Mrs. Marsden.................................Cecilia Loftus
Emma...Maria Ouspenskaya
Karl...Allen Fagan
Dr. Craig....................................James Rennie
Henry Marsden................................Earle Larimore
Nan Marsden..................................Barbara Robbins
Julia Field..................................Lee Patrick
    Acts I, II and III.—In the Marsdens' Library, New York.
    Staged by John Hayden; setting by P. Dodd Ackerman.

Henry Marsden, a wealthy alcoholic of sadistic tendencies,
smarting under the doubt of his own parentage, takes fiendish
delight in torturing his wife, Nan, who loyally sticks to him because of her love for his mother. Marsden finally advises Nan to
take Dr. Craig as her lover in the hope that she may present
him (Marsden) with an illegitimate son whom he can torture and
thus be even for the misery he suffered at the hands of his own

father. Marsden is finally shot dead by Emma, the old family servant, to save her beloveds from further humiliating tragedies.

WHATEVER GOES UP

(24 performances)

A comedy in three acts by Milton Lazarus. Produced by Crosby Gaige, Inc., at the Biltmore Theatre, New York, November 25, 1935.

Cast of characters—

Doc Harvey	Harry Tyler
A Girl	Barbara Layne
First Loafer	Frank Lindsay
Second Loafer	Philip Van Zandt
Terrance J. Sweeney	Ernest Truex
A Customer	John Davies
Second Customer	Natalie Carpenter
The Moocher	David Lesan
Mrs. Martin	Irene Cattell
Gerald	Fred Sherman
Photographer	Russell Morrison
Helen Sweeney	Peggy O'Donnell
Mrs. Sweeney	Leona Powers
First Reporter	Paul Sklar
Newsreel Interviewer	Peter Powers
Camera Man	George Peters
Assistant	Harry Jackson
Second Reporter	Robert Russell
Third Reporter	David Shelley
Sob Sister	Nondas Metcalfe
Miss Parker	Mildred Wall
Madame Lili	Annette Hoffman
Porter	W. O. McWatters
T. Russell Phelps	Raymond Bramley
Wilbur Churchill	Edward H. Robins
A Waiter	David Breen
Janitor	Frank Gabrielson
Claque Leader	Robert Russell
Agent	Jack Davis
Policeman	W. O. McWatters
Billingsby	William David
Hack	John Henry McKee
Grady	Edmon Ryan
A Man	H. H. McCollum
Detective	Ernest Woodward
Second Detective	Gordon Hamilton

Act I.—Scene 1—Cigar Store on Dyckman Street. 2—The Sweeney Flat. 3—The Sweeney Suite in the Waldorf. Act II.—Scene 1—The Sweeney Suite. 2—Broadcasting Studio of Station WSWY. Act III.—Scene 1—Sweeney Suite. 2—Dyckman Street Drug Store.
Staged by Arthur Sircom; settings by Bradford Ashworth.

Terrance J. Sweeney, clerking in a chain cigar store, takes a sweepstakes ticket in payment of a two-dollar loan. The ticket wins $150,000. After he has recovered, Sweeney, at his wife's dictation, engages a suite at the Waldorf, a social secretary for the family, and is successfully pursued by an army of confidence men and grafters. Induced by his wife's uncle, Banker Wilbur Churchill, to invest in a radio station Sweeney is amazed to discover it a fake. He finally loses half his winnings to the banker crook, pays two thirds of the other half to the government, settles his hotel bills and comes out with $6,000.

THE RAGGED EDGE

(8 performances)

A melodrama in three acts by Mary Heathfield. Produced by A. H. Woods, Ltd., at the Fulton Theatre, New York, November 25, 1935.

Cast of characters—

Dot Whalen	Nancy Dover
Landers	Frank Monroe
Rodney Cole, Jr.	Glen Boles
Rodney Cole, Sr.	Robert Harrison
Judy Farraday	Lillian Emerson
Agatha Drake	Clara Palmer
Eleanor Dunham	Dorothy Bernard
Fenwick	Edward Lester
Tom Drake	Frederick Graham
Dawson Webb	Leo Curley
Russell Parker	Percy Kilbride
Jake	Wylie Adams
Bill Craigie	Glen Boles
Pike Reardon	Edward Craven
Henry Farraday	Nicholas Joy

Act I.—Scene 1—Country Home of Rodney Cole. 2—Cole's Library, New York City. 3—Russ Parker's Shack Near the Hudson River. Act II.—Scenes 1 and 2—Cole's Library. 3—Parker's Shack. Act III.—Scene 1—Cole's Library. 2—Parker's Shack.
Staged by A. H. Van Buren; settings by Nicholas Yellenti.

Rodney Cole, Jr., for whom his father is holding in trust a half million dollar legacy, decides waiting is not worth while and kills himself. Father, having spent most of the legacy, is forced either to find a double for his son or confess his embezzlement. He finds the double in Bill Craigie of the hoodlum Craigies. Bill, a good sort at base, fills the role admirably, even to the extent of winning the dead boy's sweetheart. When he is exposed he takes a reward and goes to Australia for rejuvenation purposes. The idea being that the girl will wait.

* FIRST LADY

(238 performances)

A comedy in three acts by Katharine Dayton and George S. Kaufman. Produced by Sam H. Harris at the Music Box, New York, November 26, 1935.

Cast of characters—

Sophy Prescott.................................Diantha Pattison
Charles..James Seeley
Emmy Paige..Helen Brooks
Lucy Chase Wayne....................................Jane Cowl
Stephen Wayne...................................Stanley Ridges
Belle Hardwick.....................................Jessie Busley
Mrs. Ives..Regina Wallace
Ann Forrester...Rita Vale
A Congressman's Wife.........................Margherita Sargent
Her Friend......................................Leslie Bingham
The Baroness......................................Ulla Kazanova
Señor Ortega.....................................Armand Cortes
A Chinese..Hon. Wu
A General.......................................Donald McKenzie
Mrs. Creevey.......................................Ethel Wilson
Mrs. Davenport...................................Lillian Norton
Senator Keane.....................................Judson Laire
Tom Hardwick....................................Thomas Findlay
Irene Hibbard.......................................Lily Cahill
Bleecker.......................................John M. Troughton
Carter Hibbard....................................Oswald Yorke
George Mason..Frank Dae
Ellsworth T. Ganning..............................Florenz Ames
Jason Fleming......................................Don Beddoe
Herbert Sedgwick................................George Parsons
Guests at the Reception, Butlers, etc.: Isis Brinn, Susan Powers,
     Charles LaRue, Daniel Ocko, Naoe Kondo and Bradford Hunt.
     Acts I and III.—The Secretary of State's Home, Washington,
D. C. Act II.—Scene 1—Carter Hibbard's Study. 2—Secretary of
State's Home.
     Staged by George S. Kaufman; settings by Donald Oenslager.

See page 134.

STICK-IN-THE-MUD

(9 performances)

A comedy in three acts by Frederick Hazlitt Brennan. Produced by Jack Curtis and Carleton Hoagland, by arrangement
with Saul Burston, at the 48th Street Theatre, New York, November 26, 1935.

Cast of characters—

Buttinhead Adams..................................Rex Ingram
Cap'n Dan Minor...............................Dudley Clements
Lucy Hough.......................................Sylvia Field
Mrs. J. E. B. Drumwright.........................Maida Reade
Mrs. Emma Hamble..............................Clare Woodbury
Lew Hamble......................................Geoffrey Bryant
Paw Meriwether..................................Thomas Mitchell
Adrian Reed....................................Bruce MacFarlane
Mrs. Austin Lacey................................Alice Fleming
Judith Lacey.....................................Doris Dudley
Mr. Hoskins.....................................Hale Norcross
Chauffeur...Jose Ferrer
Musicians.................................. { Geoffrey Lind
                                            { Winton Sears
                                            { Howard Newman
     Acts I, II and III.—Grand Salon of Steamboat Dixie Belle Which
Has Been Aground at Pike County Landing, Missouri, for Thirty-
One Years.
     Staged by Thomas Mitchell; setting by P. Dodd Ackerman.

Thirty-one years before the curtain rises the "Dixie Belle" had gone aground at Pike County Landing. Capt. Dan Minor has lived on her ever since and collected an assortment of friends, including Paw Meriwether, who fishes through a hatch in the living room. Others are Lucy Hough, the unwed mother of Adrian Reed's child. Adrian would marry Lucy, but objects to being forced to do so by Capt. Dan's shotgun and is also doubtful of his pilot's salary being enough to support a family. When Captain Dan arranges a damage suit settlement with the Burlington railroad he finances Lucy's wedding and sets Adrian up in the tow-boat business.

* BOY MEETS GIRL

(235 performances)

A comedy in three acts by Bella and Samuel Spewack. Produced by George Abbott at the Cort Theatre, New York, November 27, 1935.

Cast of characters—

Robert Law	Allyn Joslyn
Larry Toms	Charles McClelland
J. Carlyle Benson	Jerome Cowan
Rosetti	Everett H. Sloane
Mr. Friday (C. F.)	Royal Beal
Peggy	Peggy Hart
Miss Crews	Lea Penman
Rodney Bevan	James MacColl
Green	Garson Kanin
Slade	Maurice Sommers
Susie	Joyce Arling
A Nurse	Helen Gardner
Doctor	Perry Ivins
Chauffeur	Edison Rice
Young Man	Philip Faversham
Studio Officer	George W. Smith
Cutter	Robert Foulk
Another Nurse	Marjorie Lytell
Major Thompson	John Clarke

Act I.—Mr. Friday's Office, the Royal Studios in Hollywood. Act II.—Scene 1—Neighborhood Theatre. 2 and 3—Mr. Friday's Office. Act III.—Scene 1—A Hospital Corridor. 2—In Your Home. 3—Mr. Friday's Office.

Staged by George Abbott; settings by Arne Lundborg.

See page 204.

ONE GOOD YEAR

(215 performances)

A comedy in two acts by Stephen Gross and Lin S. Root. Produced by Al Rosen at the Lyceum Theatre, New York, November 27, 1935.

Cast of characters—

Dr. Emelia Hansen	Hilda Spong
Julie Compton	Mary Sargent
Anne	Gertrude Flynn
Anthony Blake	Edward Woods
Robert Carlyle	Russ Brown
J. H. Weaver	Richard S. Bishop
Sarah	Doro Merande
Mrs. Cellini	Genevieve Belasco
Henry Compton	Hans Robert
Richard Patton	Guy Woolford
Tom Shanley	Joseph Vitale
Reverend Parker	Anthony Joachim

Acts I, II and III.—Living Room of Anne Haven's House, Sweetwater, Connecticut.

Staged by George Rosener; setting by Karle O. Amend.

Anne Haven, young and ambitious music student, is about to be dispossessed of her Connecticut home because she cannot meet a payment on a loan. Julie Compton, her frivolous neighbor, is eager to be a mother but dare not. Anne suggests that she (Anne) have the baby, with a eugenically selected father, on payment of $3,000, a part to be applied to her loan, the rest to help her through a year of music in Paris. One of three proposed mates for Anne is accepted, but later supplanted by a young composer, Anthony Blake, who has taken to piano tuning during the depression. Anne falls in love with the father of her child, and Mrs. Compton is surprised in the last act to discover that, anyway, she is going to be a mother herself.

HOW BEAUTIFUL WITH SHOES

(8 performances)

A drama in three acts by Wilbur Daniel Steele and Anthony Brown. Produced by Anthony Laudati at the Booth Theatre, New York, November 28, 1935.

Cast of characters—

Wale Herter	Norman Williams
Ruby Herter	Harry Bellaver
Bilbo Rittenhouse	Marion Willis
Mrs. Doggett	Nell Harrison
Sil Tooker	Mary Fletcher
Mare Doggett	Marie Brown
Wyker Adams	Ralph Riggs
Joe	Michael Lettice
Humble Jewett	Myron McCormick
Judge Kinsaugh	Burke Clarke
Henry Deeds	Charles F. Holden
Bill Deeds	Will Henry
Dr. Orrison	Earl Mitchell
Pop Herter	George Colan
Bobo Rielly	Bobo Rielly
Buck Johnson	Buck Johnson
Jodie Marlowe	Jodie Marlowe

Wedding Guests: Beatrice Cole, Elsa Beamish, Elizabeth Wilde,

Laura Windsor, Lillian Williams, Betty Fouche, Westley Addy, Norman Leavitt, Franklin Davis, Sandy Strouse, Edward Andrews, Elmer Oettinger.
Acts I and III.—Doggett Living Room. Act II.—Scene 1—Top Rock. 2 and 3—Wyker's Cabin. Act III.—Doggett's Living Room.
Staged by Anthony Brown; settings by P. Dodd Ackerman.

Mare Doggett, shy and inarticulate, is to marry Ruby Herter, strong and overbearing. In the midst of the wedding preparations, word comes that a dangerous lunatic (Humble Jewett) has escaped the asylum and is haunting the vicinity. The wedding party goes lunatic hunting, leaving the bride-to-be about to take a bath. In comes the lunatic, a mild madman crazed by a search for beauty that shall pass understanding. He sees it expressed in the simple Mare and loves her. When the natives take him and shut him in jail he sets fire to the place, kills the sheriff and escapes. On a mountain top he finds Mare again and continues his love making, frequently in the language of the "Songs of Solomon"—"How beautiful are thy feet with shoes, O Prince's daughter!" The lunatic is shot down by a drunken pursuer, but Mare will have nothing more to do with her bridegroom.

WEEP FOR THE VIRGINS

(9 performances)

A drama in three acts by Nellise Child. Produced by The Group Theatre, Inc., at the 46th Street Theatre, New York, November 30, 1935.

Cast of characters—

Homer Jobes	Art Smith
Oscar Sigsmund	J. E. Bromberg
Mrs. Bean	Margaret Barker
Ruby Jobes	Ruth Nelson
Danny Stowe	Alexander Kirkland
Mr. Walters	Tony Kraber
Clarice Jobes	Paula Miller
Cecilia Jobes	Evelyn Varden
Mrs. Walters	Hildur Lanmark
Violet Jobes	Phoebe Brand
Gladys Semp	Mildren Van Dorn
Grandma Jobes	Eunice Stoddard
Rita Elsbeth	Hilda Reis
Piano Player	William Nichols
Hap Nichols	Jules Garfield
Peggy	Virginia Stevens
Belle (The Strawberry Tart)	Marie Hunt
Nancy Kruger	Dorothy Patten
Mrs. Carsons	Margaret Barker

Sailors, Waitresses, Girls, Wedding Guests, Fish Butchers, Cannery Girls, etc.: Wilhelmina Barton, Mara Alexander, Natalie Harmon, Frances Hayes, Hal James, Robert Johnson, Victor Kraft, Edward Kogan.
Act I.—Scene 1—The Jobes' Kitchen, Cannery Court, near Fish Harbor in San Diego. 2—The Strawberry Tart's. 3—Bedroom. Act II.

—The Jobes' Kitchen. Act III.—Scenes 1 and 2—Jobes' Kitchen. 3—Cannery Court.
Staged by Cheryl Crawford; settings by Boris Aronson.

Cecilia Jobes, out of burlesque and married to Homer Jobes, an employee of a fish cannery in San Diego, is determined to rule the lives of her three daughters, Ruby, Clarice and Violet, to her own advantage and satisfaction. Ruby she dedicates to house-keeping, Clarice to a career in Hollywood and Violet to a profit-able marriage. In result Ruby is seduced by a sailor, Violet is hunted by the police after she bashes the head of an admirer she was trying to rob, and Clarice, tired of training and dieting for a career, marries Oscar Sigsmund, a man as old as her father and almost as dirty, who buys her for $200 and a promise she can eat all the sweets she wants to. The shallow and selfish mother adds it all to her martyrdom.

ROSMERSHOLM

(8 performances)

A play in four acts by Henrik Ibsen; revised translation by Eva Le Gallienne. Revived by Eva Le Gallienne at the Shubert Theatre, New York, December 2, 1935.

Cast of characters—

Rebecca West	Eva Le Gallienne
Madame Helseth	Leona Roberts
Professor Kroll	Averell Harris
Johannes Rosmer	Donald Cameron
Ulric Brendel	Hugh Buckler
Peter Mortensgard	Walter Beck

Acts I, III and IV.—Sitting Room at Rosmersholm. Act II.—Johannes Rosmer's Study.
Staged by Eva Le Gallienne; settings by Irene Sharaff.

Rebecca West, idealist, seeking to inspire the intellectual emancipation of Johannes Rosmer, a former minister of the gospel, so works upon the sensitive mind of Mrs. Rosmer that the latter is driven to self-destruction. Miss West continues her mis-sion in the case of Rosmer, but fails rather ignobly when scandal threatens and she sees in conventional marriage the death of love. Convinced of their joint defeat Rebecca joins Rosmer in a suicide pact. Together they go over the millrace where Mrs. Rosmer had died. . . . A notable production of "Rosmersholm" was made by Mrs. Fiske in 1908, with George Arliss as Brendel, Bruce McRae the Rosmer, Fuller Mellish as Kroll and Albert Bruning the Mortensgaard. The play was first produced in America in 1904, with Florence Kahn as the Rebecca.

CAMILLE

(7 performances)

A drama in four acts by Alexandre Dumas, fils, translated by Henriette Metcalf. Revived by Eva Le Gallienne at the Shubert Theatre, New York, December 4, 1935.

Cast of characters—

```
Baron De Varville...............................Averell Harris
Nanine..........................................Marion Evensen
Nichette........................................Florida Friebus
Marguerite Gautier............................Eva Le Gallienne
Olympe.......................................Eva Leonard Boyne
Saint Gaudens...................................Sayre Crawley
Prudence........................................Leona Roberts
Servants.........................Pedro Galvan, William Phillips
Gaston Rieux....................................Donald Cameron
Armand Duval....................................Richard Waring
Count De Giray....................................Walter Beck
Gustave..........................................Kendall Clark
M. Duval.........................................Hugh Buckler
Arthur......................................William S. Phillips
The Doctor........................................Walter Beck
Anais.........................................Genevieve Frizzell
```

Act I.—Marguerite Gautier's Boudoir. Act II.—Living Room in Marguerite's Villa at Auteuil, Near Paris. Act III.—A Salon in Olympe's House in Paris. Act IV.—Marguerite's Bedroom.

Staged by Eva Le Gallienne; settings by Aline Bernstein.

Miss Le Gallienne has kept the Dumas, fils, drama in her repertory since she first revived it at the Civic Repertory Theatre in 1931.

MAY WINE

(213 performances)

A musical play in two acts by Frank Mandel, adapted from a novel, "The Happy Alienist," by Eric von Stroheim and Wallace Smith; music by Sigmund Romberg; lyrics by Oscar Hammerstein II; orchestration by Don Walker. Produced by Laurence Schwab at the St. James Theatre, New York, December 5, 1935.

Cast of characters—

```
Liesl.............................................Lee Childs
Sergeant.......................................Tones Chapman
Policemen.......Edward Gallaway, Leonard Berry, Chester Herman
Musicians............................Bela Lublov, Charles Palloy
Gypsy......................................Marie Louise Quevli
Drunk.........................................Maury Tuckerman
The Lovers...................Earle R. MacVeigh and Betty Kerr
Inspector Schnorrheim.............................Roy Gordon
Mr. Whalley...................................Mitchell Harris
Prof. Johann Volk................................Walter Slezak
Willi Zimmerkopf................................Robert Sloane
Baron Kuno Adelhorst.......................Walter Woolf King
Herr Schmidt......................................Carlo Conte
```

Hans..Victor Casmore
Father..Mitchell Harris
Mother..Inga Hill
Son..Radley Collins
Daughter.......................................Marian Huntley
Waiter...Maury Tuckerman
Domino Players................Leonard Berry, Edward Gallaway
Marie—Baroness Von Schlewitz....................Nancy McCord
Vere Huber..............................Daphne Warren-Wilson
Page Boy......................................Radley Collins
People in Box........................Tones Chapman, Lee Childs
Karl...Clifford Menz
Strollers................Flora Laney, Leonard Berry, Devona Doxie
Josef...Robert C. Fischer
Uncle Pishka...................................Leo G. Carroll
Mr. Runtschli...............................Earle R. MacVeigh
Peasant Couple.....................Leonard Berry, Jessie Graham
Kathi...Inga Hill
Dancers............................Alice Dudley and Jack Cole
Friedl..Vera Van
Pawnbroker....................................Victor Casmore
Dr. Von Schlager.............................Mitchell Harris
Dr. Herbst....................................Leonard Berry
Dr. Karpis.....................................Carlo Conte
Passers-by...........................Inga Hill, Tones Chapman
Shopgirls...................Marie Louise Quevli, Marian Huntley
Newsboy.......................................Radley Collins
    Act I.—Scene 1—Inspector Schnorrheim's Office. 2 and 7—Professor Volk's Living Room. 3—Barber Shop. 4—Prater Café. 5—The Benefit Performance. 6—Marie's Room. 8—The Railroad Station. 9—Hotel Schildersturn Bridal Suite and Courtyard. Act II.—Scene 10—Bridal Suite. 11—Willi Zimmerkopf's Studio. 12, 16 and 18—Volk's Living Room. 13—Night Club. 14—Volk's Study. 15—Pawn Shop and Conference Room. 17—Marie's Dressing Room.
    Staged by Jose Ruben; settings by Raymond Sovey; costumes by Kay Morrison.

Prof. Johann Volk, successful, rich and absent-minded, falls deeply in love with Marie, the Baroness Von Schlewitz, being openly encouraged by Baron Kuno Adelhorst. Baron Kuno also loves Marie but is not married to her. He thinks between them they can get the professor's money and then return to their own affair. After they are married Marie, noting how noble the professor is, even when forgetful, comes to love him and does not want either to harm him or return to Kuno. Believing he has been deceived, Professor Volk sets out to shoot Marie dead but misses, hitting a wax replica he has had made of her instead.

A SUNNY MORNING

(1 performance)

A comedy in one act by Serafin and Joaquin Alvarez Quintero, translated by Harley Granville-Barker. Revived by Eva Le Gallienne at the Shubert Theatre, New York, December 7, 1935.

Cast of characters—
    Dona Laura...................................Eva Le Gallienne
    Petra.......................................Marion O'Neil

```
Don  Gonzalo..........................................Walter  Beck
Juanito...............................................Kendall  Clark
     Scene—A Park in Madrid.
     Staged by Eva Le Gallienne; setting by Aline Bernstein.
```

Followed by—

THE WOMEN HAVE THEIR WAY

A comedy in two acts by Serafin and Joaquin Alvarez Quintero, translated by Helen and Harley Granville-Barker.

Cast of characters—

```
Don  Julian  Figueredo.............................Hugh  Buckler
Santita............................................Genevieve  Frizell
Adolfo  Adalid.....................................Richard  Waring
Dieguilla......................................Eva  Leonard  Boyne
Concha  Puerto.....................................Leona  Roberts
Guitarra...........................................Pedro  Galvan
Pilar..............................................Marion  O'Neil
Angela.............................................Florida  Friebus
Pepe  Lora.....................................William  S.  Phillips
Dona  Helen  Zurita..............................Marion  Evensen
Juanita  La  Rosa...............................Eva  Le  Gallienne
Don  Cecilio.......................................Sayre  Crawley
A  Young  Peasant  Girl............................Amy  Chandler
The  Sacristan  of  San  Antonio......................Walter  Beck
     Acts I and II.—Don Julian's House in Andalusia.
     Staged by Eva Le Gallienne.
```

Produced by Eva Le Gallienne originally at the Civic Repertory Theatre in 1930. (Best Plays, 1929-30.)

PARADISE LOST

(73 performances)

A drama in three acts by Clifford Odets. Produced by The Group Theatre at the Longacre Theatre, New York, December 9, 1935.

Cast of characters—

```
Leo  Gordon....................................Morris  Carnovsky
Clara..............................................Stella  Adler
Ben................................................Walter  Coy
Julie.............................................Sanford  Meisner
Pearl..............................................Joan  Madison
Gus  Michaels......................................Roman  Bohnen
Libby  Michaels................................Blanche  Gladstone
Sam  Katz..........................................Luther  Adler
Bertha.............................................Frieda  Altman
Kewpie.............................................Elia  Kazan
Mr.  Pike..........................................Grover  Burgess
Mr.  May...........................................Bob  Lewis
Schnabel.......................................Louis  G.  Latzer
Rogo..............................................Vincent  Sherman
Lucille............................................Julie  Laurence
Felix..............................................Herbert  Ratner
Phil  Foley........................................Lewis  Leverett
```

Milton...Paul Morrison
Newspaper Men................................ { Bernard Kisner
                                              { Jacob Sandler
Two Homeless Men............................ { Russell Collins
                                              { William Challee
Detectives..................................... { George Pembroke
                                               { Jack Carr

Acts I, II and III.—The Gordon Home. An American City.
Staged by Harold Clurman; setting by Boris Aronson.

Leo Gordon, Clara, his wife, and Ben and Julie, their children, share a two-family house with Leo's partner in the leather goods business, Sam Katz and his wife, Bertha. Gordon is conservative, idealistic, weak. Katz is radical and strong. There is constant conflict between them which results eventually in the ruin of the business. The family also crashes. Ben, the son, marries a trollop named Libby, who takes up with a taxi racketeer, Kewpie. Ben purposely puts himself in the way of crime and a policeman's bullet. Julie, the daughter, remains a frustrated spinster because her pianist lover cannot afford to marry her. Out of the general crash Leo extracts a philosophy of optimism. Through suffering the people will learn; through learning they will rebuild the world to meet their own needs. "The world's at its morning!" he cries exultantly at the end.

THIS OUR HOUSE

(2 performances)

A drama in two acts by Joel W. Schenker and Allan Fleming. Produced by Christopher Noel at the 58th Street Theatre, New York, December 10, 1935.

Cast of characters—

Giorgio...Benedict McQuarrie
Olimpio Margio...................................Sherling Oliver
Beatrice Cenci....................................Edith Atwater
Putana...Margherite Norris
Giovanni..Elvin Field
Lucrezia Cenci...................................Helen Holmes
Bernardo Cenci...................................Ben Starkie
Salvatore...Henry Buckler
Pedro...Richard Huett
Father Simon.....................................Halliam Bosworth
Francesco Cenci..................................Ian MacLaren
Cardinal Silvestri................................Edward Jephson
Porzia..Agnes Marc
Sbirro..Harold McGee
Judges.. { John Osborne
                                                { Harry Irvine
                                                { Courtney White
Prince Colonna...................................Fred Leslie
Warder...Franklin Klein
Jailer..Richard Allen

Act I.—In the Palace. Act II.—A Courtroom.
Staged by James Light; settings by Edward Eddy.

Beatrice Cenci, subjected to new indignities on the return of her vicious father, Francesco, from a term in prison, arranges with her lover, Olimpio Margio, for Francesco's murder. Arrested with the rest of the family, Beatrice is forced finally to a confession through the threatened torture of her younger brother, Bernardo. She goes to the block, passing the Cenci hate on to Bernardo.

GHOSTS

(First engagement 45 performances; return 36. Total 81)

A play in three acts by Henrik Ibsen. Revived by Luther Greene at the Empire Theatre, New York, December 12, 1935.

Cast of characters—

Regina..Ona Munson
Jacob Engstrand.................................Raymond O'Brien
Pastor Manders....................................McKay Morris
Mrs. Alving....................................Madame Nazimova
Oswald Alving.....................................Harry Ellerbe
    Acts I, II and III.—Mrs. Alving's Estate on One of the Larger Fjords of Western Norway.
    Staged by Madame Nazimova; setting by Stewart Chaney.

"Ghosts" was first produced in America at the Berkeley Lyceum, New York, January 5, 1894. Ida Jeffreys Goodfriend was the Mrs. Alving, Courteney Thorpe the Oswald. Important revivals have been those of 1899, with Mary Shaw as Mrs. Alving; 1915, with Alberta Gallatin as Mrs. Alving and Robert Whittier as Oswald; 1917, with Mrs. Shaw and Jose Ruben; 1926, by the Actors' Theatre, with Lucille Watson as Mrs. Alving and Jose Ruben the Oswald, and that of 1927, with Mrs. Fiske the Mrs. Alving and Theodore St. John the Oswald. In 1931 Mrs. Patrick Campbell played Mrs. Alving to the Oswald of Tom Douglas in San Francisco and Los Angeles.

LIBEL

(159 performances)

A drama in three acts by Edward Wooll. Produced by Gilbert Miller at the Henry Miller Theatre, New York, December 20, 1935.

Cast of characters—

Associate...Lewis Dayton
William Bale......................................Charles Francis
Sir Wilfred Kelling, K.C., M.P..................Ernest Lawford
The Hon. Sir Arthur Tuttington.................Frederick Leister

Thomas Foxley, K.C..............................Wilfrid Lawson
Sir Mark Loddon, Bart. M.P.........................Colin Clive
Lady Enid Loddon..................................Joan Marion
Sarah Carleton.......................................Helen Goss
George Hemsby......................................Colin Hunter
Patrick Buckingham..............................Arthur Vinton
Emile Flordon..................................Boris Marshalov
Admiral Fairfax Loddon.........................Robert Benjamin
Captain Gerald Loddon.............................Larry Johns
General Winterton, C.B...........................Edward Oldfield
Lady Agatha Winterton............................Emily Gilbert
Major Brampton............................Neville Heber-Percy
Numero Quinze..................................Robert Simmons
Ushers....................................... { Robert LeSueur
                                              { Charles Wellesley
    Acts I, II and III.—King's Bench Court at the Royal Courts of
Justice in London.
    Staged by Otto Ludwig Preminger; setting by Raymond Sovey.

Sir Mark Loddon was a victim of shell shock in the war. Some
years after his discharge, and following his marriage to Lady
Enid, Sir Mark stands for Parliament. During the campaign an
opposition weekly accuses him of being an impostor who had
murdered the real Loddon and assumed his name, title, fortune
and fiancée. Sir Mark sues for libel, but because of his inability
to remember events occurring before the war, as well as because
of a strong chain of circumstantial evidence against him, he
stands in danger of defeat until he is able finally to prove his
identity.

THE SEASON CHANGES

(8 performances)

A comedy in three acts by Arthur Richman. Produced by Robert Milton at the Booth Theatre, New York, December 23, 1935.

Cast of characters—

Bessie...................................Beatrice Hendricks
Mildred Lanning....................................Phyllis Joyce
Hedwig...Hope Landin
Alice Lanning.......................................Doris Dudley
Rita Glenn..................................Zamah Cunningham
Frank Glenn......................................Nicholas Joy
Theodore Biglin...............................James Spottswood
Jim Farrington ....Eliot Cabot
    Acts I, II and III.—Mildred Lanning's Country Place in New
Hampshire.
    Staged by Robert Milton; setting by Gretl Urban.

Alice Lanning meets and is fascinated by Jim Farrington. When
she discovers that he is a married man she listens to his explanation of a separation from his wife and agrees to wait until he
divorces the first Mrs. Farrington and marries her. Mildred Lanning, Alice's mother, is at first seriously disturbed by her daughter's decision, but later becomes entirely acquiescent. At which

surprising change Alice loses interest in Farrington and calls her marriage off. She will stay at home with her mother.

ROMEO AND JULIET

(15 performances)

A tragedy in twenty-three scenes by William Shakespeare. Revived by Katharine Cornell at the Martin Beck Theatre, New York, December 23, 1935.

Cast of characters—

Escalus, Prince of Verona	Reynolds Evans
Paris	John Cromwell
Montague	Arthur Chatterton
Capulet	Charles Dalton
An Old Man	Joseph Roeder
Romeo	Maurice Evans
Mercutio	Ralph Richardson
Benvolio	Tyrone Power, Jr.
Tybalt	Irving Morrow
Friar Laurence	Charles Waldron
Friar John	David Orrick
Balthasar	Shelton Earp
Sampson	David Orrick
Peter	David Vivian
Gregory	Robert Champlain
Abraham	Grant Gordon
An Apothecary	Joseph Roeder
Officer	Carl Allan
Lady Montague	Alice John
Lady Capulet	Irby Marshal
Juliet	Katharine Cornell
Nurse to Juliet	Florence Reed

Citizens of Verona, Kinsfolk of Both Houses, Maskers, Watchmen, Attendants and Guards: Evelyn Abbott, Charlotte Fitch, Anne Froelick, Lois Jameson, Ruth March, Harriott Marshall, Gabrielle Morgan, Albert Allen, John Cornell, Richard Graham, William Roehrick, Hudson Shotwell, Kurt Steinbart and Fred Thompson.

Chorus....................................Ralph Richardson
Part I.—Scenes 1 and 11—A Public Place in Verona, Mantua. 2 and 4—In Capulet's House. 3 and 8—Street in Verona. 5—By the Wall of Capulet's House. 6 and 9—Capulet's Orchard. 7 and 10—Friar Laurence's Cell. Part II.—Scenes 12, 15, 18 and 20—Juliet's Bedroom. 13, 16 and 22—Friar Laurence's Cell. 14, 17 and 19—In Capulet's House. 21—Street in Mantua. 23—Tomb of the Capulets.
Staged by Guthrie McClintic; settings and costumes by Jo Mielziner; dances directed by Martha Graham, fencing by Georges Santelli.

Miss Cornell began her 1935-36 season by reviving "Romeo and Juliet," which she had produced the previous season, for a short road tour. In her reorganized company the principal changes in cast were the Romeo, Mercutio, and Nurse. Maurice Evans and Ralph Richardson, both members at one time of the Shakespearean company at the Old Vic in London, were brought over for Romeo and Mercutio respectively, and Florence Reed succeeded Blanche Yurka as Nurse. Two weeks in New York at holiday time concluded the tour, and Miss Cornell put "Joan of Arc" in rehearsal for early Spring production.

GEORGE WHITE'S SCANDALS

(110 performances)

A revue in two acts by George White, William K. Wells and Howard A. Shiebler; lyrics by Jack Yellen; music by Ray Henderson; orchestrations by Russell Bennett and Conrad Salinger. Produced by George White at the New Amsterdam Theatre, New York, December 25, 1935.

Principals engaged—

Rudy Vallée
Bert Lahr
Willie and Eugene Howard
Hal Ford
Richard Lane
Sam, Ted, Ray
Cliff Edwards
Edgar Battler
Harold Willard
Jimmy Shea
Gus Raymond
James Howard
Ann Laxton
Verna Long

Gracie Barrie
Jane Cooper
Estelle Jayne
Peggy Moseley
Stanley Twins
Vivian Porter
Jean Gale
Claire McQuillen
Helene Miller
Lois Eckhart
Laura Shevlin
Alice Carleton
Edna Page
Alma Saunders

Apollo Quartette

Staged by George White; settings by Russell Patterson and Walter Jagemann; costumes created by Charles Le Maire; dance ensembles by Russell Markert; orchestra directed by Tom Jones.

*VICTORIA REGINA

(198 performances)

A drama in three acts by Laurence Housman. Produced by Gilbert Miller at the Broadhurst Theatre, New York, December 26, 1935.

Cast of characters—

A Footman	Alfred Halton
Lord Conyngham	E. Bellenden-Clarke
Archbishop of Canterbury	Harry Plimmer
A Maidservant	Mary Austin
Duchess of Kent	Babette Feist
Victoria	Helen Hayes
Lord Melbourne	Lewis Casson
Prince Albert	Vincent Price
Prince Ernest	George Macready
Mr. Richards	Albert Froom
Mr. Anson	Oswald Marshall
1st Queen's Gentleman	Arthur Gould-Porter
A Court Usher	Edward Martin
Lady Muriel	Mary Heberden
Lady Grace	Renee Macredy
Lady-in-Waiting	Mary Newnham-Davis

2nd Queen's Gentleman......................Fothringham Lysons
Mr. Oakley..James Bedford
Duchess of Sutherland...........................Cherry Hardy
Lady Jane......................................Helen Trenholme
General Grey..Tom Woods
3rd Queen's Gentleman...........................Edward Jones
John Brown.....................................James Woodburn
Lord Beaconsfield................................George Zucco
A Footman......................................Robert Von Rigel
Sir Arthur Bigge..............................Herschel Martin
An Imperial Highness..............................Felix Brown
His Royal Highness..............................Gilbert McKay
1st Princess.......................................Mary Forbes
2nd Princess......................................Shirley Gale
3rd Princess...................................Elizabeth Munn
Members of the Royal Family, Footman and Court Officials: Jean
     Stephenson, William Packer, Willis Duncan, Alan Bandler, Guy
     Moneypenny.
     Act I.—Scene 1—Entrance Hall at Kensington Palace, England
(1837). 2 and 3—Sitting Room at Windsor Castle (1838 and 1839).
4—Prince Albert's Dressing Room at Windsor (1840). Act II.—
Scenes 1 and 4—Prince Albert's Writing Room at Buckingham Palace
(1842 and 1861). 2—Room in Buckingham (1842). 3—Drawing Room
at Windsor (1846). Act III.—Scene 1—Garden Tent at Balmoral
Castle (1877). 2—Buckingham (1897).
     Staged by Gilbert Miller; settings by Rex Whistler.

See page 169.

CONTINENTAL VARIETIES

(9 performances)

A revue in two acts. Produced by Henry Carson at the Masque
Theatre, New York, December 26, 1935.

Principals engaged—

Lucienne Boyer   King Lan Chew
Pils and Tabet   Paal and Leif Rocky
Georges Andre Martin   Iza Volpin's Ensemble
Helen Gray

TAPESTRY IN GRAY

(24 performances)

A drama in three acts by Martin Flavin. Produced by B. P.
Schulberg at the Shubert Theatre, New York, December 27, 1935.

Cast of characters—

Iris Nordgren......................................Elissa Landi
A Servant..Henry Vincent
Dr. Stephen Macklin..............................Minor Watson
Doctor Marius.....................................Arnold Korff
Erik Nordgren...................................Melvyn Douglas
A Ballet Dancer...................................Alice Sherbon
The Ballet Master.............................Michael Visaroff
MacManus...Jack Lescoulie
A Medical Corps Major............................Franklyn Fox
Stretcher Bearer................................Edgar Murdock
Young Medical Corps Officer......................George Lamar
Old Medical Corps Officer........................Byron Russell

A Waiter.....................................Auguste Aramini
An Editor....................................Frederick Forrester
A Ship's Steward.............................George Bleasdale
Iris' Maid..................................Audrey Barlow
Another Waiter..............................Joseph Olney
A Street Walker.............................Miriam Battista
A Hotel Porter.............................Alan Morrill
A Patient...................................Paul Gallo
A Nurse....................................Muriel Brassler
Erik Nordgren, Jr..........................Howard Sherman
Governess..................................Cornelia Bell
A Policeman................................Jack Harwood
A Hospital Nurse...........................Norma Downey
Surgical Nurse.............................Helene Bush
Anaesthetist...............................Mildred Van Dorn
Another Patient............................C. Russell Sage
Gunman.....................................Claude Carey
A Woman....................................June Leslie
A Beggar...................................Samuel Roland
Coroner's Office Man.......................Arling Alcine
Soldiers, Hospital Orderlies, Waiters, Stewards, Dancers and Pedes-
    trians: Milo Boulton, Herschel Cropper, Larney Goodkind,
    William Hunter, Starr West Jones, Robert Gray, Owen Russell,
    William Robertson, Theodore Paul.
    Act I.—First Aid Dressing Station on Battlefield in France; Mili-
tary Hospital; Bistrot in Boulogne; Dock on Waterfront. Act II.—
Deck of Ocean Liner; Street Café, Paris; Hotel Room. Act III.—
Balcony in Italy; Laboratory, Office, Night Club and Waterfront
Dock.
    Staged by Marion Gering; settings by Donald Oenslager.

Stephen Macklin and Erik Nordgren were fellow medical students. Macklin specialized in microscopy, Nordgren in surgery.
In the Great War Macklin had half his face torn away. Nordgren, coming accidentally upon him, patched him up and left
him in hospital with orders not to loosen his bandages. Iris, a
nurse, disobeyed orders. Macklin was terribly scarred. Iris, dis-
charged, on her way back to Paris meets and stays temporarily
with Nordgren. Later she would kill herself but Nordgren saves
and marries her. When Macklin comes back into their lives Iris
is jealous. In her possessiveness she forces Nordgren to give up
his friendship for Macklin. Nordgren suffers a loss of confidence
and skill. In the end he kills himself. Macklin goes to China to
fight a plague. Iris is left with her sins and her conscience.

HELL FREEZES OVER

(25 performances)

A tragedy in three acts by John Patrick. Produced by George
Kondolf at the Ritz Theatre, New York, December 28, 1935.

Cast of characters—

Swede......................................Frank Tweddell
Allan......................................Louis Calhern
Tommy......................................Richard Abert
Ace..George Tobias

Sparks..John Litel
John..Lee Baker
Clark...Myron McCormick
    Acts I, II and III.—Interior of the Wrecked Dirigible "White
Hope" Somewhere on the Polar Plateau.
    Staged by Joshua Logan; setting by John Root.

The dirigible "White Hope," carrying a party of explorers to
the South Pole, crashes in the ice wastes. All but seven of the
party are killed. The survivors die variously before the evening
is over. Two by exposure when they go in search of relief; two
by gunshot wounds when they discover that one, Allan, had
seduced the wife of another, Sparks, and they try to beat each
other to the draw; two by poison, administered by the doctor of
the expedition to a boy with a crushed leg and to himself. The
last of the party dies by starvation, he being left handcuffed to
the wreck by the duelists.

TOMORROW'S A HOLIDAY

(8 performances)

A drama in three acts adapted by Romney Brent from the
German of Leo Perutz and Hans Adler. Produced by John Golden
in association with Joseph Schildkraut at the Golden Theatre,
New York, December 30, 1935.

Cast of characters—

Ella Heffner..Doris Dalton
Colonel Geyer...Cyril Scott
Toni Heffner..Curt Bois
Paul Siebert..King Calder
Otto Eltz...Donald Foster
Baron Traising..................................Joseph Schildkraut
A Girl...Kathleen Moran
Robert Heym..William David
Countess Melnitz.................................Millicent Hanley
Station Master...................................Maurice Freeman
Ernesto Trivelli.................................Raymond Bramley
Dr. Schirmer...Jack Leslie
Mitzi..Janet Fox
Scheibel...Charles Halton
Planner..James La Curto
Brosig...Robert Burton
Oppen..Gage Clark
A Patient...S. Miller Kent
A Butler..Royal Stout
A Nurse...Mary Power
Other Parts Played by: Winifred Johnston, Charles Walton, William
    Forman, Henry Sherwood, Herbert Duffy, Carl Urbont, Leon
    Stern, Mavis Walsh, Stephen John, Ben Roberts, Charles Martin,
    Victor Colton, Joseph Singer, Richard Salasian, William Pike and
    Donald MacMillan.
    Acts I and III.—The Heffner Home, Vienna. Act II.—Scene 1—
An Office in a Railroad Station. 2—A Café. 3—Room in the Jockey
Club.
    Staged by George S. Kaufman; settings by Woodman Thompson.

Toni Heffner, a minor bank executive, is short 8,000 kronen in his accounts. The company examiner is to go over the books the next day, which is a holiday, and Toni cannot raise the money to cover the shortage. Baron Traising, a friend with gambling connections, agrees to try poker. He wins enough, but being taunted as a quitter by the losers, stakes the pile on a cut of the cards and loses. Toni faces the examiner expecting jail, but the Baron has sat in at another and later game and the day is saved.

MID-WEST

(22 performances)

A drama in three acts by James Hagan. Produced by Messrs. Shubert at the Booth Theatre, New York, January 7, 1936.

Cast of characters—

Beulah Zanhiser	Jean Adair
Hilda Zanhiser	Bernadine Hayes
Tooteboy Zanhiser	Van Heflin
Reverend Carr	Frank Wilcox
C. D. Aker	Cliff Heckinger
Jim Meed	Edgar Nelson
Luke Zanhiser	Curtis Cooksey
Fred Zanhiser	Don Dillaway
Bigwash Rowell	John Alexander
Jipinweed Bandy	Walter Baldwin
Roy Meeker	David Byrne
Ed Hendee	Eugene Keith
Doc Tanner	Dodson Mitchell
Lee Bragg	Richard Taber

Acts I, II and III.—The Farm of Luke Zanhiser in Middle-West. Staged by Melville Burke; setting by Watson Barratt.

Luke and Beulah Zanhiser have reared a family on a drought-ridden mid-Western farm and struggled through many years of discouraging experiences. Two sons have been lost in the war, one daughter is dead, another married and living in California. A third son, Fred, is restless at home and a fourth, Tooteboy, for whom the most sacrifices were made, is back from an eastern college preaching communism to the field hands. When Tooteboy is about to organize a strike the neighbors organize a vigilante group and hang him. Fred and his wife decide to go to Detroit. Leaving Luke and Beulah to begin life all over again on the farm.

O EVENING STAR

(5 performances)

A comedy in prologue and three acts by Zoe Akins. Produced by Harry Moses at the Empire Theatre, New York, January 8, 1936.

Cast of characters—

An Auctioneer	Foster J. Williams
Ellis Charteris	Frank Fenton
Agnes Jessey	Merle Maddern
The Auctioneer's Assistant	George Justin
A Woman	Grace Fox
Amy Bellaire	Jobyna Howland
Ronald Bland	Anderson Lawlor
Richard	Biacouren Yoshiwara
Dr. Wolfram	Hans Hansen
Frau Wolfram	Edith Andree
Alice Whitridge	Whitney Bourne
Mr. Howard	Frank Conroy
Mrs. Hopper	Vera Hurst
Madame Marie	Josie Intropidi
Lillian Bunn	Joan Engel
Dr. Boyd	James Todd
The Studio Gate Keeper	Jack Ball
The Studio Guard	Ross Chetwynd
Miss Leland	Mary Howes
Ben Martin	Eddie Albert
Ed	Ezra Stone
The Assistant Director	O. Z. Whitehead
The Actress Playing "Hannah"	Ethel Intropidi
The Camera Man	B. D. Krans
The Actor Playing "The Half Breed"	Alexander Micone
The Professor	Edward Jephson
Mr. Strassberg	Edward Emerson
Walter	Regis Joyce
The Radio Announcer	Patterson Greene
Edward Sothern Paul	John Raby

People at the Auction—Studio Personnel, etc.: Sara Floyd, Myrtle Ross, Quina Bilotti, Carrie Weller, Emily Draper, Virginia Gregori, Annette Robinson, Jenny Mac, Maxine Marlowe, Ada Elliott, George Lambert, Joe Fields, Earl Talbot, Richard Ogden, Larry Williams, Al Fields.

Prologue.—Amy Bellaire's House, Riverside Drive, New York, 1917. Act I.—Agnes Jessey's House, Hollywood, 1931. Act II.—Scene 1—Amy Bellaire's Flat, Hollywood. 2—Outside Gate of Motion Picture Studio. 3—On the Set. Act III.—Scenes 1 and 3—Amy Bellaire's House on Hill overlooking Hollywood. 2—Radio Announcer's Desk.

Staged by Leontine Sagan; settings by Stewart Chaney.

Amy Bellaire, one-time toast of the town in musical comedy, is reduced to bankruptcy and forced to auction her possessions in New York in 1917. Fifteen years later she is penniless in Hollywood, forgotten in the profession, looking for work as an extra in pictures. Engaged to play a pioneer mother in a Western story Amy has a chance to substitute for the leading woman. She burlesques the scene, catches the eye of the company head, is signed to a contract and eventually stages a sensational comeback. A few months after her triumph she dies of cancer.

TRULY VALIANT

(1 performance)

A drama in three acts by Irving Stone. Produced by Gustav Blum in association with Ernest W. Mandeville at the 49th Street Theatre, New York, January 9, 1936.

Cast of characters—

Esa Cranby, Ph.D. ....Ian Maclaren
Martha Cranby......................................Martha Mayo
Dale Cranby..Alan Handley
Berna Bowen.....................................Margot Stevenson
    Acts I, II and III.—Living Room of Professor Cranby's Home
near a Western University.
    Staged by Gustav Blum; setting by Louis Bromberg.

Berna Bowen, student, comes to the home of Prof. Esa Cranby
to serve as maid, be tutored by the professor and work her way
through college. Dale Cranby, the professor's undergraduate son,
falls in love with Berna and she with him. When Dale proposes
marriage Berna is forced to confess an affair with the professor,
as a result of which she is to bear a child. Prof. Cranby is willing
to divorce his wife and abandon his career to marry Berna. Martha Cranby, the wife, insists he shall go on with his career and let
her care for the child. Dale Cranby is willing to forgive and forget
all, taking his little half-brother into his home with Berna.
Which, by promise, he does.

GRANITE

(8 performances)

A drama in four acts by Clemence Dane. Revived by Charles
Hammerslough at the Vanderbilt Theatre, New York, January
13, 1936.

Cast of characters—

Penny Holt..Phyllis Welch
Jordan Morris..................................Len D. Hollister
Judith ....Mary Morris
Prosper ....Byron McGrath
The Nameless Man.............................Robert H. Gordon
A Clergyman...Jack Soanes
    Acts I, II, III and IV.—Living Room of Farm on Lundy Island.
    Staged by Charles Hammerslough; setting by Clark Robinson.

For many years Judith Morris has lived as the wife of Jordan
Morris on the island of Lundy, off the English coast. Lundy is a
granite rock onto which Jordan lures passing ships by putting
out false lights, salvaging the cargoes washed ashore. Judith,
mad with loneliness, desperately in love with Prosper Morris, a
visiting brother of Jordan's, promises her soul to the devil if she
may enjoy Prosper's favor. A Stranger washed ashore from a
stranded convict ship overhears Judith's prayer. He agrees, in
payment for food and shelter, to kill any man who abuses her. In
time the Stranger kills Jordan Morris, permitting Judith's marriage with Prosper. As Prosper also grows brutal and avaricious

the Stranger topples him off the cliff. Leaving Judith to Lundy and the Stranger.

I WANT A POLICEMAN

(47 performances)

A comedy in two acts by Rufus King and Milton Lazarus. Produced by Francis Curtis and Richard Myers at the Lyceum Theatre, New York, January 14, 1936.

Cast of characters—

Eric Davidson	Dudley Hawley
Karl	Con MacSunday
Fern Davidson	Sylvia Field
Police Commissioner Baldwin	Paul Huber
Alfaro	Weldon Heyburn
John Davidson	Eric Wollencott
Jepson	Harold Morfet
Dennis	Clinton Sundberg
Charles Talbot	Wendy Atkin
Eleanore Breen	Estelle Winwood
Lady Breen	Larry Bolton
Cotswold	Barry Sullivan
Captain Lynch	Frederick Graham
Arthur Semple	

Act I.—Scene 1—Eric Davidson's Bedroom, Oldhampton, L. I. 2—Police Headquarters. 3—Telephone Booth. 4 and 5—Living Room at Oldhampton. Act II.—Scene 1—Police Headquarters. 2 and 4—Living Room at Oldhampton. 3—Fern's Bedroom.
Staged by Arthur Sircom; settings by Cleon Throckmorton.

Eric Davidson, dying, steals the diary of his second wife, Fern Davidson. The diary contains uncomplimentary references to himself, and he intends sending it to the police. In a struggle for copies of the pages Davidson is shot with the revolver he draws on Fern. Police investigation and circumstantial evidence place the crime on Fern. She looks guilty until curtain time, when the real murderer is revealed in John Davidson, a goofy son of Eric by his first wife. John hated his father because of his treatment of his mother.

RUSSET MANTLE

(117 performances)

A comedy in three acts by Lynn Riggs. Produced by Jerome Mayer and Murray Jay Queen at the Masque Theatre, New York, January 16, 1936.

Cast of characters—

Horace Kincaid	Jay Fassett
Pablo	Harry Bellaver
Susanna Kincaid	Evelyn Varden

Effie Rowley.....................................Margaret Douglass
Manuelita...Helen Craig
Kay Rowley......................................Martha Sleeper
Scoot ....James Larmore
John Galt...John Beal
Mrs. Fawcett.....................................Clare Woodbury
Salvador ....Chief Bear
Dr. Brown.......................................Frederick Barton
    Acts I and III.—Portal of Kincaid Ranch in Santa Fe. Act II.—
The Chicken House.
    Staged by Robert Ross; settings by Donald Oenslager.

John Galt, a young poet tramping the West, applies at the New
Mexico farm of Horace Kincaid for work. Kincaid takes him on
provisionally. Kay Rowley, visiting niece of the Kincaids and
something of a social rebel, is attracted to Galt and he to her.
Their youthful disgust with the failures of the older generation
lead them into an expression of their own freedom which results
in the usual biological consequences. John is ready to face the
world an unmarried father. Kay hesitates about giving up her
luxuries as the daughter of a Louisville banker, but goes finally
with John.

A ROOM IN RED AND WHITE

(25 performances)

A drama in eight scenes by Roy Hargrave with the assistance of
Laura Adair and Thomas Schofield. Produced by Dwight Deere
Wiman and George Kondolf at the 46th Street Theatre, New
York, January 18, 1936.

Cast of characters—

Lawrence Crandall.............................Richard Kendrick
Joan Haviland......................................Louise Platt
Beatrice Crandall.................................Chrystal Herne
Philip Crandall.....................................Leslie Adams
Elinor Humphreys................................Brenda Dahlen
Robert Humphreys................................Joshua Logan
Marion Mellon.....................................Ivy Troutman
John Mellon...Karl Stall
Stewart ....William Sanders
Peter Mansky.......................................Tenen Holtz
    Scenes—Crandall Drawing Room.
    Staged by Roy Hargrave; setting by Jo Mielziner; gowns by
Elizabeth Hawes.

Philip Crandall is mad. His chief obsession is that his wife,
Beatrice, deliberately and continuously deceives him. In retaliation he treats Beatrice brutally in private and with marked kindness in public and she shields him from exposure. When Philip's
madness spreads to include his son Lawrence, whom he links in
unnatural friendship to his mother, Lawrence and Beatrice decide
their only escape is to make way with Philip. They trick him into

the writing of a suicide note and put arsenic in his coffee. After Philip dies in torment Lawrence and Beatrice discover that he was a victim of cancer, which could account for his madness and would have probably taken his life within a short time.

RUTH DRAPER

(9 performances)

A repertory of dramatic sketches. Presented at the Booth Theatre, New York, January 19, 1936.

Sketches—

At a Children's Party in Philadelphia
Three Women and Mr. Clifford
A Miner's Wife
In a Church in Italy
The Italian Lesson
A Dalmatian Peasant in the Hall of a New York Hospital
Doctors
Vive la France
A Quiet Morning in Bed
On a Porch in a Maine Coast Village
Three Breakfasts
Le Retour de l'Aveugle
The Debutante
In a Railroad Station on the Western Plains

ETHAN FROME

(120 performances)

A drama in prologue, three acts and epilogue by Owen and Donald Davis, suggested by a previous dramatization by Lowell Barrington of a novel of the same name by Edith Wharton. Produced by Max Gordon at the National Theatre, New York, January 21, 1936.

Cast of characters—

Harmon Gow	John Winthrop
A Young Man	Oliver Barbor
Ethan Frome	Raymond Massey
Zenobia Frome	Pauline Lord
Dennis Eady	Tom Ewell
Mattie Silver	Ruth Gordon
Jotham	Francis Pierlot
Ed Varnum	Charles Henderson
Ned Hale	W. Dana Hardwick
Ruth Varnum	Sylvia Weld
Mrs. Hale	Marie Falls

Citizens of Starkfield: Catherine Carey, Virgilia Chew, Virginia Frank, Beatrice Graham, Eddie James, Pam Lawrence, Evelyn Monte, William Morris, Ella Morrice, George Parkes, Arthur Rosen, Elmira Sessions, Tom Tempest, Jessie Wilson

Prologue.—Outside Frome Farmhouse near Starkfield, Northern
New England. Act I.—Scene 1—Farmhouse Kitchen. 2—Outside
Vestry of Starkfield Congregational Church. 3—Crest of Hill. 4—
Outside Farmhouse. Act II.—Scene 1—Bedroom. 2 and 3—Kitchen.
Act III.—Scene 1—Bedroom. 2—Kitchen. 3—Crest of Hill. Epilogue
—Kitchen.
Staged by Guthrie McClintic; settings by Jo Mielziner.

See page 321.

THE ILLUSTRATORS' SHOW

(5 performances)

A revue in two parts assembled by the Society of Illustrators,
amplified and edited by Tom Weatherly; music and lyrics by
Frank Loesser and Irving Actman. Produced by Tom Weatherly
at the 48th Street Theatre, New York, January 22, 1936.

Principals engaged—

Helen Lynd	Earl Oxford
Niela Goodelle	Robert Berry
Phyllis Cameron	Otto Soglow
Davenie Watson	Fred Cooper
Elizabeth Houston	Joe Donatello
Norman Lind	Dan Harden
Edward Mowen	O. Z. Whitehead
Betty Gillette	William Houston

Gomez and Winona

Staged by Tom Weatherly; dances and musical numbers by Carl
Randall; sketches by Allen Delano; music directed by Gene Salzer;
settings by Arne Lundborg from designs by the Society of Illustrators; costumes by Carl Sidney; curtain by Russell Patterson.

THE PURITAN

(4 performances)

A tragedy in two acts adapted by Chester Erskin from Liam
O'Flaherty's novel. Produced by Mr. Erskin at the Belmont
Theatre, New York, January 23, 1936.

Cast of characters—

Mrs. Kelly....................................Caroline Newcomb
Mr. Fitzgerald....................................Gerard Hayden
Francis Ferriter....................................Denis O'Dea
By permission of The Abbey Theatre Players of Dublin
Dr. Michael O'Leary..................................Jack Hartley
Policeman ....Mitchel Harris
Callahan ....Gordon Nelson
Lavan ....Gavin Muir
Patrick Corish....................................Philip Bishop
Vesey.......................................George R. Taylor
Mrs. Ferriter....................................Catherine Proctor
Aunt Mary......................................Elwynn Harvey
Professor Mellett..................................J. P. Wilson

Agnes Mellett................................Beatrice Hendricks
Priest...George R. Taylor
Kitty ....Gertrude Flynn
Waiter.......................................Lawrence M. Hurdle
Madge ....Ruth Chorpenning
Lizzie ....Vera Mellish
Mrs. Shea...Marie Hunt
Moran ....Charles Gerrard
Act I.—Scene 1—Hallway in Rooming House, Dublin, Ireland. 2—
Francis Ferriter's Room. 3—Teresa Burke's Sitting Room. 4—Office
of Patrick Corish, Newspaper Editor. 5—Superintendent's Office at
Police Headquarters. 6—Professor Mellett's Home. Act II.—Scene
1—Francis Ferriter's Room. 2—A Church. 3—Back Room in a Pub.
4—Brothel Parlor. 5—Bedroom in the Brothel. 6—Teresa Burke's
Bedroom.
    Staged by Chester Erskin; settings by C. M. Williams.

Francis Ferriter, ruled by the religious zeal of a fanatic, kills
Kitty, a prostitute, in the hope of saving her soul, following his
discovery that she is the victim of a rich man's son. Hounded by
the police and his conscience, he seeks relief in prayer and at the
confessional. Convinced finally that his murderous impulse was
stimulated by his own repressed lust and jealousy, Francis stabs
himself to death.

LADY PRECIOUS STREAM

(105 performances)

A drama in four acts by S. I. Hsiung. Produced by Morris Gest
at the Booth Theatre, New York, January 27, 1936.

Cast of characters—

Honorable Reader...................................Mai-Mai Sze
Property Men.........................Norman Stuart, Jesse Wynne
His Excellency Wang Yun, the Prime Minister.....Clarence Derwent
Madam Wang ....Molly Pearson
Su, The Dragon General..........................Henry Morrell
Wei, the Tiger General............................Detmar Poppen
Golden Stream......................................Helen Kimm
Silver Stream.....................................Marcella Abels
Precious Stream.................................Helen Chandler
Her Maid.......................................Sally Fitzpatrick
Hsieh Ping-Kuei.............................Bramwell Fletcher
Suitors....Preston Tuttle, Will Claire, Slater Barkentin, Harry Selby
The Princess of the Western Regions..............Natalie Schafer
Ma Ta...Albert Whitley
Kiang Hai.......................................Preston Tuttle
Maids to the Princess.................Joan Adrian, Lilian Dushell,
                              Joan Miller, Sally Fitzpatrick
General Mu.......................................Henry Morrell
Executioner ....Gilbert Ralston
The Minister of Foreign Affairs.......................Will Claire
Act I.—Garden of Prime Minister. Act II.—Cave of Hsieh Ping-
Kuei. Act III.—Part 1—The Western Regions. 2—The Cave. Act
IV.—Part 1—Garden of the Prime Minister. 2—Temporary Court of
King of the Western Regions.
    Staged by Dr. Hsiung; costumes designed by Mei Lan-Fang.

Lady Precious Stream is the youngest daughter of Wang
Yun, the Prime Minister. Scorning a choice of three noble young

suitors selected by her father, her ladyship decides to marry Hsieh Ping-Kuei, her father's gardener, who is both acrobat and poet. Following a short honeymoon in a cave, Hsieh is sent to the Western Provinces, where he becomes a great General in the wars and later King of the West. When, eighteen years later, the politicians would marry him to a Western Princess, Hsieh returns to Lady Precious Stream and, finding her still loyal, resumes his position as her husband, becomes the ruler of all China. Arranging the marriage of the Western Princess with an amorous Minister of Foreign Affairs, Hsieh and Lady Precious Stream are in a fair way to live happily ever after.

* CALL IT A DAY

(170 performances)

A comedy in three acts by Dodie Smith. Produced by the Theatre Guild, Inc., at the Morosco Theatre, New York, January 28, 1936.

Cast of characters—

Dorothy Hilton	Gladys Cooper
Roger Hilton	Philip Merivale
Vera	Valerie Cossart
Ann Hilton	Jeanne Dante
Martin Hilton	John Buckmaster
Catherine Hilton	Florence Williams
Cook	Florence Edney
Mrs. Milsom	Lillian Brennard Tonge
Paul Francis	Glenn Anders
Ethel Francis	Frances Williams
Muriel Weston	Viola Roache
Frank Haines	Lawrence Grossmith
Elsie Lester	Esther Mitchell
Beatrice Gwynne	Claudia Morgan
Alistair Brown	William Packer
Joan Collett	Mary Mason

Act I.—Scene 1—Roger and Dorothy Hilton's Bedroom in Their House in St. John's Wood, London. 2—Kitchen. 3—Dining Room. Act II.—Scene 1—Paul Francis' Studio in Holland Park. 2—Frank Haines' Flat in Jermyn Street. 3—Roger Hilton's Office in Grey's Inn. Act III.—Scene 1—Back Garden of Hilton House. 2—Ann and Catherine Hilton's Bedroom. 3—Roger and Dorothy Hilton's Bedroom. Staged by Tyrone Guthrie; settings by Lee Simonson.

See page 277.

ZIEGFELD FOLLIES

(115 performances)

A musical revue in two parts. Produced at the Winter Garden, New York, January 30, 1936.

Principals engaged—

Fannie Brice
Josephine Baker
Gertrude Niesen
Harriet Hoctor
Cherry Preisser
June Preisser
Eve Arden
Judy Canova

Bob Hope
Stan Kavanagh
Hugh O'Connell
Duke McHale
Rodney McLennan
John Hoysradt
Nicholas Brothers
California Varsity Eight

Staged by John Murray Anderson; settings by Vincente Minelli.

PRODUCTIONS BY THE FEDERAL THEATRE PROJECT

WALK TOGETHER CHILLUN

(29 performances)

A drama in two acts by Frank Wilson. Produced by the Negro
Theatre Unit of the Federal Theatre Project of the WPA at the
Lafayette Theatre, New York, February 2, 1936.

Cast of characters—

Judge Walters.................................J. Francis O'Reilly
Dr. Stratton...................................Cornelius Donnelly
K. C. Hawkes...................................Bertram Miller
Jim Manderville................................John Hayden
Bessie Holden..................................Be-Be Townsend
Mr. Primero....................................Percy Verwayne
Reverend Smiley................................Oliver Foster
Martha Ray Browne..............................Hilda Offley
Eli Jackson....................................Gus Smith
Alexander......................................Charles Taylor
Aubrey Gladman.................................Julian Costello
Hot Rock.......................................Abner Dorsey
Blibbie Jones..................................Alonzo Bosen
Old Face.......................................Al Watts
Tiny...Alberta Perkins
Henry..Hudson Prince
Hermantine.....................................Christola H. Williams
Blibbie's Wife.................................Wilhelmina Williams
Willy James....................................Lionel Monagas
Mrs. Stallings.................................Frances Smith
Southerners: Sidney Easten, Mary Goodwin, Hilda French, William
   Cumberpatch, Otis Morse, Ida Roley, Aimee Bates, Irene Elling-
   ton, Henry Williams, Marguerite Perry, Evelyn Davis, Josephine
   Heathman, Effie McDowell, Jean Cutler, Chauncey Worrell, Theo-
   dore Howard, Louis Godfrey, Emanuel Middleton, Milton Lacy,
   Louis Gilbert, Howard Taylor, Harold Taylor, Hilda Bell.
Northerners: Juanita Baker, Sadie Ricks, Virginia Girvin, Walter
   Duke, Helen Carter, Myrtle Simms, Merrit Smith, Walter Brogs-
   dale, Hallie Howard, Lena Halsey, Harry G. Grant, Essie Frier-
   son, Nancy Hunt, Ella Emanuel, James Wright, Jose Miralda,
   Ethel Millner.
Musicians: Roy Holland, Gabriel Brown, Joseph N. Breen, Virgil
   Van Clive.
   Act I.—Scene 1—The Board Room, Mechanics Hall. 2—Eli's
Shack. 3—Recreation Room, St. David's Church. Act II.—Scene 1—
Bland's Barn. 2—Eli's Shack. 3—Board Room, Mechanics Hall. 4—
St. David's Church.
   Staged by Frank Wilson and J. De Witt Spencer under the super-
vision of John Houseman; settings by Manuel Easman; choral arrange-
ment and direction by Leonard De Paur.

To do necessary work in a Northern village a hundred Negroes are imported from the South because they work for little money. Arriving in the North the Southern blacks are boycotted by their own people as interlopers and by the whites as inferiors. The plea is for racial unity.

JEFFERSON DAVIS

(3 performances)

A drama in three acts by John McGee. Produced by the Federal Theatre Project at the Biltmore Theatre, New York, February 18, 1936.

Cast of characters—

Burton Harrison, Secretary to Jefferson Davis	Thomas Carnahan
Robert, a slave, Davis' personal servant	Louis Gibbs
Robert Barnwell, Senator from South Carolina	Halbert Brown
Henry Graham, Physician to Davis	William Mulligan
Varina Davis	Mrs. William Courtleigh
Jefferson Davis	Guy Standing, Jr.
C. C. Clay, Jr., of Alabama	Robert Toms
William Seward, of New York	James Houston
Senator Grimes, of Iowa	Oscar Schoemaker
Governor Moore, of Alabama	Harry McKee
William Yancey, of Alabama	Ray Rawlings
Robert Toombs, Secretary of State	Charles Douglass
Alexander H. Stephens, Vice-President of the Confederacy	Charles Peyton Glockner
Leroy Walker, Secretary of War	William Parke, Jr.
Judah P. Benjamin, Attorney General	Harry Golson
William Mallory, Secretary of the Navy	Lawrence Stanhope
J. H. Reagan, of Texas	Wilbur DeRouge
Constance Cary, of Baltimore	Mildred Byron
Hetty Cary, of Baltimore	Virginia Barrie
Mary Chestnut, of Charleston	Jean Newcombe
Gen. P. T. Beauregarde	Lawrence O'Brien
Gen. Joseph Johnston	F. Clay Cody
Gen. Robert E. Lee	George Duthie
Henry Foote, of Tennessee	Frederick Smith
Senator Wigfall, of Texas	Ray Rawlings
Senator Rhett, of South Carolina	William Mulligan
Governor Smith, of Virginia	Earl Mayo
J. C. Breckenridge	Ray Southwick

Act I.—Scene 1—Jefferson Davis' Office, Washington. 2—Before the Exchange Hotel, Montgomery, Alabama. 3—Room in White House. Act II.—Scene 1—Costume Ball, Richmond, Va. 2 and 5—Office of Jefferson Davis, Richmond. 3 and 6—Morning Room in White House. 4—Capitol Building, Richmond. 7—Metropolitan Hall, Richmond. Act III.—Scene 1—Morning Room in White House, Richmond. 2—Room in House of Colonel J. Taylor Wood at Greensboro, North Carolina. Epilogue—Hollywood Cemetery, Richmond.

Staged by Henry Stillman and Charles Schofield under supervision of Kay McKay; settings by Cleon Throckmorton and costumes designed by Ivan Glidden built in Federal Theatre Workshop.

An episodic and sympathetic recital of decisive moments in the life of the President of the Confederacy through which the attitude of the South before and through the Civil War is defended and the political intrigues that destroyed faith in Jefferson Davis are exposed.

AMERICAN HOLIDAY

(20 performances)

A play in three acts by Edwin L. and Albert Barker. Produced by the Popular Price Theatre, Federal Theatre Project, at the Manhattan Theatre, New York, February 21, 1936.

Cast of characters—

Orvie Gibbs	Ronald Brogan
Marcia Hollister	Elizabeth Morgan
Clem Ferris	John Junior
Newt Sproegel	George Probert
Neal McCarter	Edward Forbes
Bessie Kinnealy	Gladys Parke
Joe Lash	Jon Lormer
Miss Mary	Julia Fassett
Mrs. Huggins	Bessie English
Mr. Huggins	George MacEntee
Jack Hollister	Whitner Bissell
Dr. Rudd	Louis Frohoff
George Manley	James Fallon
Sheriff Tom Dillard	Walter Lawrence
Mrs. McCarter	Lois Bolton
Hanvey Hollister	Henry Buckler
Charles Copenhaver	Leopold Badia
Julianna Copenhaver	Elinor Flynn
Ike	Charles Wagenheim
A Guest	Martin Noble
Jimmie Ward	Tom Greenway
Ripley	Jack Egan
State Senator Gibbs	Bert Wilcox
Burke	Dan Tobin
First Alienist	Doan Borup
Second Alienist	Charles Burrows
Whoopee Ruby Somers	Janet Rathbun
Man with Balloons	Alan Wallace
Blaine	Lewis McMichael
Miss Larue	Suzanne Caubaye
Rev. Sweet	Walter Plinge
Orvie's Aunt	Pearl Hight
Orvie's Uncle	Charles Esdale
Mr. Epstein	Alfred Allegro
Messenger boy	Paul Jacchia

Acts I, II and III.—Lobby of Hollister House in Middletown, County Seat in Central United States.

Staged by Halstead Welles, Lucius More Cook and Agnes Morgan under supervision of Edward Goodman; settings by Tom Adrian Cracraft.

A girl is killed. A boy is accused of her murder. Newspaper reporters sensationalize every circumstantial incident. The story becomes a national scandal, "the crime of the century." The town of Middletown, where action centers, is turned into a bedlam of notoriety and jammed with special correspondents, press photographers, and publicity-seeking celebrities. The boy is acquitted at the trial and joins an evangelist for a lecture tour of the country. Middletown is practically ruined by the crime circus.

A WOMAN OF DESTINY

(35 performances)

A play in three acts by Samuel Jesse Warshawsky. Produced by the Managers Try Out Theatre of the WPA Federal Theatre Project under the supervision of George Miller and Otto Metzger at the Willis Theatre, New York, March 2, 1936.

Cast of characters—

Dick Harmon	Horace Head
Bob Stillman	J. Warren Lyons
President Cumberland	Robert Harrison
Secretary of State Williamson	Tom Morrison
Senator Mora	Walter Green
Chief Justice Burke	Carlton Macy
Secretary of Treasury Bright	Howard Hall
Postmaster General Watson	John F. Morrissey
Secretary of Labor Boyle	Lee Beggs
Secretary of the Interior Maclennon	Robert Conness
Secretary of War Sherman	Henry Sherwood
Ambassador Leonid Korakin	Boris Korlin
Ambassador Takahiro Maru	Frank Verigun
Newspaper Reporters	Theodore Collins George C. Mantell Ralph Simone
"Buttons"	Kermit Augustine
Radio Announcer	Joseph Guthrie
Kathryn Lawrence	Terry Carlson
Gene Goodwin	Robert Perry
Stephen Talmadge	William Roselle
Sam Wright	George Zorn
Melrock	George Henry Trader
Bishop Grimshaw	Fuller Mellish
Art Sullivan	Roger Quinlan
Ruth Goodwin	Alice Cavanaugh
Mrs. Rice	Dorothy Raymond
Constance Goodwin	Alexandra Carlisle
Marcus Roseheim	William Malville
Bannister	William Brady
Stoneleigh	Wilfred Clark
Roger Harmon	Walter Scott Weeks
Murray Hoyt	Dillon M. Deasey

Act I.—Reception Room of Constance Goodwin's Suite, Tenth Floor Chicago Hotel. Act II.—Scene 1—Executive Office, President of U. S., Washington, D. C. 2—Garden outside Home of Constance Goodwin, Washington, D. C. Act III.—Cabinet Room.
Staged by Edward Vail; settings by Cleon Throckmorton.

Mrs. Constance Goodwin, flanked by powerful politicians, publishers, and a strong woman's delegation, deadlocks the National Republican Convention by her efforts to include an anti-war plank in the party platform. The opposition agrees to the platform, and nominates Mrs. Goodwin for Vice-President. The Party is swept into office. The opposition, led by Roger Harmon, continues to cry for a breakup of the Far Eastern Alliance. The assassination of the American Ambassador forces the President to declare war with Japan. He dies of a heart attack, and Mrs. Goodwin, now President, determines to affect peace. Deserted by her Cabinet, she contacts the Japanese Emperor, appeals to his reason and personal desire for peace. The Emperor and Mrs. Goodwin agree to withdraw their armed forces and thus avert war.

CHALK DUST

(51 performances)

A drama in three acts by Harold A. Clarke and Maxwell Nurnberg. Produced by the Experimental Theatre of the Federal Theatre Project at the Experimental Theatre, New York, March 4, 1936.

Cast of characters—

Dr. Harriman.....................................Herschel Cropper
Mr. Madison......................................George Smithfield
Mr. Fuller...William Hitch
Miss Kittredge..Faith Avery
Miss Duffy......................................Georgiana Brand
Miss Strang......................................Lida McMillan
Miss Sherwood...............................Katherine Standing
Kaplan ....Shimen Ruskin
Brown ....Frederic Giuliano
Mr. Allen Rogers.............................Mitchell Grayson
Miss Bohn..Eugenia Woods
Mr. Dana...John Adair
Miss Murtagh....................................Bertha Willsea
Miss Williams...................................Violet McKinley
Miss Merriweather..............................Lisa Rembova
Dr. Basingstoke...................................Alan MacAteer
The Elevator Man..................................John Carr
Mr. Phipps......................................Jerome Sheldon
Doozek ....George Yesner
Mr. Westbrook.................................George Pembroke
Miss McInerney.................................Dorothy Readick
Pupils: Amelia Romano, Beth Cantreau, Frances Victory, Trudy Goldrich, Louise Kirby, Eleanor Scherr, George Yesner, Roslyn Gilbert, Maryn Myers, Arthur Singer, Monty Ash, Richard Huett.
Teachers: Dorothy Nolan, Ymske Tyssen, Minnie Lithgow, Philip C. Jones, Gordon Fitts.
Acts I, II and III.—Central High School in American City.
Staged by Virgil Geddes and James Light; settings by Howard Bay.

Teachers Sherwood and Rogers protest the regimentation of high school instructors. Because of their activities they are forced to suffer the belittling and degrading of their love romance through the malicious gossip and political influences obtaining in a high school organization.

CONJUR MAN DIES

(24 performances)

A comedy in three acts by Rudolph Fisher. Produced by The Negro Theatre of the Federal Theatre Project at the Lafayette Theatre, New York, March 11, 1936.

Cast of characters—

Dr. John Archer	Lionel Monagas
Bubber Brown	William Brown
Jinx Jenkins	Irving Ellis
Detective Sergeant Perry Dart	Dooley Wilson
Aramintha Snead	Estelle Hemsley
Martha Crouch	Dorothy Paul
Hanks	Paul Johnson
Brady	Jay Mondaaye
Samuel Crouch	Louis Sharp
Smitty	Phil Thomas
Brooks	Walter Brogsdale
Dr. Winkler	Bertram Miller
Small	Emanuel Middleton
Landlady	Jaqueline Martin
Easley Jones	George Spelvin
Spider Webb	Percy Verwayne
Doty Hicks	Wardell Saunders
Entertainer	Francis Smith
Tynes, Fingerprint Man	Julian Costello
M'Gana Frimbo	Fritz Weller
Man on the Stoop	Walter Duke
Girl	Mozelle Holmes

Cabaret Patrons: Rose Poindexter, Mary Goodwin, Aselean Lynch, Almee Bates, Ethel Drayton, Leona Hemmingway, Josephine Heathman, Virginia Girvin, Maud Ward, Gena May Brown, Ernest Brown, Roy Holland, Louie Godfrey, Alonzo Bozan, Abner Dorsey, Clarence Fotter, Charles Collins, and William Cumberbatch.

Singers (Under the direction of Stanley Bennett): Josephine Heathman, Virginia Girvin, Frances Smith, Lavinia Turner, Estella Miller, Leona Hemmingway, Alonzo Bozan, Abner Dorsey, Louis Godfrey, Roy Holland, Milton Lacey and Adolph Henderson.

Act I—Scene 1—Crouch's Undertaking Parlor. 2—Frimbo's Bedroom. 3—Frimbo's Waiting Room. 4—Forty Club Cabaret. Act II.—Scenes 1 and 3—Street. 2—West 130th Street. 4—Forty Club Cabaret. 5—Frimbo's Black Room. Act III—Scenes 1 and 5—Street. 2—Frimbo's Cellar. 3—Dr. Archer's Office. 4—Frimbo's Black Room.

Staged by Augustus Smith and Joe Losey; settings by Manuel Easman.

M'Gana Frimbo, conjur man, is found dead in his studio, a wound on the side of his head, a handkerchief stuffed in his mouth. Investigations are begun by Dr. John Archer, scientist, and Detective Sergeant Perry Dart, assisted by Bubber Brown, an eager but dumb amateur sleuth. In the middle of the proceedings the conjur man apparently appears in the flesh. It may have been his assistant who was killed. During a recovery séance Frimbo is shot and stays shot.

THE LIVING NEWSPAPER

A series of news sketches written by a staff of seventy reporters and writers under the supervision of Morris Watson and Howard Cushman and dramatized by Arthur Arent and fifteen dramatists. Produced by The Federal Theatre under the supervision of Morris Watson, Ned Glass and John Brennan at the Biltmore Theatre, March 14, 1936. William Randolph, Jr., as narrator, headed a cast of 100 actors.

TRIPLE-A PLOWED UNDER

(85 performances)

Scene 1—War and Inflation. 2—Deflation. 3—Farmer to Worker. 4—Farmer's Holiday. 5—Milk Prices. 6—Farmers Organize. 7—Milk Strike. 8—Farm Sale. 9—Farmers' National Relief Conference. 10—Crops Burned. 11—Birth of Triple-A. 12—Commodities Skyrocket. 13—Drought. 14—Sharecroppers. 15—Detroit Meat Strike. 16—The Sherwood Case. 17—Supreme Court. 18—The Big "Steal." 19—Soil Conservation. 20—Finale.

Staged by Joe Losey and H. Gordon Graham; settings by Hjalmer Hermanson; music by Lee Wainer.

1935

(34 performances)

Produced May 12, 1936.

Scene 1—New Year's Eve. 2 and 11—The Great American Public. 3—Hauptmann. 4—Wagner-Connery Act. 5—Public Enemies. 6—Armament. 7—Barbara Hutton Weds. 8—Deboe Hanging. 9—Trivia. 10—Dutch Schultz. 12—Huey Long. 13—Olympics. 14—John Lewis. 15—Science. 16—China Clipper. 17—Herndon. 18—Finale.

Staged by H. Gordon Graham; settings by Hjalmar Hermanson; music by Lee Wainer.

The first of the Living Newspaper series, "Ethiopia," was rehearsed but withdrawn on advice from Washington.

MURDER IN THE CATHEDRAL

(38 performances)

A poetic drama in two parts by T. S. Eliot; music by A. Lehman Engel. Produced by The Popular Price Theatre, Federal Theatre Project, at the Manhattan Theatre, New York, March 20, 1936.

Cast of characters—

First woman of Canterbury.........................Iona Bright
Second woman of Canterbury.......................Georgia Harvey
Third woman of Canterbury........................Minnie Stanley
Fourth woman of Canterbury....................Camelia Campbell
Fifth woman of Canterbury........................Barna Ostertag
Sixth woman of Canterbury...........................Mabel Paige
Seventh woman of Canterbury.....................Helen Morrow
Eighth woman of Canterbury..........................Mary Roth
Ninth woman of Canterbury......................Bessie English
Tenth woman of Canterbury....................Charlotte Gloer
First priest....................................Robert Williamson
Second priest.......................................Harry Sothern
Third priest...Louis Prohoff
Herald ....David Friedkin
Archbishop Thomas à Becket.......................Harry Irvine
First tempter.....................................Tom Greenway
Second tempter....................................Joseph Draper
Third tempter.......................................George LeSoir
Fourth tempter.......................................Robert Bruce

First knight...Roger DeKoven
Second knight...................................Stephen Courtleigh
Third knight...Jon Lormer
Fourth knight....................................Frederick Tozere
Singing Chorus: Leopold Badia, John Battie, John James, Maria
    LaPorta, Vladimir Lepidinsky, Leo Nash, Peter Skrefstad, Alan
    Wallace, Chorus of the Negro Youth Theatre and Members of the
    Gilbert and Sullivan Operetta Company, Municipal Theatre
    Project.
Parts 1 and 2—In and about the Cathedral of Canterbury.
Staged by Edward Goodman and Halstead Welles; settings by Tom
Adrian Cracraft.

Thomas à Becket, Archbishop of Canterbury, following a six-year exile in France, returns to England after a partial reconciliation with King Henry II. Becket, having infuriated Henry through his utter devotion to the church, is made conscious of his impending defeat by the continued harassments put upon him by the King. He comes to accept martyrdom with grace and spiritual satisfaction, is murdered on the steps of the Cathedral by Henry's order and goes to his heavenly reward mourned by the flock which was devoted to him.

IN HEAVEN AND EARTH

(38 performances)

A play in three acts by Arthur Goodman and Washington Pezet. Produced by The Managers Try Out Theatre of the Federal Theatre Project of the WPA at the Willis Theatre, New York, March 26, 1936, under the supervision of Otto Metzger.

Cast of characters—

Dr. Joel Littlefield...................................Allan Tower
Judith Littlefield...............................Marguerite Walker
Bill Watts..Phil Brandon
Diana Hollister Littlefield........................Mary Hutchinson
Dr. Ronald Littlefield................................Carl Emory
Arthur Littlefield....................................Jack Effrat
Sarah ....Edith Harcourt
Claire Stanton...................................Louise Kirtland
Mrs. Stanton......................................Gwen Burrows
Mr. Stanton.....................................Herbert Dobbins
Alex Cranford, Jr. ....Mayon Pate
    Acts I, II and III.—Dr. Joel Littlefield's Home at Silver Mine,
Connecticut.
    Staged by J. J. White; settings by Rollo Wayne and Cleon Throck-
morton.

Dr. Joe Littlefield, eminent psychiatrist, is writing a book to prove his theory of "returning personality." Claire Stanton, a former patient of the doctor's, has an auto accident in front of the doctor's home and is brought in unconscious. The doctor, obsessed with the idea that she resembles his dead wife, whom he has loved dearly, hypnotizes her before she regains consciousness.

When she does she believes herself to be his wife, Lenore. Little-field is certain she's Lenore. Confronted by her family and her fiance, Alex Cranford, she persists in her illusions. Ronald, the doctor's son, attempts to hypnotize her and she pretends to be herself so she might break her engagement with Alex. Judith, the doctor's daughter, in a jealous rage attacks and knocks her down. She loses consciousness once more. Ronald begs his father to return her to her normal personality. He does so. She returns to consciousness as Claire Stanton.

* MACBETH

(56 performances)

Shakespeare's tragedy arranged in three acts and eight scenes by Orson Welles. Produced by the Negro division of the Federal Theatre Project under the supervision of John Houseman at the Lafayette Theatre, Harlem, New York, April 9, 1936.

Cast of characters—

Duncan	Service Bell
Malcolm	Wardell Saunders
Macduff	Maurice Ellis
Banquo	Canada Lee
Macbeth	Jack Carter
Ross	Frank David
Lennox	Thomas Anderson
Siward	Archie Savage
First Murderer	George Nixon
Second Murderer	Kenneth Renwick
The Doctor	Lawrence Chenault
The Priest	Al Watts
First Messenger	Philandre Thomas
Second Messenger	J. B. Johnson
The Porter	J. Lewis Johnson
Seyton	Larri Lauria
A Lord	Charles Collins
First Captain	Lisle Grenidge
Second Captain	Gabriel Brown
First Chamberlain	Halle Howard
Second Chamberlain	William Cumberbatch
First Court Attendant	Albert McCoy
Second Court Attendant	George Thomas
First Page Boy	Viola Dean
Second Page Boy	Hilda French
Lady Macduff	Marie Young
Lady Macbeth	Edna Thomas
The Duchess	Alma Dickson
The Nurse	Virginia Girvin
Young Macduff	Bertram Holmes
Daughter of Macduff	Wanda Macy
Fleance	Carl Crawford
Hecate	Eric Burroughs
First Witch	Wilhelmina Williams
Second Witch	Josephine Williams
Third Witch	Zola King
Witch Doctor	Abdul

Scenes laid in Jungles of Mythical Island Resembling Haiti in the West Indies.
Staged by Orson Welles; costumes and settings by Nat Karson; lighting by A. H. Feder.

A West Indian version of the Shakespeare tragedy with the text unaltered, the "jungle" scenes in which the witches figure extravagantly expanded and the cast put in fancy dress that suggested a garden party given by Eugene O'Neill's Emperor Jones to show off his court.

THE MISER

(3 performances)

The Molière play adapted by Alfred Saxe. Revived by the One-Act Experimental Theatre of the WPA Federal Theatre Project at the Experimental Theatre, New York, May 13, 1936.

Cast of characters—

Harpagon (The Miser)	William Lee
Valere (His Valet)	Curt Conway
Frosine (Matchmaker)	Virginia Devetzko
Master Jacques (His Cook)	Ben Ross
La Fleche (Servant)	Perry Bruskin
Brindavoine (Servant)	Vito Scozzari
La Merluche	Anne Gold

The action takes place in the Miser's Home. The 17th Century.
Staged by Alfred Saxe and Peter Hyun; settings by Samuel Leve.

Valere is in love with Elise. Harpagon, Elise's miserly father, opposes the match. Cleante, Elise's brother, and Marianne, his sweetheart, agree to help the lovers. Cleante's valet discovers Harpagon's treasure hidden in the garden. Cleante promises to restore the treasure to Harpagon on condition that he and Valere be permitted to marry Marianne and Elise. Harpagon consents.

Followed by—

SNICKERING HORSES

By EMJO BASSHE

Cast of characters—

Bob Leslie	Muni Diamond
Mr. Fullerton	Harry Golson
Professor	Robert Crozier
Rev. Tucker	Charles Peyton
Judge	Oliver Putnam
Mrs. Terrace	Joyce Weaver
Corporal	Ashley Buck

Orderly ....Bert Norton
Red Cross Man...................................Vincenzo Rocco
Workers (1917)..................Milton Williams, Elliot Beeman
Workers (1936)........Lester Palmer, William Atlee, George Hass
Veterans: Harry Lessin, Richard Le Monier, John Crotty, Robert
  Saidler
Group of Young Workers (1936): Milton Williams, Lester Palmer,
  Clarence Redd, Earl Robinson, Ben Ross, Mary George, Vir-
  ginia Devetzko, Bella Gould, Ann Goldfarb, Perry Bruskin,
  George Hass, Elliot Beeman, Charles Bronson, John Berry, Anne
  Zolna, Robert Saidler, Daniel Sayer, Nathan Malkin, Mary
  Kukawski, Lucy Kikoler, Manuel Rothstein.
  The action takes place in the Fullerton Meat Packing Plant some-
where in the United States and in the trenches during the World
War.
  Staged by Maurice Clark; settings by Samuel Leve.

When war is declared the Soldier is asked to take the place of
the Meat Packer so the Meat Packer can stay at home and fulfill
his patriotic duty of supplying the army with meat. The Soldier
agrees. At the front he is permanently disabled. At home the patri-
ots sing cheerful songs, make appeals for funds, and condemn all
conscientious objectors to the war as slackers. The Soldier is sent
home. The Meat Packer buys him artificial arms to replace those
he has lost taking the Meat Packer's place. The Soldier draws his
own conclusions.

Followed by—

THE GREAT CATHERINE

By GEORGE BERNARD SHAW

Cast of characters—

Potiomkin ....David Kerman
Varenka ....Roslyn Harvey
Sergeant ....Gregory Robins
Edstaston ....Yisrol Libman
Catherine ....Eda Reis
Maryshkin ....Paul Stein
Maestro ....William Lee
Dashkoff ....Jane Kim
Page ....Vito Scozzari
Hairdresser....................................Harry Lessin
Manicurists............................Mary George, Bella Gould
Soldiers..........................Manuel Rothstein, Max Manes
Slipper Maids.....................Elizabeth Guise, Nella Seymour
Courtiers: Elliot Beeman, Ann Goldfarb, Vincenzo Rocco, Robert
  Saidler, Nathan Malkin, Bert Norton, Lucy Kikoler, George Hass
  Scene 1—1776—Potiomkin's Bureau in the Winter Palace, St.
Petersburg. 2—Catherine's Bedroom. 3—Clair's Room. 4—Small
Room.
  Staged by Alfred Saxe and Brett Warren; settings by Samuel
Leve; music by Earl Robinson and M. I. Arnheim.

* CLASS OF '29

(29 performances)

A drama in three acts by Orrie Lashin and Milo Hastings. Produced by the Popular Price Theatre of the WPA Federal Theatre Project under the supervision of Edward Goodman and Helen Arthur at the Manhattan Theatre, New York, May 15, 1936.

Cast of characters—

Ken Holden	Jan Ullrich
Ted Brooks	Ben Starkie
Tippy Sayre	Allen Nourse
Martin Peterson	Robert Bruce
Laura Stevens	Marjorie Brown
Kate Allen	Helen Morrow
Lucille Brown	Olive Stanton
Bishop Holden	Harry Irvine
Stanley Prescott	Edward Forbes
Policeman	Jon Lormer
Case Worker	Marjorie Dalton
Miss Donovan	Edna Archer Crawford

Act I.—Scene 1—Basement Apartment. 2—Business Office. Acts II and III.—Basement Apartment.

Staged by Lucius Moore Cook, Agnes Morgan and Halsted Welles; settings by Tom Adrian Cracroft.

Ken, Tippy, Ted and Martin, representing the "Lost Generation" that was graduated at the beginning of the great depression, struggle variously for a footing in the social order. Ken, an architect, searches unsuccessfully for a job for six years; then his father, a Bishop of the church, buys him a job without his knowing it. Tippy organizes a dog washing and walking business. Ted allows his girl friend, who is working, to support him and Martin, an illustrator, goes actively communistic—until he sells a sketch to the *New Yorker*. Ken discovers his father's deceit and is pitifully crushed; Ted's girl, hoping to rehabilitate him, gets him a job as an elevator pilot. The thought of becoming a menial wearing a monkey's uniform so unnerves Ted that he throws himself in front of a subway train. Tippy goes on walking dogs. The problem remains. It may take a revolution to correct it finally.

* BATTLE HYMN

(24 performances)

A drama in three acts, three prologues and an epilogue by Michael Blankfort and Michael Gold. Produced by the Federal Theatre Works Progress Administration at the Experimental Theatre, May 22, 1936.

Cast of characters—

Owen Brown	Michael Cisney
Ruth Scott	Mary Morrison
Mary Brown	Lida MacMillan
Frederick Brown	Edward Segal
Salmon Brown	George Ward
Oliver Brown	Joseph Pevney
Watson Brown	Anthony Heathe
John Brown	Grover Burgess
Jason Brown	William Triest
Mr. Hickey	Horace Casselberry
Shields Green	George Whittington
Joe	Philip Hilton
Slave Mother	Gant Mitchell
Slave Woman	Ringgold Watts
Rev. Romney	Donald Barrie
Manny Buell	Sidney Vereker
August Bondi	Mony Ash
First Sheriff	Charles P. Thompson
Second Sheriff	Richard Huett
Bill Larkin	Curtis Parker
Joshua Larkin	R. Henry Handon
Bill Doyle	James J. Coyle
Drury Doyle	Cortell Ramey
Dutch Sherman	Philip Woodward
John Kagi	Arthur Spencer
Mrs. Kagi	Ruth Marcusson
Dolly Thompson	Robin Radin
William Lloyd Garrison	Lewis Paul
Gerrit Smith	Leslie Hunt
Ralph Waldo Emerson	Allan MacAteer
David Thoreau	Lee Hillery
Frank Sanborn	Herbert Rudley
Maria	Agnes Gildea
Aaron Stevens	Charles P. Thompson
Albert Hazlett	James J. Coyle
John Cook	David Palmer
Charles Tidd	Philip Woodward
Captain Hugh Forbes	William Burbridge
Mrs. Huffmaster	Margery Christian

In Prologues and Epilogue: Arthur Spenser, Alan MacAteer, Leslie Hunt, Richard Huett, Cortell Ramey, Lewis Paul, James J. Coyle, Brandt Peters, Donald Barrie, Harry Bonnick, Katherine Arden, Rose Cooper, Richard Huett, Lucia Lull, David Palmer, Robin Radin, Hilda Reis, Amelia Romano, Alfreda Sill, Arthur Shackett, Aldeah Wise, George Yessner.

Neighbors, Wedding Guests: Katherine Arden, Hattie Cline, Ora Day, Georgia Graham, Ruth Forst, Agnes Gildea, Agnes Delano, Lada Ladova, Gita Lurie, Manny Manisoff, Brandt Peters, Hilda Reis, Gerald Stone, Helen Wainright, Laura Strassman, Jeffrey Warnick, Florence Warren, Ann Peters, Peter White.

Act I.—John Brown's Home, Richfield, Ohio. 1854. Act II.—Scene 1—At the Kansas Border. 2, 3 and 4—John Brown's Cabin, Ossawatomie, Kansas. 1855. Act III.—Scene 1—Home of Gerrit Smith, Peterboro, N. Y. 1859. 2 and 3—Cellar and Living Room of John Brown's House near Harper's Ferry.

Staged by Vincent Sherman; dances by Georgie Graham; settings by Howard Bay.

John Brown, in his Ohio home, is running escaping slaves through to Canada, being assisted by his sons, who are eager for him to move West and join the fight of the free staters in Kansas. Old John moves to Kansas, comes to accept the feel of the rifle in his hands as a sign from God that he should avenge the wrongs of humankind, wipes out the Doyles and moves on to Harper's Ferry for the raids that brought about his defeat.

OTHER FEDERAL THEATRE ACTIVITIES

The first production of the American Historical Unit was "The Ballad of Davy Crockett" by Hoffman Hays, directed by Mr. Hays and John Lyman and presented the first week in January at Columbia University, followed by a tour of the New York City circuit.

The Yiddish Unit gave 15 performances of "We Live and Laugh," a musical revue by Alfred Kreymborg, J. L. Peretz and others; directed by Judah Bleich and Zvee Scooler at the Public Theatre, New York, May 8, 1935. It was still running on June 15.

The Poetic Division produced "The Dance of Death," a satirical play in verse by W. H. Auden, musical numbers by Clair Leonard, at the Adelphi Theatre, New York City, May 19 to June 6, 1935. Directed by Alfred Kreymborg.

The Children's Unit produced "The Emperor's New Clothes," by Charlotte Chorpenning out of a Hans Christian Andersen fairy tale, at the Adelphi Theatre, June 2, 1935. It became a part of the portable theatre repertory for the summer.

A Marionette Festival, "Stars on Strings," started May 26 at the Chanin Theatre, opening with "The Birthday Party," followed by "The Dragon Zne Zee," an original Chinese fantasy by Carl Glick.

"Master of Solitaire" by Jean Lee Latham with all-Negro cast at Hotel Commodore, New York, June 2.

THE SAP RUNS HIGH

(23 performances)

A comedy in three acts by H. T. Porter and Alfred Henri White. Produced by Milton R. Kroopf at the Bijou Theatre, New York, February 4, 1936.

Cast of characters—

Norma	Betty Lancaster
Mrs. Jennings	Marie Nordstrom
John J. Jennings	James Bell
Junior Jennings	Joe Brown, Jr.
Kenneth Robbins	Gordon Oliver
Stephenson	J. Francis Robertson
Dixon	O. Anthony Hughes
Keeler	Royal Dana Tracy
Service Man	O. Z. Whitehead
Mme. Clarice	Mildred Shay
Helga	Muriel Hutchison
Crowder	John Vosburgh
Goldfarb	Robert Leonard

Lizette ....Frances Nabors
Acts I, II and III.—The Jennings Home at Rosemore, L. I.
Staged by Theodore J. Hammerstein; settings by Karle O. Amend.

John J. Jennings, a victim of the depression, has been reduced to doing the housework while his wife supports the family as the proprietress of a beauty salon. Supposedly worthless stock held by Jennings suddenly achieves great value. Promotors would buy it up at a dollar a share, paying $25,000 down. Jennings spends the down payment wildly, including a water front lot investment. Again the stock is proved valueless, but the real estate is bought by the government for an airboat harbor.

FRESH FIELDS

(80 performances)

A comedy in three acts by Ivor Novello. Produced by Richard Aldrich and Alfred de Liagre, Jr., at the Empire Theatre, New York, February 10, 1936.

Cast of characters—

Miss Swaine....................................Audrey Ridgwell
Ludlow ....Philip Tonge
Lady Lilian Bedworthy............................Mary Sargent
Lady Mary Crabbe.............................Margaret Anglin
Tim Crabbe.....................................Derek Fairman
Mrs. Pidgeon...............................Jessamine Newcombe
Una Pidgeon......................................Agnes Doyle
Tom Larcomb......................................Boyd Davis
Lady Strawholme..................................Lilian Talbot
Acts I, II and III.—Drawing Room of Lady Mary Crabbe's London Home.
Staged by Alfred de Liagre, Jr.; settings by George S. Steele.

Lady Mary Crabbe and Lady Lilian Bedworthy, her sister, gentlewomen with no money and a great house in London on their hands, agree to take a trio of lower middle class Australians as paying guests. The adventure leads to many extravagant adventures, and ends with Lady Bedworthy marrying Tom Larcomb, one of the Australians, and Lady Crabbe's son Derek falling in love with Una Pidgeon, another.

ALICE TAKAT

(8 performances)

A drama in three acts adapted by Jose Ruben from the Hungarian of Dezso Szomory. Produced by Ed Wynn at the Golden Theatre, New York, February 10, 1936.

Cast of characters—

Zuard Takat	Nicholas Joy
Kitty Lindeman	Peggy Shannon
Alice Takat	Mady Christians
Karl Helvet	Russell Hardie
Max Durak	Lloyd Gough
Miss Haus	Florence Earle
Professor Glotz	Leo Curley
Ludwig	Emmett Rogers
Homer Horeb	Percy Ames
Fritz	A. G. Andrews
A Patient	Al Baron
George Kroos	John Emery
Mrs. Helvet	Kate Mayhew
Prof. Tardy Kroos	Arnold Korff
Mrs. Baneyi	Edna West
Mrs. Dubra	Florence Auer
Mrs. Gantz	Marjorie Wood

Act I.—Scene 1—Living Quarters of Dr. Takat in Prof. Glotz's Hospital in Berlin. 2—Special Ward in Hospital. Act II.—Scene 1— Waiting Room in Professor Kroos' Home in Budapest. 2—Dining Room in Professor Kroos' House. Act III.—Living Room in Mrs. Helvet's House in Bede Falu, a Suburb.

Staged by Frank Merlin; settings by Raymond Sovey.

Alice Takat, a personable young doctor in a Budapest hospital, knowing that a well-loved friend is dying of an incurable malady, deliberately gives him an overdose of morphine. The "mercy killing" being discovered, Karl Helvet, a young chemist in love with Alice, assumes the crime and is sentenced to ten years in prison. Some months later Alice, on a holiday, meets and is attracted to George Kroos. An affair with Kroos is followed by the unexpected release of Helvet from prison. Alice, still in love with Helvet, is conscious that she is to bear Kroos a child. Helvet nobly agrees to expand his protection of Alice to include the adoption of the expected infant.

CO-RESPONDENT UNKNOWN

(121 performances)

A comedy in three acts by Mildred Harris and Harold Goldman. Produced by McKenna, Mayer and Mielziner at the Ritz Theatre, New York, February 11, 1936.

Cast of characters—

Martin Bishop	James Rennie
Sylvia Farren	Ilka Chase
Bessie	Marietta Canty
Vincent Cummings	Richard Sterling
Claire Hammond	Phyllis Povah
Pete Edney	Ralph MacBane
Jessica	Alice Buchanan
Donald	Tom Bate
Murray Carson	Martin Wolfson
Hattie	Peggy Conklin
Tony	Edward Marr

Waiter ....Charles Scot
   Act I.—Living Room of Mr. and Mrs. Martin Bishop in the East
Fifties. Acts II and III.—Martin's Studio in Gramercy Park.
   Staged by Kenneth MacKenna; settings by Jo Mielziner.

Sylvia Farren, a popular actress, returns from a long tour to
find her husband, Martin Bishop, a rising economist, practically
in the arms of Claire Hammond, a book reviewer who has admired
his writings. A divorce is agreed upon and a co-respondent engaged to provide the evidence. The co-respondent (Hattie), being a simple child of nature, and maternally minded, discover-
ing that Martin is feeling ill following the adventure of posing as
a deceiver, decides the least she can do is to remain the night and
take care of him. Next morning Sylvia and Claire both visit
Martin's rooms and find him breakfasting quite happily with the
unknown co-respondent. The situation so angers the mistress that
she leaves in disgust. Which so pleases Sylvia that she is induced
to consider forgiving Martin.

AMONG THOSE SAILING

(7 performances)

A comedy in three acts by Laura Walker. Produced by A. J.
McGoldrick at the Longacre Theatre, New York, February 11,
1936.

Cast of characters—

Hodges..Harold de Becker
Sybil Marsh.......................................Ruth Weston
Calvert Hunter....................................Ted Trevor
Arthur Curtis ....William Harrigan
Marie Curtis......................................Selena Royle
Gilbert ....Allan Fagan
   Act I.—Scene 1—Mrs. Marsh's Suite on Board "S.S. Aquitania."
2—Living Room of Arthur Curtis's House, Oyster Bay, L. I. Act
II.—Arthur Curtis's Living Room.   Act III.—Scene 1—Living
Room. 2—Mrs. Marsh's Suite on "Aquitania."
   Staged by Robert Milton; settings by P. Dodd Ackerman.

Sylvia Marsh and Calvert Hunter find themselves attacked by
the usual sea madness aboard ship. Before they can consummate
a determination to make the most of opportunity Hunter discovers that Sylvia is the sister of a lady now married who had at
one time shared his love, but left him. Having been once bitten
he is pretty shy, but follows Sylvia to her sister's home. There
the old friendship with the sister is renewed and the husband becomes furiously jealous. Divorce for two and unhappiness for four
is narrowly averted. One reconciliation and one renewal of vows
follow.

BLACK WIDOW

(7 performances)

A drama in three acts by Samuel John Park. Produced by Thomas Kilpatrick at the Mansfield Theatre, New York, February 12, 1936.

Cast of characters—

Dr. Emma Koloich	Lucille LaVerne
Detective Sergeant Whaler	King Calder
Carl Koloich	Stanley Smith
Detective Garner	Keenan Wynn
Patrolman	Bruce Desmond
Medical Examiner Lorris	Walter Davis
Katherine	Joanna Roos
Professor	A. H. VanBuren
Jennie Mason	Michael Stone

Acts I, II and III.—Basement Reception Room of Doctor Emma Koloich in a Mid-Western City.

Staged by Miriam Doyle; setting by Louis Kennel.

Dr. Emma Koloich has been under surveillance by the police for years. Young women in trouble have been known to enter her office and disappear completely. The installation of an over-size incinerator intensifies police suspicion. Having made way with one girl's body, Dr. Emma dumps another into an acid bath and is about to rid herself of the irritation of her son's fiancée the same way when she is hemmed in and threatened with arrest. Her final acts of violence include the stabbing of her partner in crime, a chemist who had helped her murder her husband, and with whom she has been living for fifteen years. She then jumps into her own vat, which was cunningly concealed beneath the fire-box of the furnace.

* END OF SUMMER

(137 performances)

A comedy in three acts by S. N. Behrman. Produced by the Theatre Guild, Inc., at the Guild Theatre, New York, February 17, 1936.

Cast of characters—

Will Dexter	Shepperd Strudwick
Mrs. Wyler	Mildred Natwick
Paula Frothingham	Doris Dudley
Robert	Kendall Clark
Leonie Frothingham	Ina Claire
Sam Frothingham	Minor Watson
Dr. Kenneth Rice	Osgood Perkins
Dennis McCarthy	Van Heflin
Dr. Dexter	Herbert Yost

Boris, Count Mirsky..................................Tom Powers
    Acts I, II and III.—Living Room of Bay Cottage, the Frothing-
ham's Summer Place in Northern Maine.
    Staged by Philip Moeller; setting by Lee Simonson.

See page 101.

COME ANGEL BAND

(2 performances)

A drama in three acts by Dudley Nichols and Stuart Anthony.
Produced by Eugene Walter at the 46th Street Theatre, New
York, February 18, 1936.

Cast of characters—

Queenie Shannon..................................Clarice Cornell
Parson Edwards.....................................Burke Clarke
Tab Moseley.....................................J. Hammond Daly
Fate Shannon....................................Curtis Cooksey
Beulah Shannon......................................Iris Whitney
Zeke Shannon...Elvin Field
Peter Shannon.......................................Robert Woods
Thomas Shannon..................................Lester Lonergan, 3rd
Faith Shannon.......................................Joyce Gates
"Doc" McCord..................................George R. Taylor
Hode Hearn..Robert Pitkin
Selah Hearn.......................................Eleanor Lynn
Bird...Elisha Cook, Jr.
Judge Oscar Brazzle..............................Arthur Griffin
Sheriff Garr......................................Frank Wilcox
Claude Waters.....................................Arthur Barrows
Deputy Sheriff Trip...............................Richard Taber
Bos Prouty..Edgar Nelson
Wart Swain......................................Joseph Eggerton
Phid Hammock......................................Frank Conlan
Biscuit..J. Louis Johnson
Bailiff...Frederick Maynar
Jury Foreman......................................Victor Esker
Clerk...Walter Wagner
The Chauncey Northern Singers—Director, Chauncey Northern.
    Act I.—Family Burial Plot of the Shannons. Act II.—Scene 1—
Barnyard of Hode Hearn. 2—Parlor of Fate Shannon. Act III.—
Scene 1—Brush Arbor Courthouse on the Banks of the Attamaha
River. 2—Attamaha County Jail—Sheriff's Office and Condemned
Cell.
    Staged by Melville Burke; settings by Watson Barratt.

Fate Shannon, having buried four wives, bargains over the
grave of the last one at her funeral for a fifth. He gives Hode
Hearn a team of mules, a wagon and a quantity of elderberry
wine for his fifteen-year-old daughter, Selah. A neighborhood boy
named Bird, deeply in love with Selah, invades the nuptial
chamber on Selah's wedding night and stabs Hode to death with
a pitchfork. Selah and Bird escape to the swamps, where they
keep house until the posse finds them. Bird is tried and sentenced
to be hanged. A sympathetic sheriff permits Selah to spend Bird's
last night with him in his cell.

SEARCHING FOR THE SUN

(5 performances)

A drama in three acts by Dan Totheroh. Produced by Albert Ingalls, Jr., at the 58th Street Theatre, New York, February 19, 1936.

Cast of characters—

Red		Roger Blankenship
Tony		Paul Birris
Pat	Boys of the Road	Lewis Luke
Skin		Charles Henry
Ed		Richard Hunter

Fletch...Whitford Kane
Hattie...Leona Roberts
Dot..Olive Deering
Matt...Edwin Philips
Peg-Leg..Charles Niemeyer
Buck...Jazzbo Williams
Texas..Jack Warren
Alf...Vernon Crane
Cutler..Joseph Curtin
Rusty...J. Richard Jones
Purdy...Emerson Treacy
A Frightened Boy...............................Richard Hunter
A Derelict.......................................Thomas Fisher
Steve Rapson................................Roger Blankenship
Happy...Happy Robinson
Organist.......................................Eleanor Wendall
Head of the Mission..............................Walter Beck
A Woman in Fairmead..........................Georgia Simmons

Act I.—Scene 1—By the Side of a Country Road. 2 and 3—A Jungle. Act II.—Scene 1—A Natural Clearing in a Wood. 2—A Place Among Rocks Along a Large River in the South. 3—The Interior of an Empty Box Car. Act. III.—Scene 1—Interior of a Private Mission in Milwaukee. 2—Jungle. 3—Street Outside Ross Home in Fairmead, Ohio.

Staged by Julius Evans and Joan Hathaway; settings by Cleon Throckmorton.

Matt and Dot are victims of the depression. They meet in a hobo jungle in which Matt is at the head of a group of road boys roaming the country in search of work. Dot has run away from an unhappy Ohio home, also in search of a job. Matt, being attracted, tries to fight down the softening influences of Dot's femininity. Dot, hoping to hold Matt back from a try at banditry, accepts him as her lover to keep him in camp. After a three-day honeymoon Matt returns to the holdup racket. Dot follows helplessly after. When Matt discovers Dot is to bear him a child he jumps out of a box car door and disappears. Later, his better nature aroused in a "lousy mission," he returns to Dot in time for the accouchement. With the baby they go back to Dot's home seeking a chance at decent citizenship. The home is broken up and the family scattered. They must return to the road.

HALLOWE'EN

(12 performances)

A comedy in three acts by Henry Myers. Produced by William de Mille at the Vanderbilt Theatre, New York, February 20, 1936.

Cast of characters—

```
Arnold.............................................Ian  MacLaren
Amelia..............................................Edith  King
Dr. Behrens...................................Aristides de Leoni
Joan............................................... Mary Hone
Edith..........................................Zamah  Cunningham
Paul....................................................John  Seager
Father  Macklin................................Robert T. Haines
Dr.  Moore...........................................Maurice Wells
     Acts I, II and III.—A New England Inn.
     Staged by William de Mille; setting by Louis Kennel.
```

Joan, a psychic long conscious of being possessed of strange powers, finds herself in New England with her mother, Edith, and her fiancé, Paul. She insists that they spend Hallowe'en at an inn which legend declares to have been at one time the head-quarters of Satan himself and the scene of the execution of many witches. At the inn Joan recognizes in the keeper, Arnold, a fellow psychic. At the witching hour Arnold becomes the reincarnated Satan and Joan's body is possessed by the soul of a witch eager to renew her allegiance to the Evil One. Edith and Paul accept the aid of Dr. Behrens, a Jewish rabbi, and Father Macklin, a Catholic priest. These two, bringing their altar symbols, proceed to exorcise the evil spirits. Father Macklin sprinkles the exits with holy water. Dr. Behrens draws a protective circle about the good folk. The Devil refuses to budge. The situation becomes a contest of prayer and the Lord's Prayer wins.

THE DEVIL OF PEI-LING

(11 performances)

A melodrama in three acts dramatized by Howard Chenery from Herbert Asbury's novel. Produced by O. E. Wee, Inc., at the Adelphi Theatre, New York, February 20, 1936.

Cast of characters—

```
Dr. Jerry Smith...................................Robert Shayne
Hendricks........................................Clem  Wilenchick
Dorothy Crawford................................Nancy  Haswin
Professor  Jerome Deeger.......................Halliam  Bosworth
Inspector Tommy Conroy...........................Edgar Mason
```

Officer Murphy.................................. ....John Alexander
Paul Silvio...Craig Ward
Neenah...Elizabeth Langille
Officer Johnson....................................Kent Thurber
Miss Collins....................................Annette Robinson
    Acts I, II and III.—Curio Room of Professor Jerome Deeger's
Home in a Large American City.
    Staged by Seth Arnold; setting by Karl Amend.

Professor Deeger brings into his American home an ancient
Chinese idol which, from the evidence, is able to step out of
character and snap people's necks. Also put a spell upon them.
Dr. Jerry Smith, in love with Dorothy Crawford, the idol's pet
victim, is able finally to solve the mystery and save Dorothy for
himself.

MAINLY FOR LOVERS

(8 performances)

A comedy in three acts by Philip Johnson. Produced by Richard
W. Krakeur and B. Charles-Dean at the 48th Street Theatre,
New York, February 21, 1936.

Cast of characters—
Poynter..Edgar Kent
Helen Storer.......................................Dorothy Gish
Sarah Traille....................................Rachel Hartzell
Cedric Norreys....................................Leo G. Carroll
Roger Storer...................................Arthur Margetson
    Acts I, II and III.—Living Room of Helen Storer's Country
House in England During a Week-End in June.
    Staged by Harry Wagstaff Gribble; setting by Clark Robinson.

Helen and Roger Storer have been separated for seven years.
He had refused to give up his Egyptology and she had bitten his
finger in a tantrum. Helen's sister Sarah, with Helen's experience
before her, is fearful of marriage. She is thinking of accepting her
sweetheart, Cedric Norreys, as a lover by way of experiment
before she makes up her mind. Roger Storer returns from Egypt
to ask Helen to give him a divorce. She agrees on promise that
for one week-end he will act the devoted husband, to prove to
Sarah that wedded bliss is possible. The agreement made, the
Storers proceed to fight their way through the week-end. Sarah is
stronger than ever for her planned experiment. Roger and Cedric,
after sitting up all night in the library, evolve a plan satisfying
both the women.

*LOVE ON THE DOLE

(129 performances)

A drama in three acts by Ronald Gow and Walter Greenwood based on a novel of the same name by Walter Greenwood. Produced by Maurice Barber at the Shubert Theatre, New York, February 24, 1936.

Cast of characters—

Sally Hardcastle	Wendy Hiller
Sarah Hardcastle	Marga Ann Deighton
Larry Meath	Brandon Peters
Harry Hardcastle	Alexander Grandison
Henry Hardcastle	Dodson Mitchell
Mrs. Jike	Carrie Weller
Mrs. Dorbell	Marie de Becker
Mrs. Bull	Helen Strickland
Mrs. Barlow	Selma Hall
Mr. Barlow	Stanley G. Wood
Policeman	Jock McGraw
Helen Hawkins	Rita Davies
Newspaper Boy	Johnny Cort
Sam Grundy	Ross Chetwynd
Charlie	George Bleasdale
Pat O'Leary, an Agitator	Barry Macollum

Acts I and III.—The Hardcastles' Kitchen in Hanky Park.
Act II.—Scenes 1 and 2—A Back Entry in Hanky Park. 3—The Moors.

Staged by Reginald Bach; settings by Nicholas Yellenti.

Sally Hardcastle, helping her family through the economic depression that brought about the dole, is in love with Larry Meath, a modest agitator for the rights of working men. Larry is killed in a labor riot. His death serves as a last straw of discouragement added to the load Sally is carrying. Defiantly she decides that in a cockeyed world only those are saved who save themselves. She goes to live with Sam Grundy, the gambler, ostensibly as his housekeeper. Thereafter she is able to help support her father, mother and brother, who can find no work nor make ends meet on the dole.

THE POSTMAN ALWAYS RINGS TWICE

(72 performances)

A drama in two acts by James M. Cain. Produced by Jack Curtis at the Lyceum Theatre, New York, February 25, 1936.

Cast of characters—

Nick Papadakis	Joseph Greenwald
Cora Papadakis	Mary Philips
Frank Chambers	Richard Barthelmess
A State Trooper	John Kearney

```
A Policeman........................................Joseph Cotton
Walter Sackett....................................Dudley Clements
Manny Katz........................................Charles Halton
A Secretary.......................................May Holsman
An Insurance Adjuster.............................Walter Vonnegut
Another State Trooper.............................Al. Cunningham
A Priest..........................................Philip Ryder
Matron............................................Queena Belotti
```
    Act I.—Scenes 1 and 3—Nick's Lunchroom, Near Los Angeles,
California. 2, 4 and 5—Kitchen of Lunchroom. Act II.—Scene 1—
A Bridge Abutment. 2—A Hospital Room. 3—Sackett's Office. 4—
Lunchroom. 5—A Beach. 6—Along a Road. 7—A Courtroom. 8—A
Cell.
    Staged by Robert Sinclair; settings by Jo Mielziner.

Frank Chambers, a bad boy roaming the road, stops at the
refreshment stand of Nick Papadakis and, on seeing Mrs. Cora
Papadakis, decides to stay on as Nick's helper. Frank and Cora,
mutually fascinated, decide to be rid of Nick. Cora tries killing
Nick with a blunt instrument while he is in the bath. This failing,
Frank conceives the idea of plying Nick with wine, loading him
in his automobile and running the automobile over a cliff. Thus
Nick is killed. Frank and Cora are arrested and acquitted of
the charge of murder. Some time later Frank and Cora are motor-
ing when Frank runs the car into a telegraph pole, kills Cora
and is, on his former police record, convicted of her murder on
circumstantial evidence and hung.

THREE WISE FOOLS

(9 performances)

A comedy in three acts by Austin Strong. Revived by John
Golden at the Golden Theatre, New York, March 1, 1936.

Cast of characters—
```
Mr. Theodore Findley.............................William Gillette
Judge James Trumbull.............................James Kirkwood
Doctor Richard Gaunt.............................Charles Coburn
Miss Fairchild...................................Elizabeth Love
Mrs. Saunders....................................Isabel Irving
Poole............................................Brandon Tynan
Gordon Schuyler..................................William Post, Jr.
John Crawshay....................................John Blair
Douglas..........................................Sydney Booth
Benjamin Surratt.................................Scott Moore
Clancy...........................................Victor Colton
Gray.............................................John McKee
Policeman........................................Robert Burton
```
    Acts I, II and III.—Living Room in Home of the Three Wise
Fools, Washington Square, New York.
    Staged by Austin Strong.

The Messrs. Findley, Trumbull and Gaunt, three aging bachelors, are confronted with the appearance of a pretty young girl
named Fairchild who comes to them with a letter from her dead

mother asking that they look after her. The three bachelors, all of whom were at one time in love with the mother, agree to adopt the orphaned daughter. Shortly thereafter Miss Fairchild is seemingly involved in a plot to rob the bachelors and assist the escape of a fellow conspirator with a police record. The situation is happily cleared up, and Miss Fairchild marries the nephew of one of her guardians. The play was originally produced in 1919 with Harry Davenport, Claude Gillingwater and William Ingersoll as the bachelors and Helen Menken as the heroine.

DEAR OLD DARLING

(16 performances)

A comedy in two acts by George M. Cohan. Produced by Mr. Cohan at the Alvin Theatre, New York, March 2, 1936.

Cast of characters—

Calvin Miller	George M. Cohan
Gertrude Collins	Ruth Shepley
Acton	Reynolds Denniston
Jane Mayo	Marian Shockley
Joseph Leggitt	Charles D. Brown
Mrs. Mayo	Theresa Maxwell Canover
Julia Taylor	Edna M. Holland
Clarence Wheeler	Ben Lackland
Gesso	M. Hirano
L. B. Stewart	Joseph Sweeney
McDevitt	Joseph R. Garry
Captain Cramer	Walter Gilbert
John Mayo	Forrest Orr
Dolan	Jack Williams
Hogan	Dan Carey

Act I.—The Miller Home in an American City. Act II.—Scenes 1 and 3—The Miller Home. 2—The Mayo Apartment.
Staged by Sam Forrest; settings by Oden Waller.

Calvin Miller, rich and retired, meets Jane Mayo, youthful and vivacious, on a trans-Atlantic crossing. Calvin, being generous and susceptible, is nice to Jane and is somewhat startled when he finds her and her mother following him around the continent. Back in America it is not easy for Calvin to explain to the Widow Collins, whom he expects to marry, the attentions of Jane. Complications develop when the Mayos seek to force a money settlement with Calvin on the charge of his having compromised young Jane. The conspiracy is exposed and the Miller-Collins romance resumed.

SWEET ALOES

(24 performances)

A drama in three acts by Jay Mallory. Produced by Lee Ephraim at the Booth Theatre, New York, March 4, 1936.

Cast of characters—

```
Miss Esther Warren.................................Elliot Mason
Rose...............................................Marjorie Martyn
Miss Alice Dodd....................................Ruth Vivian
Belinda Warren.....................................Evelyn Laye
Tubbs Barrow,......................................Rex Harrison
Lord Farrington.................................,....Charles Bryant
Clara..............................................Myra Hampton
Jim Baker..........................................John Litel
Johnson............................................Henry Vincent
Florence Cudahy....................................Doris Dalton
Maid...............................................Elizabeth Chase
Hon. Robert Melford (Later Lord Farrington)........John Emery
Lady Farrington ...................................Joyce Carey
```
Act I.—Miss Warren's House in Pyxley, a Village in Leicestershire, England. Acts II and III.—Jim Baker's Apartment on Park Avenue, New York.
Staged by Tyrone Guthrie; settings by Raymond Sovey.

Belinda Warren is to bear Robert Melford, son of Lord Farrington, a child. Seeking a way out of her difficulty with the least possible scandal, Belinda listens to a proposition made her by Lord Farrington. If she will have the child and leave it to be adopted by the invalid wife of Melford, that it may be brought up as an heir to the Farrington line, his lordship will finance the accouchement and Belinda's retirement to America. Belinda, following the birth of a boy, sails for America and in due time is married to an upright and successful New York attorney, Jim Baker. Made miserably unhappy by worry for the fate of her abandoned offspring, Belinda's mind is cleared of her obsessions by meeting the Melfords and having a heart-to-heart talk with Lady Melford.

THE FIELDS BEYOND

(3 performances)

A drama in three acts by Francis Bosworth. Produced by Raymond Hewitt at the Mansfield Theatre, New York, March 6, 1936.

Cast of characters—

```
Dr. Reynolds, D.D..................................Herbert Duffy
Maud Reynolds......................................Merle Maddern
Vera Reynolds......................................Helen Claire
Roberta Reynolds...................................Jean Briggs
Imogene Clark......................................Helen Ray
```

```
Philip Cameron....................................Reed Brown, Jr.
Karn von Ornsdorf................................Richard Abert
Dr. Richard Sawyer..............................Joseph Roeder
Howard Lansing, D.D............................Clarence Chase
Donald Cummings, Ph.D.........................Clayton Collyer
Ellen Cummings, Ph.D...........................Laura Norton
Emaline.........................................Lenore Lonergan
Harvey Merkle...................................Jack Gilchrist
Gertrude Merkle............................Gwendoline Williams
```
    Acts I, II and III.—Living Room in Home of Dr. Reynolds, President of Watertown College in the Midwest.
    Staged by Milton Smith; setting by Horace Armistead.

Philip Cameron, come to teach English at Watertown college, is maneuvered into marrying the president's daughter, Vera Reynolds. He soon finds his marriage incompatible, but is held strictly to it, again by the maneuvering of the evil-minded mother-in-law and the clinging-vine defense of Vera. Cameron finally breaks his bonds, even facing Mrs. Reynolds' malicious suggestion that he harbors an unnatural affection for one of his boy students, and makes good his escape in the cause of intellectual integrity.

SAINT JOAN

(89 performances)

A chronicle play in six scenes and an epilogue by George Bernard Shaw. Revived by Katharine Cornell at the Martin Beck Theatre, March 9, 1936.

Cast of characters—

```
Captain Robert de Baudricourt....................Joseph Holland
His Steward.......................................Arthur Chatterton
Joan, the Maid..................................Katharine Cornell
Bertrand de Poulengy...........................Tyrone Power, Jr.
Archbishop of Rheims............................Charles Waldron
Monseigneur de la Tremouille......................Charles Dalton
Page to the Dauphin............................Robert Champlain
Gilles de Rais..................................David Vivian
Captain la Hire.................................Barry Kelly
The Dauphin....................................Maurice Evans
Duchess de la Tremouille..............Ruth March or Lois Jameson
Dunois.........................................Kent Smith
Page to Dunois.................................Edward Ryan, Jr.
Earl of Warwick................................Brian Aherne
Chaplain John de Stogumber.....................George Coulouris
Page to Warwick................................John Payne
Cauchon, Bishop of Beauvais...................Eduardo Ciannelli
John Lemaitre, Inquisitor......................Arthur Byron
Canon John d'Estivet............................Joseph Holland
Brother Martin Ladvenu.........................John Cromwell
Canon de Courcelles............................Irving Morrow
The Executioner................................Barry Kelly
An English Soldier..............................Charles Dalton
A Gentleman of 1920............................Arthur Chatterton
```
    Court Ladies: Hilde Albers, Anne Froelick.
    Courtiers and Soldiers: Richard Graham, David Orrick, William Roehrick, Hudson Shotwell, Kurt Stenbart.
    Scene 1—Castle of Voucoulers. 2—Antechamber and Throne Room at Chinon. 3—Bank of River Loire near Orleans. 4—Earl of War-

wick's Tent in English Camp. 5—Ambulatory of Rheims Cathedral.
6—Hall in Castle at Rouen. Epilogue—Bedroom in Château of
Charles VII.
  Staged by Guthrie McClintic; settings by Jo Mielziner.

The complete text of the Shaw drama, from the appearance of
Joan at Voucoulers with the message of her voices, her appearance at Chinon and her winning of Dunois' support, through her
successful campaign to see the Dauphin crowned at Rheims.
Follows her defeat at Compiègne, her capture by the Burgundians,
her trial by the inquisition and her sentence to the stake. An
epilogue, on an anniversary of her later canonization, those who
had known her in her life appear in the spirit (and the Dauphin's
dream) to beg Joan to remain dead and a saint, lest by returning
to life she again be denied by a stupid world. (Best Plays,
1923-24.)

STAR SPANGLED

(23 performances)

A comedy in three acts by Robert Ardrey. Produced by Arthur
Hopkins at the Golden Theatre, New York, March 10, 1936.

Cast of characters—

Mrs. Mary Dzieszienewski	Natasha Boleslavsky
Gregory Smith	George Tobias
Stan Jena	Millard Mitchell
Vincent Chenevski	Garson Kanin
Anna La France	Marjorie Lytell
Professor Jake Niebieski	Ivan Triesault
Czysko	Michael Visaroff
Steve	Donald Arbury
Masters	Edward Craven

  Acts I, II and III.—The Dzieszienewski Parlor in Polish District,
Northwest Side of Chicago.
  Staged by Arthur Hopkins; setting by Raymond Sovey.

Mary Dzieszienewski, widow, has three sons: Gregory, who is
serving time in Michigan City penitentiary; Vincent, who is cam-
paigning for a seat in the legislature, and Stan, who is a dumb
ball player in the Texas league. Greg gets out of prison through
the sewer and comes home for a week-end vacation in which he
hopes to bump off Czysko, Polish-American boss, who was responsible for his conviction. Vincent, hoping to buy Czysko's influence, doesn't want him bumped off. There is a good deal of
excitement keeping Greg and Czysko apart until Greg has to get
back to prison. He could have stayed longer, but he had borrowed a gun from the vice-president of the prisoners' killers' society, and the owner had planned to shoot his way out Sunday
afternoon.

CASE OF CLYDE GRIFFITHS

(19 performances)

A drama in two parts by Erwin Piscator and Lena Goldschmidt, dramatized from Theodore Dreiser's book, "The American Tragedy." Produced by The Group Theatre and Milton Shubert at the Ethel Barrymore Theatre, New York, March 13, 1936.

Cast of characters—

Speaker	Morris Carnovsky
Clyde Griffiths	Alexander Kirkland
Roberta Alden	Phoebe Brand
Sondra Finchley	Margaret Barker
Titus Alden	Art Smith
Mrs. Alden	Ruth Nelson
Emily Alden	Paula Miller
Samuel Griffiths	Roman Bohnen
Mrs. Samuel Griffiths	Virginia Stevens
Gilbert Griffiths	Walter Coy
Bella Griffiths	Kay Laughlin
Josiah Babs	Gerrit Kraber
Wiggham	Sanford Meisner

Working Men ... Elia Kazan, Grover Burgess, William Challee, Jules Garfield, Anthony Ross

Working Girls ... Eunice Stoddard, Ruth Nelson, Dorothy Patten, Paula Miller, Virginia Stevens, Helen Walpole, Kay Laughlin, Illah Lange

Orrin Short	Bob Lewis
Party Guests	Whitney Bourne, Beatrice Cole, Paul Morrison, Wendell Phillips, Jerome Thor
Doctor	Luther Adler
District Attorney	Lewis Leverett
Mrs. Asa Griffiths	Dorothy Patten

Staged by Lee Strasberg; settings by Watson Barratt.

In this rearrangement of "An American Tragedy" (Best Plays, 1926-27) the story of Clyde Griffiths, who seduced Roberta Alden and then drowned her that he might be free to marry Sondra Finchley, is told in terms of Greek tragedy, with Fate (the economic law) as the victim's Nemesis. A Speaker, representing Chorus, stands in the orchestra pit and serves as interpreter of the drama and the influences working through it.

* IDIOT'S DELIGHT

(97 performances)

A comedy in three acts by Robert E. Sherwood. Produced by The Theatre Guild, Inc., at the Shubert Theatre, New York, March 24, 1936.

Cast of characters—

```
Dumptsy..........................................George Meader
Signor Palota....................................Stephen Sandes
Donald Navadel...................................Barry Thomson
Pittaluga.......................................S. Thomas Gomez
Auguste..........................................Edgar Barrier
Captain Locicero...............................Edward Raquello
Dr. Waldersee.................................Sydney Greenstreet
Mr. Cherry....................................Bretaigne Windust
Mrs. Cherry......................................Jean Macintyre
Harry Van..........................................Alfred Lunt
Shirley.........................................Jacqueline Paige
Beulah...........................................Connie Crowell
Edna.............................................Frances Foley
Francine............................................Etna Ross
Elaine..........................................Marjorie Baglin
Bebe..............................................Ruth Timmons
1st Officer........................................Alan Hewitt
2nd Officer.......................................Winston Ross
3rd Officer.......................................Gilmore Bush
4th Officer.....................................Tomasso Tittoni
Quillery.........................................Richard Whorf
Signor Rossi......................................Le Roi Operti
Signora Rossi..............................Ernestine De Becker
Major...........................................Murry O'Neill
Anna................................................Una Val
Irene............................................Lynn Fontanne
Achille Weber...................................Francis Compton
```

Musicians: Gerald Kunz, Max Rich, Joseph Knopf.

Acts I, II and III.—Cocktail Lounge in Hotel Monte Gabrielle in Italian Alps, Near Frontiers of Switzerland and Austria.

Staged by Bretaigne Windust; supervised by Alfred Lunt and Lynn Fontanne; dances directed by Morgan Lewis; setting by Lee Simonson.

See page 67.

BITTER STREAM

(61 performances)

A drama in three acts by Victor Wolfson based on "Fontamara," a novel by Ignazio Silone. Produced by The Theatre Union at the Civic Repertory Theatre, New York, March 30, 1936.

Cast of characters—

```
Pelino.............................................Carlo Conte
Sorcanera........................................Frances Bavier
Losurdo..........................................Robert Harris
Michel Zompa....................................Charles Jordan
Della Croce.......................................Walter Beck
Baldissera........................................Frank Conlan
Elvira.....................................Lili Eisenlohr Valenty
Berardo......................................Albert Van Dekker
Teofilo..........................................David Hoffman
Maid...........................................Millicent Green
Lisabetta.....................................Hester Sondergaard
The Promoter's Wife............................Marjorie Wood
Scarpone........................................Vincent Sherman
Don Abacchio................................Malcolm Lee Beggs
Promoter.........................................Sidney Packer
Don Circonstanza..................................Lee J. Cobb
Blackshirt........................................Jerry Sylvan
```

```
Fillipo.............................................Sydney  Mason
Farmers From Sulmona........................ {Franklin  Heller
                                             {Harry  Levian
Inspector...........................................Manart  Kippen
The Stranger.......................................John  Boruff
Blackshirt........................................Franklin  Heller
Santo...............................................Carlo  Conte
Rosalia...........................................Millicent  Green
Angelina..........................................Marjorie  Wood
Goriano...........................................Harry  Levian
Prison Guard...............................Malcolm  Lee  Beggs
Farmer.............................................P.  A.  Xantho
Blackshirts, Farmers: Harry Davis, Sidney Packer, Edward Mann,
    Sam Gordon, Rolla Normund, Paul Marian, Billy Dunkley.
Women of Fontamara: Regina Kahn, Lizzie Cubitt.
    Act I.—Scene 1—Fontamara  Square. 2—Promoter's House at
Fucino. 3—Alley at Avezzano. Act II.—Fontamara Square. Act III.—
Scenes 1, 2 and 3—Prison at Fucina. 4—Fontamara Square.
    Staged by Jacob Ben-Ami and Charles Friedman; settings by
Cleon Throckmorton.
```

Berardo, a lumbering, ignorant but socially minded farmer of Fontamara, joins with his fellows in a rebellion against the Fascisti and the orders of Il Duce taking small patches of land away from little farmers and giving them to big farmers who can use the land "for the good of the state." Berardo, thrown into jail as a suspect, meets an organizer for the underground union that is protesting the autocracy of Il Duce. Through this organizer Berardo comes to see that, while he, working alone, can be of little help to the cause, if he were to substitute for the organizer and be executed in the organizer's place, the work will go forward. Berardo voluntarily confesses himself an agent of the underground union and is executed. He lives in the minds of the farmers a martyr to the cause.

A GILBERT AND SULLIVAN SERIES

THE MIKADO

(19 performances)

Operetta in two acts by W. S. Gilbert; music by Arthur Sullivan. Revived by S. M. Chartock at the Majestic Theatre, New York, April 10, 1936.

Cast of characters—

```
The Mikado of Japan...........................William  Danforth
Nanki-Poo..........................................Roy  Cropper
Ko-Ko.............................................Frank  Moulan
Pooh-Bah.......................................Herbert  Waterous
Pish-Tush.........................................George  Hirose
Yum-Yum...........................................Vivian  Hart
Pitti-Sing.......................................Frances  Baviello
```

Peep-Bo..Dean Dickens
Katisha..Vera Ross
Ladies of the Mikado's Suite: The Misses Jane Ann Edwards,
    Dorothy Forsythe, Geraldine Bork, Marion Ross.
The Mikado's Bodyguard: Joseph Olney, Norman Van Emburgh,
    David Milton and John Willard.
Ensemble of School Girls, Nobles, Guards, Coolies: Evelyn Adler,
    Elfrida Anabel, Mildred Burke, Kay Curl, Margaret Henzel,
    Emily Marsh, Celia Schiffrin, Gertrude Wandon, Georgia Dieter,
    Edith Maison, Jean Matus, Frances Wade, Bruce Barclay,
    August Loring, Joseph Olney, Paul Curtis, LeRoy McLean,
    David Milton, John Moore, John Cardini, Siegfried Langer and
    Joseph Scandur.
    Act I.—Courtyard of Ko-Ko's Official Residence. Act II.—Ko-Ko's
Garden.
    Staged by Frank Moulan.

In early July Lodewick Vroom also offered a revival of "The
Mikado." The last revival previous to this season's showings was
by the D'Oyly Carte Opera Company at the Martin Beck Theatre,
New York, beginning September 17, 1934. Earlier the same year
Mr. Chartock revived the operetta with few changes in characters
from this year's cast. John Cherry played Ko-Ko; Allen Waterous,
Pish-Tush; Vivian Hart, Pitti-Sing; Laura Ferguson, Peep-Bo,
and Hizi Koyke, Yum-Yum.

PIRATES OF PENZANCE

(8 performances)

An operetta in two acts by W. S. Gilbert; music by Arthur Sullivan. Revived by S. M. Chartock at the Majestic Theatre, New
York, April 20, 1936.

Cast of characters—

Richard.......................................Herbert Waterous
Samuel...John Eaton
Frederic..Roy Cropper
Major General Stanley............................Frank Moulan
Edward...William Danforth
Mabel...Vivian Hart
Kate..Dean Dickens
Edith...Frances Baviello
Isabel...Gertrude Waldon
Ruth...Vera Ross
General Stanley's Daughters, Pirates, Policemen, etc.
    Act I.—A Rocky Shore Off Cornwall. Act II.—A Ruined Abbey.
    Staged by Frank Moulan.

Last sung on Broadway in July of this season, revived by
Lodewick Vroom. Previous to that revival there was one by
S. M. Chartock in April, 1934, with many of the same cast. Allen
Waterous was then the Samuel, John Cherry the Stanley, Frances
Baviello the Kate, Laura Ferguson the Edith and Olga Schu-
macher the Isabel.

TRIAL BY JURY

(16 performances)

An operetta in one scene by W. S. Gilbert; music by Arthur Sullivan. Revived by S. M. Chartock at the Majestic Theatre, New York, April 27, 1936.

Cast of characters—

```
The Learned Judge.................................Frank Moulan
Foreman of the Jury............................Herbert Waterous
Defendant.............................................Roy Cropper
Counsel.................................................John Eaton
Usher.........................................William Danforth
Plaintiff..........................................Vivian Hart
Jurors, Bridesmaids.
    Scene—The Court of Exchequer.
    Staged by Frank Moulan.
```

Revived in July of this season by Lodewick Vroom. The last previous revival was during the D'Oyly Carte Opera Company season beginning September 3, 1934.

H.M.S. PINAFORE

(16 performances)

An operetta in one scene by W. S. Gilbert; music by Arthur Sullivan. Revived by S. M. Chartock at the Majestic Theatre, New York, April 27, 1936.

Cast of characters—

```
The Right Hon. Sir Joseph Porter, K.C.B............Frank Moulan
Captain Corcoran......................................John Eaton
Ralph Rackstraw.....................................Roy Cropper
Dick Deadeye....................................William Danforth
Bill Bobstay....................................Herbert Waterous
Josephine...........................................Vivian Hart
Little Buttercup (Mrs. Cripps)........................Vera Ross
Hebe..............................................Dean Dickens
First Lord's Sisters, His Cousins and His Aunts, Sailors, etc.
    Scene—Deck of H.M.S. "Pinafore," off Portsmouth, England.
    Staged by Frank Moulan.
```

Revived in July of this season by Lodewick Vroom. The last previous revival was during the D'Oyly Carte Opera Company season beginning September 3, 1934.

IOLANTHE

(8 performances)

Operetta in two acts by W. S. Gilbert; music by Arthur Sullivan. Revived by S. M. Chartock at the Majestic Theatre, New York, May 4, 1936.

Cast of characters—

Lord Chancellor	William Danforth
Earl of Mountararat	Bertram Peacock
Earl of Tolloller	Roy Cropper
Private Willis	Herbert Waterous
Strephon	John Eaton
Queen of the Fairies	Vera Ross
Iolanthe	Dean Dickens
Celia	Frances Baviello
Leila	George Dieter
Fleta	Gertrude Waldon
Phyllis	Vivian Hart

Chorus of Fairies, Earls, Viscounts, Lords, Barons, Peers.
Act I.—An Arcadian Landscape. Act II.—Palace Yard, Westminster.
Staged by Frank Moulan.

The last previous revival was by the D'Oyly Carte Opera Company in September, 1934.

* ON YOUR TOES

(73 performances)

A revue in two acts by Richard Rodgers, George Abbott and Lorenz Hart. Produced by Dwight Deere Wiman at the Imperial Theatre, New York, April 11, 1936.

Cast of characters—

Phil Dolan II	Dave Jones
Lil Dolan	Ethel Hampton
Phil Dolan III	Tyrone Kearney
Lola	Betty Jane Smith
New Year	Betty Jane Smith
Sergei Alexandrovitch	Monty Woolley
Control Man	Russ Milton
Announcer	Henry Dick
Footmen	Beau Tilden, William Baker
Peggy Porterfield	Luella Gear
Junior	Ray Bolger
Frankie Frayne	Doris Carson
Sidney Cohen	David Morris
Vera Barnova	Tamara Geva
Anushka	Mae Noble
Constantine Morrossine	Demetrios Vilan
Mischka	Valery Streshnev
Vassilli	Robert Sidney
Dimitri	Basil Galahoff
Leon	Harold Haskin
Call Boy	Harry Peterson

In the "Princess Zenobia" Ballet:

Princess Zenobia	Tamara Geva
Beggar	Demetrios Vilan
Old Prince	William Baker
Young Prince	George Church
A Singer	Earle MacVeigh
A Waiter	Jack Quinn
Snoopy	William Wadsworth
A Policeman	Robert Forsythe
A Nurse	Frances Nevins
First Thug	Nick Dennis
Second Thug	Louis Walsh

In "Slaughter on Tenth Avenue"
```
Hoofer.......................................Ray Bolger
Strip Tease Girl.............................Tamara Geva
Big Boss.....................................George Church
```
Act I.—Scenes 1 and 3—Vaudeville Stage. 2—Dressing Room. 4—
Broadcasting Studio. 5—Sergei's Bedroom. 6—Classroom of Knicker-
bocker University, WPA Extension. 7—Vera's Apartment. 8—Central
Park. 9—Green Room, Cosmopolitan Opera House. 10—Dressing
Room. 11—La Princesse Zenobia Ballet. 12—In Front of Curtain.
13—Backstage. Act II.—Scene 1—Planetarium Roof Garden. 2 and
6—Opera House Stage. 3—Green Room. 4—In Front of Curtain.
5—Ballet of "Slaughter on Tenth Avenue."
    Staged by Worthington Miner; choreography by George Balanchine;
settings by Jo Mielziner; costumes by Irene Sharaff.

Phil Dolan III, the youngest of the Three Dolans, is taken out
of the family vaudeville act by his mother, who insists that
he should be educated. As a result Phil grows up a music teacher
instead of a hoofer. But a music teacher with the dance urge.
He longs to do something in the interpretive ballet line. While
he is teaching in a WPA extension course a student submits a
ballet called "Slaughter on Tenth Avenue." Phil is thrilled. Takes
it to Alexandrovitch of the ballet; arranges for its production;
goes on as a super to learn interpretive dancing; meets Vera
Barnova and learns about life; saves the ballet by jumping in as
leading dancer; goes back to the small town girl, Frankie Frayne,
who had loved him all the time.

BROADWAY SHO-WINDOW

A vaudeville revue in two parts assembled by Eugene Conrad.
Produced by Gus Edwards at the Broadway Theatre, New York,
April 12, 1936.

Principals engaged—

Ed Lowry	Armida
Mark Plant	Milton Charleston
Joe Cook, Jr.	Al Verdi
Billy Ambrose	Ruth Ambrose
Danny Drayson	The Three Robbins

    Staged by Gus Edwards; settings by Clark Robinson; dances ar-
ranged by Bill Powers.

SUMMER WIVES

(8 performances)

A farce with music in three acts by Mark Linder and Dolph
Singer. Produced by Jack Linder and D. F. Wolfson at the Mansfield Theatre, New York, April 13, 1936.

Cast of characters—
```
Gertie............................................Linda Lee Hill
Mike Chisley......................................Charles Dale
```

Mel Tone..Eddie Yubell
Molly La Rue....................................Helen Charleston
Helen La Mott..................................Miriam Battista
Barney..Phil Arnold
Benny..Ben Marks
Sammy..Sam Morrison
Murray Lowen......................................Joe Smith
Jennie Green....................................Annette Hoffman
Joe Wilder.......................................Clarence Rock
Fred Bernard.....................................Milton Douglas
Dan McGillicuddy..............................Morgan Conway
Minna Salmon....................................Mary Douglas
Mrs. Roslyn Berg..............................Gertrude Mudge
Betty Pratt..Jane Walsh
Mrs. Mortimer Rich................................Fay Martin
Mr. Mortimer Rich.............................Herbert Warren
Jacob Adelman..................................Daniel Makarenko
Max...J. Raymond Savich
Page Boy...Seymour Linder
Laura..Laura Gilbert
Jack Archibald..................................Jhoreck Rai
Syd Sayre and His Orchestra
Guests, Firemen, Bell Boys, etc.: Jack Hassler, Robert Turner,
Wm. B. Newgard, John Wheeler, Max Beck, Jack Zero, Debby
Dare, Bassine Alfaux, Marjorie Joyce, Bertha Mack, Jeanne
Temple, Alma Ross, Roslyn Kay, Freya Schorr, Herbert Ritter
Lynne, Saul Daniel.
Act I.—Mike Chisley's Booking Agency, New York City. Act II.—
Porch of Lowen-Green Country Club. Act III.—Scene 1—Lover's
Lane. 2—Social Hall, Lowen-Green Country Club.
Staged by Ira Hards; settings by Mabel Buell Studio.

Mike Chisley runs a vaudeville booking agency in New York.
Murray Lowen runs the Lowen-Green Country Club upstate.
Lowen comes to Mike to hire a staff of entertainers for the summer. Mike obliges with an assortment of talent and a dance
orchestra. Lowen is being hounded by a loan shark. He saves his
country club when the police close in on the shark. Mike Chisley
takes his floor show and goes home.

LADY LUCK

(5 performances)

A comedy in three acts by Hyman Adler and R. L. Hill. Produced by Robert Sterling at the Adelphi Theatre, New York,
April 15, 1936.

Cast of characters—

Uncle Tige..Leslie King
Leander Fraley.....................................Seth Arnold
Winnie Fraley....................................Maud Richmond
Petricoff Chernioff Karonsky......................Sam Sidman
Rudy Larkin......................................Charles Eaton
Lorna Fraley......................................Eileen Myers
Alice Fraley.......................................Viola Frayne
Mark Fraley......................................James Norris
Ted McCoy...Hurst Amyx
Robin Boyd.......................................Hall Shelton
"Whip" Lash......................................Jack Harwood
Matt Corrigan..................................J. Robert Haag

Acts I, II and III.—Living Room of Fraley Home, Los Angeles.
Staged by Hyman Adler; setting by Stagecraft.

The Leander Fraleys and their three children, Lorna, Alice
and Mark, are in Hollywood and broke. Alice, an expert stenographer, is the only one working and the others sponge on her.
Alice rebels and buys herself a course in scenario writing from
Robin Boyd. The Fraley fortunes continue to sink. Alice refuses
to marry "Whip" Lash, in real estate, being in love with Boyd,
the scenario agent. Lorna Fraley is about to elope with Ted
McCoy, a no-gooder, when Robin Boyd steps in as a G-man
and puts the cuffs on McCoy as a racketeer whom he had been
trailing for days.

* BURY THE DEAD

(65 performances)

A drama in one act by Irwin Shaw. Produced by Alex Yokel
at the Ethel Barrymore Theatre, New York, April 18, 1936.

Cast of characters—

First Soldier	John O'Shaughnessy
Sergeant	Robert Williams
Second Soldier	Robert Porterfield
Third Soldier	Joseph Kramm
Fourth Soldier	Joseph Wolff
Priest	Edwin Cooper
Rabbi	Samson Gordon
Private Driscoll	Robert Thomsen
Private Morgan	David Sands
Private Dean	Douglass Parkhirst
Private Webster	James Shelburne
Private Levy	Bertram Thorn
Private Schelling	Frank Tweddell
Captain	Neill O'Malley
First General	Aldrich Bowker
Second General	France Bendtsen
Third General	George O. Taylor
Doctor	Erik Walz
Stenographer	Booth Whitfield
Bevins	Garland Smith
Charlie	Jay Adler
Reporter	Will Geer
Editor	Gordon Nelson
First Whore	Dorothy Brackett
Second Whore	Herta Ware
Radio Announcer	Erik Walz
Bess Schelling	Kathryn Grill
Mrs. Dean	Mary Perry
Joan	Rose Keane
Julia Blake	Lesley Stafford
Katharine Driscoll	Norma Chambers
Martha Webster	Paula Bauersmith
A Voice	William Hunter

Scene—Battlefield, Where Graves Are Being Dug for Soldiers
Just Killed in an Advance During Second Year of War That Is to
Begin Tomorrow.
Staged by Worthington Miner and Walter Hart; settings by
Jensen Studios.

During the second year of "the war that is to begin tomorrow" a burial detail is digging a trench for six dead soldiers. The cadavers arise in their graves and refuse to be buried. Officers of the regiment plead with them to no avail. Their womenfolk are sent for and add their pleas that the dead men please stay dead. The dead ones refuse. They have a message for the living. They climb out of the trench and start across the world to deliver it.

Preceded by—

* PRELUDE

(65 performances)

A drama in one act by J. Edward Shugrue and John O'Shaughnessy and developed by members of the Actors' Repertory Company; music by Fred Stewart.

Cast of characters—

"Blinky"..Robert Thomsen
"Basket"...Frank Tweddell
"Poppy"...Will Geer
Also: Jay Adler, Paula Bauersmith, France Bendtsen, Aldrich Bowker, Dorothy Brackett, Norma Chambers, Edwin Cooper, Zelda Cotton, Samson Gordon, Kathryn Grill, William Hunter, Rose Keane, Joseph Kramm, Gordon Nelson, Neill O'Malley, Douglass Parkhirst, Mary Perry, Robert Porterfield, Anthony Ross, David Sands, James Shelburne, Garland Smith, Lesley Stafford, Lucille Strudwick, George O. Taylor, Bertram Thorn, Erik Walz, Herta Ware, Sally Washington, Booth Whitfield, Robert Williams and Joseph Wolff.

Three soldiers crippled in the World War recall the horrors and the thrill of their adventures at the front in a vivid protest against a recurrence of a similar calamity.

ELIZABETH SLEEPS OUT

(44 performances)

A comedy in three acts by Leslie Howard. Revived by J. Emerson Smythe at the Comedy Theatre, New York, April 20, 1936.

Cast of characters—

Vane...Edward Parker
Mrs. Case...Irene Britt
May Tweedie...Marie Perrin
Elizabeth Tweedie............................Mercedes Ferrara
George Appleway...............................Frank Armstrong
Amelia Tweedie...................................Frances Turner
Worthington Smythe...............................Dudley Barry
Wrigley..Robert Bruce
    Acts I, II and III.—Drawing Room of Tweedie Mansion, Murray Hill.
    Staged by Preston Clark; setting by Jensen Studios.

Under its original title of "Murray Hill" this farce was first performed in 1927 ("Best Plays 1927-28") with Leslie Howard playing his own hero. The role is that of a rich young man who, looking into the eyes of Amelia Tweedie in a traffic jam, falls desperately in love with her, smuggles himself into her home during a memorial service for her dead aunt, is engaged to impersonate an heir from Chicago who is too drunk to attend, is finally unmasked, confesses all and wins Amelia. Mr. Howard made some effort to prevent a revival of the play, which was done under semi-professional auspices.

CYRANO DE BERGERAC

(40 performances)

Heroic comedy in five acts by Edmond Rostand, translated into English verse by Brian Hooker. Produced by Walter Hampden at the New Amsterdam Theatre, New York, April 27, 1936.

Cast of characters—

Cyrano de Bergerac............................Walter Hampden
Christian de Neuvillette..........................Wilton Graff
Comte de Guiche.................................Robert Hudson
Ragueneau.......................................Hannam Clark
Le Bret...Ernest Rowan
Ligniere...William Sauter
Carbon de Castel-Jaloux...................C. Norman Hammond
Vicomte de Valvert..........................Robert C. Schnitzer
A Marquis......................................Arthur Gilmour
Another Marquis.....................................Paul Tripp
Montfleury.....................................Gerald O'Neill
Bellerose..Marcel Dill
Jodelet...John Van Zanten
Cuigy.....................................Richard Edward Bowler
Brissaille..Milo Boulton
A Busybody..................................Mortimer H. Weldon
A Musketeer................................Richard Ellington
D'Artagnan.....................................Bernard Fabrizi
A Spanish Officer.................................Howard Galt
A Cavalier......................................Herbert Vigran
A Porter...James Malaidy
A Man...Franklin Salisbury
Another Man....................................Murray D'Arcy
A Guardsman.............................Edward Everett Hale
A Citizen...William Grier
His Son...Peter Johnston
A Pickpocket...................................Harvey Sayers
Bertrandou.......................................Walter Plinge
A Capuchin.......................................George Thorp
Pages............................Edwin Ross and Michel Wardell
Roxane......................................Katharine Warren
Her Duenna.......................................Mabel Moore
Lise...Constance Pelissier
An Orange Girl....................................Sela Krebs
A Flower Girl.......................................Clare Mason
A Soubrette......................................Laura Barrett
A Comedienne.......................................Albon Lewis
Another Comedienne.......................Laura Eliza Windsor

Mother Marguerite de Jesus........................Joanna Dorman
Sister Marthe....................................Margaret Watson
Sister Claire ....Mildred Vail
A Nun ....Eliza Connolly
Cadets of Gascoyne: William Grier, Richard Edward Bowler, Milo
    Boulton, Marcel Dill, Edward Everett Hale, Truman Quevli,
    Bernard Fabrizi.
Poets: Mortimer H. Weldon, Franklin Salisbury, Harvey Sayers,
    John Van Zanten, Henry Lase.
Intellectuals and Precieuses: Albon Lewis, Laura Barrett, Laura Eliza
    Windsor, Mildred Starkweather and Jane Weldon.
Citizens, Musketeers, Thieves, Pastry-Cooks, Actors, Musicians, Span-
    ish Soldiers, Spectators, etc.: Jack Harling, Jack Penwell, Her-
    bert Treitel, Franklin Webb, Geoffrey Lind, Richard Ross, George
    Marsh, Boris Ulmar and Rose Le Gant.
    Act I.—A Performance at the Hotel de Bourgoyne, Paris. Act II.
    —The Bakery of the Poets. Act III.—Roxane's Kiss. Act IV.—
The Cadets of Gascoyne. Act V.—Cyrano's Gazette.
    Staged by Walter Hampden; settings by Claude Bragdon.

Last played on Broadway for 16 performances in December,
1932, when it was revived by Walter Hampden with much the
same cast as that of this season. The original American production was made by Richard Mansfield in 1898, with Margaret
Anglin as Roxane. The first Hampden revival was in 1923, with
Carroll McComas the Roxane.

* PRE-HONEYMOON

(52 performances)

A comedy in three acts by Alford Van Ronkel and Anne Nichols. Produced by Anne Nichols at the Lyceum Theatre, New
York, April 30, 1936.

Cast of characters—

Pearl ....Georgette Harvey
Virginia Barnard...............................Jessie Royce Landis
Mr. Bell..Franklyn Fox
Joe Dukes...Louis Jean Heydt
Senator Dexter....................................Clyde Fillmore
Millie Marlowe..................................Marjorie Peterson
Jean Hammond.......................................Sylvia Field
Ken Arnold..Roy Roberts
Ace ....Morgan Stuart
Murphy ....Thomas P. Dillon
Sweeney ....Allen H. Fagan
Mr. Jones ....Pass Le Noir
Nurse ....Millicent Manners
    Acts I, II and III.—Studio apartment of Virginia Barnard.
    Staged by the authors; setting by Cirker and Robbins.

Virginia Barnard, engaged to marry U. S. Senator Dexter, goes
to Miami on a pre-honeymoon business trip, renting her New
York apartment to two girl friends of Senator Dexter's son Joe,
who is supposed to be in Europe. One of the girls, Millie Marlowe, is a bubble dancer in a night club. The Senator, seeing
Millie, thinks also to take a pre-honeymoon flier while his fiancée

is away. Millie announces her engagement to the Senator; Millie's boy friend, Ken Arnold, tries to break up the affair by smuggling himself into Millie's room in pajamas and calling the Senator to come see; Millie calls a policeman and the hotel proprietor sends in the house detective. Complications until 11 P.M. Then Virginia returns and reclaims the Senator.

PARNELL

(32 performances)

A drama in three acts by Elsie Schauffler. Revived by Pierce-Power-Waters at the 48th Street Theatre, New York, May 4, 1936.

Cast of characters—

Katharine O'Shea	Edith Barrett
Mrs. Benjamin Wood	Effie Shannon
Mrs. Annie Steele	Enid Cooper
Clara Wood	Phyllis Connard
Captain William Henry O'Shea	John Emery
The O'Gorman Mahon	Gordon Burby
Timothy Healy	Winston O'Keefe
Thomas Murphy	Barry Macollum
Michael Davitt	Whitford Kane
Montagu Harrison	Gage Clark
Parnell	Dennis King
Gladstone	Alexander Frank
Mr. Stanley	Harry Redding
John Redmond	Clement O'Loghlen
1st Leader	Hugh Bigelow
2nd Leader	Charles Trexler
3rd Leader	William Swetland

Act I.—Scenes 1 and 3—Katharine O'Shea's Drawing Room at Eltham, Nine Miles from London in 1880. 2—Committee Room 15, House of Commons. Act II.—Drawing Room at Eltham. Act III.—Scene 1—Gladstone's Study, 10 Downing Street. 2—Committee Room 15. 3—Drawing Room at Eltham, 1890.

Staged from Guthrie McClintic's original direction by Robinson Smith and Frederick Ayer, assisted by Winston O'Keefe. Settings and costumes by Stewart Chaney.

"Parnell" was produced originally on November 5, 1935, at the Ethel Barrymore Theatre, as will be seen by a reference to the earlier pages of this volume. The engagement was brought to a close because of a poorly adjusted overhead expense. With new principals, and some changes in cast, the play was restaged in May as above noted.

A PRIVATE AFFAIR

(28 performances)

A comedy in three acts by Gaston Valcourt. Produced by Albert Bannister at the Masque Theatre, New York, May 14, 1936.

Cast of characters—

Nautica Bartlett.................................Florence Britton
Madge Forrester...................................Helen Raymond
Mrs. Simon Bartlett...............................Nelly Malcolm
Laura Hamilton.....................................Betty Linley
Bertha ....Andree Corday
A Young Man...Oscar Shaw
Jimmy Mansard..................................Charles Campbell
Col. Rufus Rhinebeck............................George Graham
Leo Hamilton......................................A. J. Herbert
Agent de Police...................................Royal C. Stout

    Acts I, II and III.—Living Room of the Duchesse de Tarascon's Chalet in the Swiss Alps.
    Staged by Albert Bannister; settings by United Studios.

Nautica Bartlett and three lady friends rent a Swiss chalet for the summer and grow lonesome for masculine companionship. A young man enters the chalet in the guise of a gentleman burglar and is immediately surrounded. The young man collects the ladies' jewels in fun and takes on Nautica in earnest, revealing himself finally as the son of the lady who owns the chalet in search of certain important papers.

* NEW FACES OF 1936

(31 performances)

A musical revue in two acts; lyrics by June Sillman, Edwin Gilbert and Bickley Reichner; music by Alexander Fogarty and Irvin Graham; sketches by Mindret Lord and Everett Marcy. Produced by Leonard Sillman at the Vanderbilt Theatre, New York, May 19, 1936.

Principals engaged—

Jack Smart
Tom Rutherford
Jack Blair
George Byron
Robert Burton
Robert Bard
Van Johnson
Karl Swenson
Arthur Hughes
Mischa Pompianov
Cliff Allen
Imogene Coca
Katherine Mayfield
Irene Moore
Gerry Probst
Helen Craig
Marion Pierce
June Blair
Elizabeth Wilde
Jean Bellows
Gloria Rondell
Billie Haywood

    Staged by Leonard Sillman; sketches directed by Anton Bundsmann; dances by Ned McGurn; music by Ray Kavanaugh; settings and costumes by Stewart Chaney.

THE COUNTY CHAIRMAN

(8 performances)

A comedy in four acts by George Ade. Revived by The Players at the National Theatre, May 25, 1936.

Cast of characters—

Honorable Jim Hackler, County Chairman..........Charles Coburn
Tilford Wheeler...............................Alexander Kirkland
Elias Rigby...Forrest Orr
Riley Cleaver.................................Lyster Chambers
Wilson Prewitt...................................George Christie
Jupiter Pettaway................................Ben Lackland
Sassafras Livingstone...........................James Kirkwood
Joseph Whittaker...................................Ben Smith
Uncle Eck Milbury.............................Parker Fennelly
Jefferson Briscoe.......................................Jay Fassett
Vance Jimmison...................................Arthur Allen
Cal Barcus.....................................Houston Richards
"Chub" Tolliver.......................................Jackie Kelk
Henry ....James La Curto
Glabe Overton...............................Philip F. Broughton
Amos Whitney....................................Harold McGee
D. Montgomery....................................John C. King
Lucy Rigby...Rose Hobart
Mrs. Elias Rigby....................................Mary Ryan
Mrs. Jefferson Briscoe...........................Eda Heinemann
Lorena Watkins...............................Dorothy Stickney
"Chick" Elzey.....................................Linda Watkins
Antioch Peerless Quartette—Carl Mathieu, Walter Scanlon, Paul
    Parks, Thomas Montgomery.
    Act I.—In Front of Jimmison's Store, Main Street, Antioch. Act
II.—Court House Grove. Act III.—Hackler's Law Office. Act IV.—
Town Hall on Election Night.
    Staged by Sam Forrest; settings by W. Oden Waller.

Jim Hackler, county chairman, maneuvers the nomination of his young law partner, Tilford Wheeler, for the office of prosecuting attorney, to run against Elias Rigby of the opposition. Tilford, in love with Rigby's daughter, Lucy, agrees to keep personalities out of the campaign. In the heat of a picnic debate he breaks his promise. Lucy tries to give Tilford up, but is won back when Tilford wins the election and she learns the truth about certain underhand dealings of her father. "The County Chairman" was first produced in Chicago in 1903, after preliminary performances in South Bend, Ind. Macklyn Arbucle played Hackler, a part that afterward fell to both Theodore Hamilton and Theodore Roberts. The comedy role of Sassafras Livingstone was played by the minstrels, Willis P. Sweatman and George Thatcher.

TO MY HUSBAND

(16 performances)

A comedy in three acts by William H. Fulham. Produced by Joe Byron Totten at the Belmont Theatre, New York, June 1, 1936.

Cast of characters—

Elliott Vane...................................Donald McClelland
Sarah Vane...Julie Benell
Harry Chase...King Calder

Trudy ....Jane Farrell
Nora Vane.......................................Madeline Grey
Iris Swann.......................................Madeleine Clive
Timothy ....Master Warren Mills
    Acts I, II and III.—Living Room of the Vanes' Home, West-
chester, New York.
    Staged by Joe Byron Totten; setting by Jules Laurentz.

Elliott Vane, married for seven years to Sarah, who has presented him with three children, decides that he needs a change
of domestic routine. He will divorce Sarah and marry Iris Swann,
a dancer. Sarah has a different plan. She is perfectly willing to
give Elliott a divorce, and goes so far as to invite Iris Swann to
dinner to talk the matter over. At dinner she tells Iris that she
is not only welcome to Elliott, but to the house with all its
atrocious furniture and the three children as well. Unhappily the
children are coming down with the whooping cough. Sarah plans
a career for herself, but when the children call she goes back to
her job and Iris swishes out of the picture.

OFF BROADWAY

The Theatre Union gave a series of Sunday performances at the Civic Repertory Theatre opening January 12, 1936, with a program of four one-act plays: "Hymn to the Rising Sun" and "Unto Such Glory," by Paul Green; "Private Hicks," by Albert Maltz, and "Angelo Herndon," by Elizabeth England and Joseph North. "Running Dogs," by John Wexley, directed by Anthony Brown; "A Letter to the President," by George Sklar and Paul Peters with music by Jerome Moross; "Picket Line" as it might be written by Shakespeare, Noel Coward and Chekov, and several dance satires opened February 16. The "Let Freedom Ring" company presented "Over Here," by Walter B. Hare, and "Bury the Dead," by Irwin Shaw, at the Civic Repertory Theatre under the auspices of the New Theatre League, March 14 and 15 (later moving uptown) and on May 2, "Ten Million Others" by David Danzig, staged by Clem Wilenchick.

The Theatre of Action produced "The Crime" by Michael Blankfort, directed by Alfred Saxe and Elia Kazan, and "The Green Bundle," by Paul Peters, opening its seventh season March 1, 1936. The Theatre Collective took over the Provincetown Theatre March 21 and opened with three one-act plays, "Private Hicks," by Albert Maltz, "You Can't Change Human Nature," by Philip Stevenson, directed by Lasar Galpern, and "The Pastry-baker," by Lope de Vega, adapted from the Spanish by M. Jagendorf. These plays were repeated March 27 and played for the week following.

"The Drift," by Paul and Claire Sifton, a labor play, was given three performances May 28, 29 and 30, 1936, at the Community Center.

The Artef Players Collective opened their season with "The Reapers," by Siskind Liev, at the President Theatre, New York, October 5, 1935. It was directed by Benno Schneider with settings by M. Solotaroff, and was followed by a series of productions including "Haunch, Paunch and Jowl," adapted by Khaver Paver from a dramatization by Donald Davis and Samuel Ornitz; "Hirsch Lekert," a Soviet historic drama; "Artef Variety Show" and "Recruits."

"A Million Torments," by Valentine Katayev, translated and

adapted from the Russian by Charles Malamuth, was produced by the Forum Theatre, Inc., at the Heckscher Theatre, January 15, 1936, staged by Saul Morris with settings by Fred Shapiro.

"The Wild Man" by Jacob Gordin was played at the Public Theatre by Luther Adler in June, 1935. This was a part made famous by his father, Jacob. And at the Second Avenue Theatre "Matinee Wife" ran for 200 performances.

Joseph Lawren organized the French Players, with Guy de Vestal directing, and produced Alfred Savoir's "Bluebeard's Eighth Wife" January 26, 1936, at the Heckscher Theatre, followed by several other plays in the French language. The Teatro D'Arte opened its sixth season October 6, 1935, at the Longacre Theatre with "Quo Vadis," arranged and directed by Commendatore Giuseppe Sterni. This was followed by Alfred Capus's four-act comedy, "The Adventurer," November 10, 1935, and an Italian translation of Louis N. Parker's "The Cardinal," by Camillo Antona Traversi, at the Ritz Theatre, December 7, 1935, and the Dumas "The Three Guardsmen," in February of 1936. The Teatro Italia presented "Africanella," an Italian war drama written by Comm. Clemente Giglio, at the Venice Theatre in early January, "Maria Rosa" in May, and "The Train of Death" at the Comedy.

The Lighthouse Players opened their 13th season under the direction of Phillis Marschall with a farce, "Speak for Yourself, Joan," by Wall Spence.

A Chamberlain Brown stock company played three weeks at the Downtown National Theatre.

Gus Edwards produced "Broadway Sho-Window," a vaudeville revue in two acts with sketches and lyrics by Eugene Conrad, settings by Clark Robinson and dances arranged by Bill Powers at the Broadway Theatre April 12. Joe Cook, Jr., Danny Drayson, Ruth and Billy Ambrose, The Three Robbins, Al Verdi, Ed Lowry, Armida and Mark Plant were in the cast.

The Snarks' twenty-seventh annual production, March 16, 17 and 18, at the Heckscher Theatre, was "The Leaping Sword," a Japanese fantasy by Post Wheeler with Robert Ross directing and Robert Woods designing the sets.

There were a number of revivals. The Irish Repertory Players revived Lennox Robinson's "Far Off Hills" in January with Irwin McIver, Janice Hughes, Grace Cahill and Larry Murphy in the cast, and Sean O'Casey's "Juno and the Paycock," staged by J. Augustus Keogh, at the Heckscher Theatre, May 21, 22 and 23. The Re Gamey Players, directed by Giana Re Gamey, revived Ibsen's "Ghosts" at the Actor's Lounge Theatre October 2, 1935, with Robert Christie, a young British actor, as Pastor Manders, Marjorie Wolff as Regina, Fred Olmstead as Engstrand and Owell Elliott as Oswald. "Murder in the Old Red Barn" was revived by Harry Bannister, John Krimsky and Lucius Beebe at the American Music Hall, February 1, 1936. The settings were designed by Frank Ambros and Stephen Golding. Paul and Virginia Gillmore revived "No Mother to Guide Her" at the Cherry Lane, June 4, 1936.

Catharine A. Bamman launched the seventh edition of "Sunday Nights at 9" November 10, 1935, at the Barbizon-Plaza Theatre with Felicia Sorel in dance portraits, Shirley Booth in a satire on first night audiences, Helen Howe in a monologue, Dwight Weist, impersonator, Clifford Naudahl, Vandy Cape and the Yale Puppeteers on the program. The series continued intermittently throughout the season. The Metropolitan Players started their third edition of "Nine O'Clock Revue" at the Heckscher Theatre, July 7, 1935.

Louise Alice Williams presented her annual "Evenings in Dixie" at the Barbizon-Plaza Theatre October 23, 1935; Michael Strange appeared in a recital of poetic stories accompanied by Elsa Moegle at the Town Hall, November 20, 1935, and Mrs. Richard Mansfield gave a series of Shakespearian readings in December at the Christodora House.

Clare Tree Major's Children's Theatre Company opened its season at the Barbizon-Plaza Theatre, October 19, 1935, with "Robin Hood," followed by "Hans Brinker," November 9; "Alice in Wonderland," December 28; "Beauty and the Beast," February 1; "Heidi," February 29; and "The Secret Garden," April 4.

The Children's Theatre of Columbia presented a series of marionette performances at the McMillin Academy Theatre, opening with Sue Hastings' Group in "Cinderella," November 2, 1935, and following with the Kingsland Marionettes in "The Prince and the Goblins" and "The Donkey and His Friends," November 16; Sue Hastings' "Aladdin," November 30; Kingsland's "Rapunzel" and "Beppo's Circus," December 14; Tony Sarg's "A Connecticut Yankee," December 28; Sue Hastings' "The Prince and the Magic Sword," February 15, 1936; Tatterman's "The Glowing Bird," February 29; Remo Buffano's "The Three Bears" and "Julius Cæsar's Circus," March 14; and Sue Hastings' "Peter Rabbit," March 28.

The Yale Puppeteers presented a musical comedy, "Mr.

Noah," and a topical review at the Bayes Theatre from December 22 to December 28, 1935, with Michael Myerberg as producer.

The Federal Theatre Project gave a Marionette Festival at the Chanin Theatre May 26 to May 30, 1936, presenting "The Birthday Party," "A Trip Around the World," "The Dragon Zne Zee," an original Chinese fantasy by Carl Glick, with Remo Bufano as director. The Federal Theatre also gave some 2,600 free performances in hospitals, schools and other public institutions. June 2, 1936, "Stars on Strings" (marionette) began at the Biltmore Theatre, continuing until June 6, 1936.

STATISTICAL SUMMARY

(LAST SEASON PLAYS WHICH ENDED RUNS AFTER JUNE 16, 1935)

Plays	Number Performances	Plays	Number Performances
Accent on Youth	229	Personal Appearance	501
Anything Goes	420	Petticoat Fever	137
Awake and Sing	209	Petrified Forest	197
Ceiling Zero	104	Sketch Book	207
Fly Away Home	204	Something Gay	72
Kind Lady	102	Till the Day I Die	136
Old Maid, The	305	Waiting for Lefty	168
Parade	40	Young Go First, The	39

LONG RUNS ON BROADWAY

To June 15, 1936

(Plays marked with asterisk were still playing June 15, 1936)

Plays	Number Performances	Plays	Number Performances
Abie's Irish Rose	2,532	Kiki	600
Lightnin'	1,291	Blossom Time	592
*Tobacco Road	1,094	*Three Men on a Horse	591
The Bat	867	Show Boat	572
The Ladder	789	The Show-Off	571
The First Year	760	Sally	570
Seventh Heaven	704	Strictly Dishonorable	557
Peg o' My Heart	692	Good News	551
East Is West	680	The Music Master	540
Irene	670	The Boomerang	522
*Children's Hour	667	Blackbirds	518
A Trip to Chinatown	657	Sunny	517
Rain	648	The Vagabond King	511
The Green Pastures	640	The New Moon	509
Is Zat So	618	Shuffle Along	504
Student Prince	608	Personal Appearance	501
Broadway	603	Bird in Hand	500
Adonis	603	Sailor, Beware!	500
Street Scene	601		

DRAMA CRITICS' CIRCLE AWARD

In October, 1935, New York drama critics met and revived a Drama Critics' Circle that had ceased to function through lack of interest. At this meeting it was decided, as a help to the constructive work of the critical fraternity, to vote each year upon "The best new play written by an American playwright and produced in New York," and, if a selection could be made that should be practically unanimous, to award a silver plaque designed by Henry Varnum Poor to the dramatist whose work was thus favored. Seventeen members were elected to membership. It was agreed that five dissenting votes would nullify a choice. At a meeting in March the Circle voted on five plays placed in nomination by the full membership. These plays were Maxwell Anderson's "Winterset," Robert Sherwood's "Idiot's Delight," S. N. Behrman's "End of Summer," Katharine Dayton's and George Kaufman's "First Lady," Sidney Kingsley's "Dead End" and Owen and Donald Davis' "Ethan Frome." A choice was made on the fifth ballot, when "Winterset" received fourteen of the seventeen votes cast. Three dissenters named "Idiot's Delight" as their preference. A month later the Pulitzer Prize committee, continuing the annual award first given in 1918, named the Sherwood comedy as its choice for 1935-36.

In the organization of the New York Drama Critics' Circle (see frontispiece) Mr. Hammond represented the New York *Herald Tribune*, Mr. Lockridge the New York *Evening Sun*, Mr. Gabriel the New York *American*, Mr. Anderson the New York *Journal*, Mr. Bolton the New York *Morning Telegraph*, Mr. Field the Brooklyn *Times*, Mr. Brown the New York *Evening Post*, Mr. Pollock the Brooklyn *Eagle*, George Jean Nathan both *Vanity Fair* and *Life*, Mr. Mantle the New York *Daily News*, Mr. Garland the New York *World-Telegram*, Mr. Allen New York *Women's Wear* and Mr. Atkinson the New York *Times*.

A pictorial record of the ceremonies attending the awarding of the plaque to Mr. Anderson show the playwright receiving the award from Brooks Atkinson, president of the Critics' Circle, and a snap of Burgess Meredith and Margot as they were broadcasting a scene from the prize-winning drama, "Winterset."

PULITZER PRIZE WINNERS

"For the original American play performed in New York which shall best represent the educational value and power of the stage in raising the standard of good morals, good taste and good manners."—The Will of Joseph Pulitzer, dated April 16, 1904.

In 1929 the advisory board, which, according to the terms of the will, "shall have the power in its discretion to suspend or to change any subject or subjects . . . if in the judgment of the board such suspension, changes or substitutions shall be conducive to the public good," decided to eliminate from the above paragraph relating to the prize-winning play the words "in raising the standard of good morals, good taste and good manners."

The committee awards to date have been:

1917-18—Why Marry? by Jesse Lynch Williams
1918-19—None
1919-20—Miss Lulu Bett, by Zona Gale
1920-21—Beyond the Horizon, by Eugene O'Neill
1921-22—Anna Christie, by Eugene O'Neill
1922-23—Icebound, by Owen Davis
1923-24—Hell-bent fer Heaven, by Hatcher Hughes
1924-25—They Knew What They Wanted, by Sidney Howard
1925-26—Craig's Wife, by George Kelly
1926-27—In Abraham's Bosom, by Paul Green
1927-28—Strange Interlude, by Eugene O'Neill
1928-29—Street Scene, by Elmer Rice
1929-30—The Green Pastures, by Marc Connelly
1930-31—Alison's House, by Susan Glaspell
1931-32—Of Thee I Sing, by George S. Kaufman, Morrie Ryskind, Ira and George Gershwin
1932-33—Both Your Houses, by Maxwell Anderson
1933-34—Men in White, by Sidney Kingsley
1934-35—The Old Maid, by Zoe Akins
1935-36—Idiot's Delight, by Robert E. Sherwood

PREVIOUS VOLUMES OF BEST PLAYS

Plays chosen to represent the theatre seasons from 1909 to 1934 are as follows:

1909-1919

"The Easiest Way," by Eugene Walters. Published by G. W. Dillingham, New York; Houghton Mifflin Co., Boston.

"Mrs. Bumpstead-Leigh," by Harry James Smith. Published by Samuel French, New York.

"Disraeli," by Louis N. Parker. Published by Dodd, Mead and Co., New York.

"Romance," by Edward Sheldon. Published by the Macmillan Co., New York.

"Seven Keys to Baldpate," by George M. Cohan. Published by Bobbs-Merrill Co., Indianapolis, as a novel by Earl Derr Biggers; as a play by Samuel French, New York.

"On Trial," by Elmer Reizenstein. Published by Samuel French, New York.

"The Unchastened Woman," by Louis Kaufman Anspacher. Published by Harcourt, Brace and Howe, Inc., New York.

"Good Gracious Annabelle," by Clare Kummer. Published by Samuel French, New York.

"Why Marry?" by Jesse Lynch Williams. Published by Charles Scribner's Sons, New York.

"John Ferguson," by St. John Ervine. Published by the Macmillan Co., New York.

1919-1920

"Abraham Lincoln," by John Drinkwater. Published by Houghton Mifflin Co., Boston.

"Clarence," by Booth Tarkington. Published by Samuel French, New York.

"Beyond the Horizon," by Eugene G. O'Neill. Published by Boni & Liveright, Inc., New York.

"Déclassée," by Zoe Akins. Published by Liveright, Inc., New York.

"The Famous Mrs. Fair," by James Forbes. Published by Samuel French, New York.

"The Jest," by Sem Benelli. (American adaptation by Edward Sheldon.)

"Jane Clegg," by St. John Ervine. Published by Henry Holt & Co., New York.

"Mamma's Affair," by Rachel Barton Butler. Published by Samuel French, New York.

"Wedding Bells," by Salisbury Field. Published by Samuel French, New York.

"Adam and Eva," by George Middleton and Guy Bolton. Published by Samuel French, New York.

1920-1921

"Deburau," adapted from the French of Sacha Guitry by H. Granville Barker. Published by G. P. Putnam's Sons, New York.

"The First Year," by Frank Craven. Published by Samuel French, New York.

"Enter Madame," by Gilda Varesi and Dolly Byrne. Published by G. P. Putnam's Sons, New York.

"The Green Goddess," by William Archer. Published by Alfred A. Knopf, New York.

"Liliom," by Ferenc Molnar. Published by Boni & Liveright, New York.

"Mary Rose," by James M. Barrie. Published by Charles Scribner's Sons, New York.

"Nice People," by Rachel Crothers. Published by Charles Scribner's Sons, New York.

"The Bad Man," by Porter Emerson Browne. Published by G. P. Putnam's Sons, New York.

"The Emperor Jones," by Eugene G. O'Neill. Published by Boni & Liveright, New York.

"The Skin Game," by John Galsworthy. Published by Charles Scribner's Sons, New York.

1921-1922

"Anna Christie," by Eugene G. O'Neill. Published by Boni & Liveright, New York.

"A Bill of Divorcement," by Clemence Dane. Published by the Macmillan Company, New York.

"Dulcy," by George S. Kaufman and Marc Connelly. Published by G. P. Putnam's Sons, New York.

"He Who Gets Slapped," adapted from the Russian of Leonid Andreyev by Gregory Zilboorg. Published by Brentano's, New York.

"Six Cylinder Love," by William Anthony McGuire.

"The Hero," by Gilbert Emery.

"The Dover Road," by Alan Alexander Milne. Published by Samuel French, New York.

"Ambush," by Arthur Richman.

"The Circle," by William Somerset Maugham.

"The Nest," by Paul Geraldy and Grace George.

1922-1923

"Rain," by John Colton and Clemence Randolph. Published by Liveright, Inc., New York.

"Loyalties," by John Galsworthy. Published by Charles Scribner's Sons, New York.

"Icebound," by Owen Davis. Published by Little, Brown & Company, Boston.

"You and I," by Philip Barry. Published by Brentano's, New York.

"The Fool," by Channing Pollock. Published by Brentano's, New York.

"Merton of the Movies," by George Kaufman and Marc Connelly, based on the novel of the same name by Harry Leon Wilson.

"Why Not?" by Jesse Lynch Williams. Published by Walter H. Baker Co., Boston.

"The Old Soak," by Don Marquis. Published by Doubleday, Page & Company, New York.

"R.U.R.," by Karel Capek. Translated by Paul Selver. Published by Doubleday, Page & Company.

"Mary the 3d," by Rachel Crothers. Published by Brentano's, New York.

1923-1924

"The Swan," translated from the Hungarian of Ferenc Molnar by Melville Baker. Published by Boni & Liveright, New York.

"Outward Bound," by Sutton Vane. Published by Boni & Liveright, New York.

"The Show-off," by George Kelly. Published by Little, Brown & Company, Boston.

"The Changelings," by Lee Wilson Dodd. Published by E. P. Dutton & Company, New York.

"Chicken Feed," by Guy Bolton. Published by Samuel French,

New York and London.

"Sun-Up," by Lula Vollmer. Published by Brentano's, New York.

"Beggar on Horseback," by George Kaufman and Marc Connelly. Published by Boni & Liveright, New York.

"Tarnish," by Gilbert Emery. Published by Brentano's, New York.

"The Goose Hangs High," by Lewis Beach. Published by Little, Brown & Company, Boston.

"Hell-bent fer Heaven," by Hatcher Hughes. Published by Harper Bros., New York.

1924-1925

"What Price Glory?" by Laurence Stallings and Maxwell Anderson. Published by Harcourt, Brace & Co., New York.

"They Knew What They Wanted," by Sidney Howard. Published by Doubleday, Page & Company, New York.

"Desire Under the Elms," by Eugene G. O'Neill. Published by Boni & Liveright, New York.

"The Firebrand," by Edwin Justus Mayer. Published by Boni & Liveright, New York.

"Dancing Mothers," by Edgar Selwyn and Edmund Goulding.

"Mrs. Partridge Presents," by Mary Kennedy and Ruth Warren. Published by Samuel French, New York.

"The Fall Guy," by James Gleason and George Abbott. Published by Samuel French, New York.

"The Youngest," by Philip Barry. Published by Samuel French, New York.

"Minick," by Edna Ferber and George S. Kaufman. Published by Doubleday, Page & Company, New York.

"Wild Birds," by Dan Totheroh. Published by Doubleday, Page & Company, New York.

1925-1926

"Craig's Wife," by George Kelly. Published by Little, Brown & Company, Boston.

"The Great God Brown," by Eugene G. O'Neill. Published by Boni & Liveright, New York.

"The Green Hat," by Michael Arlen.

"The Dybbuk," by S. Ansky, Henry G. Alsberg-Winifred Katzin translation. Published by Boni & Liveright, New York.

"The Enemy," by Channing Pollock. Published by Brentano's,

New York.

"The Last of Mrs. Cheyney," by Frederick Lonsdale. Published by Samuel French, New York.

"Bride of the Lamb," by William Hurlbut. Published by Boni & Liveright, New York.

"The Wisdom Tooth," by Marc Connelly. Published by George H. Doran & Company, New York.

"The Butter and Egg Man," by George Kaufman. Published by Boni & Liveright, New York.

"Young Woodley," by John Van Druten. Published by Simon and Schuster, New York.

1926-1927

"Broadway," by Philip Dunning and George Abbott. Published by George H. Doran Company, New York.

"Saturday's Children," by Maxwell Anderson. Published by Longmans, Green & Company, New York.

"Chicago," by Maurine Watkins. Published by Alfred A. Knopf, Inc., New York.

"The Constant Wife," by William Somerset Maugham. Published by George H. Doran Company, New York.

"The Play's the Thing," by Ferenc Molnar and P. G. Wodehouse. Published by Brentano's, New York.

"The Road to Rome," by Robert Emmet Sherwood. Published by Charles Scribner's Sons, New York.

"The Silver Cord," by Sidney Howard. Published by Charles Scribner's Sons, New York.

"The Cradle Song," translated from the Spanish of G. Martinez Sierra by John Garrett Underhill. Published by E. P. Dutton & Company, New York.

"Daisy Mayme," by George Kelly. Published by Little, Brown & Company, Boston.

"In Abraham's Bosom," by Paul Green. Published by Robert M. McBride & Company, New York.

1927-1928

"Strange Interlude," by Eugene G. O'Neill. Published by Boni & Liveright, New York.

"The Royal Family," by Edna Ferber and George Kaufman. Published by Doubleday, Doran & Company, New York.

"Burlesque," by George Manker Watters. Published by Doubleday, Doran & Company, New York.

"Coquette," by George Abbott and Ann Bridgers. Published by Longmans, Green & Company, New York, London, Toronto.

"Behold the Bridegroom," by George Kelly. Published by Little, Brown & Company, Boston.

"Porgy," by DuBose Heyward. Published by Doubleday, Doran & Company, New York.

"Paris Bound," by Philip Barry. Published by Samuel French, New York.

"Escape," by John Galsworthy. Published by Charles Scribner's Sons, New York.

"The Racket," by Bartlett Cormack. Published by Samuel French, New York.

"The Plough and the Stars," by Sean O'Casey. Published by the Macmillan Company, New York.

1928-1929

"Street Scene," by Elmer Rice. Published by Samuel French, New York.

"Journey's End," by R. C. Sheriff. Published by Brentano's, New York.

"Wings Over Europe," by Robert Nichols and Maurice Browne. Published by Covici-Friede, New York.

"Holiday," by Philip Barry. Published by Samuel French, New York.

"The Front Page," by Ben Hecht and Charles MacArthur. Published by Covici-Friede, New York.

"Let Us Be Gay," by Rachel Crothers. Published by Samuel French, New York.

"Machinal," by Sophie Treadwell.

"Little Accident," by Floyd Dell and Thomas Mitchell.

"Gypsy," by Maxwell Anderson.

"The Kingdom of God," by G. Martinez Sierra; English version by Helen and Harley Granville-Barker. Published by E. P. Dutton & Company, New York.

1929-1930

"The Green Pastures," by Marc Connelly (adapted from "Ol' Man Adam and His Chillun," by Roark Bradford). Published by Farrar & Rinehart, Inc., New York.

"The Criminal Code," by Martin Flavin. Published by Horace Liveright, New York.

"Berkeley Square," by John Balderstone. Published by the Macmillan Company, New York.

"Strictly Dishonorable," by Preston Sturges. Published by Horace Liveright, New York.

"The First Mrs. Fraser," by St. John Ervine. Published by the Macmillan Company, New York.

"The Last Mile," by John Wexley. Published by Samuel French, New York.

"June Moon," by Ring W. Lardner and George S. Kaufman. Published by Charles Scribner's Sons, New York.

"Michael and Mary," by A. A. Milne. Published by Chatto & Windus, London.

"Death Takes a Holiday," by Walter Ferris (adapted from the Italian of Alberto Casella). Published by Samuel French, New York.

"Rebound," by Donald Ogden Stewart. Published by Samuel French, New York.

1930-1931

"Elizabeth the Queen," by Maxwell Anderson. Published by Longmans, Green & Co., New York.

"Tomorrow and Tomorrow," by Philip Barry. Published by Samuel French, New York.

"Once in a Lifetime," by George S. Kaufman and Moss Hart. Published by Farrar and Rinehart, New York.

"Green Grow the Lilacs," by Lynn Riggs. Published by Samuel French, New York and London.

"As Husbands Go," by Rachel Crothers. Published by Samuel French, New York.

"Alison's House," by Susan Glasgow. Published by Samuel French, New York.

"Five-Star Final," by Louis Weitzenkorn. Published by Samuel French, New York.

"Overture," by William Bolitho. Published by Simon & Schuster, New York.

"The Barretts of Wimpole Street," by Rudolf Besier. Published by Little, Brown & Company, Boston.

"Grand Hotel," adapted from the German of Vicki Baum by W. A. Drake.

1931-1932

"Of Thee I Sing," by George S. Kaufman and Morrie Ryskind; music and lyrics by George and Ira Gershwin. Published by Alfred Knopf, New York.

"Mourning Becomes Electra," by Eugene G. O'Neill. Published by Horace Liveright, Inc., New York.

"Reunion in Vienna," by Robert Emmet Sherwood. Published

by Charles Scribner's Sons, New York.

"The House of Connelly," by Paul Green. Published by Samuel French, New York.

"The Animal Kingdom," by Philip Barry. Published by Samuel French, New York.

"The Left Bank," by Elmer Rice. Published by Samuel French, New York.

"Another Language," by Rose Franken. Published by Samuel French, New York.

"Brief Moment," by S. N. Behrman. Published by Farrar & Rinehart, New York.

"The Devil Passes," by Ben W. Levy. Published by Martin Secker, London.

"Cynara," by H. M. Harwood and R. F. Gore-Browne. Published by Samuel French, New York.

1932-1933

"Both Your Houses," by Maxwell Anderson. Published by Samuel French, New York.

"Dinner at Eight," by George S. Kaufman and Edna Ferber. Published by Doubleday, Doran & Co., Inc., Garden City, New York.

"When Ladies Meet," by Rachel Crothers. Published by Samuel French, New York.

"Design for Living," by Noel Coward. Published by Doubleday, Doran & Co., Inc., Garden City, New York.

"Biography," by S. N. Behrman. Published by Farrar & Rinehart, Inc., New York.

"Alien Corn," by Sidney Howard. Published by Charles Scribner's Sons, New York.

"The Late Christopher Bean," adapted from the French of René Fauchois by Sidney Howard. Published by Samuel French, New York.

"We, the People," by Elmer Rice. Published by Coward-McCann, Inc., New York.

"Pigeons and People," by George M. Cohan.

"One Sunday Afternoon," by James Hagan. Published by Samuel French, New York.

1933-1934

"Mary of Scotland," by Maxwell Anderson. Published by Doubleday, Doran & Co., Inc., Garden City, N. Y.

"Men in White," by Sidney Kingsley. Published by Covici, Friede, Inc., New York.

"Dodsworth," by Sinclair Lewis and Sidney Howard. Published by Harcourt, Brace & Co., New York.

"Ah, Wilderness," by Eugene O'Neill. Published by Random House, New York.

"They Shall Not Die," by John Wexley. Published by Alfred A. Knopf, New York.

"Her Master's Voice," by Clare Kummer. Published by Samuel French, New York.

"No More Ladies," by A. E. Thomas.

"Wednesday's Child," by Leopold Atlas. Published by Samuel French, New York.

"The Shining Hour," by Keith Winter. Published by Doubleday, Doran & Co., Inc., Garden City, New York.

"The Green Bay Tree," by Mordaunt Shairp. Published by Baker International Play Bureau, Boston, Mass.

1935-1936

"Winterset," by Maxwell Anderson. Published by Anderson House, Washington, D. C.

"Idiot's Delight," by Robert Emmet Sherwood. Published by Charles Scribner's Sons, New York.

"End of Summer," by S. N. Behrman. Published by Random House, New York.

"First Lady," by Katharine Dayton and George S. Kaufman. Published by Random House, New York.

"Victoria Regina," by Laurence Housman. Published by Samuel French, Inc., New York and London.

"Boy Meets Girl," by Bella and Samuel Spewack. Published by Random House, New York.

"Dead End," by Sidney Kingsley. Published by Random House, New York.

"Call It a Day," by Dodie Smith. Published by Samuel French, Inc., New York and London.

"Ethan Frome," by Owen Davis and Donald Davis. Published by Charles Scribner's Sons, New York.

"Pride and Prejudice," by Helen Jerome. Published by Doubleday, Doran & Co., Garden City, New York.

WHERE AND WHEN THEY WERE BORN

Abbott, George ....Hamburg, N. Y. 1895
Abel, Walter ....St. Paul, Minn. 1898
Aborn, Milton ....Marysville, Cal. 1864
Adams, Maude ....Salt Lake City, Utah 1872
Adler, Stella ....New York 1904
Aherne, Brian ....King's Norton, England ..1902
Akins, Zoe ....Humansville, Mo. 1886
Alexander, Katherine ....Arkansas 1901
Alexander, Ross ....Brooklyn, N. Y. 1904
Allanby, Peggy ....New York 1905
Allen, Adrianne ....Manchester, England 1907
Allen, Viola ....Huntsville, Ala. 1869
Ames, Robert ....Hartford, Conn. 1893
Ames, Winthrop ....North Easton, Mass. 1871
Anders, Glenn ....Los Angeles, Cal. 1890
Anderson, Judith ....Australia 1898
Anderson, Maxwell ....Atlantic City, Pa. 1888
Andrews, Ann ....Los Angeles, Cal. 1895
Anglin, Margaret ....Ottawa, Canada 1876
Anson, A. E. ....London, England 1879
Anspacher, Louis K. ....Cincinnati, Ohio 1878
Arling, Joyce ....Memphis, Tenn. 1908
Arliss, George ....London, England 1868
Arthur, Julia ....Hamilton, Ont. 1869
Astaire, Fred ....Omaha, Neb. 1899
Atwell, Roy ....Syracuse, N. Y. 1880
Atwill, Lionel ....London, England 1885

Bainter, Fay ....Los Angeles, Cal. 1892
Baker, Lee ....Michigan 1880
Bankhead, Tallulah ....Huntsville, Ala. 1902
Banks, Leslie J. ....West Derby, England 1890
Barbee, Richard ....Lafayette, Ind. 1887
Barrett, Edith ....Roxbury, Mass. 1904
Barrie, James Matthew ......Kirriemuir, N. B. 1860
Barry, Philip ....Rochester, N. Y. 1896
Barrymore, Ethel ....Philadelphia, Pa. 1879

527

Barrymore, John ....Philadelphia, Pa. 1882
Barrymore, Lionel ....London, England 1878
Bates, Blanche ....Portland, Ore. 1873
Baxter, Lora ....New York 1907
Beatty, Roberta ....Rochester, N. Y. 1900
Beecher, Janet ....Chicago, Ill. 1884
Behrman, S. N. ....Worcester, Mass. 1893
Bell, James ....Suffolk, Va. 1891
Ben-Ami, Jacob ....Minsk, Russia 1890
Bennett, Richard ....Cass County, Ind. 1873
Bennett, Wilda ....Asbury Park, N. J. 1894
Bergner, Elizabeth ....Vienna 1901
Berlin, Irving ....Russia 1888
Best, Edna ....Sussex, England 1900
Binney, Constance ....Philadelphia, Pa. 1900
Blackmer, Sidney ....Salisbury, N. C. 1896
Boland, Mary ....Detroit, Mich. 1880
Bolger, Ray ....Dorchester, Mass. 1906
Bondi, Beulah ....Chicago, Ill. 1892
Bordoni, Irene ....Paris, France 1895
Brady, Alice ....New York 1892
Brady, William A. ....San Francisco, Cal. 1863
Brady, William A., Jr. ....New York 1900
Braham, Horace ....London, England 1896
Brent, Romney ....Saltillo, Mex. 1902
Brian, Donald ....St. Johns, N. F. 1877
Brice, Fannie ....Brooklyn, N. Y. 1891
Broadhurst, George H. ....England 1866
Broderick, Helen ....New York 1891
Bromberg, J. Edward ....Hungary 1903
Bruce, Nigel ....San Diego, Cal. 1895
Bryant, Charles ....England 1879
Buchanan, Jack ....England 1892
Buchanan, Thompson ....Louisville, Ky. 1877
Buckler, Hugh ....Southampton, England ...1886
Burke, Billie ....Washington, D. C. 1885
Burton, Frederick ....Indiana 1871
Byington, Spring ....Colorado Springs, Colo. ...1898
Byron, Arthur ....Brooklyn, N. Y. 1872

Cabot, Eliot ....Boston, Mass. 1899
Cagney, James ....New York 1904

Cahill, Lily ....Texas 1885
Cahill, Marie ....Brooklyn, N. Y. 1871
Calhern, Louis ....New York 1895
Cantor, Eddie ....New York 1894
Campbell, Mrs. Patrick ......England 1865
Carle, Richard ....Somerville, Mass. 1871
Carlisle, Alexandra ....Yorkshire, England 1886
Carminati, Tullio ....Zara, Dalmatia 1894
Carpenter, Edward Childs ....Philadelphia, Pa. 1871
Carr, Alexander ....Russia 1878
Carroll, Earl ....Pittsburgh, Pa. 1892
Carter, Mrs. Leslie ....Lexington, Ky. 1862
Catlett, Walter ....San Francisco, Cal. 1889
Cawthorne, Joseph ....New York 1868
Chandler, Helen ....Charleston, N. C. 1906
Chaplin, Charles Spencer .....London 1889
Chase, Ilka ....New York 1900
Chatterton, Ruth ....New York 1893
Cherry, Charles ....England 1872
Christians, Mady ....Vienna, Austria 1907
Churchill, Burton ....Toronto, Can. 1876
Claire, Ina ....Washington, D. C. 1892
Clarke, Marguerite ....Cincinnati, Ohio 1887
Cliffe, H. Cooper ....England 1862
Clifford, Kathleen ....Charlottesville, Va. 1887
Clive, Colin ....St. Malo, France 1900
Coburn, Charles ....Macon, Ga. 1877
Coghlan, Gertrude ....England 1879
Coghlan, Rose ....Petersborough, England ...1850
Cohan, George M. ....Providence, R. I. 1878
Cohan, Georgette ....Los Angeles, Cal. 1900
Colbert, Claudette ....Paris 1905
Collier, Constance ....Windsor, England 1882
Collier, William ....New York 1866
Collinge, Patricia ....Dublin, Ireland 1894
Collins, José ....London, England 1896
Colt, Ethel Barrymore ....Mamaroneck, N. Y. 1911
Colt, John Drew ....New York 1914
Conklin, Peggy ....Dobbs Ferry, N. Y. 1912
Connolly, Walter ....Cincinnati, Ohio 1888
Conroy, Frank ....London, England 1885
Cook, Joe ....Evansville, Ind. 1890

Cooper, Gladys ....Lewisham, England 1888
Cooper, Violet Kemble ....London, England 1890
Cornell, Katharine ....Buffalo, N. Y. 1900
Corrigan, Emmett ....Amsterdam, Holland 1871
Corthell, Herbert ....Boston, Mass. 1875
Cossart, Ernest ....Cheltenham, England 1876
Courtenay, William ....Worcester, Mass. 1875
Courtleigh, William ....Guelph, Ont. 1869
Coward, Noel ....England 1899
Cowl, Jane ....Boston, Mass. 1887
Craven, Frank ....Boston, Mass. 1880
Crews, Laura Hope ....San Francisco, Cal. 1880
Crosman, Henrietta ....Wheeling, W. Va. 1865
Crothers, Rachel ....Bloomington, Ill. 1878
Cumberland, John ....St. John, N. B. 1880
Cummings, Constance ....Seattle, Wash. 1911

Dale, Margaret ....Philadelphia, Pa. 1880
Dalton, Charles ....England 1864
Daly, Blyth ....New York 1902
Danforth, William ....Syracuse 1869
Daniels, Frank ....Dayton, Ohio 1860
Davis, Donald ....New York 1907
Davis, Owen ....Portland, Me. 1874
Davis, Owen, Jr. ....New York 1910
Dawn, Hazel ....Ogden, Utah 1891
Day, Edith ....Minneapolis, Minn. 1896
De Angelis, Jefferson ....San Francisco, Cal. 1859
Dean, Julia ....St. Paul, Minn. 1880
De Cordoba, Pedro ....New York 1881
Dillingham, Charles B. ......Hartford, Conn. 1868
Dinehart, Allan ....Missoula, Mont. 1889
Dixey, Henry E. ....Boston, Mass. 1859
Dixon, Jean ....Waterbury, Conn. 1905
Dodson, John E. ....London, England 1857
Doro, Marie ....Duncannon, Pa. 1882
D'Orsay, Lawrence ....England 1860
Dressler, Eric ....Brooklyn, N. Y. 1900
Dressler, Marie ....Cobourg, Canada 1869
Drew, Louise ....New York 1884
Duncan, Augustin ....San Francisco 1873

Hedman, Martha ....Sweden 1888
Heggie, O. P. ....Australia 1879
Heineman, Eda ....Japan 1891
Heming, Violet ....Leeds, England 1893
Hepburn, Katharine ....Hartford, Conn. 1907
Herbert, Evelyn ....Brooklyn, N. Y. 1900
Herne, Chrystal ....Dorchester, Mass. 1883
Hobert, Rose ....New York 1906
Hodge, William ....Albion, N. Y. 1874
Hopkins, Arthur ....Cleveland, Ohio 1878
Hopkins, Miriam ....Bainbridge, Ga. 1904
Hopper, de Wolf ....New York 1858
Hopper, Edna Wallace ....San Francisco, Cal. 1874
Holmes, Taylor ....Newark, N. J. 1872
Howard, Leslie ....London, England 1890
Howard, Sydney ....Oakland, Cal. 1891
Hull, Henry ....Louisville, Ky. 1893
Hunter, Glenn ....Highland Mills, N. Y. 1896
Huston, Walter ....Toronto 1884
Hutchinson, Josephine ......Seattle, Wash. 1898

Inescort, Frieda ....Hitchin, Scotland 1905
Ingram, Rex ....Dublin, Ireland 1892
Irving, Isabel ....Bridgeport, Conn. 1871
Irwin, May ....Whitby, Ont. 1862

Janis, Elsie ....Delaware, Ohio 1889
Joel, Clara ....Jersey City, N. J. 1890
Johann, Zita ....Hungary 1904
Jolson, Al ....Washington, D. C. 1883
Johnston, Moffat ....Edinburgh, Scotland 1886

Kaufman, George S. ....Pittsburgh, Pa. 1889
Keane, Doris ....Michigan 1885
Keith, Robert ....Scotland 1899
Kelly, Walter C. ....Mineville, N. Y. 1875
Kennedy, Madge ....Chicago, Ill. 1890
Kerrigan, J. M. ....Dublin, Ireland 1885
Kerr, Geoffrey ....London, England 1895
Kershaw, Willette ....Clifton Heights, Mo. 1890
King, Dennis ....Coventry, England 1897

Kingsford, Walter ....England 1876
Kingsley, Sydney ....New York 1906
Kirkland, Alexander ....Mexico City 1904
Kosta, Tessa ....Chicago, Ill. 1893
Kruger, Alma ....Pittsburgh, Pa. 1880
Kruger, Otto ....Toledo, Ohio 1895

Lackaye, Wilton ....Virginia 1862
Larimore, Earl ....Portland, Oregon 1899
Larrimore, Francine ....Russia 1898
La Rue, Grace ....Kansas City, Mo. 1882
Lauder, Harry ....Portobello, England 1870
Laughton, Charles ....Scarborough, England 1899
Lawrence, Gertrude ....London 1898
Lawton, Thais ....Louisville, Ky. 1881
Lean, Cecil ....Illinois 1878
Lederer, Francis ....Karlin, Prague 1906
Le Gallienne, Eva ....London, England 1900
Leiber, Fritz ....Chicago, Ill. 1884
Leontovich, Eugenie ....Moscow, Russia 1894
Levey, Ethel ....San Francisco, Cal. 1881
Lewis, Mabel Terry ....London, England 1872
Lillie, Beatrice ....Toronto, Canada 1898
Logan, Stanley ....Earlsfield, England 1885
Loraine, Robert ....New Brighton, England ...1876
Lord, Pauline ....Hanford, Cal. 1890
Lorraine, Lillian ....San Francisco, Cal. 1892
Lou-Tellegen ....Holland 1881
Love, Montagu ....Portsmouth, Hants 1877
Lowell, Helen ....New York 1866
Lunt, Alfred ....Milwaukee, Wis. 1893

Mack, Andrew ....Boston, Mass. 1863
Mack, Willard ....Ontario, Canada 1873
Macdonald, Donald ....Denison, Texas 1898
Mackay, Elsie ....London, England 1894
MacKellar, Helen ....Canada 1896
Marlowe, Julia ....Caldbeck, England 1870
Marshall, Herbert ....London, England 1890
Massey, Raymond ....Toronto, Canada 1896
Matthews, A. E. ....Bridlington, England 1869

Matthison, Edith Wynne ......England 1875
Maude, Cyril ....London, England 1862
McClintic, Guthrie ....Seattle, Wash. 1893
McCormick, Myron ....Albany, Indiana 1906
McIntyre, Frank ....Ann Arbor, Mich. 1879
Meek, Donald ....Glasgow, Scotland 1880
Meighan, Thomas ....Pittsburgh, Pa. 1879
Melba, Nellie ....Melbourne, Australia 1866
Menken, Helen ....New York 1901
Mercer, Beryl ....Seville, Spain 1882
Merivale, Philip ....Rehutia, India 1886
Miller, Gilbert ....New York 1884
Miller, Marilyn ....Findlay, Ohio 1898
Mitchell, Grant ....Columbus, Ohio 1874
Mitchell, Thomas ....Elizabeth, N. J. 1892
Mitzi (Hajos) ....Budapest 1891
Moore, Grace ....Del Rio, Tenn. 1901
Moore, Victor ....Hammonton, N. J. 1876
Moran, Lois ....Pittsburgh, Pa. 1909
Morgan, Claudia ....New York 1912
Morgan, Helen ....Danville, Ill. 1900
Morgan, Ralph ....New York City 1889
Morris, Mary ....Boston 1894
Morris, McKay ....San Antonio, Texas 1890
Muni, Paul ....Lemberg, Austria 1895

Nagel, Conrad ....Keokuk, Iowa 1897
Nash, Florence ....Troy, N. Y. 1888
Nash, Mary ....Troy, N. Y. 1885
Nazimova, Alla ....Crimea, Russia 1879
Nielsen, Alice ....Nashville, Tenn. 1876
Nolan, Lloyd ....San Francisco, Cal. 1903
Nugent, J. C. ....Miles, Ohio 1875
Nugent, Elliott ....Dover, Ohio 1900

O'Connell, Hugh ....New York 1891
Odets, Clifford ....Philadelphia 1906
Olcott, Chauncey ....Buffalo, N. Y. 1862
O'Neill, Eugene Gladstone .....New York 1888
O'Neill, Nance ....Oakland, Cal. 1875

Overman, Lynne ....Maryville, Mo. 1887

Painter, Eleanor ....Iowa 1890
Pawle, Lenox ....London, England ....'...1872
Pemberton, Brock ....Leavenworth, Kansas 1885
Pennington, Ann ....Philadelphia, Pa. 1898
Perkins, Osgood ....Boston, Mass. 1892
Philips, Mary ....New London, Conn. 1901
Pickford, Mary ....Toronto 1893
Pollock, Channing ....Washington, D. C. 1880
Post, Guy Bates ....Seattle, Wash. 1875
Power, Tyrone ....London, England 1869
Powers, James T. ....New York 1862
Pryor, Roger ....New York City 1901

Quartermaine, Leon ....Richmond, England 1876

Rains, Claude ....London, England 1889
Rambeau, Marjorie ....San Francisco, Cal. 1889
Rathbone, Basil ....Johannesburg 1892
Reed, Florence ....Philadelphia, Pa. 1883
Rennie, James ....Toronto, Canada 1890
Revelle, Hamilton ....Gibraltar 1872
Richman, Charles ....Chicago, Ill. 1870
Ridges, Stanley ....Southampton, England 1891
Ring, Blanche ....Boston, Mass. 1876
Ring, Frances ....New York 1882
Robson, May ....Australia 1868
Rogers, Mary ....Rogers, Ark. 1916
Roos, Joanna ....Brooklyn, N. Y. 1901
Ross, Thomas W. ....Boston, Mass. 1875
Royle, Selena ....New York 1905
Ruben, José ....Belgium 1886
Rumann, Siegfried ....Hamburg, Germany 1879
Russell, Annie ....Liverpool, England 1864

Sanderson, Julia ....Springfield, Mass. 1887
Sands, Dorothy ....Cambridge, Mass. 1900
Santley, Joseph ....Salt Lake City 1889
Sawyer, Ivy ....London, England 1897
Scheff, Fritzi ....Vienna, Austria 1879

Schildkraut, Joseph ....Bucharest, Roumania 1896
Scott, Cyril ....Ireland 1866
Segal, Vivienne ....Philadelphia, Pa. 1897
Selwyn, Edgar ....Cincinnati, Ohio 1875
Serrano, Vincent ....New York 1870
Shannon, Effie ....Cambridge, Mass. 1867
Shepley, Ruth ....New York 1889
Sherman, Lowell ....San Francisco, Cal. 1885
Sherwood, Robert Emmet .....New Rochelle, N. Y. 1896
Sidney, George ....New York 1876
Sidney, Sylvia ....New York 1910
Sinclair, Arthur ....Dublin, Ireland 1883
Sitgreaves, Beverly ....Charleston, S. C. 1867
Skelly, Hal ....Allegheny, Pa. 1891
Skinner, Cornelia Otis ....Chicago 1902
Skinner, Otis ....Cambridgeport, Mass. 1857
Smith, Ben ....Waxahachie, Texas 1905
Smith, Queenie ....New York 1898
Sondergaard, Gale ....Minnesota 1899
Sothern, Edward H. ....New Orleans, La. 1859
Spong, Hilda ....Australia 1875
Stahl, Rose ....Montreal, Canada 1872
Standing, Sir Guy ....London 1873
Starr, Frances ....Oneonta, N. Y. 1886
Stickney, Dorothy ....Dickinson, N. D. 1903
Stone, Fred ....Denver, Colo. 1873
Stone, Dorothy ....New York 1905
Strudwick, Sheppard ....North Carolina 1905
Sullavan, Margaret ....Norfolk, Va. 1910
Sunderland, Nan ....Fresno, Cal. 1898
Sydney, Basil ....London 1894

Taliaferro, Edith ....New York 1892
Taliaferro, Mabel ....New York 1887
Tanguay, Eva ....Middletown, Conn. 1878
Taylor, Laurette ....New York 1884
Tearle, Conway ....New York 1878
Tell, Alma ....New York 1892
Tell, Olive ....New York 1894
Terris, Norma ....Columbus, Kansas 1904
Thomas, Augustus ....St. Louis, Mo. 1859
Thomas, Frankie ....New York 1922

Thomas, John Charles .... Baltimore, Md. 1887
Thorndyke, Dame Sybil ...... Gainsborough, England ... 1882
Tobin, Genevieve .... New York 1901
Tobin, Vivian .... New York 1903
Toler, Sidney .... Warrensburg, Mo. 1874
Tone, Franchot .... Niagara Falls, N. Y. 1907
Truex, Ernest .... Red Hill, Mo. 1890
Tynan, Brandon .... Dublin, Ireland 1879

Ulric, Lenore .... New Ulm, Minn. 1897

Vallée, Rudy .... Island Pond, Vermont ... 1902
Varesi, Gilda .... Milan, Italy 1887
Victor, Josephine .... Hungary 1891

Waldron, Charles .... New York 1877
Walker, June .... New York 1904
Walker, Charlotte .... Galveston, Texas 1878
Walter, Eugene .... Cleveland, Ohio 1874
Warfield, David .... San Francisco, Cal. 1866
Warwick, Robert .... Sacramento, Cal. 1878
Ware, Helen .... San Francisco, Cal. 1877
Waterous, Herbert .... Flint, Mich. 1863
Watkins, Linda .... Boston, Mass. 1908
Watson, Minor .... Marianna, Ark. 1889
Webb, Clifton .... Indiana 1891
Weber, Joseph .... New York 1867
Welford, Dallas .... Liverpool, England 1874
Westley, Helen .... Brooklyn, N. Y. 1879
Westman, Nydia .... White Plains, N. Y. 1906
Whiffen, Mrs. Thomas ...... London, England 1845
White, George .... Toronto, Canada 1890
Whiteside, Walker .... Logansport, Ind. 1869
Whorf, Richard .... Winthrop, Mass. 1908
William, Warren .... Aitkin, Minn. 1896
Williams, Hope .... New York City 1901
Wilson, Francis .... Philadelphia, Pa. 1854
Wiman, Dwight Deere ...... Moline, Ill. 1895
Winwood, Estelle .... England 1883
Witherspoon, Cora .... New Orleans, La. 1891
Wood, Peggy .... Brooklyn, N. Y. 1894

NECROLOGY

June 16, 1935—June 15, 1936

Adams, Leslie, actor, 49. Played stock, vaudeville and burlesque twenty years before Broadway debut in "Carry Nation"; following Broadway success appeared in "Goodbye Again," "As Thousands Cheer," "Life's Too Short," "A Room in Red and White"; died while rehearsing leading role in "Left Turn." Born Stark, Fla.; died New York City, March 26, 1936.

Alison, George, actor, 70. Came to America with Mr. and Mrs. W. H. Kendal in 1892; stock leading man for years; supported Helen Hayes in "Pollyanna," Lynn Fontanne in "Dulcy," Ethel Barrymore in "The Kingdom of God"; last engagements in "Dinner at Eight" and "Merrily We Roll Along." Born London; died Norwalk, Conn., January 15, 1936.

Ames, Percy, actor, 62. Came to New York with the Kendals; supported Lily Langtry, Laurette Taylor; last appearances in "Something Gay" and "Alice Takat." Born Brighton, England; died New York City, March 29, 1936.

Asche, Oscar (Vasco Marenas), English actor, producer and dramatist, 65. Wrote and produced many plays and acted in most of them; began with F. R. Benson; wrote and played in "Chu Chin Chow" which ran five years in London; supported Ellen Terry and Sir Herbert Tree in Shakespearean repertory; leads in "Iris," "Trilby," "Resurrection," etc.; wrote and played in "Kismet." Born Geelong, Australia; died London, March 23, 1936.

Berlein, Annie Mack, actress, 85. Played Ophelia to Edwin Booth's Hamlet, Juliet to his Romeo; supported Joseph Jefferson, Lotta, Maggie Mitchell, Margaret Illington and John Barrymore; last appearance touring in "Little Accident." Born Dublin, Ireland; died New York City, June 22, 1935.

Brady, William A., Jr., theatrical producer, 35. Son of William A. Brady, producer, and Grace George, actress; commenced career in 1923 by staging "The Enchanted Cottage" and "Chains"; associated with Dwight Deere Wiman from 1925 to 1930 in productions of "The Road to Rome," "A Most

Immoral Lady," "Paolo and Francesca," etc.; last production "Too Many Boats" in 1934; married Katherine Alexander, 1926. Born New York City; died Colt's Neck, New Jersey, September 26, 1935.

Braslau, Sophie, opera singer, 43. One of the first American born singers to attain eminence in Metropolitan Opera; ten years with Metropolitan. Born New York City; died New York City, December 22, 1935.

Breese, Edmund, actor, 64. Forty years on American stage; first appearance Eureka Springs, Ark., in "My Awful Dad"; last appearance few days before death in "Night of January 16"; played Shylock to Madame Rhea's Portia; supported James O'Neill in "Monte Cristo," Robert Edeson in "Strongheart," Otis Skinner and Ada Rehan in "Taming of the Shrew"; most famous role John Burkett Ryder in "The Lion and the Mouse." Born Brooklyn; died New York City, April 6, 1936.

Broadhurst, Thomas W., novelist and playwright, 78. Brother of George H. Broadhurst; author of stage version of "Evangeline"; wrote "Butterflies," "The Golden Fleece," etc. Born Old Wedensfield, England; died New York City, May 1, 1936.

Brown, Martin, actor and playwright, 51. Quit acting career to write plays; best known included "Cobra," "A Very Good Young Man," "The Love Child" and "The Claw and the Wing." Born Montreal, Canada; died New York City, February 13, 1936.

Brown-Potter, Cora Urquhart, actress, 76. World wide fame as actress after Bishop Potter, her husband's uncle, objected to her use of name; supported Kyrle Bellew in Shakespearian and standard repertory; played Juliet before the Emperor of Japan; retired in 1912. Born New Orleans; died Beaulieu-sur-Mer, France, February 12, 1936.

Carlisle, Alexandra (Alexandra Swift), actress, 50. After playing five years successfully in England made American debut in 1908 in "The Mollosc" with Joseph Coyne; returned to England for succession of leading roles; came back to America in "The Marriage Game" in 1913, remaining in this country thereafter, playing prominent roles, starring in "The Country Cousin"; became interested in politics and seconded the nomination of Calvin Coolidge for president in 1920; married out of the profession and retired for six years; returned to the New York stage in "Criminal at Large" in 1932; received American Academy award for superior diction in 1932. Born London; died New York City, April 21, 1936.

Donnelly, Leo, stage and vaudeville comedian, 57. Last played in "The Milky Way" in 1934; best remembered in the Potash and Perlmutter comedies; co-author with Paul Gerard Smith of "White Lights." Born Philadelphia, Pa.; died Atlantic City, New Jersey, August 21, 1935.

Doyle, John T., actor, 62. On stage 42 years; played in several George Cohan comedies; supported many stars; appeared for years in vaudeville with his wife, Marion Willard Doyle, in sketches of his own authorship. Born St. Louis, Mo.; died New York City, October 16, 1935.

Eckstein, Louis, opera patron, 70. Director of Metropolitan Opera Association of New York; sponsor of Ravinia (Ill.) opera for more than twenty years; published Red Book, Green Book and Blue Book. Born Milwaukee, Wis.; died Chicago, Ill., November 21, 1935.

Elliot, Arthur, actor, 78. Member of Fanny Davenport's repertoire company; later with Daniel Frohman, John Drew, Ethel Barrymore, William Faversham, etc.; last New York appearance (1922) in "The Fool." Born India; died Bennington, Vermont, April 17, 1936.

Frawley, T. Daniel, actor and producer, 72. Favorite juvenile of the 90's; with Denman Thompson in original production of "The Old Homestead"; organized Frawley Stock Company in San Francisco; toured the Orient; recently on radio as "Old Ranger" in "Death Valley Days." Born Washington, D. C.; died Tottenville, Staten Island, N. Y., April 26, 1936.

Freel, Aleta, actress, 28. Went on stage after graduating from Smith College; played in "Springtime for Henry," "Three Times the Hour," "Double Door," etc. Married Ross Alexander. Born Jersey City, N. J.; died Hollywood, Calif., December 7, 1935.

Gilbert, John (Pringle), actor, 38. Romantic leading man of stage and screen; prominent in support of Greta Garbo; scored in "The Big Parade," "The Merry Widow," "Desert Nights," etc.; gained publicity as husband of Olivia Burwell, Leatrice Joy, Ina Claire and Virginia Bruce. Born Logan, Utah; died Beverly Hills, Calif., January 9, 1936.

Glassford, David, actor, 70. Came to New York in 1905 with "The Walls of Jericho"; toured Canada with Phyllis Neilson-Terry in "The Land of Promise" in 1918; with Lunt and Fontanne in "Taming of the Shrew" when he died. Born

Sydney, Australia; died New York City, October 17, 1935.

Glendinning, Ernest, actor, 52. Played 300 roles in 33 years on American stage; supported Annie Russell, John Drew, Alla Nazimova, etc.; toured in all-star cast of "Jim the Penman"; popular in "Prunella"; last appearance in May, 1935, in the Players' revival of "Seven Keys to Baldpate." Born Ulverston, England; died South Coventry, Conn., May 17, 1936.

Greet, Sir Philip (Ben), English actor-manager, 78. Supported Minnie Palmer in "My Sweetheart" and Mary Anderson in "Romeo and Juliet" in London; organized companies for classic revivals in open air; toured United States 1902 to 1914, reviving "Everyman" as well as Shakespearian repertory. Born on Training Ship in the Thames, London; died London, May 17, 1936.

Grein, J. T., dramatic critic, 72. Dean of London play reviewers; founded the Independent Theatre in 1891; president Playgoers' Club, Liverpool Playgoers' Society and Critics' Circle. Born Amsterdam, Holland; died London, England, July 10, 1935.

Hammond, Percy, dramatic critic, 63. Leading American play reviewer for thirty-five years on Chicago *Evening Post*, Chicago *Tribune* and New York *Herald Tribune;* author of "But—Is It Art?" and many magazine articles. Born Cadiz, Ohio; died New York City, April 25, 1936.

Hardy, Sam, stage and screen comedian, 52. Active on stage 25 years; two years in "Kiki"; two years in Ziegfeld's "Follies." Born New Haven, Conn., died Hollywood, Calif., October 16, 1935.

Hazzard, John E. (Jack), author and actor, 54. Debut on Broadway stage (1901) in "The Man from Mexico"; last appearance in "Champagne, Sec"; wrote "Turn to the Right" with Winchell Smith, "Go to It" with John Golden and Anne Caldwell and "Nunkie" with Kenneth Webb. Born New York City; died Great Neck, L. I., New York, December 2, 1935.

Heggie, O. P., actor, 59. Came to America in 1907 with Ellen Terry in "Nance Oldfield"; returned in 1912 in "The New Sin"; played in support of John Barrymore in "Justice"; prominent in "Androcles and the Lion," "The Truth About Blayds"; in pictures mostly after 1927. Born South Australia; died Hollywood, Calif., February 7, 1936.

Hopper, De Wolf, comedian, 77. Debut in "Our Boys" at 20; best remembered as star in musical shows; "Wang," "El

Capitan," etc., and in Gilbert and Sullivan revivals; famous also for the recitation of "Casey at the Bat" and his record as the husband of Helen Gardner, Ida Mosher, Edna Wallace, Nella Bergen, Elda Furry and Lilian Glaser in the order of selection. Born New York City; died Kansas City, Mo., September 23, 1935.

Howland, Jobyna, actress, 56. Started career in western stock companies; model for Charles Dana Gibson's "Gibson Girl"; played Flavia in "Rupert of Hentzau"; was popular in "The Gold Diggers" and Ziegfeld's "Kid Boots"; tried stardom in "A Texas Nightingale" and "O, Evening Star," written for her by Zoe Akins. Born Indianapolis, Ind.; died Los Angeles, Calif., June 7, 1936.

Huban, Eileen, actress, 38. Played with New York Irish Players in "Lonesome Like"; later was in "Crops and Croppers," "Dark Rosaleen," "Paddy the Next Best Thing," "Hindle Wakes" and the Players' production of "Troilus and Cressida." Born Loughrea, Ireland; died New York City, October 22, 1935.

Ingersoll, William, actor, 74. Played more than 800 roles in fifty-five years on American stage; began with Boston Museum Stock Company in 1882; supported Margaret Mather, Marie Wainwright, Nat Goodwin, Ethel Barrymore, Mrs. Fiske, etc.; played stock in Washington, Denver, Salt Lake City, Richmond, Providence, Pittsburgh and Philadelphia; last engagement with William Gillette in a revival of "Three Wise Fools." Born Lafayette, Indiana; died Hollywood, Calif., May 7, 1936.

Johnston, Moffat, actor, 49. Distinguished for Shakespearean roles in England prior to New York appearance with Theatre Guild in 1922 in "Back to Methusaleh"; played Polonius to John Barrymore's Hamlet and Macduff to James K. Hackett's Macbeth; appeared for the Players in revivals of "Becky Sharp" and "The Way of the World." Born Edinburgh, Scotland; died Norwalk, Conn., November 3, 1935.

Kelly, Harry, comedian, 63. Started as boy clown and contortionist at 7; played successfully in "His Honor the Mayor," "The Deacon and the Lady," "Little Nemo," in several editions of "Artists and Models" and Ziegfeld "Follies." Born New York City; died New York City, March 19, 1936.

Kendal, Dame (Madge Robertson), English actress, 86. Became star at 17; played Little Eva in "Uncle Tom's Cabin" in England in 1855; played Rosalind to W. H. Kendal's Or-

lando, marrying Kendal during rehearsals; appeared with
E. A. Sothern in London in "Our American Cousin"; first
American appearance in 1889 in "A Scrap of Paper"; be-
came Dame Commander of the Order of the British Empire
in 1927. Born Lincolnshire, England; died Chorley Wood,
Hertfordshire, England, September 4, 1935.

Klaw, Marc, producer, 78. Began in the late seventies as a theatrical lawyer, being hired by Daniel Frohman to prosecute
pirates of "Hazel Kirke"; as a touring manager met A. L.
Erlanger and formed a play-producing partnership; with
Erlanger, Frohman, Hayman, Nixon, Zimmerman and Jefferson organized the Theatrical Syndicate that increased in
power until it exercised control over practically all the important stars and theatres in America; syndicate later dissolved; Klaw and Erlanger quarreled in 1919 and severed
business relations shortly after; Klaw continued as an independent producer; built the Klaw Theatre in New York;
sold it in 1927, and retired to live in England. Born
Paducah, Ky.; died Hassocks, Sussex, England, June 14,
1936.

Landau, David, actor, 57. Began career in stock in 1900; best
remembered as the father in "Street Scene"; played Stanton
in "Abraham Lincoln" and Stonewall Jackson in "Robert E.
Lee"; started screen career in 1931. Born Philadelphia;
died Los Angeles, Calif., September 20, 1935.

Lean, Cecil, comedian, 57. Last appearance in "The Bishop Mis-
behaves," touring East with wife, Cleo Mayfield; first prom-
inence (1903) with Frank Daniels in "Miss Simplicity";
New York debut in "The Soul Kiss"; prominent in "The
Time, the Place and the Girl," "Honeymoon Trail," "Bright
Eyes," "No, No, Nanette," etc. Born London, Ontario,
Canada; died New York City, July 18, 1935.

Leigh, Philip, actor, 55. Member of Theatre Guild company for
several years; played Rizzio, the secretary, with Helen Hayes
in "Mary of Scotland"; had parts in "Strange Interlude,"
"Peer Gynt," "He Who Gets Slapped," etc. Born Surrey,
England; died New York City, June 19, 1935.

Loraine, Robert, actor, 59. Bernard Shaw laid success of "Man
and Superman" in America to his acting; starred in fifty
plays; first appearance in New York, "To Have and to
Hold" (1901); last appearance "Times Have Changed"
(1935); gained fame as an aviator in World War. Born
New Brighton, England; died London, December 23, 1935.

Macdonald, Ballard, songwriter, 52. Wrote lyrics and librettos for several Ziegfeld "Follies" and George White "Scandals"; wrote "Trail of the Lonesome Pine," "Beautiful Ohio," etc. Born Portland, Oregon; died Forest Hills, L. I., November 17, 1935.

McCarthy, Justin Huntly, novelist and playwright, 75. Best known for "If I Were King," originally played by E. H. Sothern; later made into operetta, "The Vagabond King," sung by Dennis King; journalist and later Member of Parliament. Born London, England; died Putney, England, March 21, 1936.

McCullough, Paul T., comedian, 52. Member of famous comedy team of Clark and McCullough, who played together thirty years; most successfully in "Music Box Revue," "The Ramblers," "Strike Up the Band," and "Walk a Little Faster." Born Springfield, Ohio; died Boston, Mass., March 25, 1936.

Meltzer, Charles Henry, music and dramatic critic, 83. Adapted "The Sunken Bell," "Rodion the Student," and "Hannele" from the German; drama critic of New York *Herald* and New York *Morning World;* music critic of New York *American;* translated libretti of 22 operas into English. Born London, England; died New York City, January 14, 1936.

Miller, Marilyn, actress and dancer, 37. Started with parents and sisters (The Five Columbians) in vaudeville at five; subsequently became famous musical comedy star; remembered in Ziegfeld's "Follies," and in "Sally," "Rosalie," "Smiles" and "Sunny"; tried drama with "Peter Pan"; first New York appearance "The Passing Show of 1914"; last, "As Thousands Cheer." Born Findley, Ohio; died New York City, April 7, 1936.

Mitchell, Langdon Elwyn, poet and playwright, 73. Son of famous author, Silas Weir Mitchell; first play "In the Season" produced in London, 1893; adapted "Becky Sharp" and "Pendennis"; wrote "The New York Idea" for Mrs. Fiske. Born Philadelphia, Pa.; died Philadelphia, Pa., October 21, 1935.

Palmer, Minnie, actress, 76. The "Pocket Venus" of the 80's; stage debut in "Le Pavillon Rouge" in Brooklyn; last appearance with Frank Bacon in "Lightnin' "; became internationally famous as Tina in "My Sweetheart." Born Philadelphia, Pa.; died Bay Shore, L. I., May 21, 1936.

Pawle, J. Lennox, actor, 63. First appearance at Margate, England (1890), with George Arliss and Frank Gillmore in company; came to America with "Pomander Walk"; played in Belasco and Frohman companies and Shubert musicals; was Mr. Dick in the screened "David Copperfield." Born London, England; died Hollywood, Calif., February 22, 1936.

Robyn, Dr. Alfred G., organist and composer, 75. Wrote music for "The Yankee Consul," "Gypsy Girl," "Yankee Tourist," etc. Born St. Louis; died New York City, October 18, 1935.

Rogers, Will, philosopher comedian, 56. Started to build what became a world wide reputation as Cowboy Bill in "Hands Up" in 1915; later in "Town Topics," "The Passing Show of 1917," Ziegfeld "Follies," "Midnight Frolics," "Three Cheers," etc.; wrote "Rogerisms," "The Illiterate Digest," and "Letters of a Self-made Diplomat"; made lecture tours; was Mayor of Beverly Hills, Hollywood, Calif., and popular comedian of the films; killed in airplane accident while touring Alaska with Wiley Post. Born Olagah, Indian Territory; died Point Barrow, Alaska, August 15, 1935.

Rothafel, Samuel Lionel (Roxy), 53. Radio and moving picture promoter; pioneer in development of motion picture presentations; associated with building of Strand, Rialto, Rivoli and Capitol theatres, New York. Born Stillwater, Minn.; died New York City, January 13, 1936.

Russell, Annie, actress, 72. Favorite on American stage for many years; debut in "Miss Multon" Montreal, Canada, 1872; first appearance in New York as Josephine in "HMS Pinafore," 1898; won success in "Hazel Kirke"; starred by Daniel Frohman in "Esmeralda" when she was 17; played in "A Gilded Fool" and "David Garrick" with Nat Goodwin; after tour in "The Thirteenth Chair" in 1918 left the stage; later years spent at Rollins College, Winter Park, Fla., to which the Annie Russell Theatre was donated by Mrs. Edward Bok; last appearance at Rollins College as Mrs. Malaprop in "The Rivals." Born Liverpool, England; died Winter Park, Fla., January 16, 1936.

Schauffler, Elsie T., playwright, 47. Author of three plays: "Champagne Supper," "Handicap," and "Parnell," which was in rehearsal in New York when the author died. Born Baltimore, Maryland; died New York City, October 24, 1935.

Scotti, Antonio, opera star, 70. Educated by Madame Paganini for debut at Malta (1889) as Amonasro in "Aïda"; member of Metropolitan Opera Company for 33 years; remembered particularly for his Scarpia in "Tosca" and his Don Giovanni in "The Barber of Seville." Born Naples, Italy; died Naples, February 26, 1936.

Smith, Harry Bache, librettist and lyric writer, 75. Most prolific librettist of three decades; wrote alone or in collaboration 300 musical plays and 6,000 songs; with Reginald de Koven wrote "The Begum," "Don Quixote," "Robin Hood," "The Serenade," "The Fortune Teller," etc.; collaborated with Victor Herbert, Jerome Kern, John Philip Sousa, Franz Lehar, Irving Berlin, Sigmund Romberg, Ivan Caryl, Oscar Strauss and others. Born Buffalo, New York; died Atlantic City, New Jersey, January 1, 1936.

Steck, Olga, prima donna, 38. Sang light opera roles in Wilbur Opera Company and in many musical comedies; last appeared in "The Serenade" at Jolson Theatre, New York, 1930. Born California; died San Francisco, Calif., December 18, 1935.

Thurston, Howard, magician, 66. Contemporary of Hermann the Great, and predecessor of Houdini; many exciting world tours; numbered among his patrons were the Emperor and Empress of China, Emperor of Japan, Sultan of Java, Shah of Persia, etc. Born Columbus, Ohio; died Miami Beach, Fla., April 13, 1936.

Wilson, Francis, comedian, 81. Popular star in comic opera for thirty years; founder and first president of Actors' Equity Association; sang Cadeaux in "Erminie" for 1,256 performances; after a career of light opera turned to farce, "The Mountain Climber," "The Bachelor's Baby," etc.; lectured for several years, particularly on Eugene Field, John Wilkes and Edwin Booth and Joseph Jefferson; wrote several books including "The Eugene Field I Knew" and "Joseph Jefferson"; in May, 1896, joined Nat Goodwin, W. H. Crane, Robert Tabor, Mrs. John Drew, Julia Marlowe and Joseph Jefferson in an all star revival of "The Rivals"; retired in 1926, except for a last appearance as Père Marlotte in "The Little Father of the Wilderness" for the Players. Born Philadelphia; died New York City, October 7, 1935.

THE DECADES' TOLL

(Persons of Outstanding Prominence in the Theatre Who Have Died in Recent Years)

	Born	Died
Aborn, Milton	1864	1933
Bacon, Frank	1864	1922
Baker, George Pierce	1866	1935
Belasco, David	1856	1931
Bernhardt, Sarah	1845	1923
Coghlan, Rose	1851	1932
Crabtree, Charlotte (Lotta)	1847	1924
Crane, William H.	1845	1928
De Koven, Reginald	1861	1920
De Reszke, Jean	1850	1925
Dillingham, Charles Bancroft	1868	1934
Ditrichstein, Leo	1865	1928
Dressler, Marie	1869	1934
Drew, John	1853	1927
Du Maurier, Sir Gerald	1873	1934
Duse, Eleanora	1859	1924
Fiske, Minnie Maddern	1865	1932
Galsworthy, John	1867	1933
Goodwin, Nathaniel	1857	1920
Greet, Sir Philip (Ben)	1858	1936
Hawtrey, Sir Charles	1858	1923
Herbert, Victor	1859	1924
Hopper, De Wolf	1858	1935
Lackaye, Wilton	1862	1932
Mantell, Robert Bruce	1854	1928
Miller, Henry	1858	1926
Morris, Clara	1848	1925
O'Neill, James	1850	1920
Patti, Adelina	1843	1919
Pinero, Sir Arthur Wing	1855	1934
Rejane, Gabrielle	1857	1920
Rogers, Will	1879	1935
Russell, Annie	1864	1936

	Born	Died
Russell, Lillian	1861	1922
Sembrich, Marcella	1859	1935
Shaw, Mary	1860	1929
Smith, Winchell	1862	1933
Sothern, Edwin Hugh	1859	1933
Terry, Ellen	1848	1928
Thomas, Augustus	1857	1934
Warde, Frederick	1851	1935
Wilson, Francis	1854	1935
Ziegfeld, Florenz	1869	1932

INDEX OF AUTHORS

INDEX OF PLAYS AND CASTS